THOMSON

SOUTH-WESTERN

Survey of Accounting, 2e

Carl S. Warren

Editorial Director:
Jack W. Calhoun

Vice President/Editor-in-Chief:
George Werthman

Senior Acquisitions Editor:
Sharon Oblinger

Senior Developmental Editor:
Ken Martin

Marketing Manager:
Keith Chasse

Production Editor:
Chris Hudson

Manufacturing Coordinator:
Doug Wilke

Media Development Editor:
Sally Nieman

Media Production Editor:
Robin Browning

Compositor:
GGS Information Services, Inc.

Production House:
Litten Editing and Production, Inc.

Printer:
QuebecorWorld
Versailles, Kentucky

Senior Design Project Manager:
Michelle Kunkler

Cover and Internal Designer:
Lisa Albonetti
Cincinnati, Ohio

Cover Images:
© EyeWire and © Artville, Inc.

Library of Congress Control Number:
2002117815

ISBN: 0-324-18344-5

Second Edition

Survey of Accounting

Carl S. Warren
University of Georgia

THOMSON
SOUTH-WESTERN

Australia · Canada · Mexico · Singapore · Spain · United Kingdom · United States

Preface

Survey of Accounting, 2d Edition, is designed for a one-term introductory accounting course. It provides an overview of the basic topics in financial and managerial accounting, without the extraneous accounting principles topics that must be skipped or otherwise modified to fit into a one-term course. Written for students who have no prior knowledge of accounting, this text emphasizes how accounting reports are used by managers, investors, and other business stakeholders.

New Features

The 2d Edition of the text includes new features designed to help instructors and to enhance the learning experience of students. These features include the following:

- A new chapter, "The Role of Accounting in Business," begins the text. This chapter includes an introduction to business that discusses types of businesses, forms of business, business strategies, the value chain of a business, and business stakeholders. The business activities of financing, investing, and operating are discussed, followed by an introduction to the role of accounting in business and financial statements. The chapter also includes a discussion of basic accounting concepts that will be used in later chapters.

- Based upon the discussion of business strategies in Chapter 1, "Business Strategy" items have been included in all the chapters. In addition, many of the chapters include business strategy activities as part of the assignment material.

BUSINESS STRATEGY

Not Cutting Corners

Have you ever ordered a hamburger from Wendy's and noticed that the meat patty is square? The square meat patty reflects a business strategy implemented at Wendy's by its founder, Dave Thomas. Mr. Thomas's strategy was to offer high-quality products at a fair price in a friendly atmosphere without "cutting corners"; hence, the square meat patty. In the highly competitive fast-food industry, Dave Thomas's strategy enabled Wendy's to grow to be the third largest fast-food restaurant in the world with annual sales of more than $7 billion.

Source: Douglas Martin, "Dave Thomas, 69, Wendy's Founder Dies," *The New York Times*, January 9, 2002.

■ In response to the current business environment and concern over integrity in business, "Ethics in Action" items are included throughout the text. In addition, ethics cases and activities are included as possible assignments.

■ Chapter 2 presents the cash basis of accounting. Starting the study of accounting with the cash basis is simpler than starting with the accrual basis. In addition, students can better relate to the cash basis, since it mirrors the accounting system they use in their daily lives.

Chapter 2 begins with a discussion of basic elements of all accounting systems. These basic elements include a set of standard rules of recording transactions, the accounting equation as a recording framework, and controls over the recording of transactions. Chapter 2 also includes an introductory discussion of the differences between the cash and accrual bases of accounting.

The end-of-chapter exercises and problems in Chapter 2 allow the instructor to assign the preparation of all the financial statements, including the statement of cash flows. By analyzing the effects of transactions on cash, the statement of cash flows can be easily prepared. This reinforces the Chapter 1 discussion of the three business activities of operating, investing, and financing.

■ Chapter 3 presents the accrual basis of accounting, using the continuing illustration from Chapter 2, Family Health Care. Because the accrual basis is used, adjusting entries are necessary for preparing financial statements, which contrasts with Chapter 2, where no adjusting entries were required. The importance of the matching concept under the accrual basis is also emphasized.

The end-of-chapter exercises and problems in Chapter 3 allow the instructor to assign the preparation of all the financial statements, including the statement of cash flows.

Chapter 3 includes an appendix reconciling net cash flows from operations and net income. A problem for this appendix is included in the end-of-chapter materials.

■ Chapter 4 emphasizes the differences between service and merchandising businesses. This chapter begins by comparing the financial statements of service and merchandising businesses. The determination of cost of merchandise sold is also illustrated early in the chapter. After students understand the nature of merchandising businesses, the recording of merchandising transactions is discussed and illustrated.

Chapter 4 illustrates the statement of cash flows for a merchandising business. An end-of-chapter appendix describes and illustrates how the statement of cash flows can be prepared using the indirect method. An end-of-chapter problem is included for instructors who may assign homework that requires students to prepare the statement of cash flows under the indirect method.

On January 22, collected Invoice No. 106-8 to Computer King, less 2% discount.

Trans. Date	Balance Sheet				Income Statement		
	Assets		Liabilities	Stockholders' Equity	Revenue	Expense	Net Income
Jan. 22	Cash	1,470			Sales Discounts 30		−30
	Accts. Rec.	−1,500					
Net Effect		−30		−30	30		−30
				Retained Earnings			
				(Net Income)			

■ Beginning with Chapter 4, the format for recording transactions using the accounting equation has been revised to be consistent with the earlier chapters. That is, the same format using the accounting equation is used throughout the text.

- In Chapter 7, "Fixed Assets and Intangible Assets," the discussion of asset betterments and improvements has been revised to reflect current accounting standards and practices.

- Activity-based costing is now included in Chapter 10, "Accounting Systems for Manufacturing Businesses."

- An end-of-text appendix (Appendix B) on process cost accounting using the average cost method has been added. This appendix includes exercises and problems for use as student assignment materials.

Features Retained from the 1st Edition

The 2d Edition of *Survey of Accounting* preserves the 1st Edition features that were well received by the marketplace. These features include the following:

	Assets		=	Liabilities	+	Stockholders' Equity	
				Notes		Capital	
	Cash	+	Land	=	Payable	+	Stock	
Bal.	16,000			10,000	6,000		
c.	−12,000	12,000					Purchase of land
Bal.	4,000	12,000		10,000	6,000		

- The basics of accounting are presented in an easy-to-understand manner, without using debits and credits.

- Basic accounting procedures (debits and credits) are covered in an end-of-text appendix.

- The financial statement effects of transactions are emphasized, using the accounting equation format.

- The cash and accrual bases of accounting are discussed and illustrated, using a continuing illustration, Family Health Care.

- The usefulness of the accrual basis of accounting over the cash basis in evaluating and predicting future business performance is discussed and illustrated.

- Real-world companies are illustrated throughout the text and are included in many end-of-chapter exercises, problems, and activities.

- Managerial control and reporting topics provide a basic framework for understanding how accounting systems help satisfy managerial decision-making needs and how accounting systems can be used to control business operations.

- The end-of-chapter materials contain a wide variety of assignments for students, including short exercises covering key concepts in each chapter. On average, each chapter contains 15–20 discussion questions, over 20 exercises, 5–6 problems, and 5–8 activities.

- Graphics are used to provide "pictures" of concepts described in the text.

Focus on Technology

WebTutor

Available in either WebCT™ or Blackboard® platforms, this rich course management product is a specially designed extension of the classroom experience that enlivens the course by leveraging the power of the Internet with comprehensive educational content. This powerful, turnkey solution provides the following content customized for this edition:

- E-Lectures—PowerPoint™ slides of the key topical coverage with accompanying audio explanations to provide additional learning support.

- Interactive Quizzes—Multiple-choice, true/false, and sentence completion questions, which test the students' knowledge of the chapter content and provide immediate feedback on the accuracy of their responses. These quizzes help students pinpoint areas needing additional study.

- Flashcards—A terminology quiz so that students have a complete understanding of the language that makes up the chapter content.

- Reviews of Key Concepts—Tied to each learning objective, these chapter reviews reinforce important concepts from each chapter.

- Crossword Puzzles—Test students' knowledge of the glossary.

- Quiz Bowl Game—Review of the chapter content in a Jeopardy®-type game.

Xtra!

This CD-ROM provides lecture replacement resources and access to games and interactive quizzes so that students can test their understanding of the content of the text. Free when bundled with a new text, students receive an access code so that they can receive Xtra! reinforcement in introductory accounting.

Thomson Analytics—Business School Edition

Thomson Analytics—*Business School Edition* is a Web-based portal product that provides integrated access to Thomson Financial content for the purpose of financial analysis. This is an educational version of the same financial resources used by Wall Street analysts on a daily basis! The access card will provide you with 180 days of access to **Thomson Analytics—*Business School Edition*!**

For 500 companies, this online resource provides:

- **Current and Past Company Data:** Worldscope®, which includes company profiles, financials and accounting results, market per-share data, annual information, and monthly prices going back to 1980.

- **Financial Analyst Data and Forecasts:** 1/B/E/S Consensus Estimates, which provides consensus estimates, analyst-by-analyst earnings coverage, and analysts' forecasts.

- **SEC Disclosure Statements:** Disclosure SEC Database, which includes company profiles, annual and quarterly company financials, pricing information, and earnings.

Text Web Site (http://warren.swlearning.com)

The Web site for the second edition has expanded to offer you and your students even more resources for teaching and learning. Among the many elements available to students are:

- Quizzes with feedback

- Hotlinks to many resources on the Web, including all of the Web sites listed in the text, providing a quick connection to key information

- PowerPoint™ presentation slides for review of chapter coverage

- Crossword puzzles provide fun testing of vocabulary knowledge

- Learning objectives from the chapter are repeated as a study aid to keep clear focus on the core goals

Supplements for the Instructor

The supplements described below are available on a single CD-ROM as well as in print form. In addition, except for the Test Bank, these supplements can be downloaded from the text's Web site. Visit the Warren home page (http://warren.swlearning .com) to see the power of the Internet in accounting education for both you and your students.

- **Instructor's Manual.** Each chapter contains a list of key terms, a lecture outline, transparency masters, class participation ideas, supplemental examples and illustrations, and selected group learning activities.

- **Solutions Manual.** The Solutions Manual contains answers to all questions, exercises, problems, and activities in the text.

- **Test Bank.** The Test Bank contains a wealth of short-answer questions, problems, and discussion questions, with complete solutions.

- **Computerized Test Bank.** A computerized version of the Test Bank allows instructors to quickly and easily customize tests for their students. This supplement is located on the Instructor's Resource CD-ROM with ExamView®.

- **PowerPoint™ Lecture Presentations.** These presentations enhance lecture quality and shorten preparation time. Each chapter's slides outline the chapter content and feature key exhibits from the text.

- **Instructor's Resource CD-ROM with ExamView®.** Key instructor ancillaries (Solutions Manual, Instructor's Manual, Test Bank, ExamView, and Power-Point™ presentation slides) are provided on a CD-ROM—giving instructors the ultimate tool for customizing lectures and presentations. The Test Bank files on the CD-ROM are provided in ExamView® format. This program is an easy-to-use test-creation software compatible with Microsoft® Windows. Instructors can add or edit questions, instructions, and answers and select questions (randomly or numerically) by previewing them on the screen. Instructors can also create and administer quizzes online, whether over the Internet, a local area network (LAN), or a wide area network (WAN).

Supplements for Students

Several study aids for students are available free of charge at the text's Web site (http://warren.swlearning.com). These include self-quizzes, PowerPoint slides, and hot links to related sites and materials.

Additional Resources

Inside Look: Analysis from All Angles

Accounting is in the news and in the classroom with access to this new Web site from Thomson/South-Western. The **Inside Look** access card allows the instructor and the student to utilize information related to Enron, Andersen, and other "names in the news" that involve accounting-related concerns. Well-known, popular news sources provide the background for the selected current events. Teaching tools are available to the instructor to implement class discussions, while analysis and questions are available to the student to utilize in many accounting discipline areas. This site is intended to help instructors teach and students learn about critical current issues and understand them in the context of their accounting studies. For a Demo, go to http://www.insidelook.swcollege.com.

InfoTrac® College Edition

With this resource, students can receive anytime, anywhere online access to a database of full-text articles from hundreds of popular and scholarly periodicals, such as *Newsweek, Fortune, Entrepreneur, Journal of Accountancy*, and *Nation's Business*, among others. Students can use its fast and easy search tools to find relevant news and analytical information among the tens of thousands of articles in the database—updated daily and going back as far as four years—all at a single Web site. **InfoTrac** is a great way to expose students to online research techniques, with the security that the content is academically based and reliable. An **InfoTrac College Edition** subscription card can be packaged free with new copies of this text. For more information, visit http://www.swcollege.com/infotrac/infotrac.html.

NewsEdge®

NewsEdge offers flexible delivery of news and information that meets the individual needs of your classroom. The content is derived from the world's premier news and information sources. Editorial experts sift through the clutter, delivering only the stories and updates students really need. Access this free service at http://accounting.swlearning.com.

An Introduction to Accounting, Business Processes, and ERP (by Phil Reckers, Julie Smith David, and Harriet MacCracken, all of Arizona State University)

Utilizing JD Edwards software demos, an industry-leading ERP company, students will experience an overview of the use of ERP software for accounting and business processes. They will not only learn the advantages of technology in accessing business information but will also learn to apply it in three different business models. After each module, student learning is reinforced by quizzing. Equip your students with this class-tested and easy-to-use experience to help them meet the ever-changing challenges of business and technology!

The Monopoly Game Practice Set (by Robert Knechel of University of Florida)

This fun practice set, based on Monopoly, helps students understand accounting transactions as triggered by real business events. Each student's solution is unique but easily graded.

Ethics in the Post-Enron Age (by Iris and Bruce Stuart of California State University–Fullerton)

With the Enron/Andersen debacle, ethics is becoming an increasingly important (and interesting) part of accounting education. This timely supplement contains ethics cases based on real situations in the business world. Examples include cases tied to Enron, Global Crossing, and Boston Chicken. Identifying ethical dilemmas and projecting their resolution will allow students to develop essential skills for success in their future careers.

Business & Professional Ethics for Accountants, 3e (by Leonard J. Brooks of University of Toronto)

In this supplement, interesting, real-world situations provide students with a practical understanding of appropriate values, ethical pitfalls, applicable codes of conduct, and sound ethical reasons where codes do not apply.

Acknowledgments

Many people deserve thanks for their contributions to this text. James Emig of Villanova University was an outstanding resource for his careful verification of the end-of-chapter materials. The comments of the following reviewers also influenced this edition:

John A. Armstrong
Nichols College

David Koeppen
Boise State University

Charles A. Brown
Penn State University–Erie

Donald Leonard
Nichols College

Richard Butenhoff
Waukesha County Technical College

Wendy Mahmoud
Northern Illinois University

Ronald L. Clark
Auburn University

Len Minars
University of St. Thomas

Robert Dunn
Auburn University

Les Price
Pierce College
University of Puget Sound
Seattle University

Craig Ehlert
Montana State University

Bert Zarb
Embry-Riddle Aeronautical University

Jean Hartman
University of St. Thomas

Your comments and suggestions as you use this text are sincerely appreciated.

Carl S. Warren

About the Author

CARL S. WARREN

Dr. Carl S. Warren is Professor Emeritus of Accounting at the University of Georgia, Athens. For over 25 years, Professor Warren taught all levels of classes. In recent years, he focused his teaching efforts on principles of accounting and auditing classes. He also has taught classes at the University of Iowa, Michigan State University, and University of Chicago. He received his doctorate degree (Ph.D.) from Michigan State University and his undergraduate (B.B.A.) and masters (M.A.) degrees from the University of Iowa. Professor Warren enjoys interacting and learning from colleagues on how to improve student learning. His outside interests include writing short stories and novels, painting, handball, golf, skiing, backpacking, and fly-fishing.

Brief Contents

Contents

Chapter 1

1

LEARNING OBJECTIVES

OBJECTIVE 1
Describe the types and forms of businesses, business strategies, value chains, and stakeholders.

OBJECTIVE 2
Describe the three business activities of financing, investing, and operating.

OBJECTIVE 3
Define accounting, and explain its role in business.

OBJECTIVE 4
Describe and illustrate the basic financial statements and how they interrelate.

OBJECTIVE 5
Describe eight basic accounting concepts underlying financial reporting.

OBJECTIVE 6
Describe and illustrate the use of horizontal analysis to analyze and evaluate a company's performance.

The Role of Accounting in Business

Every day, you interact with businesses. You buy a Hershey's candy bar, eat lunch at McDonald's or Burger King, order a cup of coffee from Starbucks or Seattle Coffee, or fill up your car with gas at an ExxonMobil or BP gas station. How do these businesses influence you to buy their products? What are their underlying business strategies?

As we begin our study of accounting in this chapter, we first discuss the nature, types, activities, and strategies of businesses such as these. In doing so, we describe business stakeholders and the way businesses add value for their customers (you). We conclude the chapter by discussing the role of accounting in business, including financial statements, basic accounting concepts, and how you can use financial statements to evaluate a business' performance.

The Nature of Business

OBJECTIVE   1
Describe the types and
forms of businesses,
business strategies,
value chains, and
stakeholders.

You are familiar with many large companies, such as **General Motors**, **Barnes & Noble**, and **AT&T**. You are also familiar with many local businesses, such as gas stations, grocery stores, and restaurants. You may work for one of these businesses. What do they have in common that identifies them as businesses?

In general, a **business** is an organization in which basic resources (inputs), such as materials and labor, are assembled and processed to provide goods or services (outputs) to customers.[1] Businesses come in all sizes, from a local coffee house to General Motors, which sells several billion dollars' worth of cars and trucks each year. The customers of a business are individuals or other businesses that purchase goods or services in exchange for money or other items of value. In contrast, a church is not a business because those who receive its services are not obligated to pay for them.

The objective of most businesses is to maximize profits. *Profit* is the difference between the amounts received from customers for goods or services provided and the amounts paid for the inputs used to provide the goods or services. Some businesses operate with an objective other than to maximize profits. The objective of such not-for-profit businesses is to provide some benefit to society, such as medical research or conservation of natural resources. In other cases, governmental units such as cities operate water works or sewage treatment plants on a not-for-profit basis. Our focus in this text will be on businesses operated to earn a profit. However, many of the concepts and principles also apply to not-for-profit businesses.

Types of Businesses

Three different types of businesses are operated for profit: manufacturing, merchandising, and service businesses. Each type of business has unique characteristics.

Manufacturing businesses change basic inputs into products that are sold to individual customers. Examples of manufacturing businesses and some of their products follow:

Manufacturing Business	Product
General Motors	Automobiles, trucks, vans
General Mills	Breakfast cereals
Boeing	Jet aircraft
Nike	Athletic shoes
Coca-Cola	Beverages
Sony	Stereos, televisions, radios

Merchandising businesses also sell products to customers. However, they do not make the products but purchase them from other businesses (such as manufacturers). In this sense, merchandisers bring products and customers together. Examples of merchandising businesses and some of the products they sell are shown here:

Merchandising Business	Product
Wal-Mart	General merchandise
Toys "R" Us	Toys
Barnes & Noble	Books
Best Buy	Consumer electronics
Amazon.com	Books

[1] A glossary of terms appears at the end of each chapter in the text.

Service businesses provide services rather than products to customers. These are examples of service businesses and the types of services they offer:

Service Business	Service
Disney	Entertainment
Delta Air Lines	Transportation
Marriott Hotels	Hospitality and lodging
Merrill Lynch	Financial
Sprint	Telecommunications

Forms of Business

A business is normally organized as one of three different forms: proprietorship, partnership, or corporation. A **proprietorship** is owned by one individual. More than 70% of the businesses in the United States are organized as proprietorships. The popularity of this form is due to the ease and low cost of organizing. The primary disadvantage of proprietorships is that the financial resources available to the business are limited to the individual owner's resources. Small local businesses such as hardware stores, repair shops, laundries, restaurants, and maid services are often organized as proprietorships.

As a business grows and requires more financial and managerial resources, it may become a partnership. A **partnership** is owned by two or more individuals. Like proprietorships, small local businesses such as automotive repair shops, music stores, beauty shops, and men's and women's clothing stores can be organized as partnerships. Currently, about 10% of the businesses in the United States are organized as partnerships.

Like proprietorships, a partnership can outgrow its ability to finance its operations. As a result, it can become a corporation. A **corporation** is organized under state or federal statutes as a separate legal entity. The ownership of a corporation is divided into shares of stock. A corporation issues the stock to individuals or other businesses, who then become owners, or stockholders, of the corporation.

A primary advantage of the corporate form is the ability to obtain large amounts of resources by issuing stock. For this reason, most companies that require large investments in equipment and facilities are organized as corporations. For example, **Toys "R" Us** has raised more than $800 million by issuing shares of common stock to finance its operations. Other examples of corporations include **General Motors**, **Ford**, **International Business Machines (IBM)**, **Coca-Cola**, and **General Electric**.

ETHICS IN ACTION

In a partnership, the unethical behavior of one partner can broadly impact the whole firm. A partner of **Arthur Andersen & Co.**, a major public accounting firm, pleaded guilty to obstruction of justice in the destruction of documents related to the **Enron** bankruptcy. As a result of these events, the Justice Department accused the entire firm of obstruction of justice. The questionable actions of a few had severe implications for many innocent Andersen partners and employees.

About 20% of the businesses in the United States are organized as corporations. However, since most large companies are organized as corporations, more than 90% of the total dollars of business receipts are received by corporations. Thus, corporations have a major influence on the economy.

The three types of businesses we discussed earlier—manufacturing, merchandising, and service—can be either proprietorships, partnerships, or corporations. However, because of the large amount of resources required to operate a manufacturing business, most manufacturing businesses are corporations. Likewise, most large retailers such as **Wal-Mart**, **Sears**, and **JC Penney** are corporations. Because most large businesses are corporations, they tend to dominate the economic activity in the United States. For this reason, we focus our attention in this text on the corporate form of organization. However, many of the concepts and principles we discuss also apply to proprietorships and partnerships.

Business Strategies

How does a business decide which products or services to offer its customers? For example, should **Best Buy** offer warranty and repair services to its customers? Many factors influence this decision, but ultimately it is made on the basis of whether it is consistent with the overall business strategy of the company.

A **business strategy** is an integrated set of plans and actions designed to enable the business to gain an advantage over its competitors and, in doing so, to maximize its profits. The two basic strategies a business can use are a low-cost strategy and a differentiation strategy.

Under a **low-cost strategy**, a business designs and produces products or services of acceptable quality at a cost lower than that of the competitors. **Wal-Mart** and **Southwest Airlines** are examples of businesses with a low-cost strategy. Such businesses often sell no-frills, standardized products to the most typical customer in the industry. Following this strategy, businesses must continually focus on driving costs lower.

Businesses try to achieve lower costs in a variety of ways. For example, a business can employ strict budgetary controls, use sophisticated training programs, implement simple manufacturing technologies, or enter into cost-saving supplier relationships. Such supplier relationships may involve linking the supplier's production process directly to the client's production processes to minimize inventory costs, variations in raw materials, and record keeping costs.

A primary concern of a business using a low-cost strategy is that a competitor could replicate its low costs or develop technological advances that enable it to achieve even lower costs. Another concern is that competitors could differentiate their products in such a way that customers no longer desire a standardized, no-frills product. For example, local pharmacies most often try to compete with Wal-Mart on the basis of personalized service rather than cost.

Under a **differentiation strategy**, a business designs and produces products or services that possess unique attributes or characteristics for which customers are willing to pay a premium price. For the differentiation strategy to be successful, a product or service must be truly unique or perceived as unique in quality, reliability, image, or design. To illustrate, **Maytag** attempts to differentiate its appliances on the basis of reliability, and **Tommy Hilfiger** differentiates its clothing on the basis of image.

Businesses using a differentiation strategy often implement information systems to capture and analyze customer buying habits and preferences. For example, many grocery stores such as **Kroger** and **Safeway** issue magnetic cards to preferred customers that allow the consumer to receive special discounts on purchases. In addition to establishing brand loyalty, the cards allow the stores to track consumer preferences and buying habits to use in purchasing and advertising campaigns.

One method to create differentiation is to use advertising to communicate the unique features of a product. However, making unsubstantiated claims about products or services is fraudulent. For example, the Federal Trade Commission (FTC) recently warned makers of devices and additives that claim to "improve gas mileage up to 300 percent" to cease from making such "false and grossly exaggerated" claims.

Source: Reuters English News Service, USA: FTC says gas-saving gadgets inflate online claims, April 18, 2002.

Companies can enhance differentiation by investing in manufacturing and service technologies, such as flexible manufacturing methods that allow timely product design and delivery. Some companies use marketing and sales efforts to promote product differences. Other efforts include using unique credit-granting arrangements, emphasizing personal relationships with customers, and offering extensive training and after-sales service programs for customers.

A business using a differentiation strategy wants customers to pay a premium price for the differentiated features of its products. However, a business could provide features that exceed the customers' needs. In this case, competitors may be able to offer customers less differentiated products at lower costs. Also, customers' perceptions of the differentiated features can change. As a result, customers could not be willing to continue to pay a premium price for the products. For example, as **Tommy Hilfiger** clothing becomes more commonplace, customers may become unwilling to pay a premium price for it. Over time, customers may also become better educated about the products and the value of the differentiated features. For example, **IBM** personal computers were once viewed as being differentiated on quality. However, as consumers have become better educated and more experienced with personal computers, **Dell** and **Gateway** computers have also become perceived as high quality.

A business can attempt to implement a **combination strategy** that includes elements of both the low-cost and differentiation strategies. That is, a business attempts to develop a differentiated product at competitive, low-cost price. For example, **Andersen Windows** allows customers to design their own windows through the use of its proprietary manufacturing software. By using flexible manufacturing, Andersen Windows can produce a variety of windows in small quantities with a low or moderate cost. Thus, Andersen windows sell at a higher price than standard low-cost windows but at a lower price than a fully customized window built on site.

As you might expect, a danger of a business using a combination strategy is that its products could not adequately satisfying either end of the market. That is, because its products are differentiated, it cannot establish itself as the low-cost leader, and, at the same time, its products cannot be differentiated enough that customers are willing to pay a premium price. In other words, the business can become "stuck in the middle." For example, **JC Penney** has difficulty competing as a low-cost leader against **Wal-Mart**, **Kmart**, **Goody's Family Clothing**, **Fashion USA**, **T.J. Maxx**, and **Target**. At the same time, JC Penney cannot adequately differentiate its stores and merchandise from such competitors as **The Gap**, **Old Navy**, **Eddie Bauer**, and **Talbot's** in order to charge higher prices.

A business can also attempt to implement different strategies for different markets. For example, **Toyota** segments the market for automobiles by offering the Lexus to image- and quality-conscious buyers. To reinforce this image, Toyota developed a separate dealer network. At the same time, Toyota offers a low-cost automobile, the Echo, to cost-conscious buyers.

BUSINESS STRATEGY

It's All in the Name

Intel develops and produces micro-processors for use in electronic equipment, including personal computers and organizers. Beginning with the 8086 processor and continuing with the 286, 386, and 486, Intel's processors were widely used in personal computers during the 1980s and 1990s. Intel's competitors, however, also developed and sold 386 and 486 processors. In doing so, its competitors were able to erode Intel's market share. In responding, Intel named its next micro-processor the "Pentium," rather than the 586, and registered Pentium as a trademark. By doing so, Intel prevented its competitors from selling their products as Pentiums. Thus, Intel developed a "differentiated" brand name that its competitors were unable to duplicate.

Exhibit 1 summarizes the characteristics of the low-cost, differentiation, and combination strategies. In addition, some common examples of businesses that employ each strategy are also listed.

EXHIBIT 1
Business Strategies and Industries

Business Strategy	Industry					
	Airline	Freight	Automotive	Retail	Financial Services	Hotel
Low cost	Southwest	Union Pacific	Saturn	Sam's Clubs	Schwab	Super 8
Differentiated	Virgin Atlantic	Federal Express	BMW	Talbot's	Morgan Stanley	Ritz Carlton
Combination	Delta	United Postal Service	Ford	Target	Merrill Lynch	Marriott

Value Chain of a Business

Once a business has chosen a strategy, it must implement the strategy in its value chain. A **value chain** is the way a business adds value for its customers by processing inputs into a product or service, as shown in Exhibit 2.

EXHIBIT 2   *The Value Chain*

Inputs → Business Processes → Products or Service → Customer Value

To illustrate, **Delta Air Lines'** value chain consists of taking inputs, such as people, aircraft, and equipment, and processing these inputs into a service of transporting goods and passengers throughout the world. The extent to which customers value Delta's passenger service is reflected by the air fares Delta is able to charge as well as passenger load factors (percentage of seats occupied). For example, the extent to which Delta can, on average, charge higher fares than discount airlines, such as **Air Tran**, implies that passengers value Delta's services more than Air Tran's. These services include newer, more comfortable aircraft, the ability to earn frequent flyer miles, more convenient passenger schedules, passenger lounges for frequent flyers, and international connections.

The value chain of a business can be divided into primary and supporting processes. Primary processes are those that are directly involved in creating value for customers. Examples of primary processes include manufacturing, selling, and customer service. Supporting processes are those that facilitate the primary processes. Examples of support processes include purchasing, personnel, and accounting.[2] For Delta Air Lines, primary processes include aircraft maintenance, pilot and flight attendant training, ticketing, and flight operations. Secondary processes for Delta Air Lines include the accounting and finance functions, contracting for fuel deliveries, and investor relations.

Business Stakeholders

A company's business strategy and how well the company implements it directly affect its economic performance and its stakeholders. For example, **Kmart** was unsuccessful in implementing a business strategy that would allow it to compete effectively against **Wal-Mart**. The result was that Kmart filed for bankruptcy protection in early 2002, and Kmart stakeholders, including employees, creditors, and stockholders, suffered.

A **business stakeholder** is a person or entity that has an interest in the economic performance and well-being of a business. For example, stockholders, suppliers, customers, and employees are all stakeholders in a corporation. Business stakeholders can be classified into one of the four categories illustrated in Exhibit 3.

EXHIBIT 3
Business Stakeholders

Business Stakeholder	Interest in the Business	Examples
Capital market stakeholders	Providers of major financing for the business	Banks, owners, stockholders
Product or service market stakeholders	Buyers of products or services and vendors to the business	Customers and suppliers
Government stakeholders	Collectors of taxes and fees from the business and its employees	Federal, state, and city governments
Internal stakeholders	Individuals employed by the business	Employees and managers

Capital market stakeholders provide the major financing so that the business can begin and continue its operations. Banks and other long-term creditors have an economic interest in recovering the amount they have loaned the business plus interest. Owners and stockholders want to maximize the economic value of their investments

[2]The value chain is described and illustrated in most management textbooks. A more advanced discussion of the value chain can be found in Michael E. Porter, *Competitive Advantage* (New York: The Free Press, 1985).

and thus also have an economic interest in the business. Capital market stakeholders expect to receive a return on their investments proportionate to the degree of risk they are taking on their investments. Since banks and long-term creditors have first preference to the assets in case the business fails, their risk is less than that of the owners and stakeholders, and thus their overall return is lower.

Product or service market stakeholders include customers who purchase the products or services of the business as well as the vendors who supply inputs to it. Customers have an economic interest in the continued success of the business. For example, customers of the Internet provider **@home.com** were temporarily unable to retrieve their e-mail or connect with the Internet when @home.com declared bankruptcy. Customers who purchase advance tickets on **Southwest Airlines** have an economic interest in whether Southwest will continue in business. Similarly, suppliers are stakeholders in the continued success of their customers. Suppliers may invest in technology or other capital equipment to meet a customer's buying and manufacturing specifications. If a customer fails or cuts back on purchases during downturns, suppliers could see their businesses suffer.

Various governments have an interest in the economic performance of businesses. City, county, state, and federal governments collect taxes from businesses within their jurisdictions. The better a business does, the more taxes the government can collect. In addition, workers are taxed on their wages. In contrast, workers who are laid off and are unemployed can file claims for unemployment compensation, which results in a financial burden for the government. City and state governments often provide incentives for businesses to locate in their jurisdictions.

Internal stakeholders include individuals employed by the business. The managers are those individuals who the owners have authorized to operate the business. Managers are primarily evaluated on the economic performance of the business. The managers of businesses that perform poorly are often fired by the owners. Thus, managers have an incentive to maximize the economic value of the business. Owners may offer managers salary contracts that are tied directly to how well the business performs. For example, a manager might receive a percentage of the profits or the increase in profits.

The employees provide services to the company they work for in exchange for their pay. Thus, employees have an interest in the economic performance of the business because their jobs depend on it. During business downturns, it is not unusual for a business to lay off workers for extended periods of time. In the extreme, a business can fail and its employees lose their jobs permanently. Employee labor unions often use the good economic performance of a business to argue for wage increases. In contrast, businesses often use poor economic performance to argue for employee concessions such as wage decreases.

Business Activities

OBJECTIVE   2

Describe the three business activities of financing, investing, and operating.

Regardless of whether the company is **Microsoft** or **General Motors**, all businesses are engaged in the activities of financing, investing, and operating. First, a business must obtain the necessary funds to finance the costs to organize, pay legal fees, and pay other start-up costs. Next, a business must invest funds in the necessary assets such as building and equipment to begin operations. For example, Milton Hershey, who founded Hershey Foods Corporation, invested in the German chocolate–making machinery he saw at the Chicago International Exposition. Finally, a business must utilize its assets and resources to implement its business strategy. Hershey's business strategy is to mass-produce chocolate candies at an affordable cost.

As we discuss later in this chapter, a major role of accounting is to provide stakeholders with information on the financing, investing, and operating activities of businesses. Financial statements represent one source of such information.

Financing Activities

Financing activities involve obtaining funds to begin and operate a business. Businesses seek financing through the use of the capital markets. This financing takes the form of borrowing or issuing shares of ownership. Most major businesses use both means of financing.

When a business borrows money, it incurs a liability. A **liability** is a legal obligation to repay the amount borrowed according to the terms of the borrowing agreement. For example, when you use your credit card, you incur an obligation to pay the issuer (bank). When a business borrows from a vendor or supplier, the liability is called an **account payable**. In such cases, the business is buying on credit and promising to pay according to the terms set forth by the vendor or supplier. Most vendors and suppliers require payment within a relatively short time, such as 30 days. As of December 31, 2001, **Hershey Foods Corporation** reported approximately $150 million of accounts payable.

A business can borrow money by issuing bonds. *Bonds* are sold to investors and normally require repayment with interest at a specific time in the future. Bonds are a type of long-term financing, with a face amount that is normally due years into the future. For example, **Lucent Technologies** currently has bonds due in 2028. In contrast, the interest on bonds is normally paid semiannually. Bond obligations are reported as **bonds payable**, and any interest that is due is reported as **interest payable**. Examples of well-known companies that have bonds outstanding include **American Telephone and Telegraph (AT&T)**, **John Deere**, and **Xerox**.

Most large corporations also borrow money by issuing commercial paper and negotiating lines of credit with financial institutions. *Commercial paper* refers to debt obligations that are sold to investors, such as banks and insurance companies, based on the general creditworthiness of the corporation. Similarly, lines of credit are negotiated with financial institutions in such a way that the corporation can borrow on the line of credit as needed. For example, **Hershey Foods** has a $500 million line of credit with a syndicate of banks, and, as of December 31, 2001, it had borrowed slightly more than $250 million on its credit line. When a corporation issues commercial paper or borrows on a line of credit, it incurs a note payable. A **note payable** requires the payment of the amount borrowed plus interest. Notes payable can be issued either on a short-term or a long-term basis.

A business also can finance its operations by issuing shares of ownership. For a corporation, shares of ownership are issued in the form of shares of *stock*. Although corporations may issue a variety of different types of stock, the basic type of stock issued to owners is called **common stock**. For our purposes, we will use the term **capital stock** to include all the types of stock a corporation may issue.[3] Investors who purchase the stock are referred to as **stockholders**.

---

[3]Types of stock are discussed in Chapter 8, "Liabilities and Stockholders' Equity."

The claims of creditors and stockholders on the assets of the corporation are different. In case of a corporation's liquidation or bankruptcy, creditors have first claim on its assets. Only after the creditors' claims have been satisfied can the stockholders obtain corporate assets. In addition, although creditors expect to receive timely payments of their claims, which may include interest, stockholders are not entitled to regular payments. However, many corporations distribute earnings to stockholders on a regular basis as long as the claims of creditors are being satisfied. These distributions of earnings to stockholders are called **dividends**. During 2001, **Hershey** paid stockholders almost $130 million in dividends.

Investing Activities

Once financing has been obtained, a business must use **investing activities** to obtain the necessary resources to start and operate the business. Depending on the nature of the business, a variety of different resources must be purchased. For example, Milton Hershey purchased the German chocolate–making machinery and later constructed a building to house the Hershey operations. In addition to machinery and buildings, other resources could include computers, office furnishings, trucks, and automobiles. Although most resources have physical characteristics, such as equipment, some resources are intangible in nature. For example, a business can purchase patent rights for use in a manufacturing process or product.

The resources that a business owns are called **assets**. A business may acquire assets through its financing, investing, and operating activities. Assets are acquired through financing activities when the business obtains cash through borrowing or issuing shares of stock. Assets are acquired through investing activities by purchasing resources, as in the preceding paragraph. Finally, assets can be acquired through operating activities as we describe in the next section.

Assets can be in a variety of different forms. For example, tangible assets include cash, land, property, plant, and equipment. Assets also include intangible items, such as rights to patents and rights to payments from customers. The right to payment from customers is called an **account receivable**. Other intangible assets, such as goodwill, copyrights, and patents, are often grouped and reported as a group as **intangible assets**. A business can also pay in advance for items such as insurance or rent. Such items, which are assets until they are consumed, are normally reported as **prepaid expenses**.

Operating Activities

Once resources have been acquired, a business uses **operating activities** to implement its business strategy. Hershey's strategy was to mass-produce and distribute chocolate candies at affordable prices. When Hershey sold its chocolates, it received revenue from its customers. **Revenue** is the increase in assets from selling products or services. Revenues are often identified according to their source. For example, revenues received from selling products are called *sales*. Revenues received from providing services are called *fees*.

To earn revenue, a business incurs costs, such as wages of employees, salaries of managers, rent, insurance, advertising, freight, and utilities. Costs used to earn revenue are called **expenses**. Depending on the nature of the cost, expenses can be identified in a variety of ways. For example, the cost of products sold is often referred to as the *cost of merchandise sold, cost of sales,* or *cost of goods sold.* Other expenses are often classified as either *selling expenses* or *administrative expenses.* Selling expenses include those costs directly related to selling a product or service. For example, selling expenses include costs such as sales salaries, sales commissions, freight, and advertising costs. Administrative expenses include other costs not directly related to the selling, such as officer salaries and other costs of the corporate office.

As we discuss later in this chapter, you can determine whether the business earned net income or incurred a net loss by comparing its revenues for a period with the related expenses. A **net income** results when revenues exceed expenses. A **net loss** results when expenses exceed revenues.

What Is Accounting and Its Role in Business?

OBJECTIVE 3
Define accounting, and explain its role in business.

How do stakeholders get information about the financing, investing, and operating activities of a business? The role of accounting is to provide this information. Accounting provides data for managers to use in operating the business and for other stakeholders to use in assessing the economic performance and condition of the business.

In a general sense, **accounting** can be defined as an information system that provides reports to stakeholders about the economic activities and condition of a business. We focus our discussions in this text on accounting and its role in business. However, many concepts in this text also apply to individuals, governments, and other types of organizations. For example, individuals must account for activities such as hours worked, checks written, and bills due. Stakeholders for individuals include creditors, dependents, and the government. A main interest of the government is making sure that individuals pay their proper taxes.

Accounting is sometimes called the *language of business* because it is the means by which business information is communicated to the stakeholders. For example, accounting reports summarizing the profitability of a new product help **Coca-Cola's** management decide whether to continue selling the new product. Likewise, financial analysts use accounting reports in deciding whether to recommend the purchase of Coca-Cola's stock. Banks use accounting reports in deciding the amount of credit to extend to Coca-Cola. Suppliers use accounting reports in deciding whether to offer credit to Coca-Cola for its purchases of supplies and raw materials. State and federal governments use accounting reports as a basis for assessing taxes on Coca-Cola.

As we described, accounting serves many purposes for business. A primary purpose is to summarize a firm's financial performance for external users, such as banks and governmental agencies. The branch of accounting that is associated with preparing reports for users external to the business is termed **financial accounting**. Accounting also can be used to guide management in making decisions about the business. This branch is called **managerial accounting**. Financial and managerial accounting overlap in many areas. For example, managers often use financial reports for external users in considering the impact of their decisions.

In this text, we focus on financial accounting. The two major objectives of financial accounting are

1. To report the financial condition of a business at a point in time.
2. To report changes in the financial condition of a business over a period of time.

The relationship between the two financial accounting objectives is shown in Exhibit 4. You may think of the first objective as a still photograph (snapshot) of the business and the second objective as a moving picture (video) of the business. The first objective measures the financial status of the business. Stakeholders use this measure to evaluate its financial health at a point in time. The second objective measures the change in the financial condition of the business for a period of time. Stakeholders use this measure to predict how a business may perform in the future.

EXHIBIT 4

Objectives of Financial Accounting

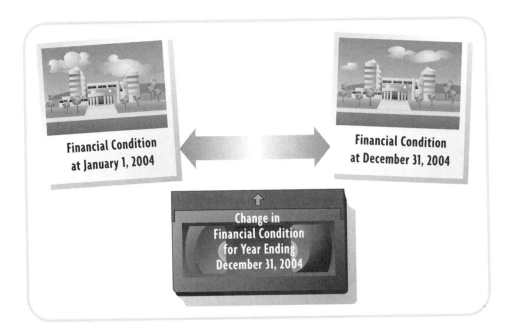

The objectives of accounting are satisfied by (1) recording the economic events affecting a business and then (2) summarizing the impact of these events on the business in financial reports, called **financial statements**. We will describe and illustrate the basic financial statements next.

Financial Statements

OBJECTIVE 4

Describe and illustrate the basic financial statements and how they interrelate.

Financial statements report the financial condition of a business at a point in time and changes in the financial condition over a period of time. The four basic financial statements and their relationship to the two objectives of financial accounting follow[4]:

[4]Instead of the retained earnings statement, companies may prepare a statement of stockholders' equity. This statement reports changes in retained earnings as well as changes in other stockholders' equity items.

Financial Statement	Financial Accounting Objective
Income statement	Reports change in financial condition
Retained earnings statement	Reports change in financial condition
Balance sheet	Reports financial condition
Statement of cash flows	Reports change in financial condition

The income statement is normally prepared first, followed by the retained earnings statement, the balance sheet, and the statement of cash flows. The nature of each statement is described here:

- **Income statement**—A summary of the revenue and the expenses for a specific period of time, such as a month or a year.

- **Retained earnings statement**—A summary of the changes in the earnings retained in the corporation for a specific period of time, such as a month or a year.

- **Balance sheet**—A list of the assets, liabilities, and stockholders' equity as of a specific date, usually at the close of the last day of a month or a year.

- **Statement of cash flows**—A summary of the cash receipts and cash payments for a specific period of time, such as a month or a year.

The four financial statements are illustrated in Exhibits 5–8. The data for the statements were adapted from the annual report of **Hershey Foods Corporation**.[5]

Income Statement

The income statement reports the change in financial condition resulting from the operations of a business. The time period covered by the income statement may vary, depending on the needs of the stakeholders. Public corporations are required to file quarterly and annual income statements with the Securities and Exchange Commission. The income statement shown in Exhibit 5 for Hershey Foods Corporation is for the year ended December 31, 2001.

EXHIBIT 5

Income Statement: Hershey Foods Corporation

HERSHEY FOODS CORPORATION
Income Statement
For the Year Ended December 31, 2001
(in thousands)

Revenues:		
Sales		$4,557,241
Expenses:		
Cost of sales	$2,665,566	
Selling and administrative	1,269,964	
Other expenses	209,077	
Interest	69,093	
Income taxes	136,385	4,350,085
Net income		$ 207,156

[5]The financial statements for Hershey Foods Corporation can be found at http://www.hersheys.com by clicking on "Investor Relations."

Since the focus of business operations is to generate revenues, the income statement begins by listing the revenues for the period. During 2001 Hershey Foods Corporation generated sales of more than $4.5 billion. These sales are listed under the revenue caption. You should note that the numbers shown in Exhibit 5 are expressed in thousands of dollars. It is common for large corporations to express their financial statements in thousands and, in some cases, millions of dollars.

Following the revenues, the expenses that were used in generating the revenues are listed. For Hershey Foods, these expenses include cost of sales, selling and administrative, other expenses, interest, and income taxes.[6] By reporting the expenses and the related revenues for a period, the expenses are said to be matched against the revenues. This is known in accounting as the *matching concept*. We will further discuss this concept later in this chapter.

When revenues exceed expenses for a period, the business has *net income*. If expenses exceed revenues, the business has a *net loss*. Reporting net income means that the business increased its net assets through its operations. That is, the assets created by the revenues coming into the business exceeded the assets used to generate the revenues. The objective of most businesses is to maximize net income or profit. A net loss means that the business decreased its net assets through its operations. A business can survive in the short run by reporting net losses, but in the long-run, it must report net income to survive.

During 2001, Hershey Foods earned net income of more than $200 million dollars. Is this good or bad? Certainly, net income is better than a net loss. However, each stakeholder must assess the economic performance of the corporation according to its own standards. For example, a creditor might be satisfied that the net income is sufficient to ensure that it will be repaid. On the other hand, a stockholder might not be satisfied if the corporation's profitability is less than that of competitors. Throughout this text, we describe various methods and analyses of assessing corporate performance.

Retained Earnings Statement

The retained earnings statement reports changes in financial condition due to changes in retained earnings during a period. **Retained earnings** is the portion of a corporation's net income that is retained in the business. A corporation may retain all of its net income for use in expanding operations, or it may pay a portion or all of its net income to stockholders as dividends. For example, high growth companies such as **Microsoft** and **Amazon.com** do not pay dividends to stockholders but retain profits for future expansion. In contrast, more mature corporations such as **Coca-Cola** and **General Electric** routinely pay their stockholders a regular dividend. Thus, investors such as retirees who desire the comfort of a routine dividend payment might invest in Coca Cola or General Electric. In contrast, younger and more aggressive growth-oriented investors might invest in Microsoft or Amazon.com.

Since retained earnings depend on net income, the time period covered by the retained earnings statement is the same period as that of the income statement. Thus, the retained earnings statement for Hershey Foods Corporation shown in Exhibit 6 is for the year ended December 31, 2001.

---

[6]Other expenses consist primarily of an asset impairment expense, which is discussed in advanced accounting texts.

EXHIBIT 6

*Retained Earnings
Statement: Hershey
Foods Corporation*

HERSHEY FOODS CORPORATION		
Retained Earnings Statement		
For the Year Ended December 31, 2001		
(in thousands)		
Retained earnings, January 1, 2001		$2,702,927
Add net income	$207,156	
Less dividends	154,750	
Increase in retained earnings		52,406
Retained earnings, December 31, 2001		$2,755,333

You should note that dividends are reported in Hershey's retained earnings statement rather than its income statement. This is done because dividends are not an expense but are a distribution of net income to stockholders. During 2001, Hershey paid dividends of approximately $155 million and retained approximately $52 million of its net income in the business. Thus, Hershey's retained earnings increased from $2,703 million to $2,755 million during 2001.

Balance Sheet

The balance sheet reports a company's financial condition as of a point in time. This is in contrast to the income statement, the retained earnings statement, and the statement of cash flows, which report changes in financial condition. The financial condition of a business as of a point in time is measured by its total assets and claims or rights to those assets. Thus, the financial condition of a business can be represented as follows:

$$\text{Assets} = \text{Claims (Rights to the Assets)}$$

The claims on the assets of a business consist of rights of creditors who have loaned money or extended credit to the business and the rights of stockholders who have invested in the business. As we discussed earlier, the rights of creditors are liabilities. The rights of stockholders are referred to as *stockholders' equity* or **owner's equity**. Thus, the assets and the claims on those assets can be presented in equation form as follows:

$$\text{Assets} = \text{Liabilities} + \text{Stockholders' Equity}$$

This equation is called the **accounting equation**. As you will discover in this and later chapters, accounting information systems are developed using this equation as their foundation.

The balance sheet, sometimes called the *statement of financial condition*, is prepared using the framework of the accounting equation. That is, assets are listed first and added to arrive at total assets. Liabilities are then listed and added to arrive at total liabilities. Stockholders' equity items are listed next and added to arrive at total stockholders' equity. Finally, the total assets must equal the combined total liabilities and stockholders' equity. In other words, the accounting equation must balance—thus, the name balance sheet. The balance sheet for Hershey Foods Corporation as of December 31, 2001, is shown in Exhibit 7.

HERSHEY FOODS CORPORATION
Balance Sheet
December 31, 2001
(in thousands)

Assets

Cash	$ 134,147
Accounts receivable	361,726
Inventories	512,134
Prepaid expenses	62,595
Property, plant, and equipment	1,534,901
Intangibles	429,128
Other assets	212,799
Total assets	$ 3,247,430

Liabilities

Accounts payable	$ 133,049
Accrued liabilities	462,901
Notes and other debt	1,245,939
Income taxes	258,337
Total liabilities	$ 2,100,226

Stockholders' Equity

Capital stock	$ 183,213
Retained earnings	2,755,333
Repurchased stock and other equity items	(1,791,342)
Total stockholders' equity	$ 1,147,204
Total liabilities and stockholders' equity	$ 3,247,430

As of December 31, 2001, Hershey had total assets of approximately $3.2 billion, to which creditors had claims of $2.1 billion and stockholders had claims of $1.1 billion. One use of the balance sheet by creditors is to determine whether the corporation's assets are sufficient to ensure that they will be paid their claims. In Hershey's case, as of December 31, 2001, the assets of the corporation exceed the creditors' claims by $1.1 billion. Thus, the creditors are reasonably ensured that their claims will be repaid.

Statement of Cash Flows

The statement of cash flows reports the change in financial condition due to the changes in cash during a period. During 2001, Hershey's net cash increased by $102 million, as shown in Exhibit 8.

Earlier in this chapter, we discussed the three business activities of financing, investing, and operating. Any changes in cash must be related to one of these three activities. Thus, the statement of cash flows is organized by reporting the changes in each of these three activities, as shown in Exhibit 8.

In the statement of cash flows, the cash flows from operating activities are reported first because they represent a primary analysis focus for most business stake-

EXHIBIT 8

Statement of Cash Flows: Hershey Foods Corporation

HERSHEY FOODS CORPORATION
Statement of Cash Flows
For the Year Ended December 31, 2001
(in thousands)

Net cash flows from operating activities	$ 706,405
Cash flows from investing activities:	
Investments in property, plant, and equipment	$(187,029)
Proceeds from sale of property, plant, and equipment	63,042
Net cash flows used in investing activities	$(123,987)
Cash flows from financing activities:	
Cash receipts from financing activities, including debt	$ 30,589
Dividends paid to stockholders	(154,750)
Repurchase of stock	(40,322)
Other, including repayment of debt	(315,757)
Net cash flows used in financing activities	$(480,240)
Net increase in cash during 2001	$ 102,178
Cash as of January 1, 2001	31,969
Cash as of December 31, 2001	$ 134,147

holders. For example, creditors are interested in determining whether the company's operating activities are generating enough positive cash flows to repay their debts. Likewise, stockholders are interested in the company's ability to pay dividends. A business cannot survive in the long term unless it generates positive cash flows from operating activities. Thus, employees, managers, and other stakeholders interested in the long-term viability of the business also focus on the cash flows from operating activities. During 2001, Hershey's operations generated a positive net cash flow of approximately $706 million.

Because of the impact that investing activities have on the operations of a business, the cash flows from investing activities are presented following the cash flows from operating activities section. Any cash receipts from selling property, plant, and equipment are reported in this section. Likewise, any purchases of property, plant, and equipment are reported as cash payments. Companies that are expanding rapidly, such as start-up companies, normally report negative net cash flows from investing activities. In contrast, companies that are downsizing or selling segments of the business could report positive net cash flows from investing activities.

As shown in Exhibit 8, Hershey reported negative net cash flows from investing activities of approximately $124 million. Of this negative net cash flow, $187 million was from the purchase of property, plant, and equipment, and approximately $63 million was related to the sale of property, plant, and equipment. Thus, it appears that Hershey is expanding operations.

Cash flows from financing activities are reported next. Any cash receipts from issuing debt or stock are reported in this section as cash receipts. Likewise, paying debt or dividends is reported as a cash payment. Business stakeholders can analyze cash flows from financing activities to determine whether a business is changing its financing policies.

As shown in Exhibit 8, Hershey paid dividends of approximately $155 million and repaid debt of approximately $316 million. Cash of approximately $31 million was received from financing activities that included additional borrowing from creditors. Finally, Hershey purchased its own stock at a cost of approximately $40 million. A company purchases its own stock if the corporate management believes its stock is undervalued or decides to provide stock to employees or managers as part of an incentive (stock option) plan.[7]

The statement of cash flows is completed by determining the increase or decrease in cash flows for the period by adding the net cash flows from operating, investing, and financing activities. Hershey reported a net increase in cash of approximately $102 million. This increase or decrease is added to or subtracted from the cash at the beginning of the period to determine the cash as of the end of the period. Thus, Hershey began the year with approximately $32 million in cash and ended the year with $134 million in cash.

So what does the statement of cash flows reveal about Hershey Foods Corporation during 2001? The statement shows that Hershey generated more than $700 million in cash flows from its operations while using cash to expand its operations and pay dividends to stockholders. Overall, Hershey appears to be in a strong operating position to generate cash and pay its creditors.

Interrelationships among Financial Statements

As we mentioned earlier, financial statements are prepared in the order of the income statement, retained earnings statement, balance sheet, and statement of cash flows. Preparing them in this order is important because the financial statements are interrelated. The Hershey Foods Corporation financial statements in Exhibits 5–8 show these interrelationships as follows[8]:

1. The income and retained earnings statements are interrelated. The net income or net loss appearing on the income statement also appears on the retained earnings statement as either an addition (net income) to or deduction (net loss) from the beginning retained earnings. To illustrate, Hershey's net income of $207,156 is also reported on the retained earnings statement as an addition to the beginning retained earnings.
2. The retained earnings statement and the balance sheet are interrelated. The retained earnings at the end of the period on the retained earnings statement also appears on the balance sheet as a part of stockholders' equity. To illustrate, Hershey's retained earnings of $2,755,333 as of December 31, 2001, is also reported on the balance sheet.
3. The balance sheet and statement of cash flows are interrelated. The cash on the balance sheet also appears as the end-of-the-period cash on the statement of cash flows. To illustrate, the cash of $134,147 reported on Hershey's balance sheet is also reported as the end-of-the-period cash on the statement of cash flows.

---

[7]We discuss the accounting for a company's purchase of its own stock in a later chapter.
[8]Depending on the method of preparing cash flows from operating activities, net income may also appear on the statement of cash flows. This interrelationship and the method of preparing the statement of cash flows, called the *indirect method*, is illustrated later in the text. In addition, as we illustrate in Chapter 2 under the cash basis of accounting, cash flow from operating activities equals net income.

The preceding interrelationships are important in analyzing financial statements and the possible impact of economic events or transactions on a business. In addition, these interrelationships serve as a check on whether the financial statements have been prepared correctly. For example, if the ending cash on the statement of cash flows doesn't agree with the balance sheet cash, an error exists.

Accounting Concepts

OBJECTIVE   5
Describe eight basic accounting concepts underlying financial reporting.

In the preceding section, we described and illustrated the four basic corporate financial statements. Just as the rules of football determine the proper manner of scoring touchdowns, accounting "rules," called **generally accepted accounting principles (GAAP)**, determine the proper content of financial statements. GAAP are necessary so that stakeholders can compare the financial condition and operating results across companies and across time. If managers of a company could prepare financial statements as they saw fit, the comparability between companies and across time periods would be difficult, if not impossible. In other words, this would be like allowing a football team to determine the point count for a touchdown every time it scored.

GAAP are established in the United States by the **Financial Accounting Standards Board (FASB)**.[9] In establishing GAAP, the FASB publishes *Statements of Financial Accounting Standards*. Understanding the concepts that support the FASB pronouncements is essential for analyzing and interpreting financial statements. We discuss eight of the most important of these concepts next.

Business Entity Concept

A business entity could be an individual, a not-for-profit organization such as a church, or a for-profit company such as a real estate agency. The **business entity concept** applies accounting to a specific entity for which stakeholders need economic data. Once the entity is identified, the accountant can determine which economic data and activities should be analyzed, recorded, and summarized in the financial statements for stakeholders.

The accounting for **Hershey Foods Corporation**, a for-profit corporation, is separated from the accounting for other entities. For example, the accounting for transactions and events of individual stockholders, creditors, or other Hershey stakeholders are not included in Hershey Foods Corporation's financial statements. Only the transactions and events of the corporation as a separate entity are included in Hershey's financial statements.

Cost Concept

The **cost concept** determines the amount initially entered into the accounting records for purchases. For example, assume that Hershey purchased land for $2 million as a site for a future plant. The cost of the land to Hershey is the amount that would be entered into the accounting records. The seller could have been asking $2.3 million

---

[9]The Securities and Exchange Commission also has authority to set accounting principles for publicly held corporations. In almost all cases, the SEC adopts the principles established by the FASB.

for the land up to the time of the sale, and the land could have been assessed for property tax purposes at $1.5 million. A month after purchasing the land, Hershey could have received an offer of $2.4 million for the land. The only amount that affects the accounting records and the financial statements, however, is the $2 million purchase price.

Going Concern Concept

In most cases, the amount of time that a business will be able to continue in operation is not known, so an assumption must be made. A business normally expects to continue operating for an indefinite period of time. This is called the **going concern concept**.

The going concern concept affects the recording of transactions and thus affects the financial statements. For example, the going concern concept justifies the use of the cost concept for recording purchases, such as the land purchased by Hershey in the preceding example. In this example, Hershey plans to build a plant on the land. Since Hershey does not plan to sell the land, reporting changes in the market value of the land is irrelevant. That is, the amount Hershey could sell the land for if it discontinued operations or went out of business is not important because Hershey plans to continue its operations.

If, however, there is strong evidence that a business is planning to discontinue its operations, the accounting records should show the values expected to be received. For example, the assets and liabilities of businesses in receivership or bankruptcy are valued from a quitting concern or liquidation point of view rather than from the going concern point of view.

Matching Concept

In accounting, revenues for a period are matched with the expenses incurred in generating those revenues. Under this **matching concept**, revenues are normally recorded at the time of the sale of the product or service. This recording of revenues is often referred to as *revenue recognition*. At the point of sale, the sale price has been agreed on, the buyer acquires ownership of the product or acquires the service, and the seller has a legal claim against the buyer for payment.

The following excerpt from the notes to Hershey's annual report describes when Hershey records sales:

> . . . . The Corporation records sales when . . . a . . . customer order with a fixed price has been received . . . the product has been shipped . . . there is no further obligation to assist in the resale of the product, and collectibility [of the account receivable] is reasonably assured.

Objectivity Concept

The **objectivity concept** requires that entries in the accounting records and the data reported on financial statements be based on objective evidence. If this concept is ignored, the confidence of users of the financial statements cannot be maintained. For example, evidence such as invoices and vouchers for purchases, bank statements for the amount of cash in the bank, and physical counts of supplies on hand support the accounting records. Such evidence is objective and verifiable. In some cases, judgments, estimates, and other subjective factors have to be used in preparing financial statements. In such situations, the most objective evidence available should be used.

Unit of Measure Concept

In the United States, the **unit of measure concept** requires that all economic data be recorded in dollars. Other relevant, nonfinancial information, such as terms of contracts, can also be recorded; however, only through using dollar amounts can the various transactions and activities of a business be measured, summarized, reported, and compared. Money is common to all business transactions, and thus the dollar is the monetary unit of measurement for reporting.

Adequate Disclosure Concept

Financial statements, including related footnotes and other disclosures, should contain all relevant data that a reader needs to understand the financial condition and performance of a business. This is called the **adequate disclosure concept**. Nonessential data should be excluded to avoid clutter. For example, the balance of each cash account is usually not reported separately. Instead, the balances are grouped together and reported as one total.

Accounting Period Concept

The process in which accounting data are recorded and summarized in financial statements is a period process. Data are recorded and the income statement, retained earnings statement, and statement of cash flows are prepared for a period of time such as a month or a year. The balance sheet is then prepared as of the end of the period. After the accounting process is completed for one period, a new one begins, and the accounting process is repeated for the new period. This process is based on the **accounting period concept**. Hershey's financial statements in Exhibits 5–8 illustrate the accounting period concept for the year ending December 31, 2001.

The financial history of a business is shown by a series of balance sheets and income statements. If the life of a business is expressed by a line moving from left to right, this series of financial statements may be graphed as follows:

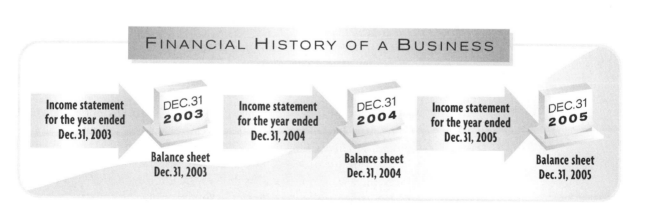

FINANCIAL HISTORY OF A BUSINESS

Income statement for the year ended Dec. 31, 2003

DEC. 31 2003

Balance sheet Dec. 31, 2003

Income statement for the year ended Dec. 31, 2004

DEC. 31 2004

Balance sheet Dec. 31, 2004

Income statement for the year ended Dec. 31, 2005

DEC. 31 2005

Balance sheet Dec. 31, 2005

Horizontal Analysis

OBJECTIVE   6

Describe and illustrate
the use of horizontal
analysis to analyze
and evaluate a
company's
performance.

The basic financial statements illustrated in this chapter are primary sources of information that financial analysts use in evaluating a company's performance. One method of analyzing financial performance is to compute the percentage of increases and decreases in related items in comparative financial statements. This type of analysis, called **horizontal analysis**, compares each item on the most recent financial statement with the related item on one or more earlier statements. The amount of the increase or decrease in each item is shown along with the percentage of increase or decrease.

To illustrate, income statements for Hershey Corporation will be used for the years ending December 31, 2001 and 2000. For analysis purposes, the statements have been condensed and adapted to emphasize the operating aspects of Hershey's performance. For example, other expenses, interest expense, and income taxes have been omitted from the income statements. This allows us to focus on the basic operating aspects of Hershey's business without being distracted by unusual items. The exclusion of income taxes helps simplify the analysis and recognizes that the amount of income taxes is largely beyond the operating control of the business. Interest expense is omitted since it deals more with the financing than the operating aspects of the business. The resulting comparative income statements are shown in Exhibit 9.

EXHIBIT 9

Comparative Income
Statements Using
Horizontal Analysis:
Hershey Foods
Corporation

HERSHEY FOODS CORPORATION
Income Statement
For the Years Ended December 31, 2001 and 2000
(in thousands)

	2001	2000	Increase (Decrease) Amount	Percent
Sales	$4,557,241	$4,220,976	$336,265	8.0%
Cost of sales	2,665,566	2,471,151	194,415	7.9
Gross profit	$1,891,675	$1,749,825	$141,850	8.1
Selling and administrative expenses	1,269,964	1,127,175	142,789	12.7
Operating income before taxes	$ 621,711	$ 622,650	$ (939)	(0.2)%

The income statements shown in Exhibit 9 report **gross profit** as sales less the cost of sales. Gross profit represents the amount that Hershey marked up the cost of its products in selling them to its customers. Gross profit is a useful performance measure in analyzing the profitability of the company's products from one period to the next.

Did Hershey improve its operations during the year ending December 31, 2001? Exhibit 9 indicates that Hershey increased its sales by 8% and that the cost of sales increased just under 8%. This combination of increases and decreases resulted in an increase in gross profit of just over 8%. Selling and administrative expenses increased significantly more than sales. This could be due to the implementation of a new advertising campaign, which could impact sales beyond just the current year.

The overall impact on operations of these changes is that operating income before taxes decreased by 0.2%. Before arriving at a final conclusion on Hershey's operating results for 2001, the reader should perform additional analyses and compare its results with the operating results of competitors.[10]

Key Points

1. **Describe the types and forms of businesses, business strategies, value chains, and stakeholders.**

   The three types of businesses operated for profit include manufacturing, merchandising, and service businesses. Such businesses may be organized as proprietorships, partnerships, or corporations. The two basic business strategies a business can use are low cost and differentiation. Sometimes a business implements a combination strategy that includes elements of both the low-cost and differentiation strategies. Once a business has chosen a strategy, it must implement the strategy in its value chain. A business's value chain is the way it adds value for its customers by processing inputs into a product or service. A company's business strategy and value chain are of interest to its stakeholders. Business stakeholders include four categories: capital market stakeholders, product or service market stakeholders, government stakeholders, and internal stakeholders.

2. **Describe the three business activities of financing, investing, and operating.**

   All businesses engage in financing, investing, and operating activities. Financing activities involve obtaining funds to begin and operate a business. Investing activities involve obtaining the necessary resources to start and operate the business. Operating activities involve using the business's resources according to its strategy.

3. **Define *accounting*, and explain its role in business.**

   Accounting is an information system that provides reports to stakeholders about the economic activities and condition of a business. Accounting is the *language of business*.

4. **Describe and illustrate the basic financial statements and how they interrelate.**

   The principal financial statements of a corporation are the income statement, the retained earnings statement, the balance sheet, and the statement of cash flows. The income statement reports a period's net income or net loss, which also appears on the retained earnings statement. The ending retained earnings reported on the retained earnings statement is also reported on the balance sheet. The ending cash balance is reported on the balance sheet and the statement of cash flows.

5. **Describe eight basic accounting concepts underlying financial reporting.**

   The eight basic accounting concepts discussed in this chapter include the business entity, cost, going concern, matching, objectivity, unit of measure, adequate disclosure, and accounting period concepts.

6. **Describe and illustrate the use of horizontal analysis to analyze and evaluate a company's performance.**

   One method of analyzing financial performance is to compute the percentage of increases and decreases in related items in comparative financial statements. This type of analysis, called *horizontal analysis*, compares each item on the most recent financial statement with the related item on one or more earlier statements.

---

[10]Additional financial statement analyses will be discussed and illustrated throughout this text.

Glossary

Account payable: The liability created when a business borrows from a vendor or supplier.

Account receivable: Right to payment from customers.

Accounting: An information system that provides reports to stakeholders about the economic activities and condition of a business.

Accounting equation: Assets = Liabilities + Stockholders' Equity.

Accounting period concept: An accounting concept in which accounting data are recorded and summarized in a period process.

Adequate disclosure concept: An accounting concept that requires financial statements to include all relevant data a reader needs to understand the financial condition and performance of a business.

Assets: The resources owned by a business.

Balance sheet: A list of the assets, liabilities, and owner's equity *as of a specific date*, usually at the close of the last day of a month or a year.

Bonds payable: A type of long-term debt financing with a face amount that is in the future with interest that is normally paid semiannually.

Business: An organization in which basic resources (inputs), such as materials and labor, are assembled and processed to provide goods or services (outputs) to customers.

Business entity concept: An accounting concept that limits the economic data in the accounting system of a specific business or entity to data related directly to the activities of that business or entity.

Business stakeholder: A person or entity who has an interest in the economic performance of a business.

Business strategy: An integrated set of plans and actions designed to enable the business to gain an advantage over its competitors and in doing so, maximize its profits.

Capital stock: Types of stock a corporation may issue.

Combination strategy: A business strategy that includes elements of both the low-cost and differentiation strategies.

Common stock: The basic type of stock issued to stockholders of a corporation.

Corporation: A business organized under state or federal statutes as a separate legal entity.

Cost concept: An accounting concept that determines the amount initially entered into the accounting records for purchases.

Differentiation strategy: A business strategy in which a business designs and produces products or services that possess unique attributes or characteristics for which customers are willing to pay a premium price.

Dividends: Distributions of the earnings of a corporation to stockholders.

Expenses: Costs used to earn revenues.

Financial Accounting Standards Board (FASB): The authoritative body that has the primary responsibility for developing accounting principles.

Financial statements: Financial reports that summarize the effects of events on a business.

Financing activities: Business activities that involve obtaining funds to begin and operate a business.

Generally accepted accounting principles (GAAP): Rules for the way financial statements should be prepared.

Going concern concept: An accounting concept that assumes a business will continue operating for an indefinite period of time.

Horizontal analysis: A method of analyzing financial performance that computes the percentage of increases and decreases in related items in comparative financial statements.

Income statement: A summary of the revenue and expenses *for a specific period of time*, such as a month or a year.

Intangible assets: Assets that are rights to future benefits such as patent or copyright rights.

Interest payable: A liability to pay interest on a due date.

Investing activities: Business activities that involve obtaining the necessary resources to start and operate the business.

Liability: The right of a creditor that represents a legal obligation to repay an amount borrowed according to terms of the borrowing agreement.

Low-cost strategy: A business strategy in which a business designs and produces products of acceptable quality at a cost lower than that of competitors.

Manufacturing: A type of business that changes basic inputs into products that are sold to individual customers.

Matching concept: An accounting concept that requires expenses of a period to be matched with the revenue generated during that period.

Merchandising: A type of business that purchases products from other businesses and sells them to customers.

Net income: The excess of revenues over expenses.

Net loss: The excess of expenses over revenues.

Note payable: A type of short- or long-term financing that requires payment of the amount borrowed plus interest.

Objectivity concept: An accounting concept that requires accounting records and data reported in financial statements be based on objective evidence.

Operating activities: Business activities that involve using the business's resources to implement its business strategy.

Owner's equity: The financial rights of the owner.

Partnership: A business owned by two or more individuals.

Prepaid expenses: An asset resulting from the prepayment of a future expense such as insurance or rent.

Proprietorship: A business owned by one individual.

Retained earnings: Net income retained in a corporation.

Retained earnings statement: A summary of the changes in the retained earnings in a corporation *for a specific period of time*, such as a month or a year.

Revenue: The increase in assets from selling products or services to customers.

Service: A type of business that provides services rather than products to customers.

Statement of cash flows: A summary of the cash receipts and cash payments *for a specific period of time*, such as a month or a year.

Stockholders: Investors who purchase stock in a corporation.

Unit of measure concept: An accounting concept requiring that economic data be recorded in dollars.

Value chain: The way a business adds value for its customers by processing inputs into a product or service.

Self-Study Questions

(Answers appear at end of chapter.)

1. A profit-making business operating as a separate legal entity and in which ownership is divided into shares of stock is known as a:
   A. proprietorship.   C. partnership.
   B. service business.   D. corporation.

2. The resources owned by a business are called:
   A. assets.
   B. liabilities.
   C. the accounting equation.
   D. stockholders' equity.

3. A listing of a business entity's assets, liabilities, and stockholders' equity as of a specific date is:
   A. a balance sheet.
   B. an income statement.
   C. a statement of owner's equity.
   D. a statement of cash flows.

4. If total assets are $20,000 and total liabilities are $12,000, the amount of stockholders' equity is:
   A. $32,000.   C. $(8,000).
   B. $(32,000).   D. $8,000.

5. If revenue was $45,000, expenses were $37,500, and dividends were $10,000, the amount of net income or net loss would be:
   A. $45,000 net income.   C. $37,500 net loss.
   B. $7,500 net income.   D. $2,500 net loss.

Discussion Questions

1. What is the objective of most businesses?

2. What is the difference between a manufacturing business and a merchandising business? Give an example of each type of business.

3. What is the difference between a manufacturing business and a service business? Is a restaurant a manufacturing business, a service business, or both?

4. Why are most large companies such as Microsoft, Pepsi, Caterpillar, and AutoZone organized as corporations?

5. Both KIA and Porche produce and sell automobiles. Describe and contrast their business strategies.

6. Assume that a friend of yours operates a family-owned pharmacy. A Super Wal-Mart that will offer pharmacy services is scheduled to open in the next several months. What business strategy would your friend use to compete with the Super Wal-Mart pharmacy?

7. How does eBay offer value to its customers?

8. A business's stakeholders can be classified into capital market, product or service market, government, and internal stakeholders. Will the interests of all the stakeholders within a classification be the same? Use bankers and stockholders of the capital market as an example in answering this question.

9. The three business activities are financing, investing, and operating. Using United Air Lines, give an example of a financing, investing, and operating activity.

10. What is the role of accounting in business?

11. Briefly describe the nature of the information provided by each of the following financial statements: the income statement, the retained earnings statement, the balance sheet, and the statement of cash flows. In your descriptions, indicate whether each of the financial statements covers a period of time or is for a specific date.

12. For the year ending February 3, 2001, The Limited Inc. had revenues of $10,104,606,000 and total expenses of $9,676,701,000. Did The Limited (a) incur a net loss or (b) realize net income?

13. What particular item of financial or operating data appears on (a) both the income statement and the retained earnings statement, (b) both the balance sheet and the retained earnings statement, and (c) both the balance sheet and statement of cash flows?

14. Lynda Lyons is the owner of Fast Delivery Service. Recently, Lynda paid interest of $3,500 to First Union on a personal loan of $60,000 that she used to begin the business. Should Fast Delivery Service record the interest payment? Explain.

15. On April 18, Neece Repair Service extended an offer of $95,000 for land that had been priced for sale at $100,000. On April 25, Neece Repair Service accepted the seller's counteroffer of $97,500. Describe how Neece Repair Service should record the cost of the land.

16. Land with an assessed value of $200,000 for property tax purposes was acquired by a business for $350,000. Seven years later, the plot of land has an assessed value of $240,000, and the business receives an offer of $400,000 for it. Should the monetary amount assigned to the land in the business records now be increased?

Exercises

EXERCISE 1-1
Types of businesses
OBJECTIVE 1

Indicate whether each of the following companies is primarily a service, merchandise, or manufacturing business. If you are unfamiliar with the company, you may use the Internet to locate the company's home page or use the finance web site of Yahoo.com.

1. Ford Motor
2. Citigroup
3. Sears, Roebuck
4. AT&T
5. H&R Block Inc.

6. **Boeing**
7. **First Union Corporation**
8. **Alcoa**
9. **CVS**
10. **Caterpillar**
11. **FedEx**
12. **Dow Chemical**
13. **The Gap**
14. **Hilton Hotels**
15. **Procter & Gamble**

EXERCISE 1–2
Business strategy
OBJECTIVE 1

Identify the primary business strategy of each of the following companies as (a) a low-cost strategy, (b) a differentiation strategy, or (c) a combination strategy. If you are unfamiliar with the company, you may use the Internet to locate the company's home page or use the finance web site of Yahoo.com.

1. **Southwest Airlines**
2. **Home Depot**
3. **BMW**
4. **Coca-Cola**
5. **Target**
6. **Goldman Sachs Group**
7. **Sara Lee**
8. **Delta Air Lines**
9. **Circuit City Stores**
10. **Maytag**
11. **Office Depot**
12. **Nike**
13. **Charles Schwab**
14. **Dollar General**
15. **General Motors**

EXERCISE 1–3
Accounting equation
OBJECTIVE 4

The total assets and total liabilities of **Toys "R" Us Inc.** and **Estee Lauder Companies Inc.** follow.

	Toys "R" Us (in millions)	Estee Lauder Companies (in millions)
Assets	$8,003	$3,219
Liabilities	4,585	1,867

Determine the stockholders' equity of each company.

EXERCISE 1–4
Accounting equation
OBJECTIVE 4

✓ a. $1,771

Determine the missing amounts (in millions) for the 2001 balance sheets (summarized below) for **The Limited Inc.**, **Federal Express Corporation**, and **Eastman Kodak Co.**

	The Limited	Federal Express	Eastman Kodak
Assets	$4,088	(b)	$13,362
Liabilities	(a)	$5,323	10,468
Stockholders' equity	2,317	4,248	(c)

EXERCISE 1-5

Net income and stockholders' equity for four businesses

OBJECTIVE 4

✓ Company Y: Net loss, ($25,000)

Four different corporations—W, X, Y, and Z—show the same balance sheet data at the beginning and end of a year. These data, exclusive of the amount of stockholders' equity, are summarized as follows:

	Total Assets	Total Liabilities
Beginning of the year	$375,000	$150,000
End of the year	$600,000	$325,000

On the basis of these data and the following additional information for the year, determine the net income (or loss) of each company for the year. (*Hint:* First determine the amount of increase or decrease in stockholders' equity during the year.)

Company W: No additional capital stock was issued and no dividends were paid.
Company X: No additional capital stock was issued, but dividends of $30,000 were paid.
Company Y: Capital stock of $75,000 was issued, but no dividends were paid.
Company Z: Capital stock of $75,000 was issued, and dividends of $30,000 were paid.

EXERCISE 1-6

Accounting equation and income statement

OBJECTIVE 4

✓ 1. $2,225,583

Staples, Inc., is a leading office products distributor with a total of 1,307 retail stores in the United States, Canada, the United Kingdom, the Netherlands, and Portugal. The following financial statement data were taken from Staples' financial statements as of February 3, 2001 and 2000:

	2001 (in thousands)	2000 (in thousands)
Total assets	$3,989,413	$3,846,076
Total liabilities	(1)	2,017,263
Total stockholders' equity	1,763,830	(2)
Retained earnings	1,008,021	948,309
Sales	$10,673,671	
Cost of goods sold	8,097,166	
Operating and other expenses	2,332,320	
Income tax expense	184,473	

a. Determine the missing data indicated for (1) and (2).
b. Using the income statement data for 2001, determine the amount of net income or loss.
c. Did Staples pay any dividends to stockholders during 2001? [*Hint:* Compare the change in retained earnings to your answer for (b).]

EXERCISE 1-7

Balance sheet and income statement items

OBJECTIVE 4

The list of selected items taken from the records of Kagy Appliance Service as of a specific date follow.

a. Identify those that would appear on the balance sheet.
b. Identify those items that would appear on the income statement.

1. Utilities Expense	6. Cash
2. Fees Earned	7. Supplies Expense
3. Supplies	8. Land
4. Wages Expense	9. Capital Stock
5. Accounts Payable	10. Wages Payable

EXERCISE 1-8
Financial statement items
OBJECTIVE 4

Identify each of the following items as (a) an asset, (b) a liability, (c) revenue, (d) expense, or (e) dividend:

1. Supplies used
2. Cash sales
3. Equipment
4. Cash paid to stockholders
5. Amounts owed vendors
6. Cash on hand
7. Wages paid employees
8. Sales commissions paid salespersons
9. Amounts due from customers
10. Note payable owed to the bank

EXERCISE 1-9
Retained earnings statement
OBJECTIVE 4

✓ Retained earnings, June 30, 2003: $393,750

Financial information related to Douma Company for the month ended June 30, 2003, is as follows:

Net income for June	$ 91,250
Dividends during June	15,000
Retained earnings, June 1, 2003	317,500

Prepare a retained earnings statement for the month ended June 30, 2003.

EXERCISE 1-10
Income statement
OBJECTIVE 4

✓ Net income: $63,800

Surgery Services was organized on April 1, 2003. A summary of the revenue and expense transactions for April follows:

Fees Earned	$165,800
Wages Expense	71,500
Miscellaneous Expense	2,250
Rent Expense	25,000
Supplies Expense	3,250

Prepare an income statement for the month ended April 30.

EXERCISE 1-11
Missing amounts from balance sheet and income statement data
OBJECTIVE 4

✓ (a) $130,250

One item is omitted in each of the following summaries of balance sheet and income statement data for four different corporations, I, II, III, and IV.

	I	II	III	IV
Beginning of the year:				
Assets	$600,000	$125,000	$100,000	(d)
Liabilities	360,000	65,000	76,000	$150,000
End of the year:				
Assets	745,000	175,000	90,000	310,000
Liabilities	325,000	55,000	80,000	170,000
During the year:				
Additional issue of capital stock	(a)	25,000	10,000	50,000
Dividends	40,000	8,000	(c)	75,000
Revenue	197,750	(b)	115,000	140,000
Expenses	108,000	32,000	122,500	160,000

Determine the missing amounts, identifying them by letter. (*Hint:* First determine the amount of increase or decrease in stockholders' equity during the year.)

EXERCISE 1-12
Balance sheets, net income
OBJECTIVE 4

✓ b. $11,330

Financial information related to Revival Interiors for August and September of 2004 is as follows:

	August 31, 2004	**September 30, 2004**
Accounts Payable	$ 3,850	$ 4,150
Accounts Receivable	8,500	9,780
Capital Stock	10,000	10,000
Retained Earnings	?	?
Cash	15,000	25,500
Supplies	750	600

a. Prepare balance sheets for Revival Interiors as of August 31 and as of September 30, 2004.
b. Determine the amount of net income for September, assuming that no additional capital stock was issued and no dividends were paid.
c. Determine the amount of net income for September, assuming that no additional capital stock was issued but dividends of $7,500 were paid.

EXERCISE 1-13
Financial statements
OBJECTIVE 4

Each of the following items is shown in the financial statements of **ExxonMobil Corporation**. Identify the financial statement (balance sheet or income statement) in which each item would appear.

a. Operating expenses
b. Crude oil inventory
c. Income taxes payable
d. Sales
e. Investments
f. Marketable securities
g. Exploration expenses
h. Notes and loans payable
i. Cash equivalents
j. Long-term debt
k. Selling expenses
l. Retained earnings
m. Equipment

EXERCISE 1-14
Statement of cash flows
OBJECTIVE 4

Indicate whether each of the following cash activities would be reported on the statement of cash flows as (a) an operating activity, (b) an investing activity, or (c) a financing activity.

1. Paid for advertising
2. Paid for office equipment
3. Issued capital stock
4. Paid officers' salaries
5. Collected accounts receivable
6. Paid for supplies
7. Paid dividends
8. Issued a note payable.
9. Paid accounts payable.
10. Sold excess office equipment.

EXERCISE 1-15
Statement of cash flows
OBJECTIVE 4

Indicate whether each of the following activities would be reported on the statement of cash flows as (a) an operating activity, (b) an investing activity, or (c) a financing activity.

1. Cash received from investment by stockholders
2. Cash paid for land
3. Cash received from fees earned
4. Cash paid for expenses

EXERCISE 1-16
Statement of cash flows
OBJECTIVE 4

Cremation Services was organized on January 1, 2004. A summary of cash flows for January follows.

✓ Net cash flow from
operating activities: $15,150

Cash receipts:
Cash received from customers	$23,500
Cash received for capital stock	90,000
Cash received from note payable	10,000

Cash payments:
Cash paid out for expenses	$ 8,350
Cash paid out for purchase of furnace	75,000
Cash paid as dividends	5,000

Prepare a statement of cash flows for the month ended January 31, 2004.

EXERCISE 1-17
*Using financial
statements*
OBJECTIVE 4

The financial statement focus of a company's stakeholders often differs. For example, some stakeholders focus primarily on the income statement, and others focus primarily on the statement of cash flows or the balance sheet. For each of the following situations, indicate which financial statement would be the likely focus for the stakeholder. Choose either the income statement, balance sheet, or the statement of cash flows and justify your choice.

Situation 1:
Assume that you are a banker for **Citigroup** (capital market stakeholder), considering whether to grant a major credit line (loan) to **Wal-Mart**. The credit line would allow Wal-Mart to borrow up to $400 million for a five-year period at the market rate of interest.

Situation 2:
Assume that you employed by **Sara Lee Corporation** (product market stakeholder) and are considering whether to extend credit for a 60-day period to a new grocery store chain that has recently opened throughout the Midwest.

Situation 3:
Assume that you are considering investing in **Amazon.com** (capital market stakeholder).

Situation 4:
Assume that you are considering taking a job (internal stakeholder) with either **Sears** or **JC Penney**.

Situation 5:
Assume that you are considering purchasing a personal computer from **Gateway**.

EXERCISE 1-18
*Financial statement
items*
OBJECTIVE 4

Starbucks Corporation purchases and roasts high-quality whole bean coffees and sells them, along with fresh, rich-brewed coffees, Italian-style espresso beverages, cold blended beverages, a variety of pastries and confections, coffee-related accessories and equipment, a selection of premium teas, and a line of compact discs, primarily through company-operated retail stores.

The following items were adapted from the annual report of Starbucks Corporation for the period ending September 30, 2001:

	In Thousands
1. Accounts payable	$ 127,905
2. Accounts receivable	90,455
3. Accrued expenses payable	244,724
4. Additions to property, plant, and equipment	384,215
5. Checks drawn in excess of bank balance	61,987
6. Cost of sales	1,112,785
7. General and administrative expenses	151,416
8. Income tax expense	107,712
9. Net cash provided by operating activities	460,826

(continued)

	In Thousands
10. Net sales	2,648,980
11. Other operating expenses	256,827
12. Other income (loss)	36,443
13. Property, plant, and equipment	1,135,784
14. Retained earnings (September 30, 2001)	589,713
15. Store operating expenses	875,473

Using the following notation, indicate on which financial statement you would find each of the 15 items:

IS   Income statement
RE   Retained earnings statement
BS   Balance sheet
SCF   Statement of cash flows

EXERCISE 1-19
Income statement
OBJECTIVE 4

✓ Net income: $181,210

Based on the **Starbucks Corporation** financial statement data in Exercise 1-18, prepare an income statement for the year ending September 30, 2001.

EXERCISE 1-20
Retained earnings statement
OBJECTIVE 4

Based on the **Starbucks Corporation** financial statement data in Exercise 1-18, prepare a retained earnings statement for the year ending September 30, 2001. The retained earnings as of October 1, 2000, was $408,503, and Starbucks paid no dividends during the year.

EXERCISE 1-21
Financial statement items
OBJECTIVE 4

The McDonald's menu of hamburgers, cheeseburgers, the Big Mac, Quarter Pounder, Filet-O-Fish, and Chicken McNuggets is familiar, but McDonald's financial statements probably are not so familiar. The following items were adapted from a recent annual report of **McDonald's Corporation**:

1. Accounts payable
2. Accrued interest payable
3. Cash
4. Cash provided by operations
5. Capital stock outstanding
6. Food and packaging costs used in operations
7. Income tax expense
8. Interest expense
9. Inventories
10. Long-term debt payable
11. Net income
12. Net increase in cash
13. Notes payable
14. Notes receivable
15. Occupancy and rent expense
16. Payroll expense
17. Prepaid expenses not yet used in operations
18. Property and equipment
19. Retained earnings
20. Sales

Identify the financial statement on which each of the preceding items would appear. An item may appear on more than one statement. Use the following notation:

IS   Income statement
RE   Retained earnings statement
BS   Balance sheet
SCF   Statement of cash flows

EXERCISE 1-22
Financial statements
OBJECTIVE 4

Aspen Realty, organized February 1, 2004, is owned and operated by Lynn Soby. How many errors can you find in the following financial statements for Aspen Realty, prepared after its second month of operations?

✓ Correct Amount of
Total Assets is $13,875

Aspen Realty
Income Statement
March 31, 2004

Sales commissions		$37,100
Operating expenses:		
Office salaries expense	$23,150	
Rent expense	7,800	
Automobile expense	1,750	
Miscellaneous expense	550	
Supplies expense	225	
Total operating expenses		33,475
Net income		$13,625

Lynn Soby
Retained Earnings Statement
March 31, 2003

Retained earnings, March 1, 2004	$ 2,450
Less dividends during March	1,000
	$ 1,450
Net income for the month	13,625
Retained earnings, March 31, 2004	$16,075

Balance Sheet
For the Month Ended March 31, 2004

Assets

Cash		$ 2,350
Accounts payable		2,300
Total assets		$ 4,650

Liabilities

Accounts receivable		$10,200
Supplies		1,325

Stockholders' Equity

Capital stock	$ 6,500	
Retained earnings	15,075	
Total liabilities and stockholders' equity		21,575
		$33,100

EXERCISE 1-23
Accounting concepts
OBJECTIVE 5

Match each of the following statements with the appropriate accounting concept. Some concepts can be used more than once, and others might not be used at all. Use the notation on the following page to indicate the appropriate accounting concept.

Accounting Concept	Notation
Accounting period concept	P
Adequate disclosure concept	D
Business entity concept	B
Cost concept	C
Going concern concept	G
Matching concept	M
Objectivity concept	O
Unit of measure concept	U

Statements

1. ____ The changes in financial condition are reported for November.
2. ____ Personal transactions of owners are kept separate from the business.
3. ____ Land worth $500,000 is reported at its original purchase price of $120,000.
4. ____ Assume that a business will continue forever.
5. ____ This concept supports relying on an independent actuary (statistician), rather than the chief operating officer of the corporation, to estimate a pension liability.
6. ____ This concept justifies recording only transactions that are expressed in dollars.
7. ____ Material litigation involving the corporation is described in a footnote.
8. ____ December utilities costs are reported as expenses along with the December revenues.
9. ____ If this concept were ignored, the confidence of users in the financial statements could not be maintained.
10. ____ Changes in the use of accounting methods from one period to the next are described in the notes to the financial statements.

EXERCISE 1-24
Business entity concept
OBJECTIVE 5

Bag-One Sports Inc. sells hunting and fishing equipment and provides guided hunting and fishing trips. Bag-One Sports Inc. is owned and operated by Marc Trailer, a well-known sports enthusiast and hunter. Marc's wife, Robin, owns and operates Red Bird Boutique Inc., a women's clothing store. Marc and Robin have established a trust fund to finance their children's college education. The trust fund is maintained by First Wyoming Bank in the name of the children, Sparrow and Trout.

For each of the following transactions, identify which of the entities listed should record the transaction in its records.

Entities

B	Bag-One Sports Inc.
F	First Wyoming Bank
R	Red Bird Boutique Inc.
X	None of the above

1. Marc received a cash advance from customers for a guided hunting trip.
2. Robin deposited a $5,000 personal check in the trust fund at First Wyoming Bank.
3. Robin purchased three dozen spring dresses from a Denver designer for a special spring sale.
4. Marc paid a local doctor for his annual physical, which was required by the worker's compensation insurance policy carried by Bag-One Sports Inc.
5. Marc paid for an advertisement in a hunters' magazine.
6. Robin purchased mutual fund shares as an investment for the children's trust.
7. Marc paid for dinner and a movie to celebrate their tenth wedding anniversary.
8. Robin donated several dresses from inventory to a local charity auction for the benefit of a women's abuse shelter.
9. Marc paid a breeder's fee for an English springer spaniel to be used as a hunting guide dog.
10. Robin paid her dues to the Young Republican's Club.

Problems

PROBLEM 1 | 1
Missing amounts from financial statements
OBJECTIVE 4

✓ a. $15,000

The financial statements at the end of Magic Realty Inc.'s first month of operations follow.

Magic Realty Inc.
Income Statement
For the Month Ended April 30, 2004

Fees earned		$ (a)
Operating expenses:		
Wages expense	$4,250	
Rent expense	1,600	
Utilities expense	(b)	
Supplies expense	900	
Miscellaneous expenses	550	
Total operating expenses		8,800
Net income		$ (c)

Magic Realty Inc.
Retained Earnings Statement
For the Month Ended April 30, 2004

Net income for April	$ (c)
Less dividends	3,000
Retained earnings, April 30, 2004	$ (d)

Magic Realty Inc.
Balance Sheet
April 30, 2004

Assets	
Cash	$ 2,900
Supplies	1,100
Land	20,000
Total assets	$ (e)

Liabilities	
Accounts payable	$ 800

Stockholders' Equity		
Capital stock	$20,000	
Retained earnings	(f)	(g)
Total liabilities and stockholders' equity		$ (h)

Magic Realty Inc.
Statement of Cash Flows
For the Month Ended April 30, 2004

Cash flows from operating activities:		
Cash received from customers	$ (i)	
Deduct cash payments for expenses and payments to creditors	9,100	
Net cash flows from operating activities		$ (j)
Cash flows from investing activities:		
Cash payment for purchase of land		(k)
Cash flows from financing activities:		
Cash received from issuing capital stock	(l)	
Deduct dividends	(m)	
Net cash flows from financing activities		(n)
Net cash flow and April 30, 2004 cash balance		$ (o)

Instructions

1. Would you classify a realty business such as Magic Realty as a manufacturing, merchandising, or service business?
2. By analyzing the interrelationships between the financial statements, determine the proper amounts for (a) through (o).

PROBLEM 1 | 2
Income statement,
retained earnings
statement, and balance
sheet

OBJECTIVE 4

✓ Net income: $40,865

Following are the amounts of the assets and liabilities of Fly Away Travel Agency at December 31, 2004, the end of the current year, and its revenue and expenses for the year. The retained earnings were $4,500 and the capital stock was $10,000 on January 1, 2004, the beginning of the current year. During the current year, dividends of $30,000 were paid.

Accounts Payable	$ 3,200
Accounts Receivable	19,500
Cash	7,200
Fees Earned	117,480
Miscellaneous Expense	1,750
Rent Expense	27,000
Supplies	1,865
Supplies Expense	2,125
Utilities Expense	10,240
Wages Expense	35,500

Instructions

1. Prepare an income statement for the current year ended December 31, 2004.
2. Prepare a retained earnings statement for the current year ended December 31, 2004.
3. Prepare a balance sheet as of December 31, 2004.

PROBLEM 1 | 3
Income statement,
retained earnings
statement, and balance
sheet

OBJECTIVE 4

✓ Net income: $395,839

The following financial data were adapted from the annual report of **Best Buy Inc.** for the period ending March 31, 2001:

	In Thousands
Accounts payable	$ 1,772,722
Accrued liabilities	827,036
Capital stock	493,786
Cash	746,879
Cost of goods sold	12,267,459
Income taxes	245,640
Interest income	37,171
Inventories	1,766,934
Goodwill	385,355
Other assets	183,370
Other liabilities	417,901
Property, plant, and equipment	1,444,172
Receivables	209,031
Retained earnings (February 26, 2000)	828,457
Sales	15,326,552
Selling, general, and administrative expenses	2,454,785

Instructions

1. Prepare Best Buy's income statement for the year ending March 31, 2001.
2. Prepare Best Buy's retained earnings statement for the year ending March 31, 2001. (*Note:* During the year, Best Buy did not pay any dividends.)
3. Prepare a balance sheet as of March 31, 2001, for Best Buy.

PROBLEM 1 | 4
Statement of cash flows
OBJECTIVE 4

✓ Net decrease in cash:
$3,844

The following cash data were adapted from the annual report of **Best Buy Inc.** for the period ending March 31, 2001. The cash balance as of April 1, 2000, was $750,723 (in thousands).

Payments for property, plant, and equipment	$657,706
Payments for purchase of other long-term assets	372,096
Payments for long-term debt	17,625
Net cash flows from operating activities	808,204
Receipts from issuing capital stock	235,379

Instructions

Prepare Best Buy's statement of cash flows for the year ending March 31, 2001.

PROBLEM 1 | 5
Financial statements, including statement of cash flows
OBJECTIVE 4

✓ Net income: $225,000

Lamar Corporation began operations on January 1, 2004, as an online retailer of computer software and hardware. The following financial statement data were taken from Lamar's records at the end of its first year of operations, December 31, 2004.

Accounts payable	$ 30,000
Accounts receivable	48,000
Cash	?
Cash receipts from operating activities	837,000
Cash payments for operating activities	700,000
Capital stock	250,000
Cost of sales	400,000
Dividends	25,000
Income tax expense	140,000
Income taxes payable	20,000
Interest expense	15,000
Inventories	90,000
Note payable due in 2010	100,000
Property, plant, and equipment	378,000
Retained earnings	?
Sales	885,000
Selling and administrative expense	105,000

Instructions

1. Prepare an income statement for the year ending December 31, 2004.
2. Prepare a retained earnings statement for the year ending December 31, 2004.
3. Prepare a balance sheet as of December 31, 2004.
4. Prepare a statement of cash flows for the year ending December 31, 2004.

Activities

Activity 1–1
Business strategy
GROUP

Assume that you are the chief executive officer for Gold Kist Inc., a national poultry producer. The company's operations include hatching chickens through the use of breeder stock and feeding, raising, and processing the mature chicks into finished products. The finished products include breaded chicken nuggets and patties and deboned, skinless and marinated chicken. Gold Kist sells its products to schools, military services, fast-food chains, and grocery stores.

In groups of four or five, discuss the following business strategy and risk issues:

1. In a commodity business like poultry production, what do you think is the dominant business strategy? What are the implications for this dominant strategy for how you would run Gold Kist? *(continued)*

2. Identify at least two major business risks for operating Gold Kist.
3. How could Gold Kist try to differentiate its products?

Activity 1-2
Ethics and professional conduct in business

Joel Phinney, president of Phinney Enterprises, applied for a $150,000 loan from Bridger National Bank. The bank requested financial statements from Phinney Enterprises as a basis for granting the loan. Joel has told his accountant to provide the bank a balance sheet. Joel has decided to omit the other financial statements because there was a net loss during the past year.

In groups of three or four, discuss the following questions:

1. Is Joel behaving in a professional manner by omitting some of the financial statements?
2. a. What types of information about their businesses would owners be willing to provide bankers? What types of information would owners not be willing to provide?
   b. What types of information about a business would bankers want before extending a loan?
   c. What common interests are shared by bankers and business owners?

Activity 1-3
Net income vs. cash flow

On January 3, 2004, Dr. Brittany North established Expert Opinion, a medical practice organized as a proprietorship. The following conversation occurred the following August between Dr. North and a former medical school classmate, Dr. Charles Ryder, at an American Medical Association convention in Bermuda.

Dr. Ryder: Brittany, good to see you again. Why didn't you call when you were in Las Vegas? We could have had dinner together.
Dr. North: Actually, I never made it to Las Vegas this year. My husband and kids went up to our Lake Tahoe condo twice, but I got stuck in New York. I opened a new consulting practice this January and haven't had any time for myself since.
Dr. Ryder: I heard about it . . . Expert . . . something . . . right?
Dr. North: Yes, Expert Opinion. My husband chose the name.
Dr. Ryder: I've thought about doing something like that. Are you making any money? I mean, is it worth your time?
Dr. North: You wouldn't believe it. I started by opening a bank account with $30,000, and my July bank statement has a balance of $180,000. Not bad for seven months—all pure profit.
Dr. Ryder: Maybe I'll try it in Las Vegas. Let's have breakfast together tomorrow and you can fill me in on the details.

Comment on Dr. North's statement that the difference between the opening bank balance ($30,000) and the July statement balance ($180,000) is pure profit.

Activity 1-4
The accounting equation

Obtain the annual reports for three well-known companies, such as **Ford Motor Co.**, **General Motors**, **IBM**, **Microsoft**, or **Amazon.com**. These annual reports can be obtained from a library or the company's 10-K filing with the Securities and Exchange Commission at http://www.sec.gov/edgar.shtml.

To obtain annual report information, key in the company name on the "Search EDGAR Archives" form. EDGAR will list the reports available for the company. Click on the 10-K (or 10-K405) report for the year you want to download. If you wish, you can save the whole 10-K report to a file and then open it with your word processor.

Examine the balance sheet for each company and determine the total assets, liabilities, and stockholders' equity. Verify that total assets equal the total of the liabilities plus stockholders' equity.

Activity 1-5
Hershey's annual report

The financial statements of **Hershey Foods Corporation** are shown in Exhibits 5 through 8 of this chapter. Based upon these statements, answer the following questions.

1. What are Hershey's sales (in thousands)?
2. What is Hershey's cost of sales (in thousands)?
3. What is Hershey's net income (in thousands)?
4. What is Hershey's percentage of the cost of sales to sales? Round to one decimal point.
5. The percentage that a company adds to its cost of sales to determine the selling price is called a *markup*. What is Hershey's markup percentage? Round to one decimal point.
6. What is the percentage of net income to sales for Hershey's? Round to one decimal point.

Activity 1-6
Income statement analysis

The following data were adapted from the December 31, 2001, financial statements of **Tootsie Roll Industries Inc.**:

	In Thousands
Sales	$423,496
Cost of goods sold	216,657
Net income	65,687

1. What is Tootsie Roll's percentage of the cost of sales to sales? Round to one decimal point.
2. The percentage a company adds to its cost of sales to determine selling price is called a *markup*. What is Tootsie Roll's markup percentage? Round to one decimal point.
3. What is the percentage of net income to sales for Tootsie Roll? Round to one decimal point.
4. Compare your answers to (2) and (3) with those of Hershey Foods Corporation in Activity 1-5. What are your conclusions?

Activity 1-7
Horizontal analysis

The following data were adapted from the January 31, 2000 and 1999, financial statements (in millions) of **Kmart Corporation**:

	For year ending....	
	2000	1999
Sales	$37,028	$35,925
Cost of sales	29,658	28,111
Selling, general, and administrative expenses	7,415	6,514

1. Prepare a horizontal analysis income statement for Kmart Corporation that includes gross profit and operating income before taxes. Round to one decimal place.
2. Comment on the results of your horizontal analysis of Kmart.

Activity 1-8
Financial analysis of Enron Corporation

Enron Corporation, headquartered in Houston, Texas, until recently provided products and services to natural gas, electricity, and communications wholesale and retail customers. Enron's operations were conducted through a variety of subsidiaries and affiliates that involve transporting gas through pipelines, transmitting electricity, and managing energy commodities. The following data were taken from Enron's December 31, 2000, financial statements.

	In Millions
Total revenues	$100,789
Total costs and expenses	98,836
Operating income	1,953
Net income	$ 979
Total assets	$ 65,503
Total liabilities	54,033
Total stockholders' equity	$ 11,470
Net cash flows from operating activities	$ 4,779
Net cash flows from investing activities	(4,264)
Net cash flows from financing activities	571
Net increase in cash	$ 1,086

At the end of 2000, the market price of Enron's stock was approximately $83 per share. As of March 15, 2002, Enron's stock was selling for $0.22 per share.

Review the preceding financial statement data and search the Internet for articles on Enron Corporation. Briefly explain why Enron's stock dropped so dramatically in such a short time.

Answers to Self-Study Questions

1. **D** A corporation, organized in accordance with state or federal statutes, is a separate legal entity in which ownership is divided into shares of stock (answer D). A proprietorship (answer A) is an unincorporated business owned by one individual. A service business (answer B) provides services to its customers. It can be organized as a proprietorship, partnership, or corporation. A partnership (answer C) is an unincorporated business owned by two or more individuals.

2. **A** The resources owned by a business are called assets (answer A). The debts of the business are called liabilities (answer B), and the equity of the owners is called owners' equity (answer D). The relationship between assets, liabilities, and owners' equity is expressed as the accounting equation (answer C).

3. **A** The balance sheet is a listing of the assets, liabilities, and owner's equity of a business at a specific date (answer A). The income statement (answer B) is a summary of the revenue and expenses of a business for a specific period of time. The retained earnings statement (answer C) summarizes the changes in retained earnings

during a specific period of time. The statement of cash flows (answer D) summarizes the cash receipts and cash payments for a specific period of time.

4. **D** The accounting equation is:

$$Assets = Liabilities + Owners' Equity$$

Therefore, if assets are $20,000 and liabilities are $12,000, stockholders' equity is $8,000 (answer D), as indicated in the following computation:

Assets	=	Liabilities + Stockholders' Equity
+$20,000	=	+$12,000 + Stockholders' Equity
+$20,000 − $12,000	=	Stockholders' Equity
+$8,000	=	Stockholders' Equity

5. **B** Net income is the excess of revenue over expenses, or $7,500 (answer B). If expenses exceed revenue, the difference is a net loss. Dividends are the opposite of the stockholders investing in the business and do not affect the amount of net income or net loss.

2

LEARNING OBJECTIVES

OBJECTIVE 1

Describe the basic elements of a financial accounting information system.

OBJECTIVE 2

Describe the cash and accrual bases of accounting.

OBJECTIVE 3

Use the cash basis of accounting to analyze, record, and summarize transactions for a corporation's first period of operations.

OBJECTIVE 4

Use the cash basis of accounting to prepare financial statements for the first period of operations.

OBJECTIVE 5

Use the cash basis of accounting for recording transactions and preparing financial statements for a second period of operations.

OBJECTIVE 6

Describe the advantages and disadvantages of the cash basis of accounting.

OBJECTIVE 7

Describe and illustrate how vertical analysis can be used to analyze and evaluate a company's performance.

The Cash Basis of Accounting

In Chapter 1 we introduced you to the nature of businesses and the basic concepts of financial statements. Financial statements are critical to the proper functioning of free-market economy. Disclosure such as that provided by financial statements is termed *financial transparency*. Financial transparency encourages individuals to invest in businesses in which they have no direct control or ability to monitor.

For example, would you be willing to invest in the stock of Lucent Technologies, Microsoft, Amazon.com, or Intel without an ability to monitor the economic performance of the company and its management? No, you wouldn't. However, financial statements provide you the transparency necessary to monitor the performance of these companies and, thus, provide you an incentive to invest in their stocks. Likewise, financial institutions such as First Union, J.P. Morgan Chase, TIAA-CREF, Bank One Corporation, and state pension and mutual funds demand financial transparency before they are willing to loan funds to businesses.

In this chapter, we continue our discussion of financial statements and their role in enhancing financial transparency. We begin by describing the basic elements of a financial accounting system that will enable the preparation of financial statements. We then distinguish types of accounting systems and illustrate the simplest form of an accounting system based on a cash basis. In doing so, this chapter serves as a foundation for our later discussions of modern-day accounting systems and financial reporting. However, throughout this discussion and the remainder of this text, you should not forget that a primary benefit of financial reporting is its role in facilitating the functioning of a free-market economy.

Elements of an Accounting System

Describe the basic elements of a financial accounting information system.

A financial accounting system is designed to produce financial statements. You should recall from Chapter 1 that the basic financial statements are the income statement, retained earnings statement, balance sheet, and statement of cash flows. So what are the basic elements of an accounting system that enable the preparation of these statements?

The basic elements of a **financial accounting system** include (1) a set of rules for determining what, when, and the amount that should be recorded for economic events, (2) a framework for preparing financial statements, and (3) one or more controls to determine whether errors could have arisen in the recording process. These basic elements are found in all financial accounting systems—from those of a local retailer or hardware store to **Microsoft**, **General Motors**, **Boeing**, and **William J. Wrigley Jr. Company**.

Rules

The set of rules for determining what, when, and the amount that should be recorded for economic events is derived from the eight concepts we discussed in Chapter 1. In addition, the set of rules depends on whether the business uses the cash basis or the accrual basis of accounting. We describe and illustrate the set of rules for the cash basis of accounting in this chapter. The set of rules for the accrual basis of accounting are described and illustrated in Chapter 3.

Framework

The accounting equation provides a framework for recording and summarizing economic events and preparing financial statements. You should recall from Chapter 1 that the accounting equation is expressed as follows:

$$\text{Assets} = \text{Liabilities} + \text{Stockholders' Equity}$$

Using this equation, accounting systems are designed to record and summarize the effects of economic events on each element of the equation. That is, an economic event is analyzed in terms of its effect on assets, liabilities, or stockholders' equity.

A **transaction** is an economic event that under generally accepted accounting principles affects an element of the accounting equation and, therefore, must be recorded. A transaction could affect only one, two, or all three elements of the accounting equation. For example, equipment purchased for cash affects only assets. That is, one asset (equipment) increases while another asset (cash) decreases. If, on the other hand, the equipment is purchased on credit, both assets (equipment) and liabilities (accounts or notes payable) increase.

By keeping a running total of the effects of transactions on each element, the equation also provides a framework for summarizing the overall effects of a series of transactions. For example, by keeping a record of increases and decreases in cash, the net change in cash for a period can be determined. Likewise, by keeping a record of sales, the total sales for the period can be determined.

Using the accounting equation as the framework for recording and summarizing transactions also facilitates preparing financial statements. This is so because the accounting equation represents all of the balance sheet elements and, thus, the financial condition of a company at a point in time. Changes in financial condition can be measured by analyzing changes in two balance sheets for two periods of time. By doing so, the income statement, retained earnings statement, and statement of cash flows can be prepared. These relationships are illustrated here for an annual accounting period ending on December 31, 2004.

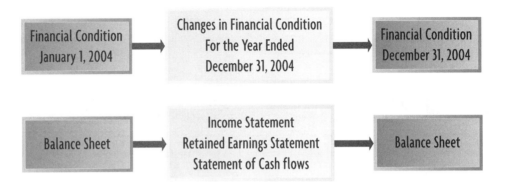

Controls

Using the accounting equation as a framework for designing an accounting system provides the control that, after recording transactions, total assets must equal total liabilities plus total stockholders' equity. If at the end of the period the equality does not hold, an error has occurred in either recording or summarizing transactions. For example, if a $10,000 purchase of equipment for cash is incorrectly recorded as an increase in both equipment and cash, the total assets will exceed the total liabilities and stockholders' equity by $20,000 at the end of the period. Likewise, if equipment was increased by $10,000 but cash was not decreased by $10,000, the total assets will exceed total liabilities and stockholders' equity by $10,000 at the end of the period. In both cases, the inequality of the equation indicates that an error has occurred in the recording process.

Before the financial statements are prepared, errors should be discovered and corrected. However, the equality of the equation at the end of the period doesn't necessarily mean that no errors have occurred. For example, assume that a business purchased $10,000 of equipment on credit and recorded the transaction as an increase in equipment of $10,000. However, instead of increasing the liabilities by $10,000, the transaction was recorded as a $10,000 decrease in cash. In this case, the accounting equation still balances, even though cash and liabilities are understated by $10,000. For this reason, accounting systems are designed with additional controls for recording and summarizing transactions. We discuss these controls in later chapters.

Cash and Accrual Bases of Accounting

OBJECTIVE   2

Describe the cash and accrual bases of accounting.

An accounting system is based on either the cash basis or the accrual basis of accounting. The accrual basis is used by large businesses and is required of publicly held corporations, such as **Amazon.com** and **Wm. J. Wrigley Jr. Company**. The cash basis of accounting is often used by individuals and small businesses.[1] For example,

[1]Some businesses use a modified-cash or tax basis of accounting. These bases of accounting are covered in advanced accounting texts.

you probably use a cash basis because your checkbook is your primary accounting record. You keep track of your deposits (cash receipts) and checks (cash payments). Periodically, the bank sends you a statement that you use to verify the accuracy of your record keeping.

Both the cash and accrual bases of accounting use the business entity, cost, going concern, objectivity, unit of measure, adequate disclosure, and accounting period concepts discussed in Chapter 1. As we discuss in the following paragraphs, the primary difference between the cash and accrual bases of accounting involves the matching concept.

BUSINESS STRATEGY

Got the Flu? Why Not Chew Some Gum?

Facing a slumping market for sugared chewing gum, such as Juicy Fruit and Doublemint, Wm. J. Wrigley Jr. Company is reinventing itself with a strategy to expand its product lines and introduce new chewing gum applications. Wrigley's new products include sugarless breath mints and more powerful flavored mint chewing gum, such as Extra Polar Ice. In addition, Wrigley is experimenting with health care applications of chewing gum. Its Health Care Division has already developed Surpass, an antacid chewing gum to compete with Rolaids and Mylanta. In addition, Wrigley is experimenting with a cold-relief chewing gum and a gum that would provide dental benefits, such as whitening teeth and reducing plaque. Given that the U.S. population is aging, the company figures that people might prefer chewing gum to taking pills for sore throats, colds, or the flu. The effects of these new strategic initiatives will ultimately be reflected in Wrigley's financial statements.

Source: Adapted from David Barboza, "A Young Heir Has New Plans at Old Company," *The New York Times,* August 28, 2001.

Using the Cash Basis of Accounting

Under the **cash basis of accounting,** a business records only transactions involving increases or decreases of its cash. To illustrate, assume that a real estate agency sells a $300,000 piece of property on December 28, 2003. In selling the property, the agency earns a commission of 8% of the selling price. However, the agency does not receive the $24,000 commission check from the attorney until January 3, 2004. Under the cash basis, the real estate agency will not record the commission (revenue) until January 3, 2004.

Under the cash basis, expenses are recorded only when cash is paid. For example, a December cellular phone bill that is paid in January would be recorded as a January expense, not a December expense. Thus, under the cash basis, the matching concept does not determine when expenses are recorded. That is, expenses are recorded when paid in cash, not necessarily in the period when the revenue is earned.

Using the Accrual Basis of Accounting

Under the **accrual basis of accounting**, revenue is recorded as it is earned regardless of when cash is received. To illustrate using the preceding example, the real estate agency records the commissions (revenue) of $24,000 as earned on December 28, 2003, even though the check (cash) is not received until January 3, 2004. Once revenue has been earned and recorded, any expenses that have been incurred in generating the revenue are recorded and thus matched against that revenue. For example, a December cellular phone bill would be recorded in December as an increase in expenses and liabilities, even though it is not paid until January. In this way, the December phone expense is matched against the revenue it helped generate in December.

Summary of Differences between the Cash and Accrual Bases of Accounting

Exhibit 1 summarizes the basic differences in recording revenue and expenses under the cash and accrual bases of accounting.

EXHIBIT 1

Cash versus Accrual Accounting

	Cash Basis	Accrual Basis
Revenue is recorded	When cash is received	When revenue is earned
Expense is recorded	When cash is paid	When expense is incurred in generating revenue

In the remainder of this chapter, we illustrate recording transactions and preparing financial statements using the cash basis of accounting. We illustrate the accrual basis of accounting in Chapter 3. Because the cash basis is simpler, it allows us to better focus on how the accounting equation is used as the framework for accounting systems. In addition, a thorough understanding of the cash basis should enhance your understanding of the accrual basis. In turn, this understanding will facilitate your ability to analyze and interpret the financial statements of publicly held corporations prepared under the accrual basis.

Using the Cash Basis for a Corporation's First Period of Operations

OBJECTIVE 3

Use the cash basis of accounting to analyze, record, and summarize transactions for a corporation's first period of operations.

Using the accounting equation as our basic framework, we illustrate the recording of transactions under the cash basis of accounting. We assume that on September 1, 2003, Lee Landry, M.D., organizes a professional corporation to practice general medicine. The business is to be known as Family Health Care, P.C. We describe each transaction or group of similar transactions during September, the first month of operations. We then describe how the accounting equation can be used to analyze the effects of the transactions on the financial condition of the business. We begin with Dr. Landry's investment to establish the business.

Transaction a.   Dr. Landry deposits $6,000 in a bank account in the name of Family Health Care, P.C., in return for shares of stock in the corporation. We refer to stock issued to the owner(s) (stockholder[s]) such as Lee Landry as *capital stock*. The effect of this transaction is to increase the asset (cash), on the left side of the equation, by $6,000. Increases are recorded as positive numbers; decreases are recorded as negative numbers. Thus, the $6,000 deposit is recorded as a positive addition to Cash. To balance the equation, the stockholders' equity (capital stock) on the right side of the equation is increased by the same amount. This $6,000 is recorded as a positive addition to Capital Stock. The effect of this transaction on Family Health Care's accounting equation follows.

	Assets	=	Stockholders' Equity	
			Capital	
	Cash	=	Stock	
a.	6,000		6,000	Investment

Note that the equation relates only to the business, Family Health Care, P.C. Lee Landry's personal assets (such as a home or a personal bank account) and personal liabilities are excluded from the equation. The business is treated as a separate entity, with cash of $6,000 and stockholders' equity of $6,000.

ETHICS IN ACTION

Unethical practices can occur in promoting the issuance of stock to stockholders. It is considered fraudulent to hide known risks from potential stockholders, use stock proceeds for purposes other than indicated, or sell counterfeit shares. For example, two people pleaded guilty for fraudulently selling $15 million of phony shares of **MindArrow Systems, Inc.** stock.

Transaction b.   Family Health Care's next transaction is to borrow $10,000 from First National Bank to finance its operations. To borrow the $10,000, Lee Landry had to pledge personal assets as security for the loan and sign a note payable in the name of Family Health Care. The note payable is a liability or a claim on assets that Family Health Care must satisfy (pay) in the future. In addition, the note payable requires the payment of interest of $100 per month until the note is due in full on September 30, 2009. At the end of September, we will record the payment of $100 of interest.

The items in the equation prior to the borrowing transaction and the effect of the borrowing transaction are shown next. The new amounts or balances of the items are also shown.

	Assets	=	Liabilities	+	Stockholders' Equity	
			Notes		Capital	
	Cash	=	Payable	+	Stock	
a.	6,000				6,000	
b.	10,000		10,000			Loan from bank
Bal.	16,000		10,000		6,000	

Observe how this transaction changed the mix of assets and liabilities but did not change Family Health Care's stockholders' equity. That is, assets minus liabilities still equal stockholders' equity of $6,000.

Transaction c.   Next, Family Health Care buys land for $12,000 cash. The land is located near a new suburban hospital that is under construction. Lee Landry plans to rent office space and equipment for several months. When the hospital is completed, Family Health Care will build on the land.

The purchase of the land changes the makeup of the assets, but it does not change the total assets. The effect of this transaction on the accounting equation follows.

	Assets			=	Liabilities	+	Stockholders' Equity	
					Notes		Capital	
	Cash	+	Land	=	Payable	+	Stock	
Bal.	16,000				10,000		6,000	
c.	−12,000		12,000					Purchase of land
Bal.	4,000		12,000		10,000		6,000	

Transactions (b) and (c) have not improved the stockholders' equity of Family Health Care. They have simply changed the mix of assets and increased the liability, notes payable. However, the objective of businesses is to improve stockholders' equity through operations.

How do businesses improve stockholders' equity? By earning revenues in excess of expenses. Revenues increase stockholders' equity through the business operations, and expenses decrease stockholders' equity. When revenues for a period exceed the expenses used to earn the revenues, the financial condition of the business will have improved. This improvement in financial condition results in an increase in the stockholders' equity of the business. Likewise, if the expenses exceed the revenues for a period of time, the stockholders' equity of the business will decrease. For this reason, transactions involving revenues and expenses are recorded as part of stockholders' equity in the accounting equation. In the following paragraphs, we illustrate the recording of revenue and expense transactions for Family Health Care.

ETHICS IN ACTION

To boost earnings prior to the end of a reporting period, managers sometimes engage in the questionable practice of "channel stuffing." Channel stuffing enhances revenue (accrual basis) by persuading a distributor to take additional products. The practice backfired for Lucent Technologies, which had to take back $452 million of equipment from distributors and reverse this amount of previously recognized revenue.

Transaction d.   During the first month of operations, Family Health Care earns patient fees of $5,500, receiving the amount in cash. These transactions increase Cash and Stockholders' Equity by $5,500, as follows.

	Assets		=	Liabilities	+	Stockholders' Equity			
	Cash	+ Land	=	Notes Payable	+	Capital Stock	+	Retained Earnings	
Bal.	4,000	12,000		10,000		6,000			
d.	5,500							5,500	Fees earned
Bal.	9,500	12,000		10,000		6,000		5,500	

Unlike transactions (b) and (c), the stockholders' equity of Family Health Care has increased by $5,500 as a result of this transaction. You should note that the increase in stockholders' equity from revenue is listed in the equation under Retained Earnings. Retained earnings is the stockholders' equity created by the business operations (revenues less expenses). Transactions affecting earnings are kept separate from transactions related to stockholders' investments (capital stock). This is useful in preparing reports to owners and creditors and in satisfying some states' legal requirements that we will discuss later in the text.

Transaction e.   For Family Health Care, the expenses paid during the month were as follows: wages, $1,125; rent, $950; utilities, $450; interest, $100; miscellaneous, $275. Miscellaneous expenses include small amounts paid for such items as postage due and newspaper and magazine purchases. This group of expense transactions reduces cash and stockholders' equity, as shown below.

	Assets		=	Liabilities	+	Stockholders' Equity			
	Cash	+ Land	=	Notes Payable	+	Capital Stock	+	Retained Earnings	
Bal.	9,500	12,000		10,000		6,000		5,500	
e.	−2,900							−1,125	Wages expense
								−950	Rent expense
								−450	Utilities expense
								−100	Interest expense
								−275	Misc. exp.
Bal.	6,600	12,000		10,000		6,000		2,600	

Transaction f.   At the end of the month, Family Health Care pays $1,500 to its stockholder (Dr. Lee Landry) as dividends. Dividends are distributions of business earnings to stockholders. Dividend payments reduce cash and stockholders' equity. The effect of this transaction is shown as follows:

	Assets		=	Liabilities	+	Stockholders' Equity			
	Cash	+ Land	=	Notes Payable	+	Capital Stock	+	Retained Earnings	
Bal.	6,600	12,000		10,000		6,000		2,600	
f.	−1,500							−1,500	Dividends
Bal.	5,100	12,000		10,000		6,000		1,100	

You should be careful not to confuse dividends with expenses. Dividends do not represent assets consumed or services used in the process of earning revenues. The decrease in stockholders' equity from dividends is listed in the equation under Retained Earnings. This is done because dividends are considered a distribution of earnings to the owner(s).

The transactions of Family Health Care are summarized as follows in Exhibit 2. The transactions are identified by letter, and the balance of each item is shown after each transaction.

EXHIBIT 2 *Family Health Care Summary of Transactions for September*

	Assets			=	Liabilities	+	Stockholders' Equity		
					Notes		Capital	Retained	
	Cash	+	Land	=	Payable	+	Stock	+ Earnings	
a.	6,000						6,000		Investment
b.	10,000				10,000				Loan from bank
Bal.	16,000				10,000		6,000		
c.	−12,000		12,000						Purchase of land
Bal.	4,000		12,000		10,000		6,000		
d.	5,500							5,500	Fees earned
Bal.	9,500		12,000		10,000		6,000	5,500	
e.	−2,900							−1,125	Wages expense
								−950	Rent expense
								−450	Utilities expense
								−100	Interest expense
								−275	Miscellaneous exp.
Bal.	6,600		12,000		10,000		6,000	2,600	
f.	−1,500							−1,500	Dividends
Bal.	5,100		12,000		10,000		6,000	1,100	

In reviewing the preceding illustration, you should note the following, which apply to all types of businesses:

1. The effect of every transaction is an increase or a decrease in one or more of the accounting equation elements.
2. The two sides of the accounting equation are always equal.
3. The stockholders' equity is increased by amounts invested by stockholders (capital stock). In addition, stockholders' equity (retained earnings) is increased by revenues and decreased by expenses. Finally, stockholders' equity (retained earnings) is decreased by dividends distributed to stockholders. The effect of these four types of transactions on stockholders' equity is illustrated in Exhibit 3.

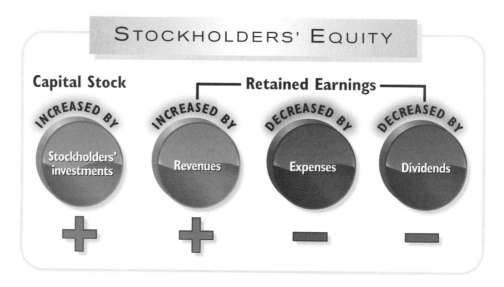

Financial Statements for a Corporation's First Period of Operations

OBJECTIVE   4

Use the cash basis of
accounting to prepare
financial statements
for the first period of
operations.

In Exhibit 2, the September transactions for Family Health Care are listed in the order that they occurred. This exhibit, however, is not very user friendly in that it does
not group and summarize similar transactions together. As we described and illustrated in Chapter 1, the accounting reports that provide this summarized information
are the financial statements.

The September financial statements for Family Health Care are illustrated in Exhibit 4. The data for the statements were taken from the transactions summary shown
in Exhibit 2. You should note that each financial statement is identified by the *name*
of the business, the *title* of the statement, and the *date* or *period of time.*

EXHIBIT 4

*Family Health Care
Financial Statements for
September*

FAMILY HEALTH CARE, P.C.		
Income Statement		
For the Month Ended September 30, 2003		
Fees earned		$5,500
Operating expenses:		
Wages expense	$1,125	
Rent expense	950	
Utilities expense	450	
Interest expense	100	
Miscellaneous expenses	275	
Total operating expenses		2,900
Net income		$2,600

EXHIBIT 4
Concluded

FAMILY HEALTH CARE, P.C.
Retained Earnings Statement
For the Month Ended September 30, 2003

Net income for September	$2,600
Less dividends	1,500
Retained earnings, September 30, 2003	$1,100

FAMILY HEALTH CARE, P.C.
Balance Sheet
September 30, 2003

Assets		
Cash		$ 5,100
Land		12,000
Total assets		$17,100
Liabilities		
Notes payable		$10,000
Stockholders' Equity		
Capital stock	$6,000	
Retained earnings	1,100	7,100
Total liabilities and stockholders' equity		$17,100

FAMILY HEALTH CARE, P.C.
Statement of Cash Flows
For the Month Ended September 30, 2003

Cash flows from operating activities:			
Cash received from customers			$ 5,500
Deduct cash payments for expenses			2,900
Net cash flow from operating activities			$ 2,600
Cash flows from investing activities:			
Cash payments for acquisition of land			$(12,000)
Cash flows from financing activities:			
Cash received from sale of cap. stock	$ 6,000		
Cash received from notes payable	10,000	$16,000	
Deduct cash dividends		1,500	
Net cash flow from financing activities			14,500
Net increase in cash			$ 5,100
September 1, 2003, cash balance			0
September 30, 2003, cash balance			$ 5,100

Income Statement

As shown in Exhibit 4, the income statement for Family Health Care reports fees earned of $5,500, total operating expenses of $2,900, and net income of $2,600. The $5,500 of fees earned was taken from the Retained Earnings column of Exhibit 2. Likewise, the expenses were summarized from the Retained Earnings column of Exhibit 2 and reported under the heading Operating Expenses. The expenses were listed in order of size, beginning with the largest expense. Miscellaneous expense is usually shown as the last item, regardless of the amount. The total operating expenses were then subtracted from the fees earned to arrive at the net income of $2,600. The effect of this net income is to increase retained earnings and stockholders' equity.

Retained Earnings Statement

Since Family Health Care has been in operation for only one month, it has no retained earnings at the beginning of September. The ending September balance is the change in retained earnings that results from net income and dividends. This change, $1,100, will be the beginning balance for October.

Balance Sheet

The amounts of Family Health Care's assets, liabilities, and stockholders' equity at the end of September appear on the last line of the summary of transactions. With the addition of a heading, the balance sheet is prepared as shown in Exhibit 4.

In the Liabilities section of Family Health Care's balance sheet, notes payable is the only liability. When there are two or more categories of liabilities, each should be listed and the total amount of liabilities reported. As with assets, liabilities should be presented in the order that they will be paid in cash. Thus, the notes payable due in 2009 will be listed after the obligations that are due in shorter time periods.

For Family Health Care, the September 30, 2003, stockholders' equity consists of $6,000 of capital stock and retained earnings of $1,100. The retained earnings amount is taken from the retained earnings statement.

Statement of Cash Flows

Family Health Care's statement of cash flows for September shows that cash increased from a zero balance at the beginning of the month to $5,100 at the end of the month. This $5,100 increase in cash was the result of cash flows from operating activities of $2,600. Family Health Care also reported net income of $2,600 for September. Under the cash basis of accounting, the net income and the cash flows from operating activities are the same. Under the accrual basis of accounting, this is normally not true.[2]

In addition to cash inflows of $2,600 from operating activities, Family Health Care spent $12,000 of cash for investing activities involving the purchase of land. This cash outflow related to investing activities was financed by an additional investment of $6,000 by Dr. Landry and $10,000 borrowed through a note payable at First National Bank. Family Health Care also distributed $1,500 in cash dividends during September.

---

[2]In Chapter 3, we discuss why net income and cash flows from operating activities differ under the accrual basis of accounting.

Using the Cash Basis for the Second Period of Operations

OBJECTIVE   5

Use the cash basis of accounting for recording transactions and preparing financial statements for a second period of operations.

To reinforce your understanding of recording transactions and preparing financial statements under the cash basis, we continue with Family Health Care's October transactions. During October, Family Health Care entered into the following transactions:

a. Received fees of $6,400 in cash.

b. Paid expenses in cash, as follows: wages, $1,370; rent, $950; utilities, $540; interest, $100; miscellaneous, $220.

c. Paid dividends of $1,000 in cash.

The preceding October transactions have been analyzed and entered into a summary of transactions for October, as shown in Exhibit 5. You should note that the summary of transactions for October begins with the ending balances as of September 30, 2003.

EXHIBIT 5 *Family Health Care Summary of Transactions for October*

	Assets		=	Liabilities	+	Stockholders' Equity			
	Cash	+ Land	=	Notes Payable	+	Capital Stock	+	Retained Earnings	
Bal.	5,100	12,000		10,000		6,000		1,100	
a.	6,400							6,400	Fees earned
Bal.	11,500	12,000		10,000		6,000		7,500	
b.	−3,180							−1,370	Wages expense
								−950	Rent expense
								−540	Utilities expense
								−100	Interest expense
								−220	Miscellaneous exp.
Bal.	8,320	12,000		10,000		6,000		4,320	
c.	−1,000							−1,000	Dividends
Bal.	7,320	12,000		10,000		6,000		3,320	

Family Health Care's financial statements for October are shown in Exhibit 6. These statements were prepared from the summary of transactions in Exhibit 5.

The income statement for October reports net income of $3,220. This is an increase of $620, or 23.8% ($620/2,600), from September's net income of $2,600. This increase in net income was due to fees increasing from $5,500 to $6,400, a $900, or 16.4% ($900/$5,500), increase from September. At the same time, total operating expenses increased only $280, or 9.7% ($280/$2,900). This suggests that Family Health Care's operations are profitable and expanding.

EXHIBIT 6

*Family Health Care
Financial Statements
for October*

FAMILY HEALTH CARE, P.C.
Income Statement
For the Month Ended October 31, 2003

Fees earned		$6,400
Operating expenses:		
Wages expense	$1,370	
Rent expense	950	
Utilities expense	540	
Interest expense	100	
Miscellaneous expenses	220	
Total operating expenses		3,180
Net income		$3,220

FAMILY HEALTH CARE, P.C.
Retained Earnings Statement
For the Month Ended October 31, 2003

Retained earnings, October 1, 2003		$1,100
Net income for October	$3,220	
Less dividends	1,000	2,220
Retained earnings, October 31, 2003		$3,320

FAMILY HEALTH CARE, P.C.
Balance Sheet
October 31, 2001

Assets		
Cash		$ 7,320
Land		12,000
Total assets		$19,320
Liabilities		
Notes payable		$10,000
Stockholders' Equity		
Capital stock	$6,000	
Retained earnings	3,320	9,320
Total liabilities and stockholders' equity		$19,320

The retained earnings statement reports an increase in retained earnings of $2,220. This increase is the result of net income ($3,220) less the dividends ($1,000) paid to Dr. Landry.

The balance sheet shows that total assets increased from $17,100 on September 30, 2003, to $19,320 on October 31. This increase of $2,220 was due to an increase in cash

EXHIBIT 6
Concluded

FAMILY HEALTH CARE, P.C.
Statement of Cash Flows
For the Month Ended October 31, 2001

Cash flows from operating activities:	
Cash received from customers	$ 6,400
Deduct cash payments for expenses	3,180
Net cash flow from operating activities	$ 3,220
Cash flows from investing activities	0
Cash flows from financing activities:	
Deduct cash dividends	(1,000)
Net increase in cash	$ 2,220
October 1, 2003 cash balance	5,100
October 31, 2001 cash balance	$ 7,320

from operations ($3,220) less the dividends ($1,000) that were paid to Dr. Landry. Total liabilities remained the same, but retained earnings and stockholders' equity increased by $2,220.

The statement of cash flows shows a net cash receipt from operations ($3,220) and a cash payment for dividends ($1,000). Recall that under the cash basis, the net income is the same as the net cash flows from operations. The ending cash balance of $7,320 also appears on the October 31 balance sheet.

Advantages and Disadvantages of the Cash Basis

OBJECTIVE 6

Describe the advantages and disadvantages of the cash basis of accounting.

The primary advantage of the cash basis of accounting is its simplicity. As shown in the illustrations for Family Health Care, it is relatively easy to use the cash basis to record and summarize transactions. In addition, the financial statements are easy to prepare, and the net income from operations is the same as the cash flows from operating activities.

The primary disadvantage of the cash basis is that revenues and expenses are not always properly matched on the income statement. This is so because revenues and expenses are recorded only when cash is received or paid. As a result, an expense can be reported in one period and its related revenue in another period, with the result that net income could be distorted. This is the primary reason that generally accepted accounting principles rely on the accrual basis of accounting. For this same reason, all publicly held corporations are required to use the accrual basis of accounting. If, on the other hand, cash receipts and payments are relatively stable and uniform over time, net income under the cash basis can approximate net income under the accrual basis. In such cases, the ease and simplicity of the cash basis could more than offset the additional costs of using the accrual basis. This is often the case for smaller businesses and individuals.

Vertical Analysis

The basic financial statements illustrated in this and the preceding chapter are primary sources of information that financial analysts and other stakeholders use in evaluating a company's performance. In Chapter 1, we illustrated horizontal analysis as one method of analyzing financial performance. Another method of analyzing comparative financial statements is to compute percentages of each item within a statement to a total within the statement. These percentages can then be compared across years. This type of analysis is called **vertical analysis**.

In vertical analysis of the balance sheet, each asset item is stated as a percentage of the total assets. Each liability and stockholders' equity item is stated as a percentage of total liabilities and stockholders' equity. To illustrate, Exhibit 7 shows comparative balance sheets for **Wm. J. Wrigley Jr. Company**, using vertical analysis.[3]

EXHIBIT 7   *Comparative Balance Sheets Using Vertical Analysis: Wm. J. Wrigley Jr. Company*

	December 31, 2001		December 31, 2000	
	Amount (thousands)	Percent	Amount (thousands)	Percent
Assets				
Cash and cash equivalents	$ 307,785	17.4%	$ 300,599	19.1%
Short-term investments	25,450	1.4	29,301	1.9
Accounts receivable	239,885	13.6	191,570	12.2
Inventories	278,981	15.8	253,291	16.1
Property, plant, and equipment	684,379	38.8	607,034	38.5
Other assets	229,168	13.0	192,945	12.3
Total assets	$1,765,648	100.0%	$1,574,740	100.0%
Liabilities				
Accounts payable	$ 91,225	5.2%	$ 73,129	4.6%
Dividends payable	42,741	2.4	39,467	2.5
Income and other taxes payable	68,467	3.9	60,976	3.9
Long-term liabilities	157,127	8.9	153,633	9.8
Other liabilities	129,891	7.4	114,638	7.3
Total liabilities	$ 489,451	27.7%	$ 441,843	28.1%
Stockholders' equity				
Total stockholders' equity	1,276,197	72.3	1,132,897	71.9
Total liabilities and stockholders' equity	$1,765,648	100.0%	$1,574,740	100.0%

To simplify, the stockholders' equity is shown as a single amount. A review of Exhibit 7 reveals no major changes in the makeup of Wrigley's December 31 balance sheets for 2001 and 2000.

[3]These financial statements have been adapted based on Securities and Exchange Commission filings.

In vertical analysis of the income statement, each item is stated as a percentage of sales. To illustrate, Exhibit 8 shows comparative income statements of Wm. J. Wrigley Jr. Company, using vertical analysis.

EXHIBIT 8

Comparative Income Statements Using Vertical Analysis Wm. J. Wrigley Jr. Company for Years Ending:

	December 31, 2001		December 31, 2000	
	Amount (thousands)	Percent	Amount (thousands)	Percent
Net sales	$2,429,646	100.0%	$2,145,706	100.0%
Cost of sales	997,054	41.1	904,266	42.1
Gross profit	$1,432,592	58.9%	$1,241,440	57.9%
Selling and administrative expenses	919,236	37.8	778,197	36.3
Operating income	$ 513,356	21.1%	$ 463,243	21.6%
Other income (expense)	14,010	0.6	16,069	0.7
Income before income taxes	$ 527,366	21.7%	$ 479,312	22.3%
Income taxes	164,380	6.8	150,370	7.0
Net income	$ 362,986	14.9%	$ 328,942	15.3%

Exhibit 8 reveals a slight decline in overall net income from 2000 to 2001 from 15.3% to 14.9% of sales. Gross profit improved from 57.9% to 58.9% of sales due to the decrease in the cost of sales from 42.1% to 41.1%. This increase in gross profit was offset by the increase in selling and administrative expenses from 36.3% to 37.8% of sales. As a result, operating income decreased from 21.6% to 21.1%. Other income and expense remained approximately the same while income taxes decreased as a percentage of sales from 7.0% to 6.8%. Further inquiry should be made as to why selling and administrative expenses increased as percentage of sales. This increase in expenses hurt what was otherwise a positive improvement in operating results.

Key Points

1. **Describe the basic elements of a financial accounting information system.**

   The basic elements of a financial accounting system include (1) a set of rules for determining what, when, and the amount that should be recorded for economic events, (2) a framework for facilitating preparation of financial statements, and (3) one or more controls to determine whether errors may have arisen in the recording process.

2. **Describe the cash and accrual bases of accounting.**

   Under the cash basis of accounting, a business records only transactions involving increases or decreases of its cash. Under the accrual basis of accounting, revenue is recorded as it is earned and expenses are recorded when they generate revenue.

3. **Use the cash basis of accounting to analyze, record, and summarize transactions for a corporation's first period of operations.**

Using the accounting equation as a basic framework, September transactions for Family Health Care are recorded using the cash basis of accounting. In doing so, (1) every transaction affects one or more elements of the accounting equation, (2) the two sides of the accounting equation are always equal, and (3) stockholders' equity is increased by issuing capital stock and revenues (retained earnings) and is decreased by expenses (retained earnings) and dividends (retained earnings).

4. **Use the cash basis of accounting to prepare financial statements for the first period of operations.**

The financial statements for Family Health Care for September, its first period of operations, are shown in Exhibit 4. Under the cash basis of accounting, the net income and the cash flows from operating activities are the same as shown in Exhibit 4.

5. **Use the cash basis of accounting for recording transactions and preparing financial statements for a second period of operations.**

Using the accounting equation as a basic framework, October transactions for Family Health Care are

recorded and are summarized in Exhibit 5. The financial statements for Family Health Care for October, its second period of operations, are shown in Exhibit 6.

6. **Describe the advantages and disadvantages of the cash basis of accounting.**

The primary advantage of the cash basis of accounting is its simplicity. In addition, the financial statements are easy to prepare, and the net income from operations is the same as the cash flows from operating activities. The primary disadvantage of the cash basis is that revenues and expenses are not always properly matched on the income statement.

7. **Describe and illustrate how vertical analysis can be used to analyze and evaluate a company's performance.**

Vertical analysis is a method of analyzing comparative financial statements in which percentages are computed for each item within a statement to a total within the statement. In vertical analysis of the balance sheet, each asset item is stated at a percentage of the total assets. Each liability and stockholders' equity item is stated at a percentage of total liabilities and stockholders' equity. In vertical analysis of the income statement, each item is stated as a percentage of sales.

Glossary

Accrual basis of accounting: A system of accounting in which revenue is recorded as it is earned and expenses are recorded when they generate revenue.

Cash basis of accounting: A system of accounting in which only transactions involving increases or decreases of the entity's cash are recorded.

Financial accounting system: A system that includes (1) a set of rules for

determining what, when, and the amount that should be recorded for economic events, (2) a framework for facilitating preparing financial statements, and (3) one or more controls to determine whether errors could have arisen in the recording process.

Transaction: An economic event that under generally accepted accounting principles affects an element of the accounting equation and, therefore, must be recorded.

Vertical analysis: A method of analyzing comparative financial statements in which percentages are computed for each item within a statement to a total within the statement.

Self-Study Questions

(Answers appear at end of chapter.)

1. The purchase of land for $50,000 cash was incorrectly recorded as an increase in land and a increase in notes payable. Which of the following statements is correct?
   A. The accounting equation will not balance because cash is overstated by $50,000.
   B. The accounting equation will not balance because notes payable are overstated by $50,000.
   C. The accounting equation will not balance because assets will exceed liabilities by $50,000.
   D. Even though a recording error has been made, the accounting equation will balance.

2. The receipt of $8,000 of cash for fees earned was recorded by Langley Consulting as an increase in cash of $8,000 and a decrease in retained earnings (revenues) of $8,000. What is the effect of this error on the accounting equation?
   A. Total assets will exceed total liabilities and stockholders' equity by $8,000.
   B. Total assets will be less than total liabilities and stockholders' equity by $8,000.
   C. Total assets will exceed total liabilities and stockholders' equity by $16,000.
   D. The error will not affect the accounting equation.

3. Assume that a lawyer bills his clients $25,000 for fees earned on April 30, 2004. The lawyer collects $18,500 of the billings during May and the remainder in June. Under the cash basis of accounting, when would the lawyer record the revenue for fees earned?
   A. April, $25,000; May, $0; and June, $0.
   B. April, $0; May $18,500; and June, $7,500.
   C. April $18,500; May, $6,500; and June, $0
   D. April $0; May, $18,500; and June, $6,500.

4. Using the information in Question 3, when would the lawyer record the revenue under the accrual basis of accounting?
   A. April, $25,000; May, $0; and June, $0.
   B. April, $0; May $18,500; and June, $7,500.
   C. April $18,500; May, $6,500; and June, $0
   D. April $0; May, $18,500; and June, $6,500.

5. Which of the following transactions changes only the mix of assets but does not affect liabilities or stockholders' equity?
   A. Borrowed $40,000 from First National Bank.
   B. Purchased land for cash.
   C. Received $3,800 for fees earned.
   D. Paid $4,000 for office salaries.

Discussion Questions

1. What are the basic elements of a financial accounting system? Do these elements apply to all businesses from a local restaurant to **General Motors**? Explain.

2. Provide an example of a transaction that affects
   (a) only one element of the accounting equation,
   (b) two elements of the accounting equation,
   (c) three elements of the accounting equation.

3. For each of the following errors, indicate whether the error would cause the accounting equation to be out of balance and, if so, indicate how it would be out of balance. (a) The purchase of land for $30,000 cash was recorded as an increase in land of $30,000 and a decrease in cash of $3,000. (b) The receipt of $4,000 for fees earned was recorded as an increase in cash of $4,000 and an increase in liabilities of $4,000. (c) The payment of wages of $2,750 was recorded as a decrease in cash of $2,750 and a decrease in retained earnings (wages expense) of $2,570.

4. Why is the cash basis rather than the accrual basis often used by individuals and small businesses?

5. Under the cash basis of accounting, what are two primary controls for determining the accuracy of a business's or individual's record keeping?

6. Assume that at the end of each month, Leister Consulting Services bills its clients for jobs completed during the month. On October 31, 2004, Leister billed its clients $45,000 for fees earned on jobs completed during October. During November, Leister collected 80% of its fees billed on October 31 and collected the remaining 20% during December. What would be recorded by Leister as fees earned during

October, November, and December under the cash basis and the accrual basis of accounting?

7. As of January 31, 2004, Wyle Construction Inc. owed its employees $5,000 for wages. Because that day falls on a Saturday, Wyle did not pay its employees until the following Monday, February 2. Under the cash basis, when would the wages expense of $5,000 be recorded? Explain.

8. Fathom Consulting Services acquired land three years ago for $25,000. On September 30, Fathom signed an agreement to sell the land for $80,000. In accordance with the sales agreement, the buyer transferred $80,000 to Fathom's bank account on October 6. Fathom uses the cash basis of accounting. (a) When would Fathom record the sale of the land? (b) How are the elements of the accounting equation affected by the sale?

9. How does the payment of dividends of $15,000 affect the three elements of the accounting equation? Is net income affected by the payment of dividends? Explain.

10. Assume that Margarita Consulting erroneously recorded the payment of $7,500 of dividends as salary expense. (a) How does this error affect the equality of the accounting equation? (b) How does this error affect the income statement, retained earnings statement, balance sheet, and statement of cash flows?

11. Assume that Blitzkrieg Realty Inc. borrowed $25,000 from First Union Bank and Trust. In recording the

transaction, Blitzkrieg erroneously recorded the receipt of $25,000 as an increase in cash, $25,000, and an increase in fees earned, $25,000. (a) How does this error affect the equality of the accounting equation? (b) How does this error affect the income statement, retained earnings statement, balance sheet, and statement of cash flows?

12. Assume that as of January 1, 2004, Palmetto Consulting has total assets of $450,000 and total liabilities of $280,000. As of December 31, 2004, Palmetto has total liabilities of $300,000 and total stockholders' equity of $225,000. (a) What was Palmetto's stockholders' equity as of December 31, 2003? (b) Assume that Palmetto did not pay any dividends during 2004. What was the amount of net income for 2004?

13. Using the January 1 and December 31, 2004, data given in Question 12, answer the following questions. (a) If Palmetto paid $18,000 of dividends during 2004, what was the amount of net income for 2004? (b) Under the cash basis, will Palmetto's cash flows from operating activities be the same as its net income?

14. The primary disadvantage of the cash basis of accounting is that revenues and expenses are not always properly matched on the income statement. Explain.

15. In Chapter 1, we described and illustrated horizontal analysis. (a) What is the difference between horizontal and vertical analysis? (b) Can horizontal and vertical analysis be used together in analyzing a company?

Exercises

EXERCISE 2–1
Accounting equation
OBJECTIVE 1

✓ a. $80,500

Determine the missing amount for each of the following:

	Assets	=	Liabilities	+	Stockholders' Equity
a.	?	=	$30,500	+	$ 50,000
b.	$360,000	=	?	+	100,000
c.	225,000	=	45,000	+	?

EXERCISE 2–2
Accounting equation
OBJECTIVE 1

✓ a. $24,100

The assets and liabilities (in millions) of **Walt Disney Company** as of September 30, 2000, were as follows:

Assets	$45,027
Liabilities	20,927

a.   Determine the stockholders' equity of Walt Disney as of September 30, 2000.

b. If assets decreased by $1,328 and stockholders' equity decreased by $1,428, what was the increase or decrease in liabilities for the year ending September 30, 2001?
c. What were the total assets, liabilities, and stockholders' equity as of September 30, 2001?
d. Based on your answer to (c), does the accounting equation balance?

EXERCISE 2–3
Accounting equation
OBJECTIVE 1

✓ a. $137

The assets and liabilities (in millions) of **Campbell Soup Co.** as of July 29, 2000, were as follows:

Assets	$5,196
Liabilities	5,059

a. Determine the stockholders' equity of Campbell Soup as of July 29, 2000.
b. If assets increased by $731 and liabilities increased by $1,115, what was the increase or decrease in stockholders' equity for the year ending July 29, 2001?
c. What were the total assets, liabilities, and stockholders' equity as of July 29, 2001?
d. Based on your answer to (c), does the accounting equation balance?

EXERCISE 2–4
Accounting equation
OBJECTIVE 1

✓ a. $303,516

One item is omitted in each of the following summaries of balance sheet and income statement data (in millions) for **General Motors** and **Coca-Cola** as of December 31, 2001 and 2000.

	General Motors	Coca-Cola
December 31, 2000:		
Assets	$323,969	$ (e)
Liabilities	(a)	(f)
Stockholders' equity	(b)	9,316
Increase (decrease) in assets, liabilities, and stockholders' equity during 2001:		
Assets	$ (20,869)	(g)
Liabilities	(31,437)	$ (467)
Stockholders' equity	10,568	(h)
December 31, 2001:		
Assets	$ (c)	$22,417
Liabilities	272,079	(i)
Stockholders' equity	(d)	11,366

Determine the amounts of the missing items (a) through (i).

EXERCISE 2–5
Accounting equation
OBJECTIVE 1

✓ b. $230,000

Jason Seagle is the sole stockholder and operator of Go-For-It, a motivational consulting business. At the end of its accounting period, December 31, 2004, Go-For-It has assets of $325,000 and liabilities of $142,000. Using the accounting equation and considering each case independently, determine the following amounts:

a. Stockholders' equity as of December 31, 2004.
b. Stockholders' equity as of December 31, 2005, assuming that assets increased by $84,000 and liabilities increased by $37,000 during 2005.
c. Stockholders' equity as of December 31, 2005, assuming that assets decreased by $8,000 and liabilities increased by $17,000 during 2005.
d. Stockholders' equity as of December 31, 2005, assuming that assets increased by $75,000 and liabilities decreased by $17,500 during 2005.

(continued)

e. Net income (or net loss) during 2005, assuming that as of December 31, 2005, assets were $425,000, liabilities were $105,000, and there were no additional investments or dividends.

EXERCISE 2-6

Effect of transactions on stockholders' equity

OBJECTIVES 1, 3, 4, 5

For **Kroger Co.,** indicate whether the following transactions would (1) increase, (2) decrease, or (3) have no effect on stockholders' equity.

a. Paid creditors.
b. Made cash sale to customers.
c. Paid interest expense.
d. Purchased store equipment.
e. Paid dividends.
f. Purchased merchandise.
g. Sold store equipment at a loss.
h. Paid store rent.
i. Paid taxes.
j. Received interest income.

EXERCISE 2-7

Effect of transactions on accounting equation

OBJECTIVES 1, 3, 4, 5

Describe how the following business transactions affect the three elements of the accounting equation.

a. Issued capital stock for cash.
b. Purchased supplies for cash.
c. Borrowed cash at local bank.
d. Received cash for services performed.
e. Paid for utilities used in the business.

EXERCISE 2-8

Effect of transactions on accounting equation

OBJECTIVES 1, 3, 4, 5

✓ a. (1) assets increase $90,000

a. A vacant lot acquired for $120,000, on which there is a balance owed of $40,000, is sold for $210,000 in cash. What is the effect of the sale on the total amount of the seller's (1) assets, (2) liabilities, and (3) stockholders' equity?
b. After receiving the $210,000 cash in (a), the seller pays the $40,000 owed. What is the effect of the payment on the total amount of the seller's (1) assets, (2) liabilities, and (3) stockholders' equity?

EXERCISE 2-9

Effect of transactions on stockholders' equity

OBJECTIVES 1, 3, 4, 5

Indicate whether each of the following types of transactions will (a) increase stockholders' equity or (b) decrease stockholders' equity:

1. Issued capital stock for cash.
2. Received cash for fees earned.
3. Paid cash for rent expense.
4. Paid cash dividends.
5. Paid cash for utilities expense.

EXERCISE 2-10

Transactions

OBJECTIVES 1, 3, 4, 5

The following selected transactions were completed by Speedy Delivery Service during May:

1. Received cash for capital stock, $25,000.
2. Borrowed $15,000 from a local bank.
3. Paid advertising expense, $800.
4. Paid rent for May, $2,500.
5. Received cash from customers, $7,250.
6. Paid creditors, $500.

7. Paid interest on note payable, $400.
8. Purchased land for future building site by paying cash of $20,000.
9. Paid a customer a $200 refund for an overcharge of services.
10. Paid cash dividends, $1,000.

Indicate the effect of each transaction on the accounting equation by listing the numbers identifying the transactions, (1) through (10), in a vertical column, and inserting at the right of each number the appropriate letter from the following list:

a. Increase in an asset, decrease in another asset.
b. Increase in an asset, increase in a liability.
c. Increase in an asset, increase in stockholders' equity.
d. Decrease in an asset, decrease in a liability.
e. Decrease in an asset, decrease in stockholders' equity.

EXERCISE 2–11
Nature of transactions
OBJECTIVES 1, 3, 4, 5

✓ b. $1,750

David Saros operates his own catering service. Summary financial data for August are presented in equation form as follows. Each line designated by a number indicates the effect of a transaction on the equation. Each increase and decrease in stockholders' equity, except transaction (4), affects net income.

	Cash	+	Land	=	Liabilities	+	Capital Stock	+	Retained Earnings
Bal.	9,500		10,000		4,350		10,000		5,150
1.	+36,000								+36,000
2.	−15,000		+15,000						
3.	−21,250								−21,250
4.	−1,500								−1,500
Bal.	7,750		25,000		4,350		10,000		18,400

a. Describe each transaction.
b. What is the amount of net decrease in cash during the month?
c. What is the amount of net increase in retained earnings during the month?
d. What is the amount of the net income for the month?
e. How much of the net income for the month was retained in the business?
f. What is the amount of net cash flows from operating activities?
g. What is the amount of net cash flows from investing activities?
h. What is the amount of net cash flows from financing activities?

EXERCISE 2–12
Net income and dividends
OBJECTIVES 4, 5

The income statement of a corporation for the month of April indicates a net income of $42,000. During the same period, $50,000 in cash dividends were paid. Would it be correct to say that the business incurred a net loss of $8,000 during the month? Discuss.

EXERCISE 2–13
Net income and stockholders' equity for four businesses
OBJECTIVES 1, 3, 4, 5

✓ Company C: Net income: $165,000

Four different corporations, A, B, C, and D, show the same balance sheet data at the beginning and end of a year. These data, exclusive of the amount of stockholders' equity, are summarized as follows:

	Total Assets	Total Liabilities
Beginning of the year	$525,000	$220,000
End of the year	970,000	425,000

On the basis of these data and the following additional information for the year, determine the net income (or loss) of each company for the year. (*Suggestion:* First determine the amount of increase or decrease in stockholders' equity during the year.)

Company A: No additional capital stock was issued, and no dividends were paid.
Company B: No additional capital stock was issued, but dividends of $50,000 were paid.
Company C: Capital stock of $75,000 was issued, but no dividends were paid.
Company D: Capital stock of $75,000 was issued, and dividends of $50,000 were paid.

EXERCISE 2-14
Missing amounts from balance sheet and income statement data
OBJECTIVES 1, 3, 4, 5

✓ a. $230,000

One item is omitted in each of the following summaries of balance sheet and income statement data for four different corporations, I, II, III, and IV.

	I	II	III	IV
Beginning of the year:				
Assets	$400,000	$ 95,000	$100,000	(d)
Liabilities	260,000	45,000	80,000	$150,000
End of the year:				
Assets	900,000	125,000	120,000	310,000
Liabilities	500,000	35,000	105,000	170,000
During the year:				
Additional issue of capital stock	(a)	22,000	10,000	50,000
Dividends	40,000	8,000	(c)	75,000
Revenue	250,000	(b)	175,000	140,000
Expenses	180,000	52,000	177,000	160,000

Determine the amounts of the missing items, identifying them by letter. (*Suggestion:* First determine the amount of increase or decrease in stockholders' equity during the year.)

EXERCISE 2-15
Net income, retained earnings, and dividends
OBJECTIVES 4, 5

✓ a. $278 increase

Use the following data (in millions) for **Campbell Soup Co.** for the year ending July 29, 2001, to answer the questions that follow the data.

Retained earnings July 29, 2000	$4,373
Retained earnings July 29, 2001	4,651
Net cash from operating activities	1,106
Net decrease in cash	3

a. Determine the net increase or decrease in retained earnings during 2001.
b. If dividends in 2001 are $371, what was the net income or loss for Campbell Soup for the year ending July 29, 2001?
c. Why doesn't your answer in (b) agree with the net cash from operating activities of $1,106 shown in the table?
d. Why doesn't the net cash from operating activities of $1,106 agree with the net decrease in cash of $3?

EXERCISE 2-16
Balance sheet, net income, and cash flows
OBJECTIVES 4, 5

✓ b. $11,000

Financial information related to Woods Interiors for September and October of 2004 is as follows:

	Sept. 30, 2004	Oct. 31, 2004
Notes Payable	$10,000	$15,000
Land	17,000	25,000
Capital Stock	6,000	9,000
Retained Earnings	?	?
Cash	18,000	27,000

a. Prepare balance sheets for Woods Interiors as of September 30 and as of October 31, 2004.
b. Determine the amount of net income for October, assuming that dividends of $2,000 were paid.
c. Determine the net cash flows from operating activities.
d. Determine the net cash flows from investing activities.
e. Determine the net cash flows for financing activities.
f. Determine the net increase or decrease in cash.

EXERCISE 2-17
Income statement
OBJECTIVES 4, 5

✓ Net income: $11,250

After its first month of operations, the following amounts were taken from the accounting records of Mata Hari Realty Inc. as of April 30, 2004. Mata Hari Realty uses the cash basis of accounting.

Capital Stock	$ 5,000
Cash	10,750
Dividends	2,000
Interest Expense	1,000
Land	18,500
Miscellaneous Expense	1,250
Notes Payable	15,000
Rent Expense	3,000
Retained Earnings	0
Salaries Expense	4,500
Sales Commissions	24,750
Utilities Expense	3,750

Prepare an income statement for the month ending April 30, 2004.

EXERCISE 2-18
Retained earnings statement
OBJECTIVES 4, 5

Using the financial data shown in Exercise 2-17 for Mata Hari Realty Inc., prepare a retained earnings statement for the month ending April 30, 2004.

EXERCISE 2-19
Balance sheet
OBJECTIVES 4, 5

✓ Total assets: $29,250

Using the financial data shown in Exercise 2-17 for Mata Hari Realty Inc., prepare a balance sheet as of April 30, 2004.

EXERCISE 2-20
Statement of cash flows
OBJECTIVES 4, 5

Using the financial data shown in Exercise 2-17 for Mata Hari Realty Inc., prepare a statement of cash flows for the month ending April 30, 2004.

EXERCISE 2-21
Effect of transactions on accounting equation
OBJECTIVES 1, 3, 4, 5

The following was adapted from the September 30, 2001, financial statements of **Lucent Technologies Inc.** Describe how each of the following transactions of Lucent Technologies would affect the three elements of its accounting equation.

a. Paid dividends.
b. Made cash sales.
c. Received cash from issuing stock.
d. Paid long-term debt.
e. Received cash proceeds from selling a portion of manufacturing operations for a gain on the sale.
f. Received cash from the issuance of long-term debt.

(continued)

g. Paid taxes.
h. Paid research and development expenses for the current year.
i. Paid employee pension expenses for the current year.
j. Purchased machinery and equipment for cash.
k. Paid officer salaries.
l. Paid selling expenses.

EXERCISE 2-22
Statement of cash flows
OBJECTIVES 4, 5

Based on the financial transactions for Lucent Technologies Inc. shown in Exercise 2-21, indicate whether the transaction would be reported in the cash flows from operating, investing, or financing section of the statement of cash flows.

Problems

PROBLEM 2 | 1
Transactions and financial statements
OBJECTIVES 1, 3, 4, 5

✓ 3. Net income: $4,475

Jay Marsh established an insurance agency on May 1, 2004, and completed the following transactions during May:

a. Opened a business bank account in the name of Frontier Insurance Inc. with a deposit of $30,000 in exchange for capital stock.
b. Borrowed $10,000 by issuing a note payable.
c. Received cash from fees earned, $8,100.
d. Paid rent on office and equipment for the month, $1,000.
e. Paid automobile expenses for month, $800, and miscellaneous expenses, $250.
f. Paid office salaries, $1,500.
g. Paid interest on the note payable, $75.
h. Purchased land as a future building site, $15,000.
i. Paid dividends, $2,000.

Instructions

1. Indicate the effect of each transaction and the balances after each transaction, using the following tabular headings:

Assets	=	Liabilities	+	Stockholders' Equity	
Cash + Land	=	Notes Payable	+	Capital Stock +	Retained Earnings

Explain the nature of each increase and decrease in stockholders' equity by an appropriate notation at the right of the amount.

2. Briefly explain why the stockholders' investments and revenues increased stockholders' equity, and why dividends and expenses decreased stockholders' equity.
3. Prepare an income statement and retained earnings statement for May.
4. Prepare a balance sheet as of May 31, 2004.
5. Prepare a statement of cash flows for May.

PROBLEM 2 | 2
Cash basis financial statements
OBJECTIVES 1, 3, 4, 5

Scott Douma established Top-Notch Computer Services on July 1, 2004. The effect of each transaction and the balances after each transaction for July are as follows:

	Assets			=	Liabilities	+	Stockholders' Equity			
					Notes		Capital		Retained	
	Cash	+	Land	=	Payable	+	Stock	+	Earnings	
a.	+18,000						+18,000			Investment
b.	+12,250								12,250	Fees earned
Bal.	30,250						18,000		12,250	
c.	−2,000								−2,000	Rent expense
Bal.	28,250						18,000		10,250	
d.	+10,000				+10,000					
Bal.	38,250				10,000		18,000		10,250	
e.	−25,000		+25,000							
Bal.	13,250		25,000		10,000		18,000		10,250	
f.	−1,150								−800	Auto expense
									−350	Misc. expense
Bal.	12,100		25,000		10,000		18,000		9,100	
g.	−2,500								−2,500	Salaries expense
Bal.	9,600		25,000		10,000		18,000		6,600	
h.	−1,000								−1,000	Dividends
Bal.	8,600		25,000		10,000		18,000		5,600	

✓ 1. Net income: $6,600

Instructions

1. Prepare an income statement for the month ended July 31, 2004.
2. Prepare a retained earnings statement for the month ended July 31, 2004.
3. Prepare a balance sheet as of July 31, 2004.
4. Prepare a statement of cash flows for the month ended July 31, 2004.

PROBLEM 2 | 3
Cash basis financial statements
OBJECTIVES 4, 5

✓ 1. Net income: $82,500

The following amounts were taken from the accounting records of Nutrition Services Inc. as of December 31, 2004. Nutrition Services began its operations on January 1, 2004, and uses the cash basis of accounting.

Capital Stock	$ 10,000
Cash	27,500
Dividends	5,000
Fees Earned	229,500
Interest Expense	1,200
Land	75,000
Miscellaneous Expense	6,800
Notes Payable	15,000
Rent Expense	24,000
Retained Earnings	0
Salaries Expense	65,000
Taxes Expense	18,000
Utilities Expense	32,000

Instructions

1. Prepare an income statement for the year ending December 31, 2004.
2. Prepare a retained earnings statement for the year ending December 31, 2004.
3. Prepare a balance sheet as of December 31, 2004.
4. Prepare a statement of cash flows for the year ending December 31, 2004.

PROBLEM 2 | 4

Cash basis financial statements

OBJECTIVES 4, 5

✓ 1. Net income: $91,500

After its second year of operations, the following amounts were taken from the accounting records of Nutrition Services Inc. as of December 31, 2005. Nutrition Services began its operations on January 1, 2004 (see Problem 2-3A) and uses the cash basis of accounting.

Capital Stock	$ 25,000
Cash	?
Dividends	15,000
Fees Earned	254,100
Interest Expense	1,600
Land	140,000
Miscellaneous Expense	7,000
Notes Payable	20,000
Rent Expense	28,000
Retained Earnings (January 1, 2005)	77,500
Salaries Expense	70,000
Taxes Expense	20,000
Utilities Expense	36,000

Instructions

1. Prepare an income statement for the year ending December 31, 2005.
2. Prepare a retained earnings statement for the year ending December 31, 2005.
3. Prepare a balance sheet as of December 31, 2005.
4. Prepare a statement of cash flows for the year ending December 31, 2005. (*Hint:* You should compare the asset and liability amounts of December 31, 2005, with those of December 31, 2004, to determine cash used in investing and financing activities. See Problem 2-3A for the December 31, 2004, balance sheet amounts.)

PROBLEM 2 | 5

Missing amounts from financial statements

OBJECTIVES 4, 5

✓ a. $13,000

The financial statements at the end of Harvest Realty Inc.'s first month of operations follow. By analyzing the interrelationships between the financial statements, fill in the proper amounts for (a) through (s).

HARVEST REALTY INC.
Income Statement
For the Month Ended March 31, 2004

Fees earned		$ (a)
Operating expenses:		
Wages expense	$3,680	
Rent expense	2,000	
Utilities expense	(b)	
Interest expense	200	
Miscellaneous expenses	440	
Total operating expenses		7,500
Net income		$ (c)

HARVEST REALTY INC.
Retained Earnings Statement
For the Month Ended March 31, 2004

Retained earnings, March 1, 2004		$ (d)
Net income for March	$5,500	
Less dividends	(e)	(f)
Retained earnings, March 31, 2004		$ (g)

HARVEST REALTY INC.
Balance Sheet
March 31, 2004

Assets

Cash		$ (h)
Land		20,000
Total assets		$26,500

Liabilities

Notes payable		$12,000

Stockholders' Equity

Capital stock	$ (i)	
Retained earnings	(j)	(k)
Total liabilities and stockholders' equity		$ (l)

HARVEST REALTY INC.
Statement of Cash Flows
For the Month Ended March 31, 2004

Cash flows from operating activities:			
Cash received from customers			$13,000
Deduct cash payments for expenses			7,500
Net cash flows from operating activities			$ (m)
Cash flows from investing activities:			
Cash payment for purchase of land			20,000
Cash flows from financing activities:			
Cash received from sale of capital stock	$10,000		
Cash received from notes payable	(n)	$ (o)	
Deduct cash dividends	1,000		
Net cash flows from financing activities			(p)
Net increase in cash			$ (q)
March 1, 2004 cash balance			(r)
March 31, 2004 cash balance			$ (s)

PROBLEM 2 | 6

Cash basis financial statements

OBJECTIVES 4, 5

Spring Creek Realty Inc., organized July 1, 2004, is operated by Bob Gibbs. What errors can you find in the following financial statements for Spring Creek Realty Inc., prepared after its first month of operations?

SPRING CREEK REALTY INC.
Income Statement
July 31, 2004

Sales commissions		$ 46,100
Operating expenses:		
Office salaries expense	$ 8,150	
Rent expense	3,800	
Automobile expense	1,750	
Dividends	1,000	
Miscellaneous expense	775	
Total operating expenses		15,475
Net income		$ 20,625

Bob Gibbs
Retained Earnings Statement
July 31, 2003

Net income for the month	20,625
Retained earnings, July 31, 2004	$ 20,625

Balance Sheet Inc.
For the Month Ended July 31, 2004

Assets		
Cash		$ 30,425
Notes payable		10,000
Total assets		$ 40,425
Liabilities		
Land		$ 20,200
Stockholders' Equity		
Capital stock	$10,000	
Retained earnings	20,625	30,625
Total liabilities and stockholders' equity		$ 50,825

SPRING CREEK REALTY INC.
Statement of Cash Flows
July 31, 2004

Cash flows from operating activities:	
Cash receipts from sales commissions	$ 46,100
Cash flows from investing activities:	
Cash payments for land	(20,200)
Cash flows from financing activities:	
Cash receipts from retained earnings	40,625
Net increase in cash during year ending March 31, 2001	$ 66,525
Cash as of July 1, 2004	0
Cash as of July 31, 2004	$ 66,525

Activities

Activity 2-1
Business strategy

G R O U P

Assume that you are considering developing a nationwide chain of women's clothing stores. You have contacted a Houston-based firm that specializes in financing new business ventures and enterprises. Such firms, called *venture capital firms*, finance new businesses in exchange for a percentage of the ownership.

1. In groups of four or five, discuss the different business strategies that you might use in your venture.
2. For each strategy you list in (1), provide an example of a real-world business using the same strategy.
3. What percentage of the ownership would you be willing to give the venture capital firm in exchange for its financing?

Activity 2-2
Cash basis of accounting

Megan Peroni and Shannon Haley both graduated from State University in May 2004. After graduation, Shannon took a job as a staff accountant in the Atlanta office of **PricewaterhouseCoopers**, an international public accounting firm. Megan began working as a manager in Arrow Electronics, a wholesale computer hardware and software company but left after only six months to start her own consulting business. The following conversation took place between Megan and Shannon at their first annual alumni function:

Megan: Shannon, good to see you again.
Shannon: Yes. It doesn't seem like it's been almost a year since we graduated.

Megan: That's for sure. It seems like only yesterday we were listening to that boring commencement speaker. I don't even remember her name . . . Monica somebody. Are you still working for PricewaterhouseCoopers?

Shannon: Yes, it's been a great year. I've worked on thirteen companies; it's been a fantastic learning experience. Each client has a different culture, management team, strategy, problems, and personality. I've learned something new every day. How about you? Are you still working for Arrow Electronics?

Megan: No, I quit after six months. My customers really didn't know what they needed for computer systems . . . so . . . I quit and started a consulting business. I feel like I'm helping my customers more now than I did before. Besides, I like being my own boss.

Shannon: What's the name of your business?

Megan: I-Chor Consulting. It's been amazing. I started with my savings of $10,000 six months ago. My last bank statement showed I've got more than $120,000—"pure profit" of $110,000 in only six months.

Shannon: That's unbelievable! If you ever need a CPA firm, keep us in mind.

Megan: Sure. What are friends for anyway?

1. Comment on Megan's statement that she's earned $110,000 "pure profit" in only six months.
2. Would the cash basis or the accrual basis of accounting be most appropriate for I-Chor?

Activity 2-3
Cash flows

Amazon.com, an Internet retailer, was incorporated in July 1994 and opened its virtual doors on the Web in July 1995. On the statement of cash flows, would you expect Amazon.com's net cash flows from operating, investing, and financing activities to be positive or negative for 1996, 1997, and 1998? Use the following format for your answers, and briefly explain your logic.

	1998	1997	1996
Net cash flows from operating activities	positive		
Net cash flows from investing activities			
Net cash flows from financing activities			

Activity 2-4
Accounting equation

Condensed financial statements for **Wm. J. Wrigley Jr. Company** for 2001 and 2000 are shown in Exhibits 7 and 8 of this chapter. Based upon these financial statements, answer the following questions:

1. Using the accounting equation, Assets = Liabilities + Stockholders' Equity, fill in the amounts for 2000. Express the amounts in thousands.
2. If during 2001 assets increased by $190,908 and liabilities increased by $47,608, determine the increase or decrease in stockholders' equity during 2001.
3. Based on your answers to (1) and (2), determine the total stockholders' equity as of December 31, 2001. Does this amount agree with Wrigley's balance sheet shown in Exhibit 7?
4. Based on Exhibit 7, what percentage of Wrigley's total assets were financed by debt during 2001? Assuming you are a long-term creditor of Wrigley, interpret this percentage in terms of the chances that you will be repaid by Wrigley.
5. Assuming that in (4) you are a short-term creditor of Wrigley, would your interpretation and analysis of your chances of being repaid change?

Activity 2-5
Vertical analysis

The following balance sheets (in millions) were adapted from the December 31, 2001 and 2000 financial statements of **Boeing Co.**:

	December 31, 2001	December 31, 2000
Assets		
Cash	$ 633	$ 1,010
Receivables	15,554	12,478
Inventories	6,920	6,852
Property, plant, and equipment	8,459	8,814
Intangible assets and goodwill	6,443	5,214
Prepaid pension cost	5,838	4,845
Other assets	4,496	3,464
Total assets	$48,343	$42,677
Liabilities and Stockholders' Equity		
Accounts payable	$13,872	$12,312
Income taxes payable	909	1,866
Notes and other liabilities	22,737	17,479
Total liabilities	$37,518	$31,657
Stockholders' equity	10,825	11,020
Total liabilities and stockholders' equity	$48,343	$42,677

1. Prepare a comparative vertical analysis of the balance sheets for 2001 and 2000.
2. Based on (1), what is your analysis of Boeing's financial condition in 2001 as compared to 2000?

Activity 2-6
Vertical analysis

The following income statement data (in thousands) for **Dell Computer Corporation** and **Gateway Inc.** were taken from their recent annual reports:

	Dell	**Gateway**
Net sales	$31,888,000	$ 6,079,524
Cost of goods sold	25,445,000	5,241,332
Gross profit	$ 6,443,000	$ 838,192
Operating expenses	3,780,000	2,022,122
Operating income (loss)	$ 2,663,000	$(1,183,930)

1. Prepare a vertical analysis of Dell's income statement.
2. Prepare a vertical analysis of Gateway's income statement.
3. Based on (1) and (2), how does Dell compare to Gateway?

Activity 2-7
Financial information

Yahoo.com's Internet finance site provides summary financial information about public companies, such as stock quotes, recent financial filings with the Securities and Exchange Commission, and recent news stories. Go to Yahoo.com's financial Web site (**http://finance .yahoo.com/**) and enter the stock symbol for Wm. J. Wrigley Jr. Company, WWY. Answer the following questions concerning Wm. J. Wrigley Jr. Company by clicking on "Profile" and "Research."

1. At what price did Wrigley's stock last trade?
2. What is the 52-week range of Wrigley's stock?
3. When was the last time Wrigley's stock hit a 52-week high?
4. Over the last six months, has there been any insider selling or buying of Wrigley's stock?
5. Who is the president of Wm. J. Wrigley Jr. Company?
6. What was the salary of the president of Wm. J. Wrigley Jr. Company?
7. What is the annual dividend of Wrigley's stock?
8. How many current broker recommendations are strong buy, buy, hold, sell, or strong sell? What is the average of the broker recommendations?

9. What is the earnings per share of stock for this year?
10. What is the earnings per share estimate for next year?

Activity 2-8
Analyzing financial information

The Business Section of the August 28, 2001, issue of *The New York Times* has an article by David Barboza, "A Young Heir Has New Plans at Old Company." Read the article and answer the following questions:

1. Is the article favorable, neutral, or unfavorable regarding future prospects for Wm. J. Wrigley Jr. Company?
2. Would you invest in Wm. J. Wrigley Jr. Company's stock based on only this article? If not, what additional information would you want?
3. Would it be a prudent investment strategy to rely on only published financial statements in deciding to invest in a company's stock?
4. What sources do you think financial analysts use in making investment decisions and recommendations?

Answers to Self-Study Questions

1. **D** Even though a recording error has been made, the accounting equation will balance (answer D). However, assets (cash) will be overstated by $50,000 and liabilities (notes payable) will be overstated by $50,000. Answer A is incorrect because although cash is overstated by $50,000, the accounting equation will balance. Answer B is incorrect because although notes payable are overstated by $50,000, the accounting equation will balance. Answer C is incorrect because the accounting equation will balance and assets will not exceed liabilities.

2. **C** Total assets will exceed total liabilities and stockholders' equity by $16,000. This happens because stockholders' equity (retained earnings) was decreased instead of increased by $8,000. Thus, stockholders' equity will be understated by a total of $16,000.

3. **D** Under the cash basis of accounting, revenues are recorded when the cash is collected, not necessarily when the fees are earned. Thus, no revenue would be recorded in April, $18,500 of revenue would be recorded in May, and $6,500 of revenue would be recorded in June (Answer D).

4. **A** Under the accrual basis of accounting, revenues are recorded when the fees are earned. Thus, $25,000 of revenue would be recorded in April and no revenue would be recorded in May or June (Answer A).

5. **B** The purchase of land for cash changes only the mix of assets but does not affect liabilities or stockholders' equity (Answer B). Borrowing cash from a bank (Answer A) increases assets and liabilities. Receiving cash for fees earned (Answer C) increases cash and stockholders' equity (retained earnings). Paying office salaries (Answer D) decreases cash and stockholders' equity (retained earnings).

Chapter 3

3

The Accrual Basis of Accounting

Do you subscribe to any magazines? Most of us subscribe to one or more, such as *Cosmopolitan, Sports Illustrated, Golf Digest, Fly Rod & Reel, Newsweek, Business Week, Barron's,* and *People*. Magazines usually require us to prepay the yearly subscription price before we receive any issues.

When should the magazine record this revenue from subscriptions? As we discussed in Chapter 2, under the cash basis of accounting, a publisher records the revenue when the cash is received. However, large corporations publish most of the popular magazines. For example, AOL Time Warner publishes more than 130 magazines including *Fortune, Time, Entertainment Weekly, People,* and *Sports Illustrated*. Large corporations such as AOL Time Warner must follow generally accepted accounting principles that require the use of the accrual basis of accounting.

In this chapter, we describe and illustrate how to account for transactions using the accrual basis of accounting. Under accrual accounting, revenues are recorded when they are earned, regardless of when the cash is actually received. Thus, AOL Time Warner records revenues from magazine subscriptions each month as its magazines are published and delivered. Because all large companies use the accrual basis of accounting, a thorough understanding of accrual basis is important for your business studies and future career.

The Accrual Basis of Accounting and the Matching Concept

In Chapter 2, we illustrated the use of the cash basis of accounting for Family Health Care for the months of September and October. In these illustrations, we used many of the accounting concepts we discussed in Chapter 1. For example, under the business entity concept, we accounted for Family Health Care as a separate entity independent of the owner-manager, Dr. Lee Landry. Under the cost concept, we recorded the purchase of land at the amount that we paid for it. Consistent with the going concern concept, we did not revalue the land for increases or decreases in its market value but retained the land in the accounting records at its original cost. We also employed the accounting period, full disclosure, objectivity, and the unit of measurement concepts in preparing financial statements for Family Health Care.

The one accounting concept that we did not emphasize in Chapter 2 was the matching concept because we used the cash basis of accounting. Transactions were recorded only when cash was received or paid. For example, when $6,000 of cash was received for Dr. Landry's initial investment in Family Health Care, the transaction was recorded as an increase in assets (cash) and an increase in stockholders' equity (capital stock). Likewise, when $10,000 cash was received from First National Bank as a loan, the transaction was recorded as an increase in assets (cash) and an increase in liabilities (notes payable). The other transactions were recorded in a similar manner as cash was received or paid. This is how individuals normally record transactions. That is, we record only the receipts and payments of cash in our personal records.

The cash basis does not emphasize the matching concept. Instead the receipt or payment of cash governs the recording process. Revenues and expenses are matched with each other only if cash from revenues is received in the same period as cash is paid for expenses. While the cash basis can work reasonably well for individuals or small businesses, it does not work well for large businesses. This is true because the timing of receiving or paying cash can vary widely with the result that net income can become meaningless under the cash basis. For example, a construction company could spend months or years developing land for a business complex or subdivision. During the development of the land, the company pays for materials, wages, insurance, and other construction items. At the same time, cash could not be received until portions of the development are sold. As a result, the company would report a series of net losses during development until sales occur. Thus, the income statement under the cash basis could provide an unrealistic picture of the company's operations. In fact, the development could be highly successful and the early losses misleading.

The accrual basis of accounting is designed to avoid misleading income statement results that could otherwise result from the timing of cash receipts and payments. At the same time, the accrual basis recognizes the importance of reporting cash flows through its emphasis on preparing the statement of cash flows.

Under the accrual basis of accounting, transactions are recorded as they occur and thus affect the accounting equation (assets, liabilities, and stockholders' equity). Since the receipt or payment of cash affects assets (cash), all cash receipts and payments are recorded in a similar manner under the accrual basis and the cash basis. However, under the accrual basis, transactions are also recorded even though cash has not been received or paid until a later point. For example, Family Health Care can provide services to patients who are covered by health insurance. It then files a claim with the insurance company for the payment. In this case, the services are said to be provided "on account." Likewise, a business can purchase supplies from a vendor with terms that allow the business to pay for the purchase within a time period, such as 10 days. In this case, the supplies are said to be purchased "on account." Each of the preceding illustrations represents a business transaction that affects elements of the accounting equation and is therefore recorded under the accrual basis *even though cash is not received or paid*.

In accounting, we often use the term *recognized* to refer to when a transaction is recorded. Thus, under the cash basis of accounting, transactions are not recognized until cash is received or paid. *Under the accrual basis of accounting, revenue is normally recognized when it is earned.* For Family Health Care, revenue is earned when services have been provided to the customer. At this point, the revenue-earning process is complete, and the customer is legally obligated to pay for the services.

Under the accrual basis, the matching concept plays an important role in determining when to record expenses. When revenues are earned and recorded, all expenses incurred in generating the revenues must also be recorded regardless of whether cash has been paid. In this way, revenues and expenses are matched and the net income or net loss for the period can be determined. This is an application of the matching concept that we discussed in Chapter 1. That is, expenses are recognized and recorded in the same period as the related revenues that they generated.

The accrual basis recognizes liabilities when the business incurs the obligation to pay for the services or goods purchased. For example, the purchase of supplies on account is recorded when the supplies are received and the business has incurred the obligation to pay for them.

BUSINESS STRATEGY

Not Cutting Corners

Have you ever ordered a hamburger from Wendy's and noticed that the meat patty is square? The square meat patty reflects a business strategy implemented at Wendy's by its founder, Dave Thomas. Mr. Thomas's strategy was to offer high-quality products at a fair price in a friendly atmosphere without "cutting corners"; hence, the square meat patty. In the highly competitive fast-food industry, Dave Thomas's strategy enabled Wendy's to grow to be the third largest fast-food restaurant in the world with annual sales of more than $7 billion.

Source: Douglas Martin, "Dave Thomas, 69, Wendy's Founder Dies," *The New York Times*, January 9, 2002.

Using the Accrual Basis of Accounting for Family Health Care's November Transactions

OBJECTIVE   2

Use the accrual basis of accounting to analyze, record, and summarize transactions.

To illustrate the accrual basis of accounting, we use the November 2003 Family Health Care transactions, which follow:

   a. On November 1, received $1,800 from ILS Company as rent for the use of Family Health Care's land as a temporary parking lot from November 2003 through March 2004.

   b. On November 1, paid $2,400 for an insurance premium on a two-year, general business policy.

   c. On November 1, paid $6,000 for an insurance premium on a six-month medical malpractice policy.

   d. Dr. Landry invested an additional $5,000 in the business in exchange for capital stock.

   e. Purchased supplies for $240 on account.

   f. Purchased $8,500 of office equipment. Paid $1,700 cash as a down payment with the remainder due in five monthly installments of $1,360, beginning December 1.

   g. Provided services of $6,100 to patients on account.

   h. Received $5,500 for services provided to patients who paid cash.

   i. Received $4,200 from insurance companies that paid on patients' accounts for services that have been provided.

   j. Paid $100 on account for supplies that had been purchased.

   k. Paid expenses during November as follows: wages, $2,790; rent, $800; utilities, $580; interest, $100; miscellaneous, $420.

   l. Paid dividends of $1,200 to stockholder (Dr. Landry).

In analyzing and recording the November transactions for Family Health Care, we use the same format as we used in Chapter 2. In so doing, we record increases and decreases for each financial statement element. These separate records in which increases and decreases in a financial statement element are referred to as **accounts**.

Transaction a.   *On November 1, received $1,800 from ILS Company as rent for the use of Family Health Care's land as a temporary parking lot from November 2003 through March 2004.* In this transaction, Family Health Care entered into a rental agreement for the use of its land. The agreement required the payment of the rental fee of $1,800 in advance.

How does this transaction affect the accounts (elements) of the accounting equation, and how should it be recorded? Since cash has been received, Cash is increased by $1,800, but what other account should be increased or decreased? Family Health Care has agreed to rent the land to ILS Company for five months and thus has incurred a liability to provide this service: rental of the land. If Family Health Care canceled the agreement on November 1, after accepting the $1,800, it would have to repay that amount to ILS Company. Thus, Family Health Care should record this transaction as an increase in cash and an increase in a liability for $1,800. Because the liability relates to rental revenue, it is recorded as unearned revenue as shown.

	Assets		=	Liabilities		+	Stockholders' Equity		
				Notes	Unearned		Capital	Retained	
	Cash	+ Land	=	Payable	+ Revenue	+	Stock	+ Earnings	
Bal.	7,320	12,000		10,000			6,000	3,320	
a.	1,800				1,800				Received rent in advance
Bal.	9,120	12,000		10,000	1,800		6,000	3,320	

As time passes, the liability will decrease, and Family Health Care will earn rental revenue. For example, at the end of November, one-fifth of the $1,800 ($360) will have been earned. Later in this chapter, we discuss how to record the $360 of earned rent revenue at the end of November.

You should note that the beginning balances shown in the preceding equation are the ending balances from October. That is, the cash balance of $7,320 is the ending cash balance as of October 31, 2003. Likewise, the other balances are carried forward from the preceding month. In this sense, the accounting equation represents a cumulative history of the financial results of the business.

Transaction b.   *On November 1, paid $2,400 for an insurance premium on a two-year, general business policy.* This umbrella policy covers a variety of possible risks to the business, such as fire and theft. By paying the premium, Family Health Care has purchased an asset, insurance coverage, in exchange for cash. Thus, the mix of assets has changed. However, the prepaid insurance coverage is unique in that it expires with the passage of time. At the end of the two-year period, the asset will have completely expired. Such assets are called *prepaid expenses* or *deferred expenses.* Thus, the purchase of the insurance coverage is recorded as prepaid insurance as shown here.

	Assets			=	Liabilities		+ Stockholders' Equity		
		Prepaid			Notes	Unearned	Capital	Retained	
	Cash	+ Insurance +	Land	= Payable +	Revenue	+	Stock	+ Earnings	
Bal.	9,120		12,000	10,000	1,800		6,000	3,320	
b.	−2,400	2,400							Paid insurance for two years
Bal.	6,720	2,400	12,000	10,000	1,800		6,000	3,320	

Later in this illustration, we discuss how such accounts are updated at the end of an accounting period to reflect the portion of the asset that has expired.

Transaction c.   *On November 1, paid $6,000 for an insurance premium on a six-month medical malpractice policy.* This transaction is similar to transaction (b) except that Family Health Care has purchased medical malpractice insurance that is renewable every six months. The transaction is recorded as follows:

	Assets			=	Liabilities		+	Stockholders' Equity		
		Prepaid			Notes	Unearned		Capital	Retained	
	Cash	+ Insurance +	Land	= Payable +	Revenue	+	Stock	+ Earnings	
Bal.	6,720	2,400	12,000	10,000	1,800		6,000	3,320	
c.	−6,000	6,000							Paid insurance for 6 months
Bal.	720	8,400	12,000	10,000	1,800		6,000	3,320	

Transaction d.   *Dr. Landry invested an additional $5,000 in the business in exchange for capital stock.* This transaction is similar to the one in which Dr. Landry initially established Family Health Care. It is recorded as follows.

	Assets			=	Liabilities		+	Stockholders' Equity	
		Prepaid			Notes	Unearned		Capital	Retained
	Cash	+ Insurance +	Land	= Payable +	Revenue	+	Stock	+ Earnings
Bal.	720	8,400	12,000	10,000	1,800		6,000	3,320
d.	5,000						5,000		Investment
Bal.	5,720	8,400	12,000	10,000	1,800		11,000	3,320

Transaction e.   *Purchased supplies for $240 on account.* This transaction is similar to transactions (b) and (c) because purchased supplies are assets until they are used up in generating revenue. Family Health Care has purchased and received the supplies and promised to pay in the near future. Such liabilities that are incurred in the normal operations of the business are called **accounts payable**. The transaction is recorded by increasing the asset supplies and increasing the liability accounts payable as shown.

	Assets				=	Liabilities			+	Stockholders' Equity	
		Prepaid				Notes	Accts.	Unearned	Capital	Retained
	Cash +	Ins.	+ Supplies +	Land	= Pay. +	Pay. +	Revenue +	Stock	+ Earnings
Bal.	5,720	8,400		12,000	10,000		1,800	11,000	3,320
e.			240			240				Purchase of supplies
Bal.	5,720	8,400	240	12,000	10,000	240	1,800	11,000	3,320

Transaction f.   *Purchased $8,500 of office equipment. Paid $1,700 cash as a down payment, with the remainder due in five monthly installments of $1,360, beginning December 1.* In this transaction, the asset office equipment is increased by $8,500, cash is decreased by $1,700, and notes payable is increased by $6,800. The transaction is recorded as follows.

		Assets				=	Liabilities			+ Stockholders' Equity	
	Cash +	Prepaid Ins. +	Supplies +	Office Equip. +	Land =	Notes Pay. +	Accts. Pay. +	Unearned Revenue +	Capital Stock +	Retained Earnings	
Bal.	5,720	8,400	240		12,000	10,000	240	1,800	11,000	3,320	
f.	−1,700			8,500		6,800					Purchase of office equip.
Bal.	4,020	8,400	240	8,500	12,000	16,800	240	1,800	11,000	3,320	

Transaction g. *Provided services of $6,100 to patients on account.* This transaction is similar to the revenue transactions that we recorded in September and October except that the services have been provided on account. Family Health Care will collect cash from the patients' insurance companies in the future. Such amounts that are to be collected in the future and that arise from the normal operations of a business are called **accounts receivable**. Since a valid claim exists against a third party, accounts receivable are assets; the transaction is recorded as shown.

			Assets				=	Liabilities			+ Stockholders' Equity	
	Cash +	Accts. Rec. +	Prepaid Ins. +	Supplies +	Office Equip. +	Land =	Notes Pay. +	Accts. Pay. +	Unearned Revenue +	Capital Stock +	Retained Earnings	
Bal.	4,020		8,400	240	8,500	12,000	16,800	240	1,800	11,000	3,320	
g.		6,100									6,100	Fees earned
Bal.	4,020	6,100	8,400	240	8,500	12,000	16,800	240	1,800	11,000	9,420	

Transaction h. *Received $5,500 for services provided to patients who paid cash.* This transaction is similar to the revenue transactions that we recorded in September and October and is recorded as shown.

			Assets				=	Liabilities			+ Stockholders' Equity	
	Cash +	Accts. Rec. +	Prepaid Ins. +	Supplies +	Office Equip. +	Land =	Notes Pay. +	Accts. Pay. +	Unearned Revenue +	Capital Stock +	Retained Earnings	
Bal.	4,020	6,100	8,400	240	8,500	12,000	16,800	240	1,800	11,000	9,420	
h.	5,500										5,500	Fees earned
Bal.	9,520	6,100	8,400	240	8,500	12,000	16,800	240	1,800	11,000	14,920	

Transaction i. *Received $4,200 from insurance companies that paid on patients' accounts for services that have been provided.* In this transaction, cash is increased and the accounts receivable is decreased by $4,200. Thus, only the mix of assets changes, and the transaction is recorded as shown.

			Assets				=	Liabilities			+ Stockholders' Equity	
	Cash +	Accts. Rec. +	Prepaid Ins. +	Supp. +	Office Equip. +	Land =	Notes Pay. +	Accts. Pay. +	Unearned Revenue +	Capital Stock +	Retained Earnings	
Bal.	9,520	6,100	8,400	240	8,500	12,000	16,800	240	1,800	11,000	14,920	
i.	4,200	−4,200										Collected cash
Bal.	13,720	1,900	8,400	240	8,500	12,000	16,800	240	1,800	11,000	14,920	

Transaction j. *Paid $100 on account for supplies that had been purchased.* This transaction reduces the cash and the accounts payable by $100 as shown.

		Assets					=		Liabilities		+	Stockholders' Equity		
		Accts.	Prepaid			Office			Notes	Accts.	Unearned	Capital	Retained	
	Cash	+ Rec.	+ Ins.	+ Supp.	+ Equip.	+ Land	=	Pay.	+ Pay.	+ Revenue	+ Stock	+ Earnings	
Bal.	13,720	1,900	8,400	240	8,500	12,000		16,800	240	1,800	11,000	14,920	
j.	−100								−100				Paid on acct.
Bal.	13,620	1,900	8,400	240	8,500	12,000		16,800	140	1,800	11,000	14,920	

Transaction k. *Paid expenses during November as follows: wages, $2,790; rent, $800; utilities, $580; interest, $100; miscellaneous, $420.* This transaction is similar to the expense transaction that we recorded for Family Health Care in September and October. It is recorded as shown.

		Assets					=		Liabilities		+	Stockholders' Equity		
		Accts.	Prepaid			Office			Notes	Accts.	Unearned	Capital	Retained	
	Cash	+ Rec.	+ Ins.	+ Supp.	+ Equip.	+ Land	=	Pay.	+ Pay.	+ Revenue	+ Stock	+ Earnings	
Bal.	13,620	1,900	8,400	240	8,500	12,000		16,800	140	1,800	11,000	14,920	
k.	−4,690											−2,790	Wages exp.
												−800	Rent exp.
												−580	Utilities exp.
												−100	Interest exp.
												−420	Misc. exp.
Bal.	8,930	1,900	8,400	240	8,500	12,000		16,800	140	1,800	11,000	10,230	

Transaction l. *Paid dividends of $1,200 to stockholder (Dr. Landry).* This transaction is similar to the dividends transactions of September and October. It is recorded as shown.

		Assets					=		Liabilities		+	Stockholders' Equity		
		Accts.	Prepaid			Office			Notes	Accts.	Unearned	Capital	Retained	
	Cash	+ Rec.	+ Ins.	+ Supp.	+ Equip.	+ Land	=	Pay.	+ Pay.	+ Revenue	+ Stock	+ Earnings	
Bal.	8,930	1,900	8,400	240	8,500	12,000		16,800	140	1,800	11,000	10,230	
l.	−1,200											−1,200	Dividends
Bal.	7,730	1,900	8,400	240	8,500	12,000		16,800	140	1,800	11,000	9,030	

The Adjustment Process

OBJECTIVE   3

Describe and illustrate the end-of-the-period adjustment process.

The accrual basis of accounting requires the accounting records to be updated prior to preparing financial statements. This updating process, called the **adjustment process**, is necessary to properly match revenues and expenses. This is an application of the matching concept.

Adjustments are necessary because, at any point in time, some accounts (elements) of the accounting equation are not up to date. For example, as time passes, prepaid insurance expires and supplies are used in operations. However, it is not efficient to record the daily expiration of prepaid insurance or the daily usage of supplies. Rather, the accounting records are normally updated just prior to the preparation of the financial statements.

You may wonder why we were able to prepare the September and October financial statements for Family Health Care in Chapter 2 without recording any adjustments. The answer is that in September and October, Family Health Care used the cash basis of accounting. Under the cash basis, no adjustments are necessary because transactions are recorded only as cash is received or paid. However, Family Health Care began using the accrual basis in November. Thus, we must now address the adjustment process.

Deferrals and Accruals

The financial statements are affected by two types of adjustments: deferrals and accruals. Whether a deferral or an accrual, each adjustment affects a balance sheet account and an income statement account.

Deferrals are created by recording a transaction in a way that delays or defers the recognition of its expense or revenue. Common examples of deferrals follow.

- **Deferred expenses** or **prepaid expenses** are items that initially were recorded as assets but are expected to become expenses over time or through the normal operations of the business. For Family Health Care, prepaid insurance is an example of a deferral that normally requires adjustment. Other examples include supplies, prepaid advertising, and prepaid interest. The tuition you pay at the beginning of each term is also an example of a deferred expense to you as a student. **McDonald's Corporation** reported more than $300 million of prepaid expenses and other current assets on a recent balance sheet.

> ### ETHICS IN ACTION
>
> Office supplies are often available to employees on a "free-issue" basis. This means employees do not have to sign for the release of office supplies but merely obtain the necessary ones from a local storage area as needed. Just because supplies are easily available, however, doesn't mean they can be taken for personal use. In many instances, employees have been terminated for taking supplies home for personal use.

- **Deferred revenues** or **unearned revenues** are items that initially were recorded as liabilities but are expected to become revenues over time or through the normal operations of the business. For Family Health Care, unearned rent is an example of a deferred revenue. Other examples include tuition received in advance by a school, an annual retainer fee received by an attorney, premiums received in advance by an insurance company, and magazine subscriptions received in advance by a publisher. On a recent balance sheet, **Microsoft Corporation** reported almost $5 billion of deferred revenue related to its software. Likewise, **AOL Time Warner** reported more than $1 billion of deferred revenue on a recent balance sheet.

Accruals are created when a revenue or expense has not been recorded at the end of the accounting period. Accruals are normally the result of revenue being earned or an expense being incurred before any cash is received or paid. For example, employees can earn wages before the end of the year but not be paid until after the year-end. That is, employee wages can be paid and recorded every Friday, but the accounting period could end on a Tuesday. Thus, at the end of the accounting period, the company owes the employees for their wages on Monday and Tuesday that will be paid on the following Friday. At the end of the accounting period, the company has incurred these wages, but they have not yet been recorded or paid. Thus, the amount of the wages for Monday and Tuesday is an accrual. Descriptions of other accruals follow.

- **Accrued expenses** or *accrued liabilities* are expenses that have been incurred but have not been recorded in the accounts. An example of an accrued expense is accrued interest on notes payable at the end of a period. Other examples include accrued utility expenses and taxes. On a recent balance sheet, **Home Depot** reported more than $600 million of accrued salaries and related expenses, almost $300 million of sales taxes payable, and more than $1 billion of other accrued expenses.

- **Accrued revenues** or *accrued assets* are revenues that have been earned but have not been recorded in the accounts. An example of an accrued revenue is the fee for services that an attorney has provided but has not billed to the client at the end of the period. Other examples include unbilled commissions by a travel agent, accrued interest on notes receivable, and accrued rent on property rented to others. On a recent balance sheet, **General Motors** reported more than $5.8 billion of accounts receivable.

Exhibit 1 summarizes the nature of deferrals and accruals and the need for adjustments in order to prepare financial statements.

Adjustments for Family Health Care

We now analyze the financial statement accounts for Family Health Care at the end of November to determine whether any adjustments are necessary. Specifically, we will focus on the following adjustment data, which are typical for most businesses.

Deferred expenses:
1. Prepaid insurance expired, $1,100.
2. Supplies used, $150.
3. Depreciation on office equipment, $160.

Deferred revenue:
4. Unearned revenue earned, $360.

Accrued expense:
5. Wages owed but not paid to employees, $220.

Accrued revenue:
6. Services provided but not billed to insurance companies, $750.

EXHIBIT 1
Deferrals and Accruals

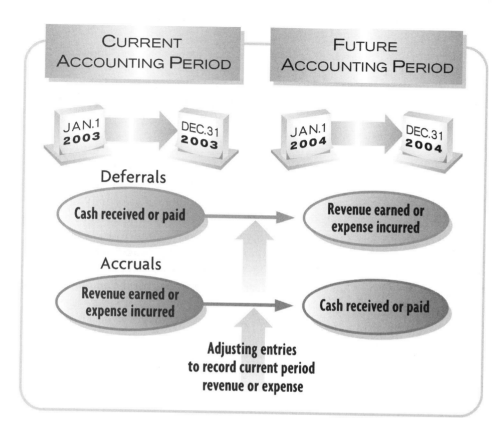

ADJUSTMENT 1 (DEFERRED EXPENSE—PREPAID INSURANCE) This first adjustment recognizes that a portion of the prepaid insurance purchased November 1 expired during November. Family Health Care prepaid two policies: a general business policy for $2,400 (transaction b) and a malpractice policy for $6,000 (transaction c). The general business policy is a two-year policy expiring at a rate of $100 ($2,400/24) per month. The malpractice policy is a six-month policy that expires at a rate of $1,000 ($6,000/6) per month. The total expired prepaid insurance is thus $1,100 ($100 + $1,000). This adjustment is recorded as shown.

			Assets				=	Liabilities			+ Stockholders' Equity		
	Cash	+ Accts. Rec. +	Prepaid Ins.	+ Supp. +	Office Equip. +	Land =	Notes Pay. +	Accts. Pay. +	Unearned Revenue +	Capital Stock +	Retained Earnings		
Bal.	7,730	1,900	8,400	240	8,500	12,000	16,800	140	1,800	11,000	9,030		
a1			−1,100								−1,100	Ins. exp.	
Bal.	7,730	1,900	7,300	240	8,500	12,000	16,800	140	1,800	11,000	7,930		

ADJUSTMENT 2 (DEFERRED EXPENSE—SUPPLIES) This adjustment recognizes the portion of the $240 of supplies purchased during November that have been used. For November, $150 of the supplies were used, leaving $90 of supplies for use during the coming months. Thus, after recording the adjustment, the accounting records should show supplies expense of $150 for November and supplies on hand (an asset) of $90. The second adjustment is recorded as shown.

	Assets					=	Liabilities			+ Stockholders' Equity		
		Accts.	Prepaid		Office			Notes	Accts.	Unearned	Capital	Retained
	Cash +	Rec. +	Ins.	+ Supp. +	Equip. +	Land =	Pay. +	Pay. +	Revenue +	Stock +	Earnings	
Bal.	7,730	1,900	7,300	240	8,500	12,000	16,800	140	1,800	11,000	7,930	
a2				−150							−150	Supplies exp.
Bal.	7,730	1,900	7,300	90	8,500	12,000	16,800	140	1,800	11,000	7,780	

ADJUSTMENT 3 (DEFERRED EXPENSE—DEPRECIATION)   This adjustment recognizes that fixed assets such as office equipment lose their ability to provide service over time. This reduction in the ability of a fixed asset to provide service is called depreciation. However, it is difficult to objectively determine the physical decline in the ability of fixed assets to provide service. For this reason, accountants estimate the amount of the cost of long-term assets that becomes expense over the asset's useful life. In a later chapter, we discuss methods of estimating depreciation. In this chapter, we simply assume that the amount of November depreciation for the office equipment is $160.

To maintain a record of the initial cost of a fixed asset for tax and other purposes, the fixed asset (office equipment) is not reduced directly. Instead, an offsetting or contra asset account, called accumulated depreciation, is included in the accounting equation. Thus, the third adjustment is recorded as shown.

	Assets						=	Liabilities			+ Stockholders' Equity		
		Accts.	Prepaid		Office	Acc.		Notes	Accts.	Unearned	Capital	Ret.	
	Cash +	Rec. +	Ins.	+ Supp. +	Equip. −	Dep. +	Land =	Pay. +	Pay. +	Revenue +	Stock +	Earn.	
Bal.	7,730	1,900	7,300	90	8,500		12,000	16,800	140	1,800	11,000	7,780	
a3						160						−160	Dep. exp.
Bal.	7,730	1,900	7,300	90	8,500	160	12,000	16,800	140	1,800	11,000	7,620	

Note that the accumulated depreciation account is subtracted in determining the total assets. To highlight the effect of this account, its balance is shown in color. We should also note three other points related to adjustment 3. First, land is not depreciated since it usually does not lose its ability to provide service. Second, the cost of the equipment can be thought of as a deferred expense since it is recognized as an expense over the equipment's useful life. Third, the cost of the fixed asset less the balance of its accumulated depreciation is called the asset's *carrying value* or *book value.* For example, the carrying value of the office equipment after the preceding adjustment is $8,340 ($8,500 − $160).

ADJUSTMENT 4 (DEFERRED REVENUE—UNEARNED RENT)   This adjustment recognizes that a portion of the unearned revenue is earned by the end of November. That is, of the $1,800 received for rental of the land for five months (November through March), one-fifth, or $360, would have been earned as of November 30. The fourth adjustment recognizes this decrease in the unearned revenue and the increase in the rental revenue as shown.

		Assets				=		Liabilities		+ Stockholders' Equity		
	Cash +	Accts. Rec. +	Prepaid Ins. +	Supp. +	Office Equip. −	Acc. Dep. +	Land =	Notes Pay. +	Accts. Pay. +	Unearned Revenue +	Capital Stock +	Ret. Earn.
Bal.	7,730	1,900	7,300	90	8,500	160	12,000	16,800	140	1,800	11,000	7,620
a4										−360		360 Rental rev.
Bal.	7,730	1,900	7,300	90	8,500	160	12,000	16,800	140	1,440	11,000	7,980

ADJUSTMENT 5 (ACCRUED EXPENSE—WAGES)

This adjustment recognizes that as of November 30, employees of Family Health Care have worked one or more days for which they have not been paid. Employees rarely are paid the same day that the accounting period ends. Thus, at the end of an accounting period, businesses normally owe wages to their employees. This is what we defined as an accrued expense earlier in our discussion. The fifth adjustment is recorded by increasing wages payable, a liability, and deducting wages expense from retained earnings, as shown.

		Assets				=			Liabilities		+ Stockholders' Equity		
	Cash +	Accts. Rec. +	Prepaid Ins. +	Supp. +	Office Equip. −	Acc. Dep. +	Land =	Notes Pay. +	Accts. Pay. +	Wages Pay +	Unearned Revenue +	Capital Stock +	Retained Earnings
Bal.	7,730	1,900	7,300	90	8,500	160	12,000	16,800	140		1,440	11,000	7,980
a5										220			−220 Wages exp.
Bal.	7,730	1,900	7,300	90	8,500	160	12,000	16,800	140	220	1,440	11,000	7,760

ADJUSTMENT 6 (ACCRUED REVENUE—FEES EARNED)

This adjustment recognizes that Family Health Care has provided services to patients that have not yet been billed. Such services are usually provided near the end of the month. This adjustment is recorded by increasing accounts receivable and fees earned as shown.

		Assets				=			Liabilities		+ Stockholders' Equity		
	Cash +	Accts. Rec. +	Prepaid Ins. +	Supp. +	Office Equip. −	Acc. Dep. +	Land =	Notes Pay. +	Accts. Pay. +	Wages Pay +	Unearned Revenue +	Capital Stock +	Retained Earnings
Bal.	7,730	1,900	7,300	90	8,500	160	12,000	16,800	140	220	1,440	11,000	7,760
a6		750											750 Fees earned
Bal.	7,730	2,650	7,300	90	8,500	160	12,000	16,800	140	220	1,440	11,000	8,510

ETHICS IN ACTION

A common type of fraud involves artificially inflating revenue. One method of inflating revenue is called "round tripping," in which a selling company (S) "lends" money to a customer company (C) to purchase a service or product without hope of reasonable repayment. S records a sale and a loan and then receives back the money it just loaned to C! This looks like a sale in the accounting records, but in reality, S is shipping product for free. The fraud is exposed when it is determined that there was no intent to repay the loan.

Family Health Care's transactions for November and the related adjustments are summarized in Exhibit 2. We will prepare Family Health Care's financial statements using this summary.

EXHIBIT 2 Family Health Care Summary of Transactions and Adjustments for November

	Cash +	Accts. Rec. +	Prepaid Ins. +	Supp. +	Office Equip. −	Acc. Dep. +	Land =	Notes Pay. +	Accts. Pay. +	Wages Pay. +	Unearned Revenue +	Capital Stock +	Ret. Earn.	
									Liabilities				**Stockholders' Equity**	
Bal.	7,320						12,000	10,000			1,800	6,000	3,320	
a.	1,800										1,800			Rental revenue
Bal.	9,120						12,000	10,000			1,800	6,000	3,320	
b.	−2,400		2,400											Paid insurance
Bal.	6,720		2,400				12,000	10,000			1,800	6,000	3,320	
c.	−6,000		6,000											Paid insurance
Bal.	720		8,400				12,000	10,000			1,800	6,000	3,320	
d.	5,000											5,000		Investment
Bal.	5,720		8,400				12,000	10,000			1,800	11,000	3,320	
e.				240					240					Purchase of supplies
Bal.	5,720		8,400	240			12,000	10,000	240		1,800	11,000	3,320	
f.	−1,700				8,500			6,800						Purchase of office equipment
Bal.	4,020		8,400	240	8,500		12,000	16,800	240		1,800	11,000	3,320	
g.		6,100											6,100	Fees earned
Bal.	4,020	6,100	8,400	240	8,500		12,000	16,800	240		1,800	11,000	9,420	
h.	5,500												5,500	Fees earned
Bal.	9,520	6,100	8,400	240	8,500		12,000	16,800	240		1,800	11,000	14,920	
i.	4,200	−4,200												Collected cash
Bal.	13,720	1,900	8,400	240	8,500		12,000	16,800	240		1,800	11,000	14,920	
j.	−100								−100					Paid on account
Bal.	13,620	1,900	8,400	240	8,500		12,000	16,800	140		1,800	11,000	14,920	
k.	−4,690												−2,790 −800 −580 −100 −420	Wages expense Rent expense Utilities expense Interest expense Misc. expense
Bal.	8,930	1,900	8,400	240	8,500		12,000	16,800	140		1,800	11,000	10,230	
l.	−1,200												−1,200	Dividends
Bal.	7,730	1,900	8,400	240	8,500		12,000	16,800	140		1,800	11,000	9,030	
a1.			−1,100										−1,100	Insurance expense
Bal.	7,730	1,900	7,300	240	8,500		12,000	16,800	140		1,800	11,000	7,930	
a2.				−150									−150	Supplies expense
Bal.	7,730	1,900	7,300	90	8,500		12,000	16,800	140		1,800	11,000	7,780	
a3.						160							−160	Dep. expense
Bal.	7,730	1,900	7,300	90	8,500	160	12,000	16,800	140		1,800	11,000	7,620	
a4.											−360		360	Rental revenue
Bal.	7,730	1,900	7,300	90	8,500	160	12,000	16,800	140		1,440	11,000	7,980	
a5.										220			−220	Wages expense
Bal.	7,730	1,900	7,300	90	8,500	160	12,000	16,800	140	220	1,440	11,000	7,760	
a6.		750											750	Fees earned
Bal.	7,730	2,650	7,300	90	8,500	160	12,000	16,800	140	220	1,440	11,000	8,510	

Financial Statements

OBJECTIVE 4

Prepare accrual-basis financial statements including a classified balance sheet.

In Chapter 2, we prepared financial statements for Family Health Care for September and October. These financial statements were prepared using the cash basis of accounting. In this section, we describe and illustrate financial statements for November using the accrual basis of accounting. We begin by introducing the classified balance sheet.

As the term implies, a **classified balance sheet** is prepared with various sections, subsections, and captions that aid in its interpretation and analysis. In the following paragraphs, we describe these sections and subsections.

Assets are resources such as physical items or rights that are owned by the business. Examples of physical assets include cash, supplies, buildings, equipment, and land. Examples of rights are patent rights or rights to services (prepaid items). Physical assets of a long-term nature are referred to as **fixed assets**. Rights that are long-term in nature are called **intangible assets**.

Assets are normally divided into classes in preparing a classified balance sheet. Three of these classes are (1) current assets, (2) fixed assets, and (3) intangible assets.

Cash and other assets that are expected to be converted to cash or sold or used up within one year or less, through the normal operations of the business, are called **current assets**. In addition to cash, the current assets normally include accounts receivable, notes receivable, supplies, and other prepaid expenses. Accounts receivable and notes receivable are current assets because they will usually be converted to cash within one year or less. **Notes receivable** are written claims against debtors who promise to pay the amount of the note and interest at an agreed-upon rate. A note receivable is the creditor's view of a note payable transaction. As shown in Exhibit 2, Family Health Care has current assets of cash, accounts receivable, prepaid insurance, and supplies as of November 30, 2003.

The **fixed assets** section can also be labeled property, plant, and equipment, or plant assets. Fixed assets include equipment, machinery, buildings, and land. Except for land, such fixed assets depreciate over a period of time, as we discussed earlier in this chapter. The cost less accumulated depreciation for each major type of fixed asset is normally reported on the classified balance sheet. As of November 30, 2003, Family Health Care's fixed assets consist of office equipment and land.

Intangible assets represent rights, such as patent rights, copyrights, and goodwill. *Goodwill* arises from factors such as name recognition, location, product quality, reputation, and managerial skill. Goodwill is reported on the balance sheet when these factors are recognized through a purchase of a company. For example, goodwill was reported by **eBay** when it purchased **PayPal**.

Liabilities are amounts owed to outsiders (creditors). Liabilities are often identified on the balance sheet by titles that include the word *payable*. Examples of liabilities include notes payable and wages payable.

Liabilities are normally divided into two classes on a classified balance sheet: (1) current liabilities and (2) long-term liabilities.

Liabilities that are due within a short time (usually one year or less) and that are to be paid out of current assets are called **current liabilities**. The most common current liabilities are notes payable and accounts payable. Other current liabilities reported on the classified balance sheet include wages payable, interest payable, taxes payable, and unearned revenue.

Liabilities that are not due for a long time (usually more than one year) are called **long-term liabilities**. Long-term liabilities are reported after the current liabilities. As long-term liabilities come due and are to be paid within one year, they are reported as current liabilities. If they are to be renewed rather than paid, they continue to be classified as long-term. When an asset is pledged as security for a long-term liability, the obligation can be called a *mortgage note payable* or a *mortgage payable.*

Family Health Care's current and long-term liabilities as of November 30, 2003, are shown in Exhibit 2. You should note that $6,800 of the notes payable is due within the next year and therefore is reported as a current liability. The remainder of the notes payable, $10,000, is not due until 2009 and thus is reported as a long-term liability. Family Health Care's other current liabilities consist of accounts payable, wages payable, and unearned revenue.

Stockholders' equity is the stockholders' rights to the assets of the business. For a corporation, the stockholders' equity consists of capital stock and retained earnings. The Stockholders' Equity section of a classified balance sheet reports each of these two financial statement accounts separately.

As reported on the income statement, revenues are the increases in the stockholders' equity as a result of providing services or selling products to customers. Examples of revenues include fees earned, fares earned, commissions revenue, interest revenue, and rent revenue.

Revenues from the primary operations of the business are normally reported separately from other revenue. For example, Family Health Care has two types of revenues for November, fees earned and rental revenue. Since the primary operation of the business is providing services to patients, rent revenue is reported under the heading Other Income.

Expenses on the income statement are assets used up or services consumed in the process of generating revenues. Expenses are matched against their related revenues to determine the net income or net loss for a period. Examples of typical expenses include wages expense, rent expense, utilities expense, supplies expense, and miscellaneous expense. Expenses not related to the primary operations of the business are sometimes reported as Other Expense. Interest expense is an example of an expense often reported separately as an Other Expense.

The November financial statements for Family Health Care are shown in Exhibit 3. These were prepared using the summary of transactions and adjustments shown in Exhibit 2.

The income statement is prepared by summarizing the revenue and expense transactions listed under the Retained Earnings column of Exhibit 2. The operating income is determined by deducting the operating expenses from the fees earned from normal operations. The other income—rental revenue—is then added to determine the net income for November.

The retained earnings statement is prepared by adding the November net income (from the income statement), less the November dividends, to the beginning amount of retained earnings. This ending amount of retained earnings is included on the balance sheet.

The capital stock amount on the balance sheet results from adding the additional investment during November to the beginning amount of capital stock. The other balance sheet amounts are the ending balances shown in Exhibit 2.

EXHIBIT 3

*Family Health Care
Financial Statements
for November*

FAMILY HEALTH CARE, P.C.
Income Statement
For the Month Ended November 30, 2003

Fees earned		$12,350
Operating expenses:		
Wages expense	$3,010	
Insurance expense	1,100	
Rent expense	800	
Utilities expense	580	
Depreciation expense	160	
Supplies expense	150	
Interest expense	100	
Miscellaneous expenses	420	
Total operating expenses		6,320
Operating income		$ 6,030
Other income:		
Rental revenue		360
Net income		$ 6,390

FAMILY HEALTH CARE, P.C.
Retained Earnings Statement
For the Month Ended November 30, 2003

Retained earnings, November 1, 2003		$3,320
Net income for November	$6,390	
Less dividends	1,200	5,190
Retained earnings, November 30, 2003		$8,510

FAMILY HEALTH CARE, P.C.
Balance Sheet
November 30, 2003

Assets

Current assets:			
Cash		$ 7,730	
Accounts receivable		2,650	
Prepaid insurance		7,300	
Supplies		90	
Total current assets			$17,770
Fixed assets:			
Office equipment	$8,500		
Less accumulated depreciation	160	$ 8,340	
Land		12,000	
Total fixed assets			20,340
Total assets			$38,110

(continued)

EXHIBIT 3
Concluded

Liabilities

Current liabilities:		
Accounts payable	$ 140	
Wages payable	220	
Notes payable	6,800	
Unearned revenue	1,440	
Total current liabilities		$ 8,600
Long-term liabilities:		
Notes payable		10,000
Total liabilities		$18,600

Stockholders' Equity

Capital stock	$11,000	
Retained earnings	8,510	19,510
Total liabilities and stockholders' equity		$38,110

FAMILY HEALTH CARE, P.C.
Statement of Cash Flows
For the Month Ended November 30, 2003

Cash flows from operating activities:		
Cash received from patients	$ 9,700	
Cash received from rental of land	1,800	$ 11,500
Deduct cash payments for expenses:		
Insurance premiums	$(8,400)	
Supplies	(100)	
Wages	(2,790)	
Rent	(800)	
Utilities	(580)	
Interest	(100)	
Miscellaneous expense	(420)	(13,190)
Net cash flow used in operating activities		$ (1,690)
Cash flows used in investing activities:		
Purchase of office equipment		(1,700)
Cash flows from financing activities:		
Additional issuance of capital stock	$ 5,000	
Deduct cash dividends	(1,200)	
Net cash flow from financing activities		3,800
Net increase in cash		$ 410
November 1, 2003 cash balance		7,320
November 30, 2003 cash balance		$ 7,730

The statement of cash flows is prepared by summarizing the cash transactions shown in the Cash column of Exhibit 2. The net cash flow from operations is computed by listing the cash receipts from revenue transactions and subtracting the cash payments for operating transactions. The purchase of the office equipment is treated as a separate cash outflow from investment activities. The receipt of the additional investment and the payment of dividends are reported as cash flows from financing activities.

Interpreting Accrual and Cash Basis Income

OBJECTIVE 5

Describe how the accrual basis of accounting enhances the interpretation of financial statements.

The financial statements of Family Health Care for November illustrate the major differences between the accrual and cash bases of accounting. Note that the $6,390 net income reported in the November income statement is different from the negative $1,690 net cash flow from operating activities reported on the November statement of cash flows.[1] This is in contrast to September and October when these amounts were the same. Under the cash basis of accounting, which Family Health Care used in those months, the net cash flow from operations is the same as the net income. In November, however, Family Health Care began using the accrual basis of accounting.

The difference between the net income (or loss) and the net cash flow from operating activities can be significant. To illustrate, we have summarized these amounts for Family Health Care here:

	Net Cash Flows from Operations	Net Income
September	$ 2,600	$2,600
October	3,220	3,220
November	(1,690)	6,390

Under the cash basis, the cash flows from operating activities and the net income for November are reported as a negative amount (loss) of $1,690. This normally is interpreted as an unfavorable trend and could imply that Family Health Care is failing. In fact, the accrual basis better reflects what is really happening to Family Health Care. Since September, revenues have more than doubled, increasing from $5,500 to $12,350, and net income has more than doubled. Thus, the accrual basis reflects Family Health Care as a very profitable, rapidly expanding business.

Such differences between the cash basis and the accrual basis illustrate why generally accepted accounting principles require the accrual basis for all but the very smallest businesses. You should recognize, however, that the net cash flows from operating activities is an important amount that is useful to readers of the financial statements. For this reason, generally accepted accounting principles require reporting cash flows. In the long run, a business will go bankrupt if it continually experiences negative cash flows from operations even though it may report net income. A business must generate positive cash flows from operations to survive. In the case of

---

[1]The difference between the net cash flows from operations and the net income can be reconciled by considering the effects of accruals and deferrals. Such a reconciliation is shown in Appendix A to this chapter.

Family Health Care, the negative cash flow from operations for November was due in large measure to prepaying insurance premiums of $8,400. Thus, the negative cash flow from operations is temporary for Family Health Care and not a matter of major concern. This illustrates the reason the financial statements must be analyzed and interpreted together rather than individually. For example, long-run profitability is best analyzed by focusing on the net income reported under the accrual basis while the availability of cash to pay debts as they become due is best analyzed by focusing on the net cash flow from operating activities.

The Accounting Cycle

OBJECTIVE   6

Describe the accounting cycle for the accrual basis of accounting.

The process that begins with the analysis of transactions and ends with the preparation of the accounting records for the next accounting period is called the **accounting cycle**. The most important output of the accounting cycle is the financial statements. The basic steps in the accounting cycle are listed here.

1. *Identifying, analyzing, and recording* the effects of transactions on the accounting equation (financial statement accounts).
2. *Identifying, analyzing, and recording* adjustment data.
3. *Preparing* financial statements.
4. *Preparing* the accounting records for the next accounting period.

We have described and illustrated steps 1–3 in this chapter. In this section, we complete the discussion of the accounting cycle by describing how the accounting records are prepared for the next accounting period.[2]

In prior illustrations, we recorded and accumulated revenue, expense, and dividend transactions under retained earnings with separate notations describing them. At the end of an accounting period, we then reviewed retained earnings and summarized the revenues and expenses so that they could be reported in the income statement. Likewise, the dividends were summarized in the retained earnings statement.

Because of the volume of transactions during a period, most businesses record revenues, expenses, and dividends as separate elements (accounts) of the accounting equation, as shown in Exhibit 4. This makes the information for preparing the financial

EXHIBIT 4 *Family Health Care Closing Process for November*

	Ret. Earn.	− Dividends	+ Fees Earned	+ Rental Rev.	− Wages Exp.	− Ins. Exp.	− Rent Exp.	− Util. Exp.	− Dep. Exp.	− Supp. Exp.	− Int. Exp.	− Misc. Exp.
Bal., Nov. 1, 2003	3,320	1,200	12,350	360	3,010	1,100	800	580	160	150	100	420
Revenue closing	12,710		−12,350	−360								
Expense closing	−6,320				−3,010	−1,100	−800	−580	−160	−150	−100	−420
	9,710	1,200	0	0	0	0	0	0	0	0	0	0
Dividends closing	−1,200	−1,200										
Bal. after closing	8,510	0	0	0	0	0	0	0	0	0	0	0

[2]An additional illustration of the complete accounting cycle for Family Health Care is shown in Appendix B.

statements more readily available. After the financial statements have been prepared, the balances of the revenue, expense, and dividend accounts are transferred to the retained earnings account. This process, which is shown in Exhibit 4 for Family Health Care, is called the **closing process**. In this way, these accounts begin each period with zero balances, and the transactions of each period are kept separate from one another.

The net amount of the revenue and expense balances transferred to the retained earnings account is the net income or net loss for the period. In this example, Family Health Care had a net income of $6,390 ($12,710 − $6,320). Because the balances of the revenue, expense, and dividend accounts are transferred to Retained Earnings, they are sometimes called *temporary accounts*.

Common-Size Financial Statements

OBJECTIVE   7

Describe and illustrate how common-size financial statements can be used to analyze and evaluate a company's performance.

Common-size financial statements are often useful in comparing one company to another. In **common-size financial statements**, all items are expressed in percentages. Such statements are useful in comparing the current period with prior periods, individual businesses, or one business with industry percentages. Industry data are often available from trade associations or financial information services.

To illustrate, common-size income statement and balance sheet data for **Wendy's** and **McDonald's Corporation** are shown in Exhibit 5.[3] The income statement data are expressed as a percentage of revenues; thus, Exhibit 5 indicates revenues for both companies as 100%. This, in turn, allows for analysis of the income statement components on a common basis. Without a common basis, it is difficult to compare companies. For example, Wendy's total operating expenses are $1,926,545,000 compared to McDonald's $10,913,300,000. Does this mean that Wendy's has an advantage because of its lower total operating expenses? Exhibit 5 reveals that this is not the case. In fact, Wendy's operating expenses are 86.2% of sales in comparison to 81.1% for McDonald's. As a result, Wendy's operating income is significantly less as a percentage of sales, 13.8%, compared to McDonald's 18.2%.

Based on Exhibit 5, further analyses are needed to determine why Wendy's operating expenses as a percentage of sales are significantly higher than McDonald's. For example, the higher operating expenses could be related to the fact that approximately 20% of Wendy's revenues come from its franchise restaurants while more than 25% of McDonald's revenues come from franchised restaurants.

Exhibit 5 also reports common-size balance sheet information for Wendy's and McDonald's. The balance sheet data are expressed as a percentage of total assets. Exhibit 5 indicates that Wendy's keeps a higher percentage of its assets in the form of cash and equivalents, 5.4%, as compared to 1.9% for McDonald's. Wendy's also has a higher percentage of receivables, inventories, and other current assets than McDonald's, and both companies have approximately the same percentage of assets in property, plant, and equipment. Exhibit 5 also reveals that Wendy's finances more of its operations through stockholders' equity, 49.6%, than does McDonald's, 42.1%.

As Exhibit 5 shows, common-size financial statements facilitate company comparisons and analyses. Such statements are often a starting point for further investigation

[3]The financial statements for Wendy's and McDonalds shown in Exhibit 5 were adapted from 10-K Securities and Exchange Commission filings.

EXHIBIT 5

Common-Size Financial Statements: Wendy's and McDonald's

	Wendy's	McDonald's
Income Statements for the Year Ending December 31, 2001		
Revenues	100.0%	100.0%
Operating expenses	86.2	81.8
Operating income	13.8%	18.2%
Other expenses	0.9	2.5
Income before taxes	12.9%	15.7%
Income taxes	4.8	4.7
Net income	8.1%	11.0%
Balance Sheets as of December 31, 2001		
Currents assets:		
Cash	5.4%	1.9%
Accounts receivable	4.0	3.9
Inventories, prepaid, and other assets	3.4	2.3
Total current assets	12.8%	8.1%
Property, plant, and equipment	79.0	76.7
Other long-term assets	8.2	15.2
Total assets	100.0%	100.0%
Current liabilities:		
Accounts payable	5.4%	3.1%
Other liabilities	8.9	6.9
Total current liabilities	14.3%	10.0%
Long-term liabilities	36.1	47.9
Stockholders' equity	49.6	42.1
Total liabilities and stockholders' equity	100.0%	100.0%

and analyses of major differences between companies in similar industries. For example, based on the preceding comparison, further inquiries could be made into why Wendy's operating expenses are a higher percentage of sales and why Wendy's maintains a higher percentage of its total assets in cash and receivables than does McDonald's.

APPENDIX A

Reconciliation: Net Cash Flows from Operations and Net Income

In Chapter 2, we illustrated financial statements for Family Health Care for September and October 2003. During September and October, Family Health Care used the cash basis of accounting. Under the cash basis of accounting, the net cash flows from operating activities shown on the statement of cash flows equals the net income shown in the income statements. For example, Exhibits 4 and 6 in Chapter 2 report net cash flows from operating activities and net income of $2,600 and $3,220 for September and October. Under the cash basis, net cash flows from operating activities always equal net income. This is not true, however, under the accrual basis of accounting.

During November and December, Family Health Care used the accrual basis of accounting. The November financial statements are illustrated in Exhibit 3 of this chapter. The December financial statements for Family Health Care are illustrated in Appendix B at the end of this chapter. The net cash flows from operating activities and net income for November and December follow.

	Net Cash Flows from Operating Activities	Net Income
November	$(1,690)	$ 6,390
December	8,760	10,825

Under the accrual basis, net cash flows from operating activities is normally not the same as net income. The difference between these two amounts can be reconciled by considering the effects of accruals and deferrals on the income statement. Exhibit 6 illustrates the November reconciliation of Family Health Care's net income with operating cash flows from operations.

EXHIBIT 6

November's Reconciliation of Net Income and Cash Flows from Operations

Net income		$ 6,390
Add:		
Depreciation expense	$ 160	
Increase in accounts payable	140	
Increase in wages payable	220	
Increase in unearned revenue	1,440	1,960
Deduct:		
Increase in accounts receivable	$(2,650)	
Increase in prepaid insurance	(7,300)	
Increase in supplies	(90)	(10,040)
Net cash flows from operating activities		$ (1,690)

In Exhibit 6, we begin with net income. We then add or deduct the effects of accruals or deferrals that influenced net income under the accrual basis of accounting but did not result in the receipt or payment of cash. By doing so, we arrive at net cash flows from operating activities.

The effect of an accrual or deferral on the income statement and net income is reflected in its net increase or decrease during the period. For example, during November depreciation expense of $160 was recorded (a deferred expense) and thus deducted in arriving at net income, yet no cash was paid. Thus, to arrive at cash flows from operations, depreciation expense is added back to net income. Likewise, accounts payable increased during November by $140 and a related expense was recorded. But again, no cash was paid. Similarly, wages payable increased during November by $220, and the related wages expense was deducted in arriving at net income. However, the $220 was not paid until the next month. Thus, for November, the increases of $140 in accounts payable and $220 in wages payable are added back to net income.

The increase of $1,440 in unearned revenue represents unearned revenue for four months for land rented to ILS Company. ISL Company initially paid Family Heath Care $1,800 in advance. Of the $1,800, one-fifth ($360) was recorded as revenue for November. However, under the cash basis, the entire $1,800 would have been recorded as revenue. Thus, $1,440 (the increase in the unearned revenue) is added back to net income to arrive at cash flows from operations.

During November, accounts receivable increased by $2,650 and thus were recorded as part of revenue in arriving at net income. However, no cash was received. Thus, this increase in accounts receivable is deducted in arriving at cash flows from operations.

The increase in prepaid insurance represents an $8,400 payment of cash for insurance premiums. During November, only $1,100 of the premiums is deducted in arriving at net income. Thus, the remaining $7,300 (the increase in prepaid insurance) is deducted in arriving at cash flows from operations. Similarly, the increase in supplies of $90 is deducted.

You could have noticed a pattern in how we reconciled net income to net cash flows from operations. First, depreciation expense was added. Next, increases in current assets related to operations were deducted, and increases in current liabilities related to operations were added. The increase in the current liability for notes payable of $6,800 was not included in the reconciliation. This is because the notes payable are related to the purchase of office equipment, which, in the statement of cash flows, is an investing activity rather than an operating activity.

During November, all current asset and liability accruals and deferrals related to operations were increases. This happened because Family Health Care used the cash basis during October and, thus, there were no deferrals or accruals at the beginning of November. In future periods, there would be both increases and decreases in these items. These increases and decreases would be added or subtracted to arrive at cash flows from operations, as shown in Exhibit 7.

EXHIBIT 7			
Reconciling Items	Net income		$XXX
	Add:		
	Depreciation expense	$XXX	
	Increases in current liabilities from operations	XXX	
	Decreases in current assets from operations	XXX	XXX
	Deduct:		
	Increases in current assets from operations	$XXX	
	Decreases in current liabilities from operations	XXX	XXX
	Net cash flows from operations		$XXX

For example, a decrease in accounts receivable implies that cash was collected and thus would be added. In contrast, a decrease in accounts payable implies that cash was paid and thus would be deducted.

APPENDIX B

Family Health Care Transactions for December: Illustrative Problem

To review the accrual accounting and the accounting cycle, we use the December transactions for Family Health Care, which are as follows:

a. Received cash of $1,900 from patients for services provided on account during November.
b. Provided services of $10,800 on account.

c. Received $6,500 for services provided for patients who paid cash.

d. Purchased supplies on account, $400.

e. Received $6,900 from insurance companies that paid on patients' accounts for services that had been provided during December.

f. Paid $310 on account for supplies that had been purchased.

g. Expenses paid during December were as follows: wages, $4,200, including $220 accrued at the end of November; rent, $800; utilities, $610; interest, $100; miscellaneous, $520.

h. Paid dividends of $1,200 to stockholder (Dr. Landry).

Instructions

1. Record the December transactions, using the following summary of transactions form. The beginning balances of December 1 have already been entered into the form. After each transaction, you should enter a balance for each item. The transactions are recorded similarly to those for November except that separate accounts are used for dividends, revenues, and expenses. In addition, you should note that in transaction (g), the $4,200 of wages paid includes wages of $220 that were accrued at the end of November. Thus, only $3,980 ($4,200 − $220) should be recorded as wages expense for December. The remaining $220 reduces the wages payable. You should also note that the balance of retained earnings on December 1, $8,510, is the balance on November 30.

		Assets							=		Liabilities			+	Stockholders' Equity	
		Accts.	Prepaid			Office	Acc.			Notes	Accts.	Wages		Unearned		Capital
	Cash +	Rec. +	Ins. +	Supp. +	Equip. −	Dep. +	Land =	Pay. +	Pay. +	Pay. +	Revenue +	Stock
Bal.	7,730	2,650	7,300	90	8,500	160	12,000	16,800	140	220	1,440	11,000

	Retained			Fees	Rental	Wages	Ins.	Rent	Util.	Dep.	Supp.	Int.	Misc.
	+ Earnings −	Dividends +	Earned +	Rev. −	Exp. −	Exp. −	Exp. −	Exp. −	Exp. −	Exp. −	Exp. −	Exp.
Bal.	8,510												

2. The adjustment data for December are as follows:

Deferred expenses:

(1) Prepaid insurance expired, $1,100.

(2) Supplies used, $275.

(3) Depreciation on office equipment, $160.

Deferred revenues:

(4) Unearned revenue earned, $360.

Accruals:

(5) Wages owed employees but not paid, $340.

(6) Services provided but not billed to insurance companies, $1,050.

Enter the adjustments in the summary of transactions. Identify each adjustment with the letter a and the number of the related adjustment item. For example, the adjustment for prepaid insurance should be identified as (a1).

(continued)

3. Prepare the December financial statements, including the income statement, retained earnings statement, balance sheet, and statement of cash flows.
4. Close the temporary accounts in the summary of transactions.
5. (Appendix A) Reconcile the December net income with the operating cash flows from operations.

Solution

1. Family Health Care Summary of Transactions for December

			Assets					=		Liabilities			Stockholders' + Equity
	Cash	Accts. + Rec.	Prepaid + Ins.	+ Supp.	Office + Equip.	Acc. − Dep.	+ Land	=	Notes Pay.	Accts. + Pay.	Wages + Pay.	Unearned + Revenue	Capital + Stock
Bal.	7,730	2,650	7,300	90	8,500	160	12,000		16,800	140	220	1,440	11,000
a.	1,900	−1,900											
Bal.	9,630	750	7,300	90	8,500	160	12,000		16,800	140	220	1,440	11,000
b.		10,800											
Bal.	9,630	11,550	7,300	90	8,500	160	12,000		16,800	140	220	1,440	11,000
c.	6,500												
Bal.	16,130	11,550	7,300	90	8,500	160	12,000		16,800	140	220	1,440	11,000
d.				400						400			
Bal.	16,130	11,550	7,300	490	8,500	160	12,000		16,800	540	220	1,440	11,000
e.	6,900	−6,900											
Bal.	23,030	4,650	7,300	490	8,500	160	12,000		16,800	540	220	1,440	11,000
f.	−310									−310			
Bal.	22,720	4,650	7,300	490	8,500	160	12,000		16,800	230	220	1,440	11,000
g.	−6,230										−220		
Bal.	16,490	4,650	7,300	490	8,500	160	12,000		16,800	230	0	1,440	11,000
h.	−1,200												
Bal.	15,290	4,650	7,300	490	8,500	160	12,000		16,800	230	0	1,440	11,000

	Retained + Earnings	− Dividends	Fees + Earned	Rental + Rev.	Wages − Exp.	Ins. − Exp.	Rent − Exp.	Util. − Exp.	Dep. − Exp.	Supp. − Exp.	Int. − Exp.	Misc. − Exp.	
Bal.	8,510												
a.													Collected cash
Bal.	8,510												
b.			10,800										Fees earned
Bal.	8,510		10,800										
c.			6,500										Fees earned
Bal.	8,510		17,300										
d.													Purch. of suppl.
Bal.	8,510		17,300										
e.													Collected cash
Bal.	8,510		17,300										
f.													Paid on account
Bal.	8,510		17,300										
g.					3,980	800	610				100	520	Paid expenses
Bal.	8,510		17,300		3,980	800	610				100	520	
h.		1,200											Paid dividends
Bal.	8,510	1,200	17,300		3,980	800	610				100	520	

2. Family Health Care Adjustments for December

	Cash +	Accts. Rec. +	Prepaid Ins. +	Supp. +	Office Equip. −	Acc. Dep. +	Land =	Notes Pay. +	Accts. Pay. +	Wages Pay. +	Unearned Revenue +	Capital Stock
					Assets			**=**		**Liabilities**		**Stockholders' + Equity**
Bal.	15,290	4,650	7,300	490	8,500	160	12,000	16,800	230	0	1,440	11,000
a1			−1,100									
Bal.	15,290	4,650	6,200	490	8,500	160	12,000	16,800	230	0	1,440	11,000
a2				−275								
Bal.	15,290	4,650	6,200	215	8,500	160	12,000	16,800	230	0	1,440	11,000
a3						160						
Bal.	15,290	4,650	6,200	215	8,500	320	12,000	16,800	230	0	1,440	11,000
a4											−360	
Bal.	15,290	4,650	6,200	215	8,500	320	12,000	16,800	230	0	1,080	11,000
a5										340		
Bal.	15,290	4,650	6,200	215	8,500	320	12,000	16,800	230	340	1,080	11,000
a6		1,050										
Bal.	15,290	5,700	6,200	215	8,500	320	12,000	16,800	230	340	1,080	11,000

	Retained Earnings −	Dividends +	Fees Earned +	Rental Rev. −	Wages Exp. −	Ins. Exp. −	Rent Exp. −	Util. Exp. −	Dep. Exp. −	Supp. Exp. −	Int. Exp. −	Misc. Exp.	
Bal.	8,510	1,200	17,300		3,980		800	610			100	520	
a1						1,100							Ins. exp.
Bal.	8,510	1,200	17,300		3,980	1,100	800	610	0	0	100	520	
a2										275			Supp. exp.
Bal.	8,510	1,200	17,300		3,980	1,100	800	610	0	275	100	520	
a3									160				Dep. exp.
Bal.	8,510	1,200	17,300		3,980	1,100	800	610	160	275	100	520	
a4				360									Rental rev.
Bal.	8,510	1,200	17,300	360	3,980	1,100	800	610	160	275	100	520	
a5					340								Wages exp.
Bal.	8,510	1,200	17,300	360	4,320	1,100	800	610	160	275	100	520	
a6			1,050										Fees earned
Bal.	8,510	1,200	18,350	360	4,320	1,100	800	610	160	275	100	520	

3.

FAMILY HEALTH CARE, P.C.
Income Statement
For the Month Ended December 31, 2003

Fees earned		$18,350
Operating expenses:		
Wages expense	$4,320	
Insurance expense	1,100	
Rent expense	800	
Utilities expense	610	
Supplies expense	275	
Depreciation expense	160	
Interest expense	100	
Miscellaneous expenses	520	
Total operating expenses		7,885
Operating income		$10,465
Other income:		
Rental revenue		360
Net income		$10,825

FAMILY HEALTH CARE, P.C.
Retained Earnings Statement
For the Month Ended December 31, 2003

Retained earnings, December 1, 2003		$ 8,510
Net income for December	$10,825	
Less dividends	1,200	9,625
Retained earnings, December 31, 2003		$18,135

FAMILY HEALTH CARE, P.C.
Balance Sheet
December 31, 2003

Assets			
Current assets:			
Cash		$15,290	
Accounts receivable		5,700	
Prepaid insurance		6,200	
Supplies		215	
Total current assets			$27,405
Fixed assets:			
Office equipment	$8,500		
Less accumulated depreciation	320	$ 8,180	
Land		12,000	
Total fixed assets			20,180
Total assets			$47,585

Liabilities

Current liabilities:		
Accounts payable	$ 230	
Wages payable	340	
Notes payable	6,800	
Unearned revenue	1,080	
Total current liabilities		$ 8,450
Long-term liabilities:		
Notes payable		10,000
Total liabilities		$18,450

Stockholders' Equity

Capital stock	$11,000	
Retained earnings	18,135	29,135
Total liabilities and stockholders' equity		$47,585

FAMILY HEALTH CARE, P.C.
Statement of Cash Flows
For the Month Ended December 31, 2003

Cash flows from operating activities:		
Cash received from patients		$15,300
Deduct cash payments for expenses:		
Supplies	$ (310)	
Wages	(4,200)	
Rent	(800)	
Utilities	(610)	
Interest	(100)	
Miscellaneous expense	(520)	(6,540)
Net cash flow from operating activities		$ 8,760
Cash flows from financing activities:		
Deduct cash dividends		(1,200)
Net increase in cash		$ 7,560
December 1, 2003 cash balance		7,730
December 31, 2003 cash balance		$15,290

4. Family Health Care Closing Process for December

Retained Earnings	− Dividends +	Fees Earned +	Rental Rev. −	Wages Exp. −	Ins. Exp. −	Rent Exp. −	Util. Exp. −	Dep. Exp. −	Supp. Exp. −	Int. Exp. −	Misc. Exp.
8,510	1,200	18,350	360	4,320	1,100	800	610	160	275	100	520
18,710		−18,350	−360								
−7,885				−4,320	−1,100	−800	−610	−160	−275	−100	−520
19,335	1,200	0	0	0	0	0	0	0	0	0	0
−1,200	−1,200										
18,135	0	0	0	0	0	0	0	0	0	0	0

5. December's Reconciliation of Net Income with Cash Flows from Operations

Net income		$10,825
Add:		
Depreciation expense	$ 160	
Decrease in prepaid insurance	1,100	
Increase in accounts payable	90	
Increase in wages payable	120	1,470
Deduct:		
Increase in accounts receivable	$(3,050)	
Increase in supplies	(125)	
Decrease in unearned revenue	(360)	(3,535)
Net cash flows from operating activities		$ 8,760

Key Points

1. Describe the accrual basis of accounting.

Under the accrual basis of accounting, revenue is recognized when it is earned. When revenues are earned and recorded, all expenses incurred in generating the revenues are recorded so that revenues and expenses are properly matched in determining the net income or loss for the period. Liabilities are recorded when a business incurs the obligation to pay for the services or goods purchased.

2. Use the accrual basis of accounting to analyze, record, and summarize transactions.

Every transaction affects one or more elements of the accounting equation, and the two sides of the equation must always be equal. Stockholders' equity is increased by issuing capital stock and revenues (retained earnings) and is decreased by expenses (retained earnings) and dividends (retained earnings).

3. Describe and illustrate the end-of-the-period adjustment process.

The accrual basis of accounting requires the accounting records to be updated prior to preparing financial statements. This updating process, called the *adjustment process*, is necessary to match revenues and expenses. The adjustment process involves two types of adjustments: deferrals and accruals. Adjustments for deferrals could involve deferred expenses or deferred revenues. Adjustments for accruals could involve accrued expenses or accrued revenues.

4. Prepare accrual-basis financial statements including a classified balance sheet.

A classified balance sheet includes sections for current assets; property, plant, and equipment (fixed assets); and intangible assets. Liabilities are classified as current liabilities or long-term liabilities. The income statement normally reports sections for revenues, operating expenses, other income and expense, and net income.

5. Describe how the accrual basis of accounting enhances the interpretation of financial statements.

The net cash flows from operating activities and net income differ under the accrual basis of accounting. Under the accrual basis, net income is a better indicator of the long-term profitability of a business. For this reason, the accrual basis of accounting is required by generally accepted accounting principles except for very small businesses. The accrual basis reports the effects of operations on cash flows through the reporting of net cash flows from operating activities on the statement of cash flows.

6. Describe the accounting cycle for the accrual basis of accounting.

The accounting cycle is the process that begins with the analysis of transactions and ends with preparing the accounting records for the next accounting period. The basic steps in the accounting cycle are (1) identifying, analyzing, and recording the effects of transactions on the accounting equation, (2) identifying, analyzing, and recording adjustment data, (3) preparing financial statements, and (4) preparing the accounting records for the next accounting period.

7. Describe and illustrate how common-size financial statements can be used to analyze and evaluate a company's performance.

Common-size financial statements are often useful in comparing one company to another. In common-size financial statements, all items are expressed in percentages. Such statements are useful in comparing the current period with prior periods, individual businesses, or one business with industry percentages.

Glossary

Account: A record in which increases and decreases in a financial statement element are recorded.

Accounting cycle: The process that begins with the analysis of transactions and ends with the preparation of the accounting records for the next accounting period.

Accounts payable: Liabilities for amounts incurred from purchases of products or services in the normal operations of a business.

Accounts receivable: An asset for amounts due from customers in the normal operations of a business.

Accruals: Revenues or expenses that have not been recorded.

Accrued expenses: Expenses that have been incurred at the end of an accounting period but have not been recorded in the accounts; sometimes called *accrued liabilities*.

Accrued revenues: Revenues that have been earned at the end of an accounting period but have not been recorded in the accounts; sometimes called *accrued assets*.

Accumulated depreciation: An offsetting or contra asset account used to record depreciation on a fixed asset.

Adjustment process: A process required by the accrual basis of accounting in which the accounts are

updated prior to preparing financial statements.

Classified balance sheet: A balance sheet prepared with various sections, subsections, and captions that aid in its interpretation and analysis.

Closing process: The process of transferring the balances of the revenue, expense, and dividends accounts to retained earnings in preparation for the next accounting period.

Common-size financial statement: A financial statement in which all items are expressed in percentages.

Current assets: Cash and other assets that are expected to be converted to cash or sold or used up through the normal operations of the business within one year or less.

Current liabilities: Liabilities that will be due within a short time (usually one year or less) and that are to be paid out of current assets.

Deferrals: Delayed recordings of expenses or revenues.

Deferred expenses: Items that are initially recorded as assets but are expected to become expenses over time or through the normal operations of the business; sometimes called *prepaid expenses*.

Deferred revenues: Items that are initially recorded as liabilities but are

expected to become revenues over time or through the normal operations of the business; sometimes called *unearned revenues*.

Depreciation: The reduction in the ability of a fixed asset to provide service.

Fixed assets: Physical assets of a long-term nature; sometimes called *plant assets*.

Intangible assets: Assets that are rights of a long-term nature.

Long-term liabilities: Liabilities that will not be due for a long time (usually more than one year).

Notes receivable: Written claims against debtors who promise to pay the amount of the note plus interest at an agreed-upon rate.

Prepaid expenses: Items that are initially recorded as assets but are expected to become expenses over time or through the normal operations of the business; often called deferred expenses.

Stockholders' equity: The stockholders' rights to the assets of a business.

Unearned revenues: Items that are initially recorded as liabilities but are expected to become revenues over time or through the normal operation of the business; often called *deferred revenues*.

Self-Study Questions

(Answers appear at end of chapter.)

1. Assume that a lawyer bills her clients $15,000 on June 30, 2004, for services rendered during June. The lawyer collects $8,500 of the billings during July and the remainder in August. Under the accrual basis of accounting, when would the lawyer record the revenue for the fees?
   A. June, $15,000; July, $0; and August, $0.
   B. June, $0; July, $6,500; and August, $8,500.
   C. June, $8,500; July, $6,500; and August, $0
   D. June, $0; July, $8,500; and August, $6,500.

2. On January 24, 2004, Niche Consulting collected $5,700 it had billed its clients for services rendered on December 31, 2003. How would you record the January 24 transaction using the accrual basis?
   A. Increase Cash, $5,700; decrease Fees Earned, $5,700.
   B. Increase Accounts Receivable, $5,700; increase Fees Earned, $5,700.
   C. Increase Cash, $5,700; decrease Accounts Receivable, $5,700.
   D. Increase Cash, $5,700; increase Fees Earned, $5,700.

3. Which of the following items represents a deferral?
   A. Prepaid Insurance
   B. Wages Payable
   C. Fees Earned
   D. Accumulated Depreciation

4. If the supplies account indicated a balance of $2,250, before adjustment on May 31, and supplies on hand at May 31 totaled $950, the adjustment would be:
   A. increase Supplies, $950; decrease Supplies Expense, $950.
   B. increase Supplies, $1,300; decrease Supplies Expense, $1,300.
   C. increase Supplies Expense, $950; decrease Supplies, $950.
   D. increase Supplies Expense, $1,300; decrease Supplies, $1,300.

5. The balance in the unearned rent account for Jones Co. as of December 31 is $1,200. If Jones Co. failed to record the adjusting entry for $600 of rent earned during December, the effect on the balance sheet and income statement for December would be:
   A. assets understated by $600; net income overstated by $600.
   B. liabilities understated by $600; net income understated by $600.
   C. liabilities overstated by $600; net income understated by $600.
   D. liabilities overstated by $600; net income overstated by $600.

Discussion Questions

1. Would **General Electric** and **Xerox** use the cash basis or the accrual basis of accounting? Explain.

2. How are revenues and expenses reported on the income statement under (a) the cash basis of accounting and (b) the accrual basis of accounting?

3. Fees for services provided are billed to a customer during 2003. The customer remits the amount owed in 2004. During which year would the revenues be reported on the income statement under (a) the cash basis? (b) the accrual basis?

4. Employees performed services in 2003, but the wages were not paid until 2004. During which year would the wages expense be reported on the income statement under (a) the cash basis and (b) the accrual basis?

5. Which of the following accounts would appear only in an accrual basis accounting system and which could appear in either a cash basis or accrual basis accounting system? (a) Capital Stock, (b) Fees Earned, (c) Accounts Payable, (d) Land, (e) Utilities Expense, and (f) Accounts Receivable.

6. Is the land balance before the accounts have been adjusted the amount that should normally be reported on the balance sheet? Explain.

7. Is the supplies balance before the accounts have been adjusted the amount that should normally be reported on the balance sheet? Explain.

8. Why are adjustments needed at the end of an accounting period?

9. What is the difference between the adjusting process and the closing process?

10. Identify the four different categories of adjustments frequently required at the end of an accounting period.

11. If the effect of an adjustment is to increase the balance of a liability account, which of the following statements describes the effect of the adjustment on the other account?
    a. Increases the balance of a revenue account.
    b. Increases the balance of an expense account.
    c. Increases the balance of an asset account.

12. If the effect of an adjustment is to increase the balance of an asset account, which of the following statements describes the effect of the adjustment on the other account?
    a. Increases the balance of a revenue account.
    b. Increases the balance of a liability account.
    c. Increases the balance of an expense account.

13. Does every adjustment have an effect on determining the amount of net income for a period? Explain.

14. (a) Explain the purpose of the two accounts, Depreciation Expense and Accumulated Depreciation. (b) Is it customary for the balances of the two accounts to be equal? (c) In what financial statements, if any, will each account appear?

15. Describe the nature of the assets that compose the following sections of a balance sheet: (a) current assets, (b) property, plant, and equipment.

16. (a) Why is the closing process required at the end of an accounting period? (b) To what account are revenue and expenses closed? (c) To what account is dividends closed?

17. (a) What are common-size financial statements? (b) Why are common-size financial statements useful in interpreting and analyzing financial statements?

Exercises

EXERCISE 3–1
Accrual basis of accounting
OBJECTIVE 2

✓ b. Net income: $6,450

Neal Hastings established Ember Services, P.C., a professional corporation, on January 1 of the current year. Ember Services offers financial planning advice to its clients. The effect of each transaction and the balances after each transaction for January are as follows. Each increase or decrease in stockholders' equity, except transaction (h), affects net income.

		Assets			=	Liabilities	+	Stockholders' Equity		
			Accounts			Accounts		Capital		Retained
	Cash	+ Receivable	+ Supplies	=		Payable	+	Stock	+	Earnings
a.	+15,000							+15,000		
b.			+1,100			+1,100				
Bal.	15,000		1,100			1,100		15,000		
c.	−775					−775				
Bal.	14,225		1,100			325		15,000		
d.	+9,000									+9,000
Bal.	23,225		1,100			325		15,000		9,000
e.	−4,500									−4,500
Bal.	18,725		1,100			325		15,000		4,500
f.			−850							−850
Bal.	18,725		250			325		15,000		3,650
g.		+2,800								+2,800
Bal.	18,725	2,800	250			325		15,000		6,450
h.	−2,000									−2,000
Bal.	16,725	2,800	250			325		15,000		4,450

a. Describe each transaction.
b. What is the amount of net income for January?

EXERCISE 3-2
Classify accruals and deferrals
OBJECTIVE 3

Classify the following items as (a) deferred expense (prepaid expense), (b) deferred revenue (unearned revenue), (c) accrued expense (accrued liability), or (d) accrued revenue (accrued asset).

1. Fees earned but not yet received.
2. Taxes owed but payable in the following period.
3. Salary owed but not yet paid.
4. Supplies on hand.
5. Fees received but not yet earned.
6. Utilities owed but not yet paid.
7. A two-year premium paid on a fire insurance policy.
8. Subscriptions received in advance by a magazine publisher.

EXERCISE 3-3
Classify adjustments
OBJECTIVE 3

The following accounts were taken from the unadjusted trial balance of O'Neil Co., a congressional lobbying firm. Indicate whether or not each account normally requires an adjusting entry. If the account normally requires an adjusting entry, use the following notation to indicate the type of adjustment:

AE   Accrued Expense
AR   Accrued Revenue
DR   Deferred Revenue
DE   Deferred Expense

To illustrate, the answers for the first two accounts follow.

Account	Answer
Dividends	Does not normally require adjustment.
Accounts Receivable	Normally requires adjustment (AR).
Accumulated Depreciation	
Cash	
Interest Payable	
Interest Receivable	
Land	
Office Equipment	
Prepaid Insurance	
Supplies Expense	
Unearned Fees	
Wages Expense	

EXERCISE 3-4
Adjustment for supplies
OBJECTIVE 3

✓ a. $1,234

Answer each of the following questions concerning supplies and the adjustment for supplies. (a) The balance in the supplies account, before adjustment at the end of the year, is $1,475. What is the amount of the adjustment if the amount of supplies on hand at the end of the year is $241? (b) The supplies account has a balance of $418, and the supplies expense account has a balance of $1,943 at December 31, 2004. If 2004 was the first year of operations, what was the amount of supplies purchased during the year?

EXERCISE 3-5
Adjustments for prepaid insurance
OBJECTIVE 3

The prepaid insurance account had a balance of $3,600 at the beginning of the year. The account was increased for $1,200 for premiums on policies purchased during the year. What is the adjustment required at the end of the year for each of the following situations: (a) the amount of unexpired insurance applicable to future periods is $3,450 and (b) the amount of insurance expired during the year is $1,875. For (a) and (b), indicate each account affected, whether the account is increased or decreased, and the amount of the increase or decrease.

EXERCISE 3-6

Adjustment for unearned revenue

OBJECTIVE 3

For the years ending June 30, 2001 and 2000, Microsoft Corporation reported unearned revenue of $4,816 million and $5,614 million, respectively. For the year ending June 30, 2001, Microsoft also reported total revenues of $19,747 million. (a) What adjustment for unearned revenue did Microsoft make at June 30, 2001? Indicate each account affected, whether the account is increased or decreased, and the amount of the increase or decrease. (b) What percentage of total revenues was the adjustment for unearned revenue?

EXERCISE 3-7

Effect of omitting adjustment

OBJECTIVE 3

At the end of March, the first month of the business year, the usual adjustment transferring rent earned to a revenue account from the unearned rent account was omitted. Indicate which items will be incorrectly stated, because of the error, on (a) the income statement for March and (b) the balance sheet as of March 31. Also indicate whether the items in error will be overstated or understated.

EXERCISE 3-8

Adjustment for accrued salaries

OBJECTIVE 3

Taylor Fork Realty Co. pays weekly salaries of $13,750 on Friday for a five-day week ending on that day. What is the adjustment at the end of the accounting period, assuming that the period ends on (a) Tuesday or (b) Wednesday? Indicate each account affected, whether the account is increased or decreased, and the amount of the increase or decrease.

EXERCISE 3-9

Determine wages paid

OBJECTIVE 3

The balances of the two wages accounts at December 31, after adjustments at the end of the first year of operations, are Wages Payable, $1,960, and Wages Expense, $87,430. Determine the amount of wages paid during the year.

EXERCISE 3-10

Effect of omitting adjustment

OBJECTIVE 3

Accrued salaries of $3,100 owed to employees for December 30 and 31 are not considered in preparing the financial statements for the year ended December 31, 2003. Indicate which items will be erroneously stated because of the error on (a) the income statement for December 2003 and (b) the balance sheet as of December 31, 2003. Also indicate whether the items in error will be overstated or understated.

EXERCISE 3-11

Effect of omitting adjustment

OBJECTIVE 3

Assume that the error in Exercise 3-10 was not corrected and that the $3,100 of accrued salaries was included in the first salary payment in January 2004. Indicate which items will be erroneously stated because of failure to correct the initial error on (a) the income statement for January 2004 and (b) the balance sheet as of January 31, 2004.

EXERCISE 3-12

Effects of errors on financial statements

OBJECTIVE 3

For a recent period, Circuit City Stores reported accrued expenses of $154,795,000. For the same period, Circuit City reported earnings before income taxes of $27,367,000. If accrued expenses had not been recorded, what would have been the earnings (loss) before income taxes?

EXERCISE 3-13

Effects of errors on financial statements

OBJECTIVE 3

The balance sheet for Ford Motor Company as of December 31, 2001, includes $23,990 million of accrued expenses as liabilities. Before taxes, Ford Motor Company reported a net loss of $7,584 million. If the accruals had not been recorded at December 31, 2001, how much would net income or net loss before taxes have been for the year ended December 31, 2001?

EXERCISE 3-14

Effects of errors on financial statements

OBJECTIVE 3

✓ b. $445,670

The accountant for Maxim Medical Co., a medical services consulting firm, mistakenly omitted adjustments for (a) unearned revenue ($10,390) and (b) accrued wages ($2,440). (a) Indicate the effect of each error, considered individually, on the income statement for the current year ended December 31. Also indicate the effect of each error on the December 31 balance sheet. Set up a table similar to the following, and record your answers by inserting the dollar amount in the appropriate spaces. Insert a zero if the error does not affect the item.

	Error (a)		Error (b)	
	Over-stated	Under-stated	Over-stated	Under-stated
1. Revenue for the year would be	$	$	$	$
2. Expenses for the year would be	$	$	$	$
3. Net income for the year would be	$	$	$	$
4. Assets at December 31 would be	$	$	$	$
5. Liabilities at December 31 would be	$	$	$	$
6. Stockholders' equity at December 31 would be	$	$	$	$

(b) If the net income for the current year had been $437,720, what would be the correct net income if the proper adjustments had been made?

EXERCISE 3-15
Adjustment for accrued fees
OBJECTIVE 3

At the end of the current year, $7,260 of fees have been earned but have not been billed to clients.

a.   What is the adjustment to record the accrued fees? Indicate each account affected, whether the account is increased or decreased, and the amount of the increase or decrease.
b.   If the cash basis rather than the accrual basis had been used, would an adjustment have been necessary? Explain.

EXERCISE 3-16
Effect of deferred revenue
OBJECTIVE 3

AOL Time Warner Inc. reported deferred revenue of $1,660 million and $1,063 million as of December 31, 2001 and 2000, respectively. For the year ending December 31, 2001, AOL Time Warner reported total revenues of $38,234 million. (a) What was the amount of the adjustment for deferred revenue for 2001? (b) What would have been total revenues under the cash basis?

EXERCISE 3-17
Adjustment for depreciation
OBJECTIVE 3

The estimated amount of depreciation on equipment for the current year is $3,000. (a) How is the adjustment recorded? Indicate each account affected, whether the account is increased or decreased, and the amount of the increase or decrease. (b) If the adjustment in (a) were omitted, which items would be erroneously stated on (1) the income statement for the year and (2) the balance sheet as of December 31?

EXERCISE 3-18
Adjustments
OBJECTIVE 3

The Purification Company is a consulting firm specializing in pollution control. The following adjustments were made for The Purification Company:

Account	Adjustments Increase (Decrease)
Accounts Receivable	$ 5,100
Supplies	(1,225)
Prepaid Insurance	(1,000)
Accumulated Depreciation—Equipment	1,800
Wages Payable	900
Unearned Rent	(2,500)
Fees Earned	5,100
Wages Expense	900
Supplies Expense	1,225
Rent Revenue	2,500
Insurance Expense	1,000
Depreciation Expense	1,800

Identify each of the six pairs of adjustments. For each adjustment, indicate the account, whether the account is increased or decreased, and the amount of the adjustment. No account is affected by more than one adjustment. Use the following format. The first adjustment is shown as an example.

Adjustment	Account	Increase or Decrease	Amount
1.	Accounts Receivable	Increase	$5,100
	Fees Earned	Increase	5,100

EXERCISE 3-19
Book value of fixed assets
OBJECTIVE 4

Cisco Systems Inc. reported Property, Plant, and Equipment of $5,029 million and Accumulated Depreciation of $2,438 million at July 28, 2001.

a. What was the book value of the fixed assets at July 28, 2001?
b. Would the book value of Cisco Systems' fixed assets normally approximate their fair market values?

EXERCISE 3-20
Classified balance sheet
OBJECTIVE 4

✓ Total assets: $96,550

Shoshone Co. offers personal weight reduction consulting services to individuals. After all the accounts have been closed on June 30, 2004, the end of the current fiscal year, the balances of selected accounts from the ledger of Shoshone Co. are as follows:

Accounts Payable	$ 8,750	Prepaid Insurance	$ 3,100
Accounts Receivable	18,725	Prepaid Rent	2,400
Accumulated Depreciation—Equipment	21,100	Retained Earnings	59,850
Capital Stock	25,000	Salaries Payable	1,750
Cash	2,150	Supplies	675
Equipment	90,600	Unearned Fees	1,200

Prepare a classified balance sheet.

EXERCISE 3-21
Classified balance sheet
OBJECTIVE 4

✓ Total assets: $1,222,503

La-Z-Boy Inc. is one of the world's largest manufacturers of furniture that is best known for its reclining chairs. The following data (in thousands) were adapted from the 2001 annual report of La-Z-Boy Inc.:

Accounts payable	$ 92,830
Accounts receivables	380,867
Accumulated depreciation	252,027
Capital stock	267,530
Cash	23,565
Income taxes payable*	11,490
Intangible assets	247,422
Inventories	257,887
Long-term debt*	5,304
Long-term debt†	196,923
Other assets*	46,457
Other assets†	35,964
Other liabilities*	51,361
Other long-term liabilities†	80,519
Notes payable*	10,380
Payroll payable*	78,550
Property, plant, and equipment	482,368
Retained earnings	427,616

For the preceding items, (*) indicates that the item is current in nature; (†) indicates that the item is long term in nature.

Prepare a classified balance sheet as of April 28, 2001.

EXERCISE 3-22
Balance Sheet
OBJECTIVE 4

List the errors you find in the following balance sheet. Prepare a corrected balance sheet.

ZIGZAG SERVICES CO.
Balance Sheet
For the Year Ended March 31, 2004

Assets		
Current assets:		
Cash	$ 3,170	
Accounts payable	4,390	
Supplies	750	
Prepaid insurance	1,600	
Land	100,000	
Total current assets		$109,910
Property, plant, and equipment:		
Building	$ 55,500	
Equipment	28,250	
Total property, plant, and equipment		$101,750
Total assets		$211,660
Liabilities		
Current liabilities:		
Accounts receivable	$ 8,390	
Accum. depr.—building	23,000	
Accum. depr.—equipment	16,000	
Net loss	10,000	
Total liabilities		$ 57,390
Stockholders' Equity		
Wages payable		$ 975
Capital stock		40,000
Retained earnings		113,295
Total stockholders' equity		$154,270
Total liabilities and stockholders' equity		$211,660

EXERCISE 3-23
Identify accounts to be closed
OBJECTIVES 3, 6

From the following list, identify the accounts that should be closed at the end of the accounting period:

a. Accounts Payable
b. Accumulated Depreciation—Buildings
c. Capital Stock
d. Depreciation Expense—Buildings
e. Dividends
f. Equipment
g. Fees Earned
h. Land
i. Salaries Expense
j. Salaries Payable
k. Supplies
l. Supplies Expense

EXERCISE 3-24
Closing process
OBJECTIVES 3, 6

During the closing process for Matrix Corporation, Retained Earnings was increased by $729,350 and decreased by $512,900 and $40,000. For the year ending July 31, 2004, dividends of $40,000 were paid. As of August 1, 2003, the balance of Retained Earnings was $405,700. (a) What was the net income or loss for the year ending July 31, 2004? (b) Prepare a retained earnings statement for the year.

EXERCISE 3-25
Closing process
OBJECTIVES 3, 6

Image Services Co. offers its services to individuals desiring to improve their personal images. After the accounts have been adjusted at January 31, the end of the fiscal year, the following balances were taken from the ledger of Image Services Co.:

Retained Earnings	$325,750	Rent Expense	$74,000
Dividends	45,000	Supplies Expense	15,500
Fees Earned	380,700	Miscellaneous Expense	4,500
Wages Expense	205,300		

Perform the closing process for (a) revenues, (b) expenses, and (c) dividends. Indicate each account closed, whether the account is increased or decreased, and the amount of the increase or decrease. Close all expenses with one transfer to Retained Earnings.

Problems

PROBLEM 3 | 1
Accrual basis accounting
OBJECTIVE 2

Papaw Health Care Inc. is owned and operated by Dr. Richard Byrne, the sole stockholder. During October 2004, Papaw Health Care entered into the following transactions:

Oct. 1 Received $4,500 from Embark Company as rent for the use of a vacant office in Papaw Health Care's building. Embark paid the rent six months in advance.
1 Paid $2,400 for an insurance premium on a one-year, general business policy.
4 Purchased supplies of $1,200 on account.
5 Collected $5,100 for services provided to customers on account.
11 Paid creditors $900 on account.
18 Dr. Byrne invested an additional $25,000 in the business in exchange for capital stock.
20 Billed patients $13,600 for services provided on account.
25 Received $3,800 for services provided to customers who paid cash.
29 Paid expenses as follows: wages, $7,000; utilities, $2,000; rent on medical equipment, $1,500; interest, $125; miscellaneous, $300.
29 Paid dividends of $3,000 to stockholder (Dr. Byrne).

Instructions

Analyze and record the October transactions for Papaw Health Care Inc. Using the following format, record each transaction as a plus or minus in the appropriate accounts. The October 1, 2004, balances are shown in the form.

	Assets							=	Liabilities			+	Stockholders' Equity	
	Cash +	Accts. Rec. +	Pre. Ins. +	Supp. +	Building −	Acc. Dep. +	Land =		Accts. Pay. +	Un. Rent +	Notes Pay. +		Wages Pay. +	Capital Stock
Bal. Oct. 1	5,800	7,500	200	310	50,000	4,000	25,000		2,150	0	20,000		0	25,000

	+	Ret. Earn. −	Dividends +	Fees Earned +	Rent Rev. −	Wages Exp. −	Utilities Exp. −	Rent Exp. −	Supplies Exp. −	Dep. Exp. −	Ins. Exp. −	Int. Exp. −	Misc. Exp.
Bal. Oct. 1		37,660	0	0	0	0	0	0	0	0	0	0	0

PROBLEM 3 | 2
Adjustment process
OBJECTIVE 3

Adjustment data for Papaw Health Care Inc. for October are as follows:

1. Insurance expired, $200.
2. Supplies on hand on October 31, $325.

3. Depreciation on building, $1,000.
4. Unearned rent revenue earned, $750.
5. Wages owed employees but not paid, $800.
6. Services provided but not billed to patients, $2,100.

Instructions

Based on the transactions recorded in October for Problem 3-1, record the adjustments for October.

PROBLEM 3 | 3
Financial statements and the closing process
OBJECTIVES 4, 6

✓ Net income: $6,140

Data for Papaw Health Care for October are provided in Problem 3-1 and Problem 3-2.

Instructions

1. Prepare an income statement, retained earnings statement, and a classified balance sheet for October. The notes payable amount is due in 2010.
2. Close the revenue, expense, and dividend accounts.

PROBLEM 3 | 4
Statement of cash flows
OBJECTIVE 4

✓ Net cash flows from operations: $(825)

Data for Papaw Health Care for October are provided in Problems 3-1, 3-2, and 3-3.

Instructions

1. Prepare a statement of cash flows for October. (*Hint:* The statement of cash flows is prepared by analyzing and summarizing the cash transactions shown in the summary of transactions for Problem 3-3.)
2. Reconcile the net cash flows from operating activities with the net income for October. (*Hint:* See Appendix A to this chapter and use adjusted balances in computing increases and decreases in accounts.)

PROBLEM 3 | 5
Adjustments and errors
OBJECTIVE 3

✓ Corrected net income: $198,225

At the end of April, the first month of operations, the following selected data were taken from the financial statements of Phil Olson, P.C., a professional services corporation owned and operated by Phil Olson, an attorney at law:

Net income for April	$187,500
Total assets at April 30	498,300
Total liabilities at April 30	67,800
Total stockholders' equity at April 30	430,500

In preparing the statements, adjustments for the following data were overlooked:

a. Unbilled fees earned at April 30, $21,500.
b. Depreciation of equipment for April, $6,000.
c. Accrued wages at April 30, $2,900.
d. Supplies used during April, $1,875.

Instructions

Determine the correct amount of net income for April and the total assets, liabilities, and stockholders' equity at April 30. In addition to indicating the corrected amounts, indicate the effect of each omitted adjustment by setting up and completing a columnar table similar to the following. Adjustment (a) is presented as an example.

	Net Income	Total Assets	Total Liabilities	Total Stockholders' Equity
Reported amounts	$187,500	$498,300	$67,800	$430,500
Corrections:				
Adjustment (a)	+21,500	+21,500	0	+21,500
Adjustment (b)	_____	_____	_____	_____
Adjustment (c)	_____	_____	_____	_____
Adjustment (d)	_____	_____	_____	_____
Corrected amounts	_____	_____	_____	_____

PROBLEM 3 | 6

Adjustment process and financial statements

OBJECTIVES 3, 4

✓ 2. Net income: $21,040

Adjustment data for Marasca Laundry Inc. for January 2004 are as follows:

a. Wages accrued but not paid at January 31, $2,100.
b. Depreciation of equipment during the year, $6,600.
c. Laundry supplies on hand at January 31, $900.
d. Insurance premiums expired, $2,800.

Instructions

1. Using the following format, record each adjustment as a plus or minus in the appropriate accounts. The January 31 balances are given.

	Assets					=	Liabilities		+	Stockholders' Equity
	Cash	+ Laundry Supplies	+ Prepaid Insurance	+ Laundry Equipment	− Acc. Dep.	=	Accounts Payable	+ Wages Payable	+	Capital Stock
Jan. 31 Balances	11,100	5,560	4,490	95,100	40,200		4,100	0		7,500

	+ Retained Earnings	− Dividends	+ Laundry Revenue	− Wages Expense	− Rent Expense	− Utilities Expense	− Dep. Expense	− Supplies Expense	− Insurance Expense	− Laundry Misc. Expense
Jan. 31 Balances	29,250	2,000	150,000	61,400	36,000	13,700	0	0	0	1,700

2. Prepare an income statement and a retained earnings statement for the year ended January 31, 2004, and a classified balance sheet as of January 31, 2004.

PROBLEM 3 | 7

Adjustment process and the closing process

OBJECTIVES 3, 4, 6

✓ 2. Net income: $45,980

Last Wishes Corporation offers legal consulting advice to death-row inmates. Adjustment data for Last Wishes Corporation for June 2004 are as follows:

a. Accrued fees revenue at June 30, $5,000.
b. Insurance expired during the year, $1,900.
c. Supplies on hand at June 30, $450.
d. Depreciation of building for the year, $1,620.
e. Depreciation of equipment for the year, $3,500.
f. Accrued salaries and wages at June 30, $1,750.
g. Unearned rent at June 30, $1,000.

Instructions

1. Using the format on the following page, record each adjustment as a plus or minus in the appropriate accounts. The June 30 balances are shown in the form.

	Cash	+	Accounts Receivable	+	Prepaid Insurance	+	Supplies	+	Land	+	Building	−	Acc. Dep. Building	+	Equipment
June 30 Balances	4,200		15,500		3,800		1,950		50,000		137,500		51,700		90,100

	−	Acc. Dep. Equip.	=	Accounts Payable	+	Salaries and Wages Payable	+	Unearned Rent	+	Capital Stock	+	Retained Earnings	−	Dividends	+	Fees Revenue
June 30 Balances		35,300		9,500		0		3,000		50,000		111,800		7,500		200,000

	+	Rent Revenue	−	Salaries and Wages Expense	−	Advertising Expense	−	Utilities Expense	−	Repairs Expense	−	Dep. Exp. Equip.	−	Insurance Expense	−	Dep. Exp. Building	−	Supplies Expense	−	Misc. Expense
June 30 Balances		0		80,000		38,200		19,000		11,500		0		0		0		0		2,050

2. Prepare an income statement and a retained earnings statement for the year ended June 30, 2004, and a classified balance sheet as of June 30, 2004.
3. Close the revenue, expense, and dividend accounts.

Activities

Activity 3-1
Business strategy

G R O U P

Assume that you and two friends are debating whether to open an automotive and service retail chain that will be called Auto-Mart. Initially, Auto-Mart will open three stores locally, but the business plan anticipates going nationwide within five years.

Currently, you and your future business partners are debating whether to focus Auto-Mart on a "do-it-yourself" or "do-it-for-me" business strategy. A "do-it-yourself" business strategy emphasizes the sale of retail auto parts that customers will use themselves to repair and service their cars. A "do-it-for-me" business strategy emphasizes the offering of mainte-nance and service for customers.

1. In groups of three or four, discuss whether to implement a "do-it-yourself" or "do-it-for-me" business strategy. List the advantages of each strategy and arrive at a conclusion as to which strategy to implement.
2. Provide examples of real-world businesses that use "do-it-yourself" or "do-it-for-me" business strategies.

Activity 3-2
Accrued revenue

The following is an excerpt from a conversation between Karen Wyer and Jim Harris just before they boarded a flight to Puerto Rico on United Airlines. They are going to Puerto Rico to attend their company's annual sales conference.

Karen: Jim, aren't you taking an accounting course at City College?
Jim: Yes, I decided it's about time I learned something about accounting. You know, our annual bonuses are based on the sales figures that come from the accounting department.
Karen: I guess I never really thought about it.
Jim: You should think about it! Last year, I placed a $250,000 order on December 23. But when I got my bonus, the $250,000 sale wasn't included. They said it hadn't been shipped until January 4, so it would have to count in next year's bonus.
Karen: A real bummer!
Jim: Right! I was counting on that bonus including the $250,000 sale.
Karen: Did you complain?

Jim: Yes, but it didn't do any good. Jacob, the head accountant, said something about matching revenues and expenses. Also, something about not recording revenues until the sale is final. I figure I'd take the accounting course and find out whether he's just jerking me around.

Karen: I never really thought about it. When do you think United Airlines will record its revenues from this flight?

Jim: Mmm . . . I guess it could record the revenue when it sells the ticket . . . or . . . when the boarding passes are taken at the door . . . or . . . when we get off the plane . . . or when our company pays for the tickets . . . or . . . I don't know. I'll ask my accounting instructor.

Discuss when United Airlines should recognize the revenue from ticket sales to properly match revenues and expenses.

Activity 3-3
Adjustments for financial statements

Several years ago, your father opened Derby Television Repair Inc. He made a small initial investment and added money from his personal bank account as needed. He withdrew money for living expenses at irregular intervals. As the business grew, he hired an assistant. He is now considering adding more employees, purchasing additional service trucks, and purchasing the building he now rents. To secure funds for the expansion, your father submitted a loan application to the bank and included the most recent financial statements (following) prepared from accounts maintained by a part-time bookkeeper.

DERBY TELEVISION REPAIR INC.
Income Statement
For the Year Ended December 31, 2004

Service revenue		$66,900
Less: Rent paid	$18,000	
Wages paid	16,500	
Supplies paid	7,000	
Utilities paid	3,100	
Insurance paid	3,000	
Miscellaneous payments	2,150	49,750
Net income		$17,150

DERBY TELEVISION REPAIR INC.
Balance Sheet
December 31, 2004

Assets	
Cash	$ 3,750
Amounts due from customers	2,100
Truck	25,000
Total assets	$30,850

Equities	
Stockholders' equity	$30,850

After reviewing the financial statements, the loan officer at the bank asked your father if he used the accrual basis of accounting for revenues and expenses. Your father responded that he did, and that is why he included the amounts due from customers account. The loan officer then asked whether or not the accounts were adjusted prior to the preparation of the statements. Your father answered that they had not been adjusted.

a. Why do you think the loan officer suspected that the accounts had not been adjusted prior to the preparation of the statements?

b. Indicate possible accounts that might need to be adjusted before an accurate set of financial statements could be prepared.

Walgreen Company and **CVS Corporation** operate national chains of drugstores that sell prescription drugs, over-the-counter drugs, and general merchandise such as greeting cards, beauty and cosmetics, household items, food, and beverages. Walgreen operates approximately 3,600 stores; CVS Corporation operates approximately 4,200 stores. The following operating data (in thousands) were adapted from the 2001 SEC 10-K filings of Walgreen and CVS.

	CVS	Walgreen
Net sales	$22,241,400	$24,623,000
Cost of sales	16,550,400	18,048,900
Gross profit	$ 5,691,000	$ 6,574,100
Selling, general, and administrative expenses	4,920,400	5,175,800
Operating income	$ 770,600	$ 1,398,300
Other income and expense	(61,000)	24,400
Income before taxes	$ 709,600	$ 1,422,700
Income taxes	296,400	537,100
Net income	$ 413,200	$ 885,600

1. Prepare common-size income statements for CVS and Walgreen.
2. Compute the average sales per store for CVS and Walgreen. Round to thousands.
3. Analyze and comment on your results in (1) and (2).
4. Broker recommendations are reported on Yahoo.com's financial Web site (http://www .finance.yahoo.com/). The recommendations are ranked as follows:

Strong buy	1
Buy	2
Hold	3
Sell	4
Strong sell	5

Based on your answer to (3), would you expect that the average broker recommendation for CVS to be higher, less favorable, lower, or more favorable than for Walgreen? Compare your assessment with the average broker recommendation on Yahoo.com's financial Web site. To find the broker recommendation, enter the stock symbols for CVS (CVS) and Walgreen (WAG) and click on "Research."

The following operating data (in thousands) were adapted from the 2001 SEC 10-K filings of Walgreen and CVS:

	CVS		Walgreen	
	2001	**2000**	**2001**	**2000**
Accounts receivable	$ 966,200	$ 824,500	$ 798,300	$ 614,500
Accounts payable	1,535,800	1,351,500	1,546,800	1,364,000
Accrued expenses payable	1,267,900	1,001,400	937,500	847,700

1. Using the preceding data, adjust the operating income for CVS and Walgreen shown in Activity 3-4 to an adjusted cash basis. (*Hint:* To convert to a cash basis, you need to compute the change in each accrual accounting item shown in the table and then either add or subtract the change to the operating income.)
2. Compute the net difference between the operating income under the accrual and cash bases.
3. Express the net difference in (2) as a percentage of operating income under the accrual basis.

4. Which company's operating income, CVS's or Walgreen's, is closer to the cash basis?
5. Do you think most analysts focus on operating income or net income in assessing the long-term profitability of a company? Explain.

Activity 3-6
Effect of events on financial statements

On September 11, 2001, two **United Air Lines** aircraft were hijacked and destroyed in terrorist attacks on the World Trade Center in New York City and in a crash near Johnstown, Pennsylvania. In addition to the loss of all passengers and crew on board the aircraft, these attacks resulted in numerous deaths and injuries to persons on the ground and massive property damage. In the immediate aftermath of the attacks, the FAA ordered all aircraft operating in the United States grounded immediately. This grounding effectively lasted for three days, and United was able to operate only a portion of its scheduled flights for several days thereafter. Passenger traffic and yields on United's flights declined significantly when flights were permitted to resume, and United refunded significant numbers of tickets for the period from September 11 to September 25.

The following data for United (in millions) were adapted from the Securities and Exchange Commission 10-K filing for the years ending December 31, 2000 and 1999:

	Year Ending December 31,	
	2000	**1999**
Operating income	$ 673	$1,342
Net income	52	1,204
Net cash flows from operating activities	2,358	2,415

1. Based on the preceding data, develop an expectation of what you believe the operating income, net income, and net cash flows from operating activities would be for United Air Lines for the year ending December 31, 2001. Use the following format for your answers:

	Year Ending December 31, 2001
Operating income	$_____
Net income	$_____
Net cash flows from operating activities	$_____

2. Would you report the loss related to the terrorist attacks separately in the income statement? If so, how?

Activity 3-7
Analysis of income and cash flows

The following data (millions) for 2001, 2000, and 1999 were taken from 10-K filings with the Securities and Exchange Commission:

	2001	**2000**	**1999**
Company A			
Revenues	$20,092	$19,889	$19,284
Operating income	5,352	3,691	3,982
Net income	3,969	2,177	2,431
Net cash flows from operating activities	4,110	3,585	3,883
Net cash flows from investing activities	(1,188)	(1,165)	(3,421)
Net cash flows from financing activities	(2,830)	(2,072)	(471)
Total assets	22,417	20,834	21,623

(continued)

	2001	**2000**	**1999**
Company B			
Revenues	$13,879	$16,741	$14,883
Operating income (loss)	(1,602)	1,637	1,318
Net income (loss)	(1,216)	828	1,208
Net cash flows from operating activities	236	2,898	2,647
Net cash flows from investing activities	(2,696)	(3,396)	(3,962)
Net cash flows from financing activities	3,306	239	2,270
Total assets	23,605	21,931	19,942
Company C			
Revenues	$ 3,122	$ 2,762	$ 1,640
Operating income (loss)	(412)	(864)	(606)
Net income (loss)	(567)	(1,411)	(720)
Net cash flows from operating activities	(120)	(130)	(91)
Net cash flows from investing activities	(253)	164	(952)
Net cash flows from financing activities	107	693	1,104
Total assets	1,638	2,135	2,466
Company D			
Revenues	$49,000	$45,352	$43,082
Operating income (loss)	2,183	1,739	1,534
Net income (loss)	877	613	247
Net cash flows from operating activities	2,281	1,548	1,838
Net cash flows from investing activities	(1,523)	(1,810)	(1,465)
Net cash flows from financing activities	(878)	280	(257)
Total assets	18,190	17,932	16,641

1. Match each of the following companies with the data for Company A, B, C, or D:

   Amazon.com
   Coca-Cola Inc.
   Delta Air Lines
   Kroger

2. Explain the logic underlying your matches.

Activity 3-8
Analysis of income statements

Home Depot and **Lowe's** operate national chains of home improvement stores that sell a wide assortment of building materials and home improvement, lawn and garden products, such as lumber, paint, wall coverings, lawn mowers, plumbing, and electrical supplies. Home Depot operates approximately 1,300 stores; Lowe's operates approximately 740 stores. The following operating data (in thousands) were adapted from the 2002 SEC 10-K filings of Home Depot and Lowe's:

	Home Depot	**Lowe's**
Net sales	$53,553,000	$22,111,108
Cost of sales	37,406,000	15,743,267
Gross profit	$16,147,000	$ 6,367,841
Operating expenses	11,215,000	4,570,053
Operating income	$ 4,932,000	$ 1,797,788
Other income and expense	25,000	(173,537)
Income before taxes	$ 4,957,000	$ 1,624,251
Income taxes	1,913,000	600,989
Net income	$ 3,044,000	$ 1,023,262

1. Prepare common-size income statements for Home Depot and Lowe's.
2. Compute the average sales per store for Home Depot and Lowe's. Round to thousands.
3. Analyze and comment on your results in (1) and (2).
4. Broker recommendations are reported on Yahoo.com's financial Web site (http://www
   .finance.yahoo.com/). The recommendations are ranked as follows:

Strong buy	1
Buy	2
Hold	3
Sell	4
Strong sell	5

   Based on your answer to (3), would you expect that the average broker recommendation
   for Home Depot to be higher, less favorable, lower, or more favorable than for Lowe's?
   Compare your assessment with the average broker recommendation on Yahoo.com's financial Web site. To find the broker recommendation, enter the stock symbols for
   Home Depot (HD) and Lowe's (LOW) and click on "Research."

Answers to Self–Study Questions

1. **A** Under the accrual basis of accounting, revenues are recorded when the services are rendered. Since the services were rendered during June, all the fees should be recorded on June 30 (Answer A). This is an example of accrued revenue. Under the cash basis of accounting, revenues are recorded when the cash is collected, not necessarily when the fees are earned. Thus, no revenue would be recorded in June, $8,500 of revenue would be recorded in July, and $6,500 of revenue would be recorded in August (Answer D). Answers B and C are incorrect and are not used under either the accrual or cash bases.

2. **C** The collection of a $5,700 accounts receivable is recorded as an increase in Cash, $5,700, and a decrease in Accounts Receivable, $5,700 (Answer C). The initial recording of the fees earned on account is recorded as an increase in Accounts Receivable and an increase in Fees Earned (Answer B). Services rendered for cash are recorded as an increase in Cash and an increase in Fees Earned (Answer D). Answer A is incorrect and would result in the accounting equation being out of balance

because total assets would exceed total liabilities and stockholders' equity by $11,400.

3. **A** A deferral is the delay in recording an expense already paid, such as prepaid insurance (answer A). Wages payable (answer B) is considered an accrued expense or accrued liability. Fees earned (answer C) is a revenue item. Accumulated depreciation (answer D) is a contra account to a fixed asset.

4. **D** The balance in the supplies account, before adjustment, represents the amount of supplies available during the period. From this amount ($2,250) is subtracted the amount of supplies on hand ($950) to determine the supplies used ($1,300). The used supplies is recorded as an increase in Supplies Expense, $1,300, and a decrease in Supplies, $1,300 (Answer D).

5. **C** The failure to record the adjusting entry increasing Rent Revenue, $600, and decreasing Unearned Rent, $600, would have the effect of overstating liabilities by $600 and understating net income by $600 (answer C).

4

LEARNING OBJECTIVES

OBJECTIVE 1
Distinguish the operating activities of a service business from those of a merchandise business.

OBJECTIVE 2
Describe and illustrate the financial statements of a merchandising business.

OBJECTIVE 3
Describe the accounting for the sale of merchandise.

OBJECTIVE 4
Describe the accounting for the purchase of merchandise.

OBJECTIVE 5
Describe the accounting for transportation costs and sales taxes.

OBJECTIVE 6
Illustrate the dual nature of merchandising transactions.

OBJECTIVE 7
Describe the accounting for merchandise shrinkage.

OBJECTIVE 8
Describe and illustrate the use of gross profit and operating income in analyzing a company's operations.

Accounting for Merchandise Operations

Merchandising has existed since the days of the traveling merchant, trade festivals, and village bartering. The way we buy goods (and services) has undergone significant changes and will continue to change with consumer tastes and technology. For example, in the past 20 years we have seen the emergence of (1) discount merchandising, (2) category killers, and (3) Internet retailing.

Wal-Mart, which led the development of discount merchandising, has become the world's largest retailer. Wal-Mart's growth is centered on providing the consumer with everyday discount pricing over a broad array of household products. Category killers include **Toys "R" Us** (toys), **Best Buy** (electronics), **Home Depot** (home improvement), and **Office Depot** (office supplies), which provide a wide selection of attractively priced goods within a particular product segment. Internet retailers such as **Amazon.com** allow time-conscious consumers to shop quickly and effortlessly.

Merchandising will undoubtedly continue to evolve as consumer lifestyles and technologies change in the future. In this chapter, we introduce you to the accounting issues unique to merchandisers. We emphasize merchandisers at this point in the text because merchandising is significant in its own right and because even nonmerchandisers have similar accounting issues to those discussed in this chapter.

Merchandise Operations

In previous chapters, we described and illustrated how businesses report their financial condition and changes in financial condition using the cash and accrual bases of accounting. In those chapters, we focused on service businesses. In this chapter, we describe and illustrate the accounting for merchandise operations.

How do the operating activities of a service business, such as a consulting firm, law practice, or architectural firm, differ from a merchandising business, such as Home Depot or Wal-Mart? The differences are best illustrated by focusing on the income statements of the two types of businesses.

The condensed income statement of **H&R Block Inc.** is shown in Exhibit 1.[1] H&R Block is a service business that primarily offers tax planning and preparation to its customers.

EXHIBIT 1

*H&R Block Income
Statement*

H&R BLOCK INC.
Condensed Income Statement
For Year Ending April 30, 2001
(in millions)

Revenue	$3,002
Operating expenses	2,537
Operating income	$ 465
Other income	8
Income before taxes	$ 473
Income taxes	196
Net income	$ 277

The condensed income statement of **Home Depot Inc.** is shown in Exhibit 2.[2] Home Depot is the world's largest home improvement retailer and the second largest retailer in the United States based on net sales volume.

The revenue activities of a service business involve providing services to customers. On the income statement for a service business, the revenues from services are reported as revenues or fees earned. The operating expenses incurred in providing services are subtracted from the revenues to arrive at operating income. Any other income or expense is then added or subtracted to arrive at income before taxes. Net income is determined by subtracting income taxes. Exhibit 1 shows that H&R Block earned operating profits of $465 million based on revenues of more than $3 billion. Adding other income and subtracting income taxes results in net income of $277 million.

In contrast, the revenue activities of a merchandising business involve the buying and selling of merchandise. A merchandise business must first purchase merchandise

[1]Adapted from H&R Block's 10-K filing with the Securities and Exchange Commission.
[2]Adapted from Home Depot's 10-K filing with the Securities and Exchange Commission.

EXHIBIT 2

Home Depot Income Statement

HOME DEPOT INC. Condensed Income Statement For the Year Ending December 28, 2001 (in millions)	
Net sales	$45,738
Cost of merchandise sold	32,057
Gross profit	$13,681
Operating expenses	9,490
Operating income	$ 4,191
Other income	26
Income before taxes	$ 4,217
Income taxes	1,636
Net income	$ 2,581

to sell to its customers. The revenue received for merchandise sold to customers less any merchandise returned or any discounts is reported as **net sales**. The related **cost of merchandise sold** is then determined and matched against the net sales. **Gross profit** is determined by subtracting the cost of merchandise sold from net sales. Gross profit gets its name from the fact that it is the profit before deducting operating expenses. Operating expenses are then subtracted in arriving at operating income. Like a service business, other income or expense is then added or subtracted to arrive at income before taxes. Subtracting income taxes yields net income.

Exhibit 2 shows that Home Depot earned a gross profit of almost $13.7 billion, based on net sales of $45.7 billion. Operating expenses reduce gross profit to an operating income of $4.2 billion. Adding other income and subtracting income taxes results in net income of $2.6 billion.

In addition to operating and income statement differences, merchandise inventory on hand (not sold) at the end of the accounting period is reported on the balance sheet as **merchandise inventory**. Since merchandise is normally sold within a year, it is reported as a current asset on the balance sheet.

Financial Statements for a Merchandising Business

OBJECTIVE 2

Describe and illustrate the financial statements of a merchandising business.

In this section, we illustrate financial statements for Online Solutions, an Internet retailer of computer hardware and software.[3] During 2006, we assume that Shannon Pence organized Online Solutions with the business strategy of offering personalized service to individuals and small businesses that are upgrading or purchasing new computer systems. Online's personal service before the sale includes a no-obligation, on-site assessment of the customer's computer needs. By providing tailor-made

---

[3]The closing process, which is not illustrated, is similar to that for a service business.

BUSINESS STRATEGY

Under One Roof

Most businesses cannot be all things to all people. Businesses must seek a position in the marketplace to serve a unique customer need. Companies that are unable to do this can be squeezed out of the marketplace. The mall-based department store has been under pressure from both ends of the retail spectrum. At the discount store end of the market, Wal-Mart has been a formidable competitor. At the high end, specialty retailers have established strong presence in identifiable niches, such as electronics and apparel. More than a decade ago, JC Penney abandoned its "hard goods," such as electronics and sporting goods, in favor of providing "soft goods" because of the emerging strength of specialty retailers in the hard good segments. JC Penney is positioning itself against these forces by *"exceeding the fashion, quality, selection, and service components of the discounter, equaling the merchandise intensity of the specialty store, and providing the selection and 'under one roof' shopping convenience of the department store."* JC Penney's merchandise strategy is focused toward customers it terms the "modern spender" and "starting outs." It views these segments as most likely to value its higher-end merchandise offered under the convenience of "one roof."

solutions, personalized service, and follow-up, Shannon believes that Online can compete effectively against larger retailers, such as Dell and Gateway. Initially, Shannon plans to grow Online Solutions regionally. If successful, Shannon plans to take the company public.

Multiple-Step Income Statement

The 2007 income statement for Online Solutions' second year as an Internet retailer is shown in Exhibit 3.[4] This form of income statement, called a **multiple-step income statement**, contains several sections, subsections, and subtotals.

Net sales for Online Solutions is determined as follows:

Sales		$720,185
Less sales returns and allowances	$6,140	
Less sales discounts	5,790	11,930
Net sales		$708,255

Sales is the total amount charged customers for merchandise sold, including cash sales and sales on account. Both sales returns and allowances and sales discounts are subtracted in arriving at net sales.

---

[4]We use the Online Solutions income statement for 2007 as a basis for illustration because, as will be shown, it allows us to better illustrate the computation of the cost of merchandise sold.

EXHIBIT 3
*Multiple-Step Income
Statement*

ONLINE SOLUTIONS
Income Statement
For Year Ended December 31, 2007

Net sales	$708,255
Cost of merchandise sold	525,305
Gross profit	$182,950
Operating expenses	105,710
Operating income	$ 77,240
Other income and expense (net)	(1,840)
Operating income before taxes	$ 75,400
Income taxes	15,000
Net income	$ 60,400

Sales returns and allowances are granted by the seller to customers for damaged or defective merchandise. For example, rather than have a buyer return merchandise, a seller may offer a $500 allowance to the customer as compensation for damaged merchandise. Sales returns and allowances are recorded when the merchandise is returned or when the allowance is granted by the seller.

Sales discounts are granted by the seller to customers for early payment of amounts owed. For example, a seller may offer a customer a 2% discount on a sale of $10,000 if the customer pays within 10 days. If the customer pays within the 10-day period, the seller receives cash of $9,800 and the buyer receives a discount of $200 ($10,000 × 0.02). Sales discounts are recorded when the customer pays the bill.

Cost of merchandise sold is the cost of the merchandise sold to customers. To illustrate the determination of the cost of merchandise sold, assume that Online Solutions purchased $340,000 of merchandise during 2006. If the inventory at December 31, 2006, the end of the year, totals $59,700, the cost of the merchandise sold during 2006 is determined as follows:

Purchases	$340,000
Less merchandise inventory, December 31, 2006	59,700
Cost of merchandise sold	$280,300

As we discussed in the preceding section, sellers can offer customers sales discounts for early payment of their bills. Such discounts are referred to as **purchase discounts** by the buyer. Purchase discounts reduce the cost of merchandise. A buyer can return merchandise to the seller (a **purchase return**), or the buyer can receive a reduction in the initial price at which the merchandise was purchased (a **purchase allowance**). Like purchase discounts, purchase returns and allowances reduce the cost of merchandise purchased during a period. In addition, transportation costs paid by the buyer for merchandise also increase the cost of merchandise purchased.

To continue the illustration, assume that during 2007 Online Solutions purchased additional merchandise of $521,980. It received credit for purchase returns and allowances of $9,100, took purchase discounts of $2,525, and paid transportation costs of $17,400. The purchase returns and allowances and the purchase discounts are deducted from the total purchases to yield the *net purchases*. The transportation costs are added to the net purchases to yield the *cost of merchandise purchased*, as follows.

Purchases		$521,980
Less: Purchases returns and allowances	$9,100	
Purchases discounts	2,525	11,625
Net purchases		$510,355
Add transportation in		17,400
Cost of merchandise purchased		$527,755

The ending inventory of Online Solutions on December 31, 2006, $59,700, becomes the beginning inventory for 2007. This beginning inventory is added to the cost of merchandise purchased to yield **merchandise available for sale**. The ending inventory, which is assumed to be $62,150, is then subtracted from the merchandise available for sale to yield the cost of merchandise sold as shown in Exhibit 4.

EXHIBIT 4   *Cost of Merchandise Sold*

Merchandise inventory, January 1, 2007			$ 59,700
Purchases		$521,980	
Less: Purchases returns and allowances	$9,100		
Purchases discounts	2,525	11,625	
Net purchases		$510,355	
Add transportation in		17,400	
Cost of merchandise purchased			527,755
Merchandise available for sale			$587,455
Less merchandise inventory, December 31, 2007			62,150
Cost of merchandise sold			$525,305

The cost of merchandise sold was determined by deducting the merchandise on hand at the end of the period from the merchandise available for sale during the period. The merchandise on hand at the end of the period is determined by taking a physical count of inventory on hand. This method of determining the cost of merchandise sold and the amount of merchandise on hand is called the periodic method of accounting for merchandise inventory. Under the **periodic inventory method**, the inventory records do not show the amount available for sale or the amount sold during the period. In contrast, under the **perpetual inventory method** of accounting for merchandise inventory, each purchase and sale of merchandise is recorded in the inventory and the cost of merchandise sold accounts. As a result, the amount of merchandise available for sale and the amount sold are continuously (perpetually) disclosed in the inventory records.

In the perpetual inventory system, the amount of merchandise available for sale and the amount sold are continuously (perpetually) disclosed in the inventory records. This is done by recording the purchase and sale of each merchandise item in its separate inventory account. These separate accounts are kept in a ledger, called a **subsidiary ledger**. The subsidiary ledger is represented in the primary ledger, called the *general ledger,* by a summarizing account, called the **controlling account**. The balance of the controlling account must equal the sum of the balances of the individual accounts in the subsidiary ledger. Thus, merchandise transactions are recorded twice. First, they are recorded in the subsidiary inventory ledger to update the detailed inventory records. Second, they are summarized and recorded in the controlling account. Controlling accounts and subsidiary ledgers are also maintained for other accounts for which daily balances or supporting details are needed. For example, subsidiary ledgers are normally maintained for accounts receivable, accounts payable, equipment, and capital stock.

Most large retailers and many small merchandising businesses use computerized perpetual inventory systems. Such systems normally use bar codes, such as the one on the back of this textbook. An optical scanner reads the bar code to record merchandise purchased and sold. Merchandise businesses using a perpetual inventory system report the cost of merchandise sold as a single line on the income statement, as shown in Exhibit 3 for Online Solutions. Merchandise businesses using the periodic inventory method report the cost of merchandise sold by using the format shown in Exhibit 4. Because of its wide use, we will use the perpetual inventory method throughout the remainder of this chapter.

Exhibit 3 shows that Online Solutions reported gross profit of $182,950 in 2007. **Operating income**, sometimes called **income from operations**, is determined by subtracting operating expenses from gross profit. Most merchandising businesses classify operating expenses as either selling expenses or administrative expenses. Expenses that are incurred directly in the selling of merchandise are **selling expenses**. They include expenses such as salespersons' salaries, store supplies used, depreciation of store equipment, and advertising. Expenses incurred in the administration or general operations of the business are **administrative expenses** or *general expenses*. Examples of these expenses are office salaries, depreciation of office equipment, and office supplies used. Credit card expense is also normally classified as an administrative expense. Although selling and administrative expenses can be reported separately, many companies report operating expenses as a single item, as shown in Exhibit 3.

As we illustrate later in this chapter, operating income is often used in financial analysis to judge the efficiency and profitability of operations. For example, operating income divided by total assets or net sales is often used in comparing merchandise businesses.

Online Solutions' income statement in Exhibit 3 also reports other income and expense. Revenue from sources other than the primary operating activity of a business is classified as **other income**. In a merchandising business, these items include income from interest, rent, and gains resulting from the sale of fixed assets.

Expenses that cannot be traced directly to operations are identified as **other expense**. Interest expense that results from financing activities and losses incurred in the disposal of fixed assets are examples of these items.

Other income and other expense are offset against each other on the income statement and are reported as a net amount, as shown in Exhibit 3. If the total of other income exceeds the total of other expense, the difference is added to income from operations. If the reverse is true, the difference is subtracted from income from operations.

Deducting income taxes from income before taxes yields the net income. As we illustrated in Chapter 3, net income or loss is closed to Retained Earnings at the end of the period.

Single-Step Income Statement

An alternate form of income statement is the **single-step income statement**. As shown in Exhibit 5, the income statement for Online Solutions deducts the total of all expenses *in one step* from the total of all revenues.

EXHIBIT 5
*Single-Step Income
Statement*

ONLINE SOLUTIONS
Income Statement
For Year Ended December 31, 2007

Revenue:		
Net sales		$708,255
Expenses:		
Cost of merchandise sold	$525,305	
Operating expenses	105,710	
Income taxes	15,000	
Other income and expense (net)	1,840	647,855
Net income		$ 60,400

The single-step form emphasizes total revenues and total expenses as the factors that determine net income. A criticism of the single-step form is that amounts such as gross profit and income from operations are not readily available for analysis.

Retained Earnings Statement

The retained earnings statement for Online Solutions is shown in Exhibit 6. This statement is prepared in the same manner that we described previously for a service business.

EXHIBIT 6
*Retained Earnings
Statement*

ONLINE SOLUTIONS
Retained Earnings Statement
For the Year Ended December 31, 2007

Retained earnings, January 1, 2007		$128,800
Net income for the year	$60,400	
Less dividends	18,000	
Increase in retained earnings		42,400
Retained earnings, December 31, 2007		$171,200

Balance Sheet

As we discussed and illustrated in previous chapters, the balance sheet may be presented in a downward sequence in three sections, beginning with the assets. This form of balance sheet is called the **report form**.[5] The 2007 balance sheet for Online Solutions is shown in Exhibit 7. In this balance sheet, note that merchandise inventory at the end of the period is reported as a current asset and that the current portion of the note payable is $5,000.

Statement of Cash Flows

The statement of cash flows for Online Solutions is shown in Exhibit 8 on page 136. It indicates that cash increased during 2007 by $11,450. This increase is generated

---

[5]The balance sheet may also be presented in an account form, with assets on the left-hand side and the liabilities and stockholders' equity on the right-hand side.

EXHIBIT 7
Balance Sheet

ONLINE SOLUTIONS
Balance Sheet
December 31, 2007

Assets

Current assets:			
Cash		$ 52,950	
Accounts receivable		76,080	
Merchandise inventory		62,150	
Office supplies		480	
Prepaid insurance		2,650	
Total current assets			$194,310
Property, plant, and equipment:			
Store equipment	$27,100		
Less accumulated depreciation	5,700	$ 21,400	
Office equipment	$15,570		
Less accumulated depreciation	4,720	10,850	
Land		20,000	
Total property, plant, and equipment			52,250
Total assets			$246,560

Liabilities

Current liabilities:		
Accounts payable	$ 22,420	
Note payable (current portion)	5,000	
Salaries payable	1,140	
Unearned rent	1,800	
Total current liabilities		$30,360
Long-term liabilities:		
Note payable (final payment due 2017)		20,000
Total liabilities		$ 50,360

Stockholders' Equity

Capital stock	$ 25,000	
Retained earnings	171,200	196,200
Total liabilities and stockholders' equity		$246,560

from a positive cash flow from operating activities of $47,120, which is partially offset by negative cash flows from investing and financing activities of $12,670 and $23,000, respectively.

The net cash flows from operating activities is shown in Exhibit 8 using a method known as the **indirect method**. This method, which reconciles net income with net cash flows from operating activities, is widely used among publicly held corporations.[6] Finally, you should note that the December 31, 2007, cash balance reported on the statement of cash flows agrees with the amount reported for cash on the December 31, 2007, balance sheet shown in Exhibit 7.

[6]The preparation of the statement of cash flows using the indirect method is further discussed and illustrated in the Appendix to this chapter.

EXHIBIT 8
*Statement of Cash Flows
for Merchandising
Business*

ONLINE SOLUTIONS		
Statement of Cash Flows		
For the Year Ended December 31, 2007		
Cash flows from operating activities:		
Net income		$ 60,400
Add: Depreciation expense—store equipment	$ 3,100	
Depreciation expense—office equipment	2,490	
Decrease in office supplies	120	
Decrease in prepaid insurance	350	
Increase in accounts payable	8,150	14,210
Deduct:		
Increase accounts receivable	$(24,080)	
Increase in merchandise inventory	(2,450)	
Decrease in salaries payable	(360)	
Decrease in unearned rent	(600)	(27,490)
Net cash flows from operating activities		$ 47,120
Cash flows from investing activities:		
Purchase of store equipment	$ (7,100)	
Purchase of office equipment	(5,570)	
Net cash flows from investing activities		(12,670)
Cash flows from financing activities:		
Payment of note payable	$ (5,000)	
Payment of dividends	(18,000)	
Net cash flows from financing activities		(23,000)
Net increase in cash		$ 11,450
January 1, 2007, cash balance		41,500
December 31, 2007, cash balance		$ 52,950

Sales Transactions

OBJECTIVE   3
Describe the
accounting for the
sale of merchandise.

In the remainder of this chapter, we illustrate transactions that affect the financial statements of a merchandising business. These transactions affect the reporting of net sales, cost of merchandise sold, gross profit, and merchandise inventory. The effect of these transactions on the accounting equation and the financial statements can be analyzed using the same format as in earlier chapters.

Cash Sales

A business can generate revenue by selling merchandise for cash. Cash sales are normally rung up (entered) on a cash register. Cash sales affect both the income statement and the balance sheet. Sales are increased on the income statement, and cash is increased on the balance sheet. Under the perpetual inventory system, the cost of the merchandise sold is recorded at the same time as the sale. This is done by increasing Cost of Merchandise Sold and decreasing Merchandise Inventory. In this way, the merchandise inventory account shows the current amount of inventory available for sale. To illustrate, assume that Computer King sells merchandise costing $1,200 for $1,800 on January 3. The effect on the accounts and financial statements follows.

Cash sales of $1,800 on January 3; cost of merchandise sold, $1,200.

Trans. Date	Balance Sheet			Income Statement		
	Assets	Liabilities	Stockholders' Equity	Revenue	Expense	Net Income
Jan. 3	Cash 1,800			Sales 1,800		1,800
Jan. 3	Merch. Inv. −1,200				Cost of Merch. Sold 1,200	−1,200
Net Effect	600		600	1,800	1,200	600
			Retained Earnings			
			(Net Income)			

ETHICS IN ACTION

Credit card fraud and identity theft are significant concerns among credit card issuers and users. One of the fastest growing credit card frauds is called *skimming*. Skimming occurs when your credit card is out of your possession during a legitimate restaurant transaction. In this scam, a server illegally swipes your credit card by using a small, hand-held scanner concealed in an apron. The hand-held scanner illegally transmits the information from the magnetic strip on your card, such as your name, card number, and routing information, to a computer. The information can then be used for making counterfeit cards.

How do retailers record sales made with the use of credit cards? Sales made to customers using credit cards issued by banks, such as MasterCard or VISA, are recorded as cash sales. The seller deposits the credit card receipts for these sales directly into its bank account as if the receipts were cash. Banks, however, charge service fees for handling credit card sales. Such service charges are recorded as an increase in Administrative Expense and a decrease in Cash.

Sales on Account

A business can sell merchandise on account. The effect of sales on account is similar to that for cash sales except that Accounts Receivable is increased instead of Cash. When the customer pays the amount, Accounts Receivable is decreased and Cash is increased.

Sales can also be made to customers using nonbank credit cards. An example of a nonbank credit card is the American Express card. Businesses must first report nonbank credit card sales to the card company before they receive cash. Therefore, such sales are recorded as sales on account. Like bank credit cards, a nonbank credit card company normally deducts a service charge before remitting the amount owed the retailer. Such service charges are recorded in the same manner as we described earlier.

Sales Discounts

The **credit terms** of a sale on account are normally indicated on the **invoice** or bill that the seller sends to the customer. An example of an invoice is shown in Exhibit 9. If payment is required on delivery, the terms are *cash* or *net cash*. Otherwise, the buyer is allowed an amount of time, known as the **credit period**, in which to pay. The credit period usually begins with the date of the sale as shown on the invoice. If payment is

EXHIBIT 9 *Invoice*

Omega Technologies	1000 Matrix Blvd. San Jose, CA. 95116-1000		
			Made in U.S.A.

| **SOLD TO** Computer King 5101 Washington Ave. Cincinnati, OH 45227-5101 | | **CUSTOMER'S ORDER NO. & DATE** 412 Jan. 10, 2007 **REFER TO INVOICE NO.** 106-8 | |

| **DATE SHIPPED** Jan. 12, 2007 | **HOW SHIPPED AND ROUTE** US Express Trucking Co. | **TERMS** 2/10, n/30 | **INVOICE DATE** Jan. 12, 2007 |
| **FROM** San Francisco | **F.O.B.** Cincinnati | **PREPAID OR COLLECT?** Prepaid | |

| **QUANTITY** 10 | **DESCRIPTION** 3COM Megahertz 10/100 Lan PC Card | **UNIT PRICE** 150.00 | **AMOUNT** 1,500.00 |

due within a stated number of days after the date of the invoice, such as 30 days, the terms are *net 30 days*. These terms may be written as *n/30*. If payment is due by the end of the month in which the sale was made, the terms are written as *n/eom*.

As a means of encouraging the buyer to pay before the end of the credit period, the seller could offer a discount, called a **sales discount**. For example, a seller may offer a 2% discount if the buyer pays within 10 days of the invoice date. If the buyer does not take the discount, the total amount is due within 30 days. These terms are expressed as *2/10, n/30* and are read as *2% discount if paid within 10 days, net amount due within 30 days*.

Sales discounts reduce the seller's sales revenue. Because managers often monitor sales discounts in deciding whether to change credit terms, we keep track of the amount by using a sales discount account. Sales Discounts is a contra (or offsetting) account to sales.

The receipt of cash on account for which a sales discount is taken is recorded by increasing Cash and Sales Discounts and decreasing Accounts Receivable. To illustrate, assume that cash is received within the discount period (10 days) from the credit sale of $1,500, shown on the invoice in Exhibit 9. The effect on the accounts and financial statements of the cash receipt is as follows:

On January 22, collected Invoice No. 106-8 to Computer King, less 2% discount.

Trans. Date	Balance Sheet				Income Statement		
	Assets		Liabilities	Stockholders' Equity	Revenue	Expense	Net Income
Jan. 22	Cash	1,470			Sales Discounts 30		−30
	Accts. Rec.	−1,500					
Net Effect		−30		−30		30	−30
				Retained Earnings			
				(Net Income)			

Sales Returns and Allowances

Merchandise that has been sold can be returned to the seller (**sales return**). In addition, because of defects or for other reasons, the seller can reduce the initial price at which the goods were sold (**sales allowance**). If the return or allowance is for a sale on account, the seller normally issues a **credit memorandum**. This memorandum is sent to the customer and indicates the amount the seller is decreasing the customer's account receivable for the return or allowance.

Sales returns and allowances reduce sales revenue. They also result in additional shipping and other expenses. Since managers often want to know the amount of returns and allowances for a period, the seller records sales returns and allowances in a separate sales returns and allowances account. Sales Returns and Allowances may be viewed as a *contra* (or *offsetting*) account to Sales.

The seller increases Sales Returns and Allowances for the amount of returns or allowances. If the original sale was on account, the seller decreases Accounts Receivable. The seller increases Merchandise Inventory and decreases Cost of Merchandise Sold for the cost of the returned merchandise.

To illustrate, assume that on January 13 Online Solutions issued a $2,000 credit memorandum to Krier Company for merchandise that was returned. The cost of the merchandise, which was sold on account, was $1,200. The effect on the accounts and financial statements of the issuance of the credit memorandum and the receipt of the returned merchandise is as follows:

On January 13 issued credit memorandum for returned merchandise sold for $2,000. The cost of the merchandise sold was $1,200.

Trans. Date	Balance Sheet			Income Statement		
	Assets	Liabilities	Stockholders' Equity	Revenue	Expense	Net Income
Jan. 13	Accts. Rec. −2,000			Sales Retns & Allow 2,000		−2,000
Jan. 13	Merch. Inv. 1,200				Cost of Merch. Sold −1,200	1,200
Net Effect	−800		−800	2,000		−800
			Retained Earnings			
			(Net Income)			

Using a perpetual inventory system, the second entry is necessary so that the merchandise inventory account is up to date and reflects the actual merchandise on hand.

What if the customer pays for the merchandise but later returns it? In this case, the seller issues a credit memorandum, and the credit can be applied against other accounts receivable owed by the customer, or cash can be refunded. If the credit memo is applied against the buyer's other receivables, the effect is similar to that just shown. If cash is refunded for merchandise returned or for an allowance, the seller increases Sales Returns and Allowances and decreases Cash.

Purchase Transactions

OBJECTIVE   4

Describe the accounting for the purchase of merchandise.

As we indicated earlier in this chapter, most large retailers and many small merchandising businesses use computerized perpetual inventory systems. Under the perpetual inventory system, the effects of purchases of merchandise on account on the accounts and financial statements are as follows:

On January 6 purchased $2,500 merchandise on account.

Trans. Date	Balance Sheet			Income Statement		
	Assets	Liabilities	Stockholders' Equity	Revenue	Expense	Net Income
Jan. 6	Mech. Inv. 2,500	Accounts Pay. 2,500				
Net Effect	2,500	2,500				

Purchase Discounts

As we mentioned in our discussion of sales transactions, a seller may offer the buyer credit terms that include a discount for early payment. The buyer refers to such discounts as **purchase discounts**, which reduce the cost of merchandise purchased. Under the perpetual inventory system, the buyer initially increases the merchandise inventory account for the amount of the invoice. When paying the invoice, the buyer decreases cash and merchandise inventory for the amount of the discount. In this way, the merchandise inventory shows the *net* cost to the buyer.

To illustrate, assume that Online Solutions purchased the $1,800 merchandise from Smith Corporation on January 6 with terms 1/15, n/30. The effects of paying the invoice within the discount period on the accounts and financial statements are as follows:

On January 21 paid invoice of $1,800, terms 1/15, n30 within the discount period.

Trans. Date	Balance Sheet			Income Statement		
	Assets	Liabilities	Stockholders' Equity	Revenue	Expense	Net Income
Jan. 21	Mech. Inv. −18	Accounts Pay. −1,800				
	Cash −1,782					
Net Effect	1,800	−1,800				

If Online Solutions does not pay within the discount period, it would record the invoice payment as a decrease in Cash and Accounts Payable for the full $1,800.

Purchase Returns and Allowances

When merchandise is returned (**purchase return**) or a price adjustment is requested (**purchase allowance**), the buyer (debtor) usually sends the seller a letter or a debit memorandum. A **debit memorandum** informs the seller of the amount the buyer proposes to decrease the account payable due the seller. It also states the reasons for the return or the request for a price reduction.

The buyer can use a copy of the debit memorandum as the basis for recording the return or allowance or wait for approval from the seller (creditor). In either case, the buyer decreases Accounts Payable and Merchandise Inventory by the amount of the memorandum.

When a buyer returns merchandise or has been granted an allowance prior to paying the invoice, the amount of the debit memorandum is deducted from the invoice amount. Any available purchase discount is then computed on the remaining amount owed. To illustrate, assume that on January 22 Online Solutions returns $5,000 of merchandise purchased from Quantum Inc. and issues an accompanying debit memorandum. The merchandise returned to Quantum on January 22 was only part of an overall purchase on January 18 of $9,000 with terms 2/10, n/30. If Online pays on January 28, it would deduct a discount of $80, or ($9,000 − $5,000) × 0.02. The effects on the accounts and financial statements of the return and payments are as follows:

On January 22 returned $5,000 of $9,000 of merchandise purchased on January 18 with terms 2/10, n/30. Paid remaining invoice amount on January 28.

Trans. Date	Balance Sheet				Income Statement		
	Assets		Liabilities	Stockholders' Equity	Revenue	Expense	Net Income
Jan. 22	Mech. Inv. −5,000		Accounts Pay. −5,000				
Jan. 28	Merch. Inv. −80		Accounts Pay. −4,000				
	Cash −3,920						
Net Effect	−9,000		−9,000				

Transportation Costs and Sales Taxes

OBJECTIVE 5
Describe the accounting for transportation costs and sales taxes.

Merchandise businesses incur transportation costs in selling and purchasing merchandise. In addition, a retailer must also collect sales taxes in most states. In this section, we briefly discuss the unique aspects of accounting for transportation costs and sales taxes.

Transportation Costs

Does the buyer or the seller pay transportation costs? It depends upon when the ownership (title) of the merchandise passes from the seller to the buyer.[7] The terms of a sale should indicate when the ownership (title) of the merchandise passes to the buyer.

[7] The transfer of ownership (title) also determines whether the buyer or seller must pay other costs, such as the cost of insurance while the merchandise is in transit.

The ownership of the merchandise could pass to the buyer when the seller delivers the merchandise to the transportation company or freight carrier. For example, **DaimlerChrysler** records the sale and the transfer of ownership of its vehicles to dealers when the vehicles are shipped. In this case, the terms are said to be **FOB (free on board) shipping point**. This term means that DaimlerChrysler is responsible for the transportation charges to the shipping point, which is where the shipment originates. The dealer then pays the transportation costs to the final destination. Such costs are part of the dealer's total cost of purchasing inventory and should be added to the cost of the inventory by debiting Merchandise Inventory.

To illustrate, assume that on January 19, Online Solutions buys merchandise from Data Max on account, $2,900, terms FOB shipping point, and prepays the transportation cost of $150. The effects on the accounts and financial statements of the purchase are as follows:

On January 19 purchased $2,900 of merchandise, FOB shipping point. Paid transportation charges of $150.

Trans. Date	Balance Sheet			Income Statement		
	Assets	Liabilities	Stockholders' Equity	Revenue	Expense	Net Income
Jan. 19	Mech. Inv. 2,900	Accounts Pay. 2,900				
Jan. 19	Merch. Inv. 150					
	Cash −150					
Net Effect	2,900	2,900				
			Retained Earnings			
			(Net Income)			

The ownership of the merchandise could pass to the buyer when the buyer receives the merchandise. In this case, the terms are said to be **FOB (free on board) destination**. This term means that the seller delivers the merchandise to the buyer's final destination, free of transportation charges to the buyer. The seller thus pays the transportation costs to the final destination. The seller increases Transportation Out or Delivery Expense, which is reported on the seller's income statement as an expense.

Sometimes FOB shipping point and FOB destination are expressed in terms of the location at which the title to the merchandise passes to the buyer. For example, if **Toyota Motor Co.'s** assembly plant in Osaka, Japan, sells automobiles to a dealer in Chicago, FOB shipping point could be expressed as FOB Osaka. Likewise, FOB destination could be expressed as FOB Chicago.

Shipping terms, the passage of title, and whether the buyer or seller pays the transportation costs are summarized in Exhibit 10.

Sales Taxes

Almost all states and many other taxing units levy a tax on sales of merchandise.[8] The liability for the sales tax is incurred when the sale is made.

At the time of a cash sale, the seller collects the sales tax. When a sale is made on account, the seller charges the tax to the buyer by increasing Accounts Receivable. The seller increases the sales account for the amount of the sale and Sales Taxes Payable for

[8]Businesses that purchase merchandise for resale to others are normally exempt from paying sales taxes on their purchases. Only final buyers of merchandise normally pay sales taxes.

EXHIBIT 10 *Transportation Terms*

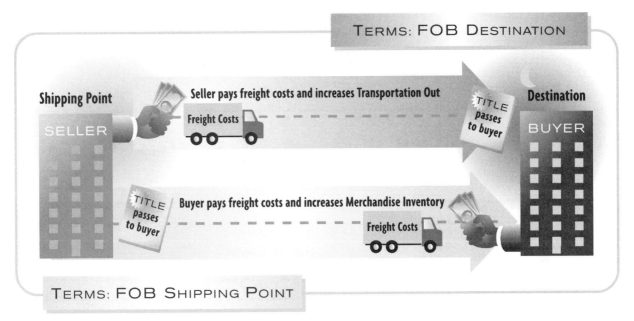

the amount of the tax. Normally on a regular basis, the seller pays the amount of the sales tax collected to the taxing unit. The seller records such a payment by decreasing Sales Taxes Payable and Cash.

Dual Nature of Merchandise Transactions

OBJECTIVE 6

Illustrate the dual nature of merchandising transactions.

Each merchandising transaction affects a buyer and a seller. In the following illustration, we show how the same transactions would be recorded by both the seller and the buyer. In this example, the seller is Scully Company and the buyer is Burton Co.

On July 1, Scully Company sold merchandise on account to Burton Co., $7,500, terms FOB destination; 2/10, n/30. The cost of the merchandise sold was $4,500.

Scully Company (Seller)

Trans. Date	Balance Sheet			Income Statement		
	Assets	Liabilities	Stockholders' Equity	Revenue	Expense	Net Income
July 1	Accts Rec. 7,500			Sales 7,500		7,500
July 1	Merch. Inv. −4,500				Cost of Merch. Sold −4,500	−4,500
Net Effect	3,000		3,000	7,500	−4,500	3,000
			Retained Earnings			
			(Net Income)			

Burton Co. (Buyer)

Trans. Date	Balance Sheet			Income Statement		
	Assets	Liabilities	Stockholders' Equity	Revenue	Expense	Net Income
July 1	Merch. Inv. 7,500	Accts. Pay. 7,500				
Net Effect	7,500	7,500				
			Retained Earnings			
			(Net Income)			

On July 5, Scully Company pays transportation charges of $300 for delivery of the merchandise sold on July1 to Burton Co.

Scully Company (Seller)

Trans. Date	Balance Sheet			Income Statement		
	Assets	Liabilities	Stockholders' Equity	Revenue	Expense	Net Income
July 5	Cash −300				Delivery Expense 300	−300
Net Effect	−300		−300			−300
			Retained Earnings			
			(Net Income)			

Burton Co. (Buyer)

No effect on the accounts and financial statements.

On July 6 Scully Company issues a credit memorandum for $1,000 for merchandise returned by Burton Co. The cost of the merchandise returned was $600.

Scully Company (Seller)

Trans. Date	Balance Sheet			Income Statement		
	Assets	Liabilities	Stockholders' Equity	Revenue	Expense	Net Income
July 6	Accts Rec. −1,000			Sales Retns. & Allow. 1,000		−1,000
July 6	Merch. Inv. 600				Cost of Merch. Sold −600	−600
Net Effect	−400		−400	−1,000	−600	−400
			Retained Earnings			
			(Net Income)			

Burton Co. (Buyer)

Trans. Date	Balance Sheet			Income Statement		
	Assets	Liabilities	Stockholders' Equity	Revenue	Expense	Net Income
July 6	Merch. Inv. −1,000	Accts. Pay. −1,000				
Net Effect	−1,000	−1,000				
			Retained Earnings			
			(Net Income)			

On July 11, Scully Company received payment from Burton Co. less discount.

Scully Company (Seller)

Trans. Date	Balance Sheet			Income Statement		
	Assets	Liabilities	Stockholders' Equity	Revenue	Expense	Net Income
July 11	Accts Rec. −6,500			Sales Discounts 130		−130
July 11	Cash 6,370					
Net Effect	−130		−130	−130		−130
			Retained Earnings			
			(Net Income)			

Burton Co. (Buyer)

Trans. Date	Balance Sheet			Income Statement		
	Assets	Liabilities	Stockholders' Equity	Revenue	Expense	Net Income
July 11	Cash −6,370	Accts. Pay. −6,500				
July 11	Merch. Inv. −130					
Net Effect	−6,500	−6,500				
			Retained Earnings			
			(Net Income)			

Merchandise Shrinkage

OBJECTIVE 7

Describe the accounting for merchandise shrinkage.

Under the perpetual inventory system, a separate merchandise inventory account is maintained in the ledger. During the accounting period, this account shows the amount of merchandise for sale at any time. However, merchandising businesses could experience some loss of inventory due to shoplifting, employee theft, or errors in recording or counting inventory. As a result, the **physical inventory** taken at the end of the accounting period could differ from the amount of inventory shown in the inventory records. Normally, the amount of merchandise for sale, as indicated by the balance of the merchandise inventory account, is higher than the total amount of merchandise counted during the physical inventory. For this reason, the difference is often called **inventory shrinkage** or *inventory shortage*. One recent study estimated that inventory shrinkage exceeds $30 billion annually in the United States.[9]

To illustrate, Online Solutions' inventory records, called the **book inventory**, indicate that $63,950 of merchandise should be available for sale on December 31, 2007. The physical inventory taken on December 31, 2007, however, indicates that only $62,150 of merchandise is actually available for sale. The inventory shrinkage for the year ending December 31, 2007, is $1,800 as shown:

December 31, 2007 unadjusted book inventory	$63,950
December 31, 2007 physical inventory	62,150
Inventory shrinkage	$ 1,800

[9]"New Study Finds U.S. Retailers Losing $32 Billion to Theft," PR Newswire, November 23, 2001.

The effect of the shrinkage on the accounts and financial statements follows.

Trans. Date	Balance Sheet			Income Statement		
	Assets	Liabilities	Stockholders' Equity	Revenue	Expense	Net Income
Dec. 31	Merch. Inv. −1,800				Cost of Merch. Sold 1,800	−1,800
Net Effect	−1,800		−1,800		1,800	−1,800
			Retained Earnings (Net Income)			

ETHICS IN ACTION

A recent survey reported that the 30 largest retail store chains have lost more than $5 billion to shoplifting and employee theft. Of this amount, only 3.45% of the losses resulted in any recovery. The stores apprehended more than 600,000 shoplifters and 78,000 dishonest employees during 2001.

Approximately one of every 27 employees was apprehended for theft from their employer. Each dishonest employee stole approximately eight times the amount stolen by shoplifters ($900 vs. $114).

Source: Jack L. Hayes International, *Fourteenth Annual Retail Theft Survey,* 2001.

After the shrinkage has been recorded, the adjusted Merchandise Inventory (book inventory) in the accounting records agrees with the actual physical inventory at the end of the period. Since no system of procedures and safeguards can totally eliminate it, inventory shrinkage is often considered a normal cost of operations. If the amount of the shrinkage is abnormally large, it can be disclosed separately on the income statement. In such cases, the shrinkage can be recorded in a separate account, such as Loss from Merchandise Inventory Shrinkage.

Gross Profit and Operating Profit Analysis

OBJECTIVE   8

Describe and illustrate the use of gross profit and operating income in analyzing a company's operations.

Gross profit and operating income are two important profitability measures that analysts use in assessing the efficiency and effectiveness of a merchandiser's operations. In this section, we use these measures to assess **JC Penney's** operating performance for the past several years.

Like many financial statement measures, sometimes referred to as *performance metrics*, gross profit and operating income are best analyzed over time as percentages rather than as amounts. Since gross profit and operating income are income statement amounts, they are normally expressed as a percentage of net sales. Doing so allows us to better analyze the operating performance over time.

Gross profit and operating profit as a percentage of net sales for JC Penney are shown in Exhibit 11. The data, shown for the past three years, are taken from the Securities and Exchange Commission annual filings (Form 10-K) for JC Penney.

As Exhibit 11 data show, the gross profit as a percentage of net sales was at its highest in fiscal 1999, dipped in fiscal 2000, and was recovered partially in fiscal 2001

EXHIBIT 11

JC Penney Operating Ratios

	For the Years Ending . . . (in millions)		
	Jan. 26, 2002	Jan. 27, 2001	Jan. 29, 2000
Net sales	$32,004	$31,846	$31,743
Cost of merchandise sold	22,789	23,031	22,286
Gross profit	$ 9,215	$ 8,815	$ 9,457
Operating expenses	8,459	8,637	8,604
Operating income	$ 756	$ 178	$ 853
Gross profit percent	28.8%	27.7%	29.8%
Operating income percent	2.4%	0.6%	2.7%

at nearly 29% of sales.[10] The gross profit improvement in fiscal 2001 was credited by Penney's management to better merchandise assortments, improved inventory productivity, and centralized buying that allowed buyers advantages in negotiating price reductions from their suppliers. Operating income as a percentage of sales followed a similar dip and then recovery trend. Operating income as a percentage of sales in fiscal 2001 was 1.8 percentage points better than the previous year (2.4% − 0.6%). The gross profit percentage improvement accounts for 1.1 percentage points (28.8% − 27.7%). The remaining 0.7 percentage point improvement was credited by Penney's management to lower catalog book and marketing costs, lower telemarketing costs, and shift from development to maintenance of JCPenney.com.

APPENDIX

Statement of Cash Flows: The Indirect Method

Online Solutions' statement of cash flows for the year ended December 31, 2007, is shown in Exhibit 8. The operating activities section of this statement was prepared using a method known as the *indirect method*. This method is used by over 90% of publicly held companies.

The use of the indirect method only affects net cash flows from operating activities. The other method of preparing the net cash flows from operating activities section is called the *direct method*. The direct method analyzes each transaction and its effect on cash flows. In contrast, the indirect method analyzes only the changes in accounts.

A major reason that the indirect method is so popular is that it is normally less costly to use. However, regardless of whether the indirect or direct method is used, the reporting of net cash flows from investing and financing activities is not affected. In this appendix, we illustrate the use of the indirect method of preparing the statement of cash flows.

The indirect method reconciles net income with net cash flows from operating activities. Net income is adjusted for the effects of accruals and deferrals that affected the net income but did not result in the receipt or payment of cash. The resulting amount is the net cash flows from operating activities.

[10]The income statement is dated at the end of the first month of the year but represents most (11 months) of the previous year's activity. Thus, a statement dated January 26, 2002, is said to be for fiscal year 2001.

The indirect method converts net income determined under the accrual basis of accounting to what it would have been under the cash basis of accounting. In other words, net cash flows from operating activities is equivalent to net income using the cash basis of accounting.

To illustrate, assume that accounts receivable increases during the period by $10,000. This increase is included in the period's revenue and thus increases net income. However, cash was not collected. Thus, an increase in accounts receivable must be deducted from net income under the indirect method. Likewise, depreciation expense is deducted in arriving at net income but does not involve any cash payments. Thus, depreciation expense is added to net income under the indirect method.

The typical adjustments to convert net income to net cash flows from operating activities, using the indirect method, are shown in Exhibit 12.

EXHIBIT 12
Indirect Method Adjustments

Net income			$XXX
Add:	Depreciation	$XXX	
	Decreases in current assets (accounts receivable, inventories, prepaid expenses)	XXX	
	Increases in current liabilities (accounts payable, notes payable, accrued expenses)	XXX	XXX
Deduct:	Increases in current assets (accounts receivable, inventories, prepaid expenses)	$XXX	
	Decreases in current liabilities (accounts payable, notes payable, accrued expenses)	XXX	XXX
Net cash flows from operating activities			$XXX

You should note that, except for depreciation, the adjustments in Exhibit 12 are for changes in the current assets and the current liabilities. This is because changes in the current assets and the current liabilities are related to operations and thus net income. For example, changes in inventories are related to sales, while changes in accounts payable are related to expenses.

Cash Flows from Operating Activities

To prepare the operating activities section for Online Solutions' statement of cash flows, we need to determine depreciation and the changes in the current assets and the liabilities during the year. This information is included in Exhibit 13, which shows the comparative balance sheets for Online Solutions as of December 31, 2007 and 2006, and related changes.

Based on Exhibit 13, the net cash flows from operating activities is shown below.

Net income			$ 60,400
Add:	Depreciation expense—store equipment	$ 3,100	
	Depreciation expense—office equipment	2,490	
	Decrease in office supplies	120	
	Decrease in prepaid insurance	350	
	Increase in accounts payable	8,150	14,210
Deduct:			
	Increase in accounts receivable	$(24,080)	
	Increase in merchandise inventory	(2,450)	
	Decrease in salaries payable	(360)	
	Decrease in unearned rent	(600)	(27,490)
Net cash flows from operating activities			$ 47,120

EXHIBIT 13 *Online Solutions' Comparative Balance Sheets*

ONLINE SOLUTIONS
Balance Sheets

	December 31, 2007	December 31, 2006	Changes Increase (Decrease)
Assets			
Current assets:			
Cash	$ 52,950	$ 41,500	$11,450
Accounts receivable	76,080	52,000	24,080
Merchandise inventory	62,150	59,700	2,450
Office supplies	480	600	(120)
Prepaid insurance	2,650	3,000	(350)
Total current assets	$194,310	$156,800	$37,510
Property, plant, and equipment:			
Land	$ 20,000	$ 20,000	$ 0
Store equipment	27,100	20,000	7,100
Accumulated depreciation—store equipment	(5,700)	(2,600)	(3,100)
Office equipment	15,570	10,000	5,570
Accumulated depreciation—office equipment	(4,720)	(2,230)	(2,490)
Total property, plant, and equipment	$ 52,250	$ 45,170	$ 7,080
Total assets	$246,560	$201,970	$44,590
Liabilities			
Current liabilities:			
Accounts payable	$ 22,420	$ 14,270	$ 8,150
Notes payable (current portion)	5,000	5,000	0
Salaries payable	1,140	1,500	(360)
Unearned rent	1,800	2,400	(600)
Total current liabilities	$ 30,360	$ 23,170	$ 7,190
Long-term liabilities:			
Notes payable (final payment due 2017)	20,000	25,000	(5,000)
Total liabilities	$ 50,360	$ 48,170	$ 2,190
Stockholders' Equity			
Capital stock	$ 25,000	$ 25,000	$ 0
Retained earnings	171,200	128,800	42,400
Total stockholders' equity	$196,200	$153,800	$42,400
Total liabilities and stockholders' equity	$246,560	$201,970	$44,590

The depreciation expense of $3,100 for store equipment is determined from the increase in the accumulated depreciation for store equipment. Likewise, the depreciation expense of $2,490 for office equipment is determined from the increase in the accumulated depreciation for office equipment. The changes in the current assets and the current liabilities are also taken from Exhibit 13.

Cash Flows Used for Investing Activities

The cash flows for investing activities section can also be prepared by analyzing the changes in the accounts shown in Exhibit 13. For Online Solutions, the cash flows used for investing activities is composed of two items. First, additional store equipment of $7,100 was purchased, as shown by the increase in the store equipment. Likewise, additional office equipment of $5,570 was purchased. Thus, cash of $12,670 was used for investing activities, as shown in Exhibit 8.

Cash Flows Used for Financing Activities

The cash flows for financing activities can also be determined from Exhibit 13. For Online Solutions, the cash flows used for financing activities is composed of two items. First, dividends of $18,000 are reported on the retained earnings statement shown in Exhibit 6. Since no dividends payable appears on the balance sheets, cash dividends of $18,000 must have been paid during the year. In addition, notes payable decreased by $5,000 during the year, so cash must have been used in paying off $5,000 of the notes. Thus, cash of $23,000 was used for financing activities, as shown in Exhibit 8.

Key Points

1. Distinguish the operating activities of a service business from those of a merchandise business.

The revenue activities of a service enterprise involve providing services to customers. In contrast, the revenue activities of a merchandising business involve the buying and selling of merchandise.

2. Describe and illustrate the financial statements of a merchandising business.

The multiple-step income statement of a merchandiser reports sales, sales returns and allowances, sales discounts, and net sales. The cost of the merchandise sold is subtracted from net sales to determine the gross profit. The cost of merchandise sold is determined by using either the periodic or perpetual inventory method. Operating income is determined by subtracting operating expenses from gross profit. Operating expenses are normally classified as selling or administrative expenses. Net income is determined by subtracting income taxes and other expense and adding other income. The income statement may also be reported in a single-step form. The retained earnings statement and the statement of cash flows are similar to those for a service business. The balance sheet reports merchandise inventory at the end of the period as a current asset.

3. Describe the accounting for the sale of merchandise.

Sales of merchandise for cash or on account are recorded by increasing Sales. The cost of merchandise sold and the reduction in merchandise inventory are also recorded for the sale. For sales of merchandise on account, the credit terms can allow sales discounts for early payment. Such discounts are recorded by the seller as an increase in Sales Discounts. Sales discounts are reported as a deduction from the amount initially recorded in Sales. Likewise, when merchandise is returned or a price adjustment is granted, the seller increases Sales Returns and Allowances. For sales on account, a subsidiary ledger is maintained for individual customer accounts receivable.

Under the perpetual inventory system, the cost of merchandise sold and the reduction of merchandise inventory on hand are recorded at the time of sale. In this way, the merchandise inventory account indicates the amount of merchandise on hand at all times. Likewise, any returned merchandise is recorded in the merchandise inventory account with a related reduction in the cost of merchandise sold.

4. **Describe the accounting for the purchase of merchandise.**

Purchases of merchandise for cash or on account are recorded by increasing Merchandise Inventory. For purchases of merchandise on account, the credit terms can allow cash discounts for early payment. Such purchase discounts are viewed as a reduction in the cost of the merchandise purchased. When merchandise is returned or a price adjustment is granted, the buyer decreases Merchandise Inventory.

5. **Describe the accounting for transportation costs and sales taxes.**

When merchandise is shipped FOB shipping point, the buyer pays the transportation costs and increases Merchandise Inventory. When merchandise is shipped FOB destination, the seller pays the transportation costs and increases Transportation Out or Delivery Expense. If the seller prepays transportation costs as a convenience to the buyer, the seller increases Accounts Receivable for the costs.

The liability for sales tax is incurred when the sale is made and is recorded by the seller as an increase in the sales taxes payable account. When the amount of the sales tax is paid to the taxing unit, Sales Taxes Payable and Cash are decreased.

6. **Illustrate the dual nature of merchandising transactions.**

Each merchandising transaction affects a buyer and a seller. The illustration in this chapter shows how the same transactions would be recorded by both.

7. **Describe the accounting for merchandise shrinkage.**

The physical inventory taken at the end of the accounting period could differ from the amount of inventory shown in the inventory records. The difference, called *inventory shrinkage*, requires an adjusting entry increasing Cost of Merchandise Sold and decreasing Merchandise Inventory. After this entry has been recorded, the adjusted Merchandise Inventory (book inventory) in the accounting records agrees with the actual physical inventory at the end of the period.

8. **Describe and illustrate the use of gross profit and operating income in analyzing a company's operations.**

Gross profit and operating income are two important profitability measures that analysts use in assessing the efficiency and effectiveness of a merchandiser's operations. Gross profit and operating income are normally analyzed over time as a percentage of net sales.

Glossary

Administrative expenses: Expenses incurred in the administration or general operations of the business.

Book inventory: The amount of inventory recorded in the accounting records.

Controlling account: The account in the general ledger that summarizes the balances of the accounts in a subsidiary ledger.

Cost of merchandise sold: The cost that is reported as an expense when merchandise is sold.

Credit memorandum: A form used by a seller to inform the buyer of the amount the seller proposes to decrease the account receivable due from the buyer.

Credit period: The amount of time the buyer is allowed in which to pay the seller.

Credit terms: Terms for payment on account by the buyer to the seller.

Debit memorandum: A form used by a buyer to inform the seller of the amount the buyer proposes to decrease the account payable due the seller.

FOB (free on board) destination: Freight terms in which the seller pays the transportation costs from the shipping point to the final destination.

FOB (free on board) shipping point: Freight terms in which the buyer pays the transportation costs from the shipping point to the final destination.

Gross profit: Sales minus the cost of merchandise sold.

Income from operations (operating income): The excess of gross profit over total operating expenses.

Indirect method: A method of preparing the statement of cash flows that reconciles net income with net cash flows from operating activities.

Inventory shrinkage: The amount by which the merchandise for sale, as indicated by the balance of the merchandise inventory account, is larger than the total amount of merchandise counted during the physical inventory.

Invoice: The bill that the seller sends to the buyer.

Loss from operations: The excess of operating expenses over gross profit.

Merchandise available for sale: The cost of merchandise available for sale to customers.

Merchandise inventory: Merchandise on hand (not sold) at the end of an accounting period.

Multiple-step income statement: A form of income statement that contains several sections, subsections, and subtotals.

Net sales: Gross sales less sales returns and allowances and sales discounts.

Other expense: Expenses that cannot be traced directly to operations.

Other income: Revenue from sources other than the primary operating activity of a business.

Periodic inventory method: The inventory method in which the inventory records do not show the amount available for sale or sold during the period.

Perpetual inventory method: The inventory system in which each purchase and sale of merchandise is recorded in an inventory account.

Physical inventory: A detailed listing of the merchandise for sale at the end of an accounting period.

Purchase discounts: Discounts taken by the buyer for early payment of an invoice.

Purchase return or allowance: From the buyer's perspective, returned merchandise or an adjustment for defective merchandise.

Report form: The form of balance sheet in which assets, liabilities, and stockholders' equity are reported in a downward sequence.

Sales: The total amount charged to customers for merchandise sold, including cash sales and sales on account.

Sales discounts: From the seller's perspective, discounts that a seller can offer the buyer for early payment.

Sales returns and allowances: From the seller's perspective, returned merchandise or an adjustment for damaged or defective merchandise.

Selling expenses: Expenses that are incurred directly in the selling of merchandise.

Single-step income statement: A form of income statement in which the total of all expenses is deducted from the total of all revenues.

Subsidiary ledger: A ledger containing individual accounts with a common characteristic.

Self-Study Questions

(Answers appear at end of chapter.)

1. If merchandise purchased on account is returned, the buyer can inform the seller of the details by issuing:
   A. a debit memorandum
   B. a credit memorandum
   C. an invoice
   D. a bill

2. If merchandise is sold on account to a customer for $1,000, terms FOB shipping point, 1/10, n/30, and the seller prepays $50 in transportation costs, the amount of the discount for early payment would be:
   A. $0   C. $10.00
   B. $5.00   D. $10.50

3. The income statement in which the total of all expenses is deducted from the total of all revenues is termed:
   A. multiple-step form   C. direct form
   B. single-step form   D. report form

4. On a multiple-step income statement, the excess of net sales over the cost of merchandise sold is called:
   A. operating income
   B. income from operations
   C. gross profit
   D. net income

5. As of December 31, 2004, Ames Corporation's physical inventory was $275,000 and its book inventory was $290,000. The effect of the inventory shrinkage on the accounts is:
   A. to increase cost of merchandise sold and inventory by $15,000.
   B. to increase cost of merchandise sold and decrease inventory by $15,000.
   C. to decrease cost of merchandise sold and increase inventory by $15,000.
   D. to decrease cost of merchandise sold and inventory by $15,000.

Discussion Questions

1. What distinguishes a merchandising business from a service business?

2. Can a business earn a gross profit but incur a net loss? Explain.

3. What is the difference between the cost of merchandise purchased and the cost of merchandise available for sale? Can they be the same amount? Explain.

4. What is the difference between the cost of merchandise available for sale and the cost of merchandise sold? Can they be the same amount? Explain.

5. Name at least three accounts that would normally appear in the financial statements of a merchandising business but would not appear in the finanicial statements of a service business.

6. How does the accounting for sales to customers using bank credit cards, such as MasterCard and VISA, differ from accounting for sales to customers using nonbank credit cards, such as American Express? Explain.

7. Sometimes a retailer will not accept American Express but will accept MasterCard or VISA. Why would a retailer accept one but not the other?

8. At some **Texaco**, **Chevron**, or **Conoco** gasoline stations, the cash price per gallon is 3 or 4 cents less than the credit price per gallon. As a result, many customers pay cash rather than use their credit cards. Why would a gasoline station owner establish such a policy?

9. Assume that you purchased merchandise with credit terms 2/10, n/30. On the date the invoice is due, you don't have the cash to pay the invoice. However, you can borrow the necessary money at an 8% annual interest rate. Should you borrow the money to pay the invoice? Explain.

10. What is the nature of (a) a credit memorandum issued by the seller of merchandise and (b) a debit memorandum issued by the buyer of merchandise?

11. Who bears the transportation costs when the terms of sale are (a) FOB shipping point and (b) FOB destination?

12. When you purchase a new car, the "sticker price" includes a "destination" charge. Are you purchasing the car FOB shipping point or FOB destination? Explain.

13. Hansen Office Equipment, which uses a perpetual inventory system, experienced a normal inventory shrinkage of $12,860. (a) What accounts would be increased and decreased to record the adjustment for the inventory shrinkage at the end of the accounting period? (b) What are some causes of inventory shrinkage?

14. Assume that Hansen Office Equipment in Question 13 experienced an abnormal inventory shrinkage of $210,500. It has decided to record the abnormal inventory shrinkage so that it would be separately disclosed on the income statement. What account would be increased for the abnormal inventory shrinkage?

Exercises

<table>
<tr><td>

EXERCISE 4-1
Determining gross profit
OBJECTIVES 1, 8

✓ a. $6,574

</td><td>

Walgreen Company operates drugstores throughout the United States, selling prescription drugs, general merchandise, cosmetics, food, and beverages. For 2001, Walgreen reported (in millions) net sales of $24,623, cost of sales of $18,049, and operating income of $1,398.

a. Determine Walgreen's gross profit.
b. Determine the gross profit as a percentage of net sales. Round to one decimal place.
c. Determine the operating income as a percentage of net sales. Round to one decimal place.

</td></tr>
<tr><td>

EXERCISE 4-2
Determining gross profit
OBJECTIVES 1, 8

</td><td>

CVS Corporation operates drugstores throughout the United States, selling prescription drugs, general merchandise, cosmetics, greeting cards, food, and beverages. For 2001, CVS reported (in millions) net sales of $22,241, cost of sales of $16,550, and operating income of $771.

</td></tr>
</table>

✓ a. $5,691

a. Determine CVS's gross profit.
b. Determine the gross profit as a percentage of net sales. Round to one decimal place.
c. Determine the operating income as a percentage of net sales. Round to one decimal place.

EXERCISE 4-3
Analyzing gross profit and operating income
OBJECTIVE 8

Based on the data shown in Exercises 4-1 and 4-2, comment on the operating performance of Walgreen in comparison to CVS.

EXERCISE 4-4
Determining gross profit
OBJECTIVES 1, 8

✓ a. $7,984

Office Depot operates a chain of office supply stores throughout the United States. For 2001, Office Depot reported (in millions) net sales of $11,154, gross profit of $3,170, and operating income of $354.

a. Determine the cost of goods sold.
b. Determine the cost of goods sold as a percentage of net sales. Round to one decimal place.
c. Determine the gross profit as a percentage of net sales. Round to one decimal place.
d. Determine the operating income as a percentage of net sales. Round to one decimal place.
e. What is the difference between the gross profit as a percentage of net sales and the operating income as a percentage of net sales? Explain.

EXERCISE 4-5
Identify items missing in determining cost of merchandise sold
OBJECTIVE 2

For (a) through (d), identify the items designated by X.

a. Purchases − (X + X) = Net Purchases.
b. Net Purchases + X = Cost of Merchandise Purchased.
c. Merchandise Inventory (beginning) + Cost of Merchandise Purchased = X.
d. Merchandise Available for Sale − X = Cost of Merchandise Sold.

EXERCISE 4-6
Cost of merchandise sold and related items
OBJECTIVE 2

✓ Cost of merchandise sold: $592,050

The following data were extracted from the accounting records of My Computers Company for the year ended November 30, 2004:

Merchandise inventory, December 1, 2003	$ 75,750
Merchandise inventory, November 30, 2004	88,200
Purchases	625,000
Purchases returns and allowances	14,500
Purchases discounts	12,950
Sales	870,625
Transportation in	6,950

a. Prepare the Cost of Merchandise Sold section of the income statement for the year ended November 30, 2004, using the periodic inventory method.
b. Determine the gross profit to be reported on the income statement for the year ended November 30, 2004.

EXERCISE 4-7
Cost of merchandise sold
OBJECTIVE 2

How many errors can you find in the following schedule of cost of merchandise sold for the current year ended December 31, 2004?

Cost of merchandise sold:			
Merchandise inventory, December 31, 2004			$ 75,000
Purchases		$500,000	
Plus: Purchases returns and allowances	$12,500		
Purchases discounts	6,500	19,000	
Gross purchases		$519,000	
Less transportation in		12,400	
Cost of merchandise purchased			506,600
Merchandise available for sale			$581,600
Less merchandise inventory, January 1, 2004			81,300
Cost of merchandise sold			$500,300

EXERCISE 4-8

Income statement for merchandiser

OBJECTIVE 2

The following expenses were incurred by a merchandising business during the year. In which expense section of the income statement should each be reported: (a) selling, (b) administrative, or (c) other?

1. Advertising expense
2. Depreciation expense on office equipment
3. Insurance expense on store equipment
4. Interest expense on notes payable
5. Office supplies used
6. Rent expense on office building
7. Salaries of office personnel
8. Salary of sales manager

EXERCISE 4-9

Determining amounts for items omitted from income statement

OBJECTIVE 2

✓ a. $10,000

Two items are omitted in each of the following four lists of income statement data. Determine the amounts of the missing items, identifying them by letter.

Sales	$298,000	$500,000	$700,000	$ (g)
Sales returns and allowances	(a)	15,000	(e)	30,500
Sales discounts	8,000	8,000	10,000	37,000
Net sales	280,000	(c)	665,000	(h)
Cost of merchandise sold	(b)	285,000	(f)	540,000
Gross profit	130,000	(d)	200,000	150,000

EXERCISE 4-10

Multiple-step income statement

OBJECTIVE 2

How many errors can you find in the following income statement?

THE FUNCTOR COMPANY
Income Statement
For the Year Ended July 31, 2004

Revenue from sales:			
Sales		$3,000,000	
Add: Sales returns and allowances	$58,000		
Sales discounts	14,500	72,500	
Gross sales			$3,072,500
Cost of merchandise sold			1,495,000
Income from operations			$1,577,500
Operating expenses:			
Selling expenses		$ 145,000	
Transportation out		5,300	
Administrative expenses		87,200	
Total operating expenses			237,500
			$1,340,000
Other expense:			
Interest revenue			47,500
Gross profit			$1,292,500

EXERCISE 4-11

Multiple-step income statement

OBJECTIVE 2

✓ a. Net income: $97,500

On August 31, 2004, the balances of the accounts appearing in the ledger of Noble Company, a furniture wholesaler, are as follows:

Administrative Expenses	$ 60,000	Office Supplies	$ 10,600
Building	512,500	Retained Earnings	558,580
Capital Stock	50,000	Salaries Payable	3,220
Cash	48,500	Sales	775,000
Cost of Merchandise Sold	450,000	Sales Discounts	20,000
Dividends	25,000	Sales Returns and Allowances	45,000
Interest Expense	7,500	Selling Expenses	95,000
Merchandise Inventory	130,000	Store Supplies	7,700
Notes Payable	25,000		

a. Prepare a multiple-step income statement for the year ended August 31, 2004.
b. Compare the major advantages and disadvantages of the multiple-step and single-step forms of income statements.

EXERCISE 4-12

Sales returns and allowances

OBJECTIVE 3

During the year, sales returns and allowances totaled $112,150. The cost of the merchandise returned was $67,300. The accountant recorded all returns and allowances by decreasing the sales account and increasing Cost of Merchandise Sold for $112,150.

Was the accountant's method of recording returns acceptable? Explain. In your explanation, include the advantages of using a sales returns and allowances account.

EXERCISE 4-13

Sales-related transactions

OBJECTIVE 3

After the amount due on a sale of $5,500, terms 2/10, n/eom, is received from a customer within the discount period, the seller consents to the return of the entire shipment. The cost of the merchandise returned was $3,380. (a) What is the amount of the refund owed to the customer? (b) Illustrate the effects on the accounts and financial statements of the return and the refund.

EXERCISE 4-14

Sales-related transactions

OBJECTIVE 3

Merchandise is sold on account to a customer for $15,000, terms FOB shipping point, 3/10, n/30. The seller paid the transportation costs of $625. Determine the following: (a) amount of the sale, (b) amount debited to Accounts Receivable, (c) amount of the discount for early payment, and (d) amount due within the discount period.

EXERCISE 4-15

Purchase-related transaction

OBJECTIVE 4

Degas Company purchased merchandise on account from a supplier for $3,500, terms 2/10, n/30. Degas Company returned $750 of the merchandise and received full credit.

a. If Degas Company pays the invoice within the discount period, what is the amount of cash required for the payment?
b. Under a perpetual inventory system, what account is decreased by Degas Company to record the return?

EXERCISE 4-16

Determining amounts to be paid on invoices

OBJECTIVE 4

Determine the amount to be paid in full settlement of each of the following invoices, assuming that credit for returns and allowances was received prior to payment and that all invoices were paid within the discount period.

	Merchandise	Transportation Paid by Seller		Returns and Allowances
a.	$4,000	—	FOB shipping point, 1/10, n/30	$1,200
b.	1,500	$50	FOB shipping point, 2/10, n/30	700
c.	9,500	—	FOB destination, n/30	400
d.	2,500	75	FOB shipping point, 1/10, n/30	600
e.	5,000	—	FOB destination, 2/10, n/30	—

EXERCISE 4-17
Purchase-related transactions
OBJECTIVE 4

A retailer is considering the purchase of 10 units of a specific item from either of two suppliers. Their offers are as follows:

a. $500 a unit, total of $5,000, 2/10, n/30, plus transportation costs of $175.
b. $510 a unit, total of $5,100, 1/10, n/30, no charge for transportation.

Which of the two offers, a or b, yields the lower price?

EXERCISE 4-18
Purchase-related transactions
OBJECTIVE 4

Citron Co., a women's clothing store, purchased $12,000 of merchandise from a supplier on account, terms FOB destination, 2/10, n/30. Citron Co. returned $3,500 of the merchandise, receiving a credit memorandum, and then paid the amount due within the discount period. Illustrate the effects on the accounts and financial statements of Citron of (a) the purchase, (b) the merchandise return, and (c) the payment.

EXERCISE 4-19
Purchase-related transactions
OBJECTIVE 4

Illustrate the effects on the accounts and financial statements of Aloha Company of the following related transactions:

a. Purchased $9,000 of merchandise from Green Co. on account, terms 2/10, n/30.
b. Paid the amount owed on the invoice within the discount period.
c. Discovered that $2,000 of the merchandise was defective and returned items, receiving credit.
d. Purchased $1,000 of merchandise from Green Co. on account, terms n/30.
e. Received a check for the balance owed from the return in (c) after deducting for the purchase in (d).

EXERCISE 4-20
Sales tax
OBJECTIVE 5

A sale of merchandise on account for $3,000 is subject to a 6% sales tax. (a) Should the sales tax be recorded at the time of sale or when payment is received? (b) What is the amount of the sale? (c) What is the amount of increase to Accounts Receivable? (d) What is the title of the account to which the $180 is recorded?

EXERCISE 4-21
Sales tax transactions
OBJECTIVE 5

Illustrate the effects on the accounts and financial statements of the following selected transactions:

a. Sold $6,000 of merchandise on account, subject to a sales tax of 5%. The cost of the merchandise sold was $3,600.
b. Paid $4,380 to the state sales tax department for taxes collected.

EXERCISE 4-22
Sales-related transactions
OBJECTIVE 3

Sterile Co., a furniture wholesaler, sells merchandise to Bawd Co. on account, $8,000, terms 2/15, n/30. The cost of the merchandise sold is $4,800. Sterile Co. issues a credit memorandum for $500 for merchandise returned and subsequently receives the amount due within the discount period. The cost of the merchandise returned is $300. Illustrate the effects on the accounts and financial statements of Sterile Co. of (a) the sale, including the cost of the merchandise sold, (b) the credit memorandum, including the cost of the returned merchandise, and (c) the receipt of the check for the amount due from Bawd Co.

EXERCISE 4-23
Purchase-related transactions
OBJECTIVE 4

Based on the data presented in Exercise 4-22, illustrate the effects on the accounts and financial statements of Bawd Co. of (a) the purchase, (b) the return of the merchandise for credit, and (c) the payment of the invoice within the discount period.

EXERCISE 4-24
Adjusting entry for merchandise inventory shrinkage
OBJECTIVE 7

Nocturnal Inc.'s perpetual inventory records indicate that $417,200 of merchandise should be on hand on October 31, 2004. The physical inventory indicates that $400,680 of merchandise is actually on hand. Illustrate the effects on the accounts and financial statements of the inventory shrinkage for Nocturnal Inc. for the year ended October 31, 2004.

EXERCISE 4-25
Gross profit and operating income
OBJECTIVE 8

Staples, Inc., operates a chain of office supply stores throughout the United States. For 2001 and 2000, Staples reported (in millions) the following operating data:

	2001	2000
Net sales	$10,674	$8,937
Cost of goods sold	8,097	6,722
Gross profit	$ 2,577	$2,215
Operating income	$ 289	$ 534

a. Compute the percentage of gross profit and operating income to net sales. Round to one decimal place.
b. Based on (a), comment on Staples' operating performance in 2001 as compared to 2000.

Problems

PROBLEM 4 | 1
Multiple-step income statement, retained earnings, and report form of balance sheet
OBJECTIVE 2

✓ 1. Net income: $100,000

The following selected accounts and their current balances appear in the ledger of Mandolin Co. for the fiscal year ended March 31, 2004:

Cash	$ 33,750	Sales	$1,275,000
Notes Receivable	120,000	Sales Returns and Allowances	23,100
Accounts Receivable	121,000	Sales Discounts	21,900
Merchandise Inventory	175,000	Cost of Merchandise Sold	775,000
Office Supplies	5,600	Sales Salaries Expense	173,200
Prepaid Insurance	3,400	Advertising Expense	43,800
Office Equipment	85,000	Depreciation Expense—	
Accumulated Depreciation—		Store Equipment	6,400
Office Equipment	12,800	Miscellaneous Selling Expense	1,600
Store Equipment	153,000	Office Salaries Expense	84,150
Accumulated Depreciation—		Rent Expense	31,350
Store Equipment	34,200	Depreciation Expense—	
Accounts Payable	55,600	Office Equipment	12,700
Salaries Payable	2,400	Insurance Expense	3,900
Note Payable		Office Supplies Expense	1,300
(final payment due 2013)	56,000	Miscellaneous Administrative	
Capital Stock	75,000	Expense	1,600
Retained Earnings	395,750	Interest Revenue	11,000
Dividends	35,000	Interest Expense	6,000

Instructions

1. Prepare a multiple-step income statement.
2. Prepare a retained earnings statement.
3. Prepare a report form of balance sheet, assuming that the current portion of the note payable is $7,500.
4. Briefly explain how multiple-step and single-step income statements differ.

PROBLEM 4 | 2
Single-step income statement and retained earnings statement
OBJECTIVE 2

Selected accounts and related amounts for Mandolin Co. for the fiscal year ended March 31, 2004, are presented in Problem 4-1.

Instructions

1. Prepare a single-step income statement.
2. Prepare a retained earnings statement.

PROBLEM 4 | 3
Sales-related transactions
OBJECTIVES 3, 5

The following selected transactions were completed by Fastball Supply Co., which sells office supplies primarily to wholesalers and occasionally to retail customers:

July   2   Sold merchandise on account to Magnolia Co., $10,500, terms FOB destination, 2/10, n/30. The cost of the merchandise sold was $6,000.
       4   Sold merchandise on account to McNutt Co., $2,800, terms FOB shipping point, n/eom. The cost of merchandise sold was $1,800.
     12   Received check for amount due from Magnolia Co. for sale on July 2.
     16   Sold merchandise on account to Westpark Co., $12,000, terms FOB shipping point, 1/10, n/30. The cost of merchandise sold was $7,200.
     18   Issued credit memorandum for $3,000 to Westpark Co. for merchandise returned from sale on July 16. The cost of the merchandise returned was $1,800.
     26   Received check for amount due from Westpark Co. for sale on July 16 less credit memorandum of July 18 and discount.
     31   Received check for amount due from McNutt Co. for sale of July 4.
     31   Paid Fast Delivery Service $1,050 for merchandise delivered during July to customers under shipping terms of FOB destination.

Instructions

Illustrate the effects of each of the preceding transactions on the accounts and financial statements of Fastball Supply Co. Identify each transaction by date.

PROBLEM 4 | 4
Purchase-related transactions
OBJECTIVES 4, 5

The following selected transactions were completed by Bushwhack Company during October of the current year:

Oct.   4   Purchased merchandise from Picadilly Co., $7,500, terms FOB destination, 2/10, n/30.
      6   Issued debit memorandum to Picadilly Co. for $1,000 of merchandise returned from purchase on October 4.
     14   Paid Picadilly Co. for invoice of October 4 less debit memorandum of October 6 and discount.
     19   Purchased merchandise from Ivy Co., $5,000, terms FOB shipping point, n/eom.
     19   Paid transportation charges of $120 on October 19 purchase from Ivy Co.
     31   Paid Ivy Co. for invoice of October 19.

Instructions

Illustrate the effects of each of the preceding transactions on the accounts and financial statements of Bushwhack Company. Identify each transaction by date.

PROBLEM 4 | 5
Sales-related and purchase-related transactions for seller and buyer
OBJECTIVES 3, 4, 5, 6

The following selected transactions were completed during July between Snap Company and Buckle Co.:

July   1   Snap Company sold merchandise on account to Buckle Co., $11,750, terms FOB destination, 2/15, n/eom. The cost of the merchandise sold was $7,000.
      2   Snap Company paid transportation costs of $350 for delivery of merchandise sold to Buckle Co. on July 1.

(continued)

July 　5　Snap Company sold merchandise on account to Buckle Co., $17,500, terms FOB shipping point, n/eom. The cost of the merchandise sold was $10,000.

　　　6　Buckle Co. returned $2,000 of merchandise purchased on account on July 1 from Snap Company. The cost of the merchandise returned was $1,200.

　　　9　Buckle Co. paid transportation charges of $200 on July 5 purchase from Snap Company.

　　16　Buckle Co. paid Snap Company for purchase of July 1 less discount and less return of July 6.

　　31　Buckle Co. paid Snap Company on account for purchase of July 5.

Instructions

Illustrate the effects of each of the preceding transactions on the accounts and financial statements of (1) Snap Company and (2) Buckle Co. Identify each transaction by date.

PROBLEM 4 | 6
Statement of Cash Flows Using Indirect Method
APPENDIX

For the year ending December 31, 2004, Seamless Systems Inc. reported net income of $30,200 and paid dividends of $9,000. Comparative balance sheets as of December 31, 2004 and 2003, are as follows:

SEAMLESS SYSTEMS INC.
Balance Sheets

	December 31, 2004	December 31, 2003	Changes Increase (Decrease)
Assets			
Current assets:			
Cash	$ 26,475	$ 20,750	$ 5,725
Accounts receivable	38,040	26,000	12,040
Merchandise inventory	31,075	29,850	1,225
Office supplies	240	300	(60)
Prepaid insurance	1,325	1,500	(175)
Total current assets	$ 97,155	$ 78,400	$18,755
Property, plant, and equipment:			
Land	$ 10,000	$ 10,000	$ 0
Store equipment	13,550	10,000	3,550
Accumulated depreciation—store equipment	(2,850)	(1,300)	(1,550)
Office equipment	7,785	5,000	2,785
Accumulated depreciation—office equipment	(2,360)	(1,115)	(1,245)
Total property, plant, and equipment	$ 26,125	$ 22,585	$ 3,540
Total assets	$123,280	$100,985	$22,295
Liabilities			
Current liabilities:			
Accounts payable	$ 11,210	$ 7,135	$ 4,075
Notes payable (current portion)	2,500	2,500	0
Salaries payable	570	750	(180)
Unearned rent	900	1,200	(300)
Total current liabilities	$ 15,180	$ 11,585	$ 3,595
Long-term liabilities:			
Notes payable (final payment due 2009)	10,000	12,500	(2,500)
Total liabilities	$ 25,180	$ 24,085	$ 1,095
Stockholders' Equity			
Capital stock	$ 12,500	$ 12,500	$ 0
Retained earnings	85,600	64,400	21,200
Total stockholders' equity	$ 98,100	$ 76,900	$21,200
Total liabilities and stockholders' equity	$123,280	$100,985	$22,295

✓ 1. Net cash flow from
operating activities: $23,560

Instructions

1. Prepare a statement of cash flows, using the indirect method.
2. Why is depreciation added to net income in determining net cash flows from operating activities? Explain.

Activities

Activity 4-1

Ethics and professional conduct in business

E T H I C S

On October 1, 2004, Couperin Company, a garden retailer, purchased $15,000 of corn seed, terms 2/10, n/30, from Kernel Co. Even though the discount period had expired, Bryant Harness subtracted the discount of $300 when he processed the documents for payment on October 15, 2004.

Discuss whether Bryant Harness behaved in a professional manner by subtracting the discount even though the discount period had expired.

Activity 4-2

Purchases discounts and accounts payable

The Movie Store Co. is owned and operated by Amy Lell. The following is an excerpt from a conversation between Amy Lell and Tammi Beach, the chief accountant for The Movie Store.

Amy: Tammi, I've got a question about this recent balance sheet.

Tammi: Sure, what's your question?

Amy: Well, as you know, I'm applying for a bank loan to finance our new store in Three Forks, and I noticed that the accounts payable are listed as $130,000.

Tammi: That's right. Approximately $100,000 of that represents amounts due our suppliers, and the remainder is miscellaneous payables to creditors for utilities, office equipment, supplies, etc.

Amy: That's what I thought. But as you know, we normally receive a 2% discount from our suppliers for earlier payment, and we always try to take the discount.

Tammi: That's right. I can't remember the last time we missed a discount.

Amy: Well, in that case, it seems to me the accounts payable should be listed minus the 2% discount. Let's list the accounts payable due suppliers as $98,000, rather than $100,000. Every little bit helps. You never know. It might make the difference between getting the loan and not.

How would you respond to Amy Lell's request?

Activity 4-3

Analysis of gross profit and operating income

Federated Department Stores, Inc., is one of the leading operators of full-line department stores in the United States, operating under the names **Bloomingdale's**, **The Bon Marche**, **Burdines**, **Goldsmith's**, **Lazarus**, **Macy's**, and **Rich's**. The following operating data (in millions) for the past three years is taken from Federated's income statement:

	For the Years Ended		
	Feb. 2, 2002	**Feb. 3, 2001**	**Jan. 29, 2000**
Net sales	$15,651	$16,638	$16,029
Cost of merchandise sold	9,584	9,955	9,576
Operating expenses	4,801	4,912	4,760

1. Compute the gross profit for each year.
2. Compute the operating income for each year.

(continued)

3. Compute the gross profit as a percentage of net sales for each year. Round to one decimal place.
4. Compute the operating income as a percentage of net sales for each year. Round to one decimal place.
5. Based on this analysis, comment on the trends in operating performance for the past three years.
6. Based upon this analysis, compare Federated's operating performance with JC Penney's performance shown in this chapter.

Activity 4-4
Sales discounts

Your sister operates Hercules Parts Company, a mail-order boat parts distributorship in its third year of operation. The following income statement was recently prepared for the year ended July 31, 2003:

HERCULES PARTS COMPANY
Income Statement
For the Year Ended July 31, 2003

Revenues:		
Net sales		$600,000
Interest revenue		5,000
Total revenues		$605,000
Expenses:		
Cost of merchandise sold	$420,000	
Selling expenses	66,000	
Administrative expenses	34,000	
Interest expense	10,000	
Total expenses		530,000
Net income		$ 75,000

Your sister is considering a proposal to increase net income by offering sales discounts of 2/15, n/30, and by shipping all merchandise FOB shipping point. Currently, no sales discounts are allowed and merchandise is shipped FOB destination. These credit terms are estimated to increase net sales by 10%. The ratio of the cost of merchandise sold to net sales is expected to be 70%. All selling and administrative expenses are expected to remain unchanged except for store supplies, miscellaneous selling, office supplies, and miscellaneous administrative expenses, which are expected to increase proportionately with increased net sales. The amounts of these preceding items for the year ended July 31, 2003, were as follows:

Store supplies expense	$5,000
Miscellaneous selling expense	2,000
Office supplies expense	1,000
Miscellaneous administrative expense	1,800

The other income and other expense items will remain unchanged. The shipment of all merchandise FOB shipping point will eliminate all transportation-out expenses, which for the year ended July 31, 2003, were $20,150.

1. Prepare a projected single-step income statement for the year ending July 31, 2004, based on the proposal.
2. a. Based on the projected income statement in (1), would you recommend the implementation of the proposed changes?
   b. Describe any possible concerns you may have related to the proposed changes described in (1).

Activity 4-5
Analysis of gross profit and operating income

Nordstrom, Inc. is a fashion specialty retailer offering a wide selection of high-quality apparel, shoes, and accessories for women, men, and children in the United States through 80 full-line Nordstrom stores, 46 Nordstrom Rack and clearance stores, 4 Faconnable boutiques, and 2 free-standing shoe stores. The following operating data (in millions) were taken from 10-K filings with the Securities and Exchange Commission:

	For Year Ending January 31		
	2002	2001	2000
Net sales	$5,634	$5,529	$5,149
Cost of goods sold	3,766	3,650	3,359
Gross profit	$1,868	$1,879	$1,790
Selling, general, admin. exp.	1,722	1,747	1,524
Operating income	$ 146	$ 132	$ 266

1. Compute gross profit as a percentage of net sales for each year. Round to one decimal place.
2. Compute operating income as a percentage of net sales for each year. Round to one decimal place.
3. Based on (1) and (2), comment on Nordstrom's operating performance.

Activity 4-6
Analysis of gross profit and operating income

Target Corporation (formerly Dayton Hudson Corporation) is a general merchandise retailer, comprised of three operating segments: **Target, Mervyn's,** and **Marshall Field's.** Target, an upscale discount chain located in 47 states, contributed 83% of the corporation's 2001 total revenues. Mervyn's, a middle-market promotional department store located in 14 states in the West, South, and Midwest, contributed 10% of total revenues. Marshall Field's (including stores formerly named Dayton's and Hudson's), a traditional department store located in 8 states in the upper Midwest, contributed 7% of total revenues. The following operating data (in millions) were taken from 10-K filings with the Securities and Exchange Commission:

	For Year Ending		
	Feb. 2 2002	Feb. 3 2001	Jan. 31 2000
Net sales	$39,888	$36,362	$33,212
Cost of goods sold	27,246	25,295	23,029
Gross profit	$12,642	$11,067	$10,183
Operating income	$ 2,680	$ 2,478	$ 2,329

1. Compute gross profit as a percentage of net sales for each year. Round to one decimal place.
2. Compute operating income as a percentage of net sales for each year. Round to one decimal place.
3. Based on (1) and (2), comment on Target's operating performance.

Activity 4-7
Comparative analysis of operating performance

Using the data provided in Activities 4-5 and 4-6, compare the operating performances of Nordstrom and Target.

Answers to Self-Study Questions

1. **A** A debit memorandum (answer A), issued by the buyer, indicates the amount the buyer proposes to debit to the accounts payable account. A credit memorandum (answer B), issued by the seller, indicates the amount the seller proposes to credit to the accounts receivable account. An invoice (answer C) or a bill (answer D), issued by the seller, indicates the amount and terms of the sale.

2. **C** The amount of discount for early payment is $10 (answer C), or 1% of $1,000. Although the $50 of transportation costs paid by the seller is debited to the customer's account, the customer is not entitled to a discount on that amount.

3. **B** The single-step form of income statement (answer B) is so named because the total of all expenses is deducted in one step from the total of all revenues. The multiple-step form (answer A) includes numerous sections and subsections with several subtotals. The report form (answer D) is a common form of the balance sheet.

4. **C** Gross profit (answer C) is the excess of net sales over the cost of merchandise sold. Operating income (answer A) or income from operations (answer B) is the excess of gross profit over operating expenses. Net income (answer D) is the final figure on the income statement after all revenues and expenses have been reported.

5. **B** The inventory shrinkage, $15,000, is the difference between the book inventory, $290,000, and the physical inventory, $275,000. The effect of the inventory shrinkage on the accounts is to increase cost of merchandise sold and decrease inventory by $15,000 (answer B).

5

LEARNING OBJECTIVES

OBJECTIVE 1
Describe and illustrate the objectives and elements of internal control.

OBJECTIVE 2
Describe and illustrate methods of preventing and detecting employee fraud.

OBJECTIVE 3
Describe and illustrate the application of internal controls to cash.

OBJECTIVE 4
Describe the nature of a bank account and its use in controlling cash.

OBJECTIVE 5
Describe and illustrate the use of a bank reconciliation in controlling cash.

OBJECTIVE 6
Describe the accounting for special-purpose cash funds.

OBJECTIVE 7
Describe and illustrate the reporting of cash and cash equivalents in the financial statements.

OBJECTIVE 8
Describe, illustrate, and interpret the cash flow to net income ratio and the cash to monthly cash expenses ratio.

Internal Control and Cash

Once a month, you could receive a bank statement that lists the deposits, withdrawals, and checks that have been added to and subtracted from your account balance. The statement could also be accompanied by your canceled checks.

New forms of payments are now arising that don't involve checks at all. Retailers, such as grocery stores, now allow customers to pay for merchandise by swiping their bank cards at checkout, causing an immediate transfer of funds out of a bank account. Banks are allowing regular monthly bills, such as utility bills, to be paid directly out of a checking account by using electronic fund transfers. Internet payments can be made by using services such as Paypal®, which will make payments to third parties directly out of a checking account. In all of these cases, you need to verify actual fund transfers with the correct amounts by comparing your bank statement with electronic invoices, receipts, and other evidence of payment.

Many banks are making real-time checking account information available on the Internet to account owners. Thus, account owners using this feature are now able to manage and control their accounts in a more timely way.

Like individuals, businesses must control their cash and other assets to guard against errors and fraud. In this chapter we will discuss how companies control their cash and other assets.

Internal Control

OBJECTIVE   1

Describe and illustrate the objectives and elements of internal control.

Internal controls are the policies and procedures used to safeguard assets, ensure accurate business information, and ensure compliance with laws and regulations. Internal controls help businesses guide their operations and prevent abuses. For example, assume that you own and manage a lawn care service. Your business uses several employee teams, and you provide each team with vehicle and lawn equipment. What are some of the issues you would face as a manager in controlling the operations of this business? Some examples follow.

- Lawn care must be provided on time.
- The quality of lawn care services must meet customer expectations.
- Employees must provide work for the hours they are paid.
- Lawn care equipment should be used for business purposes only.
- Vehicles should be used for business purposes only.
- Customers must be billed and bills collected for services rendered.

How would you address these issues? You could, for example, develop a schedule at the beginning of each day and then inspect the work at the end of the day to verify that it was completed according to quality standards. You could have "surprise" inspections by arriving on site at random times to verify that the teams are working according to schedule. You could require employees to clock in at the beginning of the day and clock out at the end of the day to make sure that they are paid for hours worked. You could require the work teams to return the vehicles and equipment to a central location to prevent unauthorized use. You could keep a log of odometer readings at the end of each day to verify that the vehicles have not been used for joy riding. You could bill customers after you have inspected the work and then monitor the collection of all receivables. All of these are examples of internal control.

Objectives of Internal Control

The objectives of internal control are to provide reasonable assurance that

1. assets are safeguarded and used for business purposes.
2. business information is accurate.
3. employees comply with laws and regulations.

Internal control can safeguard assets by preventing their theft, fraud, misuse, or misplacement. One of the most serious breaches of internal control is employee fraud. **Employee fraud** is the intentional act of deceiving an employer for personal gain. Such deception can range from purposely overstating expenses on a travel expense report to embezzling millions of dollars through complex schemes. In a separate section of this chapter, we address how to prevent and detect employee fraud.

Accurate information is necessary for operating a business successfully. The safeguarding of assets and accurate information often go hand in hand. The reason for this is that employees attempting to defraud a business also need to adjust the accounting records to hide the fraud.

Businesses must comply with applicable laws, regulations, and financial reporting standards. Examples of such standards and laws include environmental regulations, contract terms, safety regulations, and generally accepted accounting principles (GAAP).

Elements of Internal Control

How does management achieve its internal control objectives? Management is responsible for designing and applying five **elements of internal control** to meet the three internal control objectives. These elements are[1]

1. control environment.
2. risk assessment.
3. control procedures.
4. monitoring.
5. information and communication.

The elements of internal control are illustrated in Exhibit 1. In this exhibit, these elements form an umbrella over the business to protect it from control threats. The business's control environment is represented by the size of the umbrella. Risk assessment, control procedures, and monitoring are the fabric that keeps the umbrella from leaking. Information and communication links the umbrella to management. In the following paragraphs, we discuss each of these elements.

EXHIBIT 1

Elements of Internal Control

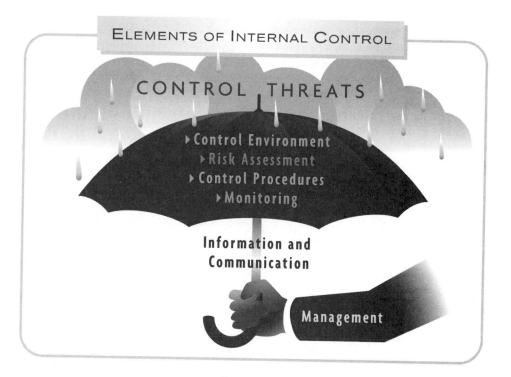

[1] *Internal Control—Integrated Framework by the Committee of Sponsoring Organizations of the Treadway Commission (COSO)*, pp. 12–14. This document provides a professionally sponsored framework for internal control.

CONTROL ENVIRONMENT   A business's control environment is the overall attitude of management and employees about the importance of controls. One factor that influences the control environment is *management's philosophy and operating style*. A management that overemphasizes operating goals and deviates from control policies could indirectly encourage employees to ignore controls. For example, the pressure to achieve revenue targets could encourage employees to fraudulently record sham sales. On the other hand, a management that emphasizes the importance of controls and encourages adherence to control policies creates an effective control environment.

The business's *organizational structure*, which is the framework for planning and controlling operations, also influences the control environment. For example, a department store chain could organize each of its stores as separate business units. Each store manager has full authority over pricing and other operating activities. In such a structure, each store manager has the responsibility for establishing an effective control environment.

Personnel policies also affect the control environment. Personnel policies involve the hiring, training, evaluation, compensation, and promotion of employees. In addition, job descriptions, employee codes of ethics, and conflict-of-interest policies are part of the personnel policies. Such policies can enhance the internal control environment if they provide reasonable assurance that only competent, honest employees are hired and retained.

To illustrate, the head of a bank's loan department perpetrated a fraud by accepting kickbacks from customers with poor credit ratings. As a result, the bank lost thousands of dollars from bad loans. After the discovery of the fraud, the bank president improved the bank's control environment by implementing a program that allowed employees to report suspicious conduct anonymously. In addition to encouraging employees to report suspicious conduct, the employees were warned that employee fraud could occur anywhere and involve anyone.

RISK ASSESSMENT   All organizations face risks. Examples of risk include changes in customer requirements, competitive threats, regulatory changes, changes in economic factors such as interest rates, and employee violations of company policies and procedures. Management should assess these risks and take necessary actions to control them so that the objectives of internal control can be achieved.

Once risks have been identified, they can be analyzed to estimate their significance, to assess their likelihood of occurring, and to determine actions that will minimize them. For example, the manager of a warehouse operation could analyze the risk of injuring employees' backs, which could give rise to lawsuits. If the manager determines that the risk is significant, the company could purchase back support braces for its warehouse employees and require them to wear the braces.

CONTROL PROCEDURES   Control procedures are established to provide reasonable assurance that business goals, including the prevention of fraud, will be achieved. In the following paragraphs, we briefly discuss control procedures that can be integrated throughout the accounting system. These procedures are listed in Exhibit 2.

EXHIBIT 2
*Internal Control
Procedures*

Hiring competent personnel, rotating duties, and requiring vacations. The successful operation of an accounting system requires procedures to ensure that people are able to perform the duties to which they are assigned. Hence, it is necessary that all accounting employees be adequately trained and supervised in performing their jobs. It could also be advisable to rotate the duties of clerical personnel and mandate vacations for nonclerical personnel. These policies encourage employees to adhere to prescribed procedures. In addition, they could result in detection of existing errors or fraud. For example, numerous cases of employee fraud have been discovered after a long-term employee who never took vacations missed work because of an illness or other unavoidable reasons.

Separating responsibilities for related operations. To decrease the possibility of inefficiency, errors, and fraud, the responsibility for related operations should be divided among two or more persons. For example, the responsibilities for purchasing, receiving, and paying for computer supplies should be divided among three persons or departments. If the same person orders supplies, verifies their receipt, and pays the supplier, the following abuses are possible:

1. Placing orders on the basis of friendship with a supplier rather than on price, quality, and other objective factors.
2. Not verifying the quantity and quality of supplies received, thus causing payment for supplies not received or poor-quality supplies.
3. Stealing supplies by the employee.
4. Carelessly verifying the validity and accuracy of invoices, thus causing the payment of false or inaccurate invoices.

The checks and balances provided by dividing responsibilities among various departments requires no duplication of effort. The business documents prepared by one department are designed to coordinate with and support those prepared by other departments.

Separating operations, custody of assets, and accounting.   Control policies should establish the responsibilities for various business activities. To reduce the possibility of errors and fraud, the responsibilities for operations, custody of assets, and accounting should be separated. The accounting records then serve as an independent check on the individuals who have custody of the assets and who engage in the business operations. For example, the employees entrusted with handling cash receipts from credit customers should not record cash receipts in the accounting records. To do so would allow employees to borrow or steal cash and hide the theft in the records. Likewise, if those engaged in operating activities also record the results of operations, they could distort the accounting reports to show favorable results. For example, a store manager whose year-end bonus is based on operating profits could be tempted to record fictitious sales to receive a larger bonus.

Implementing proofs and security measures.   Proofs and security measures should be used to safeguard assets and ensure reliable accounting data. This control procedure applies to many different techniques, such as authorization, approval, and reconciliation procedures. For example, employees who travel on company business could be required to obtain a department manager's approval on a travel request form.

Other examples of control procedures include the use of bank accounts and other measures to ensure the safety of cash and valuable documents. A cash register that displays the amount recorded for each sale and provides the customer a printed receipt can be an effective part of the internal control structure. An all-night convenience store could use the following security measures to deter robberies:

1. Locate the cash register near the door so that it is fully visible from outside the store; have two employees work late hours; employ a security guard.
2. Deposit cash in the bank daily, before 5 p.m.
3. Keep only small amounts of cash on hand after 5 p.m. by depositing excess cash in a store safe that employees on duty can't open.
4. Install cameras and alarm systems.

MONITORING   Monitoring the internal control system locates weaknesses and improves control effectiveness. The internal control system can be monitored through either ongoing efforts by management or by separate evaluations. Ongoing monitoring efforts could include observing both employee behavior and warning signs from the accounting system. The indicators shown in Exhibit 3 could be clues to internal control problems.[2]

---

[2]Edwin C. Bliss, "Employee Theft," *Boardroom Reports*, July 15, 1994, pp. 5–6.

EXHIBIT 3
*Indicators of Internal
Control Problems*

CLUES TO POTENTIAL PROBLEMS

Warning signs with regard to people

1. Abrupt change in lifestyle (without winning the lottery).
2. Close social relationships with suppliers.
3. Refusing to take a vacation.
4. Frequent borrowing from other employees.
5. Excessive use of alcohol or drugs.

Warning signs from the accounting system

1. Missing documents or gaps in transaction numbers (could mean documents are being used for fraudulent transactions).
2. An unusual increase in customer refunds (refunds may be phony).
3. Differences between daily cash receipts and bank deposits could mean receipts are being pocketed before being deposited).
4. Sudden increase in slow payments (employee may be pocketing the payment).
5. Backlog in recording transactions (possibly an attempt to delay detection of fraud).

Separate monitoring evaluations are generally performed when there are major changes in strategy, senior management, business structure, or operations. In large businesses, internal auditors who are independent of operations normally are responsible for monitoring the internal control system. Internal auditors can report issues and concerns to the audit committee of the board of directors, which is independent of management. In addition, external auditors evaluate internal control as a normal part of their annual financial statement audit.

INFORMATION AND COMMUNICATION   Information and communication are essential elements of internal control. Information about the control environment, risk assessment, control procedures, and monitoring are needed by management to guide operations and ensure compliance with reporting, legal, and regulatory requirements. Management can also use external information to assess events and conditions that impact decision making and external reporting. For example, management uses information from the Financial Accounting Standards Board (FASB) to assess the impact of possible changes in reporting standards.

Prevention and Detection of Employee Fraud

OBJECTIVE   2

Describe and illustrate methods of preventing and detecting employee fraud.

The theft of assets by employees from their employer is employee fraud. Employee fraud can involve small amounts, such as taking office supplies for personal use or making long-distance telephone calls from work. Employee fraud also can involve the theft of millions of dollars through complex schemes. For example, an employee could process payments for goods or services not received. The payments for the goods or services could be made to phantom (fictitious) companies controlled by the employee.

The following three elements are common to most employee fraud[3]:

1. An employee's perceived financial need.
2. An opportunity to use a fraudulent scheme to satisfy the need.
3. A rationalization that the fraud is justified.

For example, an employee could need cash to pay for the medical expenses of a spouse or a child. For employee fraud to occur, the employee must also have the opportunity to satisfy the need. This opportunity could involve physical access to assets such as cash or could involve the ability to obtain cash or assets by authorization of fictitious transactions. For example, the store manager of a local retail chain could have the ability to authorize the purchase of office equipment for the store as long as the amount is under $3,000. Subsequently, the store manager purchases a personal computer, has it delivered to his home address, and later sells it. The store manager could rationalize the theft as being justified because he believes that the owner is underpaying him.

In the following paragraphs, we describe and illustrate controls for preventing and detecting employee fraud. Many of these controls are similar to the control procedures that we discussed earlier in this chapter. However, the magnitude, seriousness, and frequency of employee fraud warrant a separate emphasis on controls to prevent and detect such fraud.

Preventive Controls

In trying to prevent employee fraud, a business should focus primarily on designing controls to prevent the opportunity of employees to steal assets. Businesses have little control over employees' personal financial needs and their ability to rationalize the theft of assets. Controls to prevent the opportunity of employees to steal assets can be grouped into those involving (1) physical safeguarding of assets and (2) proper authorization and approval procedures.

PHYSICAL SAFEGUARDING   Physical safeguarding of assets involves controlling the company's assets to limit an employee's ability to steal the assets. For example, in a department store, valuable inventory such as jewelry should be locked in a vault at the end of each day. Similarly, inventory in a manufacturing plant should be stored

---

[3]Donald R. Cressey, "Management Fraud, Accounting Controls, and Criminological Theory," in *Management Fraud*, Robert K. Elliott and John J. Willingham (New York: Petrocelli Books, 1980).

in a guarded, fenced-in area away from the employees' parking lot. A manufacturer could routinely inspect employees' lunch boxes and bags when they leave the plant to prevent the theft of tools. Retailers should deposit cash at least once each day, if not more frequently, to prevent the buildup of large amounts of cash on hand that could be susceptible to theft.

AUTHORIZATION AND APPROVAL   Proper authorization and approval procedures can be effectively used to prevent employee fraud. For example, the owner of a small company could prepare an approved vendor list for the purchase of supplies, merchandise, or services. Any changes to the list or purchases from vendors not on the list must be approved by the owner. This control would effectively reduce the chances that an employee could set up a "phantom vendor" who would be paid for purchases or services that were not provided. An approved vendor list would also reduce the possibility that an employee might be receiving kickbacks from vendors for purchases that are not the proper quality or the best price.

Proper authorization and approval procedures could also be used in a variety of other situations. For example, a procedure that requires a properly authorized, approved, and completed materials requisition before the release of inventory helps prevent employee theft of inventory. Likewise, proper authorization and approval procedures for hiring, firing, and increasing pay reduce the chances of theft related to overpayment of employees or the payment of fictitious employees. Finally, requiring proper supporting documentation for the payment of vendor invoices, such as an authorized purchase order and a receiving report, provides assurance that the company is paying only for goods actually received and ordered.

Detective Controls

Businesses should also design controls to detect employee fraud. These controls include periodic reviews, independent checks, and reconciliations. The effectiveness of these detective controls, however, depends on separating the custody of assets from the accounting for the assets. The separation of duties is essential for the detection of employee fraud. Otherwise, an employee could steal assets and cover up the theft by changing the accounting records.

The accounting system should also be designed so that each asset is recorded as soon as practical. By doing so, an initial accountability for the asset is established. Shortages and possible employee fraud can be detected by comparing the assets on hand with the accounting records. To illustrate, when a retailer receives inventory, a receiving report should be prepared. The receiving report includes a detailed description of the item and the quantity received. A copy of the receiving report is sent to accounting, a copy is maintained in the receiving area, and a copy accompanies the inventory to the inventory storage area or to the retail floor. In this way, if the inventory is later missing, the documentation can be traced back to determine where it was last accounted for, and the party responsible for the missing inventory can be isolated. For example, if the copy of the receiving report kept in the receiving department includes the signature of the storage supervisor, indicating that the missing inventory was delivered to storage, the receiving department is relieved of responsibility and the focus shifts to the storage area. If the storage area records indicate that the missing inventory was delivered to the sales floor, the focus then shifts to the floor area supervisor.

PERIODIC REVIEWS   Periodic reviews of the accounting records are useful in identifying unusual transactions or accounts for further investigation. For example, a review of the accounts receivable subsidiary ledger could reveal several overdue accounts from normally good customers. Further investigation could reveal that the customers in fact paid their bills but that the mail clerk or some other employee stole their payments. Likewise, a review of the payroll records could identify fictitious employees or employees who were fired or laid off months ago. The review of the payroll could also reveal unauthorized pay increases. A review of the inventory records or purchase records could reveal purchases that are not in line with normal business operations. For example, the review of the supporting documentation for a purchase of inventory, such as a freight bill, could indicate that the inventory was delivered to a residential address. Further investigation could reveal that the address is that of a purchasing agent who ordered the inventory for personal use.

INDEPENDENT CHECKS   Independent checks are useful in detecting employee fraud. Independent checks normally involve physically examining an asset or other item of interest and then comparing the results of this investigation against the accounting records. For example, inventory should be physically counted at least once a year and the results compared against the inventory that should be on hand according to the accounting records. Shoplifting results in a discrepancy between a retailer's physical inventory and its book inventory. However, wide discrepancies could also indicate employee theft. Likewise, a physical counting of fixed assets and a comparison against the subsidiary ledger for fixed assets could detect missing assets. For example, the failure to locate a microcomputer or printer could indicate employee theft. Independent checks can also be used to detect fictitious employees on the payroll. For example, if fictitious employees are suspected, the owner or a manager could be present when the payroll is distributed to employees. To receive their payroll checks, employees are asked to show identification, such as a driver's license. Any payroll checks that are not picked up represent those that are possibly related to fictitious employees.

RECONCILIATIONS   Reconciliations are useful in detecting employee theft. Reconciliations involve comparisons within the accounting records and comparisons of the accounting records with external sources of information. A reconciliation differs from an independent check in that the objective of the independent check is to determine the amount of the difference between the physical examination of an item and the accounting records. In contrast, reconciliations are based on the premise that agreement should exist and management can focus on finding and correcting differences. For example, the accounts receivable controlling account should agree with the sum of the individual balances in the customers (accounts receivable) subsidiary ledger. If the two do not agree, an error such as an incorrect recording of a transaction in a customer's account could have occurred. If an error has occurred, it must be tracked down and corrected. Similarly, businesses should reconcile the amount of recorded cash sales for the day with the amount of the daily cash deposit. Unexplained differences in reconciliations are often due to employee fraud. For example, an inability to reconcile the cash sales with the cash deposit could be the result of an employee's theft of a portion of a day's cash sales.

Risk Factors Relating to Employee Fraud

The American Institute of Certified Public Accountants has developed a set of risk factors related to employee fraud.[4] These factors are grouped into two categories: (1) susceptibility of assets to theft and (2) lack of controls.

SUSCEPTIBILITY OF ASSETS   The more assets that are susceptible to theft, the greater the opportunity and, thus, the greater the risk of employee theft. Cash is, of course, the asset most susceptible to theft. Inventories that are small in size, high in value, and high in demand are also highly susceptible to theft. Examples of such inventories include drugs, diamonds, and computer chips. Easily convertible assets, such as microcomputers that are small in size, highly marketable, or lack ownership identification, are also highly susceptible to theft.

LACK OF CONTROLS   Lack of preventive or detective controls such as we described in the preceding paragraphs increases the risk of employee fraud. The specific risk factors related to lack of controls are as follows:

1. Lack of proper record keeping for assets susceptible to theft.
2. Lack of proper segregation of duties.
3. Lack of independent checks.
4. Lack of a proper system for authorization and approval of transactions.
5. Lack of proper physical safeguarding of assets susceptible to theft.
6. Lack of timely and proper documentation for transactions.
7. Lack of proper management oversight.
8. Lack of mandatory vacations for employees in sensitive positions.
9. Lack of proper screening procedures for employees in sensitive positions.

We discussed the first six risk factors in the section on controls to prevent and detect employee fraud. The last three factors warrant additional discussion. The lack of proper management oversight provides the employee the opportunity to commit theft. The lack of mandatory vacations for employees in sensitive positions increases the risk that an employee who has stolen assets will not be caught. That is, an employee involved in stealing assets has a greater chance of getting caught when a substitute employee performs these duties. Obviously, a company that allows vacationing employees to catch up on their work when they return rather than using substitute employees defeats the purpose of requiring vacations.

Proper screening of employees who are hired for sensitive positions also helps to reduce the risk of employee theft. For example, hiring a cash register clerk who has been previously convicted of shoplifting is simply asking for trouble. However, proper hiring practices have their limits. Time and time again, employees who have been properly screened are caught stealing assets; no prior information indicated any tendencies suggesting a risk of fraud. In other words, hiring practices are not a substitute for effective preventive and detective controls for employee fraud.

---

[4]*Statement on Auditing Standards No. 82*, "Consideration of Fraud in a Financial Statement Audit" (New York: American Institute of Certified Public Accountants, 1997).

Examples of Employee Fraud

The importance of controls for preventing and detecting employee fraud can be illustrated through actual cases. In this section, we describe frauds that could have been prevented or detected before they became significant.[5]

CASE 1: FICTITIOUS INVOICES   An accounts payable clerk altered the name and address of an inactive vendor and opened a commercial account at a local bank under the assumed name. The clerk then entered fictitious invoices into the accounts payable system for payment. The clerk was able to steal thousands of dollars over several months.

Control Failure: Payments were not properly approved by an employee independent of the accounts payable (accounting) function.

Corrective Action: The company implemented a policy that required proper approval of all payments by an employee independent of the accounts payable function. In addition, an approved vendor listing for all purchases was developed. Now any purchases from a vendor not on the list must be approved by a senior manager.

CASE 2: FICTITIOUS CERTIFICATES OF DEPOSIT   A new accounts officer at a bank embezzled customer funds for more than 16 years. The officer printed his own certificates of deposit, which looked exactly like the bank's certificates. When a customer came to purchase a certificate, the officer would issue a fake certificate and pocket the customer's money. When the fake certificates matured, he would attempt to convince the customer to roll the CD over to a new, higher yielding (fake) certificate. If a customer insisted on cashing in the fake certificate, he would terminate another customer's legitimate CD and use the proceeds to pay the holder of the fake CD. Over the 16 years, the officer stole approximately $5 million.

Control Failure: The officer's transactions were not reviewed on a periodic basis, nor was he required to take vacations. The officer also handled customer cash receipts and had authority to change the accounting records of the customers.

Corrective Action: Sensitive transactions are now reviewed on a surprise basis. All employees are required to take vacations. Individuals who handle cash do not have authority to change or otherwise alter the accounting records.

CASE 3: MISSING SCHOOL FUNDS   A secretary at a middle school stole approximately $20,000 by converting student checks and activity fees to cash and by taking undeposited faculty vending machine receipts.

Control Failure: An initial accountability was never established for faculty vending machine receipts, and deposited receipts were never reconciled with vending machine usage records. A reconciliation of student checks and activity fees with student records and enrollment figures was not performed. Finally, background checks on clerical employees were not performed. The secretary had a prior criminal record.

Corrective Action: Background checks are now required on all employees of the school. An employee independent of the handling of cash, student activity fees, and student book fees performs a periodic reconciliation with attendance and enrollment

---

[5]The cases are adapted from the "Roundtable" and "Fraud Findings" sections of the *Internal Auditor* magazine, published by the Institute of Internal Auditors.

figures. Each day, vending machine receipts are collected and recorded. The receipts are periodically reconciled with machine usage.

CASE 4: PARKING TICKET SHORTAGE

Citizens of a small town could pay parking fines by inserting the ticket with the amount of the fine into a locked box outside of the town hall. An analysis later discovered that approximately $8,000 was missing over a period of 18 months.

Control Failure: The key to the locked box was readily available to a variety of employees. Thus, no one could be held responsible for the missing cash.

Corrective Action: The key to the locked box was assigned to the person collecting the cash and was kept in a safe until needed for collections. A person independent of the collections was assigned the responsibility of reconciling the parking tickets from the locked box with the cash deposits.

CASE 5: NATIONAL FLOOD INSURANCE CLAIMS

The claims agent developed fictitious claims, arranged for the claims manager to issue a check for the claim, and then recalled the checks. The claims agent then passed the checks to an accomplice, who cashed them and split the money with the claims agent. The fraud totaled approximately $85,000 before it was detected.

Control Weakness: The recalled checks were forwarded to the claims agent requesting the check for follow-up and disposition.

Corrective Action: The company implemented a procedure that prohibited recalled checks from being returned to the claims agent requesting the checks. In addition, the number of recalled checks processed by each claims agent was reviewed for unusual trends or numbers of recalled checks.

CASE 6: PAYROLL FRAUD

A payroll assistant was responsible for entering payroll hours with no review or reconciliation and for receiving, sorting, and distributing the payroll checks. These duties were assigned to the payroll assistant because he was "most familiar with the company's employees." By issuing duplicate payroll checks, the assistant stole $4,000 in two months. In addition, he submitted fictitious hours for part-time summer interns during periods when the interns were not working. The assistant then intercepted and cashed the interns' checks and thus stole another $36,000.

ETHICS IN ACTION

The following are tips for preventing employee fraud in small companies.

- Don't have the same employee write company checks and keep the books. Look for payments to vendors you don't know or payments to vendors whose names appear to be misspelled.
- If your business has a computer system, restrict access to accounting files as much as possible. Also keep a backup copy of your accounting files and store it at an off-site location.
- Be wary of anybody working in finance who declines to take vacations. He or she could be afraid that a replacement will uncover fraud.
- Require and monitor supporting documentation (such as vendor invoices) before signing checks.
- Track the number of credit card bills you sign monthly.
- Limit and monitor access to important documents and supplies, such as blank checks and signature stamps.
- Check W-2 forms against your payroll annually to make sure you aren't carrying any fictitious employees.
- Rely on yourself to spot fraud.

Source: Steve Kaufman, "Embezzlement Common at Small Companies," *Athens Daily News/Athens Banner-Herald,* March 10, 1996, p. 4D.

Control Weakness: Duties were not separated, and the payroll assistant had too much control and responsibility.

Corrective Action: The job of entering the payroll data was separated from the job of handling the payroll checks. In addition, a reconciliation of the hours worked, the employees, and the amounts paid is now performed each payroll period. Finally, the payroll clerk's computations are independently verified on a periodic basis.

Cash Controls over Receipts and Payments

Cash includes coins, currency (paper money), checks, money orders, and money on deposit that is available for unrestricted withdrawal from banks and other financial institutions. Normally, you can think of cash as anything that a bank would accept for deposit in your account. For example, a check made payable to you could normally be deposited in a bank and thus is considered cash.

We assume in this chapter that a business maintains only *one* bank account, represented in the ledger as *Cash.* In practice, however, a business can have several bank accounts, such as one for general cash payments and another for payroll. For each of its bank accounts, the business should maintain a ledger account, one of which could be called *Cash in Bank—First Bank,* for example. It should also maintain separate ledger accounts for special-purpose cash funds, such as travel reimbursements. We introduce some of these other cash accounts later in this chapter.

Because of the ease with which money can be transferred, cash is the asset most likely to be diverted and used improperly by employees. In addition, many transactions either directly or indirectly affect the receipt or the payment of cash. Businesses must therefore design and use controls that safeguard cash and control the authorization of cash transactions. In the following paragraphs, we discuss these controls.

Control of Cash Receipts

To protect cash from theft and misuse, a business must control cash from the time it is received until it is deposited in a bank. Businesses normally receive cash from two main sources: (1) customers purchasing products or services and (2) customers making payments on account. For example, fast-food restaurants, such as **McDonald's, Wendy's,** and **Burger King,** receive cash primarily from over-the-counter sales to customers. Mail-order and Internet retailers, such as **Orvis, L.L. Bean,** and **Amazon.com,** receive cash (checks) primarily through the mail and from credit card companies.

CONTROLLING CASH RECEIVED FROM CASH SALES   Regardless of the source of cash receipts, every business must properly safeguard and record its cash receipts. One of the most important controls to protect cash received in over-the-counter sales is a cash register. When a clerk (cashier) enters the amount of a sale, the cash register normally displays the amount. This is a control to ensure that the clerk has charged you the correct amount. You also receive a receipt to verify the accuracy of the amount.

At the beginning of a work shift, each cash register clerk is given a cash drawer that contains a predetermined amount of cash for making change for customers. The amount in each drawer is sometimes called a *change fund.* At the end of the shift, the clerk and the supervisor count the cash in that clerk's cash drawer. The amount of cash in each drawer should equal the beginning amount of cash plus the cash sales for the day. However, errors in recording cash sales or in making change cause the amount of cash on hand to differ from this amount. Such differences are recorded in a **cash short and over account**.

At the end of the accounting period, a positive balance in the cash short and over account is included in Miscellaneous Expense in the income statement. A negative balance is included in the Other Income section. If a clerk consistently has significant cash short and over amounts, the supervisor could require the clerk to take additional training.

After a cash register clerk's cash has been counted and recorded on a memorandum form, the cash is then placed in a store safe in the Cashier's Department until it can be deposited in the bank. The supervisor forwards the clerk's cash register tapes to the Accounting Department, where they serve as the basis for recording the transactions for the day.

BUSINESS STRATEGY

Turn Off the Light?

Kmart recently filed for bankruptcy. What happened? What went wrong?

Most analysts blame **Kmart's** problems on a strategy that relied heavily on advertising circulars to get customers into its stores. Such circulars, which are expensive to produce, accounted for 10.6% of Kmart's operating expenses, as compared to 2.2% for Target and 0.4% for Wal-Mart. In addition, Kmart continued to use its "blue-light specials" that reduced merchandise prices at periodic intervals for customers who were shopping in its stores. These specials created inventory shortages as merchandise sold out and prevented suppliers from accurately predicting customer needs. As a result, suppliers increased Kmart's prices, which in turn it passed on to customers. In contrast, **Wal-Mart** employs an "always low price" strategy for getting customers into its stores. Kmart reacted by promoting a "Blue-Light Always" program, developing a Bluelight.com Web site, and reducing its use of ad circulars. Unfortunately, Kmart's traditional customers who were used to the circulars stopped shopping at Kmart. In addition, Kmart couldn't compete with Wal-Mart's efficiency and low costs. Thus, Kmart filed for bankruptcy with the hope of reorganizing and again becoming competitive and profitable.

Source: Amy Merrick, "Expensive Ad Circulars Precipitate Kmart President's Departure," *The Wall Street Journal,* January 18, 2002; Michael Levy and Dhruv Grewal, "So Long, Kmart Shoppers," *The Wall Street Journal,* January 28, 2002; and "Blue Light Blues," *The Economist,* January 18, 2002.

Some retail companies use debit card systems to transfer and record the receipt of cash. In a debit card system, a customer pays for goods at the time of purchase by presenting a plastic card. The card authorizes the electronic transfer of cash from the customer's checking account to the retailer's bank account.

CONTROLLING CASH RECEIVED IN THE MAIL   Cash is received in the mail when customers pay their bills. This cash is usually in the form of checks and money orders. Most companies' invoices are designed so that customers return a portion of the invoice, called a *remittance advice*, with their payment. The employee who opens the incoming mail should initially compare the amount of cash received with the amount shown on the remittance advice. If a customer does not return a remittance advice, an employee prepares one. Like the cash register, the remittance advice serves as a record of cash initially received. It also helps ensure that the posting to the customer's account is accurate. Finally, as a preventive control, the employee opening the mail normally also stamps checks and money orders "For Deposit Only" in the bank account of the business.

All cash received in the mail is sent to the Cashier's Department. An employee there combines it with the receipts from cash sales and prepares a bank deposit ticket. The remittance advices and their summary totals are delivered to the Accounting Department. An accounting clerk then prepares the records of the transactions and posts them to the customer accounts.

When cash is deposited in the bank, the bank normally stamps a duplicate copy of the deposit ticket with the amount received. This bank receipt is returned to the Accounting Department, where a clerk compares the receipt with the total amount that should have been deposited. This control helps ensure that all the cash is deposited and that no cash is lost or stolen on the way to the bank. Any shortages are thus promptly detected.

Separating the duties of the Cashier's Department, which handles cash, and the Accounting Department, which records cash, is a preventive control. If Accounting Department employees were to both handle and record cash, an employee could steal cash and change the accounting records to hide the theft.

Control of Cash Payments

The control of cash payments should provide reasonable assurance that payments are made for only authorized transactions. In addition, controls should ensure that cash is used efficiently. For example, controls should ensure that all available discounts, such as purchase and trade discounts, are taken.

In a small business, an owner/manager could sign all checks based on personal knowledge of goods and services purchased. In a large business, however, employees who do not have such a complete knowledge of the transactions often prepare checks. In a large business, for example, the duties of purchasing goods, inspecting the goods received, and verifying the invoices are usually performed by different employees. These duties must be coordinated to ensure that checks for proper amounts are issued to creditors. One system used for this purpose is the voucher system.

VOUCHER SYSTEM   A **voucher system** is a set of procedures for authorizing and recording liabilities and cash payments. A **voucher** is any document that serves as proof of authority to pay cash. For example, an invoice properly approved for payment could be considered a voucher. In many businesses, however, a voucher is a special form for recording relevant data about a liability and the details of its payment.

A voucher is normally prepared after all necessary supporting documents have been received. For example, when a voucher is prepared for the purchase of goods, the voucher should be supported by the supplier's invoice, a purchase order, and a receiving report. After a voucher is prepared, it is submitted to the proper manager for approval. Once approved, the voucher is recorded in the accounts and filed by due date. On payment, the voucher is recorded in the same manner as the payment of an account payable.

A voucher system can be either manual or computerized. In a computerized system, properly approved supporting documents (such as purchase orders and receiving reports) are entered directly into computer files. At the due date, the checks are automatically generated and mailed to creditors. At that time, the voucher is automatically transferred to a paid voucher file. In some cases, payments can be made electronically rather than by check.

ELECTRONIC FUNDS TRANSFER   With rapidly changing technology, new systems are being devised to more efficiently record and transfer cash among companies. Such systems often use **electronic funds transfer (EFT)**. In an EFT system, computers, rather than paper (money, checks, etc.), are used to effect cash transactions. For example, a business can pay its employees by means of EFT. Under such a system, employees authorize the deposit of their payroll checks directly into their individual checking accounts. Each pay period, the business electronically transfers the employees' net pay to their checking accounts through the use of computer systems and telephone lines. Likewise, many companies are using EFT systems to pay their suppliers and other vendors.

Electronic funds transfer is also becoming more widely accepted by individuals. For example, **TeleCheck Services, Inc.,** offers an online real-time check payment option for purchases made over the Internet. "It is apparent from the rapid growth of online sales that many consumers are as comfortable writing checks for Internet purchases as they are at their local brick-and-mortar store," explains Steve Shaper, chief executive officer of TeleCheck.

Bank Accounts

OBJECTIVE 4
Describe the nature of a bank account and its use in controlling cash.

Most of you are familiar with bank accounts. You probably have a checking account at a local bank, credit union, savings and loan association, or other financial institution. In this section, we discuss the use of bank accounts by businesses and then their use as an additional control over cash.

Use of Bank Accounts

A business often maintains several bank accounts. For example, a business with several branches or retail outlets such as **Sears** or **The Gap** often maintains a bank account for each location. In addition, businesses usually maintain a separate bank account for payroll and other special purposes.

A major reason that businesses use bank accounts is for control purposes. Use of bank accounts reduces the amount of cash on hand at any one time. For example, many merchandise businesses deposit cash receipts twice daily to reduce the amount of cash on hand that is susceptible to theft. Likewise, the use of a payroll account enables the business to pay employees by check rather than to distribute a large amount of cash each payroll period.

In addition to reducing the amount of cash on hand, bank accounts provide an independent recording of cash transactions that can be used to verify the business's recording of transactions. That is, the use of bank accounts provides a double recording of cash transactions. The company's cash account corresponds to the bank's liability (deposit) account for the company. As we discuss and illustrate in the next section, this double recording of cash transactions allows for a reconciliation of the cash account on the company's records with the cash balance recorded by the bank.

Finally, the use of bank accounts facilitates the transfer of funds. For example, electronic funds transfer systems require bank accounts for the transfer of funds between companies. Within a company, cash can be transferred between bank accounts through the use of wire transfers. In addition, online banking through the use of the Internet allows companies to transfer funds and pay bills electronically as well as monitor their cash balances on a real-time basis.

Bank Statement

Banks usually maintain a record of all checking account transactions. A summary of all transactions, called a **bank statement**, is mailed to the depositor, usually each month. Like any account with a customer or a creditor, the bank statement shows the beginning balance, additions, deductions, and the balance at the end of the period. A typical bank statement is shown in Exhibit 4.

The depositor's checks received by the bank during the period could accompany the bank statement, perhaps arranged in the order of payment. The paid checks are stamped "Paid" with the date of payment. Other entries that the bank has made in the depositor's account are described in debit or credit memorandums enclosed with the statement.

You should note that a depositor's checking account balance *in the bank's records* is a liability. Debit memorandums issued by the bank on a depositor's account decrease the depositor's balance. Likewise, credit memorandums increase the depositor's balance. A bank issues a debit memorandum to charge (decrease) a depositor's account for service charges or for deposited checks returned because of insufficient funds. Likewise, a bank issues a credit memorandum when it increases the depositor's account for collecting a note receivable for the depositor, making a loan to the depositor, receiving a wire deposit, or adding interest to the depositor's account.

Bank Accounts as a Control over Cash

As we mentioned earlier, a bank account is one of the primary tools a business uses to control cash. For example, businesses often require that all cash receipts be initially deposited in a bank account. Likewise, businesses usually use checks or bank account transfers to make all cash payments except for very small amounts. When such a system is used, there is a double record of cash transactions—one by the business and the other by the bank.

EXHIBIT 4
Bank Statement

	MEMBER FDIC		
VALLEY NATIONAL BANK		PAGE 1	
OF LOS ANGELES			
		ACCOUNT NUMBER 1627042	

VALLEY NATIONAL BANK OF LOS ANGELES

LOS ANGELES, CA 90020-4253   (310)851-5151

MEMBER FDIC

PAGE 1

ACCOUNT NUMBER	1627042
FROM 6/30/06	TO 7/31/06
BALANCE	4,218.60
22 DEPOSITS	13,749.75
52 WITHDRAWALS	14,698.57
3 OTHER DEBITS AND CREDITS	90.00CR
NEW BALANCE	3,359.78

POWER NETWORKING
1000 Belkin Street
Los Angeles, CA 90014-1000

* — — CHECKS AND OTHER DEBITS — — — *			— — DEPOSITS — — *	— — DATE — — *	— BALANCE — — *
819.40	122.54		585.75	07/01	3,862.41
369.50	732.26	20.15	421.53	07/02	3,162.03
600.00	190.70	52.50	781.30	07/03	3,100.13
25.93	160.00		662.50	07/05	3,576.70
921.20	NSF 300.00		503.18	07/07	2,858.68
32.26	535.09		932.00	07/29	3,404.40
21.10	126.20		705.21	07/30	3,962.31
	SC 18.00		MS 408.00	07/30	4,352.31
26.12	1,615.13		648.72	07/31	3,359.78

EC — ERROR CORRECTION	OD — OVERDRAFT
MS — MISCELLANEOUS	PS — PAYMENT STOPPED
NSF — NOT SUFFICIENT FUNDS	SC — SERVICE CHARGE

* * *   * * *   * * *

THE RECONCILEMENT OF THIS STATEMENT WITH YOUR RECORDS IS ESSENTIAL.
ANY ERROR OR EXCEPTION SHOULD BE REPORTED IMMEDIATELY.

ETHICS IN ACTION

Check fraud involves counterfeiting, altering, or otherwise manipulating the information on checks in order to fraudulently cash a check. According to the National Check Fraud Center, check fraud and counterfeiting are among the fastest growing problems affecting the financial system, generating more than $10 billion in losses annually.

Criminals perpetrate the fraud by taking blank checks from your checkbook, finding a canceled check in the garbage, or removing a check you have mailed to pay bills. Consumers can prevent check fraud by carefully storing blank checks, placing outgoing mail in postal mailboxes, and shredding canceled checks.

A business can use a bank statement to compare the cash transactions recorded in its accounting records to those recorded by the bank. The cash balance shown by a bank statement is usually different from the Cash balance shown in the accounting records of the business as shown in Exhibit 5.

This difference could be the result of a delay by either party in recording transactions. For example, there is usually a time lag of one day or more between the date a check is written and the date that it is presented to the bank for payment. If the depositor

EXHIBIT 5
*Power Networking's
Records and Bank
Statement*

Bank Statement		
Beginning Balance		$ 4,218.60
Additions:		
Deposits		13,749.75
Miscellaneous		408.00
Deductions:		
Checks		14,698.57
NSF Check	$300	
Service Charge	18	318.00
Ending Balance		$ 3,359.78

Power Networking Records	
Beginning Balance	$ 4,227.60
Deposits	14,565.95
Checks	16,243.56
Ending Balance	$ 2,549.99

Power Networking should determine
the reason for the difference in
these two amounts.

mails deposits to the bank or uses the night depository, the time lag between the date of the deposit and the date that it is recorded by the bank is also probable. The bank could also debit or credit the depositor's account for transactions about which the depositor will not be informed until later.

The difference could be the result of errors made by either the business or the bank in recording transactions. For example, the business could incorrectly post to Cash a check written for $4,500 as $450. Likewise, a bank could incorrectly record the amount of a check.

Bank Reconciliation

OBJECTIVE　5
Describe and illustrate
the use of a bank
reconciliation in
controlling cash.

For effective control, the reasons for the difference between the cash balance on the bank statement and the cash balance in the accounting records should be determined by preparing a bank reconciliation. A **bank reconciliation** is a list of the items and amounts that cause the cash balance reported in the bank statement to differ from the balance of the cash account in the ledger.

A bank reconciliation is usually divided into two sections. The first section begins with the cash balance according to the bank statement and ends with the adjusted balance. The second section begins with the cash balance according to the depositor's records and ends with the adjusted balance. The two amounts designated as the adjusted balance must be equal. The content of the bank reconciliation follows.

Cash balance according to bank statement		$XXX	Cash balance according to depositor's records			$XXX
Add:　Additions by depositor not on			Add:　Additions by bank not recorded			
bank statement	$XX		by depositor		$XX	
Bank errors	XX	XX	Depositor errors		XX	XX
		$XXX				$XXX
Deduct: Deductions by depositor not on			Deduct: Deductions by bank not recorded			
bank statement	$XX		by depositor		$XX	
Bank errors	XX	XX	Depositor errors		XX	XX
Adjusted balance		$XXX	Adjusted balance			$XXX

must be equal

The following steps are useful in finding the reconciling items and determining the adjusted balance of Cash:

1. Compare each deposit listed on the bank statement with unrecorded deposits appearing in the preceding period's reconciliation and with deposit receipts or other records of deposits. *Add deposits not recorded by the bank according to the bank statement to the balance.*
2. Compare paid checks with outstanding checks appearing on the preceding period's reconciliation and with recorded checks. *Deduct checks outstanding that have not been paid by the bank according to the bank statement from the balance.*
3. Compare bank credit memorandums to the accounting records. For example, a bank would issue a credit memorandum for a note receivable and the interest that it collected for a depositor. *Add credit memorandums that have not been recorded to the depositor's records to the balance according.*
4. Compare bank debit memorandums to records of cash payments. For example, a bank normally issues debit memorandums for service charges and check-printing charges. A bank also issues debit memorandums for not-sufficient-funds checks. A *not-sufficient-funds (NSF) check* is a customer's check that was recorded and deposited but was not paid when it was presented to the customer's bank for payment. NSF checks are normally charged back to the customer as an account receivable. *Deduct debit memorandums that have not been recorded according to the depositor's records from the balance.*
5. List any errors discovered during the preceding steps. For example, if an amount has been recorded incorrectly by the depositor, the amount of the error should be added to or deducted from the cash balance according to the depositor's records. Similarly, errors by the bank should be added to or deducted from the cash balance according to the bank statement.

To illustrate a bank reconciliation, we use the bank statement for Power Networking in Exhibit 4. This bank statement shows a balance of $3,359.78 as of July 31. The cash balance in Power Networking's ledger as of the same date is $2,549.99. The following reconciling items are revealed by using the steps just outlined:

Deposit of July 31, not recorded on bank statement	$ 816.20
Checks outstanding: No. 812, $1,061.00; No. 878, $435.39; No. 883, $48.60	1,544.99
Note plus interest of $8 collected by bank (credit memorandum), not recorded in the accounting records	408.00
Check from customer (Thomas Ivey) returned by bank because of insufficient funds (NSF)	300.00
Bank service charges (debit memorandum), not recorded in the accounting records	18.00
Check No. 879 for $732.26 to Taylor Co. on account, recorded as $723.26	9.00

The bank reconciliation based on the bank statement and the reconciling items is shown in Exhibit 6.

No adjustments are necessary to the depositor's records as a result of the information included in the first section of the bank reconciliation. This section begins with the cash balance according to the bank statement. However, the bank should be notified of any errors that need to be corrected on its records.

EXHIBIT 6   *Bank Reconciliation for Power Networking*

POWER NETWORKING
Bank Reconciliation
July 31, 2006

Cash balance according to		Cash balance according to		
bank statement	$3,359.78	depositor's records		$2,549.99
Add deposit of July 31,		Add note and interest collected		
not recorded by bank	816.20	by bank		408.00
	$4,175.98			$2,957.99
		Deduct: Check returned because		
		of insufficient funds	$300.00	
Deduct outstanding checks:		Bank service charge	18.00	
No. 812	$1,061.00	Error in recording		
No. 878	435.39	Check No. 879	9.00	327.00
No. 883	48.60 1,544.99			
Adjusted balance	$2,630.99	Adjusted balance		$2,630.99

The depositor's records should be adjusted for any items in the second section of the bank reconciliation. This section begins with the cash balance according to the depositor's records. For example, adjustments should be made for any unrecorded bank memorandums and any depositor's errors. The adjustments to the accounts and their effect on the financial statements based on Power Networking's bank reconciliation are as follows:

Trans. Date	Balance Sheet			Income Statement		
	Assets	Liabilities	Stockholders' Equity	Revenue	Expense	Net Income
July 31	Cash 81	Accts Pay. −9		Interest Income 8	Misc. Expense 18	−10
	Notes Rec. −400					
	Accts Rec. 300					
Net Effect	−19	−9	−10	8	18	−10
			Retained Earnings			
			(Net Income)			

After these adjustments have been made, the cash account will have a debit balance of $2,630.99. This balance agrees with the adjusted cash balance shown on the bank reconciliation. This is the amount of cash available as of July 31 and the amount that would be reported on Power Networking's July 31 balance sheet.

Although businesses can reconcile their bank accounts in a slightly different format from what we just described, the objective is the same: to control cash by reconciling the company's records to the records of an independent outside source, the bank. In doing so, any errors or misuse of cash can be detected.

For effective control, the bank reconciliation should be prepared by an employee who does not take part in or record cash transactions. When these duties are not properly separated, mistakes are likely to occur, and it is more likely that cash will be stolen or otherwise misapplied. For example, an employee who takes part in all of these duties could prepare and cash an unauthorized check, omit it from the accounts, and omit it from the reconciliation.

Special-Purpose Cash Funds

OBJECTIVE 6

Describe the accounting for special-purpose cash funds.

It is usually not practical for a business to write checks to pay small amounts, such as postage, yet these small payments can occur often enough to add to a significant total amount. Thus, it is desirable to control such payments. For this purpose, a special cash fund, called a **petty cash fund**, is used.

In addition, businesses often use other cash funds to meet special needs, such as travel expenses for salespersons. For example, each salesperson might be given $200 for travel-related expenses. Periodically, the salesperson submits a detailed expense report and the travel funds are replenished. Also, as we discussed earlier in this chapter, retail businesses use change funds for making change for customers. Finally, most businesses use a payroll bank account to pay employees. Such cash funds are called **special-purpose funds**.

A special-purpose cash fund is initially established by first estimating the amount of cash needed for payments from the fund during a period, such as a week or a month. After necessary approvals, a check for this amount is written and cashed. The money obtained from cashing the check is then given to an employee, called the *custodian*, who is authorized to disburse monies from the fund. For control purposes, the company can place restrictions on the maximum amount and the types of payments to be made from the fund.

To illustrate, a petty cash fund of $500 is established. Each time monies are paid from petty cash, the custodian records the payment on a petty cash receipt form. At periodic intervals, or when it is depleted or reaches a minimum amount, the petty cash fund is replenished. When the fund is replenished, the accounts are adjusted by summarizing the petty cash receipts. A check is then written for this amount.

Financial Statement Reporting of Cash

OBJECTIVE 7

Describe and illustrate the reporting of cash and cash equivalents in the financial statements.

Cash is the most liquid asset, and therefore it is listed as the first asset in the Current Assets section of the balance sheet. Most companies present only a single cash amount on the balance sheet by combining all of their bank and cash fund accounts.

A company could have cash in excess of its operating needs. In such cases, the company normally invests in highly liquid investments to earn interest. These investments are called **cash equivalents**.[6] Examples of cash equivalents include U.S. Treasury bills, notes issued by major corporations (referred to as *commercial paper*), and money market funds. Companies that have invested excess cash in cash equivalents usually report *Cash and cash equivalents* as one amount on the balance sheet.

To illustrate, **Microsoft Corp.** disclosed the details of its cash and cash equivalents in the footnotes to its financial statements as follows:

In Millions/June 30	2000	2001
Cash and equivalents:		
Cash	$ 849	$1,145
Commercial paper	1,986	894
Certificates of deposit	1,017	286
U.S. government and agency securities	729	400
Corporate notes and bonds	265	1,130
Municipal securities	—	67
Cash and equivalents	4,846	3,922

Banks may require depositors to maintain minimum cash balances in their bank accounts. Such a balance is called a *compensating balance*. This requirement is often imposed by the bank as a part of a loan agreement or line of credit. A *line of credit* is a preapproved amount the bank is willing to lend to a customer on request. If significant, compensating balance requirements should be disclosed in notes to the financial statements.

Cash Ratios

OBJECTIVE   8

Describe, illustrate, and interpret the cash flow to net income ratio and the cash to monthly cash expenses ratio.

Analyzing cash and cash flows is essential to interpreting financial statements. The statement of cash flows reports cash flows from operating, investing, and financing activities. In addition, two cash ratios useful for analyzing and interpreting operating performance are (1) cash flow to net income and (2) cash to monthly cash expenses.

Ratio of Cash Flow to Net Income

The accrual basis of accounting is used by all public companies in determining and reporting net income. As we illustrate throughout this text, accrual accounting records revenues when earned and expenses when incurred, not necessarily when cash is received or paid. This process gives rise to accruals and deferrals that are updated and adjusted at the end of each reporting period. As a result, net cash flow from operations is rarely the same as net income.

When the amount of accruals and deferrals is large, the difference between net cash flows from operations and net income is also large. The effect of accruals and deferrals on net income can be measured by the ratio of net cash flows from operations to net income. Accordingly, significant changes in this ratio from year to year should be investigated for the underlying causes. For example, the implementation of a new

[6]To be classified as a cash equivalent, according to FASB *Statement 95*, the investment is expected to be converted to cash within 90 days.

accounting standard could significantly affect net income and comparability between years. On the other hand, management could change methods of estimating and recording accruals, deferrals, and depreciation. Such changes also affect the comparability of the current period's net income with prior years.

To illustrate, the ratio of cash flow to net income for **Federal Express Corporation** for 2001 and 2000 follows.

	2001	2000
Net cash flows from operations (in millions)	$1,588	$1,272
Net income	499	510
Cash flow ratio	3.2	2.5

The cash flow ratio increased from 2.5 in 2000 to 3.2 in 2001. While net cash flows from operations increased during 2001, net income decreased, and thus the cash flow ratio increased. Why did this happen? A review of the statement of cash flows for Federal Express reveals that during 2001, depreciation and amortization expense decreased by $201 million. In addition, Federal Express wrote off $102 million for the impairment of its aircraft in 2001. This expense was due to the implementation of a new accounting standard. If we adjust for these two accrual accounting effects, the revised cash flow ratio is 2.6 [$1,588/($499 − $201 + $102)]. Thus, these two accrual accounting effects on net income explain most of the change in the cash flow ratio.

Ratio of Cash to Monthly Cash Expenses

As we illustrated for Federal Express, the cash flow ratio is useful for identifying when significant changes have occurred in accrual accounting methods. Another cash ratio that is especially useful for startup companies is the ratio of cash to monthly cash expenses.

In their first few years of operations, startup companies often report losses and negative net cash flows. In these cases, the ratio of cash to monthly cash expenses is useful for assessing how long a company can continue to operate without additional financing or without generating positive cash flows from operations. In computing cash to monthly cash expenses, the amount of cash on hand can be taken from the balance sheet while the monthly cash expenses can be estimated from the Operating Activities section of the statement of cash flows.

To illustrate this ratio, we use **Pets.com**, a former online retailer of pet products. Pets.com was organized in 1999 by raising more than $90 million from private investors. Selling stock to the public in February 2000 raised an additional $77 million. For the three months ending March 31, 2000, Pets.com reported the following data (in thousands):

Revenues	$ 7,651
Net loss	(39,088)
Net cash flows from operating activities	(27,475)
Cash as of March 31, 2000	70,342

Based on the preceding data, the monthly cash expenses, sometime referred to as *cash burn*, was $9,158 per month ($27,475/3). Thus, as of March 31, 2000, the cash to monthly cash expenses ratio was 7.7 ($70,342/$9,158). In other words, as of

March 31, 2000, Pets.com would run out of cash in less than eight months unless it changed its operations or was able to raise additional financing. Failing to do either of these, the board of directors of Pets.com approved a plan of liquidation and dissolution in November 2000.

Key Points

1. Describe and illustrate the objectives and elements of internal control.

The objectives of internal control are to provide reasonable assurance that (1) assets are safeguarded and used for business purposes, (2) business information is accurate, and (3) laws and regulations are followed. The elements of internal control are the control environment, risk assessment, control procedures, monitoring, and information and communication.

2. Describe and illustrate methods of preventing and detecting employee fraud.

Controls to prevent the opportunity of employees to steal assets can be grouped into those involving (1) physical safeguarding of assets and (2) proper authorization and approval procedures. Controls to detect employee fraud include (1) periodic reviews, (2) independent checks, and (3) reconciliations.

3. Describe and illustrate the application of internal controls to cash.

One of the most important controls to protect cash received in over-the-counter sales is a cash register. A remittance advice is a preventive control for cash received through the mail. Separating the duties of handling cash and recording cash is also a preventive control. A voucher system is a control system for cash payments that uses a set of procedures for authorizing and recording liabilities and cash payments.

4. Describe the nature of a bank account and its use in controlling cash.

Businesses use bank accounts as a means of controlling cash. Bank accounts reduce the amount of cash on hand and facilitate the transfer of cash between businesses and locations. In addition, banks send monthly statements to their customers (depositors), summarizing all of the transactions for the month. The bank statement allows a business to reconcile the cash transactions recorded in the accounting records to those recorded by the bank.

5. Describe and illustrate the use of a bank reconciliation in controlling cash.

The first section of the bank reconciliation begins with the cash balance according to the bank statement. This balance is adjusted for the depositor's changes in cash that do not appear on the bank statement and for any bank errors. The second section begins with the cash balance according to the depositor's records. This balance is adjusted for the bank's changes in cash that do not appear on the depositor's records and for any depositor errors. The adjusted balances for the two sections must be equal. No adjustments are necessary on the depositor's records as a result of the information included in the first section of the bank reconciliation. However, the items in the second section require adjustments on the depositor's records.

6. Describe the accounting for special-purpose cash funds.

Businesses often use special-purpose cash funds, such as a petty cash fund or travel funds, to meet specific needs. Each fund is initially established by cashing a check for the amount of cash needed. The cash is then given to a custodian, who is authorized to disburse monies from the fund. At periodic intervals or when it is depleted or reaches a minimum amount, the fund is replenished and the disbursements are recorded.

7. Describe and illustrate the reporting of cash and cash equivalents in the financial statements.

Cash is listed as the first asset in the Current Assets section of the balance sheet. Companies that have invested excess cash in highly liquid investments usually report *Cash and cash equivalents* on the balance sheet.

8. Describe, illustrate, and interpret the cash flow to net income ratio and the cash to monthly cash expenses ratio.

Two cash ratios useful for analyzing and interpreting operating performance are (1) cash flow to net income and (2) cash to monthly cash expenses. The effect of accruals and deferrals on net income can be measured by the ratio of net cash flows from operations to net income. The ratio of cash to monthly cash expenses is useful for assessing how long a company can continue to operate without additional financing or without generating positive cash flows from operations.

Glossary

Bank reconciliation: The analysis that details the items responsible for the difference between the cash balance reported in the bank statement and the balance of the cash account in the ledger.

Bank statement: A summary of all transactions mailed to the depositor by the bank each month.

Cash: Coins, currency (paper money), checks, money orders, and money on deposit available for unrestricted withdrawal from banks and other financial institutions.

Cash equivalents: Highly liquid investments that are usually reported with cash on the balance sheet.

Cash short and over account: The account used to record the difference between the amount of cash in a cash register and the amount of cash that should be on hand according to the records.

Electronic funds transfer (EFT): A system in which computers rather than paper (money, checks, etc.) are used to effect cash transactions.

Elements of internal control: The control environment, risk assessment, control activities, information and communication, and monitoring.

Employee fraud: The intentional act of deceiving an employer for personal gain.

Internal control: The policies and procedures used to safeguard assets, ensure accurate business information, and ensure compliance with laws and regulations.

Petty cash fund: A special-purpose cash fund to pay relatively small amounts.

Special-purpose fund: A cash fund used for a special business need.

Voucher: Any document that serves as proof of authority to pay cash.

Voucher system: A set of procedures for authorizing and recording liabilities and cash payments.

Self-Study Questions

(Answers appear at end of chapter.)

1. Which of the following is *not* an element of internal control?
   A. control environment
   B. monitoring
   C. compliance with laws and regulations
   D. control procedures

2. The policies and procedures used by management to protect assets from misuse, ensure accurate business information, and ensure compliance with laws and regulations are called:
   A. internal controls
   B. monitoring

   C. information and communication
   D. risk assessment

3. In preparing a bank reconciliation, the amount of checks outstanding is:
   A. added to the cash balance according to the bank statement.
   B. deducted from the cash balance according to the bank statement.
   C. added to the cash balance according to the depositor's records.
   D. deducted from the cash balance according to the depositor's records.

4. Adjustments based on the bank reconciliation are required for:
   A. additions to the cash balance according to the depositor's records.
   B. deductions from the cash balance according to the depositor's records.
   C. both A and B.
   D. neither A nor B.

5. A petty cash fund is:
   A. used to pay relatively small amounts.
   B. established by estimating the amount of cash needed for disbursements of relatively small amounts during a specified period.
   C. reimbursed when the amount of money in the fund is reduced to a predetermined minimum amount.
   D. all of the above.

Discussion Questions

1. (a) Name and describe the five elements of internal control. (b) Is any one element of internal control more important than another?

2. How does a policy of rotating clerical employees from job to job aid in strengthening the control procedures within the control environment? Explain.

3. Why should the responsibility for a sequence of related operations be divided among different persons? Explain.

4. Why should the employee who handles cash receipts not have the responsibility for maintaining the accounts receivable records? Explain.

5. In an attempt to improve operating efficiency, one employee was made responsible for all purchasing, receiving, and storing of supplies. Is this organizational change wise from an internal control standpoint? Explain.

6. The ticket seller at a movie theater doubles as a ticket taker for a few minutes each day while the ticket taker is on a break. Which control procedure of a business's system of internal control is violated in this situation?

7. Why should the responsibility for maintaining the accounting records be separated from the responsibility for operations? Explain.

8. Assume that the accounts payable clerk for Script Inc. stole $50,000 by paying fictitious invoices for goods that were never received. The clerk set up accounts in the names of the fictitious companies and cashed the checks at a local bank. (a) Describe how the clerk could have rationalized (justified) her behavior. (b) Describe a control procedure that would have prevented or detected the fraud.

9. Before a voucher for the purchase of merchandise is approved for payment, supporting documents should be compared to verify the accuracy of the liability. Give an example of a supporting document for the purchase of merchandise.

10. The accounting clerk pays all obligations by prenumbered checks. What are the strengths and weaknesses in the internal control over cash payments in this situation?

11. The balance of Cash is likely to differ from the bank statement balance. What two factors are likely to be responsible for the difference?

12. What is the purpose of preparing a bank reconciliation?

13. Do items reported as credit memorandums on the bank statement represent (a) additions made by the bank to the depositor's balance or (b) deductions made by the bank from the depositor's balance? Explain.

14. Heifer Inc. has a petty cash fund of $500. (a) Since the petty cash fund is only $500, should Heifer Inc. implement controls over petty cash? (b) What controls, if any, could be used for the petty cash fund?

15. (a) How are cash equivalents reported in the financial statements? (b) What are some examples of cash equivalents?

Exercises

EXERCISE 5-1
Internal controls
OBJECTIVES 1, 2, 3

Connie Stevens was recently hired as the manager of Big Apple Deli, a national chain of franchised delicatessens. During her first month as store manager, Connie encountered the following internal control situations:

a. Big Apple Deli has one cash register. Prior to Connie's joining the deli, each employee working on a shift would take a customer order, accept payment, and then prepare the order. Connie made one employee on each shift responsible for taking orders and accepting the customer's payment. Other employees prepare the orders.

b. Since only one employee uses the cash register, that employee is responsible for counting the cash at the end of the shift and verifying that the cash in the drawer matches the amount of cash sales recorded by the cash register. Connie expects each cashier to balance the drawer to the penny *every* time—no exceptions.

c. Connie caught an employee putting a box of 100 single-serving bags of potato chips in his car. Not wanting to create a scene, Connie smiled and said, "I don't think you're putting those chips on the right shelf. Don't they belong inside the deli?" The employee returned the chips to the stockroom.

State whether you agree or disagree with Connie's method of handling each situation and explain your answer.

EXERCISE 5-2
Internal controls
OBJECTIVES 1, 2, 3

Summer Breeze is a retail store specializing in women's clothing. The store has established a liberal return policy for the holiday season to encourage gift purchases. Any item purchased during November and December may be returned through January 31, with a receipt, for cash or exchange. If the customer does not have a receipt, cash will still be refunded for any item under $25. If the item cost more than $25, a check is mailed to the customer.

When an item is returned, a store clerk completes a return slip, which the customer signs. The return slip is placed in a special box. The store manager visits the return counter approximately once every 2 hours to authorize the return slips. Clerks are instructed to place the returned merchandise on the proper rack on the selling floor as soon as possible.

This year, returns at Summer Breeze have reached an all-time high. There are a large number of returns under $25 without receipts.

a. How can sales clerks employed at Summer Breeze use the store's return policy to steal money from the cash register?

b. 1. What internal control weaknesses do you see in the return policy that makes cash thefts easier?

   2. Would issuing a store credit in place of a cash refund for all merchandise returned without a receipt reduce the possibility of theft? List some advantages and disadvantages of issuing a store credit in place of a cash refund.

   3. Assume that Summer Breeze is committed to the current policy of issuing cash refunds without a receipt. What changes could be made in the store's procedures regarding customer refunds to improve internal control?

EXERCISE 5-3
Internal controls for bank lending
OBJECTIVES 1, 2, 3

United Savings Bank provides loans to businesses in the community through its Commercial Lending Department. Small loans (less than $100,000) may be approved by an individual loan officer; larger loans (more than $100,000) must be approved by a board of loan officers. Once a loan is approved, the funds are made available to the loan applicant under agreed-upon terms. The president of United Savings Bank has instituted a policy whereby she has the individual authority to approve loans up to $5,000,000. The president believes that this policy will allow flexibility to approve loans to valued clients much more quickly than under the previous policy.

As an internal auditor of United Savings Bank, how would you respond to this change in policy?

EXERCISE 5-4
Internal controls
OBJECTIVES 1, 2, 3

One of the largest fraud losses in history involved a securities trader for the Singapore office of **Barings Bank**, a British merchant bank. The trader established an unauthorized account number that was used to hide $1.4 billion in losses. Even after Barings' internal auditors noted that the trader both executed trades and recorded them, management did not take action. As a result, a lone individual in a remote office bankrupted an internationally recognized firm overnight.

What general weaknesses in Barings' internal controls contributed to the occurrence and size of the fraud?

EXERCISE 5-5
Internal controls
OBJECTIVES 1, 2, 3

In the **Equity Funding** fraud, approximately $2 billion of insurance policies that were claimed to have been sold by the company were bogus. The bogus policies, which were supported by falsified policy applications, were listed along with real policies on Equity Funding's computer files (records). Equity Funding personnel, including the computer programmers, kept these files in a separate room where they were easily accessible. In addition, computer programmers and other company personnel had access to the computer.

What general weaknesses in Equity Funding's internal controls contributed to the occurrence and size of the fraud?

EXERCISE 5-6
Financial statement fraud
OBJECTIVES 1, 2, 3

The former chairman, the CFO, and the controller of **Donnkenny**, an apparel company that makes sportswear for Pierre Cardin and Victoria Jones, pleaded guilty to financial statement fraud. These managers used false entries to record fictitious sales, hid inventory in public warehouses so that it could be recorded as "sold," and required sales orders to be backdated so that the sale could be moved back to an earlier period. The combined effect of these actions caused $25 million of $40 million in quarterly sales to be phony.

a. Why might control procedures listed in this chapter be insufficient in stopping this type of fraud?
b. How could this type of fraud be stopped?

EXERCISE 5-7
Internal control of cash receipts
OBJECTIVES 1, 2, 3

The procedures used for over-the-counter receipts are as follows. At the close of each day's business, the sales clerks count the cash in their respective cash drawers, after which they determine the amount recorded by the cash register and prepare the memorandum cash form, noting any discrepancies. An employee from the cashier's office counts the cash, compares the total with the memorandum, and takes the cash to the cashier's office.

a. Indicate the weak link in internal control.
b. How can the weakness be corrected?

EXERCISE 5-8
Internal control of cash receipts
OBJECTIVES 1, 2, 3

Kathy Beal works at the drive-through window of Fletch's Burgers. Occasionally when a drive-through customer orders, Kathy fills the order and pockets the customer's money. She does not ring up the order on the cash register.

Identify the internal control weaknesses that exist at Fletch's Burgers, and discuss what can be done to prevent this theft.

EXERCISE 5-9
Internal control of cash receipts
OBJECTIVES 1, 2, 3

The mailroom employees send all remittances and remittance advices to the cashier. The cashier deposits the cash in the bank and forwards the remittance advices and duplicate deposit slips to the Accounting Department.

a.   Indicate the weak link in internal control in handling cash receipts.
b.   How can the weakness be corrected?

EXERCISE 5-10
Entry for cash sales; cash short
OBJECTIVES 1, 2, 3

The actual cash received from cash sales was $18,153.79, and the amount indicated by the cash register total was $18,178.31.

a.   What is the amount deposited in the bank for the day's sales?
b.   What is the amount recorded for the day's sales?
c.   How should the difference be recorded?
d.   If a cashier is consistently over or short, what action should be taken?

EXERCISE 5-11
Internal control of cash payments
OBJECTIVES 1, 2, 3

Fiedler Co. is a medium-size merchandising company. An investigation revealed that in spite of a sufficient bank balance, a significant amount of available cash discounts had been lost because of failure to make timely payments. In addition, it was discovered that several purchase invoices had been paid twice.

Outline procedures for the payment of vendors' invoices so that the possibilities of losing available cash discounts and of paying an invoice a second time will be minimized.

EXERCISE 5-12
Internal control of cash payments
OBJECTIVES 1, 2, 3

Herringbone Company, a communications equipment manufacturer, recently fell victim to an embezzlement scheme masterminded by one of its employees. To understand the scheme, it is necessary to review Herringbone's procedures for the purchase of services.

The purchasing agent is responsible for ordering services (such as repairs to a photocopy machine or office cleaning) after receiving a service requisition from an authorized manager. However, since no tangible goods are delivered, a receiving report is not prepared. When the Accounting Department receives an invoice billing Herringbone for a service call, the accounts payable clerk calls the manager who requested the service to verify that it was performed.

The embezzlement scheme involves Kellie Barth, the manager of plant and facilities. Kellie arranged for her uncle's company, Barth Industrial Supply and Service, to be placed on Herringbone's approved vendor list. Kellie did not disclose the family relationship.

On several occasions, Kellie submitted a requisition for services to be provided by Barth Industrial Supply and Service. However, the service requested was really not needed and was never performed. Barth would bill Herringbone for the service and then split the cash payment with Kellie.

Explain what changes should be made to Herringbone's procedures for ordering and paying for services to prevent such occurrences in the future.

EXERCISE 5-13
Bank reconciliation
OBJECTIVES 4, 5

Identify each of the following reconciling items as (a) an addition to the cash balance according to the bank statement, (b) a deduction from the cash balance according to the bank statement, (c) an addition to the cash balance according to the depositor's records, or (d) a deduction from the cash balance according to the depositor's records. (None of the transactions reported by bank debit and credit memorandums have been recorded by the depositor.)

1.   Outstanding checks, $3,512.30.
2.   Deposit in transit, $10,000.
3.   Note collected by bank, $8,000.

(continued)

4. Check for $89 incorrectly charged by bank as $98.
5. Check drawn by depositor for $200 but incorrectly recorded as $2,000.
6. Check of a customer returned by bank to depositor because of insufficient funds, $775.
7. Bank service charges, $25.

EXERCISE 5-14
Adjustments based on bank reconciliation
OBJECTIVES 4, 5

Which of the reconciling items listed in Exercise 5-13 require an entry in the depositor's accounts?

EXERCISE 5-15
Bank reconciliation
OBJECTIVES 4, 5

The following data were accumulated for use in reconciling the bank account of Juno Co. for July:

a. Cash balance according to the depositor's records at July 31, $8,530.20.
b. Cash balance according to the bank statement at July 31, $3,457.25.
c. Checks outstanding, $1,276.20.
d. Deposit in transit, not recorded by bank, $6,780.40.
e. A check for $270 in payment of an account was erroneously recorded in the check register as $720.
f. Bank debit memorandum for service charges, $18.75.

1. Prepare a bank reconciliation using the format shown in Exhibit 6.
2. Illustrate the adjustments to the accounts and their effect on the depositor's financial statements.

EXERCISE 5-16
Note collected by bank
OBJECTIVES 4, 5

Accompanying a bank statement for Lyric Company is a credit memorandum for $12,500, representing the principal ($12,000) and interest ($500) on a note that had been collected by the bank. The depositor had been notified by the bank at the time of the collection but did not record the transaction. Illustrate the adjustment to the accounts and its effect on the financial statements of the note collected by the bank.

EXERCISE 5-17
Bank reconciliation
OBJECTIVES 4, 5

✓ Adjusted balance:
$13,445

An accounting clerk for Noxious Co. prepared the following bank reconciliation:

NOXIOUS CO.
Bank Reconciliation
March 31, 2004

Cash balance according to depositor's records		$10,100.75
Add: Outstanding checks	$7,557.12	
Error by Noxious Co. in recording Check		
No. 1621 as $2,510 instead of $2,150	360.00	
Note for $2,500 collected by bank, including interest	3,000.00	10,917.12
		$21,017.87
Deduct: Deposit in transit on March 31	$6,150.00	
Bank service charges	15.75	6,165.75
Cash balance according to bank statement		$14,852.12

a. From the data in this bank reconciliation, prepare a new bank reconciliation for Noxious Co. using the format shown in Exhibit 6.
b. If a balance sheet were prepared for Noxious Co. on March 31, 2004, what amount should be reported for cash?

EXERCISE 5-18
Bank reconciliation
OBJECTIVES 4, 5

✓ Corrected adjusted
balance: $9,998.02

What errors can you find in the following bank reconciliation?

PROTRACTOR CO.
Bank Reconciliation
For the Month Ended November 30, 2004

Cash balance according to bank statement			$ 9,767.76
Add outstanding checks:			
No. 721		$ 545.95	
739		172.75	
743		459.60	
744		601.50	1,779.80
			$11,547.56
Deduct deposit of November 30, not recorded by bank			2,010.06
Adjusted balance			$10,537.50
Cash balance according to depositor's records			$ 4,363.62
Add: Proceeds of note collected by bank:			
Principal	$5,000.00		
Interest	750.00	$5,750.00	
Service charges		20.00	5,770.00
			$10,133.62
Deduct: Check returned because of			
insufficient funds		$ 635.60	
Error in recording November 10			
deposit of $3,718 as $3,178		540.00	1,175.60
Adjusted balance			$ 8,958.02

EXERCISE 5-19
*Using bank
reconciliation to
determine cash receipts
stolen*
OBJECTIVES 4, 5

Ovation Co. records all cash receipts on the basis of its cash register tapes. During November 2004, Ovation Co. discovered that one of its sales clerks had stolen an undetermined amount of cash receipts when he took the daily deposits to the bank. The following data have been gathered for November:

Cash in bank according to the general ledger	$11,573.22
Cash according to the November 30, 2004, bank statement	14,271.14
Outstanding checks as of November 30, 2004	2,901.38
Bank service charge for November	25.10
Note receivable, including interest, collected by bank in November	3,060.00

No deposits were in transit on November 30, which fell on a Sunday.

a.   Determine the amount of cash receipts stolen by the sales clerk.
b.   What accounting controls would have prevented or detected this theft?

EXERCISE 5-20
Variation in cash flows
OBJECTIVE 7

Toys "R" Us is one of the world's leading retailers of toys, children's apparel, and baby products, operating nearly 1,600 retail stores. For a recent year, Toys "R" Us reported the following net cash flows from operating activities:

First quarter ending May 5, 2001	$(437,000,000)
Second quarter ending August 4, 2001	(480,000,000)
Third quarter ending November 3, 2001	(560,000,000)
Year ending February 2, 2002	$504,000,000

Explain how Toys "R" Us can report negative net cash flows from operating activities during the first three quarters yet report net positive cash flows for the year.

EXERCISE 5-21

Cash flow to net income ratio

OBJECTIVE 8

✓ a. 2001: 1.8

Avon Products Inc. is a global manufacturer and marketer of beauty products. It distributes its products to customers in the United States through more than 450,000 independent sales representatives. The following operating results (in thousands) are for years ending December 31:

	2001	2000
Net cash flows from operating activities	$754,900	$323,900
Net income	430,000	478,400

a. Compute the ratio of cash flow to net income for each year. Round to one decimal place.
b. Is there a significant difference between the ratios for 2001 and 2000? If so, what are some possible causes for the difference?

EXERCISE 5-22

Cash flow to net income ratio

OBJECTIVE 8

✓ a. 2001: 1.4

Colgate-Palmolive is a consumer products company with the leading toothpaste brand in the United States. In addition, Colgate sells bar and liquid hand soaps, shower gels, shampoos, conditioners, deodorants, antiperspirants, and shave products. The following operating results (in millions) are for years ending December 31.

	2001	2000
Net cash flows from operating activities	$1,600	$1,536
Net income	1,147	1,064

a. Compute the ratio of cash flow to net income for each year. Round to one decimal place.
b. Is there a significant difference between the ratios for 2001 and 2000? If so, what are some possible causes for the difference?

EXERCISE 5-23

Cash to monthly cash expenses ratio

OBJECTIVE 8

During 2004, Tempura Inc. has monthly cash expenses of $40,000. On December 31, 2004, the cash balance is $720,000.

a. Compute the ratio of cash to monthly expenses.
b. Based on (a), what are the implications for Tempura Inc.?

EXERCISE 5-24

Cash to monthly cash expenses ratio

OBJECTIVE 8

EMusic.com was organized as an online music network that would allow its customers to sample and purchase music on the Internet, using the mp3 format. Through relationships with leading artists and licensing agreements with recording labels, EMusic.com offered more than 125,000 tracks of digital music for purchase. EMusic.com raised more than $80 million by issuing stock, and it reported the following financial data (in thousands) for the year ending June 30, 2000:

Net cash flows from operating activities	$(42,976)
Cash, June 30, 2000	14,591

a. Determine the monthly cash expenses. Round to the nearest dollar.
b. Determine the ratio of cash to monthly cash expenses. Round to one decimal place.
c. Based on your analysis, do you believe EMusic.com is still in business?

EXERCISE 5-25

Cash to monthly cash expenses ratio

OBJECTIVE 8

Stamps.com provides Internet-based services for mailing or shipping letters, packages, or parcels in the United States. Stamps.com permits individuals, home offices, or small businesses to print U.S. postage or shipping labels, using any ordinary PC, any ordinary inkjet or laser printer, and an Internet connection. Stamps.com reported the following financial data (in thousands) for the year ending December 31, 2001:

Net cash flows from operating activities $ (38,797)
Cash, December 31, 2001   101,703

a. Determine the monthly cash expenses. Round to the nearest dollar.
b. Determine the ratio of cash to monthly cash expenses. Round to one decimal place.
c. Based on your analysis, do you believe Stamps.com is still in business?

Problems

PROBLEM 5 | 1
Evaluating internal control of cash
OBJECTIVES 1, 2, 3

Gambrel Company recently installed the following procedures:

a. Along with petty cash expense receipts for postage, office supplies, and so on, several postdated employee checks are in the petty cash fund.
b. The accounts payable clerk prepares a voucher for each disbursement. The voucher along with the supporting documentation is forwarded to the treasurer's office for approval.
c. At the end of each day, an accounting clerk compares the duplicate copy of the daily cash deposit slip with the deposit receipt obtained from the bank.
d. The bank reconciliation is prepared by the cashier who works under the supervision of the treasurer.
e. At the end of the day, cash register clerks are required to use their own funds to make up any cash shortages in their registers.
f. All mail is opened by the mail clerk, who forwards all cash remittances to the cashier. The cashier prepares a listing of the cash receipts and forwards a copy of the list to the accounts receivable clerk for recording in the accounts.
g. After necessary approvals have been obtained for the payment of a voucher, the treasurer signs and mails the check. The treasurer then stamps the voucher and supporting documentation as paid and returns the voucher and supporting documentation to the accounts payable clerk for filing.
h. At the end of each day, any deposited cash receipts are placed in the bank's night depository.

Instructions

Indicate whether each of the procedures of internal control over cash represents (1) a strength or (2) a weakness. For each weakness, explain why it exists.

PROBLEM 5 | 2
Evaluating internal control
OBJECTIVES 1, 2, 3

The following is an excerpt from a conversation between two sales clerks, Karol Bolton and Bill Hall. Both Karol and Bill are employed by Zoom Electronics, a locally owned and operated computer retail store.

Karol: Did you hear the news?
Bill: What news?
Karol: Melanie and Richard were both arrested this morning.
Bill: What? Arrested? You're putting me on!
Karol: No, really! The police arrested them first thing this morning. Put them in handcuffs, read them their rights—the whole works. It was unreal!
Bill: What did they do?
Karol: Well, apparently they were filling out merchandise refund forms for fictitious customers and then taking the cash.
Bill: I guess I never thought of that. How did they catch them?

Karol: The store manager noticed that returns were twice that of last year and seemed to be increasing. When he confronted Melanie, she became flustered and admitted to taking the cash, apparently over $1,800 in just three months. They're going over the last six months' transactions to try to determine how much Richard stole. He apparently started stealing first.

Suggest appropriate control procedures that would have prevented or detected the theft of cash.

PROBLEM 5 | 3

Bank reconciliation

OBJECTIVES 4, 5

✓ 1. Adjusted balance: $20,395.95

The cash account for Wok Co. at November 30, 2004, indicated a balance of $16,190.95. The bank statement indicated a balance of $21,016.30 on November 30, 2004. Comparing the bank statement and the accompanying canceled checks and memorandums with the records revealed the following reconciling items:

a. Checks outstanding totaled $5,169.75.
b. A deposit of $4,189.40, representing receipts of November 30, had been made too late to appear on the bank statement.
c. The bank had collected $4,500 on a note left for collection. The face of the note was $4,000.
d. A check for $2,850 returned with the statement had been incorrectly recorded by Wok Co. as $2,580. The check was for the payment of an obligation to Kiser Co. for the purchase of office equipment on account.
e. A check drawn for $1,375 had been erroneously charged by the bank as $1,735.
f. Bank service charges for November amounted to $25.

Instructions

1. Prepare a bank reconciliation.
2. Illustrate the adjustments to the accounts and their effect on the financial statements based on the reconciliation.

PROBLEM 5 | 4

Bank reconciliation

OBJECTIVES 4, 5

✓ 1. Adjusted balance: $3,599.87

The cash account for Magneto Co. at August 1, 2004, of the current year indicated a balance of $2,705.37. During August, the total cash deposited was $21,077.75, and checks written totaled $21,770.25. The bank statement indicated a balance of $3,465.50 on August 31, 2004. Comparing the bank statement, the canceled checks, and the accompanying memorandums with the records revealed the following reconciling items:

a. Checks outstanding totaled $2,003.84.
b. A deposit of $1,148.21, representing receipts of August 31, had been made too late to appear on the bank statement.
c. The bank had collected for Magneto Co. $1,620 on a note left for collection. The face of the note was $1,500.
d. A check for $110 returned with the statement had been incorrectly charged by the bank as $1,100.
e. A check for $86 returned with the statement had been recorded by Magneto Co. as $68. The check was for the payment of an obligation to Adgate Co. on account.
f. Bank service charges for August amounted to $15.

Instructions

1. Prepare a bank reconciliation as of August 31.
2. Illustrate the adjustments to the accounts and their effect on the financial statements based on the reconciliation.

PROBLEM 5 | 5

Bank reconciliation

OBJECTIVES 4, 5

✓ 1. Adjusted balance:
$10,622.02

Kudzu Company deposits all cash receipts each Wednesday and Friday after banking hours in a night depository. The data required to reconcile the bank statement as of June 30 have been taken from various documents and records and are reproduced as follows. The sources of the data are printed in capital letters. All checks were written for payments on account.

JUNE BANK STATEMENT:

		MEMBER FDIC		
			ACCOUNT NUMBER	

AMERICAN NATIONAL BANK OF DETROIT

DETROIT, MI 48201-2500   (313)933-8547

FROM 6/01/2004	TO 6/30/2004
BALANCE	7,447.20
9 DEPOSITS	8,691.77
20 WITHDRAWALS	7,345.91
4 OTHER DEBITS AND CREDITS	2,298.70CR
NEW BALANCE	11,091.76

KUDZU COMPANY

* - - - -CHECKS AND OTHER DEBITS - - - - - * - - DEPOSITS - - * - DATE - * - - BALANCE- - *

CHECK	AMT	CHECK	AMT	DEPOSITS	DATE	BALANCE
No.731	162.15	No.738	251.40	690.25	06/01	7,723.90
No.739	60.55	No.740	237.50	1,080.50	06/02	8,806.35
No.741	495.15	No.742	501.90	854.17	06/04	8,363.47
No.743	671.30	No.744	506.88	840.50	06/09	8,025.79
No.745	117.25	No.746	298.66	MS 2,500.00	06/09	10,109.88
No.748	450.90	No.749	640.13	MS 125.00	06/09	9,143.85
No.750	276.77	No.751	299.37	896.61	06/11	9,464.32
No.752	537.01	No.753	380.95	882.95	06/16	9,429.31
No.754	449.75	No.756	113.95	1,606.74	06/18	10,472.35
No.757	407.95	No.760	486.39	897.34	06/23	10,475.35
				942.71	06/25	11,418.06
		NSF	291.90		06/28	11,126.16
		SC	34.40		06/30	11,091.76

EC — ERROR CORRECTION	OD — OVERDRAFT
MS — MISCELLANEOUS	PS — PAYMENT STOPPED
NSF — NOT SUFFICIENT FUNDS	SC — SERVICE CHARGE

* * *   * * *   * * *

THE RECONCILEMENT OF THIS STATEMENT WITH YOUR RECORDS IS ESSENTIAL.
ANY ERROR OR EXCEPTION SHOULD BE REPORTED IMMEDIATELY.

CASH ACCOUNT:	
Balance as of June 1, 2004	$7,317.40
CASH RECEIPTS FOR MONTH OF JUNE	$8,451.58

DUPLICATE DEPOSIT TICKETS:
Date and amount of each deposit in June:

Date	Amount	Date	Amount	Date	Amount
June 1	$1,080.50	June 10	$ 896.61	June 22	$897.34
3	854.17	15	882.95	24	942.71
8	840.50	17	1,246.74	29	810.06

(continued)

CHECKS WRITTEN:
Number and amount of each check issued in June:

Check No.	Amount	Check No.	Amount	Check No.	Amount
740	$237.50	747	Void	754	$249.75
741	495.15	748	$450.90	755	272.75
742	501.90	749	640.13	756	113.95
743	671.30	750	276.77	757	407.95
744	506.88	751	299.37	758	159.60
745	117.25	752	537.01	759	501.50
746	298.66	753	380.95	760	486.39

Total amount of checks issued in June $7,605.66

BANK RECONCILIATION FOR PRECEDING MONTH:

KUDZU COMPANY
Bank Reconciliation
May 31, 2004

Cash balance according to bank statement		$7,447.20
Add deposit for May 31, not recorded by bank		690.25
		$8,137.45
Deduct outstanding checks:		
No. 731	$162.15	
736	345.95	
738	251.40	
739	60.55	820.05
Adjusted balance		$7,317.40
Cash balance according to depositor's records		$7,352.50
Deduct service charges		35.10
Adjusted balance		$7,317.40

Instructions

1. Prepare a bank reconciliation as of June 30, 2004. If you discover errors in recording deposits or checks, assume that the company made the errors. Assume that all deposits are from cash sales. All checks are written to satisfy accounts payable.
2. Illustrate the adjustments to the accounts and their effect on the financial statements based on the reconciliation.
3. What is the amount of cash that should appear on the balance sheet as of June 30, 2004?
4. If in preparing the bank reconciliation you note that a canceled check for $270 has been incorrectly recorded by the bank as $720, briefly explain how the error would be included in the bank reconciliation and how it should be corrected.

Activities

Activity 5-1

Control environment of a public corporation

Adolph Coors Company is a multinational brewer, marketer, and seller of beer and other malt-based beverages. For the year ending December 31, 2001, Coors reported sales of almost $2.9 billion and net income of $123 million. For large corporations such as Coors, maintaining a strong control environment is an everyday challenge. One method of maintaining a strong control environment is to have a strong board of directors that is actively engaged in overseeing the business.

Using the Internet, access the Coors December 31, 2001, 10-K filing with the Securities and Exchange Commission. You can use the PriceWaterhouseCoopers web site, **http://edgarscan.pwcglobal.com**, to search for company filings by name. Based on the 10-K filing, answer the following questions:

1. List the members of the Board of Directors of Coors and identify whether any board member is a manager with Coors.
2. Based on your answer to (1), what percentage of the board is not part of Coors' management team? Round to one decimal place.
3. Based on your answer to (1), what percentage of the board is a member of the Coors' family? Round to one decimal place.
4. What are the primary duties and responsibilities of the Audit Committee of the Board of Directors?
5. Who makes up the Audit Committee of the Board of Directors?
6. Was the Audit Committee active throughout the year?
7. Based on your answers to (1)–(6), do you believe that the Board of Directors and the Audit Committee of the Board facilitate an effective control environment at Coors?

Activity 5-2
Responsibility for internal controls of a public corporation

CVS Corporation is a leader in the retail drugstore industry in the United States, with net sales of $22.2 billion in fiscal 2001. As of December 2001, CVS operated more than 4,000 retail and specialty pharmacy stores in 33 states and the District of Columbia.

Using the Internet, access the CVS December 29, 2001, 10-K filing with the Securities and Exchange Commission. You can use the PriceWaterhouseCoopers web site, **http://edgarscan .pwcglobal.com**, to search for company filings by name. Based on the 10-K filing, answer the following questions:

1. Who is responsible for the integrity and objectivity of the financial statements of CVS?
2. What is the CVS system of internal controls designed to accomplish?
3. In addition to management, who reviews the system of internal controls for improvements and modifications necessary because of changing business conditions?
4. Who are the independent auditors of CVS?
5. Do you think having the chief executive officer and chief financial officer of CVS serve on its Audit Committee is a good way to foster an effective control environment?
6. Do members of the management team of CVS serve on the Audit Committee of the Board of Directors?

Activity 5-3
Ethics and professional conduct in business

E T H I C S

During the preparation of the bank reconciliation for The Breadbasket Co., Lee Roberts, the assistant controller, discovered that City National Bank had incorrectly recorded a $718 check written by The Breadbasket Co. as $178. Lee has decided not to notify the bank but wait for the bank to detect the error. Lee plans to record the $540 error as Other Income if the bank fails to detect the error within the next three months.

Discuss whether Lee is behaving in a professional manner.

Activity 5-4
Ethics and professional conduct in business

E T H I C S

Devon Payne and Meredith Sibley are both cash register clerks for Mammoth Markets, and Kelley Russell is its store manager. The following is an excerpt of a conversation between Devon and Meredith:

Devon: Meredith, how long have you been working for Mammoth Markets?
Meredith: Almost five years this October. You just started two weeks ago . . . right?
Devon: Yes. Do you mind if I ask you a question?
Meredith: No, go ahead.
Devon: What I want to know is, have they always had this rule that if your cash register is short at the end of the day, you have to make up the shortage out of your own pocket?

Meredith: Yes, as long as I've been working here.

Devon: Well, it's the pits. Last week I had to pay in almost $30.

Meredith: It's not that big a deal. I just make sure that I'm not short at the end of the day.

Devon: How do you do that?

Meredith: I just short-change a few customers early in the day. There are a few jerks that deserve it anyway. Most of the time, their attention is elsewhere and they don't think to check their change.

Devon: What happens if you're over at the end of the day?

Meredith: Kelley lets me keep it as long as it doesn't get to be too large. I've not been short in over a year. I usually clear about $10 to $20 extra per day.

Discuss this case from the viewpoint of proper controls and professional behavior.

Activity 5-5

Bank reconciliation and internal control

The records of Pegasus Company indicate a March 31 Cash balance of $9,806.05, which includes undeposited receipts for March 30 and 31. The cash balance on the bank statement as of March 31 is $8,004.95. This balance includes a note of $2,500 plus $200 interest collected by the bank but not recorded by Pegasus. Checks outstanding on March 31 were as follows: No. 670, $481.20; No. 679, $510; No. 690, $616.50; No. 1996, $127.40; No. 1997, $520; and No. 1999, $851.50.

On March 3, the cashier resigned, effective at the end of the month. Before leaving on March 31, the cashier prepared the following bank reconciliation:

Cash balance per books, March 31		$ 9,806.05
Add outstanding checks:		
No. 1996	$127.40	
1997	520.00	
1999	851.50	1,198.90
		$11,004.95
Less undeposited receipts		3,000.00
Cash balance per bank, March 31		$ 8,004.95
Deduct unrecorded note with interest		2,700.00
True cash, March 31		$ 5,304.95

Calculator Tape of Outstanding Checks:

```
    0.00  *
  127.40  +
  520.00  +
  851.50  +
1,198.90  *
```

Subsequently, the owner of Pegasus Company discovered that the cashier had stolen all undeposited receipts in excess of the $3,000 on hand on March 31. The owner, a close family friend, has asked your help in determining the amount that the former cashier has stolen.

1. Determine the amount the cashier stole from Pegasus Company. Show your computations in good form.
2. How did the cashier attempt to conceal the theft?
3. a. Identify two major weaknesses in internal controls, which allowed the cashier to steal the undeposited cash receipts.
   b. Recommend improvements in internal controls so that similar types of thefts of undeposited cash receipts can be prevented.

Activity 5-6
Observe internal controls over cash

GROUP

Select a business in your community and observe its internal controls over cash receipts and cash payments. The business could be a bank or a bookstore, restaurant, department store, or other retailer. In groups of three or four, identify and discuss the similarities and differences in each business's cash internal controls.

Activity 5-7
Ratio of cash flow to net income

Home Depot, Inc., is the world's largest home improvement retailer, operating more than 1,300 stores. The following data (in millions) for the years 2002 and 2001 were taken from Home Depot's 10-K filing with the Securities and Exchange Commission:

	For Year Ending:	
	February 2, 2002	**January 28, 2001**
CASH FLOWS FROM OPERATIONS:		
Net Income	$3,044	$ 2,581
Reconciliation of Net Income to Net Cash Provided by Operations:		
Depreciation and Amortization	764	601
Increase in Receivables, net	(119)	(246)
Increase in Merchandise Inventories	(166)	(1,075)
Increase in Accounts Payable and Accrued Liabilities	2,078	754
Increase in Income Taxes Payable	272	151
Other	90	30
Net Cash Provided by Operations	5,963	2,796

1. Compute the ratio of cash flow to net income for 2002 and 2001. Round to one decimal place.
2. Using the Internet, access the February 2, 2002, Home Depot 10-K filing with the Securities and Exchange Commission. Based upon the 10-K filing, determine whether the differences between 2002 and 2001 in inventories and accounts payable are due to changes in accounting methods or operational decisions by management.

Activity 5-8
Cash to monthly cash expenses ratio

Webvan was organized as an Internet retailer offering delivery of a variety of products, including food, nonprescription drugs, housewares, pet supplies, CDs, and books. The products were offered for sale and delivery through Webvan's Webstore, which allowed customers to create a personal shopping list and schedule their deliveries. In 1999, Webvan raised more than $400 million through issuing stock to the public. The following financial data (in thousands) were reported for the years ending December 31, 2000 and 1999:

	2000	1999
Net cash flows from operating activities	$(263,080)	$(58,798)
Cash, December 31	40,293	60,220

1. Determine the monthly cash expenses for each year. Round to the nearest dollar.
2. Determine the ratio of cash to monthly cash expenses for each year. Round to one decimal place.
3. Based on your analysis of (1) and (2), do you believe Webvan is still in business?

Answers to Self-Study Questions

1. **C** Compliance with laws and regulations (answer C) is an objective, not an element, of internal control. The control environment (answer A), monitoring (answer B), control procedures (answer D), risk assessment, and information and communication are the five elements of internal control.

2. **A** The policies and procedures that are established to safeguard assets, ensure accurate business information, and ensure compliance with laws and regulations are called *internal controls* (answer A). Monitoring (answer B), information and communication (answer C), risk assessment (answer D), control environment, and control procedures are elements of internal control.

3. **B** On any specific date, the cash account in a depositor's ledger could not agree with the account in the bank's ledger because of delays and/or errors by either party in recording transactions. The purpose of a bank reconciliation, therefore, is to determine the reasons for any differences between the two account balances. All errors should then be corrected by the depositor or the bank, as appropriate. In arriving at the adjusted (correct) cash balance according to the bank statement, outstanding checks must be deducted (answer B) to adjust for checks that have been written by the depositor but that have not yet been presented to the bank for payment.

4. **C** All reconciling items that are added to and deducted from the cash balance according to the depositor's records on the bank reconciliation (answer C) require that adjustments be made by the depositor to correct errors made in recording transactions or to bring the cash account up to date for delays in recording transactions.

5. **D** To avoid the delay, annoyance, and expense that are associated with paying all obligations by check, relatively small amounts (answer A) are paid from a petty cash fund. The fund is established by estimating the amount of cash needed to pay these small amounts during a specified period (answer B), and it is then reimbursed when the amount of money in the fund is reduced to a predetermined minimum amount (answer C).

6

LEARNING OBJECTIVES

OBJECTIVE 1
Describe the common classifications of receivables.

OBJECTIVE 2
Describe the nature of uncollectible receivables.

OBJECTIVE 3
Describe methods of estimating uncollectible receivables.

OBJECTIVE 4
Describe the common classifications of inventories.

OBJECTIVE 5
Describe the three inventory cost flow assumptions and how they impact the financial statements.

OBJECTIVE 6
Compare and contrast the use of inventory costing methods.

OBJECTIVE 7
Describe how receivables and inventory are reported on the financial statements.

OBJECTIVE 8
Compute and interpret the accounts receivable and inventory turnover ratios.

Receivables and Inventories

What is the role of receivables in business? Unlike the individual consumer purchasing the CD player for cash or by MasterCard or Visa, a business normally purchases merchandise on account. That is, the seller records a receivable and invoices the buyer for payment at a later time. For example, Hershey Foods Company will record a receivable and invoice Kroger supermarkets for delivery of chocolate candy to various stores. Kroger will pay for the candy after delivery according to the terms of the invoice.

What is the role of inventory in business? From a consumer's perspective, inventory allows us to compare items, touch items, purchase on impulse, and take immediate delivery of a product on purchase. For example, at Best Buys you can inspect digital television sets before deciding which set best suits your needs and tastes. To support Wal-Mart's need for immediate product shipments, Procter & Gamble holds an inventory of Tide.® Inventory also provides protection against disruptions in production, transportation, or other processes in the value chain.[1] For example, an unexpected strike by a supplier's employees can halt production for a manufacturer or cause lost sales for a merchandiser. Inventory also allows a business to meet unexpected increases in the demand for its product.

In this chapter, we discuss accounting and reporting issues related to receivables and inventories. Specifically, the effects on the financial statements of estimating uncollectible receivables and inventory cost flow assumptions are emphasized.

[1]The value chain was defined and illustrated in Chapter 1.

Classification of Receivables

Many companies sell on credit in order to sell more services or products. The receivables that result from such sales are normally classified as accounts receivable or notes receivable. The term **receivables** includes all money claims against other entities, including people, business firms, and other organizations. These receivables are usually a significant portion of the total current assets. For example, an annual report of **La-Z-Boy Chair Company** reported that receivables made up more than 60% of La-Z-Boy's current assets.

Accounts Receivable

The most common transaction creating a receivable is selling merchandise or services on credit. The receivable is recorded as an increase to the accounts receivable account. Such **accounts receivable** are normally expected to be collected within a relatively short period, such as 30 or 60 days.

Notes Receivable

A **note receivable**, or promissory note, is a written promise to pay a sum of money on demand or at a definite time. The one to whose order the note is payable is called the *payee*, and the one making the promise is called the *maker*. The date a note is to be paid is called the *due date* or *maturity date*. The period of time between the issuance date and the due date of a short-term note may be stated in either days or months. When the term of a note is stated in days, the due date is the specified number of days after its issuance.

The interest rate on notes is normally stated in terms of a year, regardless of the actual period of time involved. Thus, the interest on $2,000 for one year at 12% is $240 (0.12 × $2,000). The interest on $2,000 for 90 days at 12% is $60 ($2,000 × 0.12 × 90/360). To simplify computations, we use 360 days per year. In practice, companies such as banks and mortgage companies use the exact number of days in a year, 365. The amount of interest is normally reported in the Other Income section of the income statement.

The amount that is due at the maturity or due date of a note receivable is its **maturity value**. The maturity value of a note is the sum of the face amount and the interest. For example, the maturity value of a $25,000, 9%, 120-day note receivable is $25,750 [$25,000 + ($25,000 × 0.09 × 120/360)].

Notes may be used to settle a customer's account receivable. A claim supported by a note has some advantages over a claim in the form of an account receivable. By signing a note, the debtor recognizes the debt and agrees to pay it according to the terms listed. A note is thus a stronger legal claim.

ETHICS IN ACTION

A sales transaction may involve "sales fraud" or "collection fraud." Sales fraud occurs when money is received in advance of the sale and the goods are either not delivered or are not what was promised. This type of fraud has occurred in **eBay** auctions where buyers must pay for the goods prior to receiving them. eBay's seller ratings help reduce the incidence of fraudulent sellers. In collection fraud, the goods are delivered to a customer that does not intend to pay for them. This type of fraud is common among customers of small businesses that fail to screen such customers by using credit reports and analyses.

Other Receivables

Other receivables are normally listed separately on the balance sheet. If they are expected to be collected within one year, they are classified as current assets. If collection is expected beyond one year, they are classified as noncurrent assets and reported under the caption Investments. *Other receivables* include interest receivable, taxes receivable, and receivables from officers or employees.

Uncollectible Receivables

OBJECTIVE 2

Describe the nature of uncollectible receivables.

In Chapter 4, we described and illustrated the accounting for transactions involving sales of merchandise or services on credit. A major issue that we have not yet discussed in recording these transactions is that some of the customers will not pay their accounts. That is, some accounts receivable will be uncollectible.

Retail businesses can shift the risk of uncollectible receivables to other companies. For example, some retailers do not accept sales on account but accept only cash or credit cards. Such policies shift the risk to the credit card companies. Other retailers, however, such as **Macy's**, **Sears**, and **JC Penney**, have issued their own credit cards.

Companies can sell their receivables to other companies. This is often the case when a company issues its own credit card. Selling receivables is called *factoring* the

---

BUSINESS STRATEGY

Coffee Anyone?

Starbucks' objective is to become the leading retailer of specialty coffee. When planning new stores, **Starbucks** focuses on high-traffic, high-visibility locations that offer convenient access for pedestrians and drivers. Starbucks varies the size and format of its stores to fit the location. As a result, you can find Starbucks in a variety of locations, including downtown and suburban retail centers, office buildings, and university campuses. In addition to its retail operations, Starbucks is also attempting to develop its brand through a number of other distribution channels. These channels include Internet and mail-order access, grocery stores and supermarkets, warehouse clubs, hotels, airlines, and restaurants. Finally, Starbucks has entered into a variety of business alliances and joint ventures. One of these joint ventures is with Pepsi for marketing a bottled coffee drink, Frappuccino. Another is with Dreyer's Grand Ice Cream for marketing premium coffee ice creams.

Source: Starbucks Corporation Form 10-K filing with the Securities and Exchange Commission for the year ending September 30, 2001.

receivables, and the buyer of the receivables is called a *factor*. An advantage of factoring is that the company selling its receivables receives immediate cash for operating and other needs. In addition, depending on the factoring agreement, some of the risk of uncollectible accounts can be shifted to the factor.

Regardless of the care used in granting credit and the collection procedures used, a part of the credit sales will not be collectible. The operating expense incurred because of the failure to collect receivables is called **uncollectible accounts expense**, *bad debts expense*, or *doubtful accounts expense*.

When does an account or a note become uncollectible? There is no general rule for determining when an account is uncollectible. A debtor's failure to pay an account according to a sales contract or to pay a note on the due date does not necessarily mean that the account is uncollectible. The debtor's bankruptcy is one of the most significant indications of partial or complete uncollectibility. Other indications include closing the customer's business and failure of repeated attempts to collect.

Estimating Uncollectible Receivables

OBJECTIVE 3

Describe methods of estimating uncollectible receivables.

The estimate of uncollectible accounts at the end of a fiscal period is based on past experience and forecasts of the future. When the general economy is doing well, the amount of uncollectible expense is normally less than it would be when the economy is doing poorly. Two methods are normally used to estimate the amount of uncollectible accounts: (1) the sales method and (2) the aging-of-receivables method.

Sales Method

The sales method of estimating uncollectible accounts emphasizes the matching of uncollectible accounts expense with the credit sales giving rise to the accounts receivable. For example, assume that from past experience it is estimated that 1% of credit sales will be uncollectible. If credit sales for the period are $300,000, the uncollectible accounts expense for the current period would be estimated as $3,000 ($300,000 $\times$ 0.01).

In the preceding example, the $3,000 is an estimate of future uncollectible accounts. The specific customer accounts that will be uncollectible will not be known until a later date. As a result, when the estimate is made at the end of the current year, specific customer accounts cannot be adjusted. As a result, a contra account for accounts receivable, **Allowance for Doubtful Accounts**, is used. The effect of the estimated uncollectible accounts of $3,000 on the accounts and financial statements follows.

Trans. Date	Balance Sheet				Income Statement		
	Assets	Liabilities	Stockholders' Equity	Revenue	Expense		Net Income
	Allow for Doubtful Accts 3,000				Uncoll. Accts Exp 3,000		−3,000
Net Effect	−3,000		−3,000			3,000	−3,000
			Retained Earnings				
			(Net Income)				

Aging-of-Receivables Method

The **aging-of-receivables method** emphasizes the current net realizable value of the receivables. The net realizable value of the receivables is the total receivables less the balance of Allowance for Doubtful Accounts. For example, if receivables total $100,000 and the balance of Allowance for Doubtful Accounts is $20,000, the net realizable value of the receivables is $80,000 ($100,000 less $20,000).

The **aging-of-receivables method** bases its estimate of uncollectible accounts on how long the accounts have been outstanding. The assumption underlying this method is that the longer an account receivable remains outstanding, the less likely it is that it will be collected. At the end of the period, the amount of uncollectible accounts is estimated by using a process called *aging the receivables*.

An aging schedule is prepared by classifying each receivable by its due date. The number of days an account is past due is determined from the due date of the account to the date the aging schedule is prepared. Exhibit 1 shows an example of a typical aging of accounts receivable. The aging schedule is completed by adding the totals in the columns to determine the total amount of receivables in each age class. A sliding scale of percentages, based on industry or company experience, is used to estimate the amount of uncollectibles in each age class, as shown in Exhibit 2.

Based on Exhibit 2, the desired balance for the Allowance for Doubtful Accounts is estimated as $3,390. Comparing this estimate with the balance of the allowance

EXHIBIT 1
Aging of Accounts Receivable

Customer	Balance	Not Past Due	Days Past Due					
			1–30	31–60	61–90	91–180	181–365	over 365
Ashby & Co.	$ 150			$ 150				
B. T. Barr	610					$ 350	$260	
Brock Co.	470	$ 470						
Saxon Woods Co.	160					160		
Total	$86,300	$75,000	$4,000	$3,100	$1,900	$1,200	$800	$300

EXHIBIT 2
Estimate of Uncollectible Accounts

Age Interval	Balance	Estimated Uncollectible Accounts	
		Percent	Amount
Not past due	$75,000	2%	$1,500
1–30 days past due	4,000	5	200
31–60 days past due	3,100	10	310
61–90 days past due	1,900	20	380
91–180 days past due	1,200	30	360
181–365 days past due	800	50	400
Over 365 days past due	300	80	240
Total	$86,300		$3,390

account before adjustment determines the amount of the uncollectible accounts expense for the period. For example, assume that the unadjusted balance of the allowance account is $510.[2] The amount of the adjustment would be $2,880 ($3,390 − $510). The effect of the estimated uncollectible accounts of $2,880 on the accounts and financial statements follows.

Trans. Date	Balance Sheet			Income Statement		
	Assets	Liabilities	Stockholders' Equity	Revenue	Expense	Net Income
	Allow for Doubtful Accts 2,880				Uncoll. Accts Exp 2,880	−2,880
Net Effect	−2,880		−2,880		2,880	−2,880
			Retained Earnings			
			(Net Income)			

After the adjustment has been recorded, the balance in the allowance account is $3,390, the desired amount. The net realizable value of the receivables is $82,910 ($86,300 − $3,390).

The percentage of uncollectible accounts varies across companies and industries. For example, in their annual reports, **JC Penney** reported 1.7% of its receivables as uncollectible, **Deere & Company** (manufacturer of John Deere tractors, etc.) reported only 1.0% of its dealer receivables as uncollectible, and **Columbia HCA Healthcare Corporation** reported 45.6% of its receivables as uncollectible.

Estimates of uncollectible accounts expense based on the aging-of-receivables method *emphasizes the current net realizable value of the receivables.* Thus, the aging method places more emphasis on the balance sheet than on the income statement. In contrast, estimates of uncollectible accounts expense based on the sales method *emphasizes the matching of uncollectible accounts expense with the related sales of the period.* Thus, the sales method places more emphasis on the income statement than on the balance sheet.

Write-Offs of Customer Accounts

When a customer's account is identified as uncollectible, it is written off against the allowance account. For example, John Parker's account of $6,000 has been determined to be uncollectible. The effect on the accounts and financial statements of writing off Parker's account is as shown:

Trans. Date	Balance Sheet			Income Statement		
	Assets	Liabilities	Stockholders' Equity	Revenue	Expense	Net Income
	Accounts Rec. −6,000					
	Allow for Doubtful Accts −6,000					
Net Effect	0					
			Retained Earnings			
			(Net Income)			

[2]To simplify, we assume that Allowance for Doubtful Accounts always has a positive balance.

The total write-offs against the allowance account during a period rarely equals the amount in the account at the beginning of the period. The allowance account will have a positive balance at the end of the period if the write-offs during the period are less than the beginning balance. It will have a negative balance if the write-offs exceed the beginning balance. However, after the end-of-period adjustment for uncollectible accounts, the allowance account should have a positive balance.

What happens if an account receivable that has been written off against the allowance account is later collected? In such cases, the account is reinstated by reversing the write-off. The cash received in payment is then recorded as a receipt on account in the normal manner. For example, assume that John Parker in the preceding example pays his account of $6,000. The effect on the accounts and financial statements of the reinstatement and collection follows:

Reinstatement:

Trans. Date	Balance Sheet				Income Statement		
	Assets		Liabilities	Stockholders' Equity	Revenue	Expense	Net Income
	Accounts Rec.	6,000					
	Allow for Doubtful Accts	6,000					
Net Effect		0					
				Retained Earnings			
				(Net Income)			

Collection:

Trans. Date	Balance Sheet				Income Statement		
	Assets		Liabilities	Stockholders' Equity	Revenue	Expense	Net Income
	Cash	6,000					
	Accounts Receivable	−6,000					
Net Effect		0					
				Retained Earnings			
				(Net Income)			

Classification of Inventories

OBJECTIVE   4

Describe the common classifications of inventories.

As discussed in Chapter 4, a merchandising company purchases products for resale, such as apparel, consumer electronics, hardware, or food items. The merchandise on hand (not sold) at the end of the period is reported as a current asset called **merchandise inventory**. Inventory sold becomes **cost of merchandise sold**, sometimes called the **cost of goods sold**. Merchandise inventory is a significant current asset for most merchandising companies, as shown:

	Merchandise Inventory as a Percentage of Current Assets	Merchandise Inventory as a Percentage of Total Assets
Wal-Mart	82%	28%
Best Buy	60	36
Home Depot	84	31
Kroger	75	22

Manufacturing companies convert raw materials into final products for sale to other businesses or directly to consumers. In contrast to a merchandising company, a manufacturing company has three types of inventory: materials, work in process, and finished goods.

Materials inventory consists of the cost of raw materials used in manufacturing a product. For example, **Hershey Foods Corporation** uses cocoa and sugar in making chocolate. The cost of cocoa and sugar held in the storage silos at the end of the period would be reported on the balance sheet as materials inventory.

Work in process inventory consists of the costs for partially completed product. These costs include the **direct materials**, which are a product's component materials that are introduced into the manufacturing process. For example, Hershey introduces cocoa and sugar in the process of making chocolate. Other costs are also added in the manufacturing process, such as direct labor and factory overhead costs. **Direct labor costs** are the wages of factory workers directly involved with making a product. **Factory overhead costs** are all factory costs other than direct labor and materials, such as equipment depreciation, supervisory salaries, and power costs. The balance sheet reports the work in process inventory at the end of the period as a current asset.

Finished goods inventory consists of the costs of direct materials, direct labor, and factory overhead for completed production. The finished goods inventory for Hershey Foods is the cost of packaged chocolate held in finished goods warehouse at the end of the period. When the finished goods are sold, the costs are transferred to the **cost of goods sold** on the income statement.

In this chapter, we illustrate inventory accounting and analysis issues from the perspective of the merchandising business. However, many of the points apply equally well to a manufacturer. The accounting for manufacturing inventories is covered in later chapters.

Inventory Cost Flow Assumptions

OBJECTIVE   5

Describe the three inventory cost flow assumptions and how they impact the income statement and balance sheet.

When you arrive in line to purchase a movie ticket, the tickets are sold on a first-in, first-out (fifo) order. That is, those who arrive first in line purchase their tickets before those who arrive later. In this section, we see how this ordering concept is used to value inventory. This issue arises when identical units of merchandise are acquired at different unit costs during a period. When the company sells one of these identical items, it must determine a unit cost for the item so that it can record the proper accounting entry. To illustrate, assume that three identical units of Item X are purchased during May:

Item X		Units	Cost
May 10	Purchase	1	$ 9
18	Purchase	1	13
24	Purchase	1	14
Total		3	$36
Average cost per unit			$12

Assume that the company sells one unit on May 30 for $20. If this unit can be identified with a specific purchase, the **specific identification method** can be used to determine the cost of the unit sold. For example, if the unit sold was purchased on May 18, the cost assigned to the unit would be $13, and the gross profit would be $7 ($20 − $13). If, however, the unit sold was purchased on May 10, the cost assigned to it would be $9, and the gross profit would be $11 ($20 − $9). The specific identification method is normally used by companies that sell relatively expensive items, such as jewelry or automobiles. For example, **Oakwood Homes Corp.**, a manufacturer and seller of mobile homes, stated in the footnotes to its annual report:

> Inventories are valued at the lower of cost or market, with cost determined using the specific identification method for new and used manufactured homes. . . .

The specific identification method is not practical unless each unit can be identified accurately. An automobile dealer, for example, may be able to use this method since each automobile has a unique serial number. For many businesses, however, identical units cannot be separately identified, and a cost flow must be assumed. That is, which units have been sold and which units are still in inventory must be assumed.

Three common cost flow assumptions are used in business. Each of these assumptions is identified with an inventory costing method, as follows.

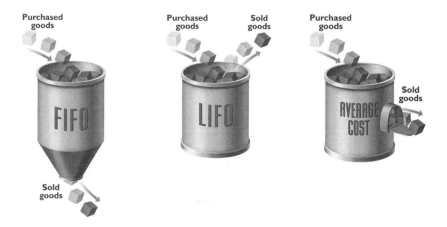

When the **first-in, first-out (fifo) method** is used, the ending inventory is made up of the most recent costs. When the **last-in, first-out (lifo) method** is used, the ending inventory is made up of the earliest costs. When the **average cost method** is used, the cost of the units in inventory is an average of the purchase costs.

To illustrate, we use the preceding example to prepare the income statement for May and the balance sheet as of May 31 for each of the cost flow methods. These financial statements are shown in Exhibit 3.

EXHIBIT 3

*Effect of Inventory
Costing Methods on
Financial Statements*

Fifo Method

Income Statement
Sales $20
Cost of merchandise sold   9
Gross profit $11

Balance Sheet
Merchandise inventory $27

Lifo Method

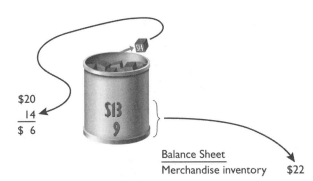

Income Statement
Sales $20
Cost of merchandise sold   14
Gross profit $ 6

Balance Sheet
Merchandise inventory $22

Average Cost Method

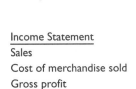
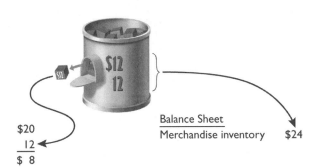

Income Statement
Sales $20
Cost of merchandise sold   12
Gross profit $ 8

Balance Sheet
Merchandise inventory $24

Comparing Costing Methods

OBJECTIVE   6

Compare and contrast
the use of inventory
costing methods.

As we illustrated in Exhibit 3, when prices change, the different inventory costing
methods affect the income statement and balance sheet differently. That is, the methods yield different amounts for (1) the cost of the merchandise sold for the period,
(2) the gross profit (and net income) for the period, and (3) the ending inventory.

Use of Fifo Method

When the fifo method is used during a period of inflation or rising prices, the earlier
unit costs are lower than the more recent unit costs. As shown in Exhibit 3, the fifo
method yields the lowest amount for cost of merchandise sold and the highest amount
for gross profit (and net income). It also yields the highest amount for the ending inventory. Much of the benefit of the larger amount of gross profit is lost, however, be-

cause the inventory must be replaced at ever higher prices. In fact, the balance sheet reports the ending merchandise inventory at an amount that is about the same as its current replacement cost. When the rate of inflation reaches double digits, as it did during the 1970s, the larger gross profits that result from the fifo method are often called *inventory profits* or *illusory profits*. You should note that in a period of deflation or declining prices, the effect is just the opposite.

Use of Lifo Method

When the lifo method is used during a period of inflation or rising prices, the results are opposite those of the other two methods. As shown in Exhibit 3, the lifo method yields a higher amount of cost of merchandise sold, a lower amount of gross profit, and a lower amount of inventory at the end of the period than the other two methods. The reason for these effects is that the cost of the most recently acquired units is about the same as the cost of their replacement. In a period of inflation, the more recent unit costs are higher than the earlier unit costs. Thus, it can be argued that the lifo method more nearly matches current costs with current revenues. For example, **DaimlerChrysler's** reason for changing from the fifo method to the lifo method was stated in the following footnote that accompanied its financial statements:

> DaimlerChrysler changed its method of accounting from first-in, first-out (fifo) to last-in, first-out (lifo) for substantially all of its domestic productive inventories. The change to lifo was made to more accurately match current costs with current revenues.

During periods of rising prices, using lifo offers an income tax savings. The income tax savings results because lifo reports the lowest amount of net income of the three methods. During the double-digit inflationary period of the 1970s, many businesses changed from fifo to lifo for the tax savings. However, the ending inventory on the balance sheet may be quite different from its current replacement cost. In such cases, the financial statements normally include a note stating that the estimated difference between the lifo inventory and the inventory had fifo been used. Again, you should note that in a period of deflation or falling price levels, the effects are just the opposite.

The rules used for external financial reporting need not be the same as those used for income tax reporting. One exception to this general rule is the use of lifo. If a firm elects to use lifo inventory valuation for tax purposes, the business must also use lifo for external financial reporting. This is called the **lifo conformity rule**. Thus, during periods of rising prices, using lifo offers an income tax savings. The income tax savings results from the fact that lifo reports the lowest amount of net income of the three methods in periods of rising prices. Many managers elect to use lifo because of the tax savings, even though the reported earnings will be lower.

The ending inventory on the balance sheet may be quite different from its current replacement cost (or fifo estimate). In such cases, the financial statements will include a note that states the estimated difference between the amount of lifo inventory and the amount of inventory had fifo been used. An example of such a note for the **Kmart Corporation** follows.

> The last-in, first-out (lifo) method . . . was used to determine the cost for $6,104 . . . of inventory as of fiscal year-end 2000 . . . Inventories valued on lifo were $194 . . . lower than

amounts that would have been reported using the first-in, first-out (fifo) method at fiscal year-end 2000. . . .

In periods of rising prices, the inventory under lifo would be less than under fifo, as was the case for Kmart. Again, you should note that in a period of deflation or falling price levels, the effects are just the opposite.

Use of Average Cost Method

As you might have already reasoned, the average cost method of inventory costing is, in a sense, a compromise between fifo and lifo. The effect of price trends is averaged in determining the cost of merchandise sold and the ending inventory. For a series of purchases, the average cost will be the same, regardless of the direction of price trends. For example, a complete reversal of the sequence of unit costs presented in the preceding illustration would not affect the reported cost of merchandise sold, gross profit, or ending inventory.

As you can see, the selection of an inventory costing method can have a significant impact on the financial statements. For this reason, the selection has important implications for managers and others in analyzing and interpreting the financial statements. The chart in Exhibit 4 shows the frequency with which fifo, lifo, and the average methods are used in practice.

EXHIBIT 4
Inventory Costing Methods*

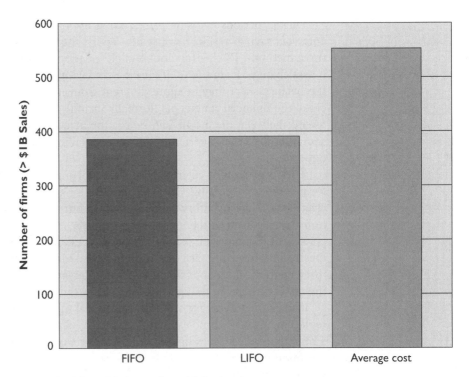

Source: Derived from Disclosure financial database.

*Firms may be counted more than once for using multiple methods.

Reporting Receivables and Inventory

OBJECTIVE 7

Describe how receivables and inventory are reported on the financial statements.

Receivables and inventory are reported as current assets on the balance sheet, as shown in Exhibit 5. In addition, generally accepted accounting principles require that supplementary information concerning these accounts be reported in the footnotes accompanying the financial statements. In this section, we focus on both the financial statement and footnote reporting requirements for receivables and inventory.

EXHIBIT 5

Receivables and Inventory in Balance Sheet

CRABTREE CO. Balance Sheet December 31, 20—		
Assets		
Current assets:		
Cash and cash equivalents		$119,500.00
Notes receivable		250,000.00
Accounts receivable	$445,000.00	
Less allowance for doubtful accounts	15,000.00	430,000.00
Interest receivable		14,500.00
Merchandise inventory—at lower of cost (first-in, first-out method) or market		216,300.00

Receivables

All receivables expected to be realized in cash within a year are presented in the Current Assets section of the balance sheet. These assets are normally listed in the order of their liquidity, that is, the order in which they are expected to be converted to cash during normal operations. The presentation of receivables on **Starbucks'** balance sheet follows.[3]

	Sept. 30, 2001	Oct. 1, 2000
ASSETS		
Current assets:		
Cash and cash equivalents	$113,237	$ 70,817
Marketable securities	107,312	61,336
Accounts receivable, net of allowances of		
$4,590 and $2,941, respectively	90,425	76,385
Inventories	221,253	201,656
Prepaid expenses and other current assets	61,698	48,040
Total current assets	$593,925	$458,234

Starbucks reports net accounts receivable of $90,425 and $76,385. The allowances for doubtful accounts of $4,590 and $2,941 are subtracted from the total accounts receivable to arrive at the net receivables. Alternatively, the allowances for each year could be shown in a note to the financial statements.

[3]Adapted from Starbucks Corporation 10-K dated September 30, 2001.

Other disclosures related to receivables are presented either on the face of the financial statements or in the accompanying notes.[4] Such disclosures include the market (fair) value of the receivables if significantly different from the reported value. In addition, if unusual credit risks exist within the receivables, the nature of the risks should be disclosed. For example, if the majority of the receivables are due from one customer or from customers located in one area of the country or one industry, these facts should be disclosed.

Starbucks did not report any unusual credit risks related to its receivables. However, the following credit risk disclosure appeared in the financial statements of **Deere & Company**:

> Credit receivables have significant concentrations of credit risk in the agricultural, industrial, lawn and grounds care, and recreational (non-Deere equipment) business sectors. . . . The portion of credit receivables related to the agricultural equipment business was 60%; that related to the industrial equipment business was 12%; that related to the lawn and grounds care equipment business was 7%; and that related to the recreational equipment business was 21%. On a geographic basis, there is not a disproportionate concentration of credit risk in any area. . . .

ETHICS IN ACTION

A company in financial distress will still try to purchase goods and services on account. In these cases, rather than "buyer beware," it is more like "seller beware." Sellers must be careful in advancing credit to such companies because trade creditors have low priority for cash payment in the event of bankruptcy. To help suppliers, third-party services specialize in evaluating financially distressed customers.

These services analyze credit risk for these firms by evaluating recent management payment decisions (who is getting paid and when), court actions (if in bankruptcy), and other supplier credit tightening or suspension actions. Such information helps a supplier monitor and tune trade credit amounts and terms with the financially distressed customer.

Inventory

Merchandise inventory is usually presented at its cost in the Current Assets section of the balance sheet, following receivables. The method of determining the cost of the inventory (fifo, lifo, or average) should be shown. It is not unusual for large businesses with varied activities to use different costing methods for different segments of their inventories. The details may be disclosed in parentheses on the balance sheet or in a footnote to the financial statements.

Inventory is valued at other than cost when (1) the cost of replacing items in inventory is below the recorded cost and (2) the inventory is not salable at normal sales prices. This latter case may be due to imperfections, shop wear, style changes, or other causes. In either situation, the method of valuing the inventories (cost or lower of cost or market) should also be disclosed on the balance sheet.

If the cost of replacing an item in inventory is lower than the original purchase cost, the **lower-of-cost-or-market (LCM) method** is used to value the inventory. *Market*, as used in *lower of cost or market*, is the cost to replace the merchandise on

---

[4]*Statements of Financial Accounting Standards, No. 105*, "Disclosures of Information about Financial Instruments with Off-Balance Sheet Risk and Financial Instruments with Concentrations of Credit Risk," and *No. 107*, "Disclosures about Fair Value of Financial Instruments" (Norwalk, CT: Financial Accounting Standards Board, 1990 and 1991).

the inventory date. This market value is based on quantities normally purchased from the usual source of supply. In businesses for which inflation is the norm, market prices rarely decline. In businesses for which technology changes rapidly (e.g., micro-computers and televisions), market declines are common. The primary advantage of the lower-of-cost-or-market method is that the gross profit (and net income) is reduced in the period in which the market decline occurred rather than waiting until the inventory is sold.

In applying the lower-of-cost-or-market method, the cost and replacement cost can be determined in one of three ways. Cost and replacement cost can be determined for (1) each item in the inventory, (2) major classes or categories of inventory, or (3) the inventory as a whole. In practice, the cost and replacement cost of each item are usually determined.

To illustrate, assume that 400 identical units of Item A are in inventory, acquired at a unit cost of $10.25 each. If at the inventory date the item would cost $10.50 to replace, the cost price of $10.25 would be multiplied by 400 to determine the inventory value. On the other hand, if the item could be replaced at $9.50 a unit, the replacement cost of $9.50 would be used for valuation purposes.

Exhibit 6 illustrates a method of organizing inventory data and applying lower-of-cost-or-market to each inventory item. The amount of the market decline, $450 ($15,520 − $15,070), may be reported as a separate item on the income statement or included in the cost of merchandise sold. Regardless, net income will be reduced by the amount of the market decline.

EXHIBIT 6

Determining Inventory at Lower of Cost or Market

Commodity	Inventory Quantity	Unit Cost Price	Unit Market Price	Cost (C)	Market (M)	Lower of C or M
A	400	$10.25	$ 9.50	$ 4,100	$ 3,800	$ 3,800
B	120	22.50	24.10	2,700	2,892	2,700
C	600	8.00	7.75	4,800	4,650	4,650
D	280	14.00	14.75	3,920	4,130	3,920
Total				$15,520	$15,472	$15,070

As you would expect, merchandise that is out of date, spoiled, or damaged or that can be sold only at prices below cost should be written down. Such merchandise should be valued at net realizable value. **Net realizable value** is the estimated selling price less any direct cost of disposal, such as sales commissions. For example, assume that damaged merchandise costing $1,000 can be sold for only $800, and direct selling expenses are estimated to be $150. This inventory should be valued at $650 ($800 − $150), which is its net realizable value.

Both the method of determining the cost of the inventory (fifo, lifo, or average) and the method of valuing the inventory (cost or the lower of cost or market) should be shown on the balance sheet. These details may be disclosed in parentheses on the balance sheet or in a footnote to the financial statements. **Starbucks'** footnote disclosure follows:

Inventories are stated at the lower of cost (primarily moving average cost) or market.

It is not unusual for large businesses with varied activities to use different costing methods for different segments of their inventories. The following note taken from the financial statements of **DaimlerChrysler** illustrates this:

> Automotive inventories are valued at the lower of cost or market. The cost of substantially all domestic automotive inventories is recorded on a Last-In, First-Out (lifo) basis. Aerospace inventories are stated at the lower of cost or market, with cost recognized on a First-In, First-Out (fifo) basis.

A company may change its inventory costing methods for a valid reason. In such cases, the effect of the change and the reason for it should be disclosed in the financial statements for the period in which the change occurred.

Turnover Ratios

OBJECTIVE   8

Compute and interpret the accounts receivable and inventory turnover ratios.

The accounts receivable and inventory turnover ratios are useful in monitoring the management of receivables and inventory. Businesses normally desire to collect receivables as promptly as possible. The cash collected from receivables improves solvency and lessens the risk of loss from uncollectible accounts. Likewise, businesses normally desire to sell inventory as quickly as possible. The cash collected from inventory improves solvency and lessens the risk of loss from obsolete or spoiled inventory.

Accounts Receivable Turnover

The **accounts receivable turnover** measures how frequently during the year the accounts receivable are being converted to cash. For example, with credit terms of 2/10, n/30 days, the accounts receivable should turn over more than 12 times per year. The accounts receivable turnover is computed as follows:

$$\text{Accounts receivable turnover} = \frac{\text{Net sales}}{\text{Average accounts receivable}}$$

The average accounts receivable can be determined by using monthly data or by simply adding the beginning and ending accounts receivable balances and dividing by 2. For example, using the following financial data for Starbucks, the 2001 accounts receivable turnover is computed as 47.6, as shown:

	Sept. 30, 2001	Oct. 1, 2000	Oct. 3, 1999
Net revenues	$2,648,980	$2,177,614	$1,680,145
Net accounts receivable	90,425	76,385	47,646

$$\text{Accounts receivable turnover} = \frac{\text{Net sales}}{\text{Average accounts receivable}}$$

$$= \frac{\$2,648,980}{(\$90,425 + \$76,385)/2} = 47.6$$

By computing the accounts receivable turnover for the prior year, shown here, we can determine whether Starbucks' management of accounts receivable has improved.

$$\text{Accounts receivable turnover} = \frac{\text{Net sales}}{\text{Average accounts receivable}}$$

$$= \frac{\$2,177,614}{(\$76,385 + \$47,646)/2} = 35.1$$

The 2000 accounts receivable turnover for Starbucks is 35.1. Thus, Starbucks improved its management of accounts receivable during 2001.

Inventory Turnover

Inventory turnover measures the relationship between the volume of goods (merchandise) sold and the amount of inventory carried during the period. It is computed as follows:

$$\text{Inventory turnover} = \frac{\text{Cost of merchandise sold*}}{\text{Average inventory}}$$

*For a manufacturing company, the numerator would be cost of goods sold.

The average inventory is computed using weekly, monthly, or annual figures. To simplify, we determine the average inventory by dividing the sum of the inventories at the beginning and end of the year by 2. As long as the amount of inventory held throughout the year is stable, this average will be accurate enough for our analysis.

To illustrate, the following data have been taken from recent annual reports for **Safeway Inc.** and **Zale Corporation**:

	Safeway Inc.	Zale Corp.
Cost of merchandise sold	$22,482,400,000	$920,003,000
Inventories:		
Beginning of year	$2,444,900,000	$571,669,000
End of year	$2,508,000,000	$630,450,000
Average	$2,476,450,000	$601,059,500
Inventory turnover	9.1	1.5

The inventory turnover is 9.1 for Safeway and 1.5 for Zale. Generally, the larger the inventory turnover, the more efficient and effective the management of the inventory. However, differences in companies and industries are too great to allow specific statements as to what is a good inventory turnover. For example, Safeway is the second largest food retailer in the United States. Because most of Safeway's inventory is perishable, we would expect it to have a high inventory turnover. In contrast, Zale Corporation is the largest specialty retailer of fine jewelry in the United States. Thus, we would expect Zale to have a lower inventory turnover than Safeway since jewelry is not perishable.

Key Points

1. **Describe the common classifications of receivables.**

   The term *receivables* includes all money claims against other entities, including people, business firms, and other organizations. Receivables are normally classified as accounts receivable, notes receivable, or other receivables.

2. **Describe the nature of uncollectible receivables.**

   Businesses attempt to limit the number and amount of uncollectible receivables primarily by investigating customer creditworthiness, using references, and performing background checks. However, regardless of the care used in granting credit and the collection procedures used, a part of credit sales will not be collectible. The operating expense incurred because of the failure to collect receivables is called *uncollectible accounts expense, bad debts expense,* or *doubtful accounts expense.*

3. **Describe methods of estimating uncollectible receivables.**

   Two methods normally used to estimate the amount of uncollectible accounts are (1) the sales method and (2) the aging-of-receivables method. The sales method emphasizes the matching of uncollectible accounts expense with the credit sales giving rise to the accounts receivable. The aging-of-receivables method emphasizes the current net realizable value of the receivables. The aging-of-receivables method bases its estimate of uncollectible accounts on how long the accounts have been outstanding. At the end of the period, the amount of uncollectible accounts is estimated by using an aging schedule. Under both methods, when a customer's account is identified as uncollectible, it is written off against the Allowance for Doubtful Accounts.

4. **Describe the common classifications of inventories.**

   The inventory of a merchandiser is called *merchandise inventory.* The cost of merchandise inventory that is sold is reported on the income statement. Manufacturers typically have three types of inventory: materials, work in process, and finished goods. When finished goods are sold, the cost is reported on the income statement as cost of goods sold.

5. **Describe the three inventory cost flow assumptions and how they impact the financial statements.**

   The three common cost flow assumptions used in business are (1) the first-in, first-out method, (2) the last-in, first-out method, and (3) the average cost method. Each method normally yields different amounts for the cost of merchandise sold and the ending merchandise inventory. Thus, the choice of a cost flow assumption directly affects the income statement and balance sheet.

6. **Compare and contrast the use of inventory costing methods.**

   During periods of inflation, the fifo method yields the lowest amount for the cost of merchandise sold, the highest amount for gross profit (and net income), and the highest amount for the ending inventory. The lifo method yields the opposite results. During periods of deflation, the preceding effects are reversed. The average cost method yields results that are between those of fifo and lifo.

7. **Describe how receivables and inventory are reported on the financial statements.**

   All receivables that are expected to be realized in cash within a year are presented in the Current Assets section of the balance sheet. Other disclosures related to receivables are presented either on the face of the financial statements or in the accompanying notes. Such disclosures include the market (fair) value of the receivables. In addition, if unusual credit risks exist within the receivables, the nature of the risks should be disclosed.

   Inventory is normally reported in the Current Assets section of the balance sheet, following receivables. Inventories are normally reported at their cost. In some cases, however, inventory is valued at other than cost. Two such cases arise when (1) the cost of replacing items in inventory is below the recorded cost and (2) the inventory is not salable at normal sales prices. Both the method of determining the cost of the inventory (fifo, lifo, or average) and the method of valuing the inventory (cost or the lower of cost or market) should be shown either on the balance sheet or in a footnote.

8. Compute and interpret the receivable and inventory turnover ratios.

The accounts receivable turnover is net sales on account divided by average accounts receivable. It measures how frequently accounts receivable are being converted into cash. The inventory turnover ratio, computed as the cost of merchandise sold divided by the average inventory, measures the relationship between the volume of goods (merchandise) sold and the amount of inventory carried during the period.

Glossary

Accounts receivable: Receivables created by selling merchandise or services on credit.

Accounts receivable turnover: Measures how frequently during the year the accounts receivable are being converted to cash.

Aging-of-receivables method: The process of analyzing the accounts receivable and classifying them according to various age groupings, with the due date being the base point for determining age.

Allowance for doubtful accounts: The contra asset account for accounts receivable.

Average cost method: The method of inventory costing that is based upon the assumption that costs should be charged against revenue by using the weighted average unit cost of the items sold.

Cost of merchandise sold: The cost of manufactured product sold; also called *cost of goods sold.*

Finished goods inventory: The costs of finished products on hand that have not been sold.

First-in, first-out (fifo) method: A method of inventory costing based on the assumption that the costs of merchandise sold should be charged against revenue in the order in which the costs were incurred.

Inventory turnover: Measures the relationship between the volume of goods (merchandise) sold and the amount of inventory carried during the period.

Last-in, first-out (lifo) method: A method of inventory costing based on the assumption that the most recent merchandise inventory costs should be charged against revenue.

Lifo conformity rule: A financial reporting rule requiring a firm that elects to use lifo inventory valuation for tax purposes to also use lifo for external financial reporting.

Lower-of-cost-or-market (LCM) method: A method of valuing inventory that reports the inventory at the lower of its cost or current market value (replacement cost).

Materials inventory: The cost of materials that have not yet entered into the manufacturing process.

Maturity value: The amount that is due at the maturity or due date of a note.

Merchandise inventory: Merchandise on hand and available for sale to customers.

Net realizable value: For a receivable, the amount of cash expected to be realized in the future. For inventory, the estimated selling price of an item of inventory less any direct costs of disposal, such as sales commissions.

Note receivable: Amounts customers owe, for which a formal, written instrument of credit has been issued.

Receivables: All money claims against other entities, including people, business firms, and other organizations.

Uncollectible accounts expense: The operating expense incurred because of the failure to collect receivables.

Work in process inventory: The direct materials costs, the direct labor costs, and the factory overhead costs that have entered into the manufacturing process, but are associated with product that has not been finished.

Self-Study Questions

(Answers appear at end of chapter.)

1. At the end of the fiscal year, before the accounts are adjusted, Accounts Receivable has a balance of $200,000 and Allowance for Doubtful Accounts has a balance of $2,500. If the estimate of uncollectible accounts determined by aging the receivables is $8,500, the amount of uncollectible accounts expense is:

    A. $2,500   C. $8,500
    B. $6,000   D. $11,000

2. At the end of the fiscal year, Accounts Receivable has a balance of $100,000 and Allowance for Doubtful Accounts has a balance of $7,000. The expected net realizable value of the accounts receivable is:
   A. $7,000   C. $100,000
   B. $93,000   D. $107,000

3. The inventory costing method that is based on the assumption that costs should be charged against revenue in the order in which they were incurred is:
   A. fifo   C. average cost
   B. lifo   D. perpetual inventory

4. The following units of a particular item were available for sale during the period:

Beginning inventory	40 units at $20
First purchase	50 units at $21
Second purchase	50 units at $22
Third purchase	50 units at $23

What is the unit cost of the 35 units on hand at the end of the period, as determined under the fifo costing method?
   A. $20   C. $22
   B. $21   D. $23

5. If merchandise inventory is being valued at cost and the price level is steadily rising, the method of costing that will yield the highest net income is:
   A. lifo   C. average
   B. fifo   D. physical

Discussion Questions

1. What are the three classifications of receivables?

2. In what section of the balance sheet should a note receivable be listed if its term is (a) 120 days and (b) 6 years?

3. If a note provides for payment of principal of $75,000 and interest at the rate of 8%, will the interest amount to $6,000? Explain.

4. Give two examples of other receivables.

5. To reduce its uncollectible accounts expense, Adang Inc. decided to stop granting credit to customers. Is this a wise decision by Adang Inc.? Explain.

6. What kind of an account (asset, liability, etc.) is Allowance for Doubtful Accounts?

7. After the accounts have been adjusted and closed at the end of the fiscal year, Accounts Receivable has a balance of $783,150 and Allowance for Doubtful Accounts has a balance of $41,694. Describe how the accounts receivable and the allowance for doubtful accounts are reported on the balance sheet.

8. A firm has consistently adjusted its allowance account at the end of the fiscal year by adding a fixed percentage of the period's net sales on account. After five years, the balance in Allowance for Doubtful Accounts has become very large in relationship to the balance in Accounts Receivable. Give two possible explanations.

9. Which of the two methods of estimating uncollectibles provides for the most accurate estimate of the current net realizable value of the receivables?

10. How do inventories of a manufacturer differ from those of a merchandiser?

11. Do the terms *fifo* and *lifo* refer to techniques used in determining quantities of the various classes of merchandise on hand? Explain.

12. Does the term *last-in* in the lifo method mean that the items in the inventory are assumed to be the most recent (last) acquisitions? Explain.

13. If merchandise inventory is being valued at cost and the price level is steadily rising, which of the three methods of costing—fifo, lifo, or average cost—will yield (a) the highest inventory cost, (b) the lowest inventory cost, (c) the highest gross profit, (d) the lowest gross profit?

14. Which of the three methods of inventory costing—fifo, lifo, or average cost—will in general yield an inventory cost most nearly approximating current replacement cost?

15. If inventory is being valued at cost and the price level is steadily rising, which of the three methods of costing—fifo, lifo, or average cost—will yield the lowest annual income tax expense? Explain.

16. Because of imperfections, an item of merchandise cannot be sold at its normal selling price. How should this item be valued for financial statement purposes?

17. How are the method of determining the cost of the inventory and the method of valuing it disclosed in the financial statements?

18. The accounts receivable and inventory turnover have increased for Nackerud Co. Are changes for the current year good or bad? Explain.

Exercises

EXERCISE 6-1
Classifications of receivables
OBJECTIVE 1

The **Boeing Company** is one of the world's major aerospace firms with operations involving commercial aircraft, military aircraft, missiles, satellite systems, and information and battle management systems. As of December 31, 2001, Boeing had $2,597 million of receivables involving U.S. government contracts and $679 million of receivables involving commercial aircraft customers, such as **Delta Air Lines** and **United Airlines**. Should Boeing report these receivables separately in the financial statements or combine them into one overall accounts receivable amount? Explain.

EXERCISE 6-2
Determine due date and interest on notes
OBJECTIVE 1

Determine the due date and the amount of interest due at maturity on the following notes:

	Date of Note	Face Amount	Term of Note	Interest Rate
a.	March 6	$10,000	60 days	9%
b.	May 20	6,000	60 days	10%
c.	June 2	7,500	90 days	12%
d.	August 30	15,000	120 days	10%
e.	October 1	12,500	60 days	12%

EXERCISE 6-3
Nature of uncollectible accounts
OBJECTIVE 2

Hilton Hotels Corporation owns and operates casinos at several of its hotels, located primarily in Nevada. At the end of one fiscal year, the following accounts and notes receivable were reported (in thousands):

Hotel accounts and notes receivable	$75,796	
Less: Allowance for doubtful accounts	3,256	
		$72,540
Casino accounts receivable	$26,334	
Less: Allowance for doubtful accounts	6,654	
		19,680

a. Compute the percentage of allowance for doubtful accounts to the gross hotel accounts and notes receivable for the end of the fiscal year.
b. Compute the percentage of the allowance for doubtful accounts to the gross casino accounts receivable for the end of the fiscal year.
c. Discuss possible reasons for the difference in the two ratios computed in (a) and (b).

EXERCISE 6-4
Estimating doubtful accounts
OBJECTIVE 3

Phoenician Co. is a wholesaler of office supplies. An aging of the company's accounts receivable on December 31, 2003, and a historical analysis of the percentage of uncollectible accounts in each age category are as follows:

Age Interval	Balance	Percent Uncollectible
Not past due	$350,000	1%
1–30 days past due	90,000	3
31–60 days past due	17,000	6
61–90 days past due	13,000	10
91–180 days past due	9,400	60
Over 180 days past due	3,600	80
	$483,000	

Estimate what the proper balance of Allowance for Doubtful Accounts should be as of December 31, 2003.

EXERCISE 6-5
Uncollectible accounts
OBJECTIVES 2, 3

Using the data in Exercise 6-4, assume that Allowance for Doubtful Accounts for Phoenician Co. had a balance of $1,891 as of December 31, 2003. Illustrate the effects of the adjustment for uncollectible accounts as of December 31, 2003, on the accounts and financial statements.

EXERCISE 6-6
Providing for doubtful accounts
OBJECTIVES 2, 3

At the end of the current year, the accounts receivable account has a balance of $775,000, and net sales for the year total $6,000,000. Determine the amount of the adjustment to provide for doubtful accounts under each of the following assumptions:

a. The allowance account before adjustment has a balance of $4,750. Uncollectible accounts expense is estimated at ¼ of 1% of net sales.
b. The allowance account before adjustment has a balance of $3,750. An aging of the accounts in the customer ledger indicates estimated doubtful accounts of $18,350.
c. The allowance account before adjustment has a balance of $5,050. Uncollectible accounts expense is estimated at ½ of 1% of net sales.
d. The allowance account before adjustment has a balance of $5,050. An aging of the accounts in the customer ledger indicates estimated doubtful accounts of $31,400.

EXERCISE 6-7
Writing off accounts receivable
OBJECTIVES 2, 3

Query.com, a computer consulting firm, decided to write off the $4,800 balance of an account owed by a customer. Later, the customer paid the written-off account in full.

a. Illustrate the effect on the accounts and financial statements of the write-off of the account.
b. Illustrate the effect on the accounts and financial statements of the subsequent collection of the written-off account.

EXERCISE 6-8
Manufacturing Inventories
OBJECTIVE 4

Qualcomm Incorporated is a leading developer and manufacturer of digital wireless telecommunications products and services. Qualcomm reported the following inventories (in thousands) on September 30, 2001, in the footnotes to its financial statements:

	September 30, 2001
Raw materials	$18,251
Work in process	3,346
Finished goods	74,266
	$95,863

a. Why does Qualcomm report three different inventories?
b. What costs are included in each of the three classes of inventory?

EXERCISE 6-9
Television costs of Walt Disney Company
OBJECTIVE 4

The **Walt Disney Company** shows "television costs" as an asset on its balance sheet. In the footnotes to its financial statements, the following television cost disclosure (in millions) was made:

	Sept. 30, 2001	Sept. 30, 2000
Television costs:		
Released, less amortization	$ 649	$ 682
Completed, not released	62	42
In-process	407	328
In development or pre-production	41	33
	$1,159	$1,085

a. Interpret the four television cost asset categories.
b. How are these classifications similar or dissimilar to the inventory classifications used in a manufacturing firm?

EXERCISE 6-10
Manufacturing inventories
OBJECTIVE 4

The inventories of **Anheuser-Busch Companies, Inc.**, on December 21, 2000, were reported on the balance sheet (in millions) as follows:

	Dec. 31, 2000
Raw materials	$347.3
Work in process	82.9
Finished goods	178.1
Total	**$608.3**

What do the three inventory classes on Anheuser-Busch's balance sheet represent?

EXERCISE 6-11
Inventory by three methods
OBJECTIVE 5

✓ b. $990

The units of an item available for sale during the year were as follows:

Jan.	1	Inventory	25 units at $24
Feb.	4	Purchase	10 units at $25
July	20	Purchase	30 units at $28
Dec.	30	Purchase	35 units at $30

There are 40 units of the item in the physical inventory at December 31. The periodic inventory system is used. Determine the inventory cost by using (a) the first-in, first-out method, (b) the last-in, first-out method, and (c) the average cost method.

EXERCISE 6-12
Inventory by three methods
OBJECTIVE 5

✓ b. $1,450

The units of an item available for sale during the year were as follows:

Jan.	1	Inventory	25 units at $48
Mar.	10	Purchase	10 units at $50
Aug.	21	Purchase	30 units at $56
Dec.	29	Purchase	35 units at $60

There are 30 units of the item in the physical inventory at December 31. The periodic inventory system is used. Determine the inventory cost by using (a) the first-in, first-out method, (b) the last-in, first-out method, and (c) the average cost method.

EXERCISE 6-13
Inventory by three methods; cost of merchandise sold
OBJECTIVE 5

✓ a. Inventory, $1,254

The units of an item available for sale during the year were as follows:

Jan.	1	Inventory	21 units at $60
Mar.	4	Purchase	29 units at $65
Aug.	7	Purchase	10 units at $68
Nov.	15	Purchase	15 units at $70

There are 18 units of the item in the physical inventory at December 31. The periodic inventory system is used. Determine the inventory cost and the cost of merchandise sold by three methods, presenting your answers in the following form:

	Cost	
Inventory Method	**Merchandise Inventory**	**Merchandise Sold**
a. First-in, first-out	$	$
b. Last-in, first-out		
c. Average cost		

EXERCISE 6-14
Inventory by three methods; cost of merchandise sold
OBJECTIVE 5

✓ a. Inventory, $2,780

The units of an item available for sale during the year were as follows:

Jan.	1	Inventory	42 units at $60
Feb.	23	Purchase	58 units at $65
Sep.	18	Purchase	20 units at $68
Dec.	10	Purchase	30 units at $70

There are 40 units of the item in the physical inventory at December 31. The periodic inventory system is used. Determine the inventory cost and the cost of merchandise sold by three methods, presenting your answers in the following form:

	Cost	
Inventory Method	**Merchandise Inventory**	**Merchandise Sold**
a. First-in, first-out	$	$
b. Last-in, first-out		
c. Average cost		

EXERCISE 6-15
Comparing inventory methods
OBJECTIVE 6

Assume that a firm separately determined inventory under fifo and lifo and then compared the results.

1. In each space following, place the correct sign—less than (<), greater than (>), or equal to (=)—for each comparison, assuming periods of rising prices.
   a. Lifo inventory   _____ Fifo Inventory
   b. Lifo cost of goods sold _____ Fifo cost of goods sold
   c. Lifo net income   _____ Fifo net income
   d. Lifo income tax   _____ Fifo income tax
2. Why would management prefer to use lifo over fifo in periods of rising prices?

EXERCISE 6-16
Receivables in the balance sheet
OBJECTIVE 7

List any errors you can find in the following partial balance sheet.

DRAGONFLY COMPANY
Balance Sheet
December 31, 2003

Assets		
Current assets:		
Cash		$ 63,750
Notes receivable	$200,000	
Less interest receivable	12,000	188,000
Accounts receivable	$376,180	
Plus allowance for doubtful accounts	30,500	406,680

EXERCISE 6-17
Lower-of-cost-or-market inventory
OBJECTIVE 7

On the basis of the following data, determine the value of the inventory at the lower of cost or market. Assemble the data in the form illustrated in Exhibit 6.

Commodity	Inventory Quantity	Unit Cost Price	Unit Market Price
X3	9	$300	$320
Y10	16	110	115
A19	12	275	260
J2	15	51	45
J8	25	96	100

EXERCISE 6-18
Merchandise inventory on the balance sheet
OBJECTIVE 7

Based on the data in Exercise 6-17 and assuming that cost was determined by the fifo method, show how the merchandise inventory would appear on the balance sheet.

EXERCISE 6-19
Accounts receivable turnover
OBJECTIVE 8

Circuit City is a national retailer of brand-name consumer electronics including televisions, DVD players, compact disc players, personal computers, printers, video games, DVD movies, and music. For the fiscal years 2002 and 2001, Circuit City reported the following (in thousands):

| | Year Ending February 28, | |
	2002	**2001**
Net sales	$12,791,468	$12,959,028
Accounts Receivable	726,541	585,761

Assume that all sales are credit sales and that the accounts receivable (in thousands) were $593,276 at March 1, 2000.

a. Compute the accounts receivable turnover for 2002 and 2001. Round to one decimal place.
b. What conclusions can be drawn from these analyses regarding Circuit City's efficiency in collecting receivables?

EXERCISE 6-20
Accounts receivable turnover
OBJECTIVE 8

The Limited Inc. sells women's and men's clothing through specialty retail stores, including **Structure, Limited, Express, Lane Bryant,** and **Lerner New York**. The Limited sells women's intimate apparel and personal care products through **Victoria's Secret** and **Bath & Body Works** stores. For the fiscal years 2002 and 2001, The Limited reported the following (in thousands):

| | Year Ending February 2, | |
	2002	**2001**
Net sales	$9,363,000	$10,105,000
Accounts receivable	79,000	94,000

Assume that the accounts receivable (in thousands) were $109,000 at the beginning of the 2001 fiscal year.

a. Compute the accounts receivable turnover for 2002 and 2001. Round to one decimal place.
b. What conclusions can be drawn from these analyses regarding The Limited's efficiency in collecting receivables?

EXERCISE 6-21
Accounts receivable turnover
OBJECTIVE 8

H.J. Heinz Company was founded in 1869 at Sharpsburg, Pennsylvania, by Henry J. Heinz. The company manufactures and markets food products throughout the world including ketchup, condiments and sauces, frozen food, pet food, soups, and tuna. For the fiscal years 2001 and 2000, H.J. Heinz reported the following (in thousands):

| | Year Ending May 2, | |
	2001	**2000**
Net sales	$9,430,422	$9,407,949
Accounts Receivable	1,383,550	1,237,804

Assume that the accounts receivable (in thousands) were $1,163,915 at the beginning of the 2000 fiscal year.

a. Compute the accounts receivable turnover for 2001 and 2000. Round to one decimal place.

b. What conclusions can be drawn from these analyses regarding Heinz's efficiency in collecting receivables?

EXERCISE 6-22
Accounts receivable turnover
OBJECTIVE 8

Use the data in Exercises 6-20 and 6-21 to analyze the accounts receivable turnover ratios of The Limited and H.J. Heinz Company.

a. Compute the average accounts receivable turnover ratio for The Limited and H.J. Heinz Company for the years shown in Exercises 6-20 and 6-21.

b. Does The Limited or H.J. Heinz Company have the higher average accounts receivable turnover ratio?

c. Explain the logic underlying your answer in (b).

EXERCISE 6-23
Inventory turnover
OBJECTIVE 8

The following data were taken from recent annual reports of **Gateway, Inc.**, a vendor of personal computers and related products, and **American Greetings Corporation**, a manufacturer and distributor of greeting cards and related products:

	Gateway	**American Greetings**
Cost of goods sold	$5,921,651,000	$757,080,000
Inventory, end of year	167,924,000	251,289,000
Inventory, beginning of the year	152,531,000	271,205,000

a. Determine the inventory turnover for Gateway and American Greetings.

b. Would you expect American Greetings' inventory turnover to be higher or lower than Gateway's? Why?

EXERCISE 6-24
Inventory turnover
OBJECTIVE 8

Kroger Co, **Albertson's Inc.**, and **Safeway Inc.** are the three largest grocery chains in the United States. Inventory management is an important aspect of the grocery retail business. The balance sheets for these three companies indicated the following inventory information (in millions):

	Fiscal 2000 **End-of-Year Balance**	**Fiscal 1999** **End-of-Year Balance**
Albertson's	$3,364	$3,481
Kroger	4,066	3,938
Safeway	2,508	2,445

The cost of goods sold (in millions) for each company during fiscal year 2000 follows:

	Cost of goods sold **for fiscal year 2000**
Albertson's	$26,336
Kroger	35,806
Safeway	22,482

a. Determine the inventory turnover for the three companies for fiscal 2000.

b. Interpret your results in (a).

Problems

PROBLEM 6 | 1
*Details of notes
receivable*
OBJECTIVE 1

✓ a. Due date, July 1;
maturity value: $12,120

Diaz Co. produces advertising videos. During the last six months of the current fiscal year, Diaz Co. received the following notes:

	Date	Face Amount	Term	Interest Rate
a.	May 17	$12,000	45 days	8%
b.	July 6	10,000	60 days	9%
c.	Aug. 1	16,500	90 days	8%
d.	Sept. 1	20,000	90 days	7%
e.	Nov. 29	18,000	60 days	9%
f.	Dec. 18	36,000	60 days	12%

Instructions

1. Determine the due date for each note, identifying each note by letter.
2. Determine the amount of interest due at maturity and the maturity value of each note, identifying each note by letter.

PROBLEM 6 | 2
*Estimating allowance for
doubtful accounts*
OBJECTIVE 3

✓ 2. $40,136

Beda Wigs Company supplies wigs and hair care products to beauty salons throughout California and the Pacific Northwest. The accounts receivable clerk for Beda Wigs prepared the following aging-of-receivables schedule as of the end of business on December 31, 2003:

Aging of Accounts Receivables
December 31, 2003

					Days Past Due			
Customer	Balance	Not Past Due	1–30	31–60	61–90	91–120	Over 120
Austin Beauty	10,000	10,000					
Blount Wigs	5,500			5,500			
Zabka's	2,900		2,900				
Totals	780,000	398,600	197,250	98,750	33,300	29,950	22,150

Beda Wigs has a past history of uncollectible accounts by age category, as follows:

Age Class	Percentage Uncollectible
Not past due	1%
1–30 days past due	4
31–60 days past due	8
61–90 days past due	15
91–120 days past due	30
Over 120 days past due	80

Instructions

1. Estimate the allowance for doubtful accounts, based on the aging-of-receivables schedule.
2. Assume that the allowance for doubtful accounts for Beda Wigs has a balance of $11,340 before adjustment on December 31, 2003. Illustrate the effect of the adjustment for uncollectible accounts on the accounts and financial statements.

(continued)

Chapter 6

3. Assume that on March 23, 2004, the Blount Wigs balance of $5,500 was written off as uncollectible. Illustrate the effects of the write-off of the Blount Wigs account on Beda's accounts and financial statements.
4. Assume that on November 2, 2004, Blount Wigs paid $3,000 on its account that had been previously written off on March 23. Illustrate the effects of the subsequent collection on the Blount Wigs account on the accounts and financial statements.

PROBLEM 6 | 3

Estimating uncollectible receivables

OBJECTIVE 3

✓ 1. 2000 (b) $14,400

For several years, Sheepshank Co.'s sales have been on a "cash only" basis. On January 1, 2000, however, Sheepshank began offering credit on terms of n/30. The amount of the adjusting entry to record the estimated uncollectible receivables at the end of each year has been ¹/₄ of 1% of credit sales, which is the rate reported as the average for the industry. Credit sales and the year-end balances in Allowance for Doubtful Accounts for the past four years are as follows:

Year	Credit Sales	Allowance for Doubtful Accounts
2000	$7,800,000	$ 5,100
2001	8,000,000	11,100
2002	8,100,000	16,850
2003	9,250,000	25,375

Carisa Parker, president of Sheepshank Co., is concerned that the method used to account for and write off uncollectible receivables is unsatisfactory. She has asked for your advice in the analysis of past operations in this area and for recommendations for change.

Instructions

1. Determine the amount of (a) the addition to Allowance for Doubtful Accounts and (b) the accounts written off for each of the four years.
2. a. Advise Carisa Parker as to whether the estimate of ¹/₄ of 1% of credit sales appears reasonable.
   b. Assume that after discussing (a) with Carisa Parker, she asked you what action might be taken to determine what the balance of Allowance for Doubtful Accounts should be at December 31, 2003, and what possible changes, if any, you might recommend in accounting for uncollectible receivables. How would you respond?

PROBLEM 6 | 4

Periodic inventory by three methods

OBJECTIVE 5, 6

✓ 1. $7,875

Details regarding the inventory of appliances at July 1, 2003, purchases invoices during the year, and the inventory count at June 30, 2004, for Sixpack Appliances are summarized as follows:

Model	Inventory, July 1	Purchases Invoices 1st	2nd	3rd	Inventory Count, June 30
A103	7 at $242	6 at $250	5 at $260	10 at $259	9
C743	6 at 80	5 at 82	8 at 89	8 at 90	7
F1010	2 at 108	2 at 110	3 at 128	3 at 130	3
H142	8 at 88	4 at 79	3 at 85	6 at 92	8
P813	2 at 250	2 at 260	4 at 271	4 at 272	5
Q661	5 at 160	4 at 170	4 at 175	7 at 180	8
W490	—	4 at 150	4 at 200	4 at 202	5

Instructions

1. Determine the cost of the inventory on June 30, 2004, by using the first-in, first-out method. Present data in columnar form, using the following headings:

Model	Quantity	Unit Cost	Total Cost

If the inventory of a particular model comprises one entire purchase plus a portion of another purchase acquired at a different unit cost, use a separate line for each purchase.

2. Determine the cost of the inventory on June 30, 2004, by the last-in, first-out method, following the procedures indicated in (1).
3. Determine the cost of the inventory on June 30, 2004, by the average cost method, using the columnar headings indicated in (1).
4. Discuss which method (fifo or lifo) would be preferred for income tax purposes in periods of (a) rising prices and (b) declining prices.

PROBLEM 6 | 5
Lower-of-cost-or-market inventory
OBJECTIVE 7

✓ Total LCM, $38,835

Data on the physical inventory of Minish Company as of December 31, 2005, are presented here.

Description	Inventory Quantity	Unit Market Price
A10	40	$ 57
B23	15	200
D82	20	140
E34	125	26
F17	18	550
H99	70	15
K41	5	390
M21	400	6
R72	100	17
T15	7	235
BD1	150	18
MS3	9	700

Quantity and cost data from the last purchase invoice of the year and the next-to-the-last purchase invoice are summarized as follows:

Description	Last Purchase Invoice Quantity Purchased	Last Purchase Invoice Unit Cost	Next-to-the-Last Purchase Invoice Quantity Purchased	Next-to-the-Last Purchase Invoice Unit Cost
A10	25	$ 60	30	$ 58
B23	30	208	20	205
D82	10	145	25	142
E34	150	25	100	24
F17	10	565	10	560
H99	100	15	100	14
K41	10	387	5	384
M21	500	6	500	6
R72	80	19	50	18
T15	5	255	4	260
BD1	100	20	75	19
MS3	7	701	6	699

Instructions

Determine the inventory at cost and at the lower of cost or market, using the first-in, first-out method. Record the appropriate unit costs on an inventory sheet and complete the pricing of the inventory. When there are two different unit costs applicable to an item, proceed as follows:

1. Draw a line through the quantity, and insert the quantity and unit cost of the last purchase.
2. On the following line, insert the quantity and unit cost of the next-to-the-last purchase.
3. Total the Cost and Market columns and insert the lower of the two totals in the Lower of C or M column. The first item on the inventory sheet has been completed as an example.

Inventory Sheet
December 31, 2005

Description	Inventory Quantity	Unit Cost Price	Unit Market Price	Total Cost (C)	Total Market (M)	Total Lower of C or M
A10	~~40~~ 25	$60	$57	$1,500	$1,425	
	15	58		870	855	
				$2,370	$2,280	$2,280

Activities

Activity 6-1
Value of receivables

The following is an excerpt from a conversation between Kay Kinder, the president and owner of Retriever Wholesale Co., and Michele Stephens, Retriever's controller. The conversation took place on January 4, 2003, shortly after Michele began preparing the financial statements for the year ending December 31, 2002.

Michele: Kay, I've completed my analysis of the collectibility of our accounts receivable. My staff and I estimate that the allowance for doubtful accounts should be somewhere between $60,000 and $90,000. Right now, the balance of the allowance account is $18,000.

Kay: Oh, no! We're already below the estimated earnings projection I gave the bank last year. We used that as a basis for convincing the bank to loan us $100,000. People there are going to be upset! Is there any way we can increase the allowance without the adjustment increasing expenses?

Michele: I'm afraid not. The allowance can be increased only by increasing the uncollectible accounts expense account.

Kay: Well, I guess we're stuck. The bank will just have to live with it. But let's increase the allowance by only $42,000. That gets us into our range of estimates with the minimum expense increase.

Michele: Kay, there is one more thing we need to discuss.

Kay: What now?

Michele: Jill, my staff accountant, noticed that you haven't made any payments on your receivable for over a year. Also, it has increased from $20,000 last year to $80,000. Jill thinks we ought to reclassify it as a noncurrent asset and report it as an "other receivable."

Kay: What's the problem? Didn't we just include it in accounts receivable last year?

Michele: Yes, but last year it was immaterial.

Kay: Look, I'll make a $60,000 payment next week. So let's report it as we did last year.

If you were Michele, how would you address Kay's suggestions?

Activity 6-2
Granting credit

GROUP

In groups of three or four, determine how credit is typically granted to customers. Interview an individual responsible for granting credit for a bank, a department store, an automobile dealer, or other business in your community. You should ask such questions as the following:

1. What procedures are used to decide whether to grant credit to a customer?
2. What procedures are used to try to collect from customers who are delinquent in their payments?
3. Approximately what percentage of customers' accounts are written off as uncollectible in a year?

Summarize your findings in a report to the class.

Activity 6-3
Lifo and inventory flow

The following is an excerpt from a conversation between John Lacy, the warehouse manager for Leconte Wholesale Co., and its accountant, Leanne Huskey. Leconte Wholesale operates a large regional warehouse that supplies produce and other grocery products to grocery stores in smaller communities.

John: Leanne, can you explain what's going on here with these monthly statements?

Leanne: Sure, John. How can I help you?

John: I don't understand this last-in, first-out inventory procedure. It just doesn't make sense.

Leanne: Well, what it means is that we assume that the last goods we receive are the first ones sold. So the inventory is made up of the items we purchased first.

John: Yes, but that's my problem. It doesn't work that way! We always distribute the oldest produce first. Some of that produce is perishable! We can't keep any of it very long or it'll spoil.

Leanne: John, you don't understand. We only assume that the products we distribute are the last ones received. We don't actually have to distribute the goods in this way.

John: I always thought that accounting was supposed to show what really happened. It all sounds like "make believe" to me! Why not report what really happens?

Respond to John's concerns.

Activity 6-4
Compare inventory cost flow assumptions

GROUP

In groups of three or four, examine the financial statements of a well-known retailing business. You may obtain the financial statements you need from one of the following sources:

1. Your school or local library.
2. The investor relations department of the company.
3. The company's Web site on the Internet.
4. EDGAR (Electronic Data Gathering, Analysis, and Retrieval), the electronic archives of financial statements filed with the Securities and Exchange Commission. SEC documents can be retrieved using the EdgarScan service from PricewaterhouseCoopers at http://edgarscan.pwcglobal.com. To obtain annual report information, type in a company name in the appropriate space. EdgarScan will list the reports available to you for the company you've selected. Select the most recent annual report filing, identified as a 10-K or 10-K405. EdgarScan provides an outline of the report, including the separate financial statements. You can double-click the income statement and balance sheet for the selected company into an Excel spreadsheet for further analysis.

Determine the cost flow assumption(s) that the company is using for its inventory and whether the company is using the lower-of-cost-or-market rule. Prepare a written summary of your findings.

Activity 6-5
Fifo vs. lifo

The following footnote was taken from the 2001 financial statements of **Walgreen Co.**:

> Inventories are valued on a . . . last-in, first-out (lifo) cost . . . basis. At August 31, 2001 and 2000, inventories would have been greater by $637,600,000 and $574,800,000 respectively, if they had been valued on a lower of first-in, first-out (fifo) cost or market basis.

Additional data are as follows:

Earnings before income taxes, 2001	$1,422,700,000
Total lifo inventories, August 31, 2001	3,482,400,000

Based on the preceding data, determine (a) what the total inventories at August 31, 2001, would have been, using the fifo method, and (b) what the earnings before income taxes for the year ended August 31, 2001, would have been if fifo had been used instead of lifo.

Activity 6-6
Accounts receivable turnover

Best Buy Company is a specialty retailer of consumer electronics, including personal computers, entertainment software, and appliances. Best Buy operates retail stores in addition to the BestBuy.com, MediaPlay.com, OnCue.com, and MagnoliaHiFi.com Web sites. For the fiscal years ending March 3, 2002 and 2001, Best Buy reported the following (in millions):

	Year Ending March 3,	
	2002	**2001**
Net sales	$19,597	$15,327
Accounts receivable at end of year	247	209

Assume that all sales are credit sales and that the accounts receivable (in millions) were $189 at the beginning of the 2001 fiscal year.

1. Compute the accounts receivable turnover for 2002 and 2001. Round to one decimal place.
2. What conclusions regarding Best Buy's efficiency in collecting receivables can be drawn from (1)?
3. Based on (1), how many days does it take Best Buy to convert its receivables to cash in 2002?
4. For its fiscal years ending in 2002 and 2001, **Circuit City** has an accounts receivable turnover of 19.5 and 22.0, respectively. Compare Best Buy's efficiency in collecting receivables with that of Circuit City. (*Note:* The data for Circuit City's 2002 and 2001 fiscal years are shown in Exercise 6-19.)
5. What assumption did we make for the Circuit City and Best Buy ratio computations that might distort the two company ratios and therefore cause the ratios not to be comparable?

Activity 6-7
Accounts receivable turnover

Earthlink, Inc., is a nationwide Internet service provider (ISP). Earthlink provides a variety of services to its customers, including narrowband access, broadband or high-speed access, and Web hosting services. For the years ending December 31, 2001 and 2000, Earthlink reported the following (in thousands):

	Year Ending December 31,	
	2001	**2000**
Net sales	$1,244,928	$986,630
Accounts receivable at end of year	40,624	49,568

Assume that all sales are credit sales and that the accounts receivable (in thousands) were $16,367 at January 1, 2000.

1. Compute the accounts receivable turnover for 2001 and 2000. Round to one decimal place.
2. What conclusions can be drawn from (1) regarding Earthlink's efficiency in collecting receivables?

3. Given the nature of Earthlink's operations, do you believe its accounts receivable would be higher or lower than a typical manufacturing company, such as **Boeing** or **Kellogg**? Explain.

Activity 6-8
Accounts receivable turnover

The accounts receivable turnover ratio varies across companies, depending on the nature of the company's operations. For example, an accounts receivable turnover of 6.0 for an Internet services provider is unacceptable but might be excellent for a manufacturer of specialty milling equipment. A list of well-known companies follows.

Alcoa
AutoZone
Barnes & Noble
Coca-Cola
Delta Air Lines
Gillette
Home Depot
IBM
Kroger
Maytag Corporation
Wal-Mart
Whirlpool

1. Using the PriceWaterhouseCoopers web site, http://edgarscan.pwcglobal.com, look up each of the preceding companies by entering the first letters of their names. Click on each company's name and then scroll down the page to find each company's accounts receivable turnover ratio.
2. Categorize each of the preceding companies as to whether its turnover ratio is above or below 15.
3. Based on (2), identify a characteristic of companies with accounts receivable turnover ratios above 15.

Activity 6-9
Inventory ratios for Dell and HP

Dell Computer Corporation and **Hewlett-Packard Company (HP)** are both manufacturers of computer equipment and peripherals. However, the two companies follow two different strategies. Dell follows a build-to-order strategy, allowing the consumer to order the computer from a web page. The order is then manufactured and shipped to the customer within days of the order. In contrast, HP follows a build-to-stock strategy, by which the computer is first built for inventory and then sold from inventory to retailers, such as **Best Buy**. The following financial statement information is provided for Dell and HP for a recent fiscal year (in millions):

	Dell	HP
Inventory, beginning of period	$ 391	$ 5,699
Inventory, end of period	400	5,204
Cost of goods sold	25,445	28,370

The two strategies are indicated in the difference between the inventory turnover and number of days' sales in inventory ratio for the two companies.

a. Determine the inventory turnover ratio for each company.
b. Interpret the difference between the ratios for the two companies.

Answers to Self–Study Questions _____

1. **B** The estimate of uncollectible accounts, $8,500 (answer C), is the amount of the desired balance of Allowance for Doubtful Accounts after adjustment. The amount of the current provision to be made for uncollectible accounts expense is thus $6,000 (answer B), which is the amount that must be added to the Allowance for Doubtful Accounts balance of $2,500 (answer A), so that the account will have the desired balance of $8,500.

2. **B** The amount expected to be realized from accounts receivable is the balance of Accounts Receivable, $100,000, less the balance of Allowance for Doubtful Accounts, $7,000, or $93,000 (answer B).

3. **A** The fifo method (answer A) is based on the assumption that costs are charged against revenue in the order in which they were incurred. The lifo method (answer B) charges the most recent costs incurred against revenue, and the average cost method (answer C) charges a weighted average of unit costs of items sold against revenue. The perpetual inventory system (answer D) is a system and not a method of costing.

4. **D** The fifo method of costing is based on the assumption that costs should be charged against revenue in the order in which they were incurred (first-in, first-out). Thus, the most recent costs are assigned to inventory. The 35 units would be assigned a unit cost of $23 (answer D).

5. **B** When the price level is steadily rising, the earlier unit costs are lower than recent unit costs. Under the fifo method (answer B), these earlier costs are matched against revenue to yield the highest possible net income. A physical inventory (answer D) is a count of the merchandise, not a method of costing.

7

LEARNING OBJECTIVES

OBJECTIVE 1
Define, classify, and account for the cost of fixed assets.

OBJECTIVE 2
Compute depreciation using the straight-line and declining-balance methods.

OBJECTIVE 3
Describe the accounting for depletion of natural resources.

OBJECTIVE 4
Describe the accounting for the disposal of fixed assets.

OBJECTIVE 5
Classify fixed asset costs as either capital expenditures or revenue expenditures.

OBJECTIVE 6
Describe accounting for intangible assets.

OBJECTIVE 7
Describe how depreciation expense is reported in an income statement, and prepare a balance sheet that includes fixed assets and intangible assets.

OBJECTIVE 8
Analyze the utilization of fixed assets.

Fixed Assets and Intangible Assets

Fixed assets are key elements of implementing a business's strategy. Businesses need fixed assets to operate. For example, a manufacturer needs equipment to make its product. Since equipment and other fixed assets use significant business resources, managers must clearly understand their business objectives and strategies before making significant purchases.

A business strives to have the right quantity and the right type of fixed assets. Overinvesting in fixed assets can lead a company into financial difficulty. For example, **Renaissance Cruise Lines**, the world's fifth largest leisure cruise line, expanded aggressively during the late 1990s. The company declared bankruptcy in late 2001 because it was unable to book enough passengers on its 10 ships to be profitable. Many argue that some Internet companies (e.g., **Pets.com**, **eToys**, and **Webvan**) failed because they invested significant resources in fixed assets without a clear strategy for earning profits. In contrast, underinvesting in fixed assets can limit a business. For example, **Pacific Gas and Electric Co.** underinvested in power-generating equipment, resulting in electricity shortages in portions of California.

In this chapter, we illustrate accounting for fixed asset acquisitions, use, and dispositions. We also illustrate tools for analyzing a business's effectiveness in managing fixed assets. Finally, we describe accounting for intangible assets.

Nature of Fixed Assets

OBJECTIVE   1

Define, classify, and
account for the cost of
fixed assets.

Why is a "major purchase" different than other expenditures that you make? More
than likely, the purchase is expensive and long-lived. As a result, you are careful when
making this type of purchase. The same is true for a business. A business makes "major purchases" of equipment, furniture, tools, machinery, buildings, and land. These
assets, which are called **fixed assets**, are long-term or relatively permanent assets.
They are *tangible assets* because they exist physically. They are owned and used by the
business and are not offered for sale as part of normal operations. Other descriptive
titles for these assets are *plant assets* or *property, plant, and equipment.*

The fixed assets of a business can be a significant part of its total assets. Exhibit 1
shows the percentage of fixed assets to total assets for some select companies, divided
between service, manufacturing, and merchandising firms. As you can see, the fixed
assets for most firms comprise a significant proportion of their total assets. In contrast, **Computer Associates** is a consulting firm that relies less on fixed assets to deliver value to customers.

EXHIBIT 1

*Fixed Assets as a
Percentage of Total
Assets—Selected
Companies*

	Fixed Assets as a Percentage of Total Assets
Service Firms	
Pacific Gas and Electric Co.	47%
Sprint Corporation	59
Computer Associates	6
Manufacturing Firms	
Sun Microsystems Inc.	15
Boeing Co.	21
E.I. DuPont De Nemours & Co.	36
Merchandising Firms	
Barnes & Noble Inc.	49
Kroger Company	48
Wal-Mart Stores Inc.	52

Classifying Costs

Exhibit 2 displays questions that help classify costs. If the purchased item is long lived,
it should be *capitalized*, which means it should appear on the balance sheet as an asset. Otherwise, the cost should be reported as an expense on the income statement.
Capitalized costs are normally expected to last more than a year. If the asset is also
used for a productive purpose that involves a repeated use or benefit, it should be
classified as a fixed asset, such as land, buildings, or equipment. An asset need not actually be used on an ongoing basis or even often. For example, standby equipment for
use in the event of a breakdown of regular equipment or for use only during peak periods is included in fixed assets. Fixed assets that have been abandoned or are no
longer used should not be classified as a fixed asset.

Fixed assets are owned and used by the business and are not offered for resale.
Long-lived assets held for resale are not classified as fixed assets but should be listed
on the balance sheet in a section entitled *investments*. For example, undeveloped land
acquired as an investment for resale would be classified as an investment, not land.

EXHIBIT 2
Classifying Costs

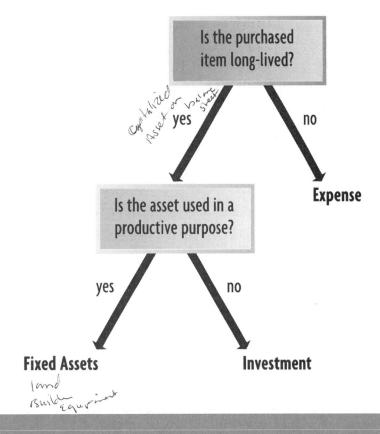

Is the purchased item long-lived?

— yes *(handwritten: Capitalized Asset on balance sheet)* → Is the asset used in a productive purpose?
— no → **Expense**

Is the asset used in a productive purpose?
— yes → **Fixed Assets** *(handwritten: land, Building, Equipment)*
— no → **Investment**

BUSINESS STRATEGY

Hub-and-Spoke or Point-to-Point?

Southwest Airlines uses a simple fare structure featuring low, unrestricted, unlimited, everyday coach fares. These fares are possible by Southwest's use of a point-to-point rather than hub-and-spoke business strategy. United, Delta, and American employ a hub-and-spoke strategy in which an airline establishes major hubs that serve as connecting links to other cities. For example, Delta has established major connecting hubs in Atlanta, Cincinnati, and Salt Lake City. In contrast, Southwest focuses on point-to-point service between selected cities with more than 300 one-way, nonstop city pairs with an average length of 500 miles and average flying time of 1.5 hours. As a result,

Southwest minimizes connections, delays, and total trip time. Southwest also focuses on serving conveniently located satellite or downtown airports, such as Dallas Love Field, Houston Hobby, and Chicago Midway. Because these airports are normally less congested than hub airports, Southwest is better able to maintain high employee productivity and reliable ontime performance. This operating strategy permits the company to achieve high asset utilization of its fixed assets, such as its 737 aircraft. For example, aircraft are scheduled to spend only 25 minutes at the gate, thereby reducing the number of aircraft and gate facilities that would otherwise be required.

The Cost of Fixed Assets

The costs of acquiring fixed assets include all amounts spent to get the asset in place and ready for use. For example, freight costs and the costs of installing equipment are included as part of the asset's total cost. Exhibit 3 summarizes some of the common costs of acquiring fixed assets. These costs should be recorded by increasing the related fixed asset account, such as Land,[1] Building, Land Improvements, and Machinery and Equipment.

Only costs necessary for preparing a long-lived asset for use should be included as a cost of the asset. Unnecessary costs that do not increase the asset's usefulness are recorded as an expense. For example, the following costs are included as expenses:

- Vandalism.

- Mistakes in installation.

- Uninsured theft.

- Damage during unpacking and installing.

- Fines for not obtaining proper permits from governmental agencies.

Accounting for Depreciation

OBJECTIVE   2

Compute depreciation using the straight-line and declining-balance methods.

As we have discussed in earlier chapters, land has an unlimited life and therefore can provide unlimited services. On the other hand, other fixed assets such as equipment, buildings, and land improvements lose their ability over time to provide services. As a result, the costs of equipment, buildings, and land improvements should be transferred to expense accounts in a systematic manner during their expected useful lives. This periodic transfer of cost to expense is called **depreciation**.

The adjustment for depreciation is usually made at the end of each month or at the end of the year. This adjustment increases *Depreciation Expense* and the *contra asset* account entitled *Accumulated Depreciation* or *Allowance for Depreciation*. The use of a contra asset account allows the original cost to remain unchanged in the fixed asset account.

Factors that cause a decline in a fixed asset's ability to provide services may be identified as physical depreciation or functional depreciation. *Physical depreciation* occurs from wear and tear from use and from the effects of weather conditions. *Functional depreciation* occurs when a fixed asset is no longer able to provide services at the level for which it was intended. Advances in technology have made functional depreciation an increasingly important cause of depreciation. For example, a personal computer made in the 1980s is not able to provide an Internet connection.

The term *depreciation* as used in accounting is often misunderstood because the same term is also used in business to mean a decline in the market value of an asset. However, the amount of a fixed asset's unexpired cost reported in the balance sheet usually does not agree with the amount that could be realized from its sale. Fixed assets are held for use in a business rather than for sale. Since the business is assumed

---

[1]As discussed here, land is assumed to be used only as a location or site, not for its mineral deposits or other natural resources.

EXHIBIT 3
Costs of Acquiring Fixed Assets

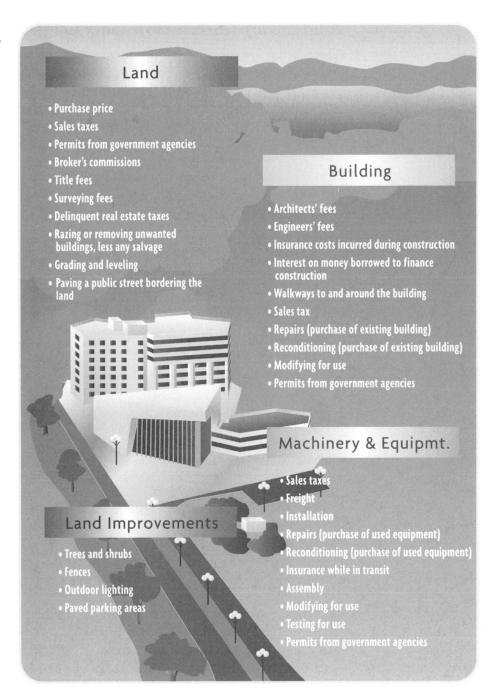

Land

- Purchase price
- Sales taxes
- Permits from government agencies
- Broker's commissions
- Title fees
- Surveying fees
- Delinquent real estate taxes
- Razing or removing unwanted buildings, less any salvage
- Grading and leveling
- Paving a public street bordering the land

Building

- Architects' fees
- Engineers' fees
- Insurance costs incurred during construction
- Interest on money borrowed to finance construction
- Walkways to and around the building
- Sales tax
- Repairs (purchase of existing building)
- Reconditioning (purchase of existing building)
- Modifying for use
- Permits from government agencies

Machinery & Equipmt.

- Sales taxes
- Freight
- Installation
- Repairs (purchase of used equipment)
- Reconditioning (purchase of used equipment)
- Insurance while in transit
- Assembly
- Modifying for use
- Testing for use
- Permits from government agencies

Land Improvements

- Trees and shrubs
- Fences
- Outdoor lighting
- Paved parking areas

to be a going concern, a decision to dispose of a fixed asset is based mainly on the usefulness of the asset to the business, not on its market value.

Another common misunderstanding is that depreciation provides cash needed to replace fixed assets as they wear out. This misunderstanding probably occurs because depreciation, unlike most expenses, does not require an outlay of cash in the period in which it is recorded. The cash account is neither increased nor decreased by the periodic entries that transfer the cost of fixed assets to depreciation expense accounts.

Factors in Computing Depreciation Expense

Three factors are considered in determining the amount of depreciation expense to be recognized each period. These three factors are (1) the fixed asset's initial cost, (2) its expected useful life, and (3) **residual value**, its estimated value at the end of its useful life. Residual value is also called *scrap value, salvage value,* or *trade-in value.* Exhibit 4 shows the relationship among the three factors and the periodic depreciation expense.

EXHIBIT 4
*Factors That Determine
Depreciation Expense*

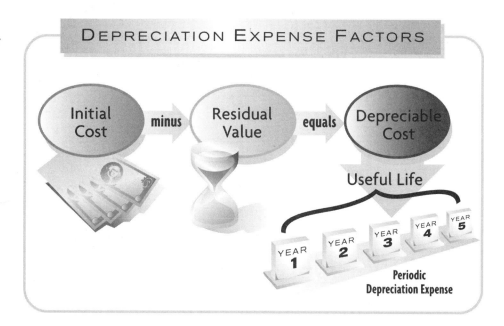

A fixed asset's residual value at the end of its expected useful life must be estimated at the time the asset is placed in service. If a fixed asset is expected to have little or no residual value when it is taken out of service, its initial cost should be spread over its expected useful life as depreciation expense. If, however, a fixed asset is expected to have a significant residual value, the difference between its initial cost and its residual value, called the asset's *depreciable cost,* is the amount that is spread over the asset's useful life as depreciation expense.

A fixed asset's *expected useful life* must also be estimated at the time the asset is placed in service. Estimates of expected useful lives are available from various trade associations and other publications. It is not uncommon for different companies to have different useful lives for similar assets. For example, the primary useful life for buildings is 50 years for **JC Penney Co.**, but varies from 10 to 40 years for **Tandy Corporation**, which operates **Radio Shack**. For federal income tax purposes, the Internal Revenue Service (IRS) has established guidelines for useful lives. For example, the IRS useful life guideline for most vehicles is 5 years, and the designated life for most machinery and equipment is 7 years. These guidelines are also helpful in determining depreciation for financial reporting purposes.

Guidelines are also necessary for determining when an asset is placed into and out of service. In practice, many businesses assume that assets placed in or taken out of service during the first half of a month are treated as if the event occurred on the first day of *that* month. That is, these businesses compute depreciation on these assets for the entire month. Likewise, all fixed asset additions and deductions during the second half of a month are treated as if the event occurred on the first day of the *next* month. We will follow this practice in this chapter.

A business is not required to use a single method of computing depreciation for all of its depreciable assets. The methods used in the accounts and financial statements may also differ from the methods used in determining income taxes and property taxes.

STRAIGHT-LINE METHOD   The **straight-line method** provides for the same amount of depreciation expense for each year of the asset's useful life. For example, assume that the cost of a depreciable asset is $24,000, its estimated residual value is $2,000, and its estimated life is 5 years. The annual depreciation is computed as follows:

$$\frac{\$24,000 \text{ cost} - \$2,000 \text{ estimated residual value}}{5 \text{ years estimated life}} = \frac{\$4,400 \text{ annual}}{\text{depreciation}}$$

When an asset is used for only part of a year, the annual depreciation is prorated. For example, assume that the fiscal year ends on December 31 and that the asset in the preceding example is placed in service on October 1. The depreciation for the first fiscal year of use would be $1,100 ($4,400 × 3/12).

For ease in applying the straight-line method, the annual depreciation may be converted to a percentage of the depreciable cost. This percentage is determined by dividing 100% by the number of years of useful life. For example, a useful life of 20 years converts to a 5% rate (100%/20), 8 years converts to a 12.5% rate (100%/8), and so on.[2] In the preceding example, the annual depreciation of $4,400 can be computed by multiplying the depreciable cost of $22,000 by 20% (100%/5).

The straight-line method is simple and widely used. It provides a reasonable transfer of costs to periodic expense when the asset's use and the related revenues from its use are about the same from period to period.

DECLINING-BALANCE METHOD   The **declining-balance method** provides for a declining periodic expense over the estimated useful life of the asset. To apply this method, the annual straight-line depreciation rate is doubled. For example, the declining-balance rate for an asset with an estimated life of 5 years is 40%, which is double the straight-line rate of 20% (100%/5).

For the first year of use, the cost of the asset is multiplied by the declining-balance rate. After the first year, the declining **book value** or *net book value* (initial asset cost minus accumulated depreciation) of the asset is multiplied by this rate. To illustrate, the annual declining-balance depreciation for an asset with an estimated 5-year life and a cost of $24,000 is shown on the following page.

---

[2]The depreciation rate may also be expressed as a fraction. For example, the annual straight-line rate for an asset with a 3-year useful life is 1/3.

Year	Cost	Accum. Depr. at Beginning of Year	Book Value at Beginning of Year	Rate	Depreciation for Year	Book Value at End of Year
1	$24,000		$24,000.00	40%	$9,600.00	$14,400.00
2	24,000	$ 9,600.00	14,400.00	40	5,760.00	8,640.00
3	24,000	15,360.00	8,640.00	40	3,456.00	5,184.00
4	24,000	18,816.00	5,184.00	40	2,073.60	3,110.40
5	24,000	20,889.60	3,110.40	—	1,110.40	2,000.00

You should note that when the declining-balance method is used, the estimated residual value is *not* considered in determining the depreciation rate. It is also ignored in computing the periodic depreciation. However, the asset should not be depreciated below its estimated residual value. In the preceding example, the estimated residual value was $2,000. Therefore, the depreciation for the fifth year is $1,110.40 ($3,110.40 − $2,000.00) instead of $1,244.16 (40% × $3,110.40).

In the example, we assumed that the first use of the asset occurred at the beginning of the fiscal year. This is normally not the case in practice, however, and depreciation for the first partial year of use must be computed. For example, assume that this asset was in service at the end of the *third* month of the fiscal year. In this case, only a portion ($9/12$) of the first full year's depreciation of $9,600 is allocated to the first fiscal year. Thus, depreciation of $7,200 ($9/12$ × $9,600) is allocated to the first partial year of use. The depreciation for the second fiscal year is then $6,720 [40% × ($24,000 − $7,200)].

Comparing Depreciation Methods

The straight-line method provides for the same periodic amounts of depreciation expense over the life of the asset. An **accelerated depreciation method** is a depreciation method that provides for a higher depreciation amount in the first year of the asset's use, followed by a gradually declining amount of depreciation. The declining-balance method is an example. It is most appropriate when the decline in an asset's productivity or earning power is greater in the early years of its use than in later years. Furthermore, using this method is often justified because repairs tend to increase with the age of an asset. The reduced amounts of depreciation in later years are thus offset to some extent by increased repair expenses.

The periodic depreciation amounts for the straight-line method and the declining-balance method are compared in Exhibit 5. This comparison is based on an asset cost of $24,000, an estimated life of 5 years, and an estimated residual value of $2,000.

Depreciation for Federal Income Tax

The Internal Revenue Code specifies the *Modified Accelerated Cost Recovery System (MACRS)* for use by businesses in computing depreciation for tax purposes. MACRS specifies eight classes of useful life and depreciation rates for each class. The two most common classes, other than real estate, are the 5-year class and the 7-year class.[3] The 5-year class includes automobiles and light-duty trucks, and the 7-year class includes most machinery and equipment. The depreciation deduction for these two classes is similar to that computed using the declining-balance method.

[3]Real estate is in 27$\frac{1}{2}$-year classes and 31$\frac{1}{2}$-year classes and is depreciated by the straight-line method.

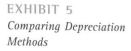

EXHIBIT 5
Comparing Depreciation Methods

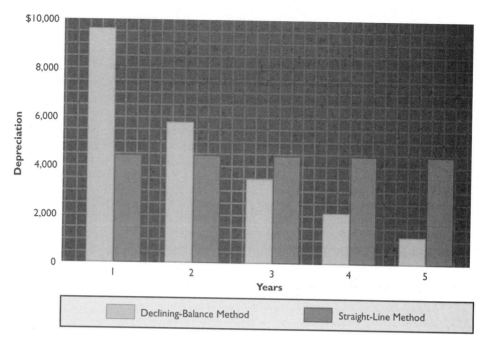

In using the MACRS rates, residual value is ignored, and all fixed assets are assumed to be put in and taken out of service in the middle of the year. For the 5-year-class assets, depreciation is spread over six years, as shown in the following MACRS schedule of depreciation rates:

Year	5-Year-Class Depreciation Rates
1	20.0%
2	32.0
3	19.2
4	11.5
5	11.5
6	5.8
	100.0%

To simplify its record keeping, a business sometimes uses the MACRS method for both financial statement and tax purposes. This is acceptable if MACRS does not result in significantly different amounts than would have been reported using one of the depreciation methods discussed earlier in this chapter.

Using MACRS for both financial statement and tax purposes could, however, hurt a business. In one case, a business that had used MACRS depreciation for its financial statements lost a $1 million order because its fixed assets had low book values. The bank viewed these low book values as inadequate, so it would not loan the business the amount needed to produce the order.[4]

[4]Lee Berton, "Do's and Don'ts," *The Wall Street Journal*, June 10, 1988, p. 34R.

Natural Resources

OBJECTIVE   3

Describe the
accounting for
depletion of natural
resources.

The fixed assets of some businesses include timber, metal ores, minerals, or other natural resources. As these businesses harvest or mine and then sell these resources, a portion of the cost of acquiring them must increase an expense account. This process of transferring the cost of natural resources to an expense account is called **depletion**. The amount of depletion is determined by multiplying the quantity extracted during the period by the depletion rate. This rate is computed by dividing the cost of the mineral deposit by its estimated size.

To illustrate, assume that a business paid $400,000 for the mining rights to a mineral deposit estimated at 1,000,000 tons of ore. The depletion rate is $0.40 per ton ($400,000/1,000,000 tons). If 90,000 tons are mined during the year, the periodic depletion is $36,000 (90,000 tons × $0.40). The effect of recording depletion on the accounts and financial statements follows:

Trans. Date	Balance Sheet			Income Statement		
	Assets	Liabilities	Stockholders' Equity	Revenue	Expense	Net Income
	Accumulated Depletion 36,000				Depletion Exp 36,000	−36,000
Net Effect	−36,000		−36,000		36,000	−36,000
			Retained Earnings			
			(Net Income)			

Like the accumulated depreciation account, Accumulated Depletion is a *contra asset* account. It is reported on the balance sheet as a deduction from the cost of the mineral deposit.

Fixed Asset Disposals

OBJECTIVE   4

Describe the
accounting for the
disposal of fixed
assets.

Fixed assets that are no longer useful may be discarded, sold, or traded[5] for other fixed assets. The details of the entry to record a disposal will vary. In all cases, however, the book value of the asset is removed from the accounts. This is done by decreasing the asset's accumulated depreciation account for its balance on the date of disposal and decreasing the asset account for the cost of the asset.

Discarding Fixed Assets

A fixed asset is not removed from the accounts only because it has been fully depreciated. If the asset is still used by the business, the cost and accumulated depreciation remain in the ledger. This maintains accountability for the asset in the ledger. If the book value of the asset is removed from the ledger, the accounts contain no evidence of the asset's continued existence. In addition, the cost and the accumulated depreciation data on such assets are often needed for property tax and income tax reports.

[5]Accounting for fixed asset exchanges (trades) is a topic covered in advanced accounting courses.

When fixed assets are no longer useful to the business and have no residual or market value, they are discarded. To illustrate, assume that an item of equipment acquired at a cost of $25,000 is fully depreciated with no salvage value at December 31, the end of the preceding fiscal year. On February 14, the equipment is discarded. The effect on the accounts and financial statements is as follows:

Trans. Date	Balance Sheet				Income Statement		
	Assets		Liabilities	Stockholders' Equity	Revenue	Expense	Net Income
2/14	Equipment	−25,000					
	Acc Dep—Equipment	−25,000					
Net Effect		0					
				Retained Earnings			
				(Net Income)			

If an asset has not been fully depreciated, depreciation should be recorded prior to removing it from service and from the accounting records. To illustrate, assume that equipment costing $6,000 is depreciated at an annual straight-line rate of 10%. In addition, assume that on December 31 of the preceding fiscal year, the accumulated depreciation balance, after adjusting entries, is $4,750. Finally, assume that the asset is removed from service on the following March 24. The effect of recording depreciation for the three months of the current period and discarding the asset is as shown:

To record current depreciation on equipment discarded ($600 × 3/12).

Trans. Date	Balance Sheet				Income Statement		
	Assets		Liabilities	Stockholders' Equity	Revenue	Expense	Net Income
3/24	Acc Dep—Equipment	150				Dep Exp—Equip 150	−150
Net Effect		−150		−150		150	−150
				Retained Earnings			
				(Net Income)			

To write off equipment discarded.

Trans. Date	Balance Sheet				Income Statement		
	Assets		Liabilities	Stockholders' Equity	Revenue	Expense	Net Income
3/24	Equipment	−6,000				Loss on Disposal 1,100	−1,100
	Acc Dep—Equipment	−4,900					
Net Effect		−1,100		−1,100		1,100	−1,100
				Retained Earnings			
				(Net Income)			

The loss of $1,100 is recorded because the balance of the accumulated depreciation account ($4,900) is less than the balance in the equipment account ($6,000). Losses on the discarding of fixed assets are nonoperating items and are normally reported in the Other Expense section of the income statement.

Selling Fixed Assets

The effect of selling a fixed asset is similar to that for discarding an asset except that the cash or other asset received is also recorded. If the selling price is more than the book value of the asset, the transaction results in a gain. If the selling price is less than the book value, there is a loss. For example, **H.J. Heinz Company** recognized a gain of $18.2 million on the sale of an office building in the United Kingdom because the selling price exceeded the book value.

To illustrate a sale transaction, assume that equipment is acquired at a cost of $10,000 and is depreciated at an annual straight-line rate of 10%. The building is sold for cash on October 12 of the eighth year of its use. The balance of the accumulated depreciation account as of the preceding December 31 is $7,000. The effect on the accounts and financial statements of updating the depreciation for the nine months of the current year is as follows:

To record current depreciation on equipment sold ($10,000 × 3⁄4 × 10%).

Trans. Date	Balance Sheet			Income Statement		
	Assets	Liabilities	Stockholders' Equity	Revenue	Expense	Net Income
10/12	Acc Dep—Equipment 750				Dep Exp—Equip 750	−750
Net Effect	−750		−750		750	−750
			Retained Earnings			
			(Net Income)			

After the current depreciation is recorded, the book value of the asset is $2,250 ($10,000 − $7,750). The effect of the sale on the accounts and financial statements, assuming three different selling prices, is as follows:

Equipment sold for $2,250. No gain or loss.

Trans. Date	Balance Sheet			Income Statement		
	Assets	Liabilities	Stockholders' Equity	Revenue	Expense	Net Income
10/12	Cash 2,250					
	Equipment −10,000					
	Acc Dep—Equip −7,750					
Net Effect	0					
			Retained Earnings			
			(Net Income)			

Equipment sold for $1,000. Loss of $1,250.

Trans. Date	Balance Sheet			Income Statement		
	Assets	Liabilities	Stockholders' Equity	Revenue	Expense	Net Income
10/12	Cash 1,000				Loss on Sale of Equip 1,250	−1,250
	Equipment −10,000					
	Acc Dep—Equip −7,750					
Net Effect	−1,250		−1,250		1,250	−1,250
			Retained Earnings			
			(Net Income)			

Equipment sold for $3,000. Gain of $750.

Trans. Date	Balance Sheet				Income Statement		
	Assets		Liabilities	Stockholders' Equity	Revenue	Expense	Net Income
10/12	Cash	3,000				Gain on Sale of Equip 750	750
	Equipment	−10,000					
	Acc Dep—Equip	−7,750					
Net Effect		750		750		750	750
				Retained Earnings (Net Income)			

Capital and Revenue Expenditures

OBJECTIVE　5

Classify fixed asset costs as either capital expenditures or revenue expenditures.

The costs incurred for fixed assets can be classified into four stages: preliminary, preacquisition, acquisition or construction, and in-service. These stages are illustrated in Exhibit 6.

EXHIBIT 6
Fixed Asset Project Stages

| Preliminary Stage | Preacquisiton Stage | Acquisition or Construction Stage | In-service Stage |

The *preliminary stage* occurs before management believes acquiring a fixed asset is probable. During this stage, a company may conduct feasibility studies, marketing studies, and financial analyses to determine the viability of a fixed asset acquisition. These costs are not associated with a particular fixed asset, so they must be treated as revenue expenditures.[6] A **revenue expenditure** is a cost that benefits only the current period and is recorded by increasing an expense account.

At the *preacquisition stage*, acquiring the fixed asset has become probable but has not yet occurred. Costs that are incurred during this stage, such as surveys, zoning, and engineering studies, can be associated with a specific fixed asset and should be treated as a capital expenditure. As we stated previously, **capital expenditures** are the costs of acquiring, constructing, adding, or replacing fixed assets.

During the *acquisition* or *construction stage*, the acquisition has occurred or construction has begun, but the fixed asset is not yet ready for use. Costs directly identified with the fixed asset during this stage should be capitalized in a construction in progress account. General and administrative costs should *not* be allocated to fixed asset acquisition or construction for capitalization. These costs are increased to the

---

[6]Payments made to acquire options to purchase fixed assets should be capitalized.

appropriate general and administrative expense account. When the fixed asset is ready for use, the capitalized costs should be transferred from construction in progress to the related fixed asset account.

During the *in-service stage*, the fixed asset is complete and ready for use. During this stage, the fixed asset should be depreciated as described in the previous section. In addition, normal, recurring, or periodic repairs and maintenance activities related to fixed assets during this stage should be charged to maintenance expense for the period. Costs incurred to either acquire additional components of fixed assets or replace existing components of fixed assets should be capitalized, as described next.

An in-service stage fixed asset may include one or more components. A *component* is a tangible portion of a fixed asset that can be separately identified as an asset and depreciated over its own separate expected useful life. For example, the roof and elevator bank of a building could be identified as components that are depreciated separately from the building itself. When a company *acquires* or *constructs a new component*, the costs should be capitalized as described for the previous project stages. Once installed, the component would be depreciated over its useful service life. For example, on April 1, Boxter Company purchased and installed a new crane within a warehouse for $150,000. This cost would be capitalized as a separate component by increasing Equipment—Crane and decreasing Cash.

A company can also *replace a component*. Replacements are accounted for in two steps. First, the book value of the replaced component increases Depreciation Expense and Accumulated Depreciation. That is, the fixed asset component is recognized as being fully depreciated on replacement. In addition, any costs to remove the old component should be charged to expense. Second, the identifiable direct costs associated with the new component are then capitalized. To illustrate, assume that Boxter removes a warehouse roof on August 1 at a cost of $1,000. As of August 1, the old roof has a remaining book value (initial cost less accumulated depreciation) of $9,000.[7] On August 5, the new roof is completed at a cost of $60,000 and is estimated to have a 20-year life, which is the remaining life of the building. First, the cost of removing the old roof must be expensed, and the book value of the replaced roof must be completely depreciated. The effect on the accounts and financial statements of removing the old roof and depreciating its remaining book value is as shown:

Removing old roof at a cost of $1,000.

Trans. Date	Balance Sheet				Income Statement		
	Assets		Liabilities	Stockholders' Equity	Revenue	Expense		Net Income
8/1	Cash	−1,000				Removal Exp	1,000	−1,000
Net Effect		−1,000					1,000	−1,000
				Retained Earnings				
				(Net Income)				

[7]The depreciation expense would be adjusted to reflect depreciation to August 1, as illustrated previously for asset disposals.

Depreciation of remaining book value of old roof.

Trans. Date	Balance Sheet			Income Statement		
	Assets	Liabilities	Stockholders' Equity	Revenue	Expense	Net Income
8/1	Acc Dep—Roof 9,000				Dep Exp—Roof 9,000	−9,000
Net Effect	−9,000		−9,000		9,000	−9,000
			Retained Earnings			
			(Net Income)			

The depreciation of the remaining book value of the old roof reduces its book value to zero. Next, the cost of the new roof must be capitalized as a separate component. The effect on the accounts and financial statements of capitalizing the new roof is as shown:

Trans. Date	Balance Sheet			Income Statement		
	Assets	Liabilities	Stockholders' Equity	Revenue	Expense	Net Income
8/5	Warehouse Roof 60,000					
	Cash −60,000					
Net Effect	0					
			Retained Earnings			
			(Net Income)			

Using the straight-line method, the new roof will be depreciated over 20 years at $3,000 per year ($60,000/20 years).

Intangible Assets

OBJECTIVE   6

Describe the accounting for intangible assets.

Patents, copyrights, trademarks, and goodwill are **intangible assets**: long-lived assets that are useful in the operations of a business and are not held for sale because they do not exist physically.

The basic principles of accounting for intangible assets are like those described earlier for fixed assets. The major concerns are determining (1) the initial cost and (2) the **amortization**—the amount of cost to transfer to expense. Amortization results from the passage of time or a decline in the usefulness of the intangible asset.

Patents

Manufacturers may acquire **patents**, exclusive rights to produce and sell goods with one or more unique features. The federal government issues such rights to inventors. These rights continue in effect for 20 years. A business may purchase patent rights from others or obtain patents developed by its own research and development efforts.

The initial cost of a purchased patent, including any related legal fees, is recorded by increasing an asset account. This cost is written off, or amortized, over the years of the patent's expected usefulness. This period of time may be less than the remaining legal life of the patent. A patent's estimated useful life may also change as technology or consumer tastes change.

The straight-line method is normally used to determine the periodic amortization. Amortization is recorded by increasing an expense account and directly decreasing the patents account. A separate contra asset account is usually *not* used for intangible assets.

To illustrate, assume that at the beginning of its fiscal year, a business acquires patent rights for $100,000. The patent had been granted 6 years earlier by the Federal Patent Office. Although the patent will not expire for 14 years, its remaining useful life is estimated as 5 years. The effect of the amortization of the patent at the end of the fiscal year follows:

Trans. Date	Balance Sheet				Income Statement		
	Assets		Liabilities	Stockholders' Equity	Revenue	Expense	Net Income
12/31	Patents	−20,000				Amort Exp—Patents 20,000	−20,000
Net Effect		−20,000		−20,000		20,000	−20,000
				Retained Earnings			
				(Net Income)			

Rather than purchase patent rights, a business may incur significant costs in developing patents through its own research and development efforts. Such *research and development costs* are usually accounted for as current operating expenses in the period in which they are incurred. Expensing research and development costs is justified because the future benefits from research and development efforts are highly uncertain.

Copyrights and Trademarks

The exclusive right to publish and sell a literary, artistic, or musical composition is granted by a **copyright**. Copyrights are issued by the federal government and extend for 70 years beyond the author's death. The costs of a copyright include all costs of creating the work plus any administrative or legal costs of obtaining the copyright. A copyright that is purchased from another should be recorded at the price paid for it. Copyrights are amortized over their estimated useful lives. For example, **Sony Corporation** states the following amortization policy with respect to its artistic and music intangible assets:

ETHICS IN ACTION

Businesses must honor the copyright held by software companies by eliminating pirated software from corporate computers. The **Business Software Group (BSA)** represents the largest software companies in campaigns to investigate illegal business use of unlicensed software. The BSA estimates software industry losses of nearly $12 billion annually from software piracy. Employees using pirated software on business assets risk bringing legal penalties on themselves and their employer.

Intangibles, which mainly consist of artist contracts and music catalogs, are being amortized on a straight-line basis principally over 16 years and 21 years, respectively.

A **trademark** is a name, term, or symbol used to identify a business and its products. For example, the distinctive red-and-white **Coca-Cola** logo is an example of a trademark. Most businesses identify their trademarks with ® in their advertisements and on their products. Under federal law, businesses can protect against others using their trademarks by registering them for 10 years and renewing the registration for 10-year periods thereafter. Like a copyright, the legal costs of registering a trademark with the federal government are recorded as assets. Thus, even though the Coca-Cola trademarks are extremely valuable, they are not shown on the balance sheet because the legal costs for establishing these trademarks are immaterial. If, however, a trademark is purchased from another business, the cost of its purchase is recorded as an asset. The cost of a trademark is in most cases considered to have an indefinite useful life. Thus, trademarks are not amortized over a useful life, as are the previously discussed intangible assets. Rather, trademarks should be tested periodically for impaired value. If a trademark is impaired from competitive threats or other circumstances, the trademark should be written down and a loss recognized.

Goodwill

In business, **goodwill** refers to an intangible asset of a business that is created from favorable factors such as location, product quality, reputation, and managerial skill. Goodwill allows a business to earn a rate of return on its investment that is often in excess of the normal rate for other firms in the same business.

Generally accepted accounting principles permit goodwill to be recorded in the accounts only if it is objectively determined by a transaction. Unlike other intangible assets, goodwill is not amortized. However, a loss should be recorded if the business prospects of the acquired firm become significantly impaired. This loss would normally be disclosed in the Other Expense section of the income statement. To illustrate, **AOL Time Warner** recorded one of the largest losses in corporate history (nearly $54 billion) for the write-down of goodwill associated with the AOL and Time Warner merger. The effect of the impairment on the accounts and financial statements is as shown:

Trans. Date	Balance Sheet			Income Statement		
	Assets	Liabilities	Stockholders' Equity	Revenue	Expense	Net Income
	Goodwill −54				Loss on Impaired Goodwill 54	−54
Net Effect	−54		−54		54	−54
			Retained Earnings			
			(Net Income)			

ETHICS IN ACTION

The timing and amount of goodwill write-offs can be very subjective. Managers and their accountants should fairly estimate the value of goodwill and record its impairment when it occurs. To delay a write-down of goodwill when it is determined that the asset is impaired would be unethical.

Exhibit 7 shows the frequency of intangible asset disclosures for a sample of 600 large firms. As you can see, goodwill is the most frequently reported intangible asset because goodwill arises from merger transactions, which are very common.

Intangible Asset Category	Number of Firms
Goodwill	495
Trademarks and brand names	94
Patents	78
Customer lists	36
Technology	35
Franchises and licenses	35
Other	93

Source: *Accounting Trends & Techniques*, 55th ed. (New York: American Institute of Certified Public Accountants, 2001).
Note: Some firms have multiple disclosures.

Reporting Fixed Assets and Intangible Assets

The amount of depreciation and amortization expense for a period should be reported separately in the income statement or disclosed in a footnote. A general description of the method or methods used in computing depreciation should also be reported, as illustrated for **Sony Corporation**:

Depreciation of property, plant, and equipment is principally computed on a declining-balance method for Sony Corporation and Japanese subsidiaries and on a straight-line method for foreign subsidiary companies at rates based on estimated useful lives of assets, principally ranging from 15 years up to 50 years for buildings and from 2 years up to 10 years for machinery and equipment.

The amount of each major class of fixed assets should be disclosed in the balance sheet or the footnotes. The related accumulated depreciation should also be disclosed either by major class or in total. The fixed assets may be shown at their *book value* (cost less accumulated depreciation), which can also be described as their *net* amount. If there are too many classes of fixed assets, a single amount may be presented in the balance sheet, supported by a separate detailed listing. Fixed assets are normally presented under the more descriptive caption of *property, plant, and equipment.*

Intangible assets are usually reported in the balance sheet in a separate section immediately following the fixed assets. The balance of each major class of intangible assets should be disclosed at an amount net of the amortization taken to date. Exhibit 8 is a partial balance sheet that shows the reporting of fixed assets and intangible assets for Sony Corporation.

Analyzing Fixed Assets

Business success for many firms is influenced by the utilization of fixed assets. Fixed assets that sit idle do not generate revenue and, hence, do not provide a return on investment. Thus, analysts examine the utilization of the fixed assets. The two major types of analyses are operational utilization analysis and financial utilization analysis.

EXHIBIT 8

Fixed Assets and Intangible Assets in the Balance Sheet

SONY CORPORATION Partial Balance Sheet March 31, 2000	
	In Millions (Yen)
Property, Plant, and Equipment:	
Land	¥ 185,736
Buildings	774,372
Machinery and Equipment	1,955,015
Construction in Progress	92,787
	¥3,007,910
Less: Accumulated Depreciation	1,752,340
Net Property, Plant, and Equipment	¥1,255,570
Intangible Assets:	
Copyrights, trademarks, and other intangibles	¥ 218,496
Goodwill	293,777

Operational Utilization Analyses

The operating statistics of fixed assets for some fixed asset-intensive industries are provided by the reports filed with the Securities and Exchange Commission (SEC) and, hence, are publicly available for analysis. These operational measures are typically determined by the following general ratio:

$$\text{Operational utilization (general ratio)} = \frac{\text{Used portion of the fixed asset}}{\text{Total fixed asset capacity}}$$

The closer the operational utilization approaches 100%, the more efficient are the fixed assets. Naturally, a 100% utilization is rare; however, much smaller percentages could indicate a problem. Exhibit 9 provides the ratio name and calculation for several operational utilization ratios across a number of industries.

EXHIBIT 9

Operational Utilization Ratio Examples

Industry	Ratio Name	Ratio Calculation
Airline	Load factor	Seat miles sold/Available seat miles
Cable	Penetration	Subscribers/Potential connections on network
Hotel	Occupancy	Nights sold/Available nights
Power generation	Utilization	Net generating output/Total generating capacity

To illustrate, the occupancy rate reported to the SEC for **Starwood Hotels & Resorts** (Sheraton® and Westin® hotel brands) was 71.6%. This percentage is determined by dividing the total room nights sold by the total available nights. The available nights are the number of rooms multiplied by 365 operating days in the year. The comparable ratio for **Marriott International, Inc.** was 78.2%. We could conclude that Marriott has utilized its hotel assets more efficiently than Starwood because it sold more room nights as a percentage of available nights.

Financial Utilization Analysis

Fixed assets can also be evaluated by their ability to generate revenue, using two basic methods. The first approach determines the revenue per unit of fixed assets, and the second determines the number of revenue dollars per dollar of fixed assets.

REVENUE PER UNIT OF FIXED ASSETS   The general formula for the revenue per unit of fixed assets is determined as follows:

$$\text{Revenue per unit of fixed assets} = \frac{\text{Total revenues}}{\text{Number of fixed asset units}}$$

This type of ratio is used only when the fixed asset units in the denominator are reasonably similar. Otherwise, such a ratio is not generally meaningful. Examples of this ratio for a number of industries are shown in Exhibit 10.

Industry	Ratio Name	Ratio Calculation
Airline	Revenue per available seat mile	Total revenues/Available seat miles
Brokerage	Revenue per share traded	Total commission revenue/Total number of shares traded
Hotel	Revenue per available room night	Total revenues/Available room nights
Restaurant	Revenue per restaurant	Total revenues/Total restaurants
Retail	Revenue per square foot	Total revenues/Total square feet of retail floor space

Using the hotel industry as an example, the total number of available room nights is a physical measure of the hotel's capacity. This is a better measure of capacity than is the "number of hotels," for example, since each hotel is a different size. Each "room night" is reasonably similar; thus, the ratio can be interpreted. The revenues per available room night for Starwood and Marriott were reported to be $115 and $117, respectively. Both hotels are generating nearly the same revenue for each available room night. In contrast, **Choice Hotels International, Inc.** (Comfort Inn®, Quality Inn®, and EconoLodge® brand names) has a revenue per available room night of only $54, which is consistent with its mid-market strategy.

FIXED ASSET TURNOVER RATIO   The second asset utilization measure is called the *fixed asset turnover ratio*. The **fixed asset turnover ratio** is a measure of the number of dollars of revenue earned per dollar of fixed assets, and is calculated as:

$$\text{Fixed asset turnover} = \frac{\text{Revenue}}{\text{Average book value of fixed assets}}$$

Unlike the revenue per unit of fixed asset ratio, the fixed asset turnover ratio can be calculated for any company because it uses publicly available financial statement information. To illustrate the calculation, the following fixed asset balance sheet information (in millions) is available for Marriott:

	December 28, 2001	**December 29, 2000**
Property and equipment (net)	$2,930	$3,011

In addition, Marriott reported revenue of $10,017,000,000 for 2001. Thus, the fixed asset turnover is:

$$\text{Fixed asset turnover} = \frac{\$10,017}{(\$3,011 + 2,930)/2} = 3.37 \text{ turns}$$

For every dollar of fixed assets, Marriott earns $3.37 of revenue. The larger this ratio, the more efficiently a business is using its fixed assets. This ratio can be compared to that of other companies in the industry to evaluate overall fixed asset turnover performance. For example, the fixed asset turnover ratios for Starwood and Choice Hotels are 0.55 and 2.29, respectively. Marriott is operating its hotel assets very efficiently. Part of the explanation is Marriott's franchising strategy, which allows it to earn franchising fees without owning hotel fixed assets.

Exhibit 11 shows the fixed asset turnover ratio for a number of different businesses. The smaller ratios are associated with companies that require large fixed asset investments. The larger fixed asset turnover ratios are associated with firms that are more labor intensive and require little fixed asset investment.

EXHIBIT 11
Fixed Asset Turnover Ratios

Company	Fixed Asset Turnover Ratio
Computer Associates International Inc. (consulting)	7.36
eBay, Inc. (online auction)	3.45
International Paper Co. (paper supplies)	1.76
Manpower, Inc. (temporary employment)	56.00
Ruby Tuesday, Inc. (restaurant)	2.83
Southwest Airlines Co. (airline)	0.97
Sprint Corporation (telecommunication)	0.93

Key Points

1. Define, classify, and account for the cost of fixed assets.

Fixed assets are long-term tangible assets that are owned by a business and are used in the normal operations of the business. Examples of fixed assets are equipment, buildings, and land. The initial cost of a fixed asset includes all amounts spent to get the asset in place and ready for use. For example, sales tax, freight, insurance in transit, and installation costs are included in the cost of a fixed asset. As time passes, all fixed assets except land lose their ability to provide services. As a result, the cost of a fixed asset should be transferred to an expense account in a systematic manner during the asset's expected useful life. This periodic transfer of cost to expense is called *depreciation*.

2. Compute depreciation, using the straight-line and declining-balance methods.

In computing depreciation, three factors need to be considered: the fixed asset's (1) initial cost, (2) useful life, and (3) residual value.

The straight-line method spreads the initial cost less the residual value equally over the useful life. The declining-balance method is applied by multiplying the declining book value of the asset by twice the straight-line rate.

3. **Describe the accounting for depletion of natural resources.**

The amount of periodic depletion is computed by multiplying the amount of minerals extracted during the period by a depletion rate. The depletion rate is computed by dividing the cost of the mineral deposit by its estimated size. The entry to record depletion increases a depletion expense account and an accumulated depletion account.

4. **Describe the accounting for the disposal of fixed assets.**

The journal entries to record disposals of fixed assets vary. In all cases, however, any depreciation for the current period should be recorded and then the book value of the asset is removed from the accounts. The entry to remove the book value from the accounts decreases the asset's accumulated depreciation account and the asset account for the cost of the asset. For assets retired from service, a loss may be recorded for any remaining book value of the asset.

When a fixed asset is sold, the book value is removed and the cash or other asset received is also recorded. If the selling price is more than the book value of the asset, the transaction results in a gain; if the selling price is less than the book value, a loss occurs.

5. **Classify fixed asset costs as either capital expenditures or revenue expenditures.**

Fixed assets are acquired and used through the following four stages: preliminary, preacquistion, acquisition or construction, and in-service. The costs incurred during the preliminary stage are generally expensed, and the direct costs incurred during the preacquisition and acquisition stages are capitalized. During the in-service stage, ordinary and normal repairs are expensed, but new and replaced components are capitalized.

6. **Describe the accounting for intangible assets.**

Long-term assets that are without physical attributes but are used in the business are classified as intangible assets. Examples of intangible assets are patents, copyrights, trademarks, and goodwill. The initial cost of an intangible asset should increase an asset account. For patents, copyrights, and trademarks, this cost should be written off, or amortized, over the years of the asset's expected usefulness by increasing an expense account and decreasing the intangible asset account. Goodwill is not amortized but is written down only upon impairment.

7. **Describe how depreciation expense is reported in an income statement, and prepare a balance sheet that includes fixed assets and intangible assets.**

The amount of depreciation expense and the method or methods used in computing depreciation should be disclosed in the financial statements. In addition, each major class of fixed assets should be disclosed along with the related accumulated depreciation. Intangible assets are usually presented in the balance sheet in a separate section immediately following the fixed assets. Each major class of intangible assets should be disclosed at an amount net of the amortization recorded to date.

8. **Analyze the utilization of fixed assets.**

Business success for many firms is influenced by the utilization of their fixed assets. Fixed asset utilization can be measured using operational and financial data. Operational utilization statistics evaluate the used portion of fixed assets to the total fixed asset capacity. Financial measures of asset utilization include (1) the revenue per unit of fixed assets and (2) the fixed asset turnover ratio (sales divided by average book value of fixed assets).

Glossary

Accelerated depreciation method: A depreciation method that provides for a higher depreciation amount in the first year of the asset's use, followed by a gradually declining amount of depreciation.

Amortization: The periodic transfer of the cost of an intangible asset to expense.

Book value: The cost of a fixed asset minus accumulated depreciation on the asset.

Capital expenditures: The costs of acquiring fixed assets, adding a component, or replacing a component of fixed assets.

Copyright: An exclusive right to publish and sell a literary, artistic, or musical composition.

Declining-balance method: A method of depreciation that provides periodic depreciation expense based on the declining book value of a fixed asset over its estimated life.

Depletion: The process of transferring the cost of natural resources to an expense account.

Depreciation: The systematic periodic transfer of the cost of a fixed asset to an expense account during its expected useful life.

Fixed assets: Long-lived or relatively permanent tangible assets that are used in the normal business operations.

Fixed asset turnover ratio: A ratio that measures the number of dollars of revenue earned per dollar of fixed assets, and is calculated as total revenue divided by the average book value of fixed assets.

Goodwill: An intangible asset of a business that is created from favorable factors such as location, product quality, reputation, and managerial skill, as verified from a merger transaction.

Intangible assets: Long-lived assets that are useful in the operations of a business, are not held for sale, and are without physical qualities.

Patents: Exclusive rights to produce and sell goods with one or more unique features.

Residual value: The estimated value of a fixed asset at the end of its useful life.

Revenue expenditures: Costs that benefit only the current period or costs incurred for normal maintenance and repairs of fixed assets.

Straight-line method: A method of depreciation that provides for equal periodic depreciation expense over the estimated life of a fixed asset.

Trademark: A name, term, or symbol used to identify a business and its products.

Self-Study Questions

(Answers appear at end of chapter.)

1. Which of the following expenditures incurred in connection with acquiring machinery is a proper charge to the asset account?
   A. Freight
   B. Installation costs
   C. Both A and B
   D. Neither A nor B

2. Using the declining-balance method (twice the straight-line rate), what is the amount of depreciation for the second year of use for equipment costing $9,000 with an estimated residual value of $600 and an estimated life of 3 years?
   A. $6,000
   B. $3,000
   C. $2,000
   D. $400

3. An example of an accelerated depreciation method is:
   A. Straight-line
   B. Declining-balance
   C. Amortization
   D. Depletion

4. A component of a fixed asset with a book value of $5,000 is replaced at the beginning of the year with a new component capitalized at a cost of $40,000. The replacement component has a 5-year estimated life. How much depreciation expense is recognized for the year?
   A. $3,000
   B. $5,000
   C. $8,000
   D. $13,000

5. A company shows the book value of fixed assets at the beginning of the year of $80,000 and a balance at the end of the year of $120,000. Total revenues were $500,000 for the year. What is the fixed asset turnover ratio?
   A. 0.20
   B. 4.0
   C. 5.0
   D. 6.0

Discussion Questions

1. Which of the following qualities are characteristics of fixed assets? (a) tangible, (b) capable of repeated use in the operations of the business, (c) held for sale in the normal course of business, (d) used continuously in the operations of the business, (e) long lived

2. Penguin Office Equipment Co. has a fleet of automobiles and trucks for use by salespersons and for delivery of office supplies and equipment. Sioux City Auto Sales Co. has automobiles and trucks for sale. Under what caption would the automobiles and trucks be reported on the balance sheet of (a) Penguin Office Equipment Co. and (b) Sioux City Auto Sales Co.?

3. Spiral Co. acquired an adjacent vacant lot with the hope of selling it in the future at a gain. The lot is not intended to be used in Spiral's business operations. Where should such real estate be listed in the balance sheet?

4. Tensile Company solicited bids from several contractors to construct an addition to its office building.

The lowest bid received was for $340,000. Tensile Company decided to construct the addition itself at a cost of $325,000. What amount should be recorded in the building account?

5. Are the amounts at which fixed assets are reported in the balance sheet their approximate market values as of the balance sheet date? Discuss.

6. a. Does recognizing depreciation in the accounts provide a special cash fund for the replacement of fixed assets? Explain.
   b. Describe the nature of depreciation as the term is used in accounting.

7. Name the three factors that need to be considered in determining the amount of periodic depreciation.

8. Trigger Company purchased a machine that has a manufacturer's suggested life of 15 years. The company plans to use the machine on a special project that will last 11 years. At the completion of the project, the machine will be sold. Over how many years should the machine be depreciated?

9. Is it necessary for a business to use the same method of computing depreciation (a) for all classes of its depreciable assets and (b) in the financial statements and in determining income taxes?

10. a. Why is an accelerated depreciation method often used for income tax purposes?

b. What is the Modified Accelerated Cost Recovery System (MACRS), and under what conditions is it used?

11. For some of the fixed assets of a business, the balance in Accumulated Depreciation is exactly equal to the cost of the asset. (a) Is it permissible to record additional depreciation on the assets if they are still useful to the business? Explain. (b) When should a fixed asset be removed from the accounts?

12. In what sections of the income statement are gains and losses from the disposal of fixed assets presented?

13. Differentiate between the accounting for capital expenditures and revenue expenditures.

14. Immediately after a used truck is acquired, a new motor is installed and the tires are replaced at a total cost of $4,750. Is this a capital expenditure or a revenue expenditure?

15. How would you evaluate the effective use of fixed assets?

16. a. Over what period of time should the cost of a patent acquired by purchase be amortized?
    b. In general, what is the required treatment for research and development costs?
    c. How should goodwill be amortized?

Exercises

EXERCISE 7-1
Costs of acquiring fixed assets
OBJECTIVE 1

Tracie Klein owns and operates Walcott Print Co. During July, Walcott incurred the following costs in acquiring two printing presses. One printing press was new, and the other was used by a business that recently filed for bankruptcy.

Costs related to new printing press:

1. Sales tax on purchase price
2. Insurance while in transit
3. Freight
4. Special foundation
5. New parts to replace those damaged in unloading
6. Fee paid to factory representative for installation

Costs related to secondhand printing press:

7. Freight
8. Installation
9. Repair of vandalism during installation
10. Replacement of worn-out parts
11. Repair of damage incurred in reconditioning the press
12. Fees paid to attorney to review purchase agreement

a. Indicate which costs incurred in acquiring the new printing press should increase the asset account.
b. Indicate which costs incurred in acquiring the secondhand printing press should increase the asset account.

EXERCISE 7-2
Cost of land
OBJECTIVE 1

A company has developed a tract of land into a ski resort. The company cut the trees, cleared and graded the land and hills, and constructed ski lifts. (a) Should the tree-cutting, land-clearing, and grading costs of constructing the ski slopes increase the land account? (b) If such costs increase Land, should they be depreciated?

EXERCISE 7-3
Cost of land
OBJECTIVE 1

✓ $138,250

Birch Delivery Company acquired an adjacent lot to construct a new warehouse, paying $25,000 and giving a short-term note for $100,000. Legal fees paid were $1,750, delinquent taxes assumed were $7,500, and fees paid to remove an old building from the land were $5,500. Materials salvaged from the demolition of the building were sold for $1,500. Birch paid a contractor $412,500 to construct a new warehouse. Determine the cost of the land to be reported on the balance sheet.

EXERCISE 7-4
Nature of depreciation
OBJECTIVE 1

Yarborough Metal Casting Co. reported $575,000 for equipment and $217,500 for accumulated depreciation—equipment on its balance sheet.

Does this mean (a) that the replacement cost of the equipment is $575,000 and (b) that $217,500 is set aside in a special fund for the replacement of the equipment? Explain.

EXERCISE 7-5
Straight-line depreciation rates
OBJECTIVE 2

✓ a. 25%

Convert each of the following estimates of useful life to a straight-line depreciation rate, stated as a percentage, assuming that the residual value of the fixed asset is to be ignored: (a) 4 years, (b) 5 years, (c) 10 years, (d) 20 years, (e) 25 years, (f) 40 years, (g) 50 years.

EXERCISE 7-6
Straight-line depreciation
OBJECTIVE 2

✓ $11,750

A refrigerator used by a meat processor has a cost of $112,000, an estimated residual value of $18,000, and an estimated useful life of 8 years. What is the amount of the annual depreciation computed using the straight-line method?

EXERCISE 7-7
Depreciation by two methods
OBJECTIVE 2

✓ a. $15,400

A backhoe acquired on January 2 at a cost of $154,000 has an estimated useful life of 10 years. Assuming that it will have no residual value, determine the depreciation for each of the first two years using (a) the straight-line method and (b) the declining-balance method (at twice the straight-line rate).

EXERCISE 7-8
Depreciation by two methods
OBJECTIVE 2

✓ a. $8,100

A dairy storage tank acquired at the beginning of the fiscal year at a cost of $70,000 has an estimated residual value of $5,200 and an estimated useful life of 8 years. Determine the following amounts: (a) annual depreciation by the straight-line method and (b) depreciation for the first and second year computed by the declining-balance method (at twice the straight-line rate).

EXERCISE 7-9
Partial-year depreciation
OBJECTIVE 2

✓ a. First year, $7,350

Sandblasting equipment acquired at a cost of $64,000 has an estimated residual value of $5,200 and an estimated useful life of 6 years. It was placed in service on April 1 of the current fiscal year, which ends on December 31. Determine the depreciation for the current fiscal year and for the following fiscal year using (a) the straight-line method and (b) the declining-balance method (at twice the straight-line rate).

EXERCISE 7-10
Book value of fixed assets
OBJECTIVE 2

The following data were taken from recent annual reports of **Interstate Bakeries Corporation (IBC)**. It produces, distributes, and sells fresh bakery products nationwide through supermarkets, convenience stores, and its 67 bakeries and 1,500 thrift stores.

	Current Year	Preceding Year
Land and buildings	$388,618,000	$364,773,000
Machinery and equipment	953,625,000	894,533,000
Accumulated depreciation	447,797,000	364,791,000

a. Compute the book value of the fixed assets for the current year and the preceding year and explain the differences, if any.

b. Would you normally expect the book value of fixed assets to increase or decrease during the year?

EXERCISE 7-11
Depletion entries
OBJECTIVE 3

Anaconda Co. acquired the mineral rights of a mineral deposit estimated at 50,000,000 tons for $30,000,000. During the current year, 7,500,000 tons were mined and sold for $6,500,000.

a. Determine the amount of depletion expense for the current year.

b. Illustrate the effects of recording the depletion expense on the accounts and financial statements.

EXERCISE 7-12
Depletion entries
OBJECTIVE 3

Coeur d'Alene Mines Corporation is a North American–based silver mining company. During 2001 Coeur d'Alene Mines produced 10.9 million ounces of silver. The firm's properties had proven reserves of 88.1 million ounces on December 31, 2000. Its December 31, 2000, balance sheet indicated the following:

Operational mining properties	$113,409,000
Less accumulated depletion	(71,225,000)
Book value of mining properties	$ 42,184,000

a. Determine the amount of depletion expense for 2001.

b. Illustrate the effects of recording the 2001 depletion expense on the accounts and financial statements.

EXERCISE 7-13
Sale of fixed asset
OBJECTIVE 4

Metal recycling equipment acquired on January 3, 2001, at a cost of $117,500, has an estimated useful life of 8 years and an estimated residual value of $7,500 and is depreciated by the straight-line method.

a. What was the book value of the equipment at December 31, 2004, the end of the fiscal year?

b. Assuming that the equipment was sold on July 1, 2005, for $53,500, illustrate the effects on the accounts and financial statements of (1) depreciation for the six months of the current year ending December 31, 2005, and (2) the sale of the equipment.

EXERCISE 7-14
Disposal of fixed asset
OBJECTIVE 4

✓ b. $21,250

Equipment acquired on January 3, 2002, at a cost of $71,500, has an estimated useful life of 4 years and an estimated residual value of $4,500.

a. What was the annual amount of depreciation for the years 2002, 2003, and 2004 using the straight-line method of depreciation?
b. What was the book value of the equipment on January 1, 2005?
c. Assuming that the equipment was sold for $18,000 on January 2, 2005, illustrate the effects on the accounts and financial statements of the sale.
d. Assuming that the equipment had been sold for $23,000 instead of $18,000 on January 2, 2005, illustrate the effects of the sale on the accounts and financial statements.

EXERCISE 7-15
Capital and revenue expenditures
OBJECTIVE 5

Yeats Co. incurred the following costs related to trucks and vans used in operating its delivery service:

1. Installed a hydraulic lift on a van.
2. Removed a two-way radio from one of the trucks and installed a new radio with an increased range of communication.
3. Overhauled the engine on one of the trucks that had been purchased 4 years ago.
4. Changed the oil and greased the joints of all trucks and vans.
5. Performed annual maintenance on trucks.
6. Installed security systems on three of the newer trucks.
7. Replaced two of the trucks' shock absorbers with new shock absorbers that allow for the delivery of heavier loads.
8. Repaired a flat tire on one of the vans.
9. Rebuilt the transmission on one of the vans that had been driven only 25,000 miles. The van was no longer under warranty.
10. Tinted the back and side windows of one of the vans to discourage the theft of its contents.

Classify each of the costs as a capital expenditure or a revenue expenditure. For those costs identified as capital expenditures, classify each as an additional or replacement component.

EXERCISE 7-16
Capital and revenue expenditures
OBJECTIVE 5

Faith Inman owns and operates Yellow Ribbon Transport Co. During the past year, Faith incurred the following costs related to her 18-wheel truck:

1. Replaced the hydraulic brake system that had begun to fail during her latest trip through the Smoky Mountains.
2. Overhauled the engine.
3. Replaced a headlight that had burned out.
4. Removed the old CB radio and replaced it with a newer model with a larger range.
5. Replaced a shock absorber that had worn out.
6. Installed fog lights.
7. Installed a wind deflector on top of the cab to increase fuel mileage.
8. Modified the factory-installed turbo charger with a special-order kit designed to add 30 more horsepower to the engine performance.
9. Installed a television in the sleeping compartment of the truck.
10. Replaced the old radar detector with a newer model that detects the KA frequencies now used by many state patrol radar guns. The detector is wired directly into the cab so that it is partially hidden. In addition, Faith fastened the detector to the truck with a locking device that prevents its removal.

Classify each of the costs as a capital expenditure or a revenue expenditure. For those costs identified as capital expenditures, classify each as an additional or replacement component.

EXERCISE 7-17

Fixed asset component replacement

OBJECTIVE 5

✓ c. Depreciation Expense, $2,250

Jacobs Company replaced carpeting throughout its general offices. The old carpet was removed at a cost of $1,500 on March 15. Its book value was determined to be $6,000 on March 15. New carpet was purchased and installed during the last two weeks of March for a total cost of $45,000. The carpet is estimated to have a 15-year useful life.

a. Illustrate the effects on the accounts and financial statements of removing the old carpet
b. Illustrate the effects of the replacement of the old carpet with the new carpet on the accounts and financial statements.
c. Illustrate the effects of the December 31 adjustment for the partial-year depreciation expense for the carpet on the accounts and financial statements. Assume that Jacobs uses the straight-line method.

EXERCISE 7-18

Fixed asset component replacement

OBJECTIVE 5

✓ b. $29,000

Dale's Edge, Inc., purchased and installed an alarm system for its retail store on January 1, 1997, at a cost of $50,000. It was estimated to have a 10-year life with no salvage value. On January 1, 2004, the alarm system was replaced with one having more advanced technology. It cost $120,000 and is estimated to have a 10-year life. The removal of the old alarm system cost $2,000.

a. Determine the total depreciation expense for 2004 related to the alarm system component.
b. Determine the total expense reported in the income statement in 2004 from these transactions.

EXERCISE 7-19

Amortization entries

OBJECTIVE 6

Langohr Company acquired patent rights on January 3, 2001, for $675,000. The patent has a useful life equal to its legal life of 18 years. On January 5, 2004, Langohr successfully defended the patent in a lawsuit at a cost of $45,000.

a. Determine the patent amortization expense for the current year ended December 31, 2004.
b. Illustrate the effects of the adjusment for the 2004 amortization on the accounts and financial statements.

EXERCISE 7-20

Goodwill impairment

OBJECTIVE 6

On January 1, 2002, Delta Financial, Inc., purchased the assets of Guardsman Insurance Co. for $23,000,000, a price reflecting an $8,000,000 goodwill premium. On December 31, 2004, Delta determined that the goodwill from the Guardsman acquisition was impaired and had a value of only $2,500,000.

a. Determine the book value of the goodwill on December 31, 2004, prior to making the impairment adjusting entry.
b. Illustrate the effects on the accounts and financial statements of the December 31, 2004, adjustment for the goodwill impairment.

EXERCISE 7-21

Balance sheet presentation

OBJECTIVE 7

How many errors can you find in the partial balance sheet on the following page?

ROSEDALE COMPANY
Balance Sheet
December 31, 2004

Assets

Total current assets $397,500

	Replacement Cost	Accumulated Depreciation	Book Value
Property, plant, and equipment:			
Land	$ 75,000	$ 20,000	$ 55,000
Buildings	160,000	76,000	84,000
Factory equipment	350,000	192,000	158,000
Office equipment	120,000	77,000	43,000
Patents	80,000	—	80,000
Goodwill	45,000	5,000	40,000
Total property, plant, and equipment	$830,000	$370,000	$460,000

EXERCISE 7–22
Fixed asset turnover ratio
OBJECTIVE 8

Verizon Communications Inc. is a major telecommunication company in the United States. Its balance sheet disclosed the following information (in millions) regarding fixed assets:

	Dec. 31, 2001	Dec. 31, 2000
Plant, property and equipment	$169,586	$158,957
Less accumulated depreciation	95,167	89,453
	$ 74,419	$ 69,504

Verizon's revenue for 2001 was $67,190 million. The fixed asset turnover for the telecommunication industry averages 1.10.

a. Determine Verizon's fixed asset turnover ratio.
b. Interpret Verizon's fixed asset turnover ratio.

Problems

PROBLEM 7 | 1
Allocate payments and receipts to fixed asset accounts
OBJECTIVE 1

The following payments and receipts are related to land, land improvements, and buildings acquired for use in a wholesale ceramic business. The receipts are identified by an asterisk.

a.	Fee paid to attorney for title search	$ 3,500 —
b.	Cost of real estate acquired as a plant site: Land	200,000 —
	Building	55,000 —
c.	Delinquent real estate taxes on property, assumed by purchaser	18,750 –
d.	Cost of razing and removing building	4,800
e.	Proceeds from sale of salvage materials from old building	3,100 ⊢
f.	Special assessment paid to city for extension of water main to the property	5,000
g.	Premium on 1-year insurance policy during construction	6,600
h.	Cost of filling and grading land	29,700
i.	Cost of repairing windstorm damage during construction	1,500

(continued)

j. Cost of paving parking lot to be used by customers   12,500
k. Cost of trees and shrubbery planted   15,000
l. Architect's and engineer's fees for plans and supervision   40,000
m. Cost of repairing vandalism damage during construction   1,500
n. Interest incurred on building loan during construction   48,000
o. Cost of floodlights installed on parking lot   13,500
p. Money borrowed to pay building contractor   500,000*
q. Payment to building contractor for new building   750,000
r. Proceeds from insurance company for windstorm and vandalism damage   3,000*
s. Refund of premium on insurance policy (g) canceled after 11 months   750*

Instructions

1. Assign each payment and receipt to Land (unlimited life), Land Improvements (limited life), Building, or Other Accounts. Indicate receipts by an asterisk. Identify each item by letter, and list the amounts in columnar form, as follows:

Item	Land	Land Improvements	Building	Other Accounts

2. Determine the total increases to Land, Land Improvements, and Building.
3. The costs assigned to the land, which is used as a plant site, will not be depreciated, but the costs assigned to land improvements will be. Explain this seemingly contradictory application of the concept of depreciation.

PROBLEM 7 | 2

Compare two depreciation methods

OBJECTIVE 2

✓ 2003: straight-line depreciation, $105,000

Diamondback Company purchased packaging equipment on January 3, 2003, for $340,000. The equipment was expected to have a useful life of 3 years and a residual value of $25,000.

Instructions

Determine the amount of depreciation expense for the years ended December 31, 2003, 2004, and 2005, using (a) the straight-line method and (b) the declining-balance method (at twice the straight-line rate). Also determine the total depreciation expense for the three years by each method. The following columnar headings are suggested for recording the depreciation expense amounts:

	Depreciation Expense	
Year	Straight-Line Method	Declining-Balance Method

PROBLEM 7 | 3

Depreciation by two methods; partial years

OBJECTIVE 2

✓ a. 2003: $17,000

Newbauer Company purchased plastic laminating equipment on July 1, 2003, for $108,000. The equipment was expected to have a useful life of 3 years and a residual value of $6,000.

Instructions

Determine the amount of depreciation expense for the years ended December 31, 2003, 2004, 2005, and 2006, using (a) the straight-line method and (b) the declining-balance method (at twice the straight-line rate).

PROBLEM 7 | 4

Depreciation by two methods; sale of fixed asset

OBJECTIVES 2, 4

✓ 1. b. Year 1: $50,000 depreciation expense

New lithographic equipment acquired at a cost of $125,000 at the beginning of a fiscal year has an estimated useful life of 5 years and an estimated residual value of $10,000. The manager requested information regarding the effect of alternative methods on the amount of depreciation expense each year. On the basis of the data received, the manager selected the declining-balance method. In the first week of the fifth year, the equipment was sold for $23,000.

Instructions

1. Determine the annual depreciation expense for each of the estimated 5 years of use, the accumulated depreciation at the end of each year, and the book value of the equipment at the end of each year using (a) the straight-line method and (b) the declining-balance method (at twice the straight-line rate). The following columnar headings are suggested for each schedule:

Year	Depreciation Expense	Accumulated Depreciation, End of Year	Book Value, End of Year

2. Illustrate the effects on the accounts and financial statements for the sale.
3. Illustrate the effects on the accounts and financial statements for the sale, assuming a sales price of $11,000.

PROBLEM 7 | 5

Amortization and depletion entries

OBJECTIVES 3, 6

✓ 1. (a) $121,600

Data related to the acquisition of timber rights and intangible assets during the current year ended December 31 are as follows:

a. Timber rights on a tract of land were purchased for $480,000 on July 12. The stand of timber is estimated at 1,500,000 board feet. During the current year, 380,000 board feet of timber were cut.
b. Goodwill in the amount of $5,000,000 was purchased on January 3.
c. Governmental and legal costs of $80,000 were incurred on October 2 in obtaining a patent with an estimated economic life of 10 years. Amortization is to be for one-fourth year.

Instructions

1. Determine the amount of the amortization or depletion expense for the current year for each of the previous items.
2. Illustrate the effects on the accounts and financial statements of the adjustments for the amortization or depletion for each item.

Activities

Activity 7–1

Comparing book value and depreciation expense for two companies

Micron Technology, Inc. is in the semiconductor industry. This industry requires extensive capital investments in fabrication facilities to maintain technological competitiveness. **E. I. DuPont De Nemours & Co.** is one of the leading chemical companies in the world. DuPont requires significant investment in chemical-processing facilities. Chemical products have longer lives than do semiconductor products. The following selected fixed asset information is provided for both companies (all numbers in millions):

	Property, Plant, and Equipment Initial Cost	Accumulated Depreciation	Depreciation Expense
Micron Technology, Inc.	$ 8,199	$ 3,495	$1,050
DuPont	34,650	20,468	1,415

a. Determine the book value of the fixed assets for each company.
b. Estimate the total useful life of the fixed assets, assuming straight-line depreciation and no salvage value.
c. Estimate the percentage of accumulated depreciation to the total initial cost of property, plant, and equipment for each company.
d. Interpret the differences between Micron and DuPont from your calculations in (b) and (c).

Activity 7-2

Ethics and professional conduct in business

ETHICS

The following is an excerpt from a conversation between the chief executive officer, Lee Baker, and the chief financial officer, Maurice Townley, of Nile Group, Inc.:

Baker (CEO): Maurice, as you know, the auditors are coming in to audit our year-end financial statements pretty soon. Do you see any problems on the horizon?

Townley (CFO): Well, you know about our "famous" Hill Companies acquisition of a couple of years ago. We booked $1,000,000 of goodwill from that acquisition, and the accounting rules require us to recognize any impairment of goodwill.

Baker (CEO): Uh oh.

Townley (CFO): Yeah, right. We had to shut the old Hill Company operations down this year because those products were no longer selling. Thus, our auditor is going to insist that we write off the $1,000,000 of goodwill to reflect the impaired value.

Baker (CEO): We can't have that—at least not this year! Do everything you can to push back on this one. We just can't take that kind of a hit this year. The most we could stand is $200,000. Maurice, keep the write-off to $200,000 and promise anything in the future. Then we'll deal with that when we get there.

How should Townley respond to the CEO?

Activity 7-3

Financial vs. tax depreciation

The following is an excerpt from a conversation between two employees of Stanza Co., Geoff Haines and Allison Foster. Geoff is the accounts payable clerk, and Allison is the cashier.

Geoff: Allison, could I get your opinion on something?
Allison: Sure, Geoff.
Geoff: Do you know Kris, the fixed assets clerk?
Allison: I know who she is, but I don't know her well. Why?
Geoff: Well, I was talking to her at lunch last Monday about how she liked her job, etc. You know, the usual—and she mentioned something about having to keep two sets of books, one for taxes and one for the financial statements. That can't be good accounting, can it? What do you think?
Allison: Two sets of books? It doesn't sound right.
Geoff: It doesn't seem right to me either. I was always taught that you had to use generally accepted accounting principles. How can there be two sets of books? What can be the difference between the two?

How would you respond to Allison and Geoff if you were Kris?

Activity 7–4
Financial and operational utilization analyses in the airline industry

The financial performance of the airline industry is sensitive to aircraft utilization and cost control. The industry uses a number of common measures to evaluate financial performance, three of which follow:

Load factor = Revenue passenger miles (RPM)/Available seat miles (ASM)

Operating revenue per ASM = Operating revenue/ASM

Operating cost per ASM = Operating cost/ASM

The following table provides some operating statistics (in millions) for four passenger airlines:

	Available Seat Miles (ASM)	Revenue Passenger Miles (RPM)	Operating Revenue	Operating Cost
Northwest Airlines Inc.	103,356	79,128	$10,346	$ 9,643
Delta Air Lines Inc.	154,974	112,998	15,700	15,110
U.S. Airways Group Inc.	66,500	46,840	8,293	8,452
Southwest Airlines Inc.	59,910	42,215	5,650	4,631

a. Prepare a table showing for each airline the load factor, operating revenue per ASM, operating cost per ASM, and operating margin (profit) per ASM.
b. Interpret the results in (a) for the four airlines.

Activity 7–5
Fixed asset turnover: three industries

The following table shows the revenues and average net fixed assets (in millions) for three different companies from three different industries: retailing, manufacturing, and communications.

	Revenues	Average Net Fixed Assets
Wal-Mart Stores, Inc.	$193,295	$37,617
Alcoa, Inc.	23,090	12,850
Comcast Corp.	8,219	5,203

a. For each company, determine the fixed asset turnover ratio.
b. Explain Wal-Mart's ratio relative to those of the other two companies.

Activity 7–6
Interpreting railroad operating and financial utilization statistics

The freight statistics for the **Burlington Northern Santa Fe Corp.** for three recent years is provided from public disclosures as follows:

Freight Statistics. The following table sets forth certain freight statistics relating to rail operations for the periods indicated.

	Year Ended December 31,		
	2000	**1999**	**1998**
Revenue ton miles (millions)	491,959	493,207	469,045
Freight revenue per thousand revenue ton miles	$18.52	$18.40	$19.08
Average haul per ton (miles)	996	994	970

a. What is a *revenue ton mile*?
b. How would you interpret the trend in "freight revenue per thousand revenue ton miles" over the three years indicated?
c. Estimate the number of tons moved in 2000.
d. Estimate Burlington Northern's total revenue for 2000.

Activity 7-7
Effect of depreciation on net income

Heimlich Construction Co. specializes in building replicas of historic houses. Ami Lamb, president of Heimlich, is considering the purchase of various items of equipment on July 1, 2002, for $150,000. The equipment would have a useful life of 5 years and no residual value. In the past, all equipment has been leased. For tax purposes, Ami is considering depreciating the equipment using the straight-line method. She discussed the matter with her CPA and learned that, although the straight-line method could be elected, it was to her advantage to use the Modified Accelerated Cost Recovery System (MACRS) for tax purposes. She asked for your advice as to which method to use for tax purposes.

1. Compute depreciation for each of the years (2002, 2003, 2004, 2005, 2006, and 2007) of useful life using (a) the straight-line method and (b) MACRS. In using the straight-line method, one-half year's depreciation should be computed for 2002 and 2007. Use the MACRS rates presented in the chapter.
2. Assuming that income before depreciation and income tax is estimated to be $150,000 uniformly per year and that the income tax rate is 30%, compute the net income for each of the years 2002, 2003, 2004, 2005, 2006, and 2007, if (a) the straight-line method is used and (b) MACRS is used.
3. What factors would you present to Ami in considering a depreciation method?

Activity 7-8
Shopping for a delivery truck

G R O U P

Assume that you are planning to acquire a vehicle. In groups of three or four, go to a local dealer and identify the costs that would be incurred in acquiring the vehicle. Classify the costs as capital or revenue expenditures.

Activity 7-9
Applying for patents, copyrights, and trademarks

G R O U P

Go to the Internet and review the procedures for applying for a patent, a copyright, or a trademark. One Internet site that is useful for this purpose is:

http://www.idresearch.com

Prepare a written summary of these procedures.

Answers to Self-Study Questions

1. **C** All amounts spent to get a fixed asset (such as machinery) in place and ready for use are proper charges to the asset account. In the case of machinery acquired, the freight (answer A) and the installation costs (answer B) are both (answer C) proper charges to the machinery account.

2. **C** The periodic charge for depreciation under the declining-balance method (twice the straight-line rate) for the second year is determined by first computing the depreciation charge for the first year. The depreciation of $6,000 for the first year (answer A) is computed by multiplying the cost of the equipment, $9,000, by $2/3$ (the straight-line rate of $1/3$ multiplied by 2). The depreciation of $2,000 for the second year (answer C) is then deter-

mined by multiplying the book value at the end of the first year, $3,000 (the cost of $9,000 minus the first-year depreciation of $6,000), by $2/3$. The third year's depreciation is $400 (answer D). It is determined by multiplying the book value at the end of the second year, $1,000, by $2/3$, thus yielding $667. However, the equipment cannot be depreciated below its residual value of $600; thus, the third-year depreciation is $400 ($1,000 − $600).

3. **B** A depreciation method that provides for a higher depreciation amount in the first year of the use of an asset and a gradually declining periodic amount thereafter is called an *accelerated depreciation method*. The declining-balance method (answer B) is an example of such a method.

4. **D** The book value of the replaced component ($5,000) should be charged (increased) to depreciation expense. In addition, the new component has a full year of depreciation equal to $8,000 ($40,000/5 years). Thus, added together, the correct depreciation expense is $13,000 for the year (answer D).

5. **C** Fixed asset turnover ratio = Revenues/Average book value of fixed assets, or $500,000/[($80,000 + $120,000)/2], or 5.0 (answer C).

8

LEARNING OBJECTIVES

OBJECTIVE 1
Describe how businesses finance their operations.

OBJECTIVE 2
Describe and illustrate current liabilities, notes payable, taxes, contingencies, and payroll.

OBJECTIVE 3
Describe and illustrate the financing of operations through issuance of bonds.

OBJECTIVE 4
Describe and illustrate the financing of operations through issuance of stock.

OBJECTIVE 5
Describe and illustrate the accounting for cash and stock dividends.

OBJECTIVE 6
Describe the effects of stock splits on the financial statements.

OBJECTIVE 7
Describe financial statement reporting of liabilities and stockholders' equity.

OBJECTIVE 8
Analyze the impact of debt or equity financing on earnings per share.

OBJECTIVE 9
Analyze and interpret long-term liability position with the number of times interest charges are earned and total liabilities to total asset ratio.

Liabilities and Stockholders' Equity

Using credit to finance trade and purchase fixed assets is probably as old as commerce itself. The Babylonians were lending money as early as 1300 B.C., and the Bible indicates the use of debt in the time of Moses. The proper use of debt can help a business reach its business objectives. On the other hand, too much debt can be a financial burden that can even lead to bankruptcy. Thus, just as for individuals, businesses must manage debt carefully.

One of the basic guidelines in managing *liabilities*, or debt, is to closely match the maturity of the liability with the underlying asset. The maturity is the time period that the liability is outstanding prior to its due date. Thus, debt can be short term in nature (due within a year) or long term (due beyond one year). For example, if a business used debt to finance the purchase of a building, then the debt maturity should approximate the life of the building. Thus, the cash flows from operating the building could be used to pay back the loan over the life of the building. It would be unwise for the business to finance a building with a current liability that was due within the year. This is so because the business would need to constantly refinance the current liability over the life of the building, which would be expensive. In addition, business conditions might change, making it difficult to refinance the short-term debt, thus creating a cash crunch. It would be similar to your trying to finance the purchase of a house with your credit card rather than obtaining a mortgage.

Businesses also finance long-term operations by issuing stock. In this chapter we describe and illustrate the nature, accounting, and analysis of debt and stock. Financing the operations of a business wisely is critical to successful business management.

Financing Operations

OBJECTIVE 1

Describe how
businesses finance
their operations.

A business must finance its operations through either debt or equity. Debt financing
includes all liabilities owed by a business, including both current and long-term liabilities. For example, most businesses maintain a normal amount of accounts payable
due vendors and other suppliers. In effect, these vendors and suppliers are helping finance the business. A business may also issue notes or bonds to finance its operations.
While accounts payable normally do not include interest payments, notes and bonds
require that interest be paid periodically.

A business may also finance its operations through equity. A proprietorship or
partnership obtains equity financing from investments by the owner(s). A corporation
obtains its equity financing by issuing stock. Corporations can issue different classes
of stock with different rights and privileges, such as rights to dividend payments.

Another way to think of how businesses finance their operations is to think of the
accounting equation. In the preceding chapters, we focused primarily on the income
statement and the asset side of the balance sheet. In this chapter, we are focusing on
the right side of the accounting equation: the liabilities and stockholders' equity. We
begin by describing current liabilities, including notes payable, deferred taxes, contingencies, and payroll. We then focus on bonds payable and stock financing.

Liabilities

OBJECTIVE 2

Describe and illustrate
current liabilities,
notes payable, taxes,
contingencies, and
payroll.

Liabilities are debts owed to others. Liabilities due within a short time, usually one year,
are current liabilities. Liabilites due beyond one year are classified as long-term liabilities. In addition, in some cases a business incurs a liability if certain events occur in
the future. In this section, we describe and illustrate these various types of liabilities.

Current Liabilities

Your credit card balance is probably due within a short time, such as 30 days. Such
liabilities that are to be paid out of current assets and are due within a short time,
usually within one year, are called *current liabilities*. Most current liabilities arise from
two basic transactions:

1. Receiving goods or services prior to making payment.
2. Receiving payment prior to delivering goods or services.

An example of the first type of transaction is an account payable arising from a
purchase of merchandise for resale. An example of the second type of transaction is
unearned rent arising from the receipt of rent in advance. We described and illustrated the accounting for accounts payable and unearned liabilities in earlier chapters.
In the remainder of this section, we focus on notes payable, deferred liabilities, contingencies, and payroll-related liabilities.

Notes Payable

Notes can be issued to creditors to temporarily satisfy an account payable created
earlier. They can also be issued when merchandise or other assets are purchased. For
example, assume that a business issues a 90-day, 12% note for $1,000, dated August 1,

2004, to Murray Co. for a $1,000 overdue account. The effect on the accounts and financial statements of Murray Co. for issuing and paying the note follows.[1]

Issuing a 90-day, 12% note on account on August 1.

Trans.	Balance Sheet			Income Statement		
Date	Assets	Liabilities	Stockholders' Equity	Revenue	Expense	Net Income
8/1		Notes Payable 1,000				
		Accts Payable −1,000				
Net Effect		0				
			Retained Earnings			
			(Net Income)			

Paying of note on October 30.

Trans.	Balance Sheet			Income Statement		
Date	Assets	Liabilities	Stockholders' Equity	Revenue	Expense	Net Income
10/30	Cash −1,030	Notes Payable −1,000			Interest Expense 30	−30
Net Effect	−1,030	−1,000	−30		30	−30
			Retained Earnings			
			(Net Income)			

The interest expense is reported in the Other Expense section of the income statement for the year ended December 31, 2004. If the accounting period ends before the maturity date of the note, interest expense to the end of the period should be recorded.

Income Taxes

Under the United States Tax Code, corporations are taxable entities that must pay federal income taxes. Depending on where it is located, a corporation may also be required to pay state and local income taxes. Although we limit our discussion to federal income taxes, the basic concepts also apply to other income taxes.

Most corporations are required to pay estimated federal income taxes in four installments throughout the year. For example, assume that a corporation with a calendar-year accounting period estimates its income tax expense for the year as $84,000. The effect on the accounts and the financial statements of the first of the four estimated tax payments of $21,000 (¼ of $84,000) is as follows:

Trans.	Balance Sheet			Income Statement		
Date	Assets	Liabilities	Stockholders' Equity	Revenue	Expense	Net Income
4/15	Cash −21,000				Income Tax Exp. 21,000	−21,000
Net Effect	−21,000		−21,000		21,000	−21,000
			Retained Earnings			
			(Net Income)			

[1]The effect on the accounts and financial statements are shown for the issuer (borrower) of the note. The effects for the receiver (lender) of the note are exactly opposite those for the issuer.

At year-end, the actual taxable income and the related tax are determined. If additional taxes are owed, the additional liability is recorded. If the total estimated tax payments are more than the tax liability based on actual taxable income, the overpayment should increase Income Tax Receivable and decrease Income Tax Expense.

The **taxable income** of a corporation is determined according to the tax laws. It is often different from the income before income taxes reported in the income statement according to generally accepted accounting principles. As a result, the *income tax based on taxable income* usually differs from the *income tax based on income before taxes*. This difference may need to be allocated between various financial statement periods, depending on the nature of the items causing the differences.

Some differences between taxable income and income before income taxes are created because items are recognized in one period for tax purposes and in another period for income statement purposes. Such differences, called **temporary differences**, reverse or turn around in later years. For example, a company may use MACRS depreciation for tax purposes and the straight-line method for financial reporting purposes.

Since temporary differences reverse in later years, they do not change or reduce the total amount of taxable income over the life of a business. For example, MACRS recognizes more depreciation in the early years but less depreciation in the later years. However, the total depreciation expense is the same for MACRS and the straight-line methods over the life of the asset.

Temporary differences affect only the timing of the recognition of revenues and expenses for tax purposes. As a result, the total amount of taxes paid does not change. Only the timing of the payment of taxes is affected. In most cases, managers use tax-planning techniques so that temporary differences delay or defer the payment of taxes to later years. As a result, at the end of each year the amount of the current tax liability and the postponed (deferred) liability must be recorded.

To illustrate, assume that at the end of the first year of operations, a corporation reports $300,000 income before income taxes on its income statement. If we assume an income tax rate of 40%, the income tax expense reported on the income statement is $120,000 ($300,000 × 0.40).[2] However, to reduce the amount owed for current income taxes, the corporation uses tax planning to reduce the taxable income to $100,000. Thus, the income tax actually due for the year is only $40,000 ($100,000 × 0.40). The $80,000 ($120,000 − $40,000) difference between the two tax amounts is created by timing differences. This amount is deferred to future years. The example is summarized here.

Income tax based on $300,000 reported income at 40%	$120,000
Income tax based on $100,000 taxable income at 40%	40,000
Income tax deferred to future years	$ 80,000

The effect of the deferral on the accounts and financial statements is shown as follows:

---

[2]For purposes of illustration, the 40% tax rate is assumed to include all federal, state, and local income taxes.

Trans. Date	Balance Sheet			Income Statement		
	Assets	Liabilities	Stockholders' Equity	Revenue	Expense	Net Income
		Income Tax Pay. 40,000			Income Tax Exp. 120,000	−120,000
		Deferred Income Tax Pay. 80,000				
Net Effect		120,000	−120,000		120,000	−120,000
			Retained Earnings			
			(Net Income)			

The income tax expense reported on the income statement is the total tax, $120,000, expected to be paid on the income for the year. In future years, the $80,000 in *Deferred Income Tax Payable* will be transferred to *Income Tax Payable* as the timing differences reverse and the taxes become due.

The balance of Deferred Income Tax Payable at the end of a year is reported as a liability. The amount due within one year is classified as a current liability. The remainder is classified as a long-term liability or reported in the Deferred Liability section following the Long-Term Liabilities section.[3]

Contingent Liabilities

Some past transactions will result in liabilities if certain events occur in the future. These potential obligations are called **contingent liabilities**. For example, Ford Motor Company would have a contingent liability for the estimated costs associated with warranty work. The obligation is contingent on a future event, namely, a customer requiring warranty work on a vehicle. The obligation is the result of a past transaction, which is the original sale of the vehicle.

If the contingent liability is probable and the amount of the liability can be reasonably estimated, it should be recorded in the accounts. An example of such a liability is Ford Motor Company's vehicle warranties. These warranty costs are probable because it is known that warranty repairs will be required on some vehicles. In addition, the costs can be estimated from past warranty experience.

To illustrate, assume that during June a company sells a product for $60,000 that has a 36-month warranty for repairing defects. Past experience indicates that the average cost to repair defects is 5% of the sales price. Warranty expense of $3,000 (0.05 × $60,000) should be recorded along with an increase in estimated product warranty liabilities. By recording the warranty expense in June, revenues and expenses are properly matched in that warranty costs are recorded in the same period as the sales. When the defective product is repaired, the repair costs are recorded by decreasing the warranty liability account and decreasing cash, supplies, or other appropriate accounts.

ETHICS IN ACTION

Environmental and public health claims are quickly growing into some of the largest contingent liabilities facing companies. For example, tobacco, asbestos, and environmental clean-up claims have reached billions of dollars and have led to a number of corporate bankruptcies. Managers must be careful that today's decisions don't become tomorrow's nightmare.

[3]In some cases, a deferred tax asset can arise for tax benefits to be received in the future. Such deferred tax assets are reported as either a current or long-term asset, depending on when the benefits are expected to be realized.

Payroll

The term **payroll** refers to the amount paid to employees for the services they provide during a period. Payroll can include either salaries or wages or both. *Salary* usually refers to payment for managerial, administrative, or similar services. The rate of salary is normally expressed in terms of a month or a year. The word *wages* usually refers to payment for manual labor, both skilled and unskilled. The rate of wages is normally stated on an hourly or weekly basis. Payroll and related payroll taxes have a significant effect on the net income of most businesses. Although the amount of such expenses varies widely, it is not unusual for a business's payroll and payroll-related expenses to equal nearly one-third of its revenue.

The total earnings of an employee for a payroll period, including bonuses and overtime pay, is called **gross pay**. From this amount is subtracted one or more deductions to arrive at the net pay. **Net pay** is the amount the employer must pay the employee. The deductions for federal taxes are usually the largest deduction. Deductions may also be required for state or local income taxes. Still other deductions may be made for FICA tax, medical insurance, contributions to pensions, and for items authorized by individual employees.

ETHICS IN ACTION

Companies must guard against the fraudulent creation and cashing of payroll checks. Numerous payroll frauds involve supervisors adding fictitious employees to or failing to remove departing employees from the payroll and then cashing the check. Requiring proper authorization and approval of employee additions, removals, or changes in pay rates can minimize this type of fraud.

The FICA tax withheld from employees contributes to two federal programs. The first program, called *social security*, is for old age, survivors, and disability insurance (OASDI). The second program, called *Medicare*, is health insurance for senior citizens. The FICA tax rate and the amounts subject to the tax are established annually by law.[4]

To illustrate recording payroll, assume that McDermott Co. had a gross payroll of $13,800 for the week ending April 11. Assume that the FICA tax was 7.5% of the gross payroll and that federal and state withholding was $1,655 and $280, respectively. The effect on the accounts and financial statements of McDermott Co. of recording the payroll follows:

Trans. Date	Balance Sheet			Income Statement		
	Assets	Liabilities	Stockholders' Equity	Revenue	Expense	Net Income
4/11	Cash −10,830	FICA Tax Pay. 1,035			Wages and Salary Exp. 13,800	−13,800
		Employee Fed. Inc. Tax Pay. 1,655				
		Employee State Inc. Tax Pay. 280				
Net Effect	−10,830	2,970	−13,800		13,800	−13,800
			Retained Earnings			
			(Net Income)			

[4]The social security tax portion of the FICA tax is limited to a specific amount of the annual compensation for each individual. The 2002 limitation is $84,000. The Medicare portion is not subject to a limitation. Throughout this text, we will simplify by assuming that all compensation is within the social security limitation. By doing so, the social security and Medicare can be expressed as a single rate of 7.5%.

The FICA, federal, and state taxes withheld from the employees' earnings are not expenses to the employer. Rather, these amounts are withheld on the behalf of employees. These amounts must be remitted periodically to the appropriate state and federal agencies.

In addition to amounts withheld on behalf of employees, most employers are also subject to federal and state payroll taxes based on the amount paid their employees. Such taxes are an operating expense of the business.

Employers are required to contribute to the social security and Medicare programs for each employee. The employer must match the employee's contribution to each program. In addition, most businesses must also pay federal and state unemployment taxes.

The Federal Unemployment Tax Act (FUTA) provides for temporary payments to those who become unemployed as a result of layoffs due to economic causes beyond their control. Types of employment subject to this program are similar to those covered by FICA taxes. The FUTA tax rate and maximum earnings of each employee subject to the tax are established annually by law.

ETHICS IN ACTION

Failure to pay payroll taxes on the proper reporting dates can result in severe penalties. These penalties are put in place to dissuade business owners from financing losses from tax payments withheld from employees and due to taxing authorities. One fraudulent practice is termed "pyramiding." Pyramiding occurs when a business withholds taxes from its employees but intentionally fails to remit them to the taxing authorities. Businesses involved in pyramiding frequently file for bankruptcy to eliminate the liability and then start a new business under a different name to begin a new scheme.

State Unemployment Tax Acts (SUTA) also provide for payments to unemployed workers. The amounts paid as benefits are obtained, for the most part, from a tax levied on employers only. The employment experience and the status of each employer's tax account are reviewed annually, and the tax rates are adjusted accordingly by each state.

The employer's payroll taxes become liabilities when the related payroll is *paid* to employees. The prior payroll information of McDermott Co. indicates that the amount of FICA tax withheld is $1,035 on April 11. Since the employer must match the employees' FICA contributions, the employer's social security payroll tax will also be $1,035. Furthermore, assume that the FUTA and SUTA taxes are $145 and $25, respectively. The effect on the accounts and financial statements of McDermott Co. of recording the payroll tax liabilities for the week follows.

Trans. Date	Balance Sheet			Income Statement		
	Assets	Liabilities	Stockholders' Equity	Revenue	Expense	Net Income
4/11		FICA Tax Pay. 1,035			Payroll Tax Exp. 1,205	−1,205
		FUTA Tax Payable 145				
		SUTA Tax Payable 25				
Net Effect		1,205	−1,205		1,205	−1,205
			Retained Earnings			
			(Net Income)			

Payroll tax liabilities are paid to appropriate taxing authorities on a quarterly basis by decreasing cash and the related taxes payable.

Many companies provide their employees a variety of benefits in addition to salary and wages earned. Such **fringe benefits** can take many forms, including vacations, pension plans, and health, life, and disability insurance coverage. When the employer pays part or all of the cost of the fringe benefits, these costs must be recognized as expenses. To properly match revenues and expenses, the estimated cost of these benefits should be recorded as an expense during the period in which the employee earns the benefit. In recording the expense, the related liability is also recorded.

BUSINESS STRATEGY

People Count

Businesses that provide services to customers depend on the hiring and retaining of good employees. *Fortune* annually publishes a list of "Best Companies to Work For." In 2002, Edward Jones, a brokerage firm headquartered in St. Louis, headed the list of "Best Companies." Edward Jones rose from a ranking of 9 in 2001 to 1 in 2002.

Charles Schwab, another brokerage firm, fell from 5 to 46. For service businesses like Edward Jones and Charles Schwab, attracting and retaining employees through perks and other incentives makes good business strategy.

Source: Fortune, "Best Companies to Work For," 2002.

Bonds

OBJECTIVE   3

Describe and illustrate the financing of operations through issuance of bonds.

Many large corporations finance their operations through the issuance of bonds. A **bond** is simply a form of an interest-bearing note. Like a note, a bond requires periodic interest payments, and the face amount must be repaid at the maturity date.

A corporation that issues bonds enters into a contract, called a **bond indenture** or trust indenture, with the bondholders. A bond issue is normally divided into a number of individual bonds. Usually the face value of each bond, called the *principal*, is $1,000 or a multiple of $1,000. The interest on bonds may be payable annually, semiannually, or quarterly. Most bonds pay interest semiannually.

The prices of bonds are quoted on bond exchanges as a percentage of the bonds' face value. Thus, investors could purchase or sell AOL Time Warner bonds quoted at $109\frac{7}{8}$ for $1,098.75. Likewise, bonds quoted at 110 could be purchased or sold for $1,100.

When a corporation issues bonds, the price that buyers are willing to pay for the bonds depends on these three factors:

1. The face amount of the bonds due at the maturity date.
2. The periodic interest to be paid on the bonds.
3. The market rate of interest.

The periodic interest to be paid on the bonds is identified in the bond indenture and is expressed as a percentage of the face amount of the bond. This percentage or rate of interest is called the **contract rate** or *coupon rate*. The **market rate of interest**, sometimes called the *effective rate of interest*, is determined by transactions between buyers and sellers of similar bonds. If the contract rate of interest is the same as the market rate of interest, the bonds sell for their face amount.

To illustrate, assume that on January 1 a corporation issues for cash $100,000 of 12%, 5-year bonds, with interest of $6,000 payable semiannually. The market rate of interest at the time the bonds are issued is 12%. Since the contract rate and the market rate of interest are the same, the bonds will sell at their face amount. The effect on the accounts and financial statements of issuing the bonds, paying the semiannual interest, and paying off the bonds at the maturity date is shown here.

Issuance of bonds payable at face amount on January 1.

Trans. Date	Balance Sheet			Income Statement		
	Assets	Liabilities	Stockholders' Equity	Revenue	Expense	Net Income
1/1	Cash 100,000	Bonds Payable 100,000				
Net Effect	100,000	100,000	0			
			Retained Earnings			
			(Net Income)			

Payment of semiannual interest on June 30. (Interest: $100,000 \times 0.12 \times 1/2 = $6,000)

Trans. Date	Balance Sheet			Income Statement		
	Assets	Liabilities	Stockholders' Equity	Revenue	Expense	Net Income
6/30	Cash −6,000				Interest Exp. 6,000	−6,000
Net Effect	−6,000		−6,000		6,000	−6,000
			Retained Earnings			
			(Net Income)			

Payment of face value of bonds at maturity.

Trans. Date	Balance Sheet			Income Statement		
	Assets	Liabilities	Stockholders' Equity	Revenue	Expense	Net Income
12/31	Cash −100,000	Bonds Pay. −100,000				
Net Effect	−100,000	−100,000	0			
			Retained Earnings			
			(Net Income)			

What if the contract rate of interest differs from the market rate of interest at the time the bonds are issued? If the market rate of interest is higher than the contract rate, the sale is a **discount on bonds payable**, or less than their face amount. Why is this the case? Buyers are not willing to pay the face amount for bonds whose contract rate is lower than the market rate. The discount, in effect, represents the amount necessary to make up for the difference in the market and the contract rates of interest.

For example, if the market rate of interest was 13%, the preceding bonds would sell for $96,406.[5] The $3,594 discount ($100,000 − $96,406) can be viewed as the amount that is needed to entice investors to accept a contract rate of interest that is below the market rate. In other words, you can think of the discount as the market's way of adjusting a bond's contract rate of interest to the higher market rate of interest.

If the market rate is lower than the contract rate, the sale is a **premium on bonds payable**, or more than their face amount. In this case, buyers are willing to pay more than the face amount for bonds whose contract rate is higher than the market rate. For example, if the market rate of interest is 11%, the preceding bonds would sell for $103,769.[6] The premium of $3,769 may be viewed as the amount investors are willing to pay above the face value of the bonds to purchase bonds paying an interest rate of 12% rather than the market interest rate of 11%.

Generally accepted accounting principles require that bond discounts and premiums be amortized to interest expense over the life of the bond. The amortization of a discount increases interest expense, and the amortization of a premium reduces interest expense.

Stock

OBJECTIVE   4

Describe and illustrate the financing of operations through issuance of stock.

A major means of equity financing for a corporation is issuing stock. The equity in the assets that results from issuing stock is called *paid-in capital* or *contributed capital*. Another major means of equity financing for a corporation's operations is through retaining net income in the business, called *retained earnings*. In this section, we discuss the financing of a corporation's operations through issuing stock.

The number of shares of stock that a corporation is authorized to issue is stated in its charter. The term *issued* refers to the shares issued to the stockholders. A corporation may, under circumstances we discuss later in this chapter, reacquire some of the stock that it has issued. The stock remaining in the hands of stockholders is then called **outstanding stock**. The relationship between authorized, issued, and outstanding stock is shown in the margin.

Shares of stock are often assigned a monetary amount, called **par**. Corporations can issue stock certificates to stockholders to document their ownership. Printed on a stock certificate is the par value of the stock, the name of the stockholder, and the number of shares owned. Stock can also be issued without par, in which case it is called *no-par stock*. Some states require the board of directors to assign a **stated value** to no-par stock.

Number of shares authorized, issued, and outstanding

Because corporations have limited liability, creditors have no claim against the personal assets of stockholders. However, some state laws require that corporations maintain a minimum stockholder contribution to protect creditors. This minimum amount is called *legal capital*. The amount of required legal capital varies among the states, but it usually includes the amount of par or stated value of the shares of stock issued.

[5]The proceeds of $96,406 can be computed using present value tables. Such computations, however, are beyond the scope of our discussion in this chapter.
[6]The proceeds of $103,769 can be computed using present value tables. Such computations, however, are beyond the scope of our discussion in this chapter.

The major rights that accompany ownership of a share of stock are as follows:

1. The right to vote in matters concerning the corporation.
2. The right to share in distributions of earnings.
3. The right to share in assets on liquidation.

Common and Preferred Stock

When only one class of stock is issued, it is called **common stock**. In this case, each share of common stock has equal rights. To appeal to a broader investment market, a corporation can issue one or more classes of stock with various preference rights. A common example of such a right is the preference to dividends. Such a stock is generally called a **preferred stock**.

The dividend rights of preferred stock are usually stated in monetary terms or as a percentage of par. For example, $4 preferred stock has a right to an annual $4-per-share dividend. If the par value of the preferred stock were $50, the same right to dividends could be stated as 8% ($4/$50) preferred stock.

The board of directors of a corporation has the sole authority to distribute dividends to the stockholders. When such action is taken, the directors are said to *declare a dividend*. Since dividends are normally based on earnings, a corporation cannot guarantee dividends even to preferred stockholders. However, because they have first rights to any dividends, the preferred stockholders have a better chance of receiving regular dividends than do the common stockholders.

Some preferred stock can also be granted the right to receive regular dividends that have been passed (not declared) before any common stock dividends are paid. Such stock is called **cumulative preferred stock**, and the dividends that have been passed are said to be *in arrears*.

To illustrate how dividends on cumulative preferred stock are calculated, assume that a corporation has 1,000 shares of $4 cumulative preferred stock and 4,000 shares of common stock outstanding. Also assume that no dividends were paid in 2002 and 2003. Exhibit 1, on the following page, shows how dividends of $22,000, declared in 2004, would be distributed between the preferred and common stockholders.

Issuance of Stock

Because different classes of stock have different rights, a separate account is used for recording the amount of each class of stock issued to investors in a corporation. Stock is often issued by a corporation at a price other than its par. This happens because the par value of a stock is simply its legal capital. The price at which stock can be sold by a corporation depends on a variety of factors, such as these:

1. The financial condition, earnings record, and dividend record of the corporation.
2. Investor expectations of the corporation's potential earning power.
3. General business and economic conditions and prospects.

Normally, stock is issued for a price that is more than its par. In this case, it is sold at a **premium on stock**.[7] Thus, if stock with a par of $50 is issued for a price of $60,

---

[7] When stock is issued for a price that is less than its par, the stock is sold at a discount. Many states do not permit stock to be issued at a discount. In others, it may be done only under unusual conditions. For these reasons, we assume that stock is sold at par or at a premium in the remainder of this text.

EXHIBIT 1
*Dividends to Cumulative
Preferred Stock*

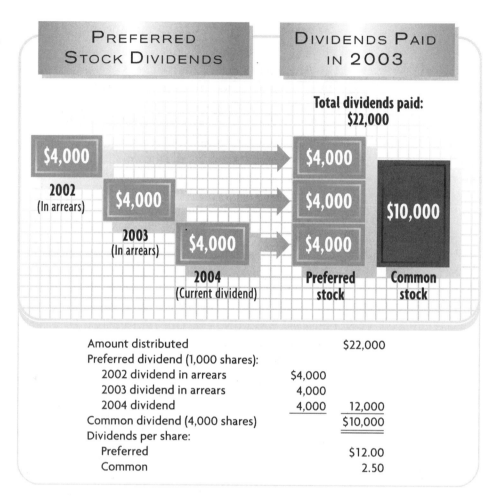

Amount distributed		$22,000
Preferred dividend (1,000 shares):		
2002 dividend in arrears	$4,000	
2003 dividend in arrears	4,000	
2004 dividend	4,000	12,000
Common dividend (4,000 shares)		$10,000
Dividends per share:		
Preferred		$12.00
Common		2.50

the stock is sold at a premium of $10. When stock is issued at a premium, Cash or another asset account is increased for the amount received. Common Stock or Preferred Stock is then increased for the par amount. The excess of the amount paid over par is a part of the total capital contributed by the stockholders of the corporation. This amount is usually recorded in an account entitled Paid-In Capital in Excess of Par.

To illustrate, assume that Caldwell Company issues 2,000 shares of $1 par preferred stock for cash at $55 on November 1. The effects on the accounts and financial statements follow:

Trans. Date	Balance Sheet				Income Statement		
	Assets	Liabilities	Stockholders' Equity		Revenue	Expense	Net Income
	Cash 110,000		Common Stock	2,000			
			Paid-In Capital in Excess of Par	108,000			
Net Effect	*110,000*			*110,000*			

When stock is issued in exchange for assets other than cash, such as land, buildings, and equipment, the assets acquired should be recorded at their fair market value. If this value cannot be objectively determined, the fair market price of the stock issued may be used.

In most states, both preferred and common stock may be issued without a par value. When no-par stock is issued, the entire proceeds are recorded in the stock account. In some states, no-par stock may be assigned a stated value per share. The stated value is recorded like a par value, and the excess of the proceeds over the stated value is recorded in a paid-in capital in excess of stated value account, similar to the recording of a premium.

Reacquired Stock

A corporation may buy its own stock to provide shares for resale to employees, for reissuing as a bonus to employees, or for supporting the market price of the stock. For example, **General Motors** bought back its common stock and stated that two primary uses of this stock would be for incentive compensation plans and employee savings plans. Stock that a corporation has once issued and then reacquires is called **treasury stock**.

The purchase of treasury stock decreases the corporation's assets and stockholders' equity. The par value and the price at which the stock was originally issued are ignored. When the stock is resold or reissued, the assets and the stockholders' equity increase.

Dividends

OBJECTIVE 5

Describe and illustrate the accounting for cash and stock dividends.

When a board of directors declares a cash dividend, it authorizes the distribution of a portion of the corporation's cash to stockholders. When a board of directors declares a stock dividend, it authorizes the distribution of a portion of its stock. In both cases, the declaration of a dividend reduces the corporation's retained earnings.

Cash Dividends

A cash distribution of earnings by a corporation to its shareholders is called a **cash dividend**. Although dividends may be paid in the form of other assets, cash dividends are the most common form.

There are usually three conditions that a corporation must meet to pay a cash dividend:

1. Sufficient retained earnings
2. Sufficient cash
3. Formal action by the board of directors

A large amount of retained earnings does not always mean that a corporation has cash available for paying dividends. Also, a corporation's board of directors is not required by law to declare dividends. This is true even if both retained earnings and cash are large enough to justify a dividend. However, most corporations try to maintain a stable dividend record to make their stock attractive to investors. Although dividends may be paid once a year or semiannually, most corporations pay dividends quarterly. In years of high profits, a corporation may declare a special or extra dividend.

You may have seen announcements of dividend declarations in financial newspapers or investor services. An example of such an announcement follows.

> On September 28, the board of directors of **Campbell Soup Co.** declared a quarterly cash dividend of $0.1575 per common share to stockholders of record as of the close of business on October 5, payable on October 31.

This announcement includes three important dates: *the date of declaration* (September 28), *the date of record* (October 5), and *the date of payment* (October 31). During the period of time between the record date and the payment date, the stock price is usually quoted as selling *ex-dividends*. This means that since the date of record has passed, a new investor will not receive the dividend.

To illustrate, assume that on *December 1* Hiber Corporation's board of directors declares the following quarterly cash dividend. The date of record is *December 10*, and the date of payment is *January 2*.

	Dividend per Share	Total Dividends
Preferred stock, $100 par, 5,000 shares outstanding	$2.50	$12,500
Common stock, $10 par, 100,000 shares outstanding	$0.30	30,000
Total		$42,500

The effect of the declaration of the dividend on the accounts and financial statements is as follows:

Trans. Date	Balance Sheet			Income Statement		
	Assets	Liabilities	Stockholders' Equity	Revenue	Expense	Net Income
12/1		Cash Dividends Pay. 42,500	Dividends 42,500			
Net Effect		42,500	−42,500			
			Retained Earnings			

Note that the date of record, December 10, does not affect the accounts or the financial statements since this date merely determines which stockholders will receive the dividend. The payment of the dividend on January 2 decreases cash and dividends payable. At the end of the period, the decrease in retained earnings is recorded when the dividends account is closed.

If a corporation holding treasury stock declares a cash dividend, the dividends are not paid on the treasury shares. To do so would place the corporation in the position of earning income through dealing with itself. For example, if Hiber Corporation in the preceding illustration had held 5,000 shares of its own common stock, the cash dividends on the common stock would have been $28,500 [(100,000 − 5,000) × $0.30] instead of $30,000.

Stock Dividends

A distribution of shares of stock to stockholders is called a **stock dividend**. Usually, such distributions are in common stock and are issued to holders of common stock. Stock dividends are different from cash dividends in that there is no distribution of cash or other assets to stockholders.

The effect of a stock dividend on the stockholders' equity of the issuing corporation is to transfer retained earnings to paid-in capital. For public corporations, the amount transferred from the retained earnings account to the paid-in capital account is normally the fair value (market price) of the shares issued in the stock dividend.[8]

A stock dividend does not change the assets, liabilities, or total stockholders' equity of the corporation. Likewise, it does not change a stockholder's proportionate interest (equity) in the corporation. For example, if a stockholder owned 1,000 of a corporation's 10,000 shares outstanding, the stockholder owns 10% (1,000/10,000) of the corporation. After declaring a 6% stock dividend, the corporation will issue 600 additional shares (10,000 shares × 0.06), and the total shares outstanding will be 10,600. The stockholder of 1,000 shares will receive 60 additional shares and will then own 1,060 shares, which is still a 10% equity.

Stock Splits

OBJECTIVE 6

Describe the effects of stock splits on the financial statements.

Corporations sometimes reduce the par or stated value of their common stock and issue a proportionate number of additional shares. When this is done, a corporation is said to have *split* its stock, and the process is called a **stock split**.

When stock is split, the reduction in par or stated value applies to all shares, including the unissued, issued, and treasury shares. A major objective of a stock split is to reduce the stock's market price per share. This, in turn, should attract more investors to enter the market for the stock and broaden the types and numbers of stockholders.

To illustrate a stock split, assume that Rojek Corporation has 10,000 shares of $100 par common stock outstanding with a current market price of $150 per share. The board of directors declares a 5-for-1 stock split, reduces the par to $20, and increases the number of shares to 50,000. The amount of common stock outstanding is $1,000,000 both before and after the stock split. Only the number of shares and the par value per share are changed. Each Rojek Corporation shareholder owns the same total par amount of stock before and after the stock split. For example, a stockholder who owned 4 shares of $100 par stock before the split (total par of $400) would own 20 shares of $20 par stock after the split (total par of $400).

Since there are more shares outstanding after the stock split, we would expect that the market price of the stock would fall. For example, in the preceding example, there would be 5 times as many shares outstanding after the split. Thus, we would expect the market price of the stock to fall from $150 to approximately $30 ($150/5).

Sometimes a firm will authorize a *reverse stock split* in which the number of shares outstanding is reduced to increase the market price of the stock. A common rationale

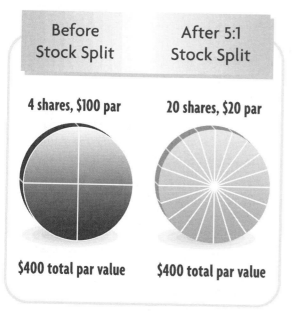

Before Stock Split

After 5:1 Stock Split

4 shares, $100 par

20 shares, $20 par

$400 total par value

$400 total par value

---

[8]The use of fair market value is justified as long as the number of shares issued for the stock dividend is small (less than 25% of the shares outstanding).

for a reverse stock split is to increase the market value of the stock above minimum listing requirements for a stock exchange. For example, NASDAQ requires a minimum market price of $1 per share. Firms that drop below the $1 market price will sometimes authorize a reverse stock split to increase the market price above the minimum requirement. **Iomega Corp.** justified its reverse 1:5 stock split when shares were trading near $1, stating:

> ... a reverse split will boost shares to above $5 each. Getting it to $5 would make it more attractive to institutional investors.

Since a stock split changes only the par or stated value and the number of shares outstanding, it is not recorded by a journal entry. Although the accounts are not affected, the details of stock splits are normally disclosed in the notes to the financial statements.

Reporting Liabilities and Stockholders' Equity

OBJECTIVE   7

Describe financial statement reporting of liabilities and stockholders' equity.

Liabilities that are expected to be paid within one year are presented in the Current Liabilities section of the balance sheet. Thus, any notes or bonds payable maturing within one year should be shown as current liabilities. However, if the notes or bonds are to be paid from noncurrent assets or if the notes or bonds are going to be refinanced, they should be reported as noncurrent liabilities. The detailed descriptions, including terms, due dates, and interest rates for notes or bonds, should be reported either on the balance sheet or in an accompanying footnote. Also, the fair market value of notes or bonds should be disclosed. Exhibit 2 illustrates the reporting of liabilities on the balance sheet.

As we discussed earlier in this chapter, some contingent liabilities are not reported on the balance sheet. Such liabilities that are probable but cannot be reasonably estimated or are only possible should be disclosed in the footnotes to the financial statements. To illustrate such a disclosure, a portion of the footnote taken from an annual report of **Philip Morris Companies, Inc.,** is shown:

> ... Pending claims related to tobacco products generally fall within three categories: (i) smoking and health cases alleging personal injury brought on behalf of individual smokers, (ii) smoking and health cases alleging personal injury and purporting to be brought on behalf of a class of plaintiffs, and (iii) health care cost recovery actions brought primarily by states and local governments seeking reimbursement for Medicaid and other health care expenditures allegedly caused by cigarette smoking. ...

Although stockholders' equity is reported on the balance sheet, significant changes in stockholders' equity during the year should also be disclosed. Changes in retained earnings are often presented in a separate retained earnings statement. Changes in paid-in capital during the year may be reported on the face of the balance sheet or in the accompanying footnotes. Some companies prepare a separate statement of stockholders' equity that includes changes in both paid-in capital and retained earnings. An example of a statement of stockholders' equity is shown in Exhibit 3 on page 300.

EXHIBIT 2

Partial Balance Sheet with Liabilities and Stockholders' Equity

ESCOE CORPORATION
Balance Sheet
December 31, 2004

Liabilities

Current liabilities:		
Accounts payable	$ 488,200	
Notes payable (9% due on March 1, 2005)	250,000	
Accrued interest payable	15,000	
Accrued salaries and wages payable	13,500	
Other accrued liabilities	9,850	
Total current liabilities		$ 776,550
Long-term liabilities:		
Debenture 8% bonds payable, due December 31, 2020		
(Market value $950,000)		1,000,000
Total liabilities		$1,776,550

Stockholders' Equity

Paid-in capital:		
Preferred 10% stock, cumulative, $50 par		
(20,000 shares authorized and issued)	$1,000,000	
Common stock, $20 par (250,000 shares authorized,		
100,000 shares issued)	2,000,000	
Additional paid-in capital in excess of par	520,000	
Total paid-in capital	$3,520,000	
Retained earnings	4,580,500	
Total	$8,100,500	
Deduct treasury stock (1,000 shares at cost)	75,000	
Total stockholders' equity		8,025,500
Total liabilities and stockholders' equity		$9,802,050

Earnings per Share

OBJECTIVE   8

Analyze the impact of debt or equity financing on earnings per share.

One of the many factors that influence the decision of whether to finance operations using debt or equity is the effect of each alternative on earnings per share. Earnings per share is a major profitability measure that is reported in the financial statements and is followed closely by the financial press. As a result, corporate managers closely monitor the impact of decisions on earnings per share.

If a corporation has issued only common stock, **earnings per share** is computed by dividing net income by the number of shares of common stock outstanding.[9] If preferred and common stock have been issued, the net income must first be reduced by the amount of preferred dividends. To illustrate, assume that Lincoln Corporation

[9]Earnings per share is further discussed in Chapter 9, "Financial Statement Analysis."

EXHIBIT 3   *Statement of Stockholders' Equity*

TELEX INC.
Statement of Stockholders' Equity
For the Year Ended December 31, 2004

	Preferred Stock	Common Stock	Paid-In Capital in Excess of Par— Common Stock	Retained Earnings	Treasury (Common) Stock	Total
Balance, January 1	$5,000,000	$10,000,000	$3,000,000	$2,000,000	$(500,000)	$19,500,000
Net income				850,000		850,000
Dividends on preferred stock				(250,000)		(250,000)
Dividends on common stock				(400,000)		(400,000)
Issuance of additional common stock		500,000	50,000			550,000
Purchase of treasury stock					(30,000)	(30,000)
Balance, December 31	$5,000,000	$10,500,000	$3,050,000	$2,200,000	$(530,000)	$20,220,000

has 100,000 shares of 9%, $100 par preferred stock and 50,000 shares of $200 par common stock outstanding. The earnings per share is computed as shown:

	2002	2001
Net income	$91,000	$76,500
Preferred dividends	9,000	9,000
	$82,000	$67,500
Shares of common stock outstanding	50,000 shares	50,000 shares
Earnings per share of common stock	$1.64	$1.35

To illustrate the possible effects of debt and equity financing on earnings per share, assume that Martin Corporation is considering the following alternative plans for financing its operations:

Plan 1: 100% financing from issuing common stock, $10 par

Plan 2: 50% financing from issuing preferred 9% stock, $50 par
50% financing from issuing common stock, $10 par

Plan 3: 50% financing from issuing 12% bonds
25% financing from issuing preferred 9% stock, $50 par
25% financing from issuing common stock, $10 par

In each case, we assume that the stocks or bonds are issued at their par or face amount. The corporation is expecting to earn $800,000 annually before deducting interest on the bonds and income taxes estimated at 40% of income. Exhibit 4 shows the effect of the three plans on the income of the corporation and the earnings per share on common stock.

EXHIBIT 4 *Effect of Alternative Financing Plans—$800,000 Earnings*

	Plan 1	Plan 2	Plan 3
12% bonds	—	—	$2,000,000
Preferred 9% stock, $50 par	—	$2,000,000	1,000,000
Common stock, $10 par	$4,000,000	2,000,000	1,000,000
Total	$4,000,000	$4,000,000	$4,000,000
Earnings before interest and income tax	$ 800,000	$ 800,000	$ 800,000
Deduct interest on bonds	—	—	240,000
Income before income tax	$ 800,000	$ 800,000	$ 560,000
Deduct income tax	320,000	320,000	224,000
Net income	$ 480,000	$ 480,000	$ 336,000
Dividends on preferred stock	—	180,000	90,000
Available for dividends on common stock	$ 480,000	$ 300,000	$ 246,000
Shares of common stock outstanding	÷ 400,000	÷ 200,000	÷ 100,000
Earnings per share on common stock	$ 1.20	$ 1.50	$ 2.46

Exhibit 4 indicates that plan 3 yields the highest earnings per share on common stock and is thus the most attractive for common stockholders. If the estimated earnings are more than $800,000, the difference between the earnings per share to common stockholders under plan 1 and plan 3 is even greater.[10] However, if smaller earnings occur, plans 2 and 3 become less attractive to common stockholders.

Analyze and Interpret Solvency

OBJECTIVE   9

Analyze and interpret long-term liability position with the number of times interest charges are earned and total liabilities to total asset ratio.

As an individual, if you have an annual salary of $50,000 per year, you should not borrow $500,000 for a new house. The reason is that your monthly income cannot support the monthly debt payments. Similarly, managers set long-term debt levels that can be supported by the company's income. The ability of a business to meet its fixed financial obligations (debts) is called **solvency**. We will describe two solvency ratios.

The first solvency ratio measures the relationship between a company's income and its interest expense on debt. The ratio is called the **number of times the interest charges are earned** during the year (or *interest coverage ratio*), and is calculated as follows:

$$\text{Number of times interest charges are earned} =$$

$$\frac{\text{Income before income tax} + \text{Interest expense}}{\text{Interest expense}}$$

The calculation uses "income *before* income tax" in the numerator because the amount available to make interest payments is not affected by taxes on income. This

[10]The higher earnings per share under plan 1 is due to a finance concept known as *leverage*. This concept is discussed further in Chapter 9, "Financial Statement Analysis."

happens because interest is deductible in determining taxable income. In interpreting the ratio, the higher the ratio, the better the chance that interest payments will continue to be made if earnings decrease. In contrast, the lower the ratio, the better the chance the company will be unable to support its required interest payments from current period earnings.[11]

To illustrate this ratio, the following financial statement information was taken from a recent annual report for **SBC Communications, Inc.,** a telecommunication company:

Interest expense	$ 1,592 million
Income before taxes	12,888 million

The number of times interest charges are earned, 9.1, is calculated using the preceding formula as follows:

$$\text{Number of times interest charges are earned} = \frac{\$12,888 \ million + \$1,592 \ million}{\$1,592 \ million}$$

The number of times interest charges are earned indicates that the creditors of SBC have their interest receipts protected by more than nine times earnings. This would be considered very adequate in most circumstances. The number of times interest charges are earned for some other companies in SBC's industry are as follows:

Telecommunication Company	Number of Times Interest Charges Are Earned
AT&T Corp.	1.82
Bellsouth Corp.	5.97
Qwest Communications	1.12
Sprint Corp.	0.29
Verizon Communications Inc.	6.11

As you can see, SBC's interest coverage appears to be one of the best in this industry. In contrast, **Sprint Corp.** and **Qwest Communications** have poor interest coverage. The reason for the poor interest coverage is either due to poor earnings (small numerator) or large interest expense (large denominator), or a combination of both. The second solvency measure helps isolate the cause.

The second solvency measure compares the total liabilities to the amount of total assets. To illustrate, assume that you borrowed $80,000 and used $20,000 of your own funds to purchase a $100,000 house. Your debt as a percentage of the total value of the house is 80% ($80,000/$100,000). In a similar way, analysts can measure a company's relative use of debt by measuring the ratio of the total liabilities to the total assets of the company. The **total liabilities to total assets ratio** is calculated as follows:[12]

[11]A similar analysis can also be applied to dividends on preferred stock. In such cases, net income would be divided by the amount of preferred dividends to yield the number of times preferred dividends were earned. This measure gives an indication of the relative assurance of continued dividend payments to preferred stockholders.

[12]The total liabilities to total stockholders' equity ratio is another common solvency measure. This ratio is algebraically related to the total liabilities to total assets ratio and thus conveys the same relative information.

$$\text{Total liabilities to total assets} = \frac{\text{Total liabilities}}{\text{Total assets}}$$

To illustrate, annual report information for SBC reported the following:

Total liabilities	$68,188 million
Total assets	98,651 million

Thus, the total liabilities to total asset ratio is as follows:

$$\frac{\$68,188 \; million}{\$98,651 \; million} = 69\%$$

This ratio should be interpreted by comparing it to the ratio for some other companies in the industry. This is done because some industries use more debt than others. The total liabilities to total assets ratio for the selected companies in the telecommunication industry is as follows:

Telecommunication Company	Total Liabilities to Total Assets Ratio
AT&T Corp.	53%
Bellsouth Corp.	67
Qwest Communications	44
Sprint Corp.	67
Verizon Communications Inc.	66

From this information we can conclude that SBC's debt at 69% of total assets is slightly higher than other companies in the industry. In addition, we can determine that neither Qwest nor Sprint is using debt excessively. Indeed, Qwest appears to be using less debt than other companies in the industry. Thus, the low number of times interest charges are earned for Qwest and Sprint appears to be caused more by low earnings rather than excessive debt.

Key Points

1. **Describe how businesses finance their operations.**

A business must finance its operations through either debt or equity. Debt financing includes all liabilities owed by a business, including both current and long-term liabilities. A corporation may also finance its operations by issuing stock. Corporations may issue different classes of stock that contain different rights and privileges, such as rights to dividend payments.

2. **Describe and illustrate current liabilities, notes payable, taxes, contingencies, and payroll.**

Liabilities that are to be paid out of current assets and are due within a short time, usually within one year, are called *current liabilities*. Most current liabilities arise from either receiving goods or services prior to making payment or receiving payment prior to delivering goods or services. Current liabilities can also arise from notes payable, taxes, contingencies, and payroll. Warranties are examples of liabilities arising from contingencies. Wages and salaries payable and employee and employer payroll taxes are examples of liabilities arising from payroll. Deferrred income taxes arise from temporary differences between taxable income and income before taxes as reported on the income statement.

3. **Describe and illustrate the financing of operations through issuance of bonds.**

Many large corporations finance their operations through the issuance of bonds. A bond is simply a form of an interest-bearing note that requires periodic interest payments and the repayment of the face amount at the maturity date. When the contract rate of interest differs from the market rate of interest, bonds are issued at discounts or premiums. The amortization of discounts and premiums affects interest expense.

4. **Describe and illustrate the financing of operations through issuance of stock.**

A corporation may finance its operations by issuing either preferred or common stock. Preferred stock has preferential rights, including the right to receive dividends ahead of the common stockholders. When stock is issued at a premium, Cash or another asset account is increased for the amount received. Common Stock or Preferred Stock is increased for the par amount. The excess of the amount paid over par is a part of the paid-in capital and is normally recorded in an account entitled Paid-In Capital in Excess of Par.

Stock that a corporation has once issued and then reacquires is called *treasury stock*. It decreases stockholders' equity.

5. **Describe and illustrate the accounting for cash and stock dividends.**

When a board of directors declares a cash dividend, it authorizes the distribution of a portion of the corporation's cash to stockholders. When a board of directors declares a stock dividend, it authorizes the distribution of a portion of the stock. In both cases, the declaration of a dividend reduces the retained earnings of the corporation.

6. **Describe the effects of stock splits on the financial statements.**

Corporations sometimes reduce the par or stated value of their common stock and issue a proportionate number of additional shares in what is called a *stock split*. Since a stock split changes only the par or stated value and the number of shares outstanding, it is not recorded. However, the details of stock splits are normally disclosed in the notes to the financial statements.

7. **Describe financial statement reporting of liabilities and stockholders' equity.**

Liabilities that are expected to be paid within one year are presented in the Current Liabilities section of the balance sheet. Notes or bonds payable not maturing within one year should be shown as noncurrent liabilities. The detailed descriptions including terms, due dates, and interest rates for notes or bonds should be reported either on the balance sheet or in an accompanying footnote. Also, the fair market value of notes or bonds should be disclosed. The notes should disclose any contingent liabilities that cannot be reasonably estimated or are only possible. Significant changes in stockholders' equity during the year should also be reported.

8. **Analyze the impact of debt or equity financing on earnings per share.**

One of the many factors that influence the decision of whether to finance operations using debt or equity is the effect of each alternative on earnings per share. If a corporation has issued only common stock, earnings per share is computed by dividing net income by the number of shares of common stock outstanding. If preferred and common stock have been issued, the net income must first be reduced by the amount of preferred dividends.

9. **Analyze and interpret long-term liability position with the number of times interest charges are earned and total liabilities to total asset ratio.**

The ability of a business to meet its fixed financial obligations (debts) is called *solvency*. Two solvency ratios are (1) the number of times the interest charges are earned and (2) the total liabilities to total assets ratio. The number of times the interest charges are earned ratio measures the chance that interest payments will continue to be made in the future. The total liabilities to total assets ratio measures percentage of assets financed by debt.

Glossary

Bond: A form of interest-bearing note used by corporations to borrow on a long-term basis.

Bond indenture: The contract between a corporation issuing bonds and the bondholders.

Cash dividend: A cash distribution of earnings by a corporation to its shareholders.

Common stock: The stock outstanding when a corporation has issued only one class of stock.

Contingent liabilities: Potential liabilities if certain events occur in the future.

Contract rate: The periodic interest to be paid on the bonds that is identified in the bond indenture; expressed as a percentage of the face amount of the bond.

Cumulative preferred stock: A class of preferred stock that has a right to receive regular dividends that have been passed (not declared) before any common stock dividends are paid.

Discount on bonds payable: The excess of the face amount of bonds over their issue price.

Earnings per share: A measure of profitability computed by dividing net income, reduced by preferred dividends, by common stockholders' equity.

Fringe benefits: Benefits provided to employees in addition to wages and salaries.

Gross pay: The total earnings of an employee for a payroll period.

Market rate of interest: The effective rate of interest at the time bonds are issued.

Maturity: The time period that the liability is outstanding prior to its due date.

Net pay: Gross pay less payroll deductions; the amount the employer is obligated to pay the employee.

Number of times the interest charges are earned: A solvency ratio that measures the ability to pay future interest charges.

Outstanding stock: The stock in the hands of stockholders.

Par: The monetary amount printed on a stock certificate.

Payroll: The total amount paid to employees for a certain period.

Preferred stock: A class of stock with preferential rights over common stock.

Premium on bonds payable: The excess of the issue price of bonds over their face amount.

Premium on stock: The excess of the issue price of a stock over its par value.

Solvency: The ability of a business to meet its fixed financial obligations (debts).

Stated value: A value, similar to par value, approved by the board of directors of a corporation for no-par stock.

Stock dividend: A distribution of shares of stock to its stockholders.

Stock split: The reduction in the par or stated value of common stock and issuance of a proportionate number of additional shares.

Taxable income: The income of a corporation that is subject to taxes as determined according to the tax laws.

Temporary differences: Differences between taxable income and income before income taxes that are created because items are recognized in one period for tax purposes and in another period for income statement purposes.

Total liabilities to total assets ratio: A solvency ratio that measures the percentage of total assets financed by debt.

Treasury stock: Stock that a corporation has once issued and then reacquires.

Self-Study Questions

(Answers appear at end of chapter.)

1. A business issued a $5,000, 60-day, 12% note to the bank. The amount due at maturity is:
   A. $4,900
   B. $5,000
   C. $5,100
   D. $5,600

2. If a corporation has outstanding 1,000 shares of $9 cumulative preferred stock of $100 par and dividends have been passed or not been paid for the preceding three years, what is the amount of preferred dividends

that must be declared in the current year before a dividend can be declared on common stock?

A. $9,000   C. $36,000

B. $27,000   D. $45,000

3. If a corporation plans to issue $1,000,000 of 12% bonds when the market rate for similar bonds is 10%, the bonds can be expected to sell at:

A. Their face amount

B. A premium

C. A discount

D. A price below their face amount

4. A corporation has issued 25,000 shares of $100 par common stock and holds 3,000 of these shares as

treasury stock. If the corporation declares a $2 per share cash dividend, what amount will be recorded as cash dividends?

A. $22,000   C. $44,000

B. $25,000   D. $50,000

5. A firm reported net income before tax of $500,000 and paid dividends of $200,000. The firm has $1,000,000 face value 10% bonds outstanding. What is the number of times interest charges are earned?

A. 3.0   C. 5.0

B. 4.0   D. 6.0

Discussion Questions

1. What two types of transactions cause most current liabilities?

2. When are short-term notes payable issued?

3. When should the liability associated with a product warranty be recorded? Discuss.

4. **Compaq Computer Corporation** reported more than $750 million of product warranties in the Current Liabilities section of a recent balance sheet. How would costs of repairing a defective product be recorded?

5. **Delta Air Lines'** SkyMiles program allows frequent flyers to earn credit toward free tickets and other amenities. (a) Does Delta Air Lines have a contingent liability for award redemption by its SkyMiles members? (b) When should a contingent liability be recorded?

6. For each of the following payroll-related taxes, indicate whether it generally applies to (1) employees only, (2) employers only, or (3) both employees and employers:

   a. Social security tax

   b. Medicare tax

   c. Federal income tax

   d. Federal unemployment compensation tax

   e. State unemployment compensation tax

7. To match revenues and expenses properly, should the expense for employee vacation pay be recorded in the period during which the vacation privilege is earned or during the period in which the vacation is taken? Discuss.

8. Identify the two distinct obligations incurred by a corporation when issuing bonds.

9. A corporation issues $10,000,000 of 6% bonds to yield an effective interest rate of 5%.

   (a) Was the amount of cash received from the sale of the bonds more or less than $10,000,000?

   (b) Identify the following amounts related to the bond issue: (1) face amount, (2) market rate of interest, (3) contract rate of interest, and (4) maturity amount.

10. The following data relate to a $1,000,000, 6% bond issue for a selected semiannual interest period:

Bond carrying amount at beginning of period	$1,150,00
Interest paid at end of period	30,000
Interest expense allocable to the period	28,750

   (a) Were the bonds issued at a discount or at a premium? (b) What expense account was decreased to amortize the discount or premium?

11. Of two corporations organized at approximately the same time and engaged in competing businesses, one issued $50 par common stock, and the other issued $1 par common stock. Do the par designations provide any indication as to which stock is preferable as an investment? Explain.

12. A stockbroker advises a client to "buy cumulative preferred stock. . . . With that type of stock, . . . [you] will never have to worry about losing the dividends." Is the broker right?

13. When a corporation issues stock at a premium, is the premium income? Explain.

14. a. In what respect does treasury stock differ from unissued stock?
    b. How should treasury stock be presented on the balance sheet?

15. A corporation reacquires 5,000 shares of its own $40 par common stock for $370,000, recording it at cost. (a) What effect does this transaction have on revenue or expense of the period? (b) What effect does it have on stockholders' equity?

16. The treasury stock in Question 15 is resold for $400,000. (a) What is the effect on the corporation's revenue of the period? (b) What is the effect on stockholders' equity?

17. A corporation with both cumulative preferred stock and common stock outstanding has a substantial balance in its retained earnings account at the beginning of the current fiscal year. Although net income for the current year is sufficient to pay the preferred dividend of $50,000 each quarter and a common dividend of $200,000 each quarter, the board of directors declares dividends only on the preferred stock. Suggest possible reasons that the board passes the dividends on the common stock.

18. An owner of 200 shares of Dunston Company common stock receives a stock dividend of 4 shares. (a) What is the effect of the stock dividend on the stockholder's proportionate interest (equity) in the corporation? (b) How does the total equity of 204 shares compare with the total equity of 200 shares before the stock dividend?

19. What is the primary purpose of a stock split?

20. The number of times interest charges are earned declined from 2 to 1.2. Is the chance that the bondholders will receive interest payments in the future increasing, decreasing, or remaining the same?

Exercises

EXERCISE 8–1
Current liabilities
OBJECTIVE 2

✓ Total current liabilities, $218,000

Net World Magazine Inc. sold 4,800 annual subscriptions of *Net World* for $45 each during December 2003. These new subscribers will receive monthly issues beginning in January 2004. In addition, the business had taxable income of $160,000 during the first calendar quarter of 2004. The federal tax rate is 35%. A quarterly tax payment will be made on April 7, 2004.

Prepare the Current Liabilities section of the balance sheet for Net World Magazine Inc. on March 31, 2004.

EXERCISE 8–2
Entries for notes payable
OBJECTIVE 2

A business issued a 60-day, 9% note for $20,000 to a creditor on account. Record the entries for (a) the issuance of the note and (b) the payment of the note at maturity, including interest.

EXERCISE 8–3
Income tax entries
OBJECTIVE 2

Illustrate the effects on the accounts and financial statements of the following selected transactions of Supernal Grave Markers Inc.:

Apr. 15 Paid the first installment of the estimated income tax for the current fiscal year ending December 31, $80,000. No entry had been made to record the liability.

Dec. 31 Recorded the estimated income tax liability for the year just ended and the deferred income tax liability, based on the April 15 transactions and the following data:

Income tax rate	40%
Income before income tax	$1,200,000
Taxable income according to tax return	850,000

EXERCISE 8-4
Deferred Income Taxes
OBJECTIVE 2

Integrated Systems, Inc., recognized service revenue of $300,000 on the financial statements in 2004. Assume, however, that the Tax Code requires this amount to be recognized for tax purposes in 2005. The taxable income amounts for 2004 and 2005 are $2,000,000 and $2,500,000, respectively. Assume a tax rate of 40%.

Illustrate the effects on the accounts and financial statements of the tax expense, deferred taxes, and taxes payable for 2004 and 2005, respectively.

EXERCISE 8-5
Accrued product warranty
OBJECTIVE 2

Precision Audio Company warrants its products for one year. The estimated product warranty is 3% of sales. Assume that sales were $600,000 for January. In February, a customer received warranty repairs requiring $310 of parts.

a. Determine the warranty liability at January 31, the end of the first month of the current year.
b. What accounts are decreased for the warranty work provided in February?

EXERCISE 8-6
Accrued product warranty
OBJECTIVE 2

✓ a. 0.77%

During a recent year, **Motorola, Inc.**, had sales of $29,398,000,000. An analysis of Motorola's product warranty payable account for the year was as follows:

Product warranty payable, January 1	$ 337,000,000
Product warranty expense	226,000,000
Warranty claims paid	(230,000,000)
Product warranty payable, December 31	$ 333,000,000

a. Determine the product warranty expense as a percentage of sales.
b. Illustrate the effects of the product warranty expense for the year on the accounts and financial statements.

EXERCISE 8-7
Contingent liabilities
OBJECTIVE 2

Several months ago, one of the plants of Endurance Battery Company experienced a hazardous materials spill. As a result, the Environmental Protection Agency (EPA) fined the company $170,000, which the company is contesting. In addition, an employee is seeking $500,000 damages related to the spill. Lastly, a homeowner has sued the company for $120,000. The homeowner lives 20 miles from the plant but believes that the incident has reduced her home's resale value by $120,000.

Endurance Battery's legal counsel believes that it is probable that the EPA fine will stand. In addition, counsel indicates that an out-of-court settlement of $250,000 has recently been reached with the employee. The final papers will be signed next week. Counsel believes that the homeowner's case is much weaker and will be decided in favor of Endurance. Other litigation related to the spill is possible, but the damage amounts are uncertain.

a. Illustrate the effects of the contingent liabilities associated with the hazardous materials spill on the accounts and financial statements.
b. Prepare a footnote disclosure relating to this incident.

EXERCISE 8-8
Contingent liabilities
OBJECTIVE 2

The following footnote accompanied recent financial statements for **eBAY, Inc.**:

... The Company was sued by Network Engineering Software, Inc. ... for the Company's alleged willful and deliberate violation of a patent. The suit seeks unspecified monetary damages as well as an injunction against the Company's operations. It also seeks treble damages and attorneys' fees and costs. The Company believes that it has meritorious defenses against this suit and intends to vigorously defend itself. The Company could be forced to incur material expenses during this defense, and if it were to lose this suit, its business would be harmed.

Was a liability recorded by eBAY, Inc., for this contingent liability? Why or why not?

EXERCISE 8-9
Calculate payroll
OBJECTIVE 2

✓ b. Net pay, $989.75

An employee earns $26 per hour and 1½ times that rate for all hours in excess of 40 hours per week. Assume that the employee worked 50 hours during the week. Assume further that the FICA tax rate was 7.5% and federal income tax to be withheld was $333.

a. Determine the gross pay for the week.
b. Determine the net pay for the week.

EXERCISE 8-10
Summary payroll data
OBJECTIVE 2

✓ (3) Total earnings, $211,000

In the following summary of data for a payroll period, some amounts have been intentionally omitted:

Earnings:	
1. At regular rate	?
2. At overtime rate	$ 32,500
3. Total earnings	?
Deductions:	
4. FICA tax	15,165
5. Income tax withheld	29,500
6. Medical insurance	3,150
7. Union dues	?
8. Total deductions	50,000
9. Net amount paid	161,000
Accounts increased:	
10. Factory Wages	121,600
11. Sales Salaries	?
12. Office Salaries	34,300

Determine the amounts omitted in lines (1), (3), (7), and (11).

EXERCISE 8-11
Payroll tax entries
OBJECTIVE 2

According to a summary of the payroll of All Sport Publishing Co., $700,000 of payroll was subject to the 7.5% FICA tax. Also, $15,000 was subject to state and federal unemployment taxes.

a. Calculate the employer's payroll taxes using the following rates: state unemployment, 4.3%; federal unemployment, 0.8%.
b. Illustrate the effect of recording the accrual of payroll taxes on the accounts and financial statements.

EXERCISE 8-12
Recording payroll and payroll taxes
OBJECTIVE 5

Tower Controls Co. had a gross salary payroll of $550,000 for the month ending March 31. The complete payroll is subject to a FICA tax rate of 7.5%. Only $20,000 of this payroll is subject to state and federal unemployment taxes of 4% and 0.5%, respectively. The federal withholding is $104,500.

a. Record the March 31 payroll.
b. Record the March 31 payroll taxes.

EXERCISE 8-13
Accrued vacation pay
OBJECTIVE 2

A business provides its employees with varying amounts of vacation time per year depending on the length of employment. The estimated amount of the current year's vacation pay is $224,400. Illustrate the effects on the accounts and financial statements of the adjustment required on January 31, the end of the first month of the current year, to accrue the vacation pay.

EXERCISE 8-14
Bond price
OBJECTIVE 3

IBM Corporation's 7% bonds due in 2025 were reported in *The Wall Street Journal* as selling for 101⅛ on April 5, 2002. Were the bonds selling at a premium or at a discount at that date? Explain.

EXERCISE 8-15
Issuing bonds
OBJECTIVE 3

Elba Co. produces and distributes fiber-optic cable for use by telecommunication companies. Elba Co. issued $12,000,000 of 15-year, 9% bonds on April 1 of the current year with interest payable on October 1 and April 1. The fiscal year of the company is the calendar year. Illustrate the effects on the accounts and financial statements of recording the following selected transactions for the current year:

Apr. 1   Issued the bonds for cash at their face amount.
Oct. 1   Paid the interest on the bonds.
Apr. 1   Paid the bonds at maturity.

EXERCISE 8-16
Dividends per share
OBJECTIVES 4, 5

✓ Preferred stock, 3rd year: $2.00

Masini Inc., a developer of radiology equipment, has stock outstanding as follows: 20,000 shares of $2 noncumulative preferred stock of $100 par and 250,000 shares of $50 par common. During its first five years of operations, the following amounts were distributed as dividends: first year, none; second year, $40,000; third year, $90,000; fourth year, $200,000; fifth year, $240,000. Determine the dividends per share on each class of stock for each of the five years.

EXERCISE 8-17
Dividends per share
OBJECTIVES 4, 5

✓ Preferred stock, 3rd year: $2.50

Mystic.com, a computer software development firm, has stock outstanding as follows: 10,000 shares of $1.50 cumulative preferred stock of $50 par and 50,000 shares of $100 par common. During its first five years of operations, the following amounts were distributed as dividends: first year, none; second year, $5,000; third year, $80,000; fourth year, $180,000; fifth year, $75,000. Calculate the dividends per share on each class of stock for each of the five years.

EXERCISE 8-18
Issuing par stock
OBJECTIVE 4

On March 10, Candler Inc., a marble contractor, issued for cash 30,000 shares of $20 par common stock at $30. On August 9, it issued for cash 5,000 shares of $100 par preferred stock at $105.

a.   Illustrate the effects on the accounts and financial statements of the March 10 and August 9 transactions.
b.   What is the total amount invested (total paid-in capital) by all stockholders as of August 9?

EXERCISE 8-19
Issuing stock for assets other than cash
OBJECTIVE 4

On February 27, Sims Corporation, a wholesaler of hydraulic lifts, acquired land in exchange for 4,000 shares of $10 par common stock with a current market price of $73. Illustrate the effects on the accounts and financial statements of the purchase of the land.

EXERCISE 8-20
Treasury stock transactions
OBJECTIVE 4

Chico Springs Inc. bottles and distributes spring water. On March 1 of the current year, Chico reacquired 5,500 shares of its common stock at $40 per share. On July 8, Chico sold 3,500 of the reacquired shares at $43 per share. The remaining 2,000 shares were sold at $39 per share on December 19.

a.   What is the balance in Paid-In Capital from Sale of Treasury Stock on December 31 of the current year?
b.   Where will the balance in Paid-In Capital from Sale of Treasury Stock be reported on the balance sheet?
c.   For what reasons might Chico Springs have purchased the treasury stock?

EXERCISE 8-21
Effect of stock split
OBJECTIVE 6

Headwaters Corporation wholesales ovens and ranges to restaurants throughout the Northwest. Headwaters Corporation, which had 30,000 shares of common stock outstanding, declared a 3-for-1 stock split (2 additional shares for each share issued).

a. What will be the number of shares outstanding after the split?
b. If the common stock had a market price of $120 per share before the stock split, what would be an approximate market price per share after the split?

EXERCISE 8-22
Effect of cash dividend and stock split
OBJECTIVES 5, 6

Indicate whether the following actions would (+) increase, (−) decrease, or (0) not affect Collier Inc.'s total assets, liabilities, and stockholders' equity:

	Assets	Liabilities	Stockholders' Equity
a. Declaring a stock dividend	___	___	___
b. Issuing stock certificates for the stock dividend declared in (a)	___	___	___
c. Declaring a cash dividend	___	___	___
d. Paying the cash dividend declared in (c)	___	___	___
e. Authorizing and issuing stock certificates in a stock split	___	___	___

EXERCISE 8-23
Effect of financing on earnings per share
OBJECTIVE 8

✓ a. $0.30

Compatriot Co., which produces and sells skiing equipment, is financed as follows:

Bonds payable, 8% (issued at face amount)	$5,000,000
Preferred $3 stock (nonparticipating), $50 par	5,000,000
Common stock, $25 par	5,000,000

Income tax is estimated at 40% of income.

Determine the earnings per share of common stock, assuming that the income before bond interest and income tax is (a) $1,000,000, (b) $1,500,000, and (c) $2,500,000.

EXERCISE 8-24
Evaluate alternative financing plans
OBJECTIVE 8

Based on the data in Exercise 8-23, discuss factors other than earnings per share that should be considered in evaluating such financing plans.

EXERCISE 8-25
Number of times interest charges earned
OBJECTIVE 9

The following data were taken from recent annual reports of **Mirage Resorts, Inc.**, which owns and operates casino-based entertainment resorts in Las Vegas and Laughlin, Nevada.

	Current Year	Preceding Year
Interest expense	$130,598,000	$ 70,350,000
Income before income tax	135,178,000	329,079,000

a. Determine the number of times interest charges were earned for the current and preceding years. Round to one decimal place.
b. What conclusions can you draw?

EXERCISE 8-26
Long-term solvency ratios for comparative years
OBJECTIVE 9

Krispy Kreme Doughnuts, Inc., manufactures and sells doughnuts. The liabilities and stockholders' equity is summarized (in millions) at the end of two recent periods as follows:

	Jan. 28, 2001	Jan. 30, 2000
Total liabilities	$45,814	$57,203
Common Stock	83,132	12,928
Retained earnings	42,547	34,827

In addition, the income statement for these two periods showed the following income before tax and interest expense information (in millions):

	Jan. 28, 2001	Jan. 30, 2000
Interest expense	$ 607	$1,525
Income before income tax	23,783	9,606

a. Determine the total liabilities to total asset ratio at the end of the two accounting periods.
b. Determine the number of times interest charges were earned for the two fiscal years.
c. Interpret the change in the two ratios across the two periods.

Problems

PROBLEM 8 | 1
Income tax allocation
OBJECTIVE 2

✓ 1. Year-end balance, 3rd year, $72,000

Differences between the accounting methods applied to accounts and financial reports and those used in determining taxable income yielded the following amounts for the first four years of a corporation's operations:

	First Year	Second Year	Third Year	Fourth Year
Income before income taxes	$300,000	$450,000	$400,000	$500,000
Taxable income	250,000	300,000	420,000	510,000

The income tax rate for each of the four years was 40% of taxable income, and each year's taxes were promptly paid.

Instructions

1. For each year, determine the amounts described by the following captions, presenting the information in the form indicated:

Year	Income Tax Expense on Income Statement	Income Tax on Tax Return for the Year	Deferred Income Tax Payable	
			Year's Addition (Deduction)	Year-End Balance

2. Total the first three amount columns.
3. Illustrate the effects of recording the current and deferred tax liabilities on the accounts and financial statements for the first year.

PROBLEM 8 | 2
Entries for payroll and payroll taxes

OBJECTIVE 2

✓ 1. (d) $43,500

The following information about the payroll for the week ended January 31 was obtained from the records of Hannah Co.:

Salaries:		Deductions:	
Sales salaries	$327,000	Income tax withheld	$104,500
Warehouse salaries	87,400	Social security tax withheld	34,800
Office salaries	165,600	Medicare tax withheld	8,700
	$580,000	U.S. savings bonds	24,400
		Group insurance	32,800

Tax rates assumed:

Social security, 6% on first $80,000 of employee annual earnings
Medicare, 1.5%
State unemployment (employer only), 3.8%
Federal unemployment (employer only), 0.8%

Instructions

1. For the January 31 payroll, determine the following amounts: (a) sales salaries expense, (b) warehouse salaries expense, (c) office salaries expense, and (d) employee FICA tax payable.
2. Illustrate the effect on the accounts and financial statements of paying and recording the January 31 payroll.
3. Determine the following amounts for the employer payroll taxes related to the January 31 payroll: (a) FICA tax payable, (b) state unemployment tax payable, and (c) federal unemployment tax payable.
4. Illustrate the effect on the accounts and financial statements of recording the liability for the January 31 payroll taxes.

PROBLEM 8 | 3
Bonds payable transactions

OBJECTIVE 3

Moresby Inc. produces and sells voltage regulators. On July 1, 2003, Moresby Inc. issued $8,000,000 of 10-year, 11% bonds priced at par. Interest on the bonds is payable semiannually on December 31 and June 30. The fiscal year of the company is the calendar year.

Instructions

1. Illustrate the effects of the issuance of the bonds on July 1, 2003, on the accounts and financial statements.
2. Illustrate the effects of the first semiannual interest payment on December 31, 2003, on the accounts and financial statements.
3. Illustrate the effects of the payment of the face value of bonds at maturity on the accounts and financial statements.
4. If the market rate of interest were 10% on July 1, 2003, would the bonds have sold at a discount or premium?

PROBLEM 8 | 4
Stock transactions for corporate expansion

OBJECTIVE 4

On January 1 of the current year, the following accounts and their balances appear in the ledger of Osaka Corp., a meat processor:

Preferred $4 Stock, $100 par (20,000 shares authorized, 7,500 shares issued)	$ 750,000
Paid-In Capital in Excess of Par—Preferred Stock	150,000
Common Stock, $50 par (100,000 shares authorized, 40,000 shares issued)	2,000,000
Paid-In Capital in Excess of Par—Common Stock	300,000
Retained Earnings	805,000

At the annual stockholders' meeting on February 20, the board of directors presented a plan for modernizing and expanding plant operations at a cost of approximately $1,200,000. The plan provided (a) that a building valued at $375,000 and the land on which it is located valued at $75,000 be acquired in accordance with preliminary negotiations by the issuance of 8,000 shares of common stock, (b) that 5,000 shares of the unissued preferred stock be issued through an underwriter, and (c) that the corporation borrow $200,000. The plan was approved by the stockholders and accomplished by the following transactions:

Mar. 7   Issued 8,000 shares of common stock in exchange for land and a building, according to the plan.
     21   Issued 5,000 shares of preferred stock, receiving $125 per share in cash from the underwriter.
     29   Borrowed $200,000 from US East National Bank, giving a 7% mortgage note.

No other transactions occurred during March.

Instructions

Illustrate the effects on the accounts and financial statements of each of the foregoing transactions.

PROBLEM 8 | 5
Dividends on preferred and common stock
OBJECTIVES 4, 5

✓ 1. Common dividends in 2001: $31,000

Magnifico Inc. owns and operates movie theaters throughout Georgia and Mississippi. Magnifico has declared the following annual dividends over a six-year period: 1999, $32,000; 2000, $65,000; 2001, $84,000; 2002, $60,000; 2003, $72,000; and 2004, $95,000. During the entire period, the outstanding stock of the company was composed of 25,000 shares of cumulative, nonparticipating, $2 preferred stock, $100 par, and 50,000 shares of common stock, $7 par.

Instructions

1. Calculate the total dividends and the per-share dividends declared on each class of stock for each of the six years. There were no dividends in arrears on January 1, 1999. Summarize the data in tabular form, using the following column headings:

Year	Total Dividends	Preferred Dividends		Common Dividends	
		Total	Per Share	Total	Per Share
1999	$32,000				
2000	65,000				
2001	84,000				
2002	60,000				
2003	72,000				
2004	95,000				

2. Calculate the average annual dividend per share for each class of stock for the six-year period.
3. Assuming that the preferred stock was sold at par and common stock was sold at $8 at the beginning of the six-year period, calculate the percentage return on initial shareholders' investment based on the average annual dividend per share (a) for preferred stock and (b) for common stock.

PROBLEM 8 | 6
Effect of financing on earnings per share
OBJECTIVE 8

Three different plans for financing a $15,000,000 corporation are under consideration by its organizers. Under each of the following plans, the securities will be issued at their par or face amount, and the income tax rate is estimated at 40% of income.

✓ 1. Plan 3: $5.20

	Plan 1	Plan 2	Plan 3
12% bonds			$ 6,250,000
Preferred $4 stock, $50 par		$ 7,500,000	5,000,000
Common stock, $30 par	$15,000,000	7,500,000	3,750,000
Total	$15,000,000	$15,000,000	$15,000,000

Instructions

1. Determine for each plan the earnings per share of common stock, assuming that the income before bond interest and income tax is $2,500,000.
2. Determine for each plan the earnings per share of common stock, assuming that the income before bond interest and income tax is $1,500,000.
3. Discuss the advantages and disadvantages of each plan.

Activities

Activity 8-1
Business strategy

GROUP

One reason that **PepsiCo** purchased **Quaker Oats** in 2001 was to acquire rights to its sports drink, Gatorade. However, Gatorade is under increasing pressure from its competitors, including **Coca-Cola's** Powerade. As a result, PepsiCo is initiating an aggressive advertising campaign to promote and grow sales of Gatorade.

In groups of 3 to 4, answer the following questions:

1. Go to the Gatorade Web site at **http://gatorade.com**. (a) How and why was Gatorade developed? (b) What is Gatorade's share of the sports drink market?
2. Drinks can be labeled as sports, lifestyle, or active thirst drinks. (a) How would you describe each of these drink labels? (b) Give an example of what you would label a sports, lifestyle, and active thirst drink.
3. Do you think PepsiCo's advertising campaign will focus on Gatorade as a sports, lifestyle, or active thirst drink? Explain.

Activity 8-2
Contingent liability disclosure

A contingent liability footnote disclosure from the **Goodyear Tire and Rubber Co.'s** December 31, 2000 financial statements is reproduced as follows:

> At December 31, 2000, the Company had recorded liabilities aggregating $78.3 million for anticipated costs related to various environmental matters, primarily the remediation of numerous waste disposal sites and certain properties sold by the Company. These costs include legal and consulting fees, site studies, the design and implementation of remediation plans, post-remediation monitoring and related activities and will be paid over several years. The amount of the Company's ultimate liability in respect of these matters may be affected by several uncertainties, primarily the ultimate cost of required remediation and the extent to which other responsible parties contribute.

On January 20, 2001 the *Buffalo News* reported the following:

> The federal government has settled its lawsuit with Goodyear Tire & Rubber Co. over contamination of the former Forest Glen mobile home park, paving the way for the recycling of the property as an industrial site.
>
> Under the settlement, filed Friday in federal court, Goodyear will pay an estimated $13 million to clean up the site to federal specifications. Goodyear also will pay more than $9 million to reimburse the federal government for its cleanup and for damage to the environment caused by the waste.[13]

[13]Source: Andrew Z. Galarneau, *Buffalo News*, p. B3, January 20, 2001.

1. How would the $78.3 million in environmental liabilities be reported on Goodyear's financial statements? Provide the journal entry.
2. How would Goodyear account for the Forest Glen cleanup payments during 2001, assuming that the cost was accrued on December 31, 2000?

Activity 8-3
General Electric bond issuance

E T H I C S

General Electric Capital, a division of General Electric, uses long-term debt extensively. In early 2002, GE Capital issued $11 billion in long-term debt to investors and within days filed legal documents to prepare for another $50 billion long-term debt issue. As a result of the $50 billion filing, the price of the initial $11 billion offering declined (due to higher risk of more debt).

Bill Gross, a manager of a bond investment fund,

denounced a "lack in candor" related to GE's recent debt deal. "It was the most recent and most egregious example of how bondholders are mistreated." Gross argued that GE was not forthright when GE Capital recently issued $11 billion in bonds, one of the largest issues ever from a U.S. corporation. What bothered Gross is that three days after the issue the company announced its intention to sell as much as $50 billion in additional debt, warrants, preferred stock, guarantees, letters of credit and promissory notes at some future date.

In your opinion, did GE Capital act unethically by selling $11 billion of long-term debt without telling those investors that a few days later it would be filing documents to prepare for another $50 billion debt offering?

Source: MARKET WEEK—Capital Markets Current Yield, Jennifer Ablan, "Gross Shakes the Bond Market; GE Calms It, a Bit," *Barron's*, March 25, 2002. (Copyright © 2002, Dow Jones & Company, Inc.)

Activity 8-4
Investing in bonds

G R O U P

Select a bond from listings that appear daily in *The Wall Street Journal*, and summarize the information related to the bond you select. Include the following information in your summary:

1. Contract rate of interest.
2. Year the bond matures.
3. Current yield (effective rate of interest).
4. Closing price of bond (indicate date).
5. Other information noted about the bond, such as whether it is a zero-coupon bond (see the Explanatory Notes to the listings).

In groups of three or four, share the information you developed about the bond you selected. As a group, select one bond in which to invest $100,000, and prepare a justification for your choice for presentation to the class. For example, your justification should include a consideration of risk and return.

Activity 8-5
Dividend information on the Internet

Yahoo's web portal provides stock market information for publicly traded companies. Go to http://finance.yahoo.com on the Internet. Enter the symbol for **Philip Morris Companies, Inc.**, using the "Symbol Lookup" feature. (Note that Philip has only one l.) Double-click on the symbol for the detailed market information for Philip Morris. Once at the detailed Philip Morris page view, answer the follow questions:

1. What is Philip Morris's historical, trailing 12 months (ttm) earnings per share?
2. What is Philip Morris's annual dividend per share?
3. What is Philip Morris's closing stock price from the previous day?
4. Calculate Philip Morris's dividend yield, using the closing stock price from (c).
5. What calendar date is the dividend "ex-dividend," and what does this mean?
6. What calendar date is the dividend date, and what does this mean?

Activity 8-6
Issuing stock

Omen Inc. began operations on January 8, 2004, with the issuance of 500,000 shares of $100 par common stock. The sole stockholders of Omen Inc. are Fay Barnes and Dr. Joseph Cawley, who organized Omen Inc. with the objective of developing a new flu vaccine. Dr. Cawley claims that the flu vaccine, which is nearing the final development stage, will protect individuals against 99% of the flu types that have been medically identified. To complete the project, Omen Inc. needs $10,000,000 of additional funds. The local banks have been unwilling to loan the funds because of the lack of sufficient collateral and the riskiness of the business.

The following is a conversation between Fay Barnes, the chief executive officer of Omen Inc., and Dr. Joseph Cawley, the leading researcher.

Barnes: What are we going to do? The banks won't loan us any more money, and we've got to have $10 million to complete the project. We are so close! It would be a disaster to quit now. The only thing I can think of is to issue additional stock. Do you have any suggestions?

Cawley: I guess you're right. But if the banks won't loan us any more money, how do you think we can find any investors to buy stock?

Barnes: I've been thinking about that. What if we promise the investors that we will pay them 2% of net sales until they have received an amount equal to what they paid for the stock?

Cawley: What happens when we pay back the $10 million? Do the investors get to keep the stock? If they do, it'll dilute our ownership.

Barnes: How about, if after we pay back the $10 million, we make them turn in their stock for $200 per share? That's twice what they paid for it, plus they would have already gotten all their money back. That's a $200 profit per share for the investors.

Cawley: It could work. We get our money, but don't have to pay any interest, dividends, or the $200 until we start generating net sales. At the same time, the investors could get their money back plus $200 per share.

Barnes: We'll need current financial statements for the new investors. I'll get our accountant working on them and contact our attorney to draw up a legally binding contract for the new investors. Yes, this could work.

In late 2004, the attorney and the various regulatory authorities approved the new stock offering, and 100,000 shares of common stock were privately sold to new investors at the stock's par of $100.

In preparing financial statements for 2004, Fay Barnes and Tanya Kuchar, the controller for Omen Inc., have the following conversation.

Kuchar: Fay, I've got a problem.

Barnes: What's that, Tanya?

Kuchar: Issuing common stock to raise that additional $10 million was a great idea. But. . . .

Barnes: But what?

Kuchar: I've got to prepare the 2004 annual financial statements, and I am not sure how to classify the common stock.

Barnes: What do you mean? It's common stock.

Kuchar: I'm not so sure. I called the auditor and explained how we are contractually obligated to pay the new stockholders 2% of net sales until $100 per share is paid. Then we may be obligated to pay them $200 per share.

Barnes: So. . . .

Kuchar: So the auditor thinks that we should classify the additional issuance of $10 million as debt, not stock! If we put the $10 million on the balance sheet as debt, we will violate our other loan agreements with the banks. And if these agreements are violated, the banks may call in all our debt immediately. If they do that, we are in deep trouble. We'll probably have to file for bankruptcy. We just don't have the cash to pay off the banks.

1. Discuss the arguments for and against classifying the issuance of the $10 million of stock as debt.

2. What do you think might be a practical solution to this classification problem?

Activity 8-7
Board of directors'
dividend decisions

Ball-Peen Inc. has paid quarterly cash dividends since 1990. These dividends have steadily increased from $0.05 per share to the latest dividend declaration of $0.40 per share. The board of directors would like to continue this trend and is hesitant to suspend or decrease the amount of quarterly dividends. Unfortunately, sales dropped sharply in the fourth quarter of 2003 because of worsening economic conditions and increased competition. As a result, the board is uncertain as to whether it should declare a dividend for the last quarter of 2003.

On November 1, 2003, Ball-Peen Inc. borrowed $500,000 from City National Bank to use in modernizing its retail stores and to expand its product line in reaction to its competition. The terms of the 10-year, 12% loan require Ball-Peen Inc. to do the following:

a. Pay monthly interest on the last day of the month.
b. Pay $50,000 of the principal each November 1, beginning in 2004.
c. Maintain a current ratio (current assets/current liabilities) of 2.
d. Maintain a minimum balance (a compensating balance) of $25,000 in its City National Bank account.

On December 31, 2003, $125,000 of the $500,000 loan had been disbursed in modernization of the retail stores and in expansion of the product line. Ball-Peen Inc.'s balance sheet as of December 31, 2003, is as follows:

BALL-PEEN INC.
Balance Sheet
December 31, 2003

Assets

Current assets:			
Cash		$ 40,000	
Marketable securities		375,000	
Accounts receivable	$ 91,500		
Less allowance for doubtful accounts	6,500	85,000	
Merchandise inventory		125,000	
Prepaid expenses		4,500	
Total current assets			$ 629,500
Property, plant, and equipment:			
Land		$150,000	
Buildings	$950,000		
Less accumulated depreciation	215,000	735,000	
Equipment	$360,000		
Less accumulated depreciation	10,000	350,000	
Total property, plant, and equipment			1,235,000
Total assets			$1,864,500

Liabilities

Current liabilities:			
Accounts payable	$ 71,800		
Notes payable (City National Bank)	50,000		
Salaries payable	3,200		
Total current liabilities		$125,000	
Long-term liabilities:			
Notes payable (City National Bank)		450,000	
Total liabilities			$ 575,000

Stockholders' Equity

Paid-in capital:			
Common stock, $20 par (50,000 shares authorized, 25,000 shares issued)	$500,000		
Excess of issue price over par	40,000		
Total paid-in capital		$540,000	
Retained earnings		749,500	
Total stockholders' equity			1,289,500
Total liabilities and stockholders' equity			$1,864,500

The board of directors is scheduled to meet January 6, 2004, to discuss the results of operations for 2003 and to consider the declaration of dividends for the fourth quarter of 2003. The chairman of the board has asked for your advice on the declaration of dividends.

1. What factors should the board consider in deciding whether to declare a cash dividend?
2. The board is considering the declaration of a stock dividend instead of a cash dividend. Discuss the issuance of a stock dividend from the point of view of (a) a stockholder and (b) the board of directors.

Activity 8-8
Long-term solvency measures for two aerospace companies

Lockheed Martin Corp. and **Northrop Grumman Corp.** are two major defense contractors. A partial balance sheet for the end of a recent fiscal year is shown as follows:

	Lockheed Martin	Northrop Grumman
Liabilities and Stockholders' Equity		
Total current liabilities	$10,175	$2,688
Long-term debt	9,065	1,605
Post-retirement benefit liabilities	1,647	1,095
Deferred income taxes	736	276
Other non-current liabilities	1,566	39
Total stockholders' equity	7,160	3,919
Total liabilities and stockholders' equity	$30,349	$9,622

The interest expense, income tax expense, and net income (before unusual items) were as follows for both companies:

Interest expense	$ 919	$175
Income tax expense	710	350
Net income	(424)	625

1. Determine the total liabilities to total assets ratio for each company.
2. Determine the number of times interest charges are earned for each company.
3. Interpret your results.

Activity 8-9
Total liabilities to total assets ratio—banking industry

The total liabilities to total assets ratio for the 12 largest bank holding companies reported to the SEC are shown in the following table. The average total liabilities to total assets ratio for the group is 92.7%. This means that the average debt held by these banks is more than 92% of their total assets, which is much more than in any other industry.

Bank Holding Company (> $10B sales)	Total Liabilities to Total Assets Ratio
Bank of America Corp.	0.918
Bank One Corp.	0.930
Citicorp	0.913
FleetBoston Financial Corp.	0.909
Household International Inc.	0.885
HSBC Holdings PLC	0.934
J P Morgan & Co. Inc.	0.951
J P Morgan Chase & Co.	0.932
Mitsubishi Tokyo Financial Group	0.955
Wachovia Corp.	0.939
Washington Mutual Inc.	0.947
Wells Fargo & Co.	0.899
Average	0.927

Why are these ratios so large?

Answers to Self-Study Questions

1. **C** The maturity value is $5,100, determined as follows:

Face amount of note	$5,000
Plus interest ($5,000 × 0.12 × 60/360)	100
Maturity value	$5,100

2. **C** If a corporation has cumulative preferred stock outstanding, dividends that have been passed for prior years plus the dividend for the current year must be paid before dividends may be declared on common stock. In this case, dividends of $27,000 ($9,000/3) have been passed for the preceding three years, and the current year's dividends are $9,000, making a total of $36,000 (answer C) that must be paid to preferred stockholders before dividends can be declared on common stock.

3. **B** Since the contract rate on the bonds is higher than the prevailing market rate, a rational investor would be willing to pay more than the face amount, or a premium (answer B), for the bonds. If the contract rate and the market rate were equal, the bonds could be expected to sell at their face amount (answer A). Likewise, if the market rate is higher than the contract rate, the bonds would sell at a price below their face amount (answer D) or at a discount (answer C).

4. **C** If a corporation that holds treasury stock declares a cash dividend, the dividends are not paid on the treasury shares. To do so would place the corporation in the position of earning income through dealing with itself. Thus, the corporation will record $44,000 (answer C) as cash dividends [(25,000 shares issued less 3,000 shares held as treasury stock) × $2 per share dividend].

5. **C** The number of times interest charges are earned is determined as ($500,000 + $100,000)/$100,000, or 6.0.

9

LEARNING OBJECTIVES

OBJECTIVE 1
Describe basic financial statement analytical procedures.

OBJECTIVE 2
Apply financial statement analysis to assess the solvency of a business.

OBJECTIVE 3
Apply financial statement analysis to assess the profitability of a business.

OBJECTIVE 4
Summarize the uses and limitations of analytical measures.

OBJECTIVE 5
Describe the contents of corporate annual reports.

Financial Statement Analysis

The Wall Street Journal (October 10, 2002) reported that the common stock of **Microsoft Corporation** was selling for $46.38 per share. If you had funds to invest, would you invest in Microsoft common stock?

Microsoft is a well-known, international company. However, **Eastern Airlines**, **Pan Am**, **Montgomery Ward**, **Woolworth's**, and **Planet Hollywood** were also well-known companies. These latter companies share the common characteristic of having declared bankruptcy!

Obviously, being well known is not necessarily a good basis for investing. By itself, knowledge that a company has a good product can also be an inadequate basis for investing in the company. Even with a good product, a company can go bankrupt for a variety of reasons, such as inadequate financing. For example, Planet Hollywood sought bankruptcy protection even though it was owned and promoted by such prominent Hollywood stars as Bruce Willis, Whoopi Goldberg, and Arnold Schwarzenegger.

How, then, does one decide on the companies in which to invest? This chapter describes and illustrates common financial data that can be analyzed to assist you in making investment decisions. In addition, the contents of corporate annual reports are also discussed.

Basic Analytical Procedures

OBJECTIVE   1

List basic financial
statement analytical
procedures.

The basic financial statements provide much of the information users need to make economic decisions about businesses. In this chapter, we illustrate how to perform a complete analysis of these statements by integrating individual analytical measures.

Analytical procedures can be used to compare items on a current statement with related items on earlier statements. For example, cash of $150,000 on the current balance sheet can be compared with cash of $100,000 on the balance sheet of a year earlier. The current year's cash can be expressed as 1.5, or 150%, of the earlier amount, or as an increase of 50% or $50,000.

Analytical procedures are also widely used to examine relationships within a financial statement. To illustrate, assume that cash of $50,000 and inventories of $250,000 are included in the total assets of $1,000,000 on a balance sheet. In relative terms, the cash balance is 5% of the total assets, and the inventories are 25% of the total assets.

In this chapter, we illustrate a number of common analytical measures. The measures are not ends in themselves. They are only guides in evaluating financial and operating data. Many other factors, such as trends in the industry and general economic conditions, should also be considered.

Horizontal Analysis

The percentage analysis of increases and decreases in related items in comparative financial statements is called **horizontal analysis**. The amount of each item on the most recent statement is compared with the related item on one or more earlier statements. The amount of increase or decrease in the item is listed, along with the percentage of increase or decrease.

Horizontal analysis can compare two statements. In this case, the earlier statement is used as the base. Horizontal analysis can also compare three or more statements. In this case, the earliest date or period can be used as the base for comparing all later dates or periods. Alternatively, each statement can be compared to the immediately preceding statement. Exhibit 1 is a condensed comparative balance sheet for two years for Lincoln Company with horizontal analysis.

We cannot fully evaluate the significance of the various increases and decreases in the items shown in Exhibit 1 without additional information. Although total assets at the end of 2004 were $91,000 (7.4%) less than at the beginning of the year, liabilities were reduced by $133,000 (30%), and stockholders' equity increased $42,000 (5.3%). It appears that the reduction of $100,000 in long-term liabilities was achieved mostly through the sale of long-term investments.

The balance sheet in Exhibit 1 can be expanded to include the details of the various categories of assets and liabilities. An alternative is to present the details in separate schedules. Exhibit 2 is a supporting schedule with horizontal analysis.

The decrease in accounts receivable could be due to changes in credit terms or improved collection policies. Likewise, a decrease in inventories during a period of increased sales could indicate an improvement in the management of inventories.

The changes in the current assets in Exhibit 2 appear favorable. This assessment is supported by the 24.8% increase in net sales shown in Exhibit 3 on page 326.

EXHIBIT 1   *Comparative Balance Sheet–Horizontal Analysis*

LINCOLN COMPANY
Comparative Balance Sheet
December 31, 2004 and 2003

	2004	2003	Increase (Decrease)	
			Amount	Percent
Assets				
Current assets	$ 550,000	$ 533,000	$ 17,000	3.2%
Long-term investments	95,000	177,500	(82,500)	(46.5)
Property, plant, and equipment (net)	444,500	470,000	(25,500)	(5.4)
Intangible assets	50,000	50,000	—	
Total assets	$1,139,500	$1,230,500	$ (91,000)	(7.4)
Liabilities				
Current liabilities	$ 210,000	$ 243,000	$ (33,000)	(13.6)
Long-term liabilities	100,000	200,000	(100,000)	(50.0)
Total liabilities	$ 310,000	$ 443,000	$(133,000)	(30.0)
Stockholders' Equity				
Preferred 6% stock, $100 par	$ 150,000	$ 150,000	—	—
Common stock, $10 par	500,000	500,000	—	—
Retained earnings	179,500	137,500	$ 42,000	30.5
Total stockholders' equity	$ 829,500	$ 787,500	$ 42,000	5.3
Total liabilities and stockholders' equity	$1,139,500	$1,230,500	$ (91,000)	(7.4)

EXHIBIT 2
Comparative Schedule of
Current Assets–
Horizontal Analysis

LINCOLN COMPANY
Comparative Schedule of Current Assets
December 31, 2004 and 2003

	2004	2003	Increase (Decrease)	
			Amount	Percent
Cash	$ 90,500	$ 64,700	$ 25,800	39.9%
Marketable securities	75,000	60,000	15,000	25.0
Accounts receivable (net)	115,000	120,000	(5,000)	(4.2)
Inventories	264,000	283,000	(19,000)	(6.7)
Prepaid expenses	5,500	5,300	200	3.8
Total current assets	$550,000	$533,000	$ 17,000	3.2

An increase in net sales does not necessarily have a favorable effect on operating performance. The percentage increase in Lincoln Company's net sales is accompanied by a larger percentage increase in the cost of goods (merchandise) sold. This has the effect of reducing gross profit. Selling expenses increased significantly, and administrative expenses increased slightly. Overall, operating expenses increased by 20.7%, whereas gross profit increased by only 19.7%.

EXHIBIT 3   *Comparative Income Statement–Horizontal Analysis*

LINCOLN COMPANY
Comparative Income Statement
For the Years Ended December 31, 2004 and 2003

	2004	2003	Increase (Decrease) Amount	Percent
Sales	$1,530,500	$1,234,000	$296,500	24.0%
Sales returns and allowances	32,500	34,000	(1,500)	(4.4)
Net sales	$1,498,000	$1,200,000	$298,000	24.8
Cost of goods sold	1,043,000	820,000	223,000	27.2
Gross profit	$ 455,000	$ 380,000	$ 75,000	19.7
Selling expenses	$ 191,000	$ 147,000	$ 44,000	29.9
Administrative expenses	104,000	97,400	6,600	6.8
Total operating expenses	$ 295,000	$ 244,400	$ 50,600	20.7
Income from operations	$ 160,000	$ 135,600	$ 24,400	18.0
Other income	8,500	11,000	(2,500)	(22.7)
	$ 168,500	$ 146,600	$ 21,900	14.9
Other expense	6,000	12,000	(6,000)	(50.0)
Income before income tax	$ 162,500	$ 134,600	$ 27,900	20.7
Income tax expense	71,500	58,100	13,400	23.1
Net income	$ 91,000	$ 76,500	$ 14,500	19.0

The increase in income from operations and in net income is favorable. However, a study of the expenses and additional analyses and comparisons should be made before reaching a conclusion as to the cause.

Exhibit 4 illustrates a comparative retained earnings statement with horizontal analysis. It reveals that retained earnings increased 30.5% for the year. The increase is due to net income of $91,000 for the year, less dividends of $49,000.

EXHIBIT 4

Comparative Retained Earnings Statement– Horizontal Analysis

LINCOLN COMPANY
Comparative Retained Earnings Statement
December 31, 2004 and 2003

	2004	2003	Increase (Decrease) Amount	Percent
Retained earnings, January 1	$137,500	$100,000	$37,500	37.5%
Net income for the year	91,000	76,500	14,500	19.0
Total	$228,500	$176,500	$52,000	29.5
Dividends:				
On preferred stock	$ 9,000	$ 9,000	—	—
On common stock	40,000	30,000	$10,000	33.3
Total	$ 49,000	$ 39,000	$10,000	25.6
Retained earnings, December 31	$179,500	$137,500	$42,000	30.5

Vertical Analysis

A percentage analysis also can be used to show the relationship of each component to the total within a single statement. This type of analysis is called **vertical analysis**. As with horizontal analysis, the statements can be prepared in either detailed or condensed form. In the latter case, additional details of the changes in individual items can be presented in supporting schedules. In such schedules, the percentage analysis can be based on either the total of the schedule or the statement total. Although vertical analysis is limited to an individual statement, its significance can be improved by preparing comparative statements.

In vertical analysis of the balance sheet, each asset item is stated as a percentage of the total assets. Each liability and stockholders' equity item is stated as a percentage of the total liabilities and stockholders' equity. Exhibit 5 is a condensed comparative balance sheet with vertical analysis for Lincoln Company.

EXHIBIT 5　*Comparative Balance Sheet–Vertical Analysis*

LINCOLN COMPANY
Comparative Balance Sheet
December 31, 2004 and 2003

	2004		2003	
	Amount	**Percent**	**Amount**	**Percent**
Assets				
Current assets	$ 550,000	48.3%	$ 533,000	43.3%
Long-term investments	95,000	8.3	177,500	14.4
Property, plant, and equipment (net)	444,500	39.0	470,000	38.2
Intangible assets	50,000	4.4	50,000	4.1
Total assets	$1,139,500	100.0%	$1,230,500	100.0%
Liabilities				
Current liabilities	$ 210,000	18.4%	$ 243,000	19.7%
Long-term liabilities	100,000	8.8	200,000	16.3
Total liabilities	$ 310,000	27.2%	$ 443,000	36.0%
Stockholders' Equity				
Preferred 6% stock, $100 par	$ 150,000	13.2%	$ 150,000	12.2%
Common stock, $10 par	500,000	43.9	500,000	40.6
Retained earnings	179,500	15.7	137,500	11.2
Total stockholders' equity	$ 829,500	72.8%	$ 787,500	64.0%
Total liabilities and stockholders equity	$1,139,500	100.0%	$1,230,500	100.0%

The major percentage changes in Lincoln Company's assets are in the current asset and long-term investment categories. In the Liabilities and Stockholders' Equity sections of the balance sheet, the highest percentage changes are in long-term liabilities and retained earnings. Stockholders' equity increased from 64% to 72.8% of total liabilities and stockholders' equity in 2004. There is a comparable decrease in liabilities.

In a vertical analysis of the income statement, each item is stated as a percent of net sales. Exhibit 6 is a condensed comparative income statement with vertical analysis for Lincoln Company.

EXHIBIT 6   *Comparative Income Statement—Vertical Analysis*

LINCOLN COMPANY
Comparative Income Statement
For the Years Ended December 31, 2004 and 2003

	2004		2003	
	Amount	Percent	Amount	Percent
Sales	$1,530,500	102.2%	$1,234,000	102.8%
Sales returns and allowances	32,500	2.2	34,000	2.8
Net sales	$1,498,000	100.0%	$1,200,000	100.0%
Cost of goods sold	1,043,000	69.6	820,000	68.3
Gross profit	$ 455,000	30.4%	$ 380,000	31.7%
Selling expenses	$ 191,000	12.8%	$ 147,000	12.3%
Administrative expenses	104,000	6.9	97,400	8.1
Total operating expenses	$ 295,000	19.7%	$ 244,400	20.4%
Income from operations	$ 160,000	10.7%	$ 135,600	11.3%
Other income	8,500	0.6	11,000	0.9
	$ 168,500	11.3%	$ 146,600	12.2%
Other expense	6,000	0.4	12,000	1.0
Income before income tax	$ 162,500	10.9%	$ 134,600	11.2%
Income tax expense	71,500	4.8	58,100	4.8
Net income	$ 91,000	6.1%	$ 76,500	6.4%

We must be careful when judging the significance of differences between percentages for the two years. For example, the decline of the gross profit rate from 31.7% in 2003 to 30.4% in 2004 is only 1.3 percentage points. In terms of dollars of potential gross profit, however, it represents a decline of approximately $19,500 (0.013 × $1,498,000).

Common-Size Statements

Horizontal and vertical analyses with both dollar and percentage amounts are useful in assessing relationships and trends in financial conditions and operations of a business. Vertical analysis with both dollar and percentage amounts is also useful in comparing one company with another or with industry averages. Such comparisons are easier to make with the use of common-size statements. In a **common-size statement**, all items are expressed in percentages.

Common-size statements are useful in comparing the current period results with those of prior periods or individual businesses or one business with industry percentages. Industry data are often available from trade associations and financial information services. Exhibit 7 is a comparative common-size income statement for two businesses.

EXHIBIT 7
*Common-Size Income
Statement*

LINCOLN COMPANY and MADISON CORPORATION
Condensed Common-Size Income Statement
For the Year Ended December 31, 2004

	Lincoln Company	Madison Corporation
Sales	102.2%	102.3%
Sales returns and allowances	2.2	2.3
Net sales	100.0%	100.0%
Cost of goods sold	69.6	70.0
Gross profit	30.4%	30.0%
Selling expenses	12.8%	11.5%
Administrative expenses	6.9	4.1
Total operating expenses	19.7%	15.6%
Income from operations	10.7%	14.4%
Other income	0.6	0.6
	11.3%	15.0%
Other expense	0.4	0.5
Income before income tax	10.9%	14.5%
Income tax expense	4.8	5.5
Net income	6.1%	9.0%

ETHICS IN ACTION

What does it take to succeed in life? The answer to this question, according to Warren Buffett, the noted investment authority, is three magic ingredients: intelligence, energy, and integrity. According to Buffett, "If you lack the third ingredient, the other two will kill you." In other words, without integrity, your intelligence and energy may very well misguide you.

Source: Eric Clifford, *University of Tennessee Torchbearer,* Summer 2003.

Exhibit 7 indicates that Lincoln Company has a slightly higher rate of gross profit than Madison Corporation. However, this advantage is more than offset by Lincoln Company's higher percentage of selling and administrative expenses. As a result, the income from operations of Lincoln Company is 10.7% of net sales, compared with 14.4% for Madison Corporation—an unfavorable difference of 3.7 percentage points.

Other Analytical Measures

In addition to the preceding analyses, other relationships can be expressed in ratios and percentages. Often, these items are taken from the financial statements and thus are a type of vertical analysis. Comparing these items with items from earlier periods is a type of horizontal analysis.

OBJECTIVE 2
Apply financial
statement analysis to
assess the solvency of
a business.

Solvency Analysis

Some aspects of a business's financial condition and operations are of more importance to some users than to others. However, all users are interested in the ability of a business to pay its debts as they are due and to earn income. The ability of a business to meet its financial obligations (debts) is called **solvency**. The ability of a business to earn income is called **profitability**.

The factors of solvency and profitability are interrelated. A business that cannot pay its debts on a timely basis could experience difficulty in obtaining credit. A lack of available credit could, in turn, lead to a decline in the business's profitability. Eventually, the business could be forced into bankruptcy. Likewise, a business that is less profitable than its competitors is likely to be at a disadvantage in obtaining credit or new capital from stockholders.

In the following paragraphs, we discuss various types of financial analyses that are useful in evaluating the solvency of a business. In the next section, we discuss various types of profitability analyses. The examples in both sections are based on Lincoln Company's financial statements presented earlier. In some cases, data from Lincoln Company's financial statements of the preceding year and from other sources are also used. These historical data are useful in assessing the past performance of a business and in forecasting its future performance. The results of financial analyses could be even more useful when they are compared with those of competing businesses and with industry averages.

Solvency analysis focuses on the ability of a business to pay or otherwise satisfy its current and noncurrent liabilities. It is normally assessed by examining balance sheet relationships, using the following major analyses:

1. Current position analysis.
2. Accounts receivable analysis.
3. Inventory analysis.
4. The ratio of fixed assets to long-term liabilities.
5. The ratio of liabilities to stockholders' equity.
6. The number of times interest charges are earned.

Current Position Analysis

To be useful in assessing solvency, a ratio or other financial measure must relate to a business's ability to pay or otherwise satisfy its liabilities. Using measures to assess a business's ability to pay its current liabilities is called **current position analysis**. Such analysis is of special interest to short-term creditors.

An analysis of a firm's current position normally includes determining the working capital, the current ratio, and the acid-test ratio. The current and acid-test ratios are most useful when analyzed together and compared to previous periods and other firms in the industry.

WORKING CAPITAL   The excess of the current assets of a business over its current liabilities is called **working capital**. The working capital is often used in evaluating a company's ability to meet currently maturing debts. It is especially useful in making monthly or other period-to-period comparisons for a company. However, amounts of working capital are difficult to assess when comparing companies of different sizes or in comparing such amounts with industry figures. For example, working capital of $250,000 could be adequate for a small local hardware store, but it would be inadequate for all of Home Depot.

CURRENT RATIO   Another means of expressing the relationship between current assets and current liabilities is the **current ratio**. This ratio is sometimes called the

working capital ratio or **bankers' ratio**. The ratio is computed by dividing the total current assets by the total current liabilities. For Lincoln Company, working capital and the current ratio for 2004 and 2003 are as follows:

	2004	2003
Current assets	$550,000	$533,000
Current liabilities	210,000	243,000
Working capital	$340,000	$290,000
Current ratio	2.6	2.2

The current ratio is a more reliable indicator of solvency than is working capital. To illustrate, assume that as of December 31, 2004, the working capital of a competitor is much more than $340,000, but its current ratio is only 1.3. Considering these facts alone, Lincoln Company, with its current ratio of 2.6, is in a more favorable position to obtain short-term credit than the competitor, which has the higher amount of working capital.

ACID-TEST RATIO   The working capital and the current ratio do not consider the makeup of the current assets. To illustrate the importance of this consideration, the current position data for Lincoln Company and Jefferson Corporation as of December 31, 2004, are as follows:

	Lincoln Company	Jefferson Corporation
Current assets:		
Cash	$ 90,500	$ 45,500
Marketable securities	75,000	25,000
Accounts receivable (net)	115,000	90,000
Inventories	264,000	380,000
Prepaid expenses	5,500	9,500
Total current assets	$550,000	$550,000
Current liabilities	210,000	210,000
Working capital	$340,000	$340,000
Current ratio	2.6	2.6

Both companies have a working capital of $340,000 and a current ratio of 2.6, but the ability of each company to pay its current debts is significantly different. Jefferson Corporation has more of its current assets in inventories. Some of these inventories must be sold and the receivables collected before the current liabilities can be paid in full. Thus, a large amount of time may be necessary to convert these inventories into cash. Declines in market prices and a reduction in demand could also impair its ability to pay current liabilities. In contrast, Lincoln Company has cash and current assets (marketable securities and accounts receivable) that can generally be converted to cash rather quickly to meet its current liabilities.

A ratio that measures the "instant" debt-paying ability of a company is called the **acid-test ratio** or **quick ratio**. It is the ratio of the total quick assets to the total current liabilities. **Quick assets** are cash and other current assets that can be quickly converted to cash. Quick assets normally include cash, marketable securities, and receivables. The acid-test ratio data for Lincoln Company are as follows:

	2004	2003
Quick assets:		
Cash	$ 90,500	$ 64,700
Marketable equity securities	75,000	60,000
Accounts receivable (net)	115,000	120,000
Total quick assets	$280,500	$244,700
Current liabilities	$210,000	$243,000
Acid-test ratio	1.3	1.0

Accounts Receivable Analysis

The size and makeup of accounts receivable change constantly during business operations. Sales on account increase accounts receivable whereas collections from customers decrease accounts receivable. Firms that grant long credit terms usually have larger accounts receivable balances than those granting short credit terms. Increases or decreases in the volume of sales also affect the balance of accounts receivable.

It is desirable to collect receivables as promptly as possible. The cash collected from receivables improves solvency. In addition, the cash generated by prompt collections from customers can be used in operations for purposes such as purchasing merchandise in large quantities at lower prices. The cash can also be used for payment of dividends to stockholders or for other investing or financing purposes. Prompt collection also lessens the risk of loss from uncollectible accounts.

ACCOUNTS RECEIVABLE TURNOVER   The relationship between credit sales and accounts receivable can be stated as the **accounts receivable turnover**. This ratio is computed by dividing net sales by the average net accounts receivable.[1] It is desirable to base the average on monthly balances, which allows for seasonal changes in sales. When such data are not available, it could be necessary to use the average of the accounts receivable balance at the beginning and the end of the year. If there are trade notes receivable as well as accounts, the two can be combined. The accounts receivable turnover data for Lincoln Company are as follows.

	2004	2003
Net sales	$1,498,000	$1,200,000
Accounts receivable (net):		
Beginning of year	$ 120,000	$ 140,000
End of year	115,000	120,000
Total	$ 235,000	$ 260,000
Average (Total/2)	$ 117,500	$ 130,000
Accounts receivable turnover	12.7	9.2

The increase in the accounts receivable turnover for 2004 indicates that there has been an improvement in the collection of receivables. This could be due to a change in the granting of credit or in collection practices, or both.

NUMBER OF DAYS' SALES IN RECEIVABLES   Another measure of the relationship between sales and accounts receivable is the **number of days' sales in receivables**. This ratio is computed by dividing the net accounts receivable at the end

[1]Alternatively, net sales on account can be used for the calculation. However, this number may not be publicly available; thus, net sales is used. When using net sales, the analyst must be aware that cash sales could impact the interpretation of the analysis.

of the year by the average daily sales.[2] Average daily sales is determined by dividing net sales by 365 days. The number of days' sales in receivables is computed for Lincoln Company as follows:

	2004	2003
Accounts receivable (net), end of year	$115,000	$120,000
Net sales	$1,498,000	$1,200,000
Average daily sales (sales/365)	$4,104	$3,288
Number of days' sales in receivables	28.0*	36.5*

*Accounts receivable ÷ Average daily sales

The number of days' sales in receivables is an estimate of the length of time (in days) that the accounts receivable have been outstanding. Comparing this measure with the credit terms provides information on the efficiency in collecting receivables. For example, assume that the number of days' sales in receivables for Grant Inc. is 40. If Grant Inc.'s credit terms are n/45, its collection process appears to be efficient. On the other hand, if Grant Inc.'s credit terms are n/30, its collection process does not appear to be efficient. A comparison with other firms in the same industry and with prior years also provides useful information. Such comparisons could indicate efficiency of collection procedures and trends in credit management.

Inventory Analysis

A business should keep enough inventory on hand to meet the needs of its customers and its operations. At the same time, however, an excessive amount of inventory reduces solvency by tying up funds. Excess inventories also increase insurance expense, property taxes, storage costs, and other related expenses. These expenses further reduce funds that could be used elsewhere to improve operations. Finally, excess inventory also increases the risk of losses because of price declines or obsolescence of the inventory. Two measures that are useful for evaluating the management of inventory are the inventory turnover and the number of days' sales in inventory.

INVENTORY TURNOVER   The relationship between the volume of goods (merchandise) sold and inventory can be stated as the **inventory turnover**. It is computed by dividing the cost of goods sold by the average inventory. If monthly data are not available, the average of the inventories at the beginning and the end of the year can be used. The inventory turnover for Lincoln Company is computed as follows:

	2004	2003
Cost of goods sold	$1,043,000	$820,000
Inventories:		
Beginning of year	$ 283,000	$311,000
End of year	264,000	283,000
Total	$ 547,000	$594,000
Average (Total/2)	$ 273,500	$297,000
Inventory turnover	3.8	2.8

The inventory turnover improved for Lincoln Company because of an increase in the cost of goods sold and a decrease in the average inventories. Differences across inventories, companies, and industries are too great to allow a general statement on

[2]Alternatively, net sales on account can be used for the calculation.

what is a good inventory turnover. For example, a firm selling food should have a higher turnover than a firm selling furniture or jewelry. Likewise, the perishable foods department of a supermarket should have a higher turnover than the soaps and cleansers department. However, each business or each department within a business has a reasonable turnover rate. A turnover lower than this rate could mean that inventory is not being managed properly.

NUMBER OF DAYS' SALES IN INVENTORY   Another measure of the relationship between the cost of goods sold and inventory is the **number of days' sales in inventory**. This measure is computed by dividing the inventory at the end of the year by the average daily cost of goods sold (cost of goods sold divided by 365). The number of days' sales in inventory for Lincoln Company is computed as follows:

	2004	2003
Inventories, end of year	$264,000	$283,000
Cost of goods sold	$1,043,000	$820,000
Average daily cost of goods sold (COGS ÷ 365 days)	$2,858	$2,247
Number of days' sales in inventory	92.4	125.9

The number of days' sales in inventory is a rough measure of the length of time it takes to acquire, sell, and replace the inventory. For Lincoln Company, there is a major improvement in the number of days' sales in inventory during 2004. However, a comparison with earlier years and similar firms would be useful in assessing Lincoln Company's overall inventory management.

Ratio of Fixed Assets to Long-Term Liabilities

Long-term notes and bonds are often secured by mortgages on fixed assets. The **ratio of fixed assets to long-term liabilities** is a solvency measure that indicates the margin of safety of the noteholders or bondholders. It also indicates the ability of the business to borrow additional funds on a long-term basis. The ratio of fixed assets to long-term liabilities for Lincoln Company is as follows:

	2004	2003
Fixed assets (net)	$444,500	$470,000
Long-term liabilities	$100,000	$200,000
Ratio of fixed assets to long-term liabilities	4.4	2.4

The major increase in this ratio at the end of 2004 is mainly due to liquidating one-half of Lincoln Company's long-term liabilities. If the company needs to borrow additional funds on a long-term basis in the future, it is in a strong position to do so.

Ratio of Liabilities to Stockholders' Equity

Claims against the total assets of a business are divided into two groups: (1) claims of creditors and (2) claims of owners. The relationship between the total claims of the creditors and owners—the **ratio of liabilities to stockholders' equity**—is a solvency measure that indicates the margin of safety for creditors. It also indicates the ability of the business to withstand adverse business conditions. When the claims of creditors are large in relation to the equity of the stockholders, there are usually significant interest payments. If earnings decline to the point where the company is unable to meet its interest payments, the business could be taken over by the creditors.

The relationship between creditor and stockholder equity is shown in the vertical analysis of the balance sheet. For example, the balance sheet of Lincoln Company in Exhibit 5 indicates that on December 31, 2004, liabilities represented 27.2% and stockholders' equity represented 72.8% of the total liabilities and stockholders' equity (100.0%). Instead of expressing each item as a percentage of the total, this relationship can be expressed as a ratio of one to the other, as follows:

	2004	2003
Total liabilities	$310,000	$443,000
Total stockholders' equity	$829,500	$787,500
Ratio of liabilities to stockholders' equity	0.37	0.56

The balance sheet of Lincoln Company shows that the major factor affecting the change in the ratio was the $100,000 decrease in long-term liabilities during 2004. The ratio at the end of both years shows a large margin of safety for the creditors.

Number of Times Interest Charges Earned

Corporations in some industries, such as airlines, normally have high ratios of debt to stockholders' equity. For such corporations, the relative risk of the debtholders is normally measured as the **number of times interest charges are earned** during the year. The higher the ratio, the lower the risk that interest payments will not be made if earnings decrease. In other words, the higher the ratio, the greater the assurance that interest payments will be made on a continuing basis. This measure also indicates the general financial strength of the business, which is of interest to stockholders and employees as well as creditors.

The amount available to meet interest charges is not affected by taxes on income. This is so because interest is deductible in determining taxable income. Thus, the number of times interest charges are earned is computed as shown here.

	2004	2003
Income before income tax	$ 900,000	$ 800,000
Add interest expense	300,000	250,000
Amount available to meet interest charges	$1,200,000	$1,050,000
Number of times interest charges earned	4	4.2

Analysis such as this can also be applied to dividends on preferred stock. In such a case, net income is divided by the amount of preferred dividends to yield the **number of times preferred dividends are earned**. This measure indicates the risk that dividends to preferred stockholders could not be paid.

Profitability Analysis

OBJECTIVE   3

Apply financial statement analysis to assess the profitability of a business.

The ability of a business to earn profits depends on the effectiveness and efficiency of its operations as well as the resources available to it. *Profitability analysis*, therefore, focuses primarily on the relationship between operating results as reported in the income statement and resources available to the business as reported in the balance sheet. Major analyses used in assessing profitability include the following:

1. Ratio of net sales to assets
2. Rate earned on total assets
3. Rate earned on stockholders' equity
4. Rate earned on common stockholders' equity
5. Earnings per share on common stock

6. Price-earnings ratio
7. Dividends per share
8. Dividend yield

Ratio of Net Sales to Assets

The **ratio of net sales to assets** is a profitability measure that shows how effectively a firm utilizes its assets. For example, two competing businesses have equal amounts of assets. If the sales of one are twice the sales of the other, the business with the higher sales is making better use of its assets.

In computing the ratio of net sales to assets, any long-term investments are excluded from total assets because such investments are unrelated to normal operations involving the sale of goods or services. Assets can be measured as the total at the end of the year, the average at the beginning and end of the year, or the average of monthly totals. The basic data and the computation of this ratio for Lincoln Company are as follows:

	2004	2003
Net sales	$1,498,000	$1,200,000
Total assets (excluding long-term investments):		
Beginning of year	$1,053,000	$1,010,000
End of year	1,044,500	1,053,000
Total	$2,097,500	$2,063,000
Average (Total/2)	$1,048,750	$1,031,500
Ratio of net sales to assets	1.4	1.2

This ratio improved during 2004, primarily due to an increase in sales volume. A comparison with similar companies or industry averages would be helpful in assessing the effectiveness of Lincoln Company's use of its assets.

Rate Earned on Total Assets

The **rate earned on total assets** measures the profitability of total assets without considering how the assets are financed. This rate is therefore not affected by whether the assets are financed primarily by creditors or stockholders.

The rate earned on total assets is computed by adding interest expense to net income and dividing this sum by the average total assets. Adding interest expense to net income eliminates the effect of whether the assets are financed by debt or equity. The rate earned by Lincoln Company on total assets is computed as follows:

	2004	2003
Net income	$ 91,000	$ 76,500
Plus interest expense	6,000	12,000
Total	$ 97,000	$ 88,500
Total assets:		
Beginning of year	$1,230,500	$1,187,500
End of year	1,139,500	1,230,500
Total	$2,370,000	$2,418,000
Average (Total/2)	$1,185,000	$1,209,000
Rate earned on total assets	8.2%	7.3%

The rate earned on total assets of Lincoln Company during 2004 improved over that of 2003. A comparison with similar companies and industry averages would be useful in evaluating Lincoln Company's profitability on total assets.

Sometimes it could be desirable to compute the **rate of income from operations to total assets**. This is especially true if significant amounts of nonoperating income and expense are reported on the income statement. In this case, any assets related to the nonoperating income and expense items should be excluded from total assets in computing the rate. In addition, using income from operations (which is before tax) has the advantage of eliminating the effects of any changes in the tax structure on the rate of earnings. When evaluating published data on rates earned on assets, you should be careful to determine the exact nature of the measure that is reported.

Rate Earned on Stockholders' Equity

Another measure of profitability is the **rate earned on stockholders' equity**. It is computed by dividing net income by average total stockholders' equity. In contrast to the rate earned on total assets, this measure emphasizes the rate of income earned on the amount invested by the stockholders.

The total stockholders' equity can vary throughout a period. For example, a business can issue or retire stock, pay dividends, and earn net income. If monthly amounts are not available, the average of the stockholders' equity at the beginning and the end of the year is normally used to compute this rate. For Lincoln Company, the rate earned on stockholders' equity is computed as follows:

	2004	2003
Net income	$ 91,000	$ 76,500
Stockholders' equity:		
Beginning of year	$ 787,500	$ 750,000
End of year	829,500	787,500
Total	$1,617,000	$1,537,500
Average (Total/2)	$ 808,500	$ 768,750
Rate earned on stockholders' equity	11.3%	10.0%

The rate earned by a business on the equity of its stockholders is usually higher than the rate earned on total assets. This occurs when the amount earned on assets acquired with creditors' funds is more than the interest paid to creditors. This difference in the rate on stockholders' equity and the rate on total assets is called **leverage**.

Lincoln Company's rate earned on stockholders' equity for 2004, 11.3%, is higher than the rate of 8.2% earned on total assets. The leverage of 3.1% (11.3% − 8.2%) for 2004 compares favorably with the 2.7% (10.0% − 7.3%) leverage for 2003. Exhibit 8 on the following page shows the 2004 and 2003 leverages for Lincoln Company.

Rate Earned on Common Stockholders' Equity

A corporation can have both preferred and common stock outstanding. In this case, the common stockholders have the residual claim on earnings. The **rate earned on common stockholders' equity** focuses only on the rate of profits earned on the amount invested by the common stockholders. It is computed by subtracting preferred dividend requirements from the net income and dividing by the average common stockholders' equity.

EXHIBIT 8
Leverage

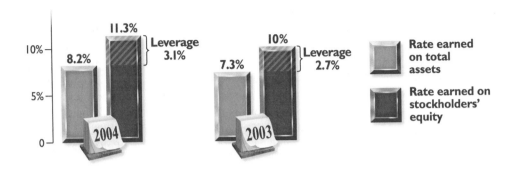

Lincoln Company has $150,000 of 6% nonparticipating preferred stock outstanding on December 31, 2004 and 2003. Thus, the annual preferred dividend requirement is $9,000 ($150,000 × 0.06). The common stockholders' equity equals the total stockholders' equity, including retained earnings, less the par of the preferred stock ($150,000). The basic data and the rate earned on common stockholders' equity for Lincoln Company are as follows:

	2004	2003
Net income	$ 91,000	$ 76,500
Preferred dividends	9,000	9,000
Remainder—identified with common stock	$ 82,000	$ 67,500
Common stockholders' equity:		
Beginning of year	$ 637,500	$ 600,000
End of year	679,500	637,500
Total	$1,317,000	$1,237,500
Average (Total/2)	$ 658,500	$ 618,750
Rate earned on common stockholders' equity	12.5%	10.9%

The rate earned on common stockholders' equity differs from the rates earned by Lincoln Company on total assets and total stockholders' equity. This occurs if there are borrowed funds and preferred stock outstanding, which rank ahead of the common shares in their claim on earnings. Thus, the concept of leverage, as we discussed in the preceding section, can also be applied to the use of funds from the sale of preferred stock as well as borrowing. Funds from both sources can be used in an attempt to increase the return on common stockholders' equity.

Earnings per Share on Common Stock

One of the profitability measures often quoted by the financial press is **earnings per share (EPS) on common stock**. It is also normally reported in the income statement in corporate annual reports. If a company has issued only one class of stock, the earnings per share is computed by dividing net income by the number of shares of stock outstanding. If preferred and common stock are outstanding, the net income is first reduced by the amount of preferred dividend requirements.[3]

---

[3]Additional details related to earnings per share were discussed in a previous chapter.

The data on the earnings per share of common stock for Lincoln Company are as follows:

	2004	2003
Net income	$91,000	$76,500
Preferred dividends	9,000	9,000
Remainder—identified with common stock	$82,000	$67,500
Shares of common stock outstanding	50,000	50,000
Earnings per share on common stock	$1.64	$1.35

Price-Earnings Ratio

Another profitability measure quoted by the financial press is the **price-earnings (P/E) ratio** on common stock. The price-earnings ratio is an indicator of a firm's future earnings prospects. It is computed by dividing the market price per share of common stock at a specific date by the annual earnings per share. To illustrate, assume that the market prices per common share are 41 at the end of 2004 and 27 at the end of 2003. The price-earnings ratio on common stock of Lincoln Company is computed as follows:

	2004	2003
Market price per share of common stock	$20.50	$13.50
Earnings per share of common stock	÷ 1.64	÷ 1.35
Price-earnings ratio on common stock	12.5	10.0

The price-earnings ratio indicates that a share of common stock of Lincoln Company was selling for 20 times the amount of earnings per share at the end of 2003. At the end of 2004, the common stock was selling for 25 times the amount of earnings per share.

Dividends per Share and Dividend Yield

Since the primary basis for dividends is earnings, **dividends per share** and earnings per share on common stock are commonly used by investors in assessing alternative stock investments. The dividends per share for Lincoln Company were $0.80 ($40,000/50,000 shares) for 2004 and $0.60 ($30,000/50,000 shares) for 2003.

Dividends per share can be reported with earnings per share to indicate the relationship between dividends and earnings. Comparing these two per share amounts indicates the extent to which the corporation is retaining its earnings for use in operations. Exhibit 9 on the following page shows these relationships for Lincoln Company.

The **dividend yield** on common stock is a profitability measure that shows the rate of return to common stockholders in terms of cash dividends. It is of special interest to investors whose main investment objective is to receive current returns (dividends) on an investment rather than an increase in the market price of the investment. The dividend yield is computed by dividing the annual dividends paid per share of common stock by the market price per share on a specific date. To illustrate, assume that

Dividends and Earnings per Share of Common Stock

the market price was 41 at the end of 2004 and 27 at the end of 2003. The dividend yield on common stock of Lincoln Company is as follows:

	2004	2003
Dividends per share of common stock	$ 0.80	$ 0.60
Market price per share of common stock	÷ 41.00	÷ 27.00
Dividend yield on common stock	1.95%	2.22%

Summary of Analytical Measures

OBJECTIVE   4

Summarize the uses and limitations of analytical measures.

Exhibit 10 presents a summary of the analytical measures that we have discussed. These measures can be computed for most medium-size businesses. Depending on the specific business being analyzed, some measures might be omitted or additional measures could be developed. The type of industry, the capital structure, and the diversity of the business's operations usually affect the measures used. For example, analysis for an airline might include revenue per passenger mile and cost per available seat as measures. Likewise, analysis for a hotel might focus on occupancy rates.

Percentage analyses, ratios, turnovers, and other measures of financial position and operating results are useful analytical measures. They are helpful in assessing a business's past performance and predicting its future. They are not, however, a substitute for sound judgment. In selecting and interpreting analytical measures, conditions peculiar to a business or its industry should be considered. In addition, the influence of the general economic and business environment should be considered.

In determining trends, the interrelationship of the measures used in assessing a business should be carefully studied. Comparable indexes of earlier periods should also be studied. Data from competing businesses can be useful in assessing the efficiency of operations for the firm under analysis. In making such comparisons, however, the effects of differences in the accounting methods used by the businesses should be considered.

EXHIBIT 10   *Summary of Analytical Measures*

	Method of Computation	Use
Solvency measures:		
Working capital	Current assets − Current liabilities	To indicate the ability to meet currently maturing obligations
Current ratio	$\dfrac{\text{Current assets}}{\text{Current liabilities}}$	
Acid-test ratio	$\dfrac{\text{Quick assets}}{\text{Current liabilities}}$	To indicate instant debt-paying ability
Accounts receivable turnover	$\dfrac{\text{Net sales}}{\text{Average accounts receivable}}$	To assess the efficiency in collecting receivables and in the management of credit
Number of days' sales in receivables	$\dfrac{\text{Accounts receivable, end of year}}{\text{Average daily sales}}$	
Inventory turnover	$\dfrac{\text{Cost of goods sold}}{\text{Average inventory}}$	To assess the efficiency in the management of inventory
Number of days' sales in inventory	$\dfrac{\text{Inventory, end of year}}{\text{Average daily cost of goods sold}}$	
Ratio of fixed assets to long-term liabilities	$\dfrac{\text{Fixed assets (net)}}{\text{Long-term liabilities}}$	To indicate the margin of safety to long-term creditors
Ratio of liabilities to stockholders' equity	$\dfrac{\text{Total liabilities}}{\text{Total stockholders' equity}}$	To indicate the margin of safety to creditors
Number of times interest charges earned	$\dfrac{\text{Income before income tax} + \text{Interest expense}}{\text{Interest expense}}$	To assess the risk to debtholders in terms of number of times interest charges were earned
Profitability measures:		
Ratio of net sales to assets	$\dfrac{\text{Net sales}}{\text{Average total assets (excluding long-term investments)}}$	To assess the effectiveness in the use of assets
Rate earned on total assets	$\dfrac{\text{Net income} + \text{Interest expense}}{\text{Average total assets}}$	To assess the profitability of the assets
Rate earned on stockholders' equity	$\dfrac{\text{Net income}}{\text{Average total stockholders' equity}}$	To assess the profitability of the investment by stockholders
Rate earned on common stockholders' equity	$\dfrac{\text{Net income} - \text{Preferred dividends}}{\text{Average common stockholders' equity}}$	To assess the profitability of the investment by common stockholders
Earnings per share on common stock	$\dfrac{\text{Net income} - \text{Preferred dividends}}{\text{Shares of common stock outstanding}}$	
Price-earnings ratio	$\dfrac{\text{Market price per share of common stock}}{\text{Earnings per share of common stock}}$	To indicate future earnings prospects, based on the relationship between market value of common stock and earnings
Dividends per share of common stock	$\dfrac{\text{Dividends}}{\text{Shares of common stock outstanding}}$	To indicate the extent to which earnings are being distributed to common stockholders
Dividend yield	$\dfrac{\text{Dividends per share of common stock}}{\text{Market price per share of common stock}}$	To indicate the rate of return to common stockholders in terms of dividends

Corporate Annual Reports

Corporations normally issue annual reports to their stockholders and other interested parties. Such reports summarize the corporation's operating activities for the past year and plans for the future. There are many variations in the order and form for presenting the major sections of annual reports. However, one section of the annual report is devoted to the financial statements, including the accompanying notes. In addition, annual reports usually include the following sections:

1. Financial Highlights
2. President's Letter to the Stockholders
3. Management Discussion and Analysis
4. Independent Auditors' Report
5. Historical Summary

Financial Highlights

The Financial Highlights section summarizes the operating results for the last year or two. It is sometimes called *Results in Brief*. It is usually presented on the first one or two pages of the annual report.

There are many variations in the format and content of the Financial Highlights section. Items such as sales, net income, net income per common share, cash dividends paid, cash dividends per common share, and the amount of capital expenditures are typically presented. In addition to these data, information about the financial position at the end of the year can be presented.

President's Letter to the Stockholders

A letter from the company president to the stockholders is also presented in most annual reports. These letters usually discuss items such as reasons for an increase or decrease in net income, changes in existing plants, purchase or construction of new plants, significant new financing commitments, social responsibility issues, and future plans.

Management Discussion and Analysis

A required disclosure in the annual report filed with the Securities and Exchange Commission is the **Management Discussion and Analysis (MDA)**. The MDA provides critical information in interpreting the financial statements and assessing the future of the company.

The MDA includes an analysis of the results of operations and discusses management's opinion about future performance. It compares the prior year's income statement with the current year's to explain changes in sales, significant expenses, gross profit, and income from operations. For example, an increase in sales can be explained by referring to higher shipment volume or stronger prices.

The MDA also includes an analysis of the company's financial condition. It compares significant balance sheet items in successive years to explain changes in liquidity and capital resources. In addition, the MDA discusses significant risk exposure.

BUSINESS STRATEGY

The Responsible Board

Recent corporate failures, such as Enron and Global Crossing, have highlighted the roles of boards of directors in executing their responsibilities. New standards for corporate governance are being suggested, such as (1) independent directors to oversee management, (2) board member expertise and education, (3) separation of the Board Chairmanship from the CEO position, (4) transparent disclosure of all board activities and transactions with the corporation (insider trades), and (5) an independent audit committee. Indeed, one study found that "audit committees of companies where financial statement fraud has occurred generally were less independent, less expert, met less often, and were less likely to have internal audit support."

Sources: R. Luke, "Inquisitive Directors: Tough Audit Questions Loom Large Since Enron," *Atlanta Journal—Constitution*, March 29, 2002; and *21st Century Governance Principles for U.S. Corporations* (Corporate Governance Center, 2002).

Independent Auditors' Report

Before issuing annual statements, all publicly held corporations are required to have an independent audit (examination) of their financial statements. For the financial statements of most companies, the CPAs who conduct the audit render an opinion on the fairness of the statements.

Historical Summary

The Historical Summary section reports selected financial and operating data of past periods, usually for 5 or 10 years. It is usually presented near the financial statements for the current year.

Key Points

1. Describe basic financial statement analytical procedures.

The analysis of percentage increases and decreases in related items in comparative financial statements is called *horizontal analysis*. The analysis of percentages of component parts to the total in a single statement is called *vertical analysis*. Financial statements in which all amounts are expressed in percentages for purposes of analysis are called *common-size statements*.

2. Apply financial statement analysis to assess the solvency of a business.

The primary focus of financial statement analysis is the assessment of solvency and profitability. All users are interested in the ability of a business to pay its debts as they come due (solvency) and to earn income (profitability). Solvency analysis is normally assessed by examining the following balance sheet relationships: (1) current position analysis, (2) accounts receivable analysis, (3) inventory analysis, (4) the ratio of fixed assets to long-term liabilities, (5) the ratio of liabilities to stockholders' equity, and (6) the number of times interest charges are earned.

3. Apply financial statement analysis to assess the profitability of a business.

Profitability analysis focuses mainly on the relationship between operating results (income statement) and resources available (balance sheet). Major analyses used in assessing profitability include (1) the ratio of net sales to assets, (2) the rate earned on total assets, (3) the rate earned on stockholders' equity, (4) the rate earned on common stockholders' equity, (5) earnings per share on common stock, (6) the price-earnings ratio, (7) dividends per share, and (8) dividend yield.

4. Summarize the uses and limitations of analytical measures.

In selecting and interpreting analytical measures, conditions peculiar to a business or its industry should be considered. For example, the type of industry, capital structure, and diversity of the business's operations affect the measures used. In addition, the influence of the general economic and business environment should be considered.

5. Describe the contents of corporate annual reports.

Corporate annual reports normally include financial statements and the following sections: Financial Highlights, President's Letter to the Stockholders, Management Discussion and Analysis, Independent Auditors' Report, and Historical Summary.

Glossary

Accounts receivable turnover: The relationship between sales and accounts receivable computed by dividing net sales by the average net accounts receivable.

Acid-test ratio: The ratio of the sum of cash, receivables, and marketable securities to current liabilities.

Common-size statement: A financial statement in which all items are expressed only in relative terms.

Current ratio: The ratio of current assets to current liabilities.

Dividend yield: A profitability measure that is computed by dividing the annual dividends paid per share of common stock by the market price per share on a specific date.

Dividends per share: The ratio of dividends paid to common stockholders divided by the number of common shares outstanding.

Earnings per share (EPS) on common stock: The profitability ratio of net income available to common shareholders to the number of common shares outstanding.

Horizontal analysis: The percentage of increases and decreases in corresponding items in comparative financial statements.

Inventory turnover: The relationship between the volume of goods sold and inventory computed by dividing the cost of goods sold by the average inventory.

Leverage: The tendency of the rate earned on stockholders' equity to vary from the rate earned on total assets because the amount earned on assets acquired through the use of funds provided by creditors varies from the interest paid to these creditors.

Management Discussion and Analysis: An annual report disclosure that

provides an analysis of the results of operations and financial condition.

Number of days' sales in inventory: The relationship between the volume of sales and inventory, computed by dividing the inventory at the end of the year by the average daily cost of goods sold.

Number of days' sales in receivables: The relationship between sales and accounts receivable, computed by dividing the net accounts receivable at the end of the year by the average daily sales.

Number of times interest charges are earned: A ratio that measures the risk that interest payments to debt holders will continue to be made if earnings decrease.

Price-earnings (P/E) ratio: The ratio of the market price per share of common stock at a specific date to the annual earnings per share.

Profitability: The ability of a firm to earn income.

Quick assets: The sum of cash, receivables, and marketable securities.

Rate earned on common stockholders' equity: A measure of profitability computed by dividing net income, reduced by preferred dividend requirements, by common stockholders' equity.

Rate earned on stockholders' equity: A measure of profitability computed by dividing net income by total stockholders' equity.

Rate earned on total assets: A measure of the profitability of assets without regard to the equity of creditors and stockholders in the assets.

Ratio of fixed assets to long-term liabilities: A solvency measure that indicates the margin of safety of the noteholders or bondholders.

Ratio of liabilities to stockholders' equity: A solvency measure that indicates the margin of safety for creditors.

Ratio of net sales to assets: A profitability measure that measures how effectively a firm utilizes its assets.

Solvency: The ability of a firm to pay its debts as they come due.

Vertical analysis: The percentage analysis of component parts in relation to the total of the parts in a single financial statement.

Working capital: The excess of total current assets over total current liabilities at some point in time.

Self-Study Questions

(Answers appear at end of chapter.)

1. What type of analysis is indicated by the following?

	Amount	Percent
Current assets	$100,000	20%
Property, plant, and equipment	400,000	80
Total assets	$500,000	100%

    A. Vertical analysis
    B. Horizontal analysis
    C. Profitability analysis
    D. Contribution margin analysis

2. Which of the following measures indicates the ability of a firm to pay its current liabilities?
    A. Working capital   C. Acid-test ratio
    B. Current ratio   D. All of the above

3. The ratio determined by dividing total current assets by total current liabilities is:
    A. current ratio   C. bankers' ratio
    B. working capital ratio D. all of the above

4. The ratio of the quick assets to current liabilities, which indicates the "instant" debt-paying ability of a firm, is the:
    A. current ratio   C. acid-test ratio
    B. working capital ratio D. bankers' ratio

5. A measure useful in evaluating the efficiency in the management of inventories is the:
    A. working capital ratio
    B. acid-test ratio
    C. number of days' sales in inventory
    D. ratio of fixed assets to long-term liabilities

Discussion Questions

1. What is the advantage of using comparative statements for financial analysis rather than statements for a single date or period?

2. The current year's amount of net income (after income tax) is 15% higher than that of the preceding year. Does this indicate an improved operating performance? Discuss.

3. How would the current and acid-test ratios of a service business compare?

4. For Lindsay Corporation, the working capital at the end of the current year is $5,000 higher than the working capital at the end of the preceding year, reported as follows:

	Current Year	Preceding Year
Current assets:		
Cash, marketable securities, and receivables	$34,000	$30,000
Inventories	51,000	32,500
Total current assets	$85,000	$62,500
Current liabilities	42,500	25,000
Working capital	$42,500	$37,500

Has the current position improved? Explain.

5. A company that grants terms of n/30 on all sales has a yearly accounts receivable turnover, based on monthly averages, of 6. Is this a satisfactory turnover? Discuss.

6. What does an increase in the number of days' sales in receivables ordinarily indicate about the credit and collection policy of the firm?

7. a. Why is it advantageous to have a high inventory turnover?
   b. Is it possible for the inventory turnover to be too high? Discuss.
   c. Is it possible to have a high inventory turnover and a high number of days' sales in inventory? Discuss.

8. What do the following data taken from a comparative balance sheet indicate about the company's ability to borrow additional funds on a long-term basis in the current year as compared to the preceding year?

	Current Year	Preceding Year
Fixed assets (net)	$175,000	$170,000
Total long-term liabilities	70,000	85,000

9. In computing the ratio of net sales to assets, why are long-term investments excluded in determining the amount of the total assets?

10. In determining the number of times interest charges are earned, why are interest charges added to income before income tax?

11. In determining the rate earned on total assets, why is interest expense added to net income before dividing by total assets?

12. a. Why is the rate earned on stockholders' equity by a thriving business ordinarily higher than the rate earned on total assets?
    b. Should the rate earned on common stockholders' equity normally be higher or lower than the rate earned on total stockholders' equity? Explain.

13. The net income (after income tax) of A. L. Gibson Inc. was $25 per common share in the latest year and $40 per common share for the preceding year. At the beginning of the latest year, the number of shares outstanding was doubled by a stock split. There were no other changes in the amount of stock outstanding. What were the earnings per share in the preceding year adjusted for comparison with the latest year?

14. The price-earnings ratio for the common stock of Essian Company was 10 at December 31, the end of the current fiscal year. What does the ratio indicate about the selling price of the common stock in relation to current earnings?

15. Why would the dividend yield differ significantly from the rate earned on common stockholders' equity?

16. Favorable business conditions can bring about certain seemingly unfavorable ratios, and unfavorable business operations can result in apparently favorable ratios. For example, Sanchez Company increased its sales and net income substantially for the current year, yet the current ratio at the end of the year is lower than at the beginning of the year. Discuss some possible causes of the apparent weakening of the current position while sales and net income have increased substantially.

17. a. What are the major components of an annual report?
    b. Indicate the purpose of the Financial Highlights section and the Management Discussion and Analysis.

Exercises

EXERCISE 9-1
Vertical analysis of income statement
OBJECTIVE 1

Revenue and expense data for Murry Cabinet Co. are as follows:

	2004	2003
Sales	$770,000	$700,000
Cost of goods sold	415,800	350,000
Selling expenses	138,600	140,000
Administrative expenses	84,700	105,000
Income tax expense	53,900	49,000

✓ 2004 net income: $77,000; 10% of sales

a. Prepare an income statement in comparative form, stating each item for both 2004 and 2003 as a percentage of sales.
b. Comment on the significant changes disclosed by the comparative income statement.

EXERCISE 9-2

Vertical analysis of income statement

OBJECTIVE 1

✓ a. Fiscal year 2000 income from operations, 8.3% of revenues

The following comparative income statement (in millions of dollars) for the fiscal years 2001 and 2000 was adapted from the annual report of **Dell Computer Corporation**:

	Fiscal Year 2001	Fiscal Year 2000
Revenues	$31,168	$31,888
Costs and expenses:		
Cost of sales	25,661	25,445
Gross profit	$ 5,507	$ 6,443
Operating expenses	3,718	3,780
Income from operations	$ 1,789	$ 2,663

a. Prepare a comparative income statement for fiscal years 2001 (ended February 1, 2002) and 2000 (ended February 2, 2001) in vertical form, stating each item as a percentage of revenues. Round to one digit after the decimal place.
b. Comment on the significant changes.

EXERCISE 9-3

Common-size income statement

OBJECTIVE 1

✓ a. Keystone net income: $218,500; 9.1% of sales

Revenue and expense data for the current calendar year for Keystone Publishing Company and for the publishing industry are as follows. The Keystone Publishing Company data are expressed in dollars. The publishing industry averages are expressed in percentages.

	Keystone Publishing Company	Publishing Industry Average
Sales	$2,450,000	101.0%
Sales returns and allowances	24,500	1.0
Cost of goods sold	850,000	40.0
Selling expenses	970,000	39.0
Administrative expenses	280,000	10.5
Other income	30,000	1.2
Other expense	40,000	1.7
Income tax expense	97,000	4.0

a. Prepare a common-size income statement comparing the results of operations for Keystone Publishing Company with the industry average. Round to one digit after the decimal place.
b. As far as the data permit, comment on significant relationships revealed by the comparisons.

EXERCISE 9-4

Vertical analysis of balance sheet

OBJECTIVE 1

Balance sheet data for Atlas Fitness Equipment Company on December 31, the end of the fiscal year, are as follows:

	2004	2003
Current assets	$180,000	$150,000
Property, plant, and equipment	340,000	330,000
Intangible assets	30,000	35,000
Current liabilities	120,000	125,000
Long-term liabilities	175,000	150,000
Common stock	50,000	40,000
Retained earnings	205,000	200,000

Prepare a comparative balance sheet for 2004 and 2003, stating each asset as a percentage of total assets and each liability and stockholders' equity item as a percentage of the total liabilities and stockholders' equity. Round to two digits after the decimal place.

EXERCISE 9–5
Horizontal analysis of the income statement
OBJECTIVE 1

Income statement data for Neon Flashlight Company for the year ended December 31, 2004 and 2003, are as follows:

	2004	2003
Sales	$400,000	$460,000
Cost of goods sold	170,000	200,000
Gross profit	$230,000	$260,000
Selling expenses	$ 70,000	$ 60,000
Administrative expenses	50,000	40,000
Total operating expenses	$120,000	$100,000
Income before income tax	$110,000	$160,000
Income tax expense	28,000	40,000
Net income	$ 82,000	$120,000

a. Prepare a comparative income statement with horizontal analysis, indicating the increase (decrease) for 2004 when compared with 2003. Round to two digits after the decimal place.

b. What conclusions can be drawn from the horizontal analysis?

EXERCISE 9–6
Current position analysis
OBJECTIVE 2

The following data were taken from the balance sheet of Precision Gears Company:

	Current Year	Preceding Year
Cash	$280,000	$265,000
Marketable securities	131,000	121,000
Accounts and notes receivable (net)	395,000	384,000
Inventories	570,000	555,000
Prepaid expenses	19,000	40,000
Accounts and notes payable (short-term)	250,000	285,700
Accrued liabilities	60,000	64,300

a. Determine for each year (1) the working capital, (2) the current ratio, and (3) the acid-test ratio.

b. What conclusions can be drawn from these data as to the company's ability to meet its currently maturing debts?

EXERCISE 9–7
Current position analysis
OBJECTIVE 2

PepsiCo, the parent company of Frito-Lay snack foods and Pepsi beverages, had the following current assets and current liabilities (in millions) at the end of two recent years:

	Current Year	Preceding Year
Cash	$ 311	$1,928
Marketable securities	83	955
Accounts and notes receivable (net)	2,453	2,150
Inventories	1,016	732
Prepaid expenses	499	486
Short-term borrowings	3,921	—
Accounts and notes payable (short-term)	3,870	3,617
Income taxes payable	123	640

✓ a. (1) Current year's current ratio, 0.55

a. Determine the (1) current ratio and (2) acid-test ratio for both years. Round to two digits after the decimal place.

b. What conclusions can you draw from these data?

EXERCISE 9-8
Current position analysis
OBJECTIVE 2

The bond indenture for the 10-year, 91/2% debenture bonds dated January 2, 2003, required working capital of $350,000, a current ratio of 1.5, and an acid-test ratio of 1.0 at the end of each calendar year until the bonds mature. At December 31, 2004, the three measures were computed as follows:

1. Current assets:

Cash	$245,000	
Marketable securities	123,000	
Accounts and notes receivable (net)	172,000	
Inventories	295,000	
Prepaid expenses	35,000	
Goodwill	150,000	
Total current assets		$1,020,000
Current liabilities:		
Accounts and short-term notes payable	$350,000	
Accrued liabilities	250,000	
Total current liabilities		600,000
Working capital		$ 420,000

2. Current ratio = 1.7 ($1,020,000/$600,000)
3. Acid-test ratio = 1.54 ($540,000/$350,000), rounded

a. Can you find any errors in the determination of the three measures of current position analysis?

b. Is the company satisfying the terms of the bond indenture?

EXERCISE 9-9
Accounts receivable analysis
OBJECTIVE 2

The following data are taken from the financial statements of Northern Expressions Company. Terms of all sales are 1/10, n/60.

✓ a. Accounts receivable turnover, current year, 7.0

	Current Year	Preceding Year
Accounts receivable, end of year	$ 222,466	$ 235,068
Monthly average accounts receivable (net)	207,143	216,667
Net sales	1,450,000	1,300,000

a. Determine for each year (1) the accounts receivable turnover and (2) the number of days' sales in receivables. Round to one digit after the decimal place.

b. What conclusions can be drawn from these data concerning accounts receivable and credit policies?

EXERCISE 9-10

Accounts receivable analysis

OBJECTIVE 2

✓ a. (1) Sears' accounts receivable turnover, 2.1

Sears and **JC Penney** are two of the largest department store chains in the United States. Both companies offer credit to their customers through their own credit card operations. Information from the financial statements for both companies for two recent years is as follows (all numbers are in millions):

	Sears	JC Penney
Sales—recent year	$41,332	$30,678
Credit card receivables—recent year balance	18,946	4,415
Credit card receivables—previous year balance	20,956	3,819

a. Determine the (1) accounts receivable turnover and (2) the number of days' sales in receivables for both companies. Round to one digit after the decimal place.
b. Compare the two companies with regard to their credit card policies.

EXERCISE 9-11

Inventory analysis

OBJECTIVE 2

✓ a. Inventory turnover, current year, 6.0

The following data were extracted from the income statement of Sierra Instruments Inc.:

	Current Year	Preceding Year
Sales	$3,600,000	$3,900,000
Beginning inventories	310,000	290,000
Cost of goods sold	2,010,000	2,400,000
Ending inventories	360,000	310,000

a. Determine for each year (1) the inventory turnover and (2) the number of days' sales in inventory. Round to two digits after the decimal place.
b. What conclusions can be drawn from these data concerning the inventories?

EXERCISE 9-12

Inventory analysis

OBJECTIVE 2

✓ a. (1) Dell inventory turnover, 75.7

Dell Computer Corporation and **Gateway Inc.** compete with each other in the personal computer market. Dell's strategy is to assemble computers according to customer phone and Internet orders rather than for inventory. Thus, for example, Dell will build and deliver a computer within four days after a customer enters an order on a Web page. Gateway, on the other hand, builds some computers prior to receiving an order and then sells from this inventory once an order is received. In addition, Gateway uses its own retail outlets to sell its computers. Following is selected financial information for both companies from a recent year's financial statements (in millions):

	Dell Computer Corporation	Gateway Inc.
Sales—fiscal 2001	$31,161	$6,080
Cost of goods sold	25,661	5,241
Inventory, beginning of fiscal 2001	400	315
Inventory, end of fiscal 2001	278	120

a. Determine for both companies (1) the inventory turnover and (2) the number of days' sales in inventory. Round to one digit after the decimal place.
b. Interpret the inventory ratios by considering Dell's and Gateway's operating strategies.

EXERCISE 9-13

Ratio of liabilities to stockholders' equity and number of times interest charges earned

The following data were taken from the financial statements of Clear Spring Water Co. for December 31, 2004 and 2003:

OBJECTIVE 2

✓ a. Ratio of liabilities to stockholders' equity, Dec. 31, 2004, 0.63

	December 31, 2004	December 31, 2003
Accounts payable	$ 150,000	$ 204,000
Current maturities of serial bonds payable	300,000	300,000
Serial bonds payable, 8%, issued 1998, due 2008	1,800,000	2,100,000
Common stock, $1 par value	100,000	100,000
Paid-in capital in excess of par	800,000	800,000
Retained earnings	2,700,000	2,200,000

The income before income tax was $252,000 and $216,000 for the years 2004 and 2003, respectively.

a. Determine the ratio of liabilities to stockholders' equity at the end of each year. Round to two digits after the decimal place.
b. Determine the number of times the bond interest charges are earned during the year for both years.
c. What conclusions can be drawn from these data as to the company's ability to meet its currently maturing debts?

EXERCISE 9–14
Profitability ratios
OBJECTIVE 3

✓ a. Rate earned on total assets, 2004, 18.7%

The following selected data were taken from the financial statements of Central States Transportation Co. for December 31, 2004, 2003, and 2002:

	December 31, 2004	December 31, 2003	December 31, 2002
Total assets	$3,200,000	$2,800,000	$2,200,000
Notes payable (10% interest)	400,000	400,000	400,000
Common stock	900,000	900,000	900,000
Preferred $12 stock, $100 par, cumulative, nonparticipating (no change during year)	500,000	500,000	500,000
Retained earnings	1,330,000	870,000	330,000

The 2004 net income was $520,000, and the 2003 net income was $600,000. No dividends on common stock were declared between 2002 and 2004.

a. Determine the rate earned on total assets, the rate earned on stockholders' equity, and the rate earned on common stockholders' equity for the years 2003 and 2004. Round to one digit after the decimal place.
b. What conclusions can be drawn from these data as to the company's profitability?

EXERCISE 9–15
Profitability ratios
OBJECTIVE 3

✓ a. 2002 rate earned on total assets, 3.36%

Ann Taylor Inc. sells professional women's apparel through company-owned retail stores. Recent financial information for Ann Taylor follows (all numbers in thousands):

	Fiscal Year Ended	
	Feb. 2, 2002	Feb. 3, 2001
Net income	$29,105	$52,363

	Feb. 2, 2002	Feb. 3, 2001	Jan. 29, 2000
Total assets	$882,986	$848,115	$765,117
Total stockholders' equity	612,129	574,029	515,622

An analysis of 63 apparel retail companies indicates an industry average rate earned on total assets of 3.2% and an average rate earned on stockholders' equity of 7.6% for fiscal year 2001 (mostly February 2, 2002–dated statements).

a. Determine the rate earned on total assets for Ann Taylor for the fiscal years ended February 2, 2002, and February 3, 2001. Round to two digits after the decimal place.
b. Determine the rate earned on stockholders' equity for Ann Taylor for the fiscal years ended February 2, 2002, and February 3, 2001. Round to two digits after the decimal place.
c. Evaluate the two-year trend for the profitability ratios determined in (a) and (b).
d. Evaluate Ann Taylor's profit performance relative to the industry.

EXERCISE 9–16

Six measures of solvency or profitability

OBJECTIVES 2, 3

✓ c. Ratio of net sales to assets, 1.14

The following data were taken from the financial statements of Austin Labs Inc. for the current fiscal year:

Property, plant, and equipment (net)		$2,500,000
Liabilities:		
Current liabilities	$ 100,000	
Mortgage note payable, 7.5%, issued 1993, due 2008	1,200,000	
Total liabilities		$1,300,000
Stockholders' equity:		
Preferred $8 stock, $100 par, cumulative, nonparticipating (no change during year)		$ 600,000
Common stock, $10 par (no change during year)		1,600,000
Retained earnings:		

Balance, beginning of year	$900,000		
Net income	500,000	$1,400,000	
Preferred dividends	$ 48,000		
Common dividends	52,000	100,000	
Balance, end of year			1,300,000
Total stockholders' equity			$3,500,000
Net sales			$5,000,000
Interest expense			$ 90,000

Assuming that long-term investments totaled $200,000 throughout the year and that total assets were $4,400,000 at the beginning of the year, determine the following: (a) ratio of fixed assets to long-term liabilities, (b) ratio of liabilities to stockholders' equity, (c) ratio of net sales to assets, (d) rate earned on total assets, (e) rate earned on stockholders' equity, and (f) rate earned on common stockholders' equity. Round to two digits after the decimal place.

EXERCISE 9–17

Five measures of solvency or profitability

OBJECTIVES 2, 3

✓ d. Price-earnings ratio, 20

The balance sheet for Aspen Properties Inc. at the end of the current fiscal year indicated the following:

Bonds payable, 12% (issued in 1993, due in 2013)	$3,000,000
Preferred $10 stock, $100 par	500,000
Common stock, $20 par	5,000,000

Income before income tax was $800,000, and income tax was $200,000 for the current year. Cash dividends paid on common stock during the current year totaled $220,000. The common stock was selling for $44 per share at the end of the year. Determine each of the following: (a) the number of times bond interest charges were earned, (b) the number of times preferred dividends were earned, (c) the earnings per share on common stock, (d) the price-earnings ratio, (e) the dividends per share of common stock, and (f) the dividend yield. Round to two digits after the decimal place.

EXERCISE 9-18
*Earnings per share,
price-earnings ratio,
dividend yield*
OBJECTIVE 3

✓ b. Price-earnings ratio, 30

The following information was taken from the financial statements of Arctic Air Conditioners Inc. for December 31 of the current fiscal year:

Common stock, $12 par value (no change during the year)	$4,800,000
Preferred $9 stock, $100 par, cumulative, nonparticipating (no change during year)	1,200,000

The net income was $588,000 and the declared dividends on the common stock were $500,000 for the current year. The market price of the common stock is $36 per share.

For the common stock, determine the (a) earnings per share, (b) price-earnings ratio, (c) dividends per share, and (d) dividend yield. Round to two digits after the decimal place.

EXERCISE 9-19
Earnings per share
OBJECTIVE 3

✓ b. Earnings per share
on common stock, $8.64

The net income reported on the income statement of Southern Pulp and Paper Co. was $2,800,000. There were 250,000 shares of $20 par common stock and 80,000 shares of $8 cumulative preferred stock outstanding throughout the current year. The income statement included two extraordinary items: a $400,000 gain from condemnation of land and a $600,000 loss arising from flood damage, both after applicable income tax. Determine the per share figures for common stock for (a) income before extraordinary items and (b) net income.

Problems

PROBLEM 9 | 1
*Horizontal analysis for
income statement*
OBJECTIVE 1

✓ 1. Sales, 30% increase

For 2004, Better Biscuit Company reported its most significant increase in net income in years. At the end of the year, John Newton, the president, is presented with the following condensed comparative income statement:

BETTER BISCUIT COMPANY
Comparative Income Statement
For the Years Ended December 31, 2004 and 2003

	2004	2003
Sales	$715,000	$550,000
Sales returns and allowances	5,000	5,000
Net sales	$710,000	$545,000
Cost of goods sold	281,250	225,000
Gross profit	$428,750	$320,000
Selling expenses	$136,400	$110,000
Administrative expenses	42,350	35,000
Total operating expenses	$178,750	$145,000
Income from operations	$250,000	$175,000
Other income	3,500	3,000
Income before income tax	$253,500	$178,000
Income tax expense	85,000	60,000
Net income	$168,500	$118,000

Instructions

1. Prepare a comparative income statement with horizontal analysis for the two-year period, using 2003 as the base year. Round to two digits after the decimal place.
2. To the extent the data permit, comment on the significant relationships revealed by the horizontal analysis prepared in (1).

PROBLEM 9 | 2
Vertical analysis for income statement

OBJECTIVE 1

✓ 1. Net income, 2004, 8.55%

For 2004, Stainless Flow Systems Inc. initiated a sales promotion campaign that included the expenditure of an additional $50,000 for advertising. At the end of the year, Edwardo Gonzalez, the president, is presented with the following condensed comparative income statement:

STAINLESS FLOW SYSTEMS INC.
Comparative Income Statement
For the Years Ended December 31, 2004 and 2003

	2004	2003
Sales	$810,000	$775,000
Sales returns and allowances	5,000	5,000
Net sales	$805,000	$770,000
Cost of goods sold	438,700	416,000
Gross profit	$366,300	$354,000
Selling expenses	$165,800	$115,800
Administrative expenses	96,600	93,400
Total operating expenses	$262,400	$209,200
Income from operations	$103,900	$144,800
Other income	2,000	1,800
Income before income tax	$105,900	$146,600
Income tax expense	37,000	51,000
Net income	$ 68,900	$ 95,600

Instructions

1. Prepare a comparative income statement for the two-year period, presenting an analysis of each item in relationship to net sales for each of the years. Round to two digits after the decimal place.
2. To the extent the data permit, comment on the significant relationships revealed by the vertical analysis prepared in (1).

PROBLEM 9 | 3
Effect of transactions on current position analysis

OBJECTIVE 2

✓ 1. Acid-test ratio, 1.45

Data pertaining to the current position of Flintstone Aggregates Inc. are as follows:

Cash	$150,000
Marketable securities	64,000
Accounts and notes receivable (net)	221,000
Inventories	294,000
Prepaid expenses	11,000
Accounts payable	204,000
Notes payable (short-term)	66,000
Accrued expenses	30,000

Instructions

1. Compute (a) the working capital, (b) the current ratio, and (c) the acid-test ratio. Round to two digits after the decimal place.
2. List the following captions on a sheet of paper:

Transaction	Working Capital	Current Ratio	Acid-Test Ratio

Compute the working capital, the current ratio, and the acid-test ratio after each of the following transactions, and record the results in the appropriate columns. Consider each transaction separately and assume that only that transaction affects the preceding data. Round to two digits after the decimal point.

a. Sold marketable securities at no gain or loss, $34,000.
b. Paid accounts payable, $60,000.
c. Purchased goods on account, $40,000.
d. Paid notes payable, $20,000.
e. Declared a cash dividend, $25,000.
f. Declared a common stock dividend on common stock, $16,500.
g. Borrowed cash from bank on a long-term note, $120,000.
h. Received cash on account, $86,000.
i. Issued additional shares of stock for cash, $100,000.
j. Paid cash for prepaid expenses, $9,000.

PROBLEM 9 | 4
Nineteen measures of solvency and profitability
OBJECTIVES 2, 3

✓ 9. Ratio of liabilities to stockholders' equity, 0.7

The comparative financial statements of Integrity Technologies Inc. are as follows. The market price of Integrity Technologies Inc. common stock was $80 on December 31, 2004.

INTEGRITY TECHNOLOGIES INC.
Comparative Retained Earnings Statement
For the Years Ended December 31, 2004 and 2003

	Dec. 31, 2004	Dec. 31, 2003
Retained earnings, January 1	$ 964,000	$ 689,000
Add net income for year	503,000	435,000
Total	$1,467,000	$1,124,000
Deduct dividends:		
On preferred stock	$ 48,000	$ 40,000
On common stock	120,000	120,000
Total	$ 168,000	$ 160,000
Retained earnings, December 31	$1,299,000	$ 964,000

INTEGRITY TECHNOLOGIES INC.
Comparative Income Statement
For the Years Ended December 31, 2004 and 2003

	2004	2003
Sales (all on account)	$6,130,000	$5,640,000
Sales returns and allowances	30,000	40,000
Net sales	$6,100,000	$5,600,000
Cost of goods sold	2,800,000	2,550,000
Gross profit	$3,300,000	$3,050,000
Selling expenses	$1,450,000	$1,440,000
Administrative expenses	1,000,000	910,000
Total operating expenses	$2,450,000	$2,350,000
Income from operations	$ 850,000	$ 700,000
Other income	40,000	30,000
	$ 890,000	$ 730,000
Other expense (interest)	157,000	85,000
Income before income tax	$ 733,000	$ 645,000
Income tax expense	230,000	210,000
Net income	$ 503,000	$ 435,000

(continued)

INTEGRITY TECHNOLOGIES INC.
Comparative Balance Sheet
December 31, 2004 and 2003

	Dec. 31, 2004	Dec. 31, 2003
Assets		
Current assets:		
Cash	$ 200,000	$ 180,000
Marketable securities	923,000	215,000
Accounts receivable (net)	350,000	365,000
Inventories	500,000	480,000
Prepaid expenses	26,000	24,000
Total current assets	$1,999,000	$1,264,000
Long-term investments	700,000	500,000
Property, plant, and equipment (net)	3,100,000	2,600,000
Total assets	$5,799,000	$4,364,000
Liabilities		
Current liabilities	$ 600,000	$ 400,000
Long-term liabilities:		
Mortgage note payable, 9%, due 2008	$ 800,000	—
Bonds payable, 8.5%, due 2012	1,000,000	$1,000,000
Total long-term liabilities	$1,800,000	$1,000,000
Total liabilities	$2,400,000	$1,400,000
Stockholders' Equity		
Preferred $8 stock, $100 par	$ 600,000	$ 500,000
Common stock, $10 par	1,500,000	1,500,000
Retained earnings	1,299,000	964,000
Total stockholders' equity	$3,399,000	$2,964,000
Total liabilities and stockholders' equity	$5,799,000	$4,364,000

Instructions

Determine the following measures for 2004, rounding to nearest single digit after the decimal point:

1. Working capital
2. Current ratio
3. Acid-test ratio
4. Accounts receivable turnover
5. Number of days' sales in receivables
6. Inventory turnover
7. Number of days' sales in inventory
8. Ratio of fixed assets to long-term liabilities
9. Ratio of liabilities to stockholders' equity
10. Number of times interest charges earned
11. Number of times preferred dividends earned
12. Ratio of net sales to assets
13. Rate earned on total assets
14. Rate earned on stockholders' equity
15. Rate earned on common stockholders' equity
16. Earnings per share on common stock
17. Price-earnings ratio
18. Dividends per share of common stock
19. Dividend yield

PROBLEM 9 | 5
Solvency and profitability trend analysis
OBJECTIVES 2, 3

Jupiter Company has provided the following comparative information:

	2004	2003	2002	2001	2000
Net income	$ 100,000	$ 150,000	$ 150,000	$ 200,000	$ 250,000
Income tax expense	30,000	45,000	45,000	60,000	75,000
Interest	144,000	138,000	138,000	126,000	120,000
Average total assets	2,300,000	2,150,000	2,000,000	1,750,000	1,500,000
Average total stockholders' equity	1,100,000	1,000,000	850,000	700,000	500,000

You have been asked to evaluate the historical performance of the company over the last five years.

Selected industry ratios have remained relatively steady for the last five years at the following levels:

	2000–2004
Rate earned on total assets	12%
Rate earned on stockholders' equity	15%
Number of times interest charges earned	3.0
Ratio of liabilities to stockholders' equity	1.5

Instructions

1. Prepare four line graphs with the ratio on the vertical axis and the years on the horizontal axis for the following four ratios (round to two digits after the decimal place):
   a. Rate earned on total assets
   b. Rate earned on stockholders' equity
   c. Number of times interest charges earned
   d. Ratio of liabilities to stockholders' equity (using average balances)
   Display both the company ratio and the industry benchmark on each graph (which should have two lines).
2. Prepare an analysis of the graphs in (1).

Activities

Activity 9–1
Ethics and professional conduct in business
ETHICS

Lee Camden, president of Camden Equipment Co., prepared a draft of the President's Letter to be included with Camden Equipment Co.'s 2004 annual report. The letter mentions a 10% increase in sales and a recent expansion of plant facilities but fails to mention the net loss of $180,000 for the year. You have been asked to review the letter for inclusion in the annual report.

How would you respond to the omission of the net loss of $180,000? Specifically, is such an action ethical?

Activity 9–2
Analysis of financing corporate growth

Assume that the president of Crest Brewery made the following statement in the President's Letter to Shareholders:

"The founding family and majority shareholders of the company do not believe in using debt to finance future growth. The founding family learned from hard experience during Prohibition and the Great Depression that debt can cause loss of flexibility and eventual loss of corporate control. The company will not place itself at such risk. As such, all future growth will be financed either by stock sales to the public or by internally generated resources."

As a public shareholder of this company, how would you respond to this policy?

Activity 9-3

Receivables and inventory turnover

Imex Computer Company has completed its fiscal year on December 31, 2004. The auditor, Sandra Blake, has approached the CFO, Travis Williams, regarding the year-end receivables and inventory levels of Imex. The following conversation takes place:

Sandra: We are beginning our audit of Imex and have prepared ratio analyses to determine whether there have been significant changes in operations or financial position. This helps us guide the audit process. This analysis indicates that the inventory turnover has decreased from 5 to 2.8, while the accounts receivable turnover has decreased from 12 to 8. I was wondering if you could explain this change in operations.

Travis: There is little need for concern. The inventory represents computers that we were unable to sell during the holiday buying season. We are confident, however, that we will be able to sell these computers as we move into the next fiscal year.

Sandra: What gives you this confidence?

Travis: We will increase our advertising and provide some very attractive price concessions to move these machines. We have no choice. Newer technology is already out there, and we have to unload this inventory.

Sandra: . . . and the receivables?

Travis: As you may be aware, the company is under tremendous pressure to expand sales and profits. As a result, we lowered our credit standards to our commercial customers so that we would be able to sell products to a broader customer base. As a result of this policy change, we have been able to expand sales by 35%.

Sandra: Your responses have not been reassuring to me.

Travis: I'm a little confused. Assets are good, right? Why don't you look at our current ratio? It has improved, hasn't it? I would think that you would view that very favorably.

Why is Sandra concerned about the inventory and accounts receivable turnover ratios and Travis' responses to them? What action could Sandra need to take? How would you respond to Travis' last comment?

Activity 9-4

Vertical analysis

The condensed income statements through income from operations for **Dell Computer Corporation** and **Apple Computer Co.** are reproduced here for recent fiscal years (numbers in millions):

	DELL COMPUTER CORPORATION For the Year Ended February 1, 2002	APPLE COMPUTER CO. For the Year Ended September 29, 2001
Sales (net)	$31,168	$5,363
Cost of sales	25,661	4,128
Gross profit	$ 5,507	$1,235
Selling, general, and administrative expense	$ 2,784	$1,138
Research and development	452	430
Special charges	482	11
Operating expenses	$ 3,718	$1,579
Income from operations	$ 1,789	$ (344)

Prepare comparative common-size statements, rounding to two digits after the whole percent. Interpret the analyses.

Activity 9-5

Common-sized statements and analysis

American Airlines Inc. is the largest passenger airline in the world. Condensed income statement information for American is as follows:

AMERICAN AIRLINES, INC.
Comparative Income Statements
For the Years Ended December 31, 2001, 2000, 1999
(in millions)

	2001	2000	1999
REVENUES	$17,484	$18,117	$16,338
EXPENSES			
Wages, salaries, and benefits	$ 7,566	$ 6,354	$ 5,747
Aircraft fuel	2,744	2,372	1,622
Depreciation and amortization	1,257	1,068	977
Other rentals and landing fees	1,113	919	867
Maintenance, materials, and repairs	979	899	833
Aircraft rentals	799	561	582
Commissions to agents	786	973	1,090
Food service	771	769	734
Other operating expenses	3,322	2,958	2,866
Special charges, net of U.S. Government grant	421	0	0
Total operating expenses	$19,758	$16,873	$15,318
OPERATING INCOME (LOSS)	($2,274)	$ 1,244	$ 1,020
OTHER INCOME (EXPENSE)	(175)	38	34
EARNINGS (LOSS) BEFORE INCOME TAXES	($2,449)	$ 1,282	$ 1,054
Income tax provision (benefit)	(887)	504	427
NET EARNINGS (LOSS)	($1,562)	$ 778	$ 627

1. Prepare common-size statements for the three comparative years.
2. Analyze the company's performance trend for the three comparative years, using the information in (1).

Activity 9-6
Common-sized statements and analysis

Merck & Co. is one of the largest global pharmaceutical companies in the world, and **Amgen, Inc.**, is one of the largest biotechnology companies in the world. Both companies provide human health products. Merck develops new products principally by discovering new chemical combinations. Amgen relies on using advanced cellular and molecular biology (gene therapies) to discover new products. Comparative condensed income statements for both companies are as follows:

MERCK & CO. and AMGEN, INC.
Comparative Income Statements
For the Year Ended Dec. 31, 2001
(in thousands)

	Merck	Amgen
Sales	$47,715,700	$4,015,700
Costs, expenses and other		
Cost of sales	28,976,500	443,000
Marketing and administrative	6,224,400	970,700
Research and development	2,456,400	865,000
Equity income from affiliates	(685,900)	2,700
Other (income) expense, net	367,100	203,100
Total expenses	$37,338,500	$2,484,500
Other income (expense):		
Interest and other income, net	490,100	168,700
Interest expense, net	(464,700)	(13,600)
Total other income	$ 25,400	$ 155,100
Income before taxes	$10,402,600	$1,686,300
Taxes on income	3,120,800	566,600
Net income	$ 7,281,800	$1,119,700

Average 2001 balances (in thousands) from the comparative balance sheets for both companies were as follows:

	Merck	Amgen
Average total assets	$42,080,800	$5,921,350
Average accounts receivable	5,238,900	443,200
Average inventory	3,300,400	330,400
Average fixed assets	12,292,750	1,863,800

1. Prepare a common-size income statement for both companies. (Round to the nearest single decimal place after the whole percent.)
2. Calculate the accounts receivable and inventory turnover for each company.
3. Analyze and compare the two companies, based on the analyses in (1) and (2).

Activity 9-7
Comparative ratio analysis

Marriott International Inc. and **Hilton Hotels Corp.** are two major owners and managers of lodging and resort properties in the United States. Abstracted income statement information (in millions) for the two companies is as follows for the year ended December 31, 2001:

	Marriott	Hilton
Operating profit before other expenses and interest:	$ 590	$ 495
Other income (expenses)	(111)	48
Interest expense	(109)	(237)
Income before income taxes	$ 370	$ 306
Income tax expense	134	130
Net income	$ 236	$ 176

Balance sheet information (in millions) is as follows for December 31, 2001:

	Marriott	Hilton
Total liabilities	$5,629	$7,498
Total stockholders' equity	3,478	1,642
Total liabilities and stockholders' equity	$9,107	$9,140

The average liabilities, stockholders' equity, and total assets for 2001 were as follows:

	Marriott	Hilton
Average total liabilities	$5,300	$7,250
Average total stockholders' equity	3,373	1,713
Average total assets	8,673	8,963

1. Determine the following ratios for both companies. (Round to the nearest two digits after the whole percent.)
   a. Rate earned on total assets
   b. Rate earned on total stockholders' equity
   c. Number of times interest charges are earned
   d. Ratio of liabilities to stockholders' equity
2. Analyze and compare the two companies, using the information in (1) and (2).

Activity 9-8
Solvency and profitability analysis

One team should obtain the latest annual report for **Wal-Mart Stores Inc.**, and the other team should obtain the latest **Kmart Corp.** annual report. These annual reports can be obtained from a library or the SEC's EDGAR service.

G R O U P

EDGAR (Electronic Data Gathering, Analysis, and Retrieval) is the electronic archive of financial statements filed with the Securities and Exchange Commission (SEC). SEC documents can be retrieved using the EdgarScan service from PricewaterhouseCoopers at http://edgarscan.pwcglobal.com. To obtain annual report information, type in a company name in the appropriate space. EdgarScan will list the reports available to you for the company you've selected. Select the most recent annual report filing, identified as a 10-K or 10-K405. EdgarScan provides an outline of the report, including the separate financial statements. You can double-click the income statement and balance sheet for the selected company into an Excel spreadsheet for further analysis.

Each team should compute the following for its company:

a. Current ratio
b. Inventory turnover
c. Rate earned on stockholders' equity
d. Rate earned on total assets
e. Net income as a percentage of sales
f. Ratio of liabilities to stockholders' equity

As a class, prepare a report comparing the two companies for the latest fiscal period.

Answers to Self–Study Questions

1. **A** Percentage analysis indicating the relationship of the component parts to the total in a financial statement, such as the relationship of current assets to total assets (20% to 100%) in the question, is called *vertical analysis* (answer A). Percentage analysis of increases and decreases in corresponding items in comparative financial statements is called *horizontal analysis* (answer B). An example of horizontal analysis is the presentation of the amount of current assets in the preceding balance sheet along with the amount of current assets at the end of the current year and with the increase or decrease in current assets between the periods expressed as a percentage. Profitability analysis (answer C) is the analysis of a firm's ability to earn income. Contribution margin analysis (answer D) is discussed in a later managerial accounting chapter.

2. **D** Various solvency measures, categorized as current position analysis, indicate a firm's ability to meet currently maturing obligations. Each measure contributes in the analysis of a firm's current position and is most useful when viewed with other measures and when compared with similar measures for other periods and for other firms. Working capital (answer A) is the excess of current assets over current liabilities; the current ratio (answer B) is the ratio of current assets to current liabilities; and the acid-test ratio (answer C) is the ratio of the sum of cash, receivables, and marketable securities to current liabilities.

3. **D** The ratio of current assets to current liabilities is usually called the *current ratio* (answer A). It is sometimes called the *working capital ratio* (answer B) or *bankers' ratio* (answer C).

4. **C** The ratio of the sum of cash, receivables, and marketable securities (sometimes called *quick assets*) to current liabilities is called the *acid-test ratio* (answer C) or *quick ratio*. The current ratio (answer A), working capital ratio (answer B), and bankers' ratio (answer D) are terms that describe the ratio of current assets to current liabilities.

5. **C** The number of days' sales in inventory (answer C), which is determined by dividing the inventories at the end of the year by the average daily cost of goods sold, expresses the relationship between the cost of goods sold and inventory. It indicates the efficiency in the management of inventory. The working capital ratio (answer A) indicates the ability of the business to meet currently maturing obligations (debt). The acid-test ratio (answer B) indicates the "instant" debt-paying ability of the business. The ratio of fixed assets to long-term liabilities (answer D) indicates the margin of safety for long-term creditors.

10

LEARNING OBJECTIVES

OBJECTIVE 1
Distinguish the activities of a manufacturing business from those of a merchandise or service business.

OBJECTIVE 2
Define and illustrate materials, factory labor, and factory overhead costs.

OBJECTIVE 3
Describe accounting systems used by manufacturing businesses.

OBJECTIVE 4
Describe and illustrate a job order cost accounting system.

OBJECTIVE 5
Use job order cost information for decision making.

OBJECTIVE 6
Diagram the flow of costs for a service business that uses a job order cost accounting system.

OBJECTIVE 7
Describe just-in-time manufacturing.

OBJECTIVE 8
Describe and illustrate the use of activity-based costing in a service business.

Accounting Systems for Manufacturing Businesses

Suppose you go down to the local bakery and buy a bagel and coffee before class. How much should the bakery charge you? The purchase price must be more than the costs of producing and serving the bagel and coffee. Moreover, the bakery needs to be able to answer additional questions, such as these:

- How many bagels must be sold in a given month and at given prices to cover costs?
- How should the price for a single bagel differ from the price for a dozen bagels?
- How many employees should be in the shop at different times of the week?
- How much should be charged for delivery service?
- Would a larger oven be a good investment?
- Should the shop stay open 24 hours per day?

All of these questions can be answered with the aid of cost information. In this chapter you will be introduced to cost concepts used in managerial accounting, which help answer questions like those above. In addition, we explore how cost information is developed and used when work is performed on a specified quantity of product.

We begin this chapter by describing managerial (or management) accounting and its relationship to financial accounting. Following this overview, we describe the organizational role of management accountants in the management process. Lastly, we introduce you to the basic cost terms and apply them within a job order cost system.

Nature of Manufacturing Businesses

Distinguish the activities of a manufacturing business from those of a merchandise or service business.

In Chapters 2 and 3, we described and illustrated accounting systems for service businesses. In Chapter 4, we described and illustrated accounting systems for merchandising businesses. In this chapter, we focus on manufacturing businesses. Examples of manufacturing businesses include General Motors and Intel Corporation.

The revenue activities of a service business involve providing services to customers. The revenue activities of a merchandising business involve the buying and selling of merchandise. In contrast, manufacturing businesses must first produce the products they sell. A manufacturing business converts materials into finished product through the use of machinery and labor.

Like merchandising businesses, a manufacturing business reports sales from selling its products. The cost of the products sold is normally reported as **cost of goods sold**, whereas a merchandising business reports these costs as cost of merchandise sold. The subtraction of the cost of goods sold from sales is reported as gross profit. Operating expenses are deducted from gross profit to arrive at net income.

Materials, products in the process of being manufactured, and finished products are reported on the manufacturer's balance sheet as inventories. Like merchandise inventory, these inventories are reported as current assets.

ETHICS IN ACTION

Management sometimes feels pressured to boost earnings by relaxing credit policies. Thus, it is able to create more sales on account but at a higher collection risk. The result is a temporary positive impact on the income statement. However, cash flow can be negatively impacted if high-credit-risk customers delay payment or are unable to pay. For example, **Lucent Technologies, Inc.**, extended billions of dollars in credit to upstart telecom companies to support its equipment sales. Loans to companies like **Winstar** and **One.Tel Ltd.** were eventually written off to the tune of $1 billion. This has prompted shareholder lawsuits accusing Lucent's directors of "mismanaging the top U.S. maker of phone equipment by lending the company's money to financially shaky customers to promote sales."

Source: "Lucent to Cut Almost Half Its Work Force: Troubled Phone Equipment Maker to Eliminate 20,000 Jobs, Take a Charge of as much as $9 Billion," *Omaha World-Herald,* July 24, 2001.

Manufacturing Cost Terms

Define and illustrate materials, factory labor, and factory overhead costs.

Managers rely on managerial accountants to provide useful cost information to support decision making. What is a cost? A **cost** is a payment of cash or its equivalent or the commitment to pay cash in the future for the purpose of generating revenues. A cost provides a benefit that is used immediately or deferred to a future period of time. If the benefit is used immediately, then the cost is an expense, such as salary expense. If the benefit is deferred, then the cost is an asset, such as equipment. As the asset is used, an expense, such as depreciation expense, is recognized.

In this section, we illustrate manufacturing costs for Goodwell Printers, a manufacturing firm. A **manufacturing business** converts materials into a finished product through the use of machinery and labor. Goodwell Printers prints textbooks, like the one you are using now. Exhibit 1 provides an overview of Goodwell Printers' text-

EXHIBIT 1

Textbook Printing Operations of Goodwell Printers

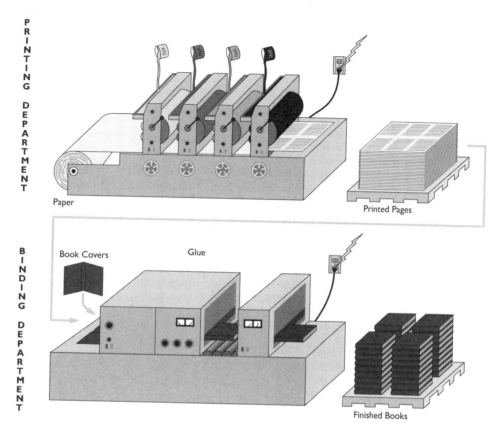

book printing operations. The Printing Department feeds large rolls of paper onto printing presses. The printing presses use electricity and ink. From the Printing Department, the printed pages are stacked and moved to the Binding Department. In the Binding Department, the pages are cut, separated, stacked, and bound to book covers. A finished book is the final output of the Binding Department.

Materials

The cost of materials that are an integral part of the product is classified as **direct materials cost**. For example, the direct materials cost for Goodwell Printers would include paper and book covers.

As a practical matter, a direct materials cost must not only be an integral part of the finished product, but it must also be a significant portion of the total cost of the product. Other examples of direct materials costs are the cost of electronic components for a TV manufacturer and tires for an automobile manufacturer.

The costs of materials that are not a significant portion of the total product cost are termed **indirect materials**. Indirect materials are considered a part of factory overhead, which we discuss later. For Goodwell Printers, the costs of ink and binding glue are classified as indirect materials.

EXAMPLES OF DIRECT MATERIALS

TELEVISION MANUFACTURER

GOODWELL PRINTERS

AUTOMOBILE MANUFACTURER

Factory Labor

The cost of wages of employees who are directly involved in converting materials into the manufactured product is classified as **direct labor cost**. The direct labor cost of Goodwell Printers includes the wages of the employees who operate the printing presses. Other examples of direct labor costs are carpenters' wages for a construction contractor, mechanics' wages in an automotive repair shop, machine operators' wages in a tool manufacturing plant, and assemblers' wages in a microcomputer assembly plant.

As a practical matter, a direct labor cost must not only be an integral part of the finished product but also must be a significant portion of the total cost of the product. For Goodwell Printers, the printing press operators' wages are a significant portion of the total cost of each book. Labor costs that do not enter directly into the manufacture of a product are termed **indirect labor** and are recorded as factory overhead. Indirect labor for Goodwell Printers might include the salaries of maintenance, plant management, and quality control personnel.

Factory Overhead Cost

Costs other than direct materials cost and direct labor cost incurred in the manufacturing process are classified as **factory overhead cost**. Factory overhead is sometimes called **manufacturing overhead** or **factory burden**. Examples of factory overhead costs, in addition to indirect materials and indirect labor, are machine depreciation, factory utilities, factory supplies, and factory insurance. In addition, payments to employees for overtime and nonproductive time (such as idle time) are considered factory

---

BUSINESS STRATEGY

Rent or Own?

You could hire a copy shop to copy a school paper rather than acquiring a copy machine to make your own copies. In the same way, companies must decide which activities they should perform and which activities they should hire other companies to perform for them. The activities that are performed internally usually require fixed assets. Fixed assets, in turn, place a firm at risk since these assets must be used to have a financial return. Thus, some firms limit internal activities to their core competencies, or those activities that provide the company a strategic comparative advantage. Under this philosophy, noncore activities are purchased from others. Sara Lee Corporation embraces this strategic philosophy by becoming "an asset-less company." That is, Sara Lee has retained only its core activities and has asked suppliers to perform its noncore activities, such as manufacturing. In contrast, General Mills, a Sara Lee competitor, owns its manufacturing facilities. This difference in strategic philosophy can be seen in the companies' respective fixed asset turnover ratios, 8.3 for Sara Lee and 4.7 for General Mills.

overhead. For many industries, factory overhead costs are becoming a larger portion of the costs of a product as manufacturing processes become more automated.

The direct materials, direct labor, and factory overhead costs are considered **product costs**, because they are associated with making a product. The costs of converting the materials into finished products consist of direct labor and factory overhead costs, which are commonly called **conversion costs**.

Cost Accounting System Overview

OBJECTIVE   3

Describe accounting systems used by manufacturing businesses.

An objective of a **cost accounting system** is to accumulate product costs. Product cost information is used by managers to establish product prices, control operations, and develop financial statements. In addition, the cost accounting system improves control by supplying data on the costs incurred by each manufacturing department or process.

There are two main types of cost accounting systems for manufacturing operations: job order cost systems and process cost systems. Each of the two systems is widely used, and any one manufacturer can use more than one type.

A **job order cost system** provides a separate record for the cost of each quantity of product that passes through the factory. A particular quantity of product is termed a *job*. A job order cost system is best suited to industries that manufacture custom goods to fill special orders from customers or that produce a high variety of products for stock. Manufacturers that use a job order cost system are sometimes called **job shops**. For example, **Warner Bros.** and other movie studios use job order cost systems to accumulate movie production and distribution costs. Costs such as actor salaries, production costs, movie print costs, and marketing costs are accumulated in a job account for a particular movie. Cost information from the job cost report can be used to control the costs of the movie while it is being produced and to determine its profitability after it has been exhibited.

Many service firms also use job order cost systems to accumulate the costs associated with providing client services. For example, an accounting firm will accumulate all of the costs associated with a particular client engagement, such as accountant time, copying charges, and travel costs. Recording costs in this manner helps the accounting firm control costs during a client engagement and determines client billing and profitability.

Under a **process cost system**, costs are accumulated for each of the departments or processes within the factory. A process system is best suited for manufacturers of units of product that are not distinguishable from each other during a continuous production process. Examples would be automobiles (**General Motors**), beverages (**Coca-Cola**), soap and cosmetics (**Procter & Gamble**), and pharmaceuticals (**Eli Lilly**).

We describe and illustrate only job order cost systems in this chapter because they are often used by service as well as manufacturing businesses. However, we will introduce many manufacturing terms and concepts that also apply to process cost systems.[1]

---

[1]Process cost accounting systems are described and illustrated in Appendix B.

Job Order Cost Systems for Manufacturing Businesses

In this section, we illustrate the job order cost system for a manufacturing firm, Goodwell Printers. The job order system accumulates manufacturing costs by job, as shown in Exhibit 2. The **materials inventory**, sometimes called **raw materials inventory**, consists of the costs of the direct and indirect materials that have not yet entered the manufacturing process. For Goodwell Printers, the materials inventory consists of paper, ink, glue, and book covers. The **work in process inventory** consists of direct materials costs, direct labor costs, and factory overhead costs that have entered the manufacturing process but are associated with products that have not been completed. Examples are the costs of Jobs 71 and 72 that are still in the printing process in Exhibit 2. Completed jobs that have not been sold are termed **finished goods inventory**. Examples are completed printed books from Jobs 69 and 70 shown in Exhibit 2. Upon sale, a manufacturer records the cost of the sale as cost of goods sold. An example is the case of *Physics* books sold to the bookstore in Exhibit 2. The *cost of goods sold* for a manufacturer is comparable to the *cost of merchandise sold* for a merchandising business.

EXHIBIT 2 *Manufacturing Costs and Jobs*

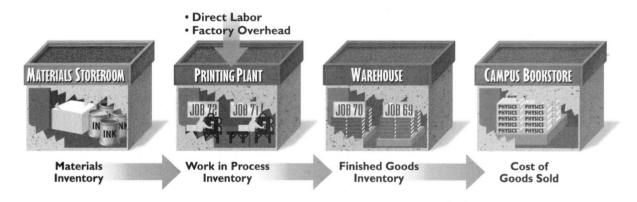

In a job order cost accounting system, perpetual inventory controlling accounts and subsidiary ledgers are maintained for materials, work in process, and finished goods inventories. Each inventory account is increased for all additions and is decreased for all deductions. The balance of each account thus represents the balance on hand.

Materials

The procedures used to purchase, store, and issue materials to production often differ among manufacturers. Exhibit 3 shows the basic information and cost flows for the paper received and issued to production by Goodwell Printers.

Purchased materials are first received and inspected by the Receiving Department. The Receiving Department personnel prepare a **receiving report** showing the quan-

EXHIBIT 3
Materials Information and Cost Flows

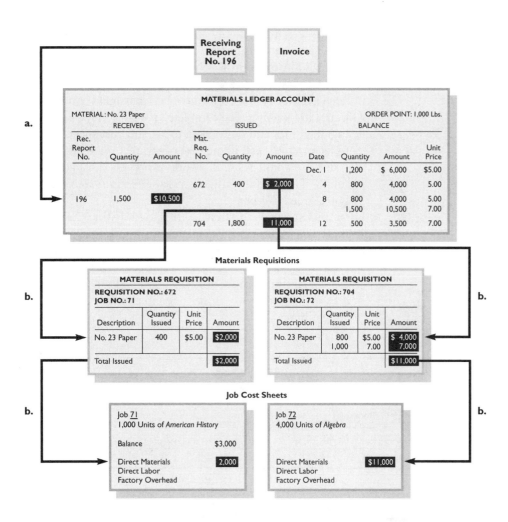

tity of materials received and their condition. Some organizations now use bar code scanning devices in place of receiving reports to record and electronically transmit incoming materials data. The receiving information and invoice are used to record the receipt and control the payment for purchased items. Receiving Report No. 196 is used as the basis for recording the increase in the materials inventory and the accounts payable. The effect on the accounts and financial statements follows:

Trans. Date	Balance Sheet			Income Statement		
	Assets	Liabilities	Stockholders' Equity	Revenue	Expense	Net Income
a.	Materials 10,500	Accts Pay 10,500				
Net Effect	*10,500*	*10,500*				
			Retained Earnings			
			(Net Income)			

The materials account in the general ledger is a controlling account. A separate account for each type of material is maintained in a subsidiary **materials ledger**.

Details as to the quantity and cost of materials received are recorded in the materials ledger on the basis of the receiving reports. A typical form of a materials ledger account is illustrated in Exhibit 3.

Materials are released from the storeroom to the factory in response to **materials requisitions** from the Production Department. An illustration of a materials requisition is in Exhibit 3. The completed requisition for each job serves as the basis for posting quantities and dollar data to the job cost sheets in the case of direct materials or to factory overhead in the case of indirect materials. **Job cost sheets**, which are illustrated in Exhibit 3, are the work in process subsidiary ledger. For Goodwell Printers, Job 71 is for 1,000 textbooks titled *American History*, while Job 72 is for 4,000 textbooks titled *Algebra*.

In Exhibit 3, the first-in, first-out costing method is used. A summary of the materials requisitions completed during the month is the basis for transferring the cost of the direct materials from the materials account in the general ledger to the controlling account for work in process. The flow of materials from the materials storeroom into production ($2,000 + $11,000) increases work in process and decreases materials inventory. The effect on the accounts and financial statements is shown here:

Trans. Date	Balance Sheet				Income Statement		
	Assets		Liabilities	Stockholders' Equity	Revenue	Expense	Net Income
b.	Materials Inventory	−13,000					
	Work in Process	13,000					
Net Effect		0					
				Retained Earnings			
				(Net Income)			

For many manufacturing firms, the direct materials cost can be more than 50% of the total cost to manufacture a product. This is the reason that controlling materials costs is very important and that many organizations are using computerized information processes that account for the flow of materials. In a computerized setting, the storeroom manager can record the release of materials into a computer, which can automatically update the subsidiary materials records.

Factory Labor

There are two primary objectives in accounting for factory labor. One objective is to determine the correct amount to be paid each employee for each payroll period. A second objective is to properly allocate factory labor costs to factory overhead and individual job orders.

The amount of time spent by an employee in the factory is usually recorded on **clock cards** or **in-and-out cards**. The amount of time spent by each employee and the labor cost incurred for each individual job are recorded on **time tickets**. Exhibit 4 shows typical time ticket forms and cost flows for direct labor for Goodwell Printers.

A summary of the time tickets at the end of each month is the basis for recording the direct and indirect labor costs incurred in production. Direct labor is posted to

EXHIBIT 4
*Labor Information and
Cost Flows*

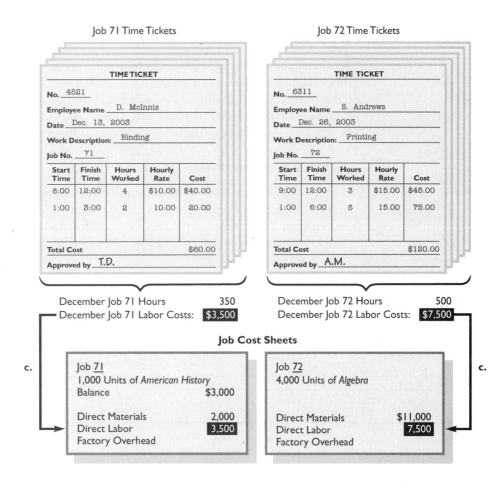

each job cost sheet, and indirect labor increases Factory Overhead.[2] Goodwell Printers incurred 850 direct labor hours on Jobs 71 and 72 during December. The total direct labor costs were $11,000, divided into $3,500 for Job 71 and $7,500 for Job 72. The labor costs that flow into production increase Work in Process and Wages Payable. The effects on the accounts and financial statements is shown below:

Trans. Date	Balance Sheet			Income Statement		
	Assets	Liabilities	Stockholders' Equity	Revenue	Expense	Net Income
c.	Work in Process 11,000	Wages Payable 11,000				
Net Effect	11,000	11,000				
			Retained Earnings			
			(Net Income)			

[2]There are a variety of methods for recording direct labor costs. In the approach illustrated in this chapter, we assume that labor costs are automatically recorded to jobs or factory overhead when incurred. Alternatively, wages could first be recorded as Factory Labor when incurred and then later distributed to jobs and factory overhead.

As with recording materials, many organizations are automating the labor-recording process. For example, in companies that build very large products, such as submarines, jet aircraft, or space vehicles, direct labor employees can be given magnetic cards, much like credit cards. These cards can be used to log in and log out of particular work assignments on particular jobs by running the card through a magnetic reader at any number of remote computer terminals. Using a similar system, **Shell Oil Company** uses a magnetic system to track the work of maintenance crews in its refineries.

Factory Overhead Cost

Factory overhead includes all manufacturing costs except direct materials and direct labor. Increases to Factory Overhead come from various sources, such as indirect materials, indirect labor, factory power, and factory depreciation. For example, the factory overhead of $4,600 incurred in December for Goodwell Printers is recorded as follows:

Trans. Date	Balance Sheet						Income Statement		
	Assets		Liabilities		Stockholders' Equity		Revenue	Expense	Net Income
d.	Factory Overhead	4,600	Wages Pay	2,000					
	Materials	−500	Utilities Pay	900					
	Acc. Depreciation	1,200							
Net Effect		2,900		2,900					
					Retained Earnings				
					(Net Income)				

ALLOCATING FACTORY OVERHEAD   Factory overhead is much different from direct labor and direct materials because it is indirectly related to the jobs. How, then, do the jobs get assigned a portion of overhead costs? The answer is through cost allocation. **Cost allocation** is the process of assigning factory overhead costs to a cost object, such as a job. The factory overhead costs are assigned to the jobs on the basis of some known measure about each job. The measure used to allocate factory overhead is frequently called an **activity base**, **allocation base**, or **activity driver**. The estimated activity base should be a measure that reflects the consumption or use of factory overhead cost. For example, the direct labor is recorded for each job using time tickets. Thus, direct labor could be used to allocate production-related factory overhead costs to each job. Likewise, direct materials costs are known about each job through the materials requisitions. Thus, materials-related factory overhead, such as Purchasing Department salaries, could logically be allocated to the job on the basis of direct materials cost.

PREDETERMINED FACTORY OVERHEAD RATE   So that job costs are currently available, factory overhead can be allocated or applied to production using a **predetermined factory overhead rate**. The predetermined factory overhead rate is calculated by dividing the estimated amount of factory overhead for the forthcoming year by the estimated activity base, such as machine hours, direct materials costs, direct labor costs, or direct labor hours.

To illustrate calculating a predetermined overhead rate, assume that Goodwell Printers estimates the total factory overhead cost to be $50,000 for the year and the activity base to be 10,000 direct labor hours. The predetermined factory overhead rate is calculated as $5 per direct labor hour, as follows:

$$\text{Predetermined factory overhead rate} = \frac{\text{Estimated total factory overhead costs}}{\text{Estimated activity base}}$$

$$\text{Predetermined factory overhead rate} = \frac{\$50,000}{10,000 \text{ direct labor hours}} = \frac{\$5 \text{ per direct}}{\text{labor hour}}$$

Why is the predetermined overhead rate calculated from estimated numbers at the beginning of the period? The answer is to ensure timely information. If a company waited until the end of an accounting period when all overhead costs are known, the allocated factory overhead would be accurate but not timely. If the cost system is to have maximum usefulness, cost data should be available as each job is completed, even though there may be a small sacrifice in accuracy. Only through timely reporting can management make needed adjustments in pricing or in manufacturing methods and achieve the best possible combination of revenue and cost on future jobs.

A number of companies are using a new product-costing approach called activity-based costing. **Activity-based costing** is a method of accumulating and allocating factory overhead costs to products using many overhead rates. Each rate is related to separate factory activities, such as inspecting, moving, and machining. A survey conducted by the Cost Management Group of the Institute for Management Accountants found that 43% of survey respondents had adopted activity-based costing and 39% were considering it. Activity-based costing is discussed and illustrated at the end of this chapter.

APPLYING FACTORY OVERHEAD TO WORK IN PROCESS   As factory overhead costs are incurred, they increase the factory overhead account, as shown previously in transaction (d). For Goodwell Printers, factory overhead costs are applied to production at the rate of $5 per direct labor hour. The amount of factory overhead applied to each job would be recorded in the job cost sheets as shown in Exhibit 5 on the following page. For example, the 850 direct labor hours used in Goodwell's December operations would all be traced to individual jobs. Job 71 used 350 labor hours, so $1,750 (350 × $5) of factory overhead would be applied to Job 71. Similarly, $2,500 (500 × $5) of factory overhead would be applied to Job 72.

The factory overhead costs applied to production are periodically recorded as increases to the work in process account and decreases to the factory overhead account. The effects of applying the $4,250 ($1,750 + $2,500) of factory overhead to production on the accounts and financial statements for Goodwell follow:

Trans. Date	Balance Sheet				Income Statement		
	Assets		Liabilities	Stockholders' Equity	Revenue	Expense	Net Income
e.	Work in Process	4,250 ·					
	Factory Overhead	−4,250					
Net Effect		0					
				Retained Earnings			
				(Net Income)			

EXHIBIT 5

*Assigning Factory
Overhead to Jobs*

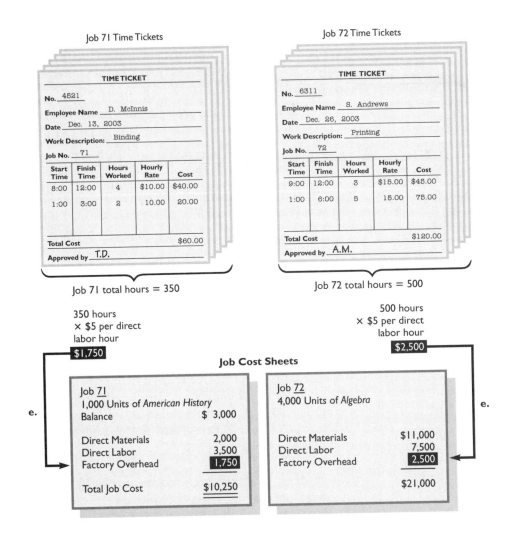

The factory overhead costs applied and the actual factory overhead costs incurred during a period usually differ. If the amount applied exceeds the actual costs incurred, the factory overhead account has a negative balance. This negative balance is described as **overapplied** or **overabsorbed** **factory overhead**. If the amount applied is less than the actual costs incurred, the account has a positive balance. This positive balance is described as **underapplied** or **underabsorbed** **factory overhead**.

If the underapplied or overapplied balance increases in only one direction and it becomes large, the balance and the overhead rate should be investigated. For example, if a large balance is caused by changes in manufacturing methods or in production goals, the factory overhead rate should be revised. On the other hand, a large underapplied balance could indicate a serious control problem caused by inefficiencies in production methods, excessive costs, or a combination of factors.

DISPOSAL OF FACTORY OVERHEAD BALANCE   The balance in the factory overhead account is carried forward from month to month. This balance should not be carried over to the next year, however, since it applies to the operations of the year just ended.

One approach for disposing of the balance of factory overhead at the end of the year is to transfer the entire balance to the cost of goods sold account.[3] To illustrate, the effects on the accounts and financial statements of eliminating an underapplied overhead balance of $150 at the end of the year for Goodwell Printers' follows:

Trans. Date	Balance Sheet			Income Statement		
	Assets	Liabilities	Stockholders' Equity	Revenue	Expense	Net Income
f.	Factory Overhead −150				Cost of Goods Sold 150	−150
Net Effect	−150				150	−150
			Retained Earnings			
			(Net Income)			

Work in Process

Costs incurred for the various jobs increase Work in Process. Goodwell Printers' job costs described in the preceding sections can be summarized as follows:

- **Direct materials, $13,000**—Work in Process increased and Materials decreased (transaction b); data obtained from summary of materials requisitions.

- **Direct labor, $11,000**—Work in Process and Wages Payable increased (transaction c); data obtained from summary of time tickets.

- **Factory overhead, $4,250**—Work in Process increased and Factory Overhead decreased (transaction e); data obtained from summary of time tickets.

The details concerning the costs incurred on each job order are accumulated in the job cost sheets. Exhibit 6 illustrates the relationship between the job cost sheets and the work in process controlling account.

In this example, Job 71 was started in November and completed in December. The beginning December balance for Job 71 represents the costs carried over from the end of November. Job 72 was started in December but was not yet completed at the end of the month. Thus, the balance of the incomplete Job 72, or $21,000, is shown on the balance sheet on December 31 as work in process inventory.

When Job 71 was completed, the direct materials costs, the direct labor costs, and the factory overhead costs were totaled and divided by the number of units produced to determine the cost per unit. If we assume that 1,000 units of a textbook titled *American History* were produced for Job 71, the unit cost would be $10.25 ($10,250/1,000).

Upon completing Job 71, the job cost sheet was removed from the cost ledger and filed for future reference. At the end of the accounting period (December), the total costs for all completed jobs during the period are determined. These costs are then

---

[3]Alternatively, the balance may be allocated among the work in process, finished goods, and cost of goods sold balances. This approach brings the accounts into agreement with the costs actually incurred, but it is more complex and adds little accuracy.

EXHIBIT 6

Job Cost Sheets and the
Work in Process
Controlling Account

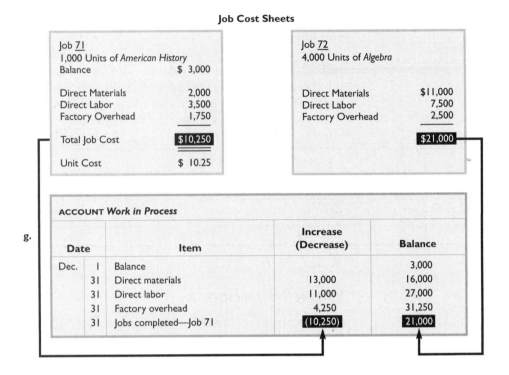

Job Cost Sheets

transferred to the finished goods inventory account. For Job 71, this transfer of costs affects the accounts and financial statements as follows:

Trans. Date	Balance Sheet				Income Statement		
	Assets		Liabilities	Stockholders' Equity	Revenue	Expense	Net Income
g.	Work in Process	−10,250					
	Finished Goods	10,250					
Net Effect		0					
				Retained Earnings			
				(Net Income)			

Finished Goods and Cost of Goods Sold

The finished goods account is a controlling account. Its related subsidiary ledger, which has an account for each product, is called the finished goods ledger or **stock ledger**. Each account in the finished goods ledger contains cost data for the units manufactured, units sold, and units on hand. Exhibit 7 illustrates an account in the finished goods ledger.

Sales and Cost of Goods Sold

Sales for a manufacturing business and a merchandising business have the same effect on the accounts and financial statements. To illustrate, assume that Goodwell Printers sold the 2,000 *American History* textbooks during December for $14 per

EXHIBIT 7 *Finished Goods Ledger Account*

ITEM: *American History*									
Manufactured			Shipped			Balance			
Job Order No.	Quantity	Amount	Ship Order No.	Quantity	Amount	Date	Quantity	Amount	Unit Cost
						Dec. 1	2,000	$20,000	$10.00
			643	2,000	$20,000	9	—	—	—
71	1,000	$10,250				31	1,000	10,250	10.25

unit.[4] These books have a cost of $10 per unit. The cost data can be obtained from the finished goods ledger. The effect of selling the 2,000 books on the accounts and financial statements is as follows:

Trans. Date	Balance Sheet				Income Statement		
	Assets		Liabilities	Stockholders' Equity	Revenue	Expense	Net Income
h.	Accounts Receivable	28,000			Sales 28,000	Cost of Goods Sold 20,000	8,000
	Finished Goods	−20,000					
Net Effect		8,000		8,000	28,000	20,000	8,000
				Retained Earnings			
				(Net Income)			

Period Costs

In addition to product costs (direct materials, direct labor, and factory overhead), businesses also have period costs. **Period costs** are expenses that are used in generating revenue during the current period and are not involved in the manufacturing process. Period costs are generally classified into two categories: selling and administrative. **Selling expenses** are incurred in marketing the product and delivering the sold product to customers. **Administrative expenses** are incurred in the administration of the business and are not related to the manufacturing or selling functions. Examples of administrative expenses include office supplies and depreciation of office equipment. Assuming Goodwell Printers incurred sales salaries of $2,000 and office salaries of $1,500, the effect on the accounts and financial statements is as follows:

Trans. Date	Balance Sheet			Income Statement		
	Assets	Liabilities	Stockholders' Equity	Revenue	Expense	Net Income
i.		Salaries Pay 3,500			Sales Salaries 2,000	−2,000
					Office Salaries 1,500	−1,500
Net Effect		3,500	−3,500		3,500	−3,500
			Retained Earnings			
			(Net Income)			

[4]The price of the textbook is the amount paid by the textbook publisher for printing the book. Printing is one small part of the total cost of the textbook. The publisher must also pay royalties, development and production costs, and selling expenses. Thus, the price of the textbook to the final user will be higher than $14.

Service companies, such as telecommunications, insurance, banking, broadcasting, and hospitality, typically have a large portion of their total costs as period costs. This is so because most service companies do not have products that can be inventoried, and, hence, they do not have product costs.

Summary of Cost Flows for Goodwell Printers

Exhibit 8 on the following page shows the cost flow through the manufacturing accounts, together with summary details of the subsidiary ledgers for Goodwell Printers. Entries in the accounts are identified by letters that refer to the summary journal entries introduced in the preceding section.

The balances of the general ledger controlling accounts are supported by their respective subsidiary ledgers. The balances of the three inventory accounts—Finished Goods, Work in Process, and Materials—represent the respective ending inventories of December 31 on the balance sheet. These balances are as follows:

Materials	$ 3,500
Work in process	21,000
Finished goods	10,250

The income statement for Goodwell Printers would be as shown in Exhibit 9.

EXHIBIT 9
Income Statement of Goodwell Printers

GOODWELL PRINTERS
Income Statement
For the Month Ended December 31, 2004

Sales		$28,000
Cost of goods sold		20,150
Gross profit		$ 7,850
Selling and administrative expenses:		
Sales salaries expense	$2,000	
Office salaries expense	1,500	
Total selling and administrative expenses		3,500
Income from operations		$ 4,350

Job Order Costing for Decision Making

OBJECTIVE   5

Use job order cost information for decision making.

The job order cost system that we developed in the previous sections can be used to evaluate an organization's cost performance. The unit costs for similar jobs can be compared over time to determine if costs are staying within expected ranges. If costs increase for some unexpected reason, the details in the job cost sheets can help discover the reasons.

To illustrate, Exhibit 10 on page 380 shows the direct materials on the job cost sheets for Jobs 144 and 163 for a furniture company. Since both job cost sheets refer to the same type and number of chairs, the direct materials cost per unit should be about the same. However, the materials cost per chair for Job 144 is $28, and for Job 163 it is $35. For some reason, materials costs have increased since the folding chairs were produced for Job 144.

EXHIBIT 8 *Flow of Manufacturing Costs for Goodwell Printers*

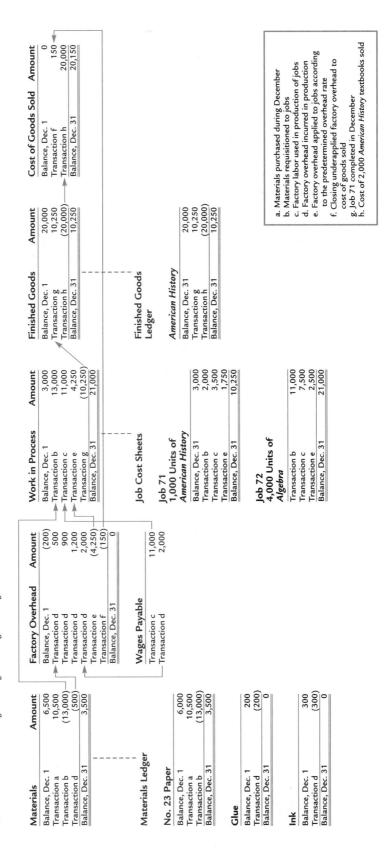

Materials	Amount
Balance, Dec. 1	6,500
Transaction a	10,500
Transaction b	(13,000)
Transaction d	(500)
Balance, Dec. 31	3,500

Materials Ledger

No. 23 Paper	Amount
Balance, Dec. 1	6,000
Transaction a	10,500
Transaction b	(13,000)
Balance, Dec. 31	3,500

Glue	
Balance, Dec. 1	200
Transaction d	(200)
Balance, Dec. 31	0

Ink	
Balance, Dec. 1	300
Transaction d	(300)
Balance, Dec. 31	0

Factory Overhead	Amount
Balance, Dec. 1	(200)
Transaction a	500
Transaction d	900
Transaction d	1,200
Transaction e	2,000
Transaction e	(4,250)
Transaction f	(150)
Balance, Dec. 31	0

Wages Payable	
Transaction c	11,000
Transaction d	2,000

Work in Process	Amount
Balance, Dec. 1	3,000
Transaction b	13,000
Transaction c	11,000
Transaction e	4,250
Transaction g	(10,250)
Balance, Dec. 31	21,000

Job Cost Sheets

Job 71 1,000 Units of American History	Amount
Balance, Dec. 1	3,000
Transaction b	2,000
Transaction c	3,500
Transaction e	1,750
Balance, Dec. 31	10,250

Job 72 4,000 Units of Algebra	
Transaction b	11,000
Transaction c	7,500
Transaction e	2,500
Balance, Dec. 31	21,000

Finished Goods	Amount
Balance, Dec. 1	20,000
Transaction g	10,250
Transaction h	(20,000)
Balance, Dec. 31	10,250

Finished Goods Ledger

American History	Amount
Balance, Dec. 31	20,000
Transaction g	10,250
Transaction h	(20,000)
Balance, Dec. 31	10,250

Cost of Goods Sold	Amount
Balance, Dec. 1	0
Transaction f	150
Transaction h	20,000
Balance, Dec. 31	20,150

a. Materials purchased during December
b. Materials requisitioned to jobs
c. Factory labor used in production of jobs
d. Factory overhead incurred in production
e. Factory overhead applied to jobs according to the predetermined overhead rate
f. Closing underapplied factory overhead to cost of goods sold
g. Job 71 completed in December
h. Cost of 2,000 *American History* textbooks sold

EXHIBIT 10
*Comparing Data from
Job Cost Sheets*

Job 144
Item: 200 folding chairs

	Materials Quantity (board feet)	Materials Price	Materials Amount
Direct materials:			
Wood	1,600	$3.50	$5,600
Direct materials per chair			$28

Job 163
Item: 200 folding chairs

	Materials Quantity (board feet)	Materials Price	Materials Amount
Direct materials:			
Wood	2,000	$3.50	$7,000
Direct materials per chair			$35

Job cost sheets can be used to investigate possible reasons for the increased cost. First, you should note that the rate for direct materials did not change. Thus, the cost increase is not related to increasing prices. What about the wood consumption? This tells us a different story. The quantity of wood used to produce 200 chairs in Job 144 is 1,600 board feet. However, Job 163 required 2,000 board feet. How can this be explained? Any one of the following explanations is possible and could be investigated further:

1. There was a new employee who was not adequately trained for cutting the wood for chairs. As a result, the employee improperly cut and scrapped many pieces.
2. The lumber was of poor quality. As a result, the cutting operator ended up using and scrapping additional pieces of lumber.
3. The cutting tools needed repair. As a result, the cutting operators miscut and scrapped many pieces of wood.
4. The operator was careless. As a result of poor work, many pieces of cut wood had to be scrapped.
5. The instructions attached to the job were incorrect. The operator cut wood according to the instructions but discovered that the pieces would not fit. As a result, many pieces had to be scrapped.

You should note that many of these explanations are not necessarily related to operator error. Poor cost performance can be the result of root causes that are outside the control of the operator.

Major electric utilities such as **Tennessee Valley Authority**, **Consolidated Edison**, and **Pacific Gas and Electric** use job order accounting to control the costs associated with major repairs and overhauls that occur during forced or planned outages. A *forced outage* is an unexpected shutdown of a power plant whereas a *planned outage* is a scheduled shutdown.

Job Order Cost Systems for Professional Service Businesses

A job order cost accounting system can be useful to the management of a professional service business in planning and controlling operations. For example, an advertising agency, an attorney, and a physician all share the common characteristic of providing services to individual customers, clients, or patients. In such cases, the customer, client, or patient can be viewed as an individual job for which costs are accumulated.

Since the "product" of a service business is service, management's focus is on direct labor and overhead costs. The cost of any materials or supplies used in rendering services for a client is usually small and is normally included as part of the overhead.

The direct labor and overhead costs of rendering services to clients are accumulated in a work in process account. This account is supported by a cost ledger. A job cost sheet is used to accumulate the costs for each client's job. When a job is completed and the client is billed, the costs are transferred to a cost of services account. This account is similar to the cost of merchandise sold account for a merchandising business or the cost of goods sold account for a manufacturing business. A finished goods account and related finished goods ledger are not necessary since the revenues associated with the services are recorded after the services have been provided. The flow of costs through a service business using a job order cost accounting system is shown in Exhibit 11.

EXHIBIT 11 *Flow of Costs Through a Service Business*

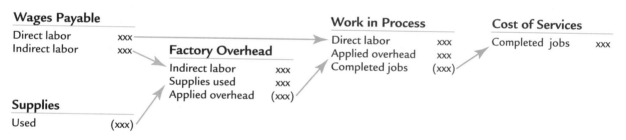

In practice, additional accounting considerations unique to service businesses could need to be considered. For example, a service business can bill clients on a weekly or monthly basis rather than waiting until a job is completed. In these situations, a portion of the costs related to each billing should be transferred from the work in process account to the cost of services account. A service business can also have advance billings that would be accounted for as deferred revenue until the services have been completed.

Just-in-Time Manufacturing Principles

The manufacturing approaches used by many companies are undergoing significant change. Companies are recognizing the need to produce products and services with high quality, low cost, and instant availability. Achieving these objectives requires a change in the methods of manufacturing products and delivering services. One approach is **just-in-time (JIT) manufacturing**, sometimes called **short-cycle** or **lean manufacturing**. It focuses on reducing time, cost, and poor quality within manufacturing processes.

Exhibit 12 lists some of the just-in-time manufacturing principles and the traditional manufacturing principles. In the following paragraphs, we briefly discuss each of the just-in-time principles.

EXHIBIT 12

Operating Principles of Just-in-Time versus Traditional Manufacturing

Issue	Just-in-Time Manufacturing	Traditional Manufacturing
Inventory	Reduces inventory.	Increases inventory to "buffer" or protect against process problems.
Lead time	Reduces lead time.	Increases lead time as a buffer against uncertainty.
Setup time	Reduces setup time.	Disregards setup time as an improvement priority.
Production layout	Emphasizes product-oriented layout.	Emphasizes process-oriented layout.
Role of the employee	Emphasizes team-oriented employee involvement.	Emphasizes work of individuals, following manager instructions.
Production scheduling policy	Emphasizes pull manufacturing.	Emphasizes push manufacturing.
Quality	Emphasizes zero defects.	Tolerates defects.
Suppliers	Emphasizes supplier partnering.	Treats suppliers as "arm's-length," independent entities.

Reducing Inventory

Supporters of just-in-time manufacturing view inventory as wasteful and unnecessary. They argue that inventory can hide underlying production problems. For example, they point out that inventory is often used to maintain sales and production levels during various production interruptions, such as machine breakdowns, manufacturing schedule changes, transportation delays, and unexpected scrap and rework. An important focus in just-in-time manufacturing is to remove these production problems so that the materials, work in process, and finished goods inventory levels can be reduced or eliminated.

The role of inventory can be explained by referring to a river. Inventory is the water in a river, while the rocks at the bottom of the river are the production problems. When the water level is high, all the rocks at the bottom of the river are hidden.

In other words, inventory hides the production problems. However, as the water level drops, the rocks become exposed, one by one. Reducing inventory reveals production problems. Once these problems are fixed, the "water level" can be reduced even further to expose more "rocks" for elimination until an efficient, effective production process is achieved.

Reducing Lead Times

Lead time, sometimes called **throughput time**, is a measure of the time that elapses between starting a unit of product into the beginning of a process and completing the unit of product. If a product begins the process at 1:00 p.m. and is completed at 5:00 p.m., the lead time is 4 hours.

Reducing lead times can be an objective for products manufactured in the plant or any other item that is produced through a process. For example, lead times could be reduced for processing sales orders, invoices, insurance applications, or hospital patients.

The total lead time can be divided into value-added and nonvalue-added time portions. Value-added lead time is the time required to actually manufacture a unit of a product. It is the conversion time for a unit. For example, value-added lead time includes the time to drill and pack parts for shipment. Nonvalue-added lead time is the time that a unit of product sits in inventories or moves unnecessarily. Nonvalue-added lead time occurs in poor production processes. In a well-functioning process, the product should spend very little time waiting in inventory because inventory is at a minimum. The product should also spend little time moving because operations are sequenced closely.

Just-in-time manufacturing attempts to make the nonvalue-added lead time very small, thereby reducing the cost and improving the speed of production. Reducing nonvalue-added lead time is often directly related to reducing inventory. Organizations that use many work in process inventory locations could discover that the percentage of nonvalue-added lead time can often approach 90% of the total lead time. Just-in-time concepts have allowed Boeing Company to slash the time it takes to deliver a commercial plane from 1½ years to 10 months.

Reducing Setup Time

A setup is the effort required to prepare an operation for a new production run. For example, a beverage company's bottling line would need to be cleaned between flavor changes. If setups are long and expensive, the production run (**batch**) must be large to recover the setup cost. Large batches increase inventory, and larger inventories add to lead time.

Emphasizing Product-Oriented Layout

Organizing work around products is called a product-oriented layout (or **product cells**) while organizing work around processes is called a process-oriented layout. Just-in-time methods favor organizing work around products rather than processes. Organizing work around products reduces the amount of materials movement, coordination between operations, and work in process inventory. As a result, lead time and production costs are reduced.

To illustrate, **Hallmark Cards** at one time processed greeting card design work through separate Art, Layout, and Preproduction Departments. These departments were organized around the processes for designing a new greeting card. Hallmark decided that this traditional method of organizing work was slowing down the designing of new cards while increasing their cost. As a result, Hallmark reorganized the greeting card design activity around each holiday. Layout, art, and preproduction activities were arranged together into single cells according to each type of holiday. Hallmark now has a Valentine's Day cell, a Mother's Day cell, and cells for other major holidays. **Sony** has also employed JIT principles by organizing a small team of four employees to completely assemble a camcorder, doing everything from soldering to testing. The new line reduces assembly time from 70 minutes to 15 minutes per camera. "There is no future in conventional conveyor lines. They are a tool that conforms to the person with the least ability," states a Sony representative.

Emphasizing Employee Involvement

Employee involvement is a management approach that grants employees the responsibility and authority to make decisions about operations rather than relying solely on management instructions. This decision-making authority requires accounting and other information to be made available to all employees.

Employee involvement uses teams organized in product cells rather than just the efforts of isolated, individual employees. Such employee teams can be **cross-trained** to perform any operation within the product cell. For example, employees learn how to operate several different machines within their product cell. Moreover, team members are trained to perform functions traditionally handled by centralized service departments. For example, direct labor employees are able to perform their own maintenance, quality control, housekeeping, and production improvement work. When direct labor employees perform such indirect functions, the distinction between direct and indirect labor cost becomes less important.

Emphasizing Pull Manufacturing

Another important just-in-time principle is to produce items only as they are needed by the customer. This principle is called **pull manufacturing** (or **make to order**). In pull manufacturing, the status of the next operation determines when products are moved or produced. If the next operation is busy, production stops so that material does not pile up in front of the busy operation. If the next operation is ready, product can be produced or moved to that operation.

The system that accomplishes pull manufacturing is often called **kanban**, which is Japanese for "cards." Electronic cards or containers signal production quantities to be filled by the feeder operation. The cards link the customer back through each stage of production. When a consumer purchases a product, a card triggers assembly of a replacement product, which in turn triggers cards to manufacture the components required for the assembly. This creates a flow of parts and products that move to the drumbeat of customer demand.

In contrast, the traditional approach is to schedule production based on forecasted customer requirements. This principle is called **push manufacturing** (or **make to stock**). In push manufacturing, product is released for manufacturing without reference to line status but according to a production schedule. The schedule "pushes" product to inventory ahead of known customer demand. As a result, manufacturers using push manufacturing generally have more inventory than those of manufacturers using pull manufacturing. As stated by one consultant, "If your manufacturing operations are still set up around guessing demand, you will forever be in a loop of producing and holding the wrong items and not having enough of what the customer actually wants."[5]

Kenney Manufacturing Company, a manufacturer of window shades, estimated that 50% of its window shade process was nonvalue added. By using pull manufacturing and changing the line layout, Kenney was able to reduce inventory by 82% and lead time by 84%.

Emphasizing Zero Defects

Just-in-time manufacturing practices strive to eliminate poor quality. Poor quality results in an increased need for inspection, more production interruptions, an increased need for rework, additional recordkeeping for scrap, a higher cost from scrap, and additional warranty costs. Thus, one of the primary objectives of just-in-time manufacturing is to improve the process so that products are made right the first time.

Emphasizing Supplier Partnering

Another just-in-time manufacturing practice is entering into long-term agreements with suppliers. Developing long-term customer/supplier relationships is called **supplier partnering**. Partnering encourages suppliers to develop a commitment to the manufacturer so that materials purchased will be high quality, low cost, and on time.

Supplier partnering often involves working to improve supplier operations by employing just-in-time principles. Thus, the just-in-time approach does not stop within the four walls of the factory but extends to the supplier's manufacturing operations as well. The result is an effective and efficient production chain that operates from raw materials to the final consumer. In addition, electronic data interchange and the Internet are used to improve the information flows between suppliers and customers. **Electronic data interchange (EDI)** is a method of using computers to electronically communicate orders, relay information, and make or receive payments from one organization to another. In addition, a supplier partner can electronically transmit engineering and design support for supplied parts.

Activity-Based Costing

OBJECTIVE   8
Describe and illustrate the use of activity-based costing in a service business.

In today's complex manufacturing systems, product costs can be distorted if inappropriate factory overhead rates are used. One way to avoid this distortion is by using the **activity-based costing (ABC) method**. This approach allocates factory overhead more accurately than does a single, plant-wide overhead rate that was illustrated earlier in this chapter.

[5]Jennifer Shah, "E-biz Requires Leaner Operation, More Integration," *Electronic Buyers News*, July 31, 2000, quoting David Rucker of TBM Institute.

The activity-based costing method uses cost of activities to determine product costs. Under this method, factory overhead costs are initially accounted for in **activity cost pools**. These cost pools are related to a given activity, such as machine usage, inspections, moving, production setups, and engineering activities.

In order to simplify, we use a service business to illustrate the principles of activity-based costing. Like manufacturing businesses, service companies need to determine the cost of services in order to make pricing, promotional, and other decisions with regard to service offerings. Many service companies find that a single overhead rate can lead to service cost distortions. Thus, many service companies are now using activity-based costing for determining the cost of providing services to customers.

To illustrate activity-based costing for a service company, assume that Hopewell Hospital uses an activity-based costing system to determine how hospital overhead is allocated to patients. Hopewell Hospital first determines the activity cost pools and then allocates the activity cost pools to patients, using activity rates. We assume that the activities of Hopewell Hospital include admitting, radiological testing, operating room, pathological testing, dietary, and laundry. Each activity cost pool has an estimated activity base measuring the output of the activity. The cost of activities is allocated to patients by multiplying the activity rate by the number of activity-base usage quantities consumed by each patient. Exhibit 13 illustrates the activity-based costing method for Hopewell Hospital.

EXHIBIT 13 *Activity-Based Costing Method—Hopewell Hospital*

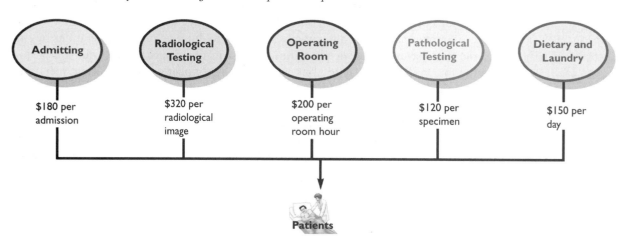

Each activity rate shown in Exhibit 13 is determined by dividing the budgeted activity cost pool by the estimated activity-base quantity. To illustrate, assume that the radiological testing activity cost pool budget is $960,000, and the total estimated activity-base quantity is 3,000 images. The activity rate of $320 per image is calculated as follows:

$$\text{Radiological testing activity rate} = \frac{\$960,000}{3,000 \text{ images}} = \$320 \text{ per image}$$

The activity rates for the other activities are determined in a similar manner. These activity rates are used to allocate costs to patients. To illustrate, assume that Mary

Wilson was a patient of the hospital. The hospital overhead cost associated with services (activities) performed for Mary Wilson is determined by multiplying the activity-base quantity for Mary Wilson's stay in the hospital by the activity rate. The sum of the costs across the activities is the total hospital overhead cost of services performed for Mary Wilson. These calculations follow.

Patient Name: Mary Wilson

Activity	Activity-Base Usage	×	Activity Rate	=	Activity Cost
Admitting	1 admission	×	$180 per admission	=	$ 180
Radiological testing	2 images	×	320 per image	=	640
Operating room	4 hours	×	200 per hour	=	800
Pathological testing	1 specimen	×	120 per specimen	=	120
Dietary and laundry	7 days	×	150 per day	=	1,050
Total					$2,790

The patient activity costs can be combined with the direct costs, such as drugs and supplies, and are reported with the revenues earned for each patient in a customer profitability report. A partial customer profitability report for Hopewell Hospital is shown in Exhibit 14.

EXHIBIT 14

Customer Profitability Report

HOPEWELL HOSPITAL
Customer (Patient) Profitability Report
For the Period Ending December 31, 2004

	Adcock, Kim	Birini, Brian	Conway, Don	Wilson, Mary
Revenues	$9,500	$21,400	$5,050	$3,300
Less patient costs:				
Drugs and supplies	$ 400	$ 1,000	$ 300	$ 200
Admitting	180	180	180	180
Radiological testing	1,280	2,560	1,280	640
Operating room	2,400	6,400	1,600	800
Pathological testing	240	600	120	120
Dietary and laundry	4,200	14,700	1,050	1,050
Total patient costs	$8,700	$25,440	$4,530	$2,990
Income from operations	$ 800	$(4,040)	$ 520	$ 310

The report in Exhibit 14 can be used by the administrators to guide decisions on pricing or service delivery. For example, there was a large loss on services provided to Brian Birini. Further investigation could reveal that services provided to Birini were out of line with what would be allowed for reimbursement by the insurance company. As a result, future losses could be avoided by lobbying for a higher insurance reimbursement or aligning the services closer to the revenues allowed by the insurance company.

Key Points

1. **Distinguish the activities of a manufacturing business from those of a merchandise or service business.**

   A manufacturing business must first produce the products it sells. A manufacturing business converts materials into a finished product through the use of machinery and labor. Materials, products in the process of being manufactured, and finished products are reported on the balance sheet as inventories under the Current Assets caption.

2. **Define and illustrate materials, factory labor, and factory overhead costs.**

   A manufacturer converts materials into a finished product by using machinery and labor. The cost of materials that are an integral part of the manufactured product is direct materials cost. The cost of wages of employees who are involved in converting materials into the manufactured product is direct labor cost. Costs other than direct materials and direct labor costs are factory overhead costs, including indirect materials and labor. Direct labor and factory overhead are termed *conversion costs*. Direct materials, direct labor, and factory overhead costs are associated with products and are called *product costs*.

3. **Describe accounting systems used by manufacturing businesses.**

   A cost accounting system accumulates product costs. The cost accounting system is used by management to determine the proper product cost for inventory valuation on the financial statements, to support product pricing decisions, and to identify opportunities for cost reduction and improved production efficiency. The two primary cost accounting systems are job order and process cost systems.

4. **Describe and illustrate a job order cost accounting system.**

   A job order cost system provides a separate record of the cost of each particular quantity of product that passes through the factory. Direct materials, direct labor, and factory overhead costs are accumulated in a subsidiary cost ledger, in which each account is represented by a job cost sheet. Work in Process is the controlling account for the cost ledger. As a job is finished, its costs are transferred to the finished goods ledger, for which Finished Goods is the controlling account.

5. **Use job order cost information for decision making.**

   Job order cost information can support pricing and cost analysis. Managers can use job cost information to identify unusual trends and areas for cost improvement.

6. **Diagram the flow of costs for a service business that uses a job order cost accounting system.**

   A cost flow diagram for a service business using a job order cost accounting system is shown in Exhibit 11. For a service business, the cost of materials or supplies used is normally included as part of the overhead. The direct labor and overhead costs of rendering services are accumulated in a work in process account. When a job is completed and the client is billed, the costs are transferred to a cost of services account.

7. **Describe just-in-time manufacturing.**

   The just-in-time manufacturing philosophy uses different principles than do traditional manufacturing methods. Just-in-time attempts to reduce lead time while traditional methods attempt to lengthen lead time to provide a time buffer for uncertainty. Just-in-time emphasizes a product-oriented production layout rather than a process-oriented layout. Just-in-time emphasizes a team-oriented work environment; the traditional approach is more individual oriented. Just-in-time views setup time reduction as a high-priority item. With reduced setup times, just-in-time manufacturers can emphasize pull manufacturing rather than push manufacturing. Just-in-time manufacturers must emphasize high quality since there is very little inventory to protect production against quality problems. Finally, just-in-time manufacturers emphasize supplier partnering to improve the quality and delivery of incoming materials.

8. **Describe and illustrate the use of activity-based costing in a service business.**

   Activity-based costing can be applied in service settings to determine the cost of individual service offerings. Service costs are determined by multiplying activity rates by the amount of activity-base quantities consumed by the customer using the service offering. Such information can support service pricing and profitability analysis.

Glossary

Activity base: A measure of activity that is related to changes in cost and is used in the denominator in calculating the predetermined factory overhead rate to assign factory overhead costs to cost objects.

Activity-based costing (ABC) method: An accounting framework based on determining the cost of activities and allocating these costs to products using activity rates.

Activity cost pools: Cost accumulations that are associated with a given activity, such as machine usage, inspections, moving, and production setups.

Conversion costs: The combination of direct labor and factory overhead costs.

Cost: A payment of cash (or a commitment to pay cash in the future) for the purpose of generating revenues.

Cost accounting system: A system used to accumulate manufacturing costs for decision-making and financial reporting purposes.

Cost allocation: The process of assigning indirect costs to a cost object, such as a job.

Cost of goods sold: The cost of the manufactured product sold.

Direct labor cost: Wages of factory workers who are directly involved in converting materials into a finished product.

Direct materials cost: The cost of materials that are an integral part of the finished product.

Electronic data interchange (EDI): An information technology that allows different business organizations to use computers to communicate orders, relay information, and make or receive payments.

Employee involvement: A philosophy that grants employees the responsibility

and authority to make their own decisions about their operations.

Factory overhead cost: All of the costs of operating the factory except for direct materials and direct labor.

Finished goods inventory: The cost of finished products on hand that have not been sold.

Finished goods ledger: The subsidiary ledger that contains the individual accounts for each kind of commodity or product produced.

Job cost sheet: An account in the work in process subsidiary ledger in which the costs charged to a particular job order are recorded.

Job order cost system: A type of cost accounting system that provides for a separate record of the cost of each particular quantity of product that passes through the factory.

Just-in-time manufacturing: A business philosophy that focuses on eliminating time, cost, and poor quality within manufacturing processes.

Lead time: The elapsed time between starting a unit of product into the beginning of a process and its completion.

Materials inventory: The cost of materials that have not yet entered into the manufacturing process.

Materials ledger: The subsidiary ledger containing the individual accounts for each type of material.

Materials requisitions: The form or electronic transmission used by a manufacturing department to authorize the issuance of materials from the storeroom.

Nonvalue-added lead time: The time that units wait in inventories, move unnecessarily, and wait during machine breakdowns.

Overapplied factory overhead: The amount of factory overhead applied in excess of the actual factory overhead costs incurred for production during a period.

Period costs: Those costs that are used up in generating revenue during the current period and that are not involved in the manufacturing process.

Predetermined factory overhead rate: The rate used to apply factory overhead costs to the goods manufactured. The rate is determined from budgeted overhead cost and estimated activity usage data at the beginning of the fiscal period.

Process cost system: A type of cost accounting system in which costs are accumulated by department or process within a factory.

Process-oriented layout: Organizing work in a plant or administrative function around processes (tasks).

Product costs: The three components of manufacturing cost: direct materials, direct labor, and factory overhead costs.

Product-oriented layout: Organizing work in a plant or administrative function around products; sometimes referred to as *product cells.*

Pull manufacturing: A just-in-time method wherein customer orders trigger the release of finished goods, which trigger production, which triggers release of materials from suppliers.

Push manufacturing: Materials are released into production and work in process is released into finished goods in anticipation of future sales.

Receiving report: The form or electronic transmission used by the receiving personnel to indicate that materials have been received and inspected.

Setup: The effort required to prepare an operation for a new production run.

Supplier partnering: A just-in-time method that views suppliers as a valuable contributor to the overall success of the business.

Time tickets: The form on which the amount of time spent by each employee and the labor cost incurred for each individual job, or for factory overhead, are recorded.

Underapplied factory overhead: The actual factory overhead costs incurred in excess of the amount of factory overhead applied for production during a period.

Value-added lead time: The time required to manufacture a unit of product or other output.

Work in process inventory: The direct materials costs, the direct labor costs, and the factory overhead costs that have entered into the manufacturing process but are associated with products that have not been finished.

Self-Study Questions

(Answers appear at end of chapter.)

1. Which of the following is not considered a cost of manufacturing a product?
   A. Direct materials cost
   B. Factory overhead cost
   C. Sales salaries
   D. Direct labor cost

2. Which of the following costs would be included as part of the factory overhead costs of a microcomputer manufacturer?
   A. The cost of memory chips
   B. Depreciation of testing equipment
   C. Wages of computer assemblers
   D. The cost of disk drives

3. For which of the following would the job order cost system be appropriate?

A. Antique furniture repair shop
B. Rubber manufacturer
C. Coal mining
D. All of the above

4. If the factory overhead account has a negative balance, factory overhead is said to be:
   A. underapplied   C. underabsorbed
   B. overapplied   D. in error

5. Which of the following is not a characteristic of the just-in-time philosophy?
   A. Product-oriented layout
   B. Push manufacturing (make to stock)
   C. Short lead times
   D. Reducing setup time as a critical improvement priority

Discussion Questions

1. If the cost of wages paid to employees who are directly involved in converting raw materials into a manufactured end product is not a significant portion of the total product cost, how would the wages cost be classified as to type of manufacturing cost?

2. How is product cost information used by managers?

3. a. Name two principal types of cost accounting systems.
   b. Which system provides for a separate record of each particular quantity of product that passes through the factory?
   c. Which system accumulates the costs for each department or process within the factory?

4. **Hewlett-Packard Company** assembles printed circuit boards in which a high volume of standardized units is assembled and tested. Is the job order cost system appropriate in this situation?

5. Which account is used in a job order cost system to accumulate direct materials, direct labor, and factory overhead applied to production costs for individual jobs?

6. How does the use of the materials requisition help control the issuance of materials from the storeroom?

7. Describe the source of the data for increasing Work in Process for (a) direct materials, (b) direct labor, and (c) factory overhead.

8. Discuss how the predetermined factory overhead rate can be used in job order cost accounting to assist management in pricing jobs.

9. a. How is a predetermined factory overhead rate calculated?
   b. Name three common bases used in calculating the rate.

10. a. What is (1) overapplied factory overhead and (2) underapplied factory overhead?
    b. If the factory overhead account has a positive balance, was factory overhead underapplied or overapplied?

11. What is the difference between a product cost and a period cost?

12. How can job cost information be used to identify cost improvement opportunities?

13. What is the benefit of just-in-time processing?

14. What are some examples of nonvalue-added lead time?

15. Why do just-in-time manufacturers favor pull or "make-to-order" manufacturing?

16. Why would a just-in-time manufacturer strive to produce zero defects?

17. How is supplier partnering different from traditional supplier relationships?

18. How can activity-based costing be used in service companies?

Exercises

EXERCISE 10-1
Classify costs as materials, labor, or factory overhead
OBJECTIVE 2

Indicate whether each of the following costs of a furniture manufacturer would be classified as direct materials cost, direct labor cost, or factory overhead cost:

a. Supervisor salaries
b. Saw blades
c. Furniture hardware
d. Wages of wood cutters
e. Wood
f. Assembly wages
g. Depreciation on woodworking machinery
h. Inspector salaries

EXERCISE 10-2
Classify costs as materials, labor, or factory overhead
OBJECTIVE 2

Indicate whether each of the following costs of the **Procter & Gamble Company** would be classified as direct materials cost, direct labor cost, or factory overhead cost:

a. Salary of process engineers
b. Depreciation on disposable diaper converting machines
c. Scents and fragrances
d. Wages of Making Department employees
e. Pulp for towel and tissue products
f. Plant manager salary of the Lima, Ohio, liquid soap plant
g. Packaging materials
h. Maintenance supplies
i. Wages paid to Packing Department employees
j. Depreciation on the St. Bernard (Cincinnati) soap plant

EXERCISE 10-3
Classify costs as product or period costs
OBJECTIVES 2, 4

Classify the following costs for **Ford Motor Company** as either a product cost or a period cost.

a. Steel
b. Stamping Department employee wages
c. Utility costs used in executive building
d. Travel costs used by sales personnel

(continued)

e. Shipping costs
f. Property taxes on Kansas City, Missouri, assembly plant
g. Glass
h. Maintenance supplies
i. Depreciation on Atlanta, Georgia, assembly plant
j. Plant manager's salary
k. CEO's salary
l. Depreciation of Dearborn, Michigan, executive building
m. Salary of marketing executive
n. Assembly employee wages
o. Tires
p. Advertising

EXERCISE 10-4

Classify factory overhead costs

OBJECTIVE 2

Which of the following items are properly classified as part of factory overhead for **John Deere & Co.**?

a. Factory supplies used in the Loudon, Tennessee, skid loader factory
b. Consultant fees for surveying production employee morale
c. Interest expense on debt
d. Amortization of patents on a new welding process
e. Sales incentive fees to dealers
f. Steel plate
g. Chief financial officer's salary
h. Property taxes on Ankeny, Iowa, components plant
i. Depreciation on Moline, Illinois, headquarters building
j. Plant manager's salary at Greenville, Tennessee, turf care products plant

EXERCISE 10-5

Concepts and terminology

OBJECTIVES 2, 4

From the choices presented in parentheses, choose the appropriate term for completing each of the following sentences:

a. An example of factory overhead is (plant depreciation, sales office depreciation).
b. Materials that are an integral part of the manufactured product are classified as (direct materials, materials inventory).
c. The balance sheet of a manufacturer would include an account for (cost of goods sold, work in process inventory).
d. Advertising expenses are usually viewed as (period, product) costs.
e. Payments of cash or its equivalent or the commitment to pay cash in the future for the purpose of generating revenues are (costs, expenses).
f. Implementing automatic factory robotics equipment normally (increases, decreases) the factory overhead component of product costs.
g. Direct labor costs combined with factory overhead costs are called (product, conversion) costs.
h. The wages of an assembly worker are normally considered a (period, product) cost.

EXERCISE 10-6

Transactions in a job order cost system

OBJECTIVE 5

Five selected transactions for the current month are indicated by letters in the following accounts in a job order cost accounting system:

Materials	Work in Process
(a) decrease	(a) increase
	(b) increase
	(c) increase
	(d) decrease

Wages Payable	**Finished Goods**
(b) increase	(d) increase
	(e) decrease

Factory Overhead	**Cost of Goods Sold**
(a) increase	(e) increase
(b) increase	
(c) decrease	

Describe each of the five transactions.

EXERCISE 10-7
Cost flow relationships
OBJECTIVE 4

✓ c. $343,000

The following information is available for the first month of operations of Asian Arts Inc., a manufacturer of craft items:

Sales	$710,000
Gross profit	220,000
Indirect labor	15,000
Indirect materials	25,000
Other factory overhead	12,000
Materials purchased	180,000
Total manufacturing costs for the period	530,000
Materials inventory, end of period	20,000

Using the preceding information, determine the following missing amounts:

a. Cost of goods sold
b. Direct materials cost
c. Direct labor cost

EXERCISE 10-8
Cost of materials issuances by FIFO method
OBJECTIVE 4

✓ b. $1,100

An incomplete subsidiary ledger of wire cable for May is as follows:

RECEIVED			ISSUED			BALANCE			
Receiving Report Number	Quantity	Unit Price	Materials Requisition Number	Quantity	Amount	Date	Quantity	Amount	Unit Price
						May 1	150	$2,700	$18.00
23	210	$20.00				May 3			
			104	250		May 5			
29	140	22.00				May 19			
			117	200		May 25			

a. Complete the materials issuances and balances for the wire cable subsidiary ledger under FIFO.
b. Determine the balance of wire cable at the end of May.
c. Determine the total amount of materials transferred to work in process for May.
d. Explain how the materials ledger might be used as an aid in maintaining inventory quantities on hand.

EXERCISE 10-9
Issuing materials
OBJECTIVE 4

Materials issued for the current month are as follows:

Requisition No.	Material	Job No.	Amount
711	Steel	511	$ 9,500
712	Copper	514	6,300
713	Plastic	526	900
714	Abrasives	Indirect	150
715	Titanium alloy	533	36,400

a. Determine the amount of materials transferred to Work in Process and Factory Overhead for the current month.
b. Illustrate the effect on the accounts and financial statements of the materials transferred in (a).

EXERCISE 10-10
Materials transactions
OBJECTIVE 4

✓ c. Fabric, $97,600

Hermitage Furniture Company (HFC) manufactures furniture. HFC uses a job order cost system. Balances on June 1 from the materials ledger are as follows:

Fabric	$45,800
Polyester filling	9,200
Lumber	95,800
Glue	2,200

The materials purchased during June are summarized from the receiving reports as follows:

Fabric	$568,500
Polyester filling	165,500
Lumber	842,200
Glue	19,100

Materials were requisitioned to individual jobs as follows:

	Fabric	Polyester Filling	Lumber	Glue	Total
Job 11	$276,700	$ 85,400	$454,800		$ 816,900
Job 12	35,800	12,300	78,900		127,000
Job 13	204,200	66,300	340,800		611,300
Factory overhead—indirect materials				$17,900	17,900
Total	$516,700	$164,000	$874,500	$17,900	$1,573,100

The glue is not a significant cost, so it is treated as indirect materials (factory overhead).

a. Determine the total purchase of materials in June.
b. Determine the amounts of materials transferred to Work in Process and Factory Overhead for the requisition of materials in June.
c. Determine the June 30 balances that would be shown in the materials ledger accounts.

EXERCISE 10-11
Entry for factory labor costs
OBJECTIVE 4

A summary of the time tickets for the current month follows:

Job No.	Amount	Job No.	Amount
101	$1,540	141	$ 1,540
122	1,610	Indirect labor	10,100
133	870	143	3,240
139	3,550	147	2,480

a. Determine the amounts of factory labor costs transferred to Work in Process and Factory Overhead for the current month.
b. Illustrate the effects on the accounts and financial statements of the factory labor costs transferred in (a).

EXERCISE 10-12
Entries for direct labor and factory overhead
OBJECTIVE 4

Colonial Homes Inc. manufactures log homes. Colonial uses a job order cost system. The time tickets from September jobs are summarized here.

Job 502	$1,680
Job 503	784
Job 504	490
Job 505	1,078
Factory supervision	1,670

Factory overhead is applied to jobs on the basis of a predetermined overhead rate of $22 per direct labor hour. The direct labor rate is $14 per hour.

a. Determine the total factory labor costs transferred to Work in Process and Factory Overhead for September.
b. Determine the amount of factory overhead applied to production for September.
c. Illustrate the effects of the factory overhead applied in (b) on the accounts and financial statements.

EXERCISE 10-13
Factory overhead rates, entries, and account balance
OBJECTIVE 4

✓ b. $25 per direct labor hour

Digital Pictures Inc. operates two factories. The company applies factory overhead to jobs on the basis of machine hours in factory 1 and on the basis of direct labor hours in factory 2. Estimated factory overhead costs, direct labor hours, and machine hours are as follows:

	Factory 1	Factory 2
Estimated factory overhead cost for fiscal year beginning April 1	$270,000	$235,000
Estimated direct labor hours for year		9,400
Estimated machine hours for year	15,000	
Actual factory overhead costs for April	$21,900	$19,400
Actual direct labor hours for April		770
Actual machine hours for April	1,260	

a. Determine the factory overhead rate for factory 1.
b. Determine the factory overhead rate for factory 2.
c. Determine the factory overhead applied to production in each factory for April.
d. Determine the balances of the factory accounts for each factory as of April 30, and indicate whether the amounts represent overapplied or underapplied factory overhead.

EXERCISE 10-14
Predetermined factory overhead rate
OBJECTIVE 4

AutoCare Body Shop uses a job order cost system to determine the cost of performing automotive body and repair work. Estimated costs and expenses for the coming period are as follows:

Auto parts	$ 520,000
Shop direct labor	384,000
Shop and repair equipment depreciation	14,800
Shop supervisor salaries	82,400
Shop property tax	23,200
Shop supplies	12,400
Advertising expense	15,200
Administrative office salaries	54,800
Administrative office depreciation expense	10,000
Total costs and expenses	$1,116,800

The average shop direct labor rate is $12 per hour. Determine the predetermined shop overhead rate per direct labor hour.

EXERCISE 10–15
*Predetermined factory
overhead rate*
OBJECTIVE 4

✓ a. $175 per hour

Elk City Medical Center has a single operating room that is used by local physicians to perform surgical procedures. The cost of using the operating room is accumulated by each patient procedure and includes the direct materials costs (drugs and medical devices), physician surgical time, and operating room overhead. On January 1 of the current year, the annual operating room overhead is estimated as follows:

Disposable supplies	$ 65,000
Depreciation expense	22,000
Utilities	16,300
Nurse salaries	168,800
Technician wages	95,400
Total operating room overhead	$367,500

The overhead costs will be assigned to procedures based on the number of surgical room hours. The Medical Center expects to use the operating room an average of 7 hours per day, 6 days per week. In addition, the operating room will be shut down two weeks per year for general repairs.

a. Determine the predetermined operating room overhead rate for the year.
b. LeVar Wilson had a 3-hour procedure on January 10. How much operating room overhead would be charged to his procedure using the rate determined in (a)?
c. During January, the operating room was used 190 hours. The actual overhead costs incurred for January were $31,800. Determine the overhead under- or overapplied for the period.

EXERCISE 10–16
*Jobs completed; cost of
unfinished jobs*
OBJECTIVE 4

✓ b. $27,500

The following account appears in the ledger after only part of the postings have been completed for March:

Work in Process

Balance, March 1	$ 19,200
Direct materials	121,400
Direct labor	52,500
Factory overhead	74,600

Jobs finished during March are summarized as follows:

Job 320	$52,100	Job 327	$28,400
Job 326	72,500	Job 350	87,200

a. Determine the cost of jobs completed.
b. Determine the cost of the unfinished jobs at March 31.

EXERCISE 10–17
*Factory costs and jobs
completed*
OBJECTIVE 4

✓ d. $22,570

Palm Printing Company began manufacturing operations on May 1. Jobs 1 and 2 were completed during the month, and all costs applicable to them were recorded on the related cost sheets. Jobs 3 and 4 are still in process at the end of the month, and all applicable costs except factory overhead have been recorded on the related cost sheets. In addition to the materials and labor charged directly to the jobs, $960 of indirect materials and $6,300 of indirect labor were used during the month. The cost sheets for the four jobs entering production during the month are as follows, in summary form:

Job 1			Job 2	
Direct materials	5,400		Direct materials	9,800
Direct labor	1,250		Direct labor	2,100
Factory overhead	1,500		Factory overhead	2,520
Total	8,150		Total	14,420

Job 3			Job 4	
Direct materials	7,200		Direct materials	1,200
Direct labor	1,600		Direct labor	350
Factory overhead			Factory overhead	

Determine each of the following operations for May operations:

a. Direct and indirect materials used.
b. Direct and indirect labor used.
c. Factory overhead applied (a single overhead rate is used based on direct labor cost).
d. Costs of completed Jobs 1 and 2.

EXERCISE 10-18
Financial statements of a manufacturing firm
OBJECTIVE 4

✓ a. Income from operations, $97,100

The following events took place for Comet Shoe Company during May 2004, the first month of operations as a producer of athletic shoes:

- Purchased $124,000 of materials.
- Used $111,300 of direct materials in production.
- Incurred $84,700 of direct labor wages.
- Applied factory overhead at a rate of 80% of direct labor cost.
- Transferred $257,000 of work in process to finished goods.
- Sold goods with a cost of $246,500.
- Sold goods for $450,000.
- Incurred $65,000 of selling expenses.
- Incurred $41,400 of administrative expenses.

a. Prepare the May income statement for Comet Shoe Company. Assume that Comet Shoe uses the perpetual inventory method.
b. Determine the inventory balances at the end of the first month of operations.

EXERCISE 10-19
Decision making with job order costs
OBJECTIVE 5

Yokohama Manufacturing Company is a job shop. The management of Yokohama uses the cost information from the job sheets to assess their cost performance. Information on the total cost, product type, and quantity of items produced is as follows:

Date	Job No.	Quantity	Product	Amount
Jan. 1	1	400	XXY	$ 4,800
Jan. 29	26	1,200	AAB	18,000
Feb. 15	43	600	AAB	9,600
Mar. 10	64	450	XXY	6,300
Mar. 31	75	900	MM	19,800
May 10	91	1,000	MM	21,000
June 20	104	400	XXY	6,800
Aug. 2	112	1,500	MM	25,500
Sept. 20	114	400	AAB	6,000
Nov. 1	126	600	XXY	10,800
Dec. 3	133	850	MM	12,750

a. Develop a graph for each product (three graphs), with Job No. (in date order) on the horizontal axis and unit cost on the vertical axis. Use this information to determine Yokohama's cost performance over time for the three products.

(continued)

b. What additional information would management require to investigate Yokohama's cost performance more precisely?

EXERCISE 10-20

Decision making with job order costs

OBJECTIVE 5

Brass Plaque Company uses a job order cost system for determining the cost to manufacture award products (plaques and trophies). Among the company's products is an engraved plaque that is awarded to participants who complete an executive education program at a local university. The company sells the plaque to the university for $12 each.

Each plaque has a brass plate engraved with the name of the participant. Engraving requires approximately 10 minutes per name. Improperly engraved names must be redone. The plate is screwed to a walnut backboard. This assembly takes approximately 5 minutes per unit. Improper assembly must be redone using a new walnut backboard.

During the first half of the year, the university had two separate executive education classes. The job cost sheets for the two separate jobs indicated the following information:

Job 223   **March 28**

	Cost per Unit	Units	Job Cost
Direct materials:			
Wood	$1.20/unit	36 units	$ 43.20
Brass	1.50/unit	36 units	54.00
Engraving labor	12.00/hr.	6.0 hrs.	72.00
Assembly labor	12.00/hr.	3.0 hrs.	36.00
Factory overhead	20.00/hr.	9.0 hrs.	180.00
			$385.20
Plaques shipped			÷ 36
Cost per plaque			$ 10.70

Job 275   **May 16**

	Cost per Unit	Units	Job Cost
Direct materials:			
Wood	$1.20/unit	42 units	$ 50.40
Brass	1.50/unit	45 units	67.50
Engraving labor	12.00/hr.	7.5 hrs.	90.00
Assembly labor	12.00/hr.	3.5 hrs.	42.00
Factory overhead	20.00/hr.	11.0 hrs.	220.00
			$469.90
Plaques shipped			÷ 40
Cost per plaque			$ 11.75

a. Why did the cost per plaque increase from $10.70 to $11.75?
b. What improvements would you recommend for Brass Plaque Company?

EXERCISE 10-21

Job order cost accounting for a service business

OBJECTIVE 6

✓ d. Cost of Services, $665,000

New Media Solutions provides advertising services for clients across the nation. New Media Solutions is presently working on four projects, each for a different client. New Media Solutions accumulates costs for each account (client) on the basis of both direct costs and allocated indirect costs. The direct costs include the charged time of professional personnel and media purchases (air time and ad space). Overhead is allocated to each project as a percentage of media purchases. The predetermined overhead rate is 30% of media purchases.

On March 1, the four advertising projects had the following accumulated costs:

	March 1 Balances
Stone Beverage	$120,000
Hampshire Bank	160,000
All-Right Rentals	60,000
SleepEzz Hotel	12,000

During March, New Media Solutions incurred the following direct labor and media pur-chase costs related to preparing advertising for each of the four accounts:

	Direct Labor	Media Purchases
Stone Beverage	$ 48,000	$150,000
Hampshire Bank	25,000	90,000
All-Right Rentals	67,000	105,000
SleepEzz Hotel	70,000	155,000
Total	$210,000	$500,000

At the end of March, both the Stone Beverage and Hampshire Bank projects were com-pleted. The cost of completed projects are increases to the cost of services account.

Determine each of the following for the month:

a. Direct labor costs
b. Media purchases
c. Overhead applied
d. Completion of Stone Beverage and Hampshire Bank projects

EXERCISE 10-22
Just-in-time principles
OBJECTIVE 7

The Chief Executive Officer (CEO) of Comfort Air Inc. has just returned from a management seminar describing the benefits of the just-in-time philosophy. The CEO issued the following statement after returning from the conference:

> This company will become a just-in-time manufacturing company. Presently, we have too much inventory. To become just-in-time we need to eliminate the excess inventory. Therefore, I want all employees to begin reducing inventories until we are just-in-time. Thank you for your cooperation.

How would you respond to the CEO's statement?

EXERCISE 10-23
Just-in-time as a strategy
OBJECTIVE 7

The American textile industry has moved much of its operations offshore in the pursuit of lower labor costs. Textile imports have risen from 2% of all textile production in 1962 to more than 60% in 2000. Offshore manufacturers make long runs of standard mass-market apparel items. These are then brought to the United States in container ships, requiring signifi-cant time between original order and delivery. As a result, retail customers must accurately forecast market demands for imported apparel items.

Assuming that you work for a U.S.-based textile company, how would you recommend responding to the low-cost imports?

EXERCISE 10-24
Lead time reduction—service company
OBJECTIVE 7

Golden Insurance Company takes 10 days to make payments on insurance claims. Claims are processed through three departments: Data Input, Claims Audit, and Claims Adjustment. The three departments are on different floors, approximately one hour apart from each other. Claims are processed in batches of 100. Each batch of 100 claims moves through the three departments on a wheeled cart. Management is concerned about customer dissatisfaction caused by the long lead time for claim payments.

How might this process be changed so that the lead time could be reduced significantly?

EXERCISE 10-25
Just-in-time principles
OBJECTIVE 7

Champion Shirt Company manufactures various styles of men's casual wear. Shirts are cut and assembled by a workforce that is paid by piece rate. This means that they are paid according to the amount of work completed during a period of time. To illustrate, if the piece rate is $0.10 per sleeve assembled and the worker assembles 700 sleeves during the day, the worker would be paid $70 (700 × $0.10) for the day's work.

The company is considering adopting a just-in-time manufacturing philosophy by organizing work cells around various types of products and employing pull manufacturing. However, no change is expected in the compensation policy. On this point, the manufacturing manager stated the following:

> Piecework compensation provides an incentive to work fast. Without it, the workers will just goof off and expect a full day's pay. We can't pay straight hourly wages—at least not in this industry.

How would you respond to the manufacturing manager's comments?

EXERCISE 10-26
Supplier partnering
OBJECTIVE 7

The Ford Tempo required more than 700 different suppliers. However, the successor to the Tempo, the Ford Contour, required only 227 different suppliers. For example, the Tempo required 12 suppliers for door panels and other interior trim pieces, while the Contour used only 3 suppliers for these parts.

Why would Ford strive to reduce the number of suppliers of parts for its products?

EXERCISE 10-27
Employee involvement
OBJECTIVE 7

Quickie Designs Inc. uses teams in the manufacture of lightweight wheelchairs. Two features of its team approach are team hiring and peer reviews. Under team hiring, the team recruits, interviews, and hires new team members from within the organization. Using peer reviews, the team evaluates each member of the team with regard to quality, knowledge, teamwork, goal performance, attendance, and safety. These reviews provide feedback to the team member for improvement.

How do these two team approaches differ from using managers to hire and evaluate employees?

EXERCISE 10-28
Activity-based costing for a hospital
OBJECTIVE 8

✓ a. Patient M, $4,555

Hope Hospital plans to use activity-based costing to assign hospital indirect costs to the care of patients. The hospital has identified the following activities and activity rates for the hospital indirect costs:

Activity	Activity Rate
Room and meals	$150 per day
Radiology	$95 per image
Pharmacy	$28 per physician order
Chemistry lab	$85 per test
Operating room	$550 per operating room hour

The records of two representative patients were analyzed using the activity rates. The activity information associated with the two patients is as follows:

	Patient M	Patient T
Number of days	7 days	3 days
Number of images	4 images	2 images
Number of physician orders	5 orders	1 order
Number of tests	6 tests	2 tests
Number of operating room hours	4.5 hours	1 hour

a. Determine the activity cost associated with each patient.
b. Why is the total activity cost different for the two patients?

EXERCISE 10-29
Activity-based costing in an insurance company
OBJECTIVE 8

Security Insurance Company carries three major lines of insurance: auto, workers' compensation, and homeowners. The company has prepared the following report for 2004:

SECURITY INSURANCE COMPANY
Product Profitability Report
For the Year Ended December 31, 2004

	Auto	Workers' Comp.	Homeowners
Premium revenue	$5,000,000	$4,000,000	$6,000,000
Less estimated claims	3,250,000	2,600,000	3,900,000
Underwriting income	$1,750,000	$1,400,000	$2,100,000
Underwriting income as a percent of premium revenue	35%	35%	35%

Management is concerned that the administrative expenses can make some of the insurance lines unprofitable. However, the administrative expenses have not been allocated to the insurance lines. The controller has suggested that the administrative expenses could be assigned to the insurance lines, using activity-based costing. The administrative expenses are composed of five activities. The activities and their rates are as follows:

	Activity Rates
New policy processing	$250 per new policy
Cancellation processing	$340 per cancellation
Claim audits	$540 per claim audit
Claim disbursements processing	$280 per disbursement
Premium collection processing	$35 per premium collected

Activity-base usage data for each line of insurance were retrieved from the corporate records and are shown below.

	Auto	Workers' Comp.	Homeowners
Number of new policies	1,100	1,200	2,600
Number of canceled policies	450	150	1,350
Number of audited claims	325	110	720
Number of claim disbursements	350	140	750
Number of premiums collected	7,400	1,200	12,000

a. Complete the product profitability report through the administrative activities. Determine the income from operations as a percentage of premium revenue, rounded to one decimal place.
b. Interpret the report.

Problems

PROBLEM 10 | 1
Classify costs
OBJECTIVES 2, 4

The following is a list of costs that were incurred in the production and sale of boats:

a. Steering wheels.
b. Commissions to sales representatives based on the number of boats sold.
c. Wood paneling for use in interior boat trim.
d. Straight-line depreciation on factory equipment.
e. Oil to lubricate factory equipment.
f. Hourly wages of assembly-line workers.
g. Cost of paving the employee parking lot.
h. Masks for use by sanders in smoothing boat hulls.
i. Cost of normal scrap from defective hulls.
j. Premiums on business interruption insurance in case of a natural disaster.

(continued)

k. Yearly cost of maintenance contract for robotics equipment.
l. Power used by sanding equipment.
m. Cost of metal hardware for boats, such as ornaments and tie-down grasps.
n. Fiberglass for producing the boat hull.
o. Salary of president of company.
p. Paint for boats.
q. Legal department costs for the year.
r. Annual fee for Jim Bo Wilks, a famous fisherman, to promote the boats.
s. Decals for boat hulls.
t. Salary of shop supervisor.
u. Executive end-of-year bonuses.
v. Cost of electrical wiring for boats.
w. Navigation and fishing instruments for boats.
x. Memberships for key executives in the Bass World Association.
y. Cost of boat for "grand prize" promotion in local bass tournament.
z. Special advertising campaign in Bass World.

Instructions

Classify each cost as either a product cost or a period cost. Indicate whether each product cost is a direct materials cost, a direct labor cost, or a factory overhead cost. Indicate whether each period cost is a selling expense or an administrative expense. Use the following tabular headings for your answer, placing an X in the appropriate column.

Product Costs			Period Costs	
Direct Materials Cost	Direct Labor Cost	Factory Overhead Cost	Selling Expense	Admin. Expense

PROBLEM 10 | 2
Schedules for unfinished jobs and completed jobs
OBJECTIVE 4

✓ 5. Work in Process balance, $87,700

Industrial Fittings Inc. uses a job order cost system. The following data summarize the operations related to production for June 2004, the first month of operations:

a. Materials purchased on account, $150,500.
b. Materials requisitioned and factory labor used:

Job	Materials	Factory Labor
No. 601	$32,400	$19,300
No. 602	18,500	14,200
No. 603	21,300	15,200
No. 604	10,400	8,900
No. 605	15,200	11,300
No. 606	28,400	17,500
For general factory use	5,300	32,400

c. Factory overhead costs incurred on account, $27,500.
d. Depreciation of machinery and equipment, $5,100.
e. The factory overhead rate is $50 per machine hour. Machine hours used:

Job	Machine Hours
No. 601	320
No. 602	205
No. 603	225
No. 604	150
No. 605	180
No. 606	300
Total	1,380

f. Jobs completed: 601, 602, 603, and 605.

g. Jobs were shipped and customers were billed as follows: Job 601, $83,200; Job 602, $54,200; Job 605, $49,100.

Instructions

1. Prepare a schedule summarizing manufacturing costs by job for June. Use the following form:

Job	Direct Materials	Direct Labor	Factory Overhead	Total

2. Prepare a schedule of jobs finished in June.
3. Prepare a schedule of jobs sold in June. What account does this schedule support for the month of June?
4. Prepare a schedule of completed jobs on hand as of June 30, 2004. What account does this schedule support?
5. Prepare a schedule of unfinished jobs as of June 30, 2004. What account does this schedule support?

PROBLEM 10 | 3
Job order cost sheet
OBJECTIVES 4, 5

Nathan Hale Furniture Company refinishes and reupholsters furniture. Nathan Hale uses a job order cost system. When a prospective customer asks for a price quote on a job, the estimated cost data are inserted on an unnumbered job cost sheet. If the offer is accepted, a number is assigned to the job, and the costs incurred are recorded in the usual manner on the job cost sheet. After the job is completed, reasons for the variances between the estimated and actual costs are noted on the sheet. The data are then available to management in evaluating the efficiency of operations and in preparing quotes on future jobs. On September 1, an estimate of $910 for reupholstering two chairs and a couch was given to Kendra Brown. The estimate was based on the following data:

Estimated direct materials:	
14 meters at $18 per meter	$252.00
Estimated direct labor:	
20 hours at $16 per hour	320.00
Estimated factory overhead (40% of direct labor cost)	128.00
Total estimated costs	$700.00
Markup (30% of production costs)	210.00
Total estimate	$910.00

On September 4, the chairs and couch were picked up from the residence of Kendra Brown, 1244 Merchants Drive, Columbus, with a commitment to return them on October 13. The job was completed on October 10.

The related materials requisitions and time tickets are summarized as follows:

Materials Requisition No.	Description	Amount
3480	9 meters at $18	$162
3492	8 meters at $18	144

Time Ticket No.	Description	Amount
H143	12 hours at $16	$192
H151	10 hours at $16	160

Instructions

1. Prepare a job order cost sheet showing the estimate given to the customer. Use the format shown below.
2. Assign number 00-10-23 to the job, record the costs incurred, and complete the job order cost sheet. Comment on the reasons for the variances between actual costs and estimated costs. For this purpose, assume that 3 meters of materials were spoiled, the factory overhead rate has been proved to be satisfactory, and an inexperienced employee performed the work.

JOB ORDER COST SHEET

Customer _____   Date _____

Address _____   Date wanted _____

_____   Date completed _____

Item _____   Job No. _____

ESTIMATE

Materials		Direct Labor		Summary	
	Amount		Amount		Amount
___ meter at $___		___ hours at $___		Direct materials	
___ meter at $___		___ hours at $___		Direct labor	
___ meter at $___		___ hours at $___		Factory overhead	
___ meter at $___		___ hours at $___		Total cost	
Total		Total			

ACTUAL

Direct Materials			Direct Labor			Summary	
Mat. Req. No.	Description	Amount	Mat. Req. No.	Description	Amount	Item	Amount
						Direct materials	
						Direct labor	
						Factory overhead	
						Total cost	
Total			Total				

PROBLEM 10 | 4

Analyzing manufacturing cost accounts

OBJECTIVE 4

✓ G. $215,865

Sawtooth Golf Equipment Company manufactures golf club sets in a wide variety of lengths and weights. The following incomplete ledger accounts refer to transactions that are summarized for August:

Materials

Aug. 1	Balance	8,000
31	Purchases	100,000
31	Requisitions	(A)

Work in Process

Aug.	1	Balance	(B)
	31	Materials	(C)
	31	Direct labor	(D)
	31	Factory overhead applied	(E)
	31	Completed jobs	(F)

Finished Goods

Aug.	1	Balance	0
	31	Completed jobs	(F)
	31	Cost of goods sold	(G)

Wages Payable

Aug. 31	Wages incurred	90,000

Factory Overhead

Aug.	1	Balance	2,000
	31	Indirect labor	(H)
	31	Indirect materials	2,500
	31	Other overhead	35,000
	31	Factory overhead applied	(E)

In addition, the following information is available:

a.   Materials and direct labor were applied to six jobs in August:

Job No.	Style	Quantity	Direct Materials	Direct Labor
Job 111	DL-8	110	$ 20,380	$15,600
Job 112	DL-18	120	25,450	19,500
Job 113	DL-11	50	14,120	11,400
Job 114	SL-101	150	9,400	4,200
Job 115	SL-110	70	27,500	24,300
Job 116	DL-14	75	4,000	3,000
Total		575	$100,850	$78,000

b.   Factory overhead is applied to each job at a rate of 70% of direct labor cost.
c.   The August 1 Work in Process balance consisted of two jobs, as follows:

Job No.	Style	Work in Process, Aug. 1
Job 111	DL-8	$18,000
Job 112	DL-18	35,000
Total		$53,000

d.   Customer jobs completed and units sold in August were as follows:

Job No.	Style	Completed in August	Units Sold in August
Job 111	DL-8	X	90
Job 112	DL-18	X	105
Job 113	DL-11	X	40

(continued)

Job No.	Style	Completed in August	Units Sold in August
Job 114	SL-101		0
Job 115	SL-110	X	55
Job 116	DL-14		0

Instructions

1. Determine the missing amounts associated with each letter. Provide supporting calculations by completing a table with the following headings:

Job No.	Quantity	Aug. 1 Work in Process	Direct Materials	Direct Labor	Factory Overhead	Total Cost	Unit Cost	Units Sold	Cost of Goods Sold

2. Determine the August 31 balances for each of the inventory accounts and factory overhead.

PROBLEM 10 | 5
Flow of costs and income statement
OBJECTIVE 4

✓ 1. Income from operations, $1,335,200

Advent Technologies Inc. (AT) is a designer, manufacturer, and distributor of software for microcomputers. A new product, Wordsmith 2004, was released for production and distribution in early 2004. In January, $450,000 was spent to design print advertisements. For the first six months of 2004, the company spent $1,500,000 promoting Wordsmith 2004 in computer trade magazines. The product was ready for manufacture on January 21, 2004.

AT uses a job order cost system to accumulate costs associated with each software title. Direct materials unit costs follow:

Blank disk	$ 8
Packaging	5
Manual	10
Total	$23

The actual production process for the software product is fairly straightforward. First, blank disks are brought to a disk-copying machine. The copying machine requires 1 hour per 1,000 disks.

After the program is copied onto the disk, the disk is brought to assembly, where assembly personnel pack the disk and manual for shipping. The direct labor cost for this work is $0.80 per unit.

The completed packages are then sold to retail outlets through a sales force. The sales force is compensated by a 10% commission on the wholesale price for all sales. In addition, salespersons are trained at a cost of $500 per individual.

Total completed production was 30,000 units during the year. Other information is as follows:

Number of salespersons	1,500
Number of software units sold in 2004	26,000
Wholesale price per unit	$200

Factory overhead cost is applied to jobs at the rate of $1,000 per copy machine hour. There were an additional 500 copied CDs, packaging, and manuals waiting to be assembled on December 31, 2004.

Instructions

1. Prepare an annual income statement for the Wordsmith 2004 product, including supporting calculations, from the preceding information.

2. Determine the balances in the finished goods and work in process inventory for the Wordsmith 2004 product on December 31, 2004.

Activities

Activity 10-1
Ethics and professional conduct in business

ETHICS

Oak Enterprises allows employees to purchase, at cost, manufacturing materials, such as metal and lumber, for personal use. To purchase materials for personal use, an employee must complete a materials requisition form, which must then be approved by the employee's immediate supervisor. Cheryl Long, an assistant cost accountant, charges the employee an amount based on Oak's net purchase cost.

Cheryl Long is in the process of replacing a deck on her home and has requisitioned lumber for personal use, which has been approved in accordance with company policy. In computing the cost of the lumber, Long reviewed all the purchase invoices for the past year. She then used the lowest price to compute the amount due the company for the lumber.

Discuss whether Cheryl behaved in an ethical manner.

Activity 10-2
Financial vs. managerial accounting

The following statement was made by the vice-president of finance of Kitty Hawk Aerospace Company: "The managers of a company should use the same information as the shareholders of the firm. When managers use the same information in guiding their internal operations as shareholders use in evaluating their investments, the managers will be aligned with the stockholders' profit objectives."

Respond to the vice-president's statement.

Activity 10-3
Classifying costs

Reliable TV Repairs provides TV repair services for the community. Gail Song's TV was not working, and she called Reliable for a home repair visit. The Reliable technician arrived at 2:00 p.m. to begin work. By 4:00 p.m. the problem was diagnosed as a failed circuit board. Unfortunately, the technician did not have a new circuit board in the truck since the technician's previous customer had the same problem, and a board was used on that visit. Replacement boards were available back at the Reliable shop. Therefore, the technician drove back to the shop to retrieve a replacement board. From 4:00 to 5:00 p.m., the Reliable technician drove the round trip to retrieve the replacement board from the shop.

At 5:00 p.m. the technician was back on the job at Song's home. The replacement procedure is somewhat complex since a variety of tests must be performed once the board is installed. The job was completed at 6:00 p.m.

Gail Song's repair bill showed the following:

Circuit board	$ 50
Labor charges	140
Total	$190

Gail Song was surprised at the bill and asked for more detail supporting the calculations. Reliable responded with the following explanations.

Cost of materials:	
Purchase price of circuit board	$40
Markup on purchase price to cover storage and handling	10
Total materials charge	$50

The labor charge per hour is detailed as follows:

2:00–3:00 p.m.	$ 30
3:00–4:00 p.m.	25
4:00–5:00 p.m.	35
5:00–6:00 p.m.	50
Total labor charge	$140

Further explanations in the differences in the hourly rates are as follows:

First hour:
Base labor rate	$15
Fringe benefits	5
Overhead (other than storage and handling)	5
Total base labor rate	$25
Additional charge for first hour of any job to cover the cost of vehicle depreciation, fuel, and employee time in transit. A 30-minute transit time is assumed.	5
	$30

Third hour:
Base labor rate	$25
The trip back to the shop includes vehicle depreciation and fuel; therefore, a charge was added to the hourly rate to cover these costs. The round trip took an hour.	10
	$35

Fourth hour:
Base labor rate	$25
Overtime premium for time worked in excess of an eight-hour day (starting at 5:00 p.m.) is equal to the base rate.	25
	$50

1. If you were in Gail Song's position, how would you respond to the bill? Are there parts of the bill that appear incorrect to you? If so, what argument would you employ to convince Reliable that the bill is too high?
2. Use the following headings to construct a table. Fill in the table by first listing the costs identified in the activity in the left-hand column. For each cost, place a check mark in the appropriate column identifying the correct cost classification. Assume that each service call is a job.

Cost	Direct Materials	Direct Labor	Overhead

Activity 10-4
Managerial analysis

The controller of the plant of Texas Molding Company prepared a graph of the unit costs from the job cost reports for Product XD. The graph appeared as follows:

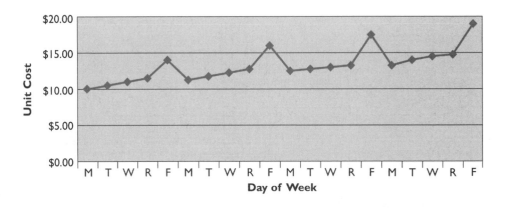

How would you interpret this information? What further information would you request?

Activity 10-5
Factory overhead rate

Silicon Inc., an electronics instrument manufacturer, uses a job order costing system. The overhead is allocated to jobs on the basis of direct labor hours. The overhead rate is now $1,000 per direct labor hour. The design engineer thinks that this is illogical. The design engineer has stated the following:

> Our accounting system doesn't make any sense to me. It tells me that every labor hour carries an additional burden of $1,000. This means that direct labor makes up only 5% of our total product cost, yet it drives all our costs. In addition, these rates give my design engineers incentives to "design out" direct labor by using machine technology, yet over the past years as we have had less and less direct labor, the overhead rate keeps going up and up. I won't be surprised if next year the rate is $1,200 per direct labor hour. I'm also concerned because small errors in our estimates of the direct labor content can have a large impact on our estimated costs. Just a 30-minute error in our estimate of assembly time is worth $500. Small mistakes in our direct labor time estimates really swing our bids around. I think this puts us at a disadvantage when we are going after business.

1. What is the engineer's concern about the overhead rate going "up and up"?
2. What did the engineer mean about the large overhead rate being a disadvantage when placing bids and seeking new business?
3. What do you think is a possible solution?

Activity 10-6
Classifying costs

G R O U P

With a group of students, visit a local copy and graphics shop or a pizza restaurant. As you observe the operation, consider the costs associated with running the business. As a group, identify as many costs as you can and classify them according to the following table headings:

Cost	Direct Materials	Direct Labor	Overhead	Selling Expenses

Activity 10-7
Just-in-time principles

Radiant Devices, Inc. manufactures electric space heaters. While the CEO, Chris Heath, is visiting the production facility, the following conversation takes place with the plant manager, Ron Daley:

Chris: As I walk around the facility, I can't help noticing all the materials inventories. What's going on?

Ron: I have found our suppliers to be very unreliable in meeting their delivery commitments. Thus, I keep a lot of materials on hand so as not to risk running out and shutting down production.

Chris: Not only do I see a lot of materials inventory, but there also seems to be a lot of finished goods inventory on hand. Why is this?

Ron: As you know, I am evaluated on maintaining a low cost per unit. The one way that I am able to reduce my unit costs is by producing as many space heaters as possible. This allows me to spread my fixed costs over a larger base. When orders are down, the production builds up as inventory, as we are seeing now. But don't worry—I'm really keeping our costs down this way.

Chris: I'm not so sure. It seems that this inventory must cost us something.

Ron: Not really. I'll eventually use the materials and we'll eventually sell the finished goods. By keeping the plant busy, I'm using our plant assets wisely. This is reflected in the low unit costs that I'm able to maintain.

If you were Heath, how would you respond to Daley? What recommendations would you provide Daley?

Answers to Self-Study Questions

1. **C** Sales salaries (answer C) is a selling expense and is not considered a cost of manufacturing a product. Direct materials cost (answer A), factory overhead cost (answer B), and direct labor cost (answer D) are costs of manufacturing a product.

2. **B** Depreciation of testing equipment (answer B) is included as part of the factory overhead costs of the microcomputer manufacturer. The cost of memory chips (answer A) and the cost of disk drives (answer D) are both considered a part of direct materials cost. The wages of microcomputer assemblers (answer C) are part of direct labor costs.

3. **A** Job order cost systems are best suited to businesses manufacturing special orders from customers, such as would be the case for a repair shop for antique furniture (answer A). A process cost system is best suited for manufacturers of homogeneous units of product, such as rubber (answer B) and coal (answer C).

4. **B** If the amount of factory overhead applied during a particular period exceeds the actual overhead costs, the factory overhead account will have a negative balance and is said to be overapplied (answer B) or overabsorbed. If the amount applied is less than the actual costs, the account will have a positive balance and is said to be underapplied (answer A) or underabsorbed (answer C). Since an "estimated" predetermined overhead rate is used to apply overhead, a negative balance does not necessarily represent an error (answer D).

5. **B** The just-in-time philosophy embraces a product-oriented layout (answer A), making lead times short (answer C), and reducing setup times (answer D). Pull manufacturing, the opposite of push manufacturing (answer B), is also a just-in-time principle.

Chapter 11

11

LEARNING OBJECTIVES

Objective 1
Classify costs according to their behavior as variable costs, fixed costs, or mixed costs.

Objective 2
Compute the contribution margin, the contribution margin ratio, and the unit contribution margin, and explain how they can be useful to managers.

Objective 3
Using the unit contribution margin, determine the break-even point and the volume necessary to achieve a target profit.

Objective 4
Using a cost-volume-profit chart and a profit-volume chart, determine the break-even point and the volume necessary to achieve a target profit.

Objective 5
Calculate the break-even point for a business selling more than one product.

Objective 6
Compute the margin of safety and the operating leverage, and explain how managers use these concepts.

Objective 7
List the assumptions underlying cost-volume-profit analysis.

Cost Behavior and Cost-Volume-Profit Analysis

What are the costs of operating your car? You normally pay a license plate (tag) fee once a year. This cost does not change, regardless of the number of miles you drive. On the other hand, the total amount you spend on gasoline during the year changes on a day-to-day basis as you drive. The more you drive, the more you spend on gasoline.

How does such operating cost information affect you? Information on how your car's operating costs behave could be relevant in planning a summer vacation. For example, you might be trying to decide between taking an airline flight or driving your car to your vacation destination. In this case, your license plate fee and annual car insurance costs will not change regardless of whether you drive your car or fly. Thus, these costs would not affect your decision. However, the estimated cost of gasoline and routine maintenance would affect your decision.

As in operating your car, not all of the costs of operating a business behave in the same way. In this chapter, we discuss commonly used methods for classifying costs according to how they change. We also discuss how management uses cost-volume-profit analysis as a tool in making decisions.

Cost Behavior

Knowing how costs behave is useful to management for a variety of purposes. For example, knowing how costs behave allows managers to predict profits as sales and production volumes change. Knowing how costs behave is also useful for estimating costs. Estimated costs, in turn, affect a variety of management decisions, such as whether to use excess machine capacity to produce and sell a product at a reduced price.

Cost behavior refers to the manner in which a cost changes as a related activity changes. To understand cost behavior, two factors must be considered. First, we must identify the activities that are thought to cause the cost to be incurred. Such activities are called **activity bases** (or **activity drivers**). Second, we must specify the range of activity over which the changes in the cost are of interest. This range of activity is called the **relevant range**.

To illustrate, hospital administrators must plan and control hospital food costs. To fully understand why food costs change, the activity that causes cost to be incurred must be identified. In the case of food costs, the feeding of patients is a major cause of these costs. The number of patients treated by the hospital would not be a good activity base since some patients are outpatients who do not stay in the hospital. The number of patients who *stay* in the hospital, however, is a good activity base for studying food costs. Once the proper activity base is identified, food costs can then be analyzed over the range of the number of patients who normally stay in the hospital (the relevant range).

Three of the most common classifications of cost behavior are variable costs, fixed costs, and mixed costs.

Variable Costs

When the level of activity is measured in units produced, direct materials and direct labor costs are generally classified as variable costs. **Variable costs** are costs that vary in proportion to changes in the level of activity. For example, assume that Jason Inc. produces stereo sound systems under the brand name of J-Sound. The parts for the stereo systems are purchased from outside suppliers for $10 per unit and are assembled in Jason Inc.'s Waterloo plant. The direct materials costs for Model JS-12 for the relevant range of 5,000 to 30,000 units of production follow.

Number of Units of Model JS-12 Produced	Direct Materials Cost per Unit	Total Direct Materials Cost
5,000	$10	$ 50,000
10,000	10	100,000
15,000	10	150,000
20,000	10	200,000
25,000	10	250,000
30,000	10	300,000

Variable costs are the same per unit, but the total variable cost changes in proportion to changes in the activity base. For Model JS-12, for example, the direct materials cost for 10,000 units ($100,000) is twice the direct materials cost for 5,000 units

($50,000). The total direct materials cost varies in proportion to the number of units produced because the direct materials cost per unit ($10) is the same for all levels of production. Thus, producing 20,000 additional units of JS-12 will increase the direct materials cost by $200,000 (20,000 × $10), producing 25,000 additional units will increase the materials cost by $250,000, and so on.

Exhibit 1 illustrates how the variable costs for direct materials for Model JS-12 behave in total and on a per-unit basis as production changes.

EXHIBIT 1 *Variable Cost Graphs*

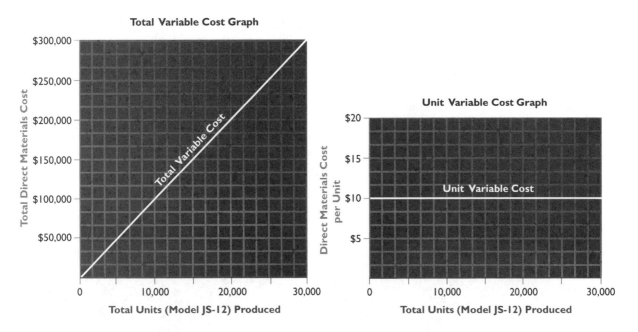

Managers use a variety of activity bases for evaluating cost behavior. The following list provides some examples of variable costs, along with their related activity bases for various types of businesses.

Type of Business	Cost	Activity Base
University	Instructor salaries	Number of classes
Passenger airline	Fuel	Number of miles flown
Manufacturing	Direct materials	Number of units produced
Hospital	Nurse wages	Number of patients
Hotel	Maid wages	Number of guests
Bank	Teller wages	Number of banking transactions
Insurance	Claim-processing salaries	Number of claims

Fixed Costs

Fixed costs are costs that remain the same in total dollar amount as the level of activity changes. To illustrate, assume that Minton Inc. manufactures, bottles, and distributes La Fleur Perfume at its Los Angeles plant. The production supervisor at the

Los Angeles plant is Jane Sovissi, who is paid a salary of $75,000 per year. The relevant range of activity for a year is 50,000 to 300,000 bottles of perfume. Sovissi's salary is a fixed cost that does not vary with the number of units produced. Regardless of the number of bottles produced within the range of 50,000 to 300,000 bottles, Sovissi receives a salary of $75,000.

Although the total fixed cost remains the same as the number of bottles produced changes, the fixed cost per bottle changes. As more bottles are produced, the total fixed costs are spread over a higher number of bottles, and thus the fixed cost per bottle decreases. This relationship for Jane Sovissi's $75,000 salary follows.

Number of Bottles of Perfume Produced	Total Salary for Jane Sovissi	Salary per Bottle of Perfume Produced
50,000	$75,000	$1.500
100,000	75,000	0.750
150,000	75,000	0.500
200,000	75,000	0.375
250,000	75,000	0.300
300,000	75,000	0.250

Exhibit 2 illustrates how the fixed cost of Jane Sovissi's salary behaves in total and on a per-unit basis as production changes.

EXHIBIT 2   *Fixed Cost Graphs*

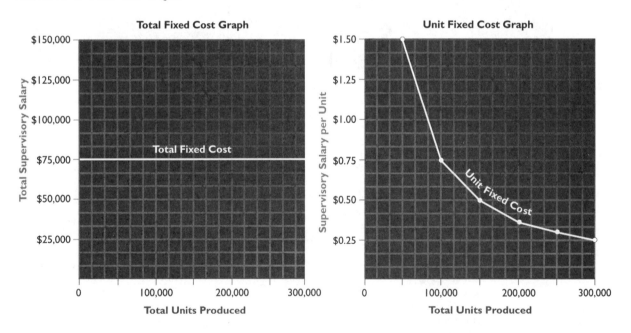

When units produced is the measure of activity, examples of fixed costs include straight-line depreciation of factory equipment, insurance on factory plant and equipment, and salaries of factory supervisors. Other examples of fixed costs and their activity bases for a variety of businesses are as follows:

Type of Business	Fixed Cost	Activity Base
University	Building depreciation	Number of students
Passenger airline	Airplane depreciation	Number of passengers
Manufacturing	Plant manager salary	Number of units produced
Hospital	Property insurance	Number of patients
Hotel	Property taxes	Number of guests
Bank	Branch manager salary	Number of customer accounts
Insurance	Computer depreciation	Number of insurance policies

Mixed Costs

A **mixed cost** has characteristics of both a variable and a fixed cost. For example, over one range of activity, the total mixed cost could remain the same. It thus behaves as a fixed cost. Over another range of activity, the mixed cost could change in proportion to changes in the level of activity. It thus behaves as a variable cost. Mixed costs are sometimes called *semivariable* or *semifixed* costs.

To illustrate, assume that Simpson Inc. manufactures sails using rented machinery. The rental charges are $15,000 per year, plus $1 for each machine hour used over 10,000 hours. If the machinery is used 8,000 hours, the total rental charge is $15,000. If the machinery is used 20,000 hours, the total rental charge is $25,000 [$15,000 + (10,000 hours × $1)], and so on. Thus, if the level of activity is measured in machine hours and the relevant range is 0 to 40,000 hours, the rental charges are a fixed cost up to 10,000 hours and a variable cost thereafter. This mixed cost behavior is shown graphically in Exhibit 3.

EXHIBIT 3
Mixed Costs

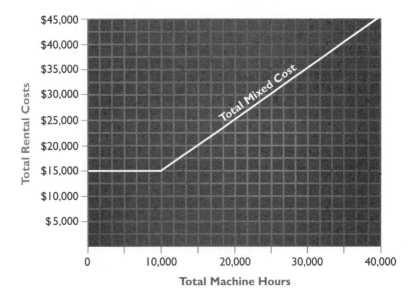

In analyses, mixed costs are usually separated into their fixed and variable components. The **high-low method** is a cost estimation technique that can be used for this purpose.[1] The high-low method uses the highest and lowest activity levels and

[1]Other methods of estimating costs, such as the scattergraph method and the least squares method, are discussed in cost accounting textbooks.

their related costs to estimate the variable cost per unit and the fixed cost component of mixed costs.

To illustrate, assume that the Equipment Maintenance Department of Kason Inc. incurred the following costs during the past five months:

	Units of Production	Total Cost
June	1,000	$45,550
July	1,500	52,000
August	2,100	61,500
September	1,800	57,500
October	750	41,250

The number of units produced is the measure of activity, and the number of units produced between June and October is the relevant range of production. For Kason Inc., the difference between the number of units produced and the difference between the total cost at the highest and lowest levels of production are as follows:

	Units of Production	Total Cost
Highest level	2,100	$61,500
Lowest level	750	41,250
Difference	1,350	$20,250

Since the total fixed cost does not change with changes in volume of production, the $20,250 difference in the total cost is the change in the total variable cost. Hence, dividing the difference in the total cost by the difference in production provides an estimate of the variable cost per unit. For Kason Inc., this estimate is $15, as shown here.

$$\text{Variable cost per unit} = \frac{\textbf{Difference in total cost}}{\textbf{Difference in production}}$$

$$\text{Variable cost per unit} = \frac{\$20,250}{1,350 \text{ units}} = \$15$$

The fixed cost is the same at both the highest and the lowest levels of production. Thus, the fixed cost can be estimated at either of these levels. This is done by subtracting the estimated total variable cost from the total cost, using the following total cost equation:

Total cost = (Variable cost per unit × Units of production) + Fixed cost

Highest level:
$61,500 = ($15 × 2,100 units) + Fixed cost
$61,500 = $31,500 + Fixed cost
$30,000 = Fixed cost

Lowest level:
$41,250 = ($15 × 750 units) + Fixed cost
$41,250 = $11,250 + Fixed cost
$30,000 = Fixed cost

The total equipment maintenance cost for Kason Inc. can thus be analyzed as a $30,000 fixed cost and a $15-per-unit variable cost. Using these amounts in the total cost equation, the total equipment maintenance cost at other levels of production can be estimated.

Summary of Cost Behavior Concepts

Examples of common variable, fixed, and mixed costs when the number of units produced is the activity base follow:

Variable Cost	Fixed Cost	Mixed Cost
Direct materials	Depreciation expense	Quality Control Department salaries
Direct labor	Property taxes	Purchasing Department salaries
Electricity expense	Officer salaries	Maintenance expenses
Sales commissions	Insurance expense	Warehouse expenses

Mixed costs contain a fixed cost component that is incurred even if nothing is produced. For analyses, the fixed and variable cost components of mixed costs should be separated.

The following table summarizes the cost behavior attributes of variable costs and fixed costs:

Cost	Effect of Changing Activity Level	
	Total Amount	Per-Unit Amount
Variable	Increases and decreases proportionately with activity level.	Remains the same regardless of activity level.
Fixed	Remains the same regardless of activity level.	Increases and decreases inversely with activity level.

BUSINESS STRATEGY

Tinkering with Success?

Lego is a privately held Danish company that built its reputation on interlocking play bricks. Since the early 1970s, generations of children have built houses, cars, and trucks with the famous bricks. However, younger and younger children are demanding more sophisticated toys. Within the toy industry, this phenomenon is known as "age compression." As a result, Lego has expanded beyond plastic bricks into ready-to-play figures and has licensed its brand name to manufacturers of wristwatches and children's apparel. In addition, Lego decided to open Legoland theme parks throughout the world, including parks outside London and San Diego, thus increasing its fixed costs. Has Lego's strategy worked? It's too soon to tell, although Lego recently reported its largest loss ever of more than $100 million.

Source: Adapted from John Tagliabue, "Lego Tinkered with Success, And Is Now Paying a Price," *The Wall Street Journal*, December 25, 2001.

Reporting Variable and Fixed Costs

Separating costs into their variable and fixed components for reporting purposes can be useful for decision making. One method of reporting variable and fixed costs is called **variable costing** or **direct costing**. Under variable costing, only the variable manufacturing costs (direct materials, direct labor, and variable factory overhead) are included in the product cost. The fixed factory overhead is an expense of the period in which it is incurred.

Cost-Volume-Profit Relationships

OBJECTIVE   2

Compute the contribution margin, the contribution margin ratio, and the unit contribution margin, and explain how they can be useful to managers.

After costs have been classified as fixed and variable, their effect on revenues, volume, and profits can be studied by using cost-volume-profit analysis. **Cost-volume-profit analysis** is the systematic examination of the relationships among selling prices, sales and production volume, costs, expenses, and profits.

Cost-volume-profit analysis provides management useful information for decision making. For example, cost-volume-profit analysis can be used in setting selling prices, selecting the mix of products to sell, choosing among marketing strategies, and analyzing the effects of changes in costs on profits. In today's business environment, management must make such decisions quickly and accurately. As a result, the importance of cost-volume-profit analysis has increased in recent years.

Contribution Margin Concept

One relationship among cost, volume, and profit is the contribution margin. The **contribution margin** is the excess of sales revenues over variable costs. The contribution margin concept is especially useful in business planning because it gives insight into the profit potential of a firm. To illustrate, the income statement of Lambert Inc. in Exhibit 4 has been prepared in a contribution margin format.

EXHIBIT 4
*Contribution Margin
Income Statement*

Sales	$1,000,000
Variable costs	600,000
Contribution margin	$ 400,000
Fixed costs	300,000
Income from operations	$ 100,000

The contribution margin of $400,000 is available to cover the fixed costs of $300,000. Once the fixed costs are covered, any remaining amount adds directly to the income from operations of the company. Think of the fixed costs as a bucket and the contribution margin as water filling the bucket. Once the bucket is filled, the overflow represents income from operations. Until the point of overflow, however, the contribution margin contributes to fixed costs (filling the bucket).

CONTRIBUTION MARGIN RATIO   The contribution margin can also be expressed as a percentage. The **contribution margin ratio**, sometimes called the **profit-**

volume ratio, indicates the percentage of each sales dollar available to cover the fixed costs and to provide income from operations. For Lambert Inc., the contribution margin ratio is 40%, as computed here:

$$\text{Contribution margin ratio} = \frac{\text{Sales} - \text{Variable costs}}{\text{Sales}}$$

$$\text{Contribution margin ratio} = \frac{\$1,000,000 - \$600,000}{\$1,000,000} = 40\%$$

The contribution margin ratio measures the effect on income from operations of an increase or a decrease in sales volume. For example, assume that the management of Lambert Inc. is studying the effect of adding $80,000 in sales orders. Multiplying the contribution margin ratio (40%) by the change in sales volume ($80,000) indicates that income from operations will increase $32,000 if the additional orders are obtained. The validity of this analysis is illustrated by the following contribution margin income statement of Lambert Inc.:

Sales	$1,080,000
Variable costs ($1,080,000 × 0.60)	648,000
Contribution margin ($1,080,000 × 0.40)	$ 432,000
Fixed costs	300,000
Income from operations	$ 132,000

Variable costs as a percentage of sales are equal to 100% minus the contribution margin ratio. Thus, in the preceding income statement, the variable costs are 60% (100% − 40%) of sales, or $648,000 ($1,080,000 × 0.60). The total contribution margin, $432,000, can also be computed directly by multiplying the sales by the contribution margin ratio ($1,080,000 × 0.40).

In using the contribution margin ratio in analysis, factors other than sales volume, such as variable cost per unit and sales price, are assumed to remain constant. If such factors change, their effect must be considered.

The contribution margin ratio is also useful in setting business policy. For example, if the contribution margin ratio of a firm is large and production is at a level below 100% capacity, a large increase in income from operations can be expected from an increase in sales volume. A firm in such a position could decide to devote more effort to sales promotion because of the large change in income from operations that will result from changes in sales volume. In contrast, a firm with a small contribution margin ratio will probably want to give more attention to reducing costs before attempting to promote sales.

UNIT CONTRIBUTION MARGIN   The unit contribution margin is also useful for analyzing the profit potential of proposed projects. The **unit contribution margin** is the number of dollars from each unit of sales available to cover fixed costs and provide income from operations. For example, a $200-per-night room at the Ritz

Carlton could have a variable cost, including maids' salaries, linens, towels, soap, and utilities, of only $25 per night and thus a high contribution margin per room. Likewise, the contribution margin per unit for **Microsoft** software will also be very high. The variable costs per unit include packaging, CDs, and copying costs. These costs are small relative to the price. In both these cases, the high contribution margin per unit is necessary to cover other costs. In the case of the hotel, its fixed costs must be covered by the high contribution margin per unit. For Microsoft, the high contribution margin is necessary to fund software development expenditures. For Lambert Inc., a unit selling price of $20 and a unit variable cost of $12 yield a unit contribution margin of $8 ($20 − $12).

The contribution margin ratio is most useful when the increase or decrease in sales volume is measured in sales dollars. The unit contribution margin is most useful when the increase or decrease in sales volume is measured in sales units (quantities). To illustrate, assume that Lambert Inc. sold 50,000 units. Its income from operations is $100,000, as shown in the following contribution margin income statement:

Sales (50,000 units × $20)	$1,000,000
Variable costs (50,000 units × $12)	600,000
Contribution margin (50,000 units × $8)	$ 400,000
Fixed costs	300,000
Income from operations	$ 100,000

If Lambert Inc.'s sales could be increased by 15,000 units, from 50,000 units to 65,000 units, its income from operations would increase by $120,000 (15,000 units × $8), as shown:

Sales (65,000 units × $20)	$1,300,000
Variable costs (65,000 units × $12)	780,000
Contribution margin (65,000 units × $8)	$ 520,000
Fixed costs	300,000
Income from operations	$ 220,000

Unit contribution margin analyses can provide useful information for managers. The preceding illustration indicates, for example, that Lambert could spend up to $120,000 for special advertising or other product promotions to increase sales by 15,000 units.

OBJECTIVE 3
Using the unit contribution margin, determine the break-even point and the volume necessary to achieve a target profit.

Mathematical Approach to Cost-Volume-Profit Analysis

Accountants use various approaches for expressing the relationship of costs, sales (volume), and income from operations (operating profit). The mathematical approach is often in practice.

The mathematical approach to cost-volume-profit analysis uses equations (1) to determine the number of units of sales necessary to achieve the break-even point in operations or (2) to determine the number of units of sales necessary to achieve a target or desired profit. We next describe and illustrate these equations and their use by management in profit planning.

Break-Even Point

The **break-even point** is the level of operations at which a business's revenues and expired costs are exactly equal. At break-even, a business has neither an income nor a loss from operations. The break-even point is useful in business planning, especially when expanding or decreasing operations.

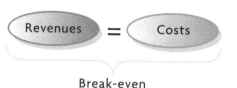

To illustrate the computation of the break-even point, assume that the fixed costs for Barker Corporation are estimated to be $90,000. The unit selling price, unit variable cost, and unit contribution margin for Barker Corporation are as follows:

Unit selling price	$25
Unit variable cost	15
Unit contribution margin	$10

The break-even point is 9,000 units, which can be computed by using the following equation:

$$\text{Break-even sales (units)} = \frac{\text{Fixed costs}}{\text{Unit contribution margin}}$$

$$\text{Break-even sales (units)} = \frac{\$90,000}{\$10} = 9,000$$

The following income statement verifies the preceding computation:

Sales (9,000 units × $25)	$225,000
Variable costs (9,000 units × $15)	135,000
Contribution margin	$ 90,000
Fixed costs	90,000
Income from operations	$ 0

The break-even point is affected by changes in the fixed costs, unit variable costs, and the unit selling price. Next, we briefly describe the effect of each of these factors on the break-even point.

EFFECT OF CHANGES IN FIXED COSTS   Although fixed costs do not change in total with changes in the level of activity, they can change because of other factors. For example, changes in property tax rates or factory supervisors' salaries change fixed costs. Increases in fixed costs raise the break-even point. Likewise, decreases in fixed costs lower the break-even point. For example, **General Motors** closed 21 plants and eliminated 74,000 jobs to lower its break-even from approximately 7 million to 5 million automobiles through the 1990s.

To illustrate, assume that Bishop Co. is evaluating a proposal to budget an additional $100,000 for advertising. Fixed costs before the additional advertising are estimated at $600,000, and the unit contribution margin is $20. The break-even point before the additional expense is 30,000 units, computed as follows:

$$\text{Break-even sales (units)} = \frac{\text{Fixed costs}}{\text{Unit contribution margin}}$$

$$\text{Break-even sales (units)} = \frac{\$600,000}{\$20} = 30,000$$

If the additional amount is spent, the fixed costs will increase by $100,000 and the break-even point will increase to 35,000 units, computed as follows:

$$\text{Break-even sales (units)} = \frac{\text{Fixed costs}}{\text{Unit contribution margin}}$$

$$\text{Break-even sales (units)} = \frac{\$700,000}{\$20} = 35,000$$

The $100,000 increase in the fixed costs requires an additional 5,000 units ($100,000/$20) of sales to break even. In other words, an increase in sales of 5,000 units is required to generate an additional $100,000 of total contribution margin (5,000 units $\times$ $20) to cover the increased fixed costs.

In a real-world example, **Warner Books** agreed to pay $7.1 million for the publishing rights to the memoirs of Jack Welch, the legendary **General Electric** chairman and CEO. Warner Books estimates it must sell about 1.5 million hardback books to break even.

EFFECT OF CHANGES IN UNIT VARIABLE COSTS   Although unit variable costs are not affected by changes in volume of activity, they can be affected by other factors. For example, changes in the price of direct materials and the wages for factory workers providing direct labor change unit variable costs. Increases in unit variable costs raise the break-even point. Likewise, decreases in unit variable costs lower the break-even point. For example, when fuel prices rise or decline, there is a direct impact on the break-even passenger load for **American Airlines**.

To illustrate, assume that Park Co. is evaluating a proposal to pay an additional 2% commission on sales to its salespeople as an incentive to increase sales. Fixed costs are estimated at $840,000, and the unit selling price, unit variable cost, and unit contribution margin before the additional 2% commission are as follows:

Unit selling price	$250
Unit variable cost	145
Unit contribution margin	$105

The break-even point is 8,000 units, computed as follows:

$$\text{Break-even sales (units)} = \frac{\text{Fixed costs}}{\text{Unit contribution margin}}$$

$$\text{Break-even sales (units)} = \frac{\$840,000}{\$105} = 8,000$$

If the sales commission proposal is adopted, variable costs increase by $5 per unit ($250 × 0.02). This increase in the variable costs decreases the unit contribution margin by $5 (from $105 to $100). Thus, the break-even point is raised to 8,400 units, computed as follows:

$$\text{Break-even sales (units)} = \frac{\text{Fixed costs}}{\text{Unit contribution margin}}$$

$$\text{Break-even sales (units)} = \frac{\$840,000}{\$100} = 8,400$$

At the original break-even point of 8,000 units, the new unit contribution margin of $100 provides only $800,000 to cover fixed costs of $840,000. Thus, an additional 400 units of sales will be required to provide the additional $40,000 (400 units × $100) contribution margin necessary to break even.

EFFECT OF CHANGES IN THE UNIT SELLING PRICE   Increases in the unit selling price lower the break-even point, while decreases in the unit selling price raise the break-even point. For example, when **The Golf Channel** went from a premium cable service price of $6.95 per month to a much lower basic cable price, its break-even point increased from 6 million to 19 million subscribers.

To illustrate, assume that Graham Co. is evaluating a proposal to increase the unit selling price of its product from $50 to $60. The following data have been gathered:

	Current	Proposed
Unit selling price	$50	$60
Unit variable cost	30	30
Unit contribution margin	$20	$30
Total fixed costs	$600,000	$600,000

The break-even point based on the current selling price is 30,000 units, computed as follows:

$$\text{Break-even sales (units)} = \frac{\text{Fixed costs}}{\text{Unit contribution margin}}$$

$$\text{Break-even sales (units)} = \frac{\$600,000}{\$20} = 30,000$$

If the selling price is increased by $10 per unit, the break-even point is decreased to 20,000 units, computed as follows:

$$\text{Break-even sales (units)} = \frac{\text{Fixed costs}}{\text{Unit contribution margin}}$$

$$\text{Break-even sales (units)} = \frac{\$600,000}{\$30} = 20,000$$

The increase of $10 per unit in the selling price increases the unit contribution margin by $10. Thus, the break-even point decreases by 10,000 units (from 30,000 units to 20,000 units).

SUMMARY OF EFFECTS OF CHANGES ON BREAK-EVEN POINT   The break-even point in sales (units) moves in the same direction as changes in the variable cost per unit and fixed costs. In contrast, the break-even point in sales (units) moves in the opposite direction to changes in the sales price per unit. A summary of the impact of these changes on the break-even point in sales (units) is shown here.

Type of Change	Direction of Change	Effect of Change on Break-Even Sales (Units)
Fixed cost	Increase	Increase
	Decrease	Decrease
Variable cost per unit	Increase	Increase
	Decrease	Decrease
Unit sales price	Increase	Decrease
	Decrease	Increase

Target Profit

At the break-even point, sales and costs are exactly equal. However, the break-even point is not the goal of most businesses. Rather, managers seek to maximize profits. By modifying the break-even equation, the sales volume required to earn a target or desired amount of profit can be estimated. For this purpose, target profit is added to the break-even equation as follows.

$$\text{Sales (units)} = \frac{\text{Fixed costs} + \text{Target profit}}{\text{Unit contribution margin}}$$

To illustrate, assume that fixed costs are estimated at $200,000, and the desired profit is $100,000. The unit selling price, unit variable cost, and unit contribution margin are as follows:

Unit selling price	$75
Unit variable cost	45
Unit contribution margin	$30

The sales volume necessary to earn the target profit of $100,000 is 10,000 units, computed as follows:

$$\text{Sales (units)} = \frac{\text{Fixed costs} + \text{Target profit}}{\text{Unit contribution margin}}$$

$$\text{Sales (units)} = \frac{\$200,000 + \$100,000}{\$30} = 10,000$$

The following income statement verifies this computation:

Sales (10,000 units × $75)	$750,000	
Variable costs (10,000 units × $45)	450,000	
Contribution margin (10,000 units × $30)	$300,000	
Fixed costs	200,000	
Income from operations	$100,000	⟵ Target profit

Graphic Approach to Cost-Volume-Profit Analysis

OBJECTIVE   4

Using a cost-volume-profit chart and a profit-volume chart, determine the break-even point and the volume necessary to achieve a target profit.

Cost-volume-profit analysis can be presented graphically as well as in equation form. Many managers prefer the graphic format because the income or loss from operations (operating profit or loss) for different levels of sales can readily be determined. Next we describe two graphic approaches that managers find useful.

Cost-Volume-Profit (Break-Even) Chart

A **cost-volume-profit chart**, sometimes called a **break-even chart**, can assist management in understanding relationships among costs, sales, and operating profit or loss. To illustrate, the cost-volume-profit chart in Exhibit 5 is based on the following data:

Unit selling price	$50
Unit variable cost	30
Unit contribution margin	$20
Total fixed costs	$100,000

EXHIBIT 5

Cost-Volume-Profit Chart

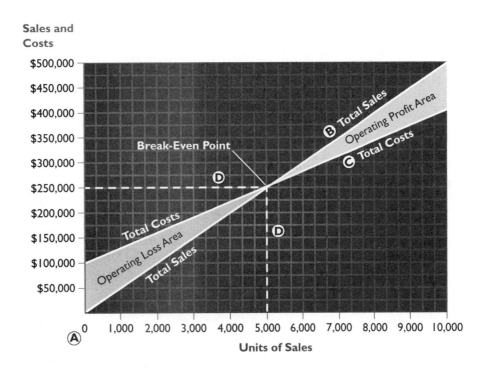

We constructed the cost-volume-profit chart in Exhibit 5 as follows:

A. Volume expressed in units of sales is indicated along the horizontal axis. The range of volume shown on the horizontal axis should reflect the *relevant range* in which the business expects to operate. Dollar amounts representing total sales and costs are indicated along the vertical axis.

B. A sales line is plotted by beginning at zero on the left corner of the graph. A second point is determined by multiplying any units of sales on the horizontal axis by the unit sales price of $50. For example, for 10,000 units of sales, the total sales is $500,000 (10,000 units × $50). The sales line is drawn upward to the right from zero through the $500,000 point.

C. A cost line is plotted by beginning with total fixed costs, $100,000, on the vertical axis. A second point is determined by multiplying any units of sales on the horizontal axis by the unit variable costs and adding the fixed costs. For example, for 10,000 units of sales, the total estimated costs would be $400,000 [(10,000 units × $30) + $100,000]. The cost line is drawn upward to the right from $100,000 on the vertical axis through the $400,000 point.

D. Horizontal and vertical lines are drawn at the point of intersection of the sales and cost lines, which is the break-even point, and the areas representing operating profit and operating loss are identified.

In Exhibit 5, the dotted lines drawn from the point of intersection of the total sales line and the total cost line identify the break-even point in total sales dollars and units. The break-even point is $250,000 of sales, which represents a sales volume of 5,000 units. Operating profits are earned when sales levels are to the right of the break-even point (operating profit area). Operating losses are incurred when sales levels are to the left of the break-even point (operating loss area).

Changes in the unit selling price, total fixed costs, and unit variable costs can be analyzed by using a cost-volume-profit chart. Using the data in Exhibit 5, assume that a proposal to reduce fixed costs by $20,000 is to be evaluated. In this case, the total fixed costs would be $80,000 ($100,000 − $20,000). As shown in Exhibit 6, the total cost line should be redrawn, starting at the $80,000 point (total fixed costs) on the vertical axis. A second point is determined by multiplying any units of sales on the horizontal axis by the unit variable costs and adding the fixed costs. For example, for

EXHIBIT 6
Revised Cost-Volume-Profit Chart

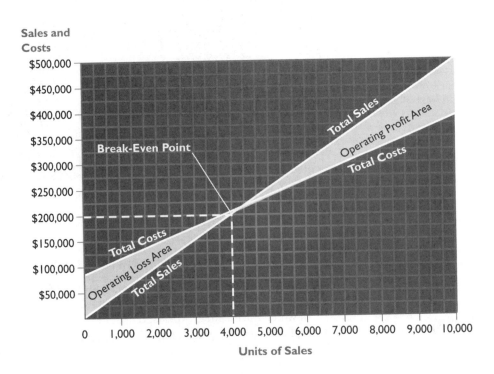

10,000 units of sales, the total estimated costs are $380,000 [(10,000 units × $30) + $80,000]. The cost line is drawn upward to the right from $80,000 on the vertical axis through the $380,000 point. The revised cost-volume-profit chart in Exhibit 6 indicates that the break-even point decreases to $200,000, or 4,000 units of sales.

Profit-Volume Chart

Another graphic approach to cost-volume-profit analysis, the **profit-volume chart**, focuses on profits. This is in contrast to the cost-volume-profit chart, which focuses on sales and costs. The profit-volume chart plots only the difference between total sales and total costs (or profits). In this way, the profit-volume chart allows managers to determine the operating profit (or loss) for various levels of operations.

To illustrate, assume that the profit-volume chart in Exhibit 7 is based on the same data as used in Exhibit 5. These data are as follows:

Unit selling price	$50
Unit variable cost	30
Unit contribution margin	$20
Total fixed costs	$100,000

The maximum operating loss is equal to the fixed costs of $100,000. Assuming that the maximum unit sales within the relevant range is 10,000 units, the maximum operating profit is $100,000, computed as follows:

Sales (10,000 units × $50)	$500,000	
Variable costs (10,000 units × $30)	300,000	
Contribution margin (10,000 units × $20)	$200,000	
Fixed costs	100,000	
Operating profit	$100,000	⟵ Maximum profit

EXHIBIT 7
Profit-Volume Chart

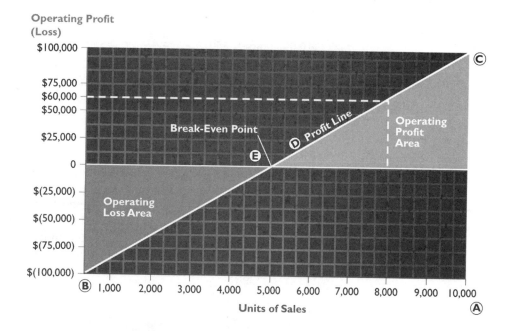

We constructed the profit-volume chart in Exhibit 7 as follows:

A. Volume expressed in units of sales is indicated along the horizontal axis. The range of volume shown on the horizontal axis should reflect the *relevant range* in which the business expects to operate. In this illustration, the maximum number of sales units within the relevant range is assumed to be 10,000 units. Dollar amounts indicating operating profits and losses are shown along the vertical axis.

B. A point representing the maximum operating loss is plotted on the vertical axis at the left. This loss is equal to the total fixed costs at the zero level of sales.

C. A point representing the maximum operating profit within the relevant range is plotted on the right.

D. A diagonal profit line is drawn connecting the maximum operating loss point with the maximum operating profit point.

E. The profit line intersects the horizontal zero operating profit line at the break-even point expressed in units of sales, and the areas indicating operating profit and loss are identified.

In Exhibit 7, the break-even point is 5,000 units of sales, which is equal to total sales of $250,000 (5,000 units X $50). Operating profit is earned when sales levels are to the right of the break-even point (operating profit area). Operating losses are incurred when sales levels are to the left of the break-even point (operating loss area). For example, at sales of 8,000 units, an operating profit of $60,000 will be earned, as shown in Exhibit 7.

The effect of changes in the unit selling price, total fixed costs, and unit variable costs on profit can be analyzed using a profit-volume chart. To illustrate, using the data in Exhibit 7, we evaluate the effect on profit of an increase of $20,000 in fixed costs. In this case, the total fixed costs are $120,000 ($100,000 + $20,000), and the maximum operating loss is also $120,000. If the maximum sales within the relevant range is 10,000 units, the maximum operating profit would be $80,000, computed as follows:

Sales (10,000 units × $50)	$500,000	
Variable costs (10,000 units × $30)	300,000	
Contribution margin (10,000 units × $20)	$200,000	
Fixed costs	120,000	
Operating profit	$ 80,000	← Revised maximum profit

A revised profit-volume chart is constructed by plotting the maximum operating loss and maximum operating profit points and drawing the revised profit line. The original and the revised profit-volume charts are shown in Exhibit 8.

The revised profit-volume chart indicates that the break-even point is 6,000 units of sales. This is equal to total sales of $300,000 (6,000 units × $50). The operating loss area of the chart has increased, while the operating profit area has decreased under the proposed change in fixed costs.

EXHIBIT 8
*Original Profit-Volume
Chart and Revised
Profit-Volume Chart*

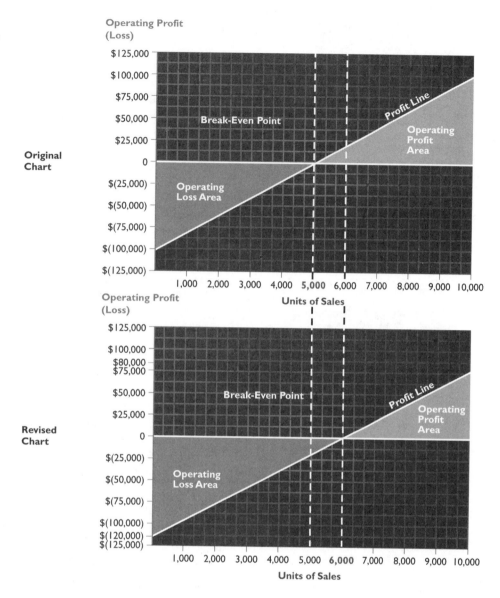

Use of Computers in Cost-Volume-Profit Analysis

With computers, the graphic approach and the mathematical approach to cost-volume-profit analysis are easy to use. Managers can vary assumptions regarding selling prices, costs, and volume and immediately see the effects of each change on the break-even point and profit. Such an analysis is called a **"what if" analysis** or **sensitivity analysis**. To illustrate, NBA franchises, such as the **Los Angeles Lakers**, analyze the effects of making the playoffs on their team's profitability. For example, assuming that the team only breaks even during the regular season, its profitability depends on making the playoffs, or basketball's so called "second season." The further the team goes into the playoffs, the greater the operating profit earned above break-even from additional ticket sales and TV revenues.

Sales Mix Considerations

OBJECTIVE   5

Calculate the break-even point for a business selling more than one product.

Most businesses sell more than one product at varying selling prices. In addition, the products often have different unit variable costs, and each product makes a different contribution to profits. Thus, the sales volume necessary to break even or to earn a target profit for a business selling two or more products depends on the sales mix. The **sales mix** is the relative distribution of sales among the various products sold by a business.

To illustrate the calculation of the break-even point for a company that sells more than one product, assume that Cascade Company sold 8,000 units of Product A and 2,000 units of Product B during the past year. The sales mix for products A and B can be expressed as percentages (80% and 20%) or as a ratio (80:20).

Cascade Company's fixed costs are $200,000. The unit selling prices, unit variable costs, and unit contribution margins for products A and B are as follows:

Product	Unit Selling Price	Unit Variable Cost	Unit Contribution Margin
A	$ 90	$70	$20
B	140	95	45

In computing the break-even point, it is useful to think of the individual products as components of one overall enterprise product. For Cascade Company, this overall enterprise product is called E. We can think of the unit selling price of E as equal to the total of the unit selling prices of products A and B, multiplied by their sales mix percentages. Likewise, we can think of the unit variable cost and unit contribution margin of E as equal to the total of the unit variable costs and unit contribution margins of products A and B, multiplied by the sales mix percentages. These computations are as follows:

Unit selling price of E: ($90 × 0.8) + ($140 × 0.2) = $100

Unit variable cost of E: ($70 × 0.8) + ($ 95 × 0.2) = $ 75

Unit contribution margin of E: ($20 × 0.8) + ($ 45 × 0.2) = $ 25

The break-even point of 8,000 units of E can be determined in the normal manner as follows:

$$\text{Break-even sales (units)} = \frac{\text{Fixed costs}}{\text{Unit contribution margin}}$$

$$\text{Break-even sales (units)} = \frac{\$200,000}{\$25} = 8,000$$

Since the sales mix for products A and B is 80% and 20%, the break-even quantity of A is 6,400 units (8,000 units × 0.80) and B is 1,600 units (8,000 units × 0.20). This analysis can be verified in the income statement shown at the top of page 433.

The effects of changes in the sales mix on the break-even point can be determined by repeating this analysis but assuming a different sales mix.

Real-world examples of the effects of sales mix include Universal Studios, Delta Air Lines, and AT&T. For example, the daily break-even attendance at **Universal**

	Product A	Product B	Total
Sales:			
6,400 units × $90	$576,000		$576,000
1,600 units × $140		$224,000	224,000
Total sales	$576,000	$224,000	$800,000
Variable costs:			
6,400 units × $70	$448,000		$448,000
1,600 units × $95		$152,000	152,000
Total variable costs	$448,000	$152,000	$600,000
Contribution margin	$128,000	$ 72,000	$200,000
Fixed costs			200,000
Income from operations			$ 0	← Break-even point

Studios theme areas depends on how many tickets were sold at an advance purchase discount rate versus the full gate rate. Likewise, the break-even point for an overseas flight of **Delta Air Lines** is influenced by the number of first class, business class, and economy class tickets sold for the flight. The weekly break-even number of long distance minutes for **AT&T** depends on the number of minutes called during day, evening, and weekend rates.

Special Cost-Volume-Profit Relationships

OBJECTIVE   6

Compute the margin of safety and the operating leverage, and explain how managers use these concepts.

Some additional relationships useful to managers can be developed from cost-volume-profit data. Two of these relationships are the margin of safety and operating leverage.

Margin of Safety

The difference between the current sales revenue and the sales at the break-even point is called the **margin of safety**. It indicates the possible decrease in sales that can occur before an operating loss results. For example, if the margin of safety is low, even a small decline in sales revenue can result in an operating loss.

If sales are $250,000, the unit selling price is $25 and sales at the break-even point are $200,000, the margin of safety is 20%, computed as follows:

$$\text{Margin of safety} = \frac{\text{Sales} - \text{Sales at break-even point}}{\text{Sales}}$$

$$\text{Margin of safety} = \frac{\$250,000 - \$200,000}{\$250,000} = 20\%$$

The margin of safety can also be stated in terms of units. In this illustration, for example, the margin of safety of 20% is equivalent to $50,000 ($250,000 × 0.20). In units, the margin of safety is 2,000 units ($50,000/$25). Thus, the current sales of $250,000 can decline $50,000, or 2,000 units, before an operating loss occurs.

Operating Leverage

The relative mix of a business's variable costs and fixed costs is measured by the **operating leverage**. It is computed as follows:

$$\text{Operating leverage} = \frac{\text{Contribution margin}}{\text{Income from operations}}$$

Since the difference between contribution margin and income from operations is the fixed cost, companies with large amounts of fixed costs generally have a high operating leverage. Thus, companies in capital-intensive industries, such as the airline and automotive industries, generally have a high operating leverage. Also, "network" businesses in which services are provided over a network that moves either goods or information have high operating leverage. Examples of network businesses include **United Airlines**, **USWEST**, **Yahoo!**, and **Union Pacific**. A low operating leverage is normal for companies in industries that are labor intensive, such as professional services. Examples of professional service businesses include **Ernst & Young**, **Merrill Lynch**, and **American Express**.

Managers can use operating leverage to measure the impact of changes in sales on income from operations. A high operating leverage indicates that a small increase in sales will yield a large percentage increase in income from operations. In contrast, a low operating leverage indicates that a large increase in sales is necessary to significantly increase income from operations. To illustrate, assume the following operating data for Jones Inc. and Wilson Inc.:

	Jones Inc.	Wilson Inc.
Sales	$400,000	$400,000
Variable costs	300,000	300,000
Contribution margin	$100,000	$100,000
Fixed costs	80,000	50,000
Income from operations	$ 20,000	$ 50,000

Both companies have the same sales, the same variable costs, and the same contribution margin. Jones Inc. has higher fixed costs than Wilson Inc. and, as a result, a lower income from operations and a higher operating leverage. The operating leverage for each company is computed as follows:

Jones Inc.	Wilson Inc.
$\text{Operating leverage} = \dfrac{\$100,000}{\$20,000} = 5$	$\text{Operating leverage} = \dfrac{\$100,000}{\$50,000} = 2$

Jones Inc.'s operating leverage indicates that, for each percentage point change in sales, income from operations will change five times that percentage. In contrast, for each percentage point change in sales, the income from operations of Wilson Inc. will change only two times that percentage. For example, if sales increased by

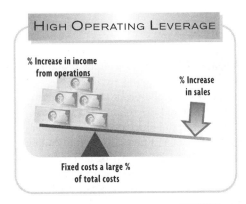

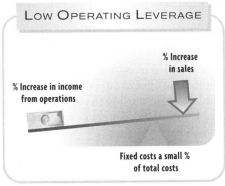

10% ($40,000) for each company, income from operations will increase by 50% (0.10 × 5), or $10,000 (0.50 × $20,000), for Jones Inc. The sales increase of $40,000 will increase income from operations by only 20% (0.10 × 2), or $10,000 (0.20 × $50,000), for Wilson Inc. The validity of this analysis is shown as follows:

	Jones Inc.	Wilson Inc.
Sales	$440,000	$440,000
Variable costs	330,000	330,000
Contribution margin	$110,000	$110,000
Fixed costs	80,000	50,000
Income from operations	$ 30,000	$ 60,000

For Jones Inc., even a small increase in sales will generate a large percentage increase in income from operations. Thus, Jones's managers may be motivated to think of ways to increase sales. In contrast, Wilson's managers might attempt to increase operating leverage by reducing variable costs and thereby change the cost structure.

Assumptions of Cost-Volume-Profit Analysis

The reliability of cost-volume-profit analysis depends on the validity of several assumptions. The primary assumptions are as follows:

1. Total sales and total costs can be represented by straight lines.
2. Within the relevant range of operating activity, the efficiency of operations does not change.
3. Costs can be accurately divided into fixed and variable components.
4. The sales mix is constant.
5. There is no change in the inventory quantities during the period.

These assumptions simplify cost-volume-profit analysis. Since they are often valid for the relevant range of operations, cost-volume-profit analysis is useful to decision making.[2]

[2]The impact of violating these assumptions is discussed in advanced accounting texts.

Key Points

1. **Classify costs according to their behavior as variable costs, fixed costs, or mixed costs.**

   Cost behavior refers to the manner in which a cost changes as a related activity changes. *Variable costs* are costs that vary in total in proportion to changes in the level of activity. *Fixed costs* are costs that remain the same in total dollar amount as the level of activity changes. A *mixed cost* has attributes of both a variable and a fixed cost.

2. **Compute the contribution margin, the contribution margin ratio, and the unit contribution margin, and explain how they can be useful to managers.**

   The contribution margin concept is useful in business planning because it gives insight into the profit potential of a firm. The contribution margin is the excess of sales revenues over variable costs. The contribution margin ratio is computed as follows:

   Contribution margin ratio =

   $$\frac{\text{Sales} - \text{Variable costs}}{\text{Sales}}$$

   The unit contribution margin is the excess of the unit selling price over the unit variable cost.

3. **Using the unit contribution margin, determine the break-even point and the volume necessary to achieve a target profit.**

   The mathematical approach to cost-volume-profit analysis uses the unit contribution margin concept and the following equations to determine the break-even point and the volume necessary to achieve a target profit for a business:

   Break-even sales (units) =

   $$\frac{\text{Fixed costs}}{\text{Unit contribution margin}}$$

   $$\text{Sales (units)} = \frac{\text{Fixed costs} + \text{Target profit}}{\text{Unit contribution margin}}$$

4. **Using a cost-volume-profit chart and a profit-volume chart, determine the break-even point and the volume necessary to achieve a target profit.**

   A cost-volume-profit chart focuses on the relationships among costs, sales, and operating profit or loss. Preparing and using a cost-volume-profit chart to determine the break-even point and the volume necessary to achieve a target profit are illustrated in this chapter.

   The profit-volume chart focuses on profits rather than on revenues and costs. Preparing and using a profit-volume chart to determine the break-even point and the volume necessary to achieve a target profit are illustrated in this chapter.

5. **Calculate the break-even point for a business selling more than one product.**

   Calculating the break-even point for a business selling two or more products is based on a specified sales mix. Given the sales mix, the break-even point can be computed using the methods illustrated for Cascade Company in this chapter.

6. **Compute the margin of safety and the operating leverage, and explain how managers use these concepts.**

   The margin of safety as a percentage of current sales is computed as follows:

   Margin of safety =

   $$\frac{\text{Sales} - \text{Sales at break-even point}}{\text{Sales}}$$

   The margin of safety is useful in evaluating past operations and in planning future operations. For example, if the margin of safety is low, even a small decline in sales revenue can result in an operating loss.

   Operating leverage is computed as follows:

   $$\text{Operating leverage} = \frac{\text{Contribution margin}}{\text{Income from operations}}$$

   Operating leverage is useful in measuring the impact of changes in sales on income from operations without preparing formal income statements. For example, a high operating leverage indicates that a small increase in sales will yield a large percentage increase in income from operations.

7. **List the assumptions underlying cost-volume-profit analysis.**

   The primary assumptions underlying cost-volume-profit analysis are as follows:

a. Total sales and total costs can be represented by straight lines.
b. Within the relevant range of operating activity, the efficiency of operations does not change.
c. Costs can be accurately divided into fixed and variable components.

d. The sales mix is constant.
e. There is no change in the inventory quantities during the period.

Glossary

Activity bases (activity drivers): Measures of an activity that is thought to cause a cost; used in analyzing and classifying cost behavior.

Break-even point: The level of business operations at which revenues and expired costs are equal.

Contribution margin: Sales less variable cost of goods sold and variable selling and administrative expenses.

Contribution margin ratio: The percentage of each sales dollar that is available to cover the fixed costs and provide income from operations.

Cost behavior: The manner in which a cost changes in relation to its activity base (driver).

Cost-volume-profit analysis: The systematic examination of the relationships among costs, expenses, sales, and operating profit or loss.

Cost-volume-profit chart: A chart used to assist management in under-

standing the relationships among costs, expenses, sales, and operating profit or loss.

Fixed costs: Costs that tend to remain the same in amount, regardless of variations in the level of activity.

High-low method: A technique that uses the highest and lowest total cost as a basis for estimating the variable cost per unit and the fixed cost component of a mixed cost.

Margin of safety: The difference between current sales revenue and the sales at the break-even point.

Mixed cost: A cost with both variable and fixed characteristics.

Operating leverage: A measure of the relative mix of a business's variable costs and fixed costs, computed as contribution margin divided by income from operations.

Profit-volume chart: A chart used to assist management in understanding

the relationship between profit and volume.

Relevant range: The range of activity over which changes in cost are of interest to management.

Sales mix: The relative distribution of sales among the various products available for sale.

Unit contribution margin: The dollars available from each unit of sales to cover fixed costs and provide income from operations.

Variable costing: A method of reporting variable and fixed costs that includes only the variable manufacturing costs in the cost of the product.

Variable costs: Costs that vary in total dollar amount as the level of activity changes.

Self-Study Questions

(Answers appear at end of chapter.)

1. Which of the following statements describes variable costs?
   A. Costs that vary on a per-unit basis as the level of activity changes.
   B. Costs that vary in total in direct proportion to changes in the level of activity.
   C. Costs that remain the same in total dollar amount as the level of activity changes.

   D. Costs that vary on a per-unit basis but remain the same in total as the level of activity changes.

2. If sales are $500,000, variable costs are $200,000, and fixed costs are $240,000, what is the contribution margin ratio?
   A. 40%   C. 52%
   B. 48%   D. 60%

3. If the unit selling price is $16, the unit variable cost is $12, and fixed costs are $160,000, what is the number of break-even sales (units)?
   A. 5,714 units   C. 13,333 units
   B. 10,000 units   D. 40,000 units

4. Based on the data presented in Question 3, how many units of sales would be required to realize income from operations of $20,000?
   A. 11,250 units   C. 40,000 units
   B. 35,000 units   D. 45,000 units

5. Based on the following operating data, what is the operating leverage?

Sales	$600,000
Variable costs	240,000
Contribution margin	$360,000
Fixed costs	160,000
Income from operations	$200,000

    A. 0.8
    B. 1.2
    C. 1.8
    D. 4.0

Discussion Questions

1. What are the three most common classifications of cost behavior?

2. Describe how total variable costs and unit variable costs behave with changes in the level of activity.

3. How would each of the following costs be classified if units produced represent the activity base?
   a. Direct labor costs
   b. Direct materials cost
   c. Electricity costs of $0.20 per kilowatt-hour

4. Describe the behavior of (a) total fixed costs and (b) unit fixed costs as the level of activity increases.

5. How would each of the following costs be classified if units produced represent the activity base?
   a. Straight-line depreciation of plant and equipment
   b. Salary of factory supervisor ($80,000 per year)
   c. Property insurance premiums of $5,000 per month on plant and equipment

6. In cost analyses, how are mixed costs treated?

7. Which of the following graphs illustrates how total variable costs behave with changes in total units produced?

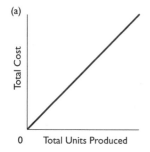

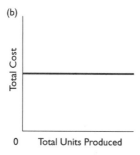

8. Which of the following graphs illustrates how unit variable costs behave with changes in total units produced?

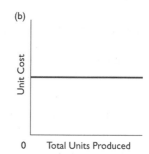

9. Which of the following graphs best illustrates fixed costs per unit as the activity base changes?

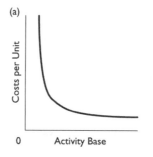

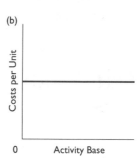

10. In applying the high-low method of cost estimation, how is the total fixed cost estimated?

11. How is contribution margin calculated?

12. If fixed costs increase, what would be the impact on the (a) contribution margin and (b) income from operations?

13. An examination of the accounting records of Hudson Company disclosed a high contribution margin ratio and production at a level below maximum capacity. Based on this information, suggest a likely means of improving income from operations. Explain.

14. What equation is used to determine the break-even point in sales units?

15. If the unit cost of direct materials is decreased, what effect will this change have on the break-even point?

16. If insurance rates are increased, what effect will this change in fixed costs have on the break-even point?

17. Both Simmons Company and Pate Company had the same sales, total costs, and income from operations for the current fiscal year, yet Simmons Company had a lower break-even point than Pate Company. Explain the reason for this difference in break-even points.

18. How does the sales mix affect the calculation of the break-even point?

19. How is the margin of safety calculated?

20. a. How is operating leverage computed?
    b. What does operating leverage measure?

Exercises

EXERCISE 11-1
Classify costs
OBJECTIVE 1

Following is a list of various costs incurred in producing frozen pizzas. With respect to the production and sale of frozen pizzas, classify each cost as either variable, fixed, or mixed.

1. Pepperoni
2. Salary of plant manager
3. Electricity costs, $0.08 per kilowatt-hour
4. Tomato paste
5. Rent on warehouse, $5,000 per month plus $5 per square foot of storage used
6. Janitorial costs, $3,000 per month
7. Hourly wages of machine operators
8. Dough
9. Hourly wages of inspectors
10. Pension cost, $0.50 per employee hour on the job
11. Property taxes, $50,000 per year on factory building and equipment
12. Property insurance premiums, $1,500 per month plus $0.005 for each dollar of property over $3,000,000
13. Packaging
14. Straight-line depreciation on the production equipment
15. Refrigerant used in refrigeration equipment

EXERCISE 11-2
Identify cost graphs
OBJECTIVE 1

The following cost graphs illustrate various types of cost behavior:

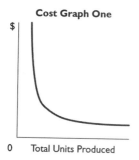

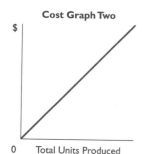

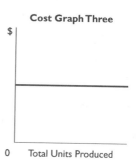

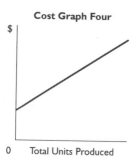

For each of the following costs, identify the cost graph that best illustrates its cost behavior as the number of units produced increases.

a. Per-unit cost of straight-line depreciation on factory equipment
b. Per-unit direct labor cost
c. Electricity costs of $2,000 per month plus $0.02 per kilowatt-hour
d. Salary of quality control supervisor, $4,000 per month
e. Total direct materials cost

EXERCISE 11–3
Identify activity bases
OBJECTIVE 1

For **The Ohio State University**, match each cost in the following table with the activity base most appropriate to it. An activity base may be used more than once or not used at all.

Cost:
1. Financial aid office salaries
2. Instructor salaries
3. Supplies
4. Housing personnel wages
5. Record office salaries
6. Admissions office salaries

Activity Base:
a. Number of enrollment applications
b. Number of financial aid applications
c. Student credit hours
d. Number of enrolled students and alumni
e. Number of students living on campus
f. Number of student/athletes

EXERCISE 11–4
Identify activity bases
OBJECTIVE 1

From the following list of activity bases for an automobile dealership, select the base that would be most appropriate for each of these costs: (1) preparation costs (cleaning, oil, and gasoline costs) for each car received, (2) salespersons' commission of 3% for each car sold, and (3) administrative costs for ordering cars.

a. Number of cars sold
b. Number of cars ordered
c. Number of cars on hand
d. Number of cars received
e. Dollar amount of cars ordered
f. Dollar amount of cars received
g. Dollar amount of cars on hand
h. Dollar amount of cars sold

EXERCISE 11–5
Identify fixed and variable costs
OBJECTIVE 1

Intuit Inc. develops and sells software products for the personal finance market, including the popular titles Quicken® and TurboTax®. Classify each of the following costs and expenses for this company as either variable or fixed to the number of units produced and sold:

a. President's salary
b. User's guides
c. Property taxes on general offices
d. Wages of telephone order assistants
e. Shipping expenses
f. Straight-line depreciation of computer equipment
g. Advertising
h. Sales commissions
i. Disks
j. Salaries of customer support personnel
k. Salaries of software developers
l. Packaging costs

EXERCISE 11-6

Relevant range and fixed and variable costs

OBJECTIVE 1

✓ a. $7

Tru-View Video Inc. manufactures video cassette cartridges within a relevant range of 200,000 to 400,000 cassettes per year. Within this range, the following partially completed manufacturing cost schedule has been prepared:

Cassettes produced	200,000	300,000	400,000
Total costs:			
Total variable costs	$1,400,000	(d)	(j)
Total fixed costs	600,000	(e)	(k)
Total costs	$2,000,000	(f)	(l)
Cost per unit:			
Variable cost per unit	(a)	(g)	(m)
Fixed cost per unit	(b)	(h)	(n)
Total cost per unit	(c)	(i)	(o)

Complete the cost schedule, identifying each cost by the appropriate letter (a) through (o).

EXERCISE 11-7

High-low method

OBJECTIVE 1

✓ a. $26.50 per unit

Tiempo Watch Company has decided to use the high-low method to estimate the total cost and the fixed and variable cost components of the total cost. The data for the highest and lowest levels of production are as follows:

	Units Produced	Total Costs
Highest level	15,000	$557,500
Lowest level	5,000	$292,500

a. Determine the variable cost per unit and the fixed cost.
b. Based on (a), estimate the total cost for 12,000 units of production.

EXERCISE 11-8

High-low method for service company

OBJECTIVE 1

✓ Fixed cost, $620,000

Bi-Coast Railroad decided to use the high-low method and operating data from the past six months to estimate the fixed and variable components of transportation costs. The activity base used by Bi-Coast Railroad is a measure of railroad operating activity, termed "gross-ton miles," which is the total number of tons multiplied by the miles moved.

	Transportation Costs	Gross-Ton Miles
January	$1,710,000	450,000
February	2,090,000	580,000
March	1,632,500	405,000
April	2,105,000	600,000
May	1,900,000	520,000
June	2,145,000	610,000

Determine the variable cost per gross-ton mile and the fixed cost.

EXERCISE 11-9

Contribution margin ratio

OBJECTIVE 2

✓ a. 25%

a. Banner Company budgets sales of $480,000, fixed costs of $90,000, and variable costs of $360,000. What is the contribution margin ratio for Banner Company?
b. If the contribution margin ratio for Manville Company is 32%, sales were $850,000, and fixed costs were $190,000, what was the income from operations?

EXERCISE 11-10

Contribution margin and contribution margin ratio

OBJECTIVE 2

✓ b. 52.46%

For a recent year, **McDonald's Corporation** had the following sales and expenses (in millions):

Sales	$12,421
Food	$ 2,997
Payroll	2,220
Occupancy (rent, depreciation, etc.)	2,722
General, selling, and administrative expenses	1,720
	$ 9,659
Income from operations	$ 2,762

Assume that the variable costs consist of food, payroll, and 40% of the general, selling, and administrative expenses.

a.   What is McDonald's contribution margin?
b.   What is McDonald's contribution margin ratio?
c.   How much would income from operations increase if same-store sales increased by $280 million for the coming year, with no change in the contribution margin ratio or fixed costs?

EXERCISE 11-11

Break-even sales and sales to realize income from operations

OBJECTIVE 3

✓ b. 15,775 units

For the current year ending March 31, Yin Company expects fixed costs of $437,600, a unit variable cost of $48, and a unit selling price of $80.

a.   Compute the anticipated break-even sales (units).
b.   Compute the sales (units) required to realize income from operations of $67,200.

EXERCISE 11-12

Break-even sales

OBJECTIVE 3

✓ a. 66,905,206 barrels

Anheuser Busch Corporation reported the following operating information for a recent year (in millions):

Net sales	$11,246
Cost of goods sold	$ 7,162
Marketing and distribution	1,958
	$ 9,120
Income from operations	$ 2,126

In addition, Anheuser Busch sold 111 million barrels of beer during the year. Assume that variable costs were 70% of the cost of goods sold and 45% of marketing and distribution expenses. Assume that the remaining costs are fixed. For the following year, assume that Anheuser Busch expects all revenue and costs to remain constant except that a new computer system and general office facility are expected to increase fixed costs by $40 million.
Rounding to the nearest cent:

a.   Compute the break-even sales (barrels) for the current year.
b.   Compute the anticipated break-even (barrels) for the following year.

EXERCISE 11-13

Break-even sales

OBJECTIVE 3

✓ a. 11,250 units

Currently, the unit selling price of a product is $165, the unit variable cost is $105, and the total fixed costs are $675,000. A proposal is being evaluated to increase the unit selling price to $180.

a.   Compute the current break-even sales (units).
b.   Compute the anticipated break-even sales (units), assuming that the unit selling price increases and all costs remain constant.

EXERCISE 11-14
Break-even analysis
OBJECTIVE 3

America Online (AOL) has fueled its growth by using aggressive promotion strategies. One of these strategies is to send CD disks to potential customers, offering free AOL service for a period of time. If AOL mailed 500,000 disks to prospective customers, offering three months free service, how many people would need to sign up for the service to break even on the cost of this campaign? Assume the following in forming your response:

Cost per disk (including mailing)	$2.50
Number of months an average new customer stays with the service	36 months
Revenue per month per account	$20

In addition, assume that the monthly variable cost of providing the AOL service to an individual customer is insignificant.

EXERCISE 11-15
Break-even analysis
OBJECTIVE 3

Nextel Communications Inc. is one of the largest digital wireless service providers in the United States. In a recent year, it had 3.6 million subscribers that generated revenue of $1,846,758,000. Costs and expenses for the year were as follows:

Cost of revenue	$ 516,393,000
Selling, general, and administrative expenses	1,550,323,000
Depreciation	832,299,000

Assume that 20% of the cost of revenue and 40% of the selling, general, and administrative expenses are variable with the number of subscribers.

a. What is Nextel's break-even number of subscribers, using the preceding data and assumptions? Round per-unit calculations to the nearest dollar.
b. How much revenue per subscriber would be sufficient for Nextel to break even if the number of subscribers remained constant?

EXERCISE 11-16
Cost-volume-profit chart
OBJECTIVE 4

✓ b. $800,000

For the coming year, Peters Inc. anticipates fixed costs of $300,000, a unit variable cost of $25, and a unit selling price of $40. The maximum sales within the relevant range are $1,600,000.

a. Construct a cost-volume-profit chart.
b. Estimate the break-even sales (dollars) by using the cost-volume-profit chart constructed in (a).
c. What is the main advantage of presenting the cost-volume-profit analysis in graphic form rather than equation form?

EXERCISE 11-17
Profit-volume chart
OBJECTIVE 4

✓ b. $300,000

Using the data for Peters Inc. in Exercise 11-16, (a) determine the maximum possible operating loss, (b) compute the maximum possible income from operations, (c) construct a profit-volume chart, and (d) estimate the break-even sales (units) by using the profit-volume chart constructed in (c).

EXERCISE 11-18
Break-even chart
OBJECTIVE 4

Name the chart on the following page and identify the items represented by the letters (a) through (f).

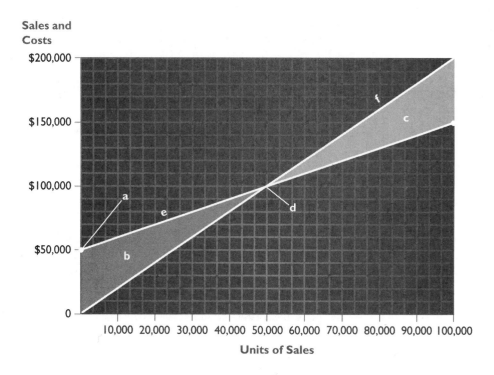

EXERCISE 11-19

Graphic approach to cost-volume-profit analysis

OBJECTIVE 4

Name the following chart, and identify the items represented by the letters (a) through (f).

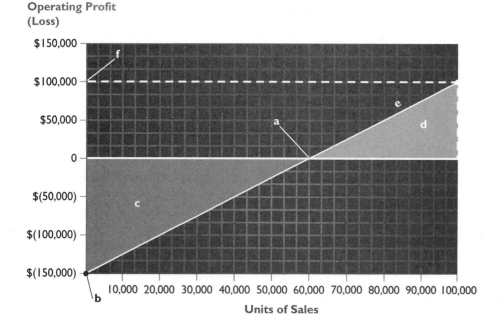

EXERCISE 11-20

Sales mix and break-even sales

OBJECTIVE 5

Tasty Snacks Inc. manufactures and sells two products, potato chips and pretzels. The fixed costs are $167,500, and the sales mix is 70% potato chips and 30% pretzels. The unit selling price and the unit variable cost for each product are as follows:

✓ a. 250,000 units

Products	Unit Selling Price	Unit Variable Cost
Potato Chips	$2.20	$1.50
Pretzels	1.70	1.10

a. Compute the break-even sales (units) for the overall product, E.

b. How many units of each product, potato chips and pretzels, would be sold at the break-even point?

EXERCISE 11-21

Break-even sales and sales mix for a service company

OBJECTIVE 5

✓ a. 48 seats

Eastern Airways provides air transportation services between New York and Miami. A single New York-to-Miami round-trip flight has the following operating statistics:

Fuel	$6,520
Flight crew salaries	3,400
Airplane depreciation	1,600
Variable cost per passenger—business class	58
Variable cost per passenger—tourist class	34
One-way ticket price—business class	400
One-way ticket price—tourist class	240

It is assumed that the fuel, crew salaries, and airplane depreciation are fixed regardless of the number of seats sold for the round-trip flight.

a. Compute the break-even number of seats sold on a single round-trip flight for the overall product. Assume that the overall product is 25% business class and 75% tourist class tickets.

b. How many business class and tourist class seats would be sold at the break-even point?

EXERCISE 11-22

Margin of safety

OBJECTIVE 6

✓ a. 1. $50,000

a. If Kelvin Company, with a break-even point at $350,000 of sales, has actual sales of $400,000, what is the margin of safety expressed (1) in dollars and (2) as a percentage of sales?

b. If the margin of safety for Moore Company was 25%, fixed costs were $600,000, and variable costs were 60% of sales, what was the amount of actual sales (dollars)? (*Hint:* Determine the break-even in sales dollars first.)

EXERCISE 11-23

Break-even and margin of safety relationships

OBJECTIVE 6

At a recent staff meeting, the question of discontinuing Product Q from the product line was being discussed. The chief financial analyst reported the following current monthly data for Product Q:

Units of sales	20,000
Break-even units	23,000
Margin of safety in units	3,000

For what reason would you question the validity of these data?

EXERCISE 11-24

Operating leverage

OBJECTIVE 6

✓ a. Duncan, 1.50

Duncan Inc. and Chow Inc. have the following operating data:

	Duncan	Chow
Sales	$550,000	$525,000
Variable costs	400,000	250,000
Contribution margin	$150,000	$275,000
Fixed costs	50,000	225,000
Income from operations	$100,000	$ 50,000

a. Compute the operating leverage for Duncan Inc. and Chow Inc.
b. How much would income from operations increase for each company if its sales increased by 20%?
c. Why is there a difference in the increase in income from operations for the two companies? Explain.

Problems

PROBLEM 11 | 1
Classify costs
OBJECTIVE 1

Franklin Furniture Company manufactures sofas for distribution to several major retail chains. The following costs are incurred in the production and sale of sofas:

a. Salesperson's salary, $12,000 plus 5% of the selling price of each sofa sold
b. Janitorial supplies, $10 for each sofa produced
c. Consulting fee of $15,000 paid to efficiency specialists
d. Rent on experimental equipment, $25 for every sofa produced
e. Springs
f. Employer's FICA taxes on controller's salary of $75,000
g. Insurance premiums on property, plant, and equipment, $5,000 per year plus $20 per $10,000 of insured value over $8,000,000
h. Salary of production vice-president
i. Fabric for sofa coverings
j. Cartons used to ship sofas
k. Straight-line depreciation on factory equipment
l. Electricity costs of $0.02 per kilowatt-hour
m. Property taxes on property, plant, and equipment
n. Hourly wages of sewing machine operators
o. Sewing supplies
p. Foam rubber for cushion fillings
q. Salary of designers
r. Wood for framing the sofas
s. Rental costs of warehouse, $10,000 per month
t. Legal fees paid to attorneys in defense of the company in a patent infringement suit, $10,000 plus $75 per hour

Instructions

Classify the preceding costs as either fixed, variable, or mixed. Use the following tabular headings and place an "X" in the appropriate column. Identify each cost by letter in the Cost column.

Cost	Fixed Cost	Variable Cost	Mixed Cost

PROBLEM 11 | 2
*Break-even sales under
present and proposed
conditions*
OBJECTIVES 2, 3

✓ 3. 210,000 units

Good Earth Garden Tools Inc., operating at full capacity, sold 292,000 units at a price of $45 per unit during 2003. Its income statement for 2003 is as follows:

Sales		$13,140,000
Cost of goods sold		8,000,000
Gross profit		$ 5,140,000
Operating expenses:		
Selling expenses	$1,500,000	
Administrative expenses	2,000,000	
Total operating expenses		3,500,000
Income from operations		$ 1,640,000

The division of costs between fixed and variable is as follows:

	Fixed	Variable
Cost of sales	25%	75%
Selling expenses	40%	60%
Administrative expenses	80%	20%

Management is considering a plant expansion program that will permit an increase of $2,250,000 in yearly sales. The expansion will increase fixed costs by $600,000 but will not affect the relationship between sales and variable costs.

Instructions

1. Determine for 2003 the total fixed costs and the total variable costs.
2. Determine for 2003 (a) the unit variable cost and (b) the unit contribution margin.
3. Compute the break-even sales (units) for 2003.
4. Compute the break-even sales (units) under the proposed program.
5. Determine the amount of sales (units) that would be necessary under the proposed program to realize the $1,640,000 of income from operations that was earned in 2003.
6. Determine the maximum income from operations possible with the expanded plant.
7. If the proposal is accepted and sales remain at the 2003 level, what will the income or loss from operations be for 2004?
8. Based on the data given, would you recommend accepting the proposal? Explain.

PROBLEM 11 | 3
Break-even sales and cost-volume-profit chart
OBJECTIVES 3, 4

✓ 1. 18,000 units

For the coming year, Colorado Shoe Company anticipates a unit selling price of $80, a unit variable cost of $50, and fixed costs of $540,000.

Instructions

1. Compute the anticipated break-even sales (units).
2. Compute the sales (units) required to realize income from operations of $84,000.
3. Construct a cost-volume-profit chart, assuming maximum sales of 40,000 units within the relevant range.
4. Determine the probable income (loss) from operations if sales total 23,000 units.

PROBLEM 11 | 4
Break-even sales and cost-volume-profit chart
OBJECTIVES 3, 4

✓ 1. 1,500 units

Last year, Lansing Company had sales of $225,000 based on a unit selling price of $180. The variable cost per unit was $100, and fixed costs were $120,000. The maximum sales within Lansing Company's relevant range are 3,000 units. Lansing Company is considering a proposal to spend an additional $40,000 on billboard advertising during the current year in an attempt to increase sales and utilize unused capacity.

Instructions

1. Construct a cost-volume-profit chart indicating the break-even sales for last year.
2. Using the cost-volume-profit chart prepared in (1), determine (a) the income from operations for last year and (b) the maximum income from operations that could have been realized during the year.
3. Construct a cost-volume-profit chart indicating the break-even sales for the current year, assuming that a noncancelable contract is signed for the additional billboard advertising. No changes are expected in the selling price or other costs.
4. Using the cost-volume-profit chart prepared in (3), determine (a) the income from operations if sales total 2,500 units and (b) the maximum income from operations that could be realized during the year.

PROBLEM 11 | 5

Sales mix and break-even sales

OBJECTIVE 5

✓ 1. 55,000 units

Data related to the expected sales of CDs and cassette tapes for Bliss Music Inc. for the current year, which is typical of recent years, are as follows:

Products	Unit Selling Price	Unit Variable Cost	Sales Mix
CDs	$18	$11	75%
Cassette tapes	12	7	25%

The estimated fixed costs for the current year are $357,500.

Instructions

1. Determine the estimated units of sales of the overall product necessary to reach the break-even point for the current year.
2. Based on the break-even sales (units) in (1), determine the unit sales of both CDs and cassette tapes for the current year.
3. Assume that the sales mix was 25% CDs and 75% cassette tapes. Compare the break-even point with that in (1). Why is it so different?

PROBLEM 11 | 6

Contribution margin, break-even sales, cost-volume-profit chart, margin of safety, and operating leverage

OBJECTIVES 2, 3, 4, 6

✓ 2. 50%

Jarvis Inc. expects to maintain the same inventories at the end of 2003 as at the beginning of the year. The total of all production costs for the year is therefore assumed to be equal to the cost of goods sold. With this in mind, the various department heads were asked to submit estimates of the costs for their departments during 2003. A summary report of these estimates is as follows:

	Estimated Fixed Cost	Estimated Variable Cost (per unit sold)
Production costs:		
Direct materials	—	$ 6.80
Direct labor	—	3.20
Factory overhead	$ 83,500	1.40
Selling expenses:		
Sales salaries and commissions	37,300	0.80
Advertising	12,500	—
Travel	3,200	—
Miscellaneous selling expense	4,200	0.50
Administrative expenses:		
Office and officers' salaries	75,400	—
Supplies	5,000	0.20
Miscellaneous administrative expense	3,900	2.10
Total	$225,000	$15.00

It is expected that 20,000 units will be sold at a price of $30 a unit. Maximum sales within the relevant range are 30,000 units.

Instructions

1. Prepare an estimated income statement for 2003.
2. What is the expected contribution margin ratio?
3. Determine the break-even sales in units.
4. Construct a cost-volume-profit chart indicating the break-even sales.
5. What is the expected margin of safety?
6. Determine the operating leverage.

Activities

Activity 11-1
Ethics and professional conduct in business
E T H I C S

Howard Skinner is a financial consultant to Golden Properties Inc., a real estate syndicate. Golden Properties Inc. finances and develops commercial real estate (office buildings). The completed projects are then sold as limited partnership interests to individual investors. The syndicate makes a profit on the sale of these partnership interests. Howard provides financial information for the offering prospectus, which is the document that provides the financial and legal details of the limited partnership offerings. In one of the projects, the bank has financed the construction of a commercial office building at a rate of 6% for the first four years, after which time the rate jumps to 10% for the remaining 26 years of the mortgage. The interest costs are one of the major ongoing costs of a real estate project. Howard has reported prominently in the prospectus that the break-even occupancy for the first four years is 60%. This is the amount of office space that must be leased to cover the interest and general upkeep costs over the first four years. The 60% break-even is very low and thus communicates a low risk to potential investors. Howard uses the 60% break-even rate as a major marketing tool in selling the limited partnership interests. Buried in the fine print of the prospectus is additional information that would allow an astute investor to determine that the break-even occupancy will jump to 85% after the fourth year because of the contracted increase in the mortgage interest rate. Howard believes prospective investors are adequately informed as to the risk of the investment.

Comment on the ethical considerations of this situation.

Activity 11-2
Break-even sales, contribution margin

"For a student, a grade of 65 percent is nothing to write home about. But for the airline . . . [industry], filling 65 percent of the seats . . . is the difference between profit and loss.

"The [economy] might be just strong enough to sustain all the carriers on a cash basis, but not strong enough to bring any significant profitability to the industry. . . . For the airlines . . . , the emphasis will be on trying to consolidate routes and raise ticket prices. . . ."

The airline industry is notorious for boom and bust cycles. Why is airline profitability very sensitive to these cycles? Do you think that during a down cycle the strategy to consolidate routes and raise ticket prices is reasonable? What would make this strategy succeed or fail? Why?

Source: Edwin McDowell, "Empty Seats, Empty Beds, Empty Pockets," *New York Times*, January 6, 1992, p. C3.

Activity 11-3
Break-even analysis

Galaxy Studios has finished a new VCR movie offering, *Keeping in Balance*. Management is now considering its marketing strategies. The following information is available:

Anticipated sales price per unit	$25
Variable cost per unit*	$5
Anticipated volume	750,000
Movie production costs	$10,000,000
Anticipated advertising	$5,000,000

*The cost of the VCR tape, packaging, and copying costs.

Two managers, Julie Wilson and Steve Harris, had the following discussion of ways to increase the profitability of this new offering.

Julie: I think we need to think of some way to increase our profitability. Do you have any ideas?

Steve: Well, I think the best strategy would be to become aggressive on price.

Julie: How aggressive?

Steve: If we drop the price to $20 per unit and maintain our advertising budget at $5,000,000, I think we will generate sales of 1,600,000 units.

Julie: I think that's the wrong way to go. You're giving too much up on price. Instead, I think we need to follow an aggressive advertising strategy.

Steve: How aggressive?

Julie: If we increase our advertising to a total of $8,000,000, we should be able to increase sales volume to 1,500,000 units without any change in price.

Steve: I don't think that's reasonable. We'll never cover the increased advertising costs.

Which strategy is best: Do nothing? Follow the advice of Julie Wilson? Or follow Steve Harris's strategy?

Activity 11–4

Variable costs and activity bases in decision making

The owner of Image4U Inc., a T-shirt printing company, is planning direct labor needs for the upcoming year. The owner has provided you with the following information for next year's plans:

	One Color	Two Color	Three Color	Four Color	Total
Number of T-shirts	300	800	900	1,000	3,000

Each color on the T-shirt must be printed one at a time. Thus, for example, a four-color T-shirt will need to be run through the silk screen operation four separate times. The total production volume last year was 2,000 T-shirts as follows.

	One Color	Two Color	Three Color	Total
Number of T-shirts	300	800	900	2,000

As you can see, the four-color T-shirt is a new product offering for the upcoming year. The owner believes that the expected 1,000-unit increase in volume from last year means that direct labor expenses should increase by 50% (1,000/2,000). What do you think?

Activity 11–5

Variable costs and activity bases in decision making

Sales volume has been dropping at Hassid Company. During this time, however, the Shipping Department manager has been under severe financial constraints. The manager knows that most of the Shipping Department's effort is related to pulling inventory from the warehouse for each order and performing the related paperwork. The paperwork involves preparing shipping documents for each order. Thus, the pulling and paperwork effort associated with each sales order is essentially the same, regardless of the size of the order. The Shipping Department manager has discussed the financial situation with senior management. Senior management has responded by pointing out that sales volume has been dropping, so that the amount of work in the Shipping Department should be dropping. Thus, senior management told the Shipping Department manager that costs should be decreasing in the department.

The Shipping Department manager prepared the following information:

Month	Sales Volume	Number of Customer Orders	Sales Volume per Order
January	$95,000	500	$190
February	93,600	520	180
March	90,100	530	170
April	90,000	600	150
May	89,900	620	145
June	85,000	625	136
July	81,900	630	130
August	80,000	640	125

Given this information, how would you respond to senior management?

Activity 11-6
Break-even analysis
GROUP

Break-even analysis is one of the most fundamental tools for managing any kind of business unit. Consider the management of your school. In a group, brainstorm some applications of break-even analysis at your school. Identify three areas where break-even analysis could be used. For each area, identify the revenues, variable costs, and fixed costs that would be used in the calculation.

Activity 11-7
Cost-volume-profit analysis

Access the portion of **Microsoft's** Web site at http://www.microsoft.com/msft that deals with investor relations. A number of features is accessible from this contents page. Go to the online analysis tools. One of these tools is a Microsoft Excel® "what-if" model. Download this model, and use Excel® (or the Excel Viewer if you don't have Excel) to open the model.

a. Use the model to project next year's net income, based on the following assumptions*:

Revenue to change by	0.12
Cost of revenue to change by	0.10
Sales and marketing to change by	0.10
Research and development to change by	0.11
General and administrative expenses to change by	0.08
Investment income	$2,000 million
Other expenses to be	$100 million
Tax rate to be	0.30
Average number of shares to be	5,500 million

*If the model has changed since this text was written, complete the projection by filling in your own assumptions required by the model.

b. Why did your net income increase a different percentage than did sales?

Answers to Self-Study Questions

1. **B** Variable costs vary in total in direct proportion to changes in the level of activity (answer B). Costs that vary on a per-unit basis as the level of activity changes (answer A) or remain constant in total dollar amount as the level of activity changes (answer C), or both (answer D), are fixed costs.

2. **D** The contribution margin ratio indicates the percentage of each sales dollar available to cover the fixed costs and provide income from operations and is determined as follows:

$$\text{Contribution margin ratio} = \frac{\text{Sales} - \text{Variable costs}}{\text{Sales}}$$

$$\text{Contribution margin ratio} = \frac{\$500,000 - \$200,000}{\$500,000}$$

$$= 60\%$$

3. **D** The break-even sales of 40,000 units (answer D) is computed as follows:

$$\text{Break-even sales (units)} = \frac{\text{Fixed costs}}{\text{Unit contribution margin}}$$

$$\text{Break-even sales (units)} = \frac{\$160,000}{\$4} = 40,000 \text{ units}$$

4. **D** Sales of 45,000 units are required to realize income from operations of $20,000, computed as follows:

$$\text{Sales (units)} = \frac{\text{Fixed costs} + \text{Target profit}}{\text{Unit contribution margin}}$$

$$\text{Sales (units)} = \frac{\$160,000 + \$20,000}{\$4} = 45,000 \text{ units}$$

5. **C** The operating leverage is 1.8, computed as follows:

$$\text{Operating leverage} = \frac{\text{Contribution margin}}{\text{Income from operations}}$$

$$\text{Operating leverage} = \frac{\$360,000}{\$200,000} = 1.8$$

12

LEARNING OBJECTIVES

OBJECTIVE 1

Prepare a differential analysis report for decisions involving

- Leasing or selling equipment.
- Discontinuing an unprofitable segment.
- Manufacturing or purchasing a needed part.
- Replacing usable fixed assets.
- Processing further or selling an intermediate product.
- Accepting additional business at a special price.

OBJECTIVE 2

Determine the selling price of a product using the total cost concept.

OBJECTIVE 3

Calculate the relative profitability of products in bottleneck production environments.

Differential Analysis and Product Pricing

Many of the decisions that you make depend on comparing the estimated costs of alternatives. The payoff from such comparisons is described in the following report from a University of Michigan study.

> *Richard Nisbett and two colleagues quizzed Michigan faculty members and university seniors on such questions as how often they walk out on a bad movie, refuse to finish a bad meal, start over on a weak term paper, or abandon a research project that no longer looks promising. They believe that people who cut their losses this way are following sound economic rules: calculating the net benefits of alternative courses of action, writing off past costs that can't be recovered, and weighing the opportunity to use future time and effort more profitably elsewhere.*
>
> *They find that among faculty members, those who use cost-benefit reasoning in this fashion— being more likely to give up on research that isn't getting anywhere or using labor-saving devices as often as possible—have higher salaries relative to their age and departments. Not surprisingly, economists are more likely to apply the approach than professors of humanities or biology.*
>
> *Among students, those who have learned to use cost-benefit analysis are apt to have far better grades than their SAT scores would have predicted. Again, the more economics courses the students have, the more likely they are to apply cost-benefit analysis outside the classroom.*
>
> *Dr. Nisbett concedes that for many Americans, cost-benefit rules often appear to conflict with such traditional principles as "never give up" and "waste not, want not."*

Managers must also consider the effects of alternative decisions on their businesses. In this chapter, we discuss differential analysis, which reports the effects of alternative decisions on total revenues and costs. We also describe and illustrate a practical approach to setting product prices. Finally, we discuss how production bottlenecks influence product mix and pricing decisions.

Source: Alan L. Otten, "Economic Perspective Produces Steady Yields," from People Patterns, *The Wall Street Journal*, March 31, 1992, p. B1.

Differential Analysis

OBJECTIVE   1

Prepare a differential analysis report for decisions involving

- Leasing or selling equipment.
- Discontinuing an unprofitable segment.
- Manufacturing or purchasing a needed part.
- Replacing usable fixed assets.
- Processing further or selling an intermediate product.
- Accepting additional business at a special price.

Planning for future operations involves decision making. For some decisions, revenue and cost data from the accounting records can be useful. However, the revenue and cost data for use in evaluating courses of future operations or choosing among competing alternatives are often not available in the accounting records and must be estimated.

Consider the following:

- The decision by **General Motors** to purchase on-board communications products from **Delphi Automotive Systems** instead of making them internally.

- The decision by **Marriott Hotels** to accept a special price from a bid placed on **priceline.com**.

- The decision by **TWA** to discontinue service to Rome, Madrid, and Barcelona.

In each of these decisions, the estimated revenues and costs were **relevant**. The relevant revenues and costs focus on the differences between each alternative. Costs that have been incurred in the past are not relevant to the decision. These costs are called **sunk costs**.

The irrelevancy of sunk cost is sometimes difficult to apply in practice. Psychologists believe this is because acknowledging a sunk cost is the same as admitting to a past mistake. For example, one study compared the playing time of players selected in the first round of the **NBA** draft with other players. The study found that poor-performing first-round draftees received more court time than players with better performance but less costly contracts. Apparently, the owners believed that they had to prove that the big contract wasn't wasted, even though it meant having the wrong players on the court.

Differential revenue is the amount of increase or decrease in revenue expected from a course of action as compared with an alternative. To illustrate, assume that certain equipment is being used to manufacture calculators, which are expected to generate revenue of $150,000. If the equipment could be used to make digital clocks, which would generate revenue of $175,000, the differential revenue from making and selling digital clocks is $25,000.

Differential cost is the amount of increase or decrease in cost that is expected from a course of action as compared with an alternative. For example, if an increase in advertising expenditures from $100,000 to $150,000 is being considered, the differential cost of the action is $50,000.

Differential income or loss is the difference between the differential revenue and the differential costs. Differential income indicates that a particular decision is expected to be profitable, and a differential loss indicates the opposite.

Differential analysis focuses on the effect of alternative courses of action on the relevant revenues and costs. For example, if a manager must decide between two alternatives, differential analysis would involve comparing the differential revenues of the two alternatives with the differential costs.

In this chapter, we discuss the use of differential analysis in analyzing the following alternatives:

1. Leasing or selling equipment.
2. Discontinuing an unprofitable segment.

3. Manufacturing or purchasing a needed part.
4. Replacing usable fixed assets.
5. Processing further or selling an intermediate product.
6. Accepting additional business at a special price.

Lease or Sell

Management could have a choice between leasing or selling a piece of equipment that is no longer needed in the business. In deciding which option is better, management can use differential analysis. To illustrate, assume that Marcus Company is considering disposing of equipment that cost $200,000 and has $120,000 of accumulated depreciation to date. Marcus Company can sell the equipment through a broker for $100,000 less a 6% commission. Alternatively, Potamkin Company (the lessee) has offered to lease the equipment for five years for a total of $160,000. At the end of the fifth year of the lease, the equipment is expected to have no residual value. During the period of the lease, Marcus Company (the lessor) will incur repair, insurance, and property tax expenses estimated at $35,000. Exhibit 1 shows Marcus Company's analysis of whether to lease or sell the equipment.

EXHIBIT 1
Differential Analysis
Report–Lease or Sell

Proposal to Lease or Sell Equipment June 22, 2006		
Differential revenue from alternatives:		
Revenue from lease	$160,000	
Revenue from sale	100,000	
Differential revenue from lease		$60,000
Differential cost of alternatives:		
Repair, insurance, and property tax expenses	$ 35,000	
Commission expense on sale	6,000	
Differential cost of lease		29,000
Net differential income from the lease alternative		**$31,000**

Note that in Exhibit 1, the $80,000 book value ($200,000 − $120,000) of the equipment is a sunk cost and is not considered in the analysis. The $80,000 is a cost that resulted from a previous decision. It is not affected by the alternatives now being considered in leasing or selling the equipment. The relevant factors to be considered are the differential revenues and differential costs associated with the lease or sell decision. This analysis is verified by the traditional analysis in Exhibit 2 on page 456.

The alternatives presented in Exhibits 1 and 2 were relatively simple. However, regardless of the complexity, the approach to differential analysis is basically the same. Two additional factors that often need to be considered are (1) differential revenue from investing the funds generated by the alternatives and (2) any income tax differential. In Exhibit 1, there could be differential interest revenue related to investing the cash flows from the two alternatives. Any income tax differential would be related to the differences in the timing of the income from the alternatives and the differences in the amount of investment income.

EXHIBIT 2
Traditional Analysis

Lease or Sell			
Lease alternative:			
Revenue from lease		$160,000	
Depreciation expense for remaining five years	$80,000		
Repair, insurance, and property tax expenses	35,000	115,000	
Net gain			$45,000
Sell alternative:			
Sales price		$100,000	
Book value of equipment	$80,000		
Commission expense	6,000	86,000	
Net gain			14,000
Net differential income from the lease alternative			**$31,000**

Many companies that manufacture expensive equipment give customers the choice of leasing the equipment. For example, construction equipment from **Caterpillar Inc.** can either be purchased outright or leased through Caterpillar's financial services subsidiary. **IBM** makes its large mainframe computers available by lease, as does **Xerox** with its copy machines.

Discontinue a Segment or Product

When a product or a department, branch, territory, or other segment of a business is generating losses, management could consider eliminating the product or segment. It is often assumed, sometimes in error, that the total income from operations of a business would be increased if the operating loss could be eliminated. Discontinuing the product or segment usually eliminates all of the product or segment's variable costs (direct materials, direct labor, sales commissions, and so on). However, if the product or segment is a relatively small part of the business, the fixed costs (depreciation, insurance, property taxes, and so on) could not decrease by discontinuing it. It is possible in this case for the total operating income of a company to decrease rather than increase by eliminating the product or segment. To illustrate, the income statement for Battle Creek Cereal Co. presented in Exhibit 3 is for a normal year ending August 31, 2006.

Because Bran Flakes incurs annual losses, management is considering discontinuing it. Total annual operating income of $80,000 ($40,000 Toasted Oats + $40,000 Corn Flakes) could seem to be indicated by the income statement in Exhibit 3 if Bran Flakes is discontinued.

Discontinuing Bran Flakes, however, would actually decrease operating income by $15,000, to $54,000 ($69,000 − $15,000). This is shown by the differential analysis report in Exhibit 4, in which we assume that discontinuing Bran Flakes would have no effect on fixed costs and expenses.

The traditional analysis in Exhibit 5 verifies the preceding differential analysis. In Exhibit 5, only the short-term (one-year) effects of discontinuing Bran Flakes are considered. When eliminating a product or segment, management should also consider the long-term effects. For example, the plant capacity made available by discontinuing Bran Flakes could be eliminated. This could reduce fixed costs. Some employees

EXHIBIT 3
Income (Loss) by Product

BATTLE CREEK CEREAL CO.
Condensed Income Statement
For the Year Ended August 31, 2006

	Corn Flakes	Toasted Oats	Bran Flakes	Total
Sales	$500,000	$400,000	$100,000	$1,000,000
Cost of goods sold:				
Variable costs	$220,000	$200,000	$ 60,000	$ 480,000
Fixed costs	120,000	80,000	20,000	220,000
Total cost of goods sold	$340,000	$280,000	$ 80,000	$ 700,000
Gross profit	$160,000	$120,000	$ 20,000	$ 300,000
Operating expenses:				
Variable expenses	$ 95,000	$ 60,000	$ 25,000	$ 180,000
Fixed expenses	25,000	20,000	6,000	51,000
Total operating expenses	$120,000	$ 80,000	$ 31,000	$ 231,000
Income (loss) from operations	$ 40,000	$ 40,000	$(11,000)	$ 69,000

EXHIBIT 4
*Differential Analysis
Report—Discontinue an
Unprofitable Segment*

Proposal to Discontinue Bran Flakes
September 29, 2006

Differential revenue from annual sales of Bran Flakes:		
Revenue from sales		$100,000
Differential cost of annual sales of Bran Flakes:		
Variable cost of goods sold	$60,000	
Variable operating expenses	25,000	85,000
Annual differential income from sales of Bran Flakes		$ 15,000

EXHIBIT 5
Traditional Analysis

Proposal to Discontinue Bran Flakes
September 29, 2006

	Bran Flakes, Toasted Oats, and Corn Flakes	Discontinue Bran Flakes*	Toasted Oats and Corn Flakes
Sales	$1,000,000	$100,000	$900,000
Cost of goods sold:			
Variable costs	$ 480,000	$ 60,000	$420,000
Fixed costs	220,000	—	220,000
Total cost of goods sold	$ 700,000	$ 60,000	$640,000
Gross profit	$ 300,000	$ 40,000	$260,000
Operating expenses:			
Variable expenses	$ 180,000	$ 25,000	$155,000
Fixed expenses	51,000	—	51,000
Total operating expenses	$ 231,000	$ 25,000	$206,000
Income (loss) from operations	$ 69,000	$ 15,000	$ 54,000

*Fixed costs do not decline with the discontinuance of Bran Flakes.

could have to be laid off, and others could have to be relocated and retrained. Furthermore, there could be a related decrease in sales of more profitable products to those customers who were attracted by the discontinued product.

Make or Buy

The assembly of many parts is often a major element in manufacturing some products, such as automobiles. These parts can be made by the product's manufacturer, or they can be purchased. For example, some of the parts for an automobile, such as the motor, can be produced by the automobile manufacturer. Other parts, such as tires, can be purchased from other manufacturers. In addition, in manufacturing motors, items such as spark plugs and nuts and bolts can be acquired from suppliers.

Nike, Inc., is a company that has made a make or buy decision. Specifically, Nike does not make shoes but buys 100% of its shoe manufacturing from outside suppliers. Nike, Inc., believes that its strengths are in designing, marketing, distributing, and selling athletic shoes. Thus, Nike focuses on the parts of the business it believes add the greatest value to the customer and thus the greatest profitability to the company.

Management uses differential costs to decide whether to make or buy a part. For example, if a part is purchased, management has concluded that it is less costly to buy the part than to manufacture it. Make or buy options often arise when a manufacturer has excess productive capacity in the form of unused equipment, space, and labor.

The differential analysis is similar, whether management is considering making a part that is currently being purchased or purchasing a part that is currently being made. To illustrate, assume that an automobile manufacturer has been purchasing instrument panels for $240 a unit. The factory is currently operating at 80% of capacity, and no major increase in production is expected in the near future. The cost per unit of manufacturing an instrument panel internally, including fixed costs, is estimated as follows:

Direct materials	$ 80
Direct labor	80
Variable factory overhead	52
Fixed factory overhead	68
Total cost per unit	$280

If the *make* price of $280 is simply compared with the *buy* price of $240, the decision is to buy the instrument panel. However, if unused capacity could be used in manufacturing the part, there would be no increase in the total amount of fixed factory overhead costs. Thus, only the variable factory overhead costs need to be considered. The relevant costs are summarized in the differential report in Exhibit 6.

*Differential Analysis
Report—Make or Buy*

Proposal to Manufacture Instrument Panels February 15, 2006		
Purchase price of an instrument panel		$240.00
Differential cost to manufacture:		
Direct materials	$80.00	
Direct labor	80.00	
Variable factory overhead	52.00	212.00
Cost savings from manufacturing an instrument panel		$ 28.00

Other possible effects of a decision to manufacture the instrument panel should also be considered. For example, increasing production in the future could require using the currently idle capacity. This decision could affect employees. It can also affect future business relations with the instrument panel supplier, which could provide other essential parts. The company's decision to manufacture instrument panels could jeopardize the timely delivery of these other parts.

Replace Equipment

The usefulness of fixed assets can be reduced long before they are considered to be worn out. For example, equipment can no longer be efficient for the purpose for which it is used. On the other hand, the equipment could not have reached the point of complete inadequacy. Decisions to replace usable fixed assets should be based on relevant costs. The relevant costs are the future costs of continuing to use the equipment versus replacement. The book values of the fixed assets being replaced are sunk costs and are irrelevant.

To illustrate, assume that a business is considering the disposal of several identical machines having a total book value of $100,000 and an estimated remaining life of five years. The old machines can be sold for $25,000. They can be replaced by a single high-speed machine at a cost of $250,000. The new machine has an estimated useful life of five years and no residual value. Analyses indicate an estimated annual reduction in variable manufacturing costs from $225,000 with the old machine to $150,000 with the new machine. No other changes in the manufacturing costs or the operating expenses are expected. The relevant costs are summarized in the differential report in Exhibit 7.

EXHIBIT 7
Differential Analysis Report—Replace Equipment

Proposal to Replace Equipment November 28, 2006		
Annual variable costs—present equipment	$225,000	
Annual variable costs—new equipment	150,000	
Annual differential decrease in cost	$ 75,000	
Number of years applicable	× 5	
Total differential decrease in cost	$375,000	
Proceeds from sale of present equipment	25,000	$400,000
Cost of new equipment		250,000
Net differential decrease in cost, 5-year total		$150,000
Annual net differential decrease in cost—new equipment		$ 30,000

Other factors are often important in equipment replacement decisions. For example, differences between the remaining useful life of the old equipment and the estimated life of the new equipment could exist. In addition, the new equipment could improve the overall quality of the product, resulting in an increase in sales volume. Additional factors could include the time value of money and other uses for the cash needed to purchase the new equipment.[1]

[1]The importance of the time value of money in equipment replacement decisions is discussed in a later chapter.

The amount of income that is forgone from an alternative use of an asset, such as cash, is called an **opportunity cost**. For example, your opportunity cost of attending school is the income forgone from lost work hours. Although the opportunity cost does not appear as a part of historical accounting data, it is useful in analyzing alternative courses of action. To illustrate, assume that the cash outlay of $250,000 for the new equipment, less the $25,000 proceeds from the sale of the present equipment, could be invested to yield a 10% return. Thus, the annual opportunity cost related to the purchase of the new equipment is $22,500 (10% × $225,000).

Process or Sell

When a product is manufactured, it progresses through various stages of production. Often a product can be sold at an intermediate stage of production, or it can be processed further and then sold. In deciding whether to sell a product at an intermediate stage or to process it further, differential analysis is useful. The differential revenues from further processing are compared to the differential costs of further processing. The costs of producing the intermediate product do not change regardless of whether the intermediate product is sold or processed further. Thus, these costs are not differential costs and are irrelevant to the decision to process further.

To illustrate, assume that a business produces kerosene in batches of 4,000 gallons. Standard amounts of 4,000 gallons of direct materials are processed, which cost $0.60 per gallon. Kerosene can be sold without further processing for $0.80 per gallon. It can be processed further to yield gasoline, which can be sold for $1.25 per gallon. Gasoline requires additional processing costs of $650 per batch, and 20% of the gallons of kerosene will evaporate during production. Exhibit 8 summarizes the differential revenues and costs in deciding whether to process kerosene to produce gasoline.

EXHIBIT 8
Differential Analysis Report—Process or Sell

Proposal to Process Kerosene Further **October 1, 2006**		
Differential revenue from further processing per batch:		
Revenue from sale of gasoline [(4,000 gallons − 800 gallons evaporation) × $1.25]	$4,000	
Revenue from sale of kerosene (4,000 gallons × $0.80)	3,200	
Differential revenue		$800
Differential cost per batch:		
Additional cost of producing gasoline		650
Differential income from further processing gasoline per batch		**$150**

The differential income from further processing kerosene into gasoline is $150 per batch. The initial cost of producing the intermediate kerosene, $2,400 (4,000 gallons × $0.60), is not considered in deciding whether to process kerosene further. This initial cost will be incurred regardless of whether gasoline is produced.

Another example of a differential decision involving further processing is the distribution of movies in a DVD format. After initial release, movie studios must decide whether to "process" movies further by releasing them in DVD format for the home market. Differential revenues and costs that are relevant to making this decision are the copying and packaging costs for the disk, marketing costs associated with promoting the disk, and anticipated revenues from selling the disk. The original movie production costs are not relevant to the decision.

Accept Business at a Special Price

Differential analysis is also useful in deciding whether to accept additional business at a special price. The differential revenue that would be provided from the additional business is compared to the differential costs of producing and delivering the product to the customer. If the company is operating at full capacity, any additional production will increase both fixed and variable production costs. If, however, the normal production of the company is below full capacity, additional business can be undertaken without increasing fixed production costs. In this case, the differential costs of the additional production are the variable manufacturing costs. If operating expenses increase because of the additional business, these expenses should also be considered.

To illustrate, assume that the monthly capacity of a sporting goods business is 12,500 basketballs. Current sales and production are averaging 10,000 basketballs per month. The current manufacturing cost of $20 per unit consists of variable costs of $12.50 and fixed costs of $7.50. The normal selling price of the product in the domestic market is $30. The manufacturer receives an offer from an exporter for 5,000 basketballs at $18 each. Production can be spread over a three-month period without interfering with normal production or incurring overtime costs. Pricing policies in the domestic market will not be affected. Simply comparing the sales price of $18 with the present unit manufacturing cost of $20 indicates that the offer should be rejected. However, by focusing only on the differential cost, which in this case is the variable cost, the decision is different. Exhibit 9 shows the differential analysis report for this decision.

EXHIBIT 9
Differential Analysis Report—Sell at Special Price

Proposal to Sell Basketballs to Exporter	
March 10, 2006	
Differential revenue from accepting offer:	
Revenue from sale of 5,000 additional units at $18	$90,000
Differential cost of accepting offer:	
Variable costs of 5,000 additional units at $12.50	62,500
Differential income from accepting offer	**$27,500**

Proposals to sell a product in the domestic market at prices lower than the normal price can require additional considerations. For example, it could be unwise to increase sales volume in one territory by price reductions if this results in lost sales volume in other areas. Manufacturers must also conform to the Robinson-Patman Act, which prohibits price discrimination within the United States unless differences in prices can be justified by different costs of serving different customers.

BUSINESS STRATEGY

People Make a Difference

Wal-Mart is the world's second largest corporation and is the world's largest private-sector employer in the world. Despite its size, Wal-Mart has stayed true to its small-town roots. Its founder, Sam Walton, set up shop in Bentonville, Arkansas, in 1962 to avoid Kmart and Sears, which dominated larger towns. To attract staff and corporate talent, he offered profit-sharing incentives, including stock options for employees. Sam Walton instilled a paternal feeling in Wal-Mart where employees are called "associates"

and are given a large degree of autonomy. Similarly, suppliers are treated as part of the family once they prove their worth and are given full access to real-time data on how their products are selling, store by store. The result of this "people make a difference" strategy is that in four decades, Wal-Mart has come to account for 60% of America's retail sales and between 7 to 8% of total consumer spending.

Source: Adapted from "Wal Around the World," *The Economist*, December 8, 2001, pp. 55–57.

Setting Normal Product Selling Prices

OBJECTIVE 2

Determine the normal selling price of a product using the total cost concept.

Differential analysis can be useful in deciding to lower selling prices for special short-run decisions, such as whether to accept business at a price lower than the normal price. In such cases, the minimum short-run price is set high enough to cover all variable costs. Any price above this minimum price will improve profits in the short run. In the long run, however, the normal selling price must be set high enough to cover all costs and expenses (both fixed and variable) and provide a reasonable profit. Otherwise, the business could not survive.

The normal selling price can be viewed as the target selling price to be achieved in the long run. The two basic approaches to setting this price are the market and cost-plus approach.

Managers using the market approach refer to the external market to determine the price using either the demand-based or the competition-based methods. Demand-based methods set the price according to the demand for the product. If there is high demand for the product, the price can be set high; lower demand can require the price to be set low. An example of setting different prices according to the demand for the product is found in the telecommunications industry, with low weekend rates and high business day rates for long-distance telephone calls.

Competition-based methods set the price according to the price offered by competitors. For example, if a competitor reduces the price, management can be required to adjust the price to meet the competition. The market-based pricing approaches are discussed in greater detail in marketing courses, so we do not expand on them here.

Managers using the cost-plus approach price the product to achieve a target profit. Managers add to the cost an amount called a **markup** so that all costs plus a profit are included in the selling price. In the following paragraphs, we describe and illustrate the cost-plus approach using the total cost concept. Product cost and variable cost concepts can also be used in applying the cost-plus approach. However, these concepts arrive at the same normal selling price as the total cost concept. For this reason, we describe and illustrate only the total cost concept.

Total Cost Concept

Using the **total cost concept**, all costs of manufacturing a product plus the selling and administrative expenses are included in the cost amount to which the markup is added. Since all costs and expenses are included in the cost amount, the dollar amount of the markup equals the desired profit.

The first step in applying the total cost concept is to determine the total cost of manufacturing the product. This cost includes the costs of direct materials, direct labor, and factory overhead and should be available from the accounting records. The next step is to add the estimated selling and administrative expenses to the total cost of manufacturing the product. The cost amount per unit is then computed by dividing the total costs by the total units expected to be produced and sold.

After the cost amount per unit has been determined, the dollar amount of the markup is determined. For this purpose, the markup is expressed as a percentage of cost. This percentage is then multiplied by the cost amount per unit. The dollar amount of the markup is then added to the cost amount per unit to arrive at the selling price.

The markup percentage for the total cost concept is determined by applying the following formula:

$$\text{Markup percentage} = \frac{\text{Desired profit}}{\text{Total costs}}$$

The numerator of the formula is only the desired profit. This is so because all costs and expenses are included in the cost amount to which the markup is added. The denominator of the formula is the total cost.

To illustrate, assume that the costs for calculators of Digital Solutions Inc. are as follows:

Variable costs:	
Direct materials	$ 3.00 per unit
Direct labor	10.00
Factory overhead	1.50
Selling and administrative expenses	1.50
Total	$16.00 per unit
Fixed costs:	
Factory overhead	$50,000
Selling and administrative expenses	20,000

Digital Solutions Inc. desires a profit equal to a 20% rate of return on assets, $800,000 of assets are devoted to producing calculators, and 100,000 units are expected to be produced and sold. The calculators' total cost is $1,670,000, or $16.70 per unit, computed as follows:

Variable costs ($16.00 × 100,000 units)		$1,600,000
Fixed costs:		
Factory overhead	$50,000	
Selling and administrative expenses	20,000	70,000
Total costs		$1,670,000
Total cost per calculator ($1,670,000/100,000 units)		$16.70

The desired profit is $160,000 (0.20 × $800,000), and the markup percentage for a calculator is 9.6%, computed as follows:

$$\text{Markup percentage} = \frac{\text{Desired profit}}{\text{Total costs}}$$

$$\text{Markup percentage} = \frac{\$160,000}{\$1,670,000} = 9.6\%$$

Based on the total cost per unit and the markup percentage for a calculator, Digital Solutions Inc. would price each calculator at $18.30 per unit as shown here.

Total cost per calculator	$16.70
Markup ($16.70 × 0.096)	1.60
Selling price	$18.30

The ability of the selling price of $18.30 to generate the desired profit of $160,000 is shown by the following income statement:

DIGITAL SOLUTIONS INC.
Income Statement
For the Year Ended December 31, 2006

Sales (100,000 units × $18.30)		$1,830,000
Expenses:		
Variable (100,000 units × $16.00)	$1,600,000	
Fixed ($50,000 + $20,000)	70,000	1,670,000
Income from operations		$ 160,000

The total cost concept of applying the cost-plus approach to product pricing is often used by contractors who sell products to government agencies. In many cases, government contractors are required by law to be reimbursed for their products on a total-cost-plus-profit basis.

A variation of the total cost concept discussed in the preceding paragraphs is the **target cost concept**. Under this concept, which was first used by the Japanese, the selling price is assumed to be set by the marketplace. The target cost is determined by *subtracting* a desired profit from the selling price. Thus, managers must design and manufacture the product to achieve its target cost. In contrast, the total cost concept discussed previously starts with a given product cost and *adds* a markup to determine the selling price. Some argue that the target cost concept could be better than the cost-plus approaches in highly competitive markets that require continual product cost reductions to remain competitive.

Activity-Based Costing

As illustrated in the preceding paragraphs, costs are important considerations in setting product prices. To more accurately measure the costs of producing and selling products, some companies use activity-based costing. **Activity-based costing** (ABC) identifies and traces activities to specific products.

Activity-based costing can be useful in making product-pricing decisions when manufacturing operations involve large amounts of factory overhead. In such cases, traditional overhead allocation using activity bases such as units produced or machine hours can yield inaccurate cost allocations. This, in turn, can result in distorted product costs and product prices. By providing more accurate product cost allocations, activity-based costing aids in setting product prices that will cover costs and expenses.

Product Profitability and Pricing under Production Bottlenecks

OBJECTIVE   3

Calculate the relative profitability of products in bottleneck production environments.

An important consideration influencing production volumes and prices is the production bottleneck. A production **bottleneck** (or **constraint**) occurs at the point in the process where the demand for the company's product exceeds the ability to produce the product. The **theory of constraints (TOC)** is a manufacturing strategy that focuses on reducing the influence of bottlenecks on a process.

Product Profitability under Production Bottlenecks

The sand in the hourglass can pass only as fast as the narrowest point in the glass will allow.

Bottleneck

When a company has a bottleneck in its production process, it should attempt to maximize its profitability subject to the influence of the bottleneck. To illustrate, assume that Snapp-Off Tool Company makes three types of wrenches: small, medium, and large. All three products are processed through a heat treatment operation, which hardens the steel tools. Snapp-Off Tool's heat treatment process is operating at full capacity and is a production bottleneck. The product contribution margin per unit and the number of hours of heat treatment used by each type of wrench are as follows:

	Small Wrench	Medium Wrench	Large Wrench
Sales price per unit	$130	$140	$160
Variable cost per unit	40	40	40
Contribution margin per unit	$ 90	$100	$120
Heat treatment hours per unit	1	4	8

The large wrench appears to be the most profitable product because its contribution margin per unit is the highest. However, the contribution margin per unit can be a misleading indicator of profitability in a bottleneck operation. The correct measure of performance is the value of each bottleneck hour, or the contribution margin per bottleneck hour. Using this measure, each product has a much different profitability when compared to the contribution margin per unit information, as shown in Exhibit 10.

EXHIBIT 10

Contribution Margin per Bottleneck Hour

	Small Wrench	Medium Wrench	Large Wrench
Sales price	$130	$140	$160
Variable cost per unit	40	40	40
Contribution margin per unit	$ 90	$100	$120
Bottleneck (heat treatment) hours per unit	÷ 1	÷ 4	÷ 8
Contribution margin per bottleneck hour	$ 90	$ 25	$ 15

The small wrench produces the most contribution margin per bottleneck (heat treatment) hour used, and the large wrench produces the smallest profit per bottleneck hour. Thus, the small wrench is the most profitable product. This information is the opposite of that implied by the unit contribution margin profit.

Product Pricing under Production Bottlenecks

Each hour of a bottleneck delivers profit to the company. When a company has a production bottleneck, the contribution margin per hour of bottleneck provides a measure of the product's relative profitability. This information can also be used to adjust the product price to better reflect the value of the product's use of a bottleneck. Products that use a large number of bottleneck hours per unit require more contribution margin than products that use few bottleneck hours per unit. For example, Snapp-Off Tool Company should increase the price of the large wrench in order to deliver more contribution margin per bottleneck hour.

To determine the price of the large wrench that would equate its profitability to the small wrench, we need to solve the following equation:

$$\text{\textbf{Contribution margin per bottleneck hour per small wrench}} = \frac{\text{\textbf{Revised price of large wrench} $-$ \textbf{Variable cost per large wrench}}}{\text{\textbf{Bottleneck hours per large wrench}}}$$

$$\$90 = \frac{\text{Revised price of large wrench} - \$40}{8}$$

$$\$720 = \text{Revised price of large wrench} - \$40$$

$$\$760 = \text{Revised price of large wrench}$$

The large wrench's price needs to be increased to $760 to deliver the same contribution margin per bottleneck hour as does the small wrench, as verified on the next page.

Revised price of large wrench	$760
Less: Variable cost per unit of large wrench	40
Contribution margin per unit of large wrench	$720
Bottleneck hours per unit of large wrench	÷ 8
Revised contribution margin per bottleneck hour	$ 90

At a price of $760, the company would be indifferent between producing and selling the small wrench or the large wrench, all else being equal. This analysis assumes that there is unlimited demand for the products. If the market were unwilling to purchase the large wrench at this price, the company should produce the small wrench.

Latrobe Steel Division of **Timken Company** originally used total cost plus a markup to price its steel products. However, Latrobe discovered that one of its machines was a bottleneck in its operation. It recalculated the profitability of its products based on the contribution margin per hour of constraint. The results showed that some products that had appeared only marginally profitable had, in fact, a high contribution margin per bottleneck hour. This analysis caused Latrobe management to change the product mix in favor of products with high contribution margins per constraint hour. Management estimated that these changes improved income from operations by 20%.

Key Points

1. Prepare a differential analysis report for decisions involving

- Leasing or selling equipment.
- Discontinuing an unprofitable segment.
- Manufacturing or purchasing a needed part.
- Replacing usable fixed assets.
- Processing further or selling an intermediate product.
- Accepting additional business at a special price.

Differential analysis reports for leasing or selling, discontinuing a segment or product, making or buying, replacing equipment, processing or selling, and accepting business at a special price are illustrated in the text. Each analysis focuses on the differential revenues and/or costs of the alternative courses of action.

2. Determine the selling price of a product using the total cost concept.

The total cost concept of applying the cost-plus approach adds a desired profit to the total costs to determine the normal selling price. The markup percentage used in applying the total cost concept is as follows:

$$\text{Markup percentage} = \frac{\text{Desired profit}}{\text{Total costs}}$$

3. Calculate the relative profitability of products in bottleneck production environments.

The profitability of a product in a bottleneck production environment is perhaps not accurately shown in the contribution margin product report. Instead, the best measure of profitability is determined by dividing the contribution margin per unit by the bottleneck hours per unit. The resulting measure indicates the product's profitability per hour of bottleneck use. This information can be used to support product pricing decisions.

Glossary

Activity-based costing: A cost allocation method that identifies activities causing the incurrence of costs and allocates these costs to products (or other cost objects) based on activity drivers (bases).

Bottleneck: A condition that occurs when product demand exceeds production capacity.

Differential analysis: The area of accounting concerned with the effect of alternative courses of action on revenues and costs.

Differential cost: The amount of increase or decrease in cost expected from a particular course of action compared with an alternative.

Differential revenue: The amount of increase or decrease in revenue expected from a particular course of action as compared with an alternative.

Markup: An amount that is added to a "cost" amount to determine product price.

Opportunity cost: The amount of income forgone from an alternative to a proposed use of cash or its equivalent.

Sunk cost: A cost that is not affected by subsequent decisions.

Target cost concept: A concept used to design and manufacture a product at a cost that will deliver a target profit for a given market-determined price.

Theory of constraints (TOC): A manufacturing strategy that attempts to remove the influence of bottlenecks (constraints) on a process.

Total cost concept: A concept used in applying the cost-plus approach to product pricing in which all the costs of manufacturing the product plus the selling and administrative expenses are included in the cost amount to which the markup is added.

Self–Study Questions

(Answers appear at end of chapter.)

1. Marlo Company is considering discontinuing a product. The costs of the product consist of $20,000 fixed costs and $15,000 variable costs. The variable operating expenses related to the product total $4,000. What is the differential cost?

   A. $19,000   C. $35,000
   B. $15,000   D. $39,000

2. Victor Company is considering disposing of equipment that was originally purchased for $200,000 and has $150,000 of accumulated depreciation to date. The same equipment would cost $310,000 to replace. What is the sunk cost?

   A. $50,000   C. $200,000
   B. $150,000   D. $310,000

3. Henry Company is considering spending $100,000 for a new grinding machine. This amount could be invested to yield a 12% return. What is the opportunity cost?

   A. $112,000   C. $12,000
   B. $88,000   D. $100,000

4. James Company uses the total cost concept in applying the cost-plus approach to product pricing. James Company desires a profit equal to a 20% rate of return on invested assets of $600,000. The costs of producing and selling 5,000 units of Product X are as follows:

Fixed costs:	
Factory overhead	$80,000
Selling and admn. exp.	25,000

Variable costs:	
Direct materials	$35
Direct labor	25
Factory overhead	12
Selling and admn. exp.	3

   What is the markup percentage for Product X?

   A. 20%   C. 42.6%
   B. 25%   D. 60%

5. Mendosa Company produces three products. All of the products use a furnace operation, which is a production bottleneck. The following information is available:

	Product 1	Product 2	Product 3
Unit volume—March	1,000	1,500	1,000
Per unit information:			
Sales price	$35	$33	$29
Variable cost	15	15	15
Contribution margin	$20	$18	$14
Furnace hours	4	3	2

   From a profitability perspective, which product should be emphasized in April's advertising campaign?

   A. Product 1   C. Product 3
   B. Product 2   D. All three

Discussion Questions

1. Explain the meaning of (a) differential revenue, (b) differential cost, and (c) differential income.

2. It was recently reported that **Exabyte**, a fast-growing (100-fold in 4 years) Colorado marketer of tape drives, has decided to purchase key components of its product from others. For example, **Sony** provides Exabyte with mechanical decks, and **Solectron** provides circuit boards. Exabyte's chief executive officer, Peter Behrendt, states, "If we'd tried to build our own plants, we could never have grown that fast or maybe survived." The decision to purchase key product components is an example of what type of decision illustrated in this chapter?

3. In the long run, the normal selling price must be set high enough to cover what factors?

4. What are the two primary approaches of setting prices?

5. What cost concept of applying the cost-plus approach to product pricing is illustrated in this chapter?

6. In using the total cost concept of applying the cost-plus approach to product pricing, what factors are included in the markup?

7. The total cost concept used in applying the cost-plus approach to product pricing includes what costs in the cost amount to which the markup is added?

8. In determining the markup percentage for the total cost concept of applying the cost-plus approach, what is included in the numerator?

9. Why could the use of ideal standards in applying the cost-plus approach to product pricing lead to setting product prices that are too low?

10. Although the cost-plus approach to product pricing can be used by management as a general guideline, what are some examples of other factors that managers should also consider in setting product prices?

11. What method of determining product cost can be appropriate in settings with a complex manufacturing process?

12. How does the target cost concept differ from cost-plus approaches?

13. What is a production bottleneck?

14. What is the appropriate measure of a product's value when a firm is operating under production bottlenecks?

Exercises

EXERCISE 12–1
Lease or sell decision
OBJECTIVE 1

✓ a. Differential revenue from lease, $14,000

Miller Construction Company is considering selling excess machinery with a book value of $250,000 (original cost of $375,000 less accumulated depreciation of $125,000) for $220,000 less a 5% brokerage commission. Alternatively, the machinery can be leased for a total of $234,000 for five years, after which it is expected to have no residual value. During the period of the lease, Miller Construction Company's costs of repairs, insurance, and property tax expenses are expected to be $23,000.

a. Prepare a differential analysis report, dated January 3, 2006, for the lease or sell decision.
b. On the basis of the data presented, is it advisable to lease or sell the machinery? Explain.

EXERCISE 12–2
Differential analysis report for a discontinued product
OBJECTIVE 1

✓ a. Differential cost of annual sales, $285,000

A condensed income statement by product line for Fresh Kola Co. indicated the following for Diet Kola for the past year:

Sales	$350,000
Cost of goods sold	225,000
Gross profit	$125,000
Operating expenses	140,000
Loss from operations	$ (15,000)

It is estimated that 20% of the cost of goods sold represents fixed factory overhead costs and that 25% of the operating expenses are fixed. Since Diet Kola is only one of many products, the fixed costs will not be materially affected if the product is discontinued.

a. Prepare a differential analysis report, dated January 3, 2006, for the proposed discontinuance of Diet Kola.
b. Should Diet Kola be retained? Explain.

EXERCISE 12–3
Differential analysis report for a discontinued product
OBJECTIVE 1

✓ a. Differential income: bowls, $48,880

The condensed product-line income statement for Bold Ceramics Company for the current year is as follows:

BOLD CERAMICS COMPANY
Product-Line Income Statement
For the Year Ended December 31, 2006

	Bowls	Plates	Cups
Sales	$150,000	$160,000	$125,000
Cost of goods sold	96,000	84,000	85,000
Gross profit	$ 54,000	$ 76,000	$ 40,000
Selling and administrative expenses	32,000	52,000	48,000
Income from operations	$ 22,000	$ 24,000	$ (8,000)

Fixed costs are 18% of the cost of goods sold and 30% of the selling and administrative expenses. Bold Ceramics assumes that fixed costs would not be materially affected if the Cups line were discontinued.

a. Prepare a differential analysis report for all three products for the current year.
b. Should the cups line be retained? Explain.

EXERCISE 12–4
Segment analysis
OBJECTIVE 1

The **Charles Schwab Corporation** is one of the more innovative brokerage and financial service companies in the United States. The company recently provided information about its major business segments as follows:

	Individual Investor	Institutional Investor	Capital Markets
Revenues	$1,955,186	$444,685	$336,350
Income from operations	402,150	92,842	81,552
Depreciation	102,903	21,115	14,459

a. How do you believe Schwab defines the difference between the Individual Investor and Institutional Investor segments?
b. Provide a specific example of a variable and fixed cost in the Individual Investor segment.
c. Estimate the contribution margin for each segment.
d. If Schwab decided to sell its Institutional Investor accounts to another company, estimate how much operating income would decline.

EXERCISE 12–5
Decision to discontinue a product
OBJECTIVE 1

On the basis of the following data, the general manager of Sole Mates Inc. decided to discontinue the Children's Shoes segment because it reduced income from operations by $20,000. What is the flaw in this decision?

SOLE MATES INC.
Product-Line Income Statement
For the Year Ended August 31, 2003

	Children's Shoes	Men's Shoes	Women's Shoes	Total
Sales	$105,000	$300,000	$500,000	$905,000
Costs of goods sold:				
Variable costs	$ 70,000	$150,000	$220,000	$440,000
Fixed costs	20,000	60,000	120,000	200,000
Total cost of goods sold	$ 90,000	$210,000	$340,000	$640,000
Gross profit	$ 15,000	$ 90,000	$160,000	$265,000
Operating expenses:				
Variable expenses	$ 28,000	$ 45,000	$ 95,000	$168,000
Fixed expenses	7,000	20,000	25,000	52,000
Total operating expenses	$ 35,000	$ 65,000	$120,000	$220,000
Income (loss) from operations	$(20,000)	$ 25,000	$ 40,000	$ 45,000

EXERCISE 12-6
Make or buy decision
OBJECTIVE 1

✓ a. Cost savings from making, $2.50 per case

Quick Computer Company has been purchasing carrying cases for its portable computers at a delivered cost of $35 per unit. The company, which is currently operating below full capacity, charges factory overhead to production at the rate of 40% of direct materials cost. The costs to produce comparable carrying cases are expected to be $18 per unit for direct materials and $10 per unit for direct labor. If Quick Computer Company manufactures the carrying cases, fixed factory overhead costs will not increase and variable factory overhead costs associated with the cases are expected to be 25% of the direct materials costs.

a. Prepare a differential analysis report, dated June 5, 2006, for the make or buy decision.
b. On the basis of the data presented, would it be advisable to make or to continue buying the carrying cases? Explain.

EXERCISE 12-7
Machine replacement decision
OBJECTIVE 1

✓ a. Annual differential income, $5,000

A company is considering replacing an old piece of machinery, which cost $500,000 and has $300,000 of accumulated depreciation to date, with a new machine that costs $450,000. The old equipment could be sold for $120,000. The variable production costs associated with the old machine are estimated to be $150,000 for 6 years. The variable production costs for the new machine are estimated to be $90,000 for 6 years.

a. Determine the differential annual income or loss from replacing the old machine.
b. What is the sunk cost in this situation?

EXERCISE 12-8
Differential analysis report for machine replacement
OBJECTIVE 1

✓ a. Annual differential increase in costs, $3,000

Custom Electronics Company assembles circuit boards by using a manually operated machine to insert electronic components. The original cost of the machine is $150,000, the accumulated depreciation is $110,000, its remaining useful life is 10 years, and its salvage value is negligible. On January 20, 2006, a proposal was made to replace the present manufacturing procedure with a fully automatic machine that will cost $350,000. The automatic machine has an estimated useful life of 10 years and no significant salvage value. For use in evaluating the proposal, the accountant accumulated the following annual data on present and proposed operations:

	Present Operations	Proposed Operations
Sales	$365,000	$365,000
Direct materials	108,000	108,000
Direct labor	59,800	—
Power and maintenance	7,500	32,800
Taxes, insurance, etc.	4,500	7,000
Selling and administrative expenses	65,000	65,000

a. Prepare a differential analysis report for the proposal to replace the machine. Include in the analysis both the net differential change in costs anticipated over the 10 years and the net annual differential change in costs anticipated.

b. Based only on the data presented, should the proposal be accepted?

c. What are some of the other factors that should be considered before a final decision is made?

EXERCISE 12-9
Decision on accepting additional business
OBJECTIVE 1

✓ a. Differential income, $36,000

American Leisure Wear Co. has an annual plant capacity of 60,000 units, and current production is 45,000 units. Monthly fixed costs are $30,000, and variable costs are $29 per unit. The present selling price is $45 per unit. On January 18, 2006, the company received an offer from Barker Company for 12,000 units of the product at $32 each. Barker Company will market the units in a foreign country under its own brand name. The additional business is not expected to affect the domestic selling price or number of sales of American Leisure Wear Co.

a. Prepare a differential analysis report for the proposed sale to Barker Company.

b. Briefly explain the reason that accepting this additional business will increase operating income.

c. What is the minimum price per unit that would produce a contribution margin?

EXERCISE 12-10
Sell or process further
OBJECTIVE 1

✓ a. $220

Hyde Lumber Company incurs a cost of $425 per hundred board feet in processing certain rough-cut lumber, which it sells for $610 per hundred board feet. An alternative is to produce finished-cut lumber at a total processing cost of $550 per hundred board feet, which can be sold for $830 per hundred board feet. For these alternatives, what is the amount of (a) the differential revenue, (b) differential cost, and (c) differential income?

EXERCISE 12-11
Sell or process further
OBJECTIVE 1

✓ c. $9.95

Star Coffee Company produces Columbian coffee in batches of 8,000 pounds, which represent the standard amount of materials required in the process. The cost is $5.00 per pound. Columbian coffee can be sold without further processing for $8.40 per pound. Columbian coffee can also be processed further to yield decaf Columbian, which can be sold for $9.60 per pound. The processing into decaf Columbian requires additional processing costs of $8,420 per batch. The additional processing will also cause a 5% loss of product due to evaporation.

a. Prepare a differential analysis report for the decision to sell or process further.

b. Should Star sell Columbian coffee or process further and sell decaf Columbian?

c. Determine the price of Decaf Columbian that would cause neither an advantage or disadvantage for processing further and selling decaf Columbian.

EXERCISE 12-12
Accepting business at a special price
OBJECTIVE 1

First Light Company expects to operate at 90% of productive capacity during May. The total manufacturing costs for May for the production of 20,000 batteries are budgeted as follows:

Direct materials	$146,000
Direct labor	65,000
Variable factory overhead	29,000
Fixed factory overhead	60,000
Total manufacturing costs	$300,000

The company has an opportunity to submit a bid for 1,000 batteries to be delivered by May 31 to a government agency. If the contract is obtained, it is anticipated that the additional activity will not interfere with normal production during May or increase the selling or administrative expenses. What is the unit cost below which First Light Company should not go in bidding on the government contract?

EXERCISE 12–13
Total cost concept of product costing
OBJECTIVE 2

✓ d. $350

ClearTalk Company uses the total cost concept of applying the cost-plus approach to product pricing. The costs of producing and selling 4,000 units of mobile phones are as follows:

Variable costs:			Fixed costs:	
Direct materials	$150.00	per unit	Factory overhead	$200,000
Direct labor	45.00		Selling and adm. exp.	100,000
Factory overhead	25.00			
Selling and adm. exp.	30.00			
Total	$250.00	per unit		

ClearTalk Company desires a profit equal to a 25% rate of return on invested assets of $400,000.

a. Determine the amount of desired profit from the production and sale of mobile phones.
b. Determine the total costs and the cost amount per unit for the production and sale of 4,000 units of mobile phones.
c. Determine the markup percentage (rounded to one decimal) for mobile phones.
d. Determine the selling price of mobile phones. Round to the nearest dollar.

EXERCISE 12–14
Total cost concept of product costing
OBJECTIVES 1, 2

✓ a. $500 gain

Assume that ClearTalk Company received an offer to sell 100 mobile phones to an agency of the state government for $225 each. No selling and administrative expenses will be incurred with the sale, and phones can be produced using existing capacity. Based on the data presented in Exercise 12-13, answer the following questions:

a. What is the differential gain or loss on the sale?
b. Should ClearTalk accept the offer?

EXERCISE 12–15
Target cost concept
OBJECTIVE 2

Toyota Motor Corporation uses the target cost concept. Assume that Toyota marketing personnel estimate that the selling price for the Camry in the upcoming model year will need to be $32,000 to be competitive. Assume further that the Camry's total manufacturing cost for the upcoming model year is estimated to be $26,000 and that Toyota requires a 20% profit margin on selling price (which is equivalent to a 25% markup on product cost).

a. What price will Toyota establish for the Camry for the upcoming model year?
b. What impact will the target cost concept have on Toyota, given the assumed information?

EXERCISE 12–16
Product decisions under bottlenecked operations
OBJECTIVE 3

✓ a. Total income from operations, $106,000

Blue Glass Company manufactures three types of safety plate glass: large, medium, and small. All three products have high demand. Thus, Blue Glass is able to sell all the safety glass that it can make. The production process includes an autoclave operation, which is a pressurized heat treatment. The autoclave is a production bottleneck. Fixed costs are $450,000. In addition, the following information is available about the three products:

	Large	Medium	Small
Sales price per unit	$230	$190	$120
Variable cost per unit	122	85	55
Contribution margin per unit	$108	$105	$ 65
Autoclave hours per unit	12	15	10
Total process hours per unit	30	25	22
Budgeted units of production	2,000	2,000	2,000

a. Determine the contribution margin by glass type and the total company income from operations for the budgeted units of production.
b. Prepare an analysis showing which product is the most profitable per bottleneck hour.

EXERCISE 12–17
Product pricing under
bottlenecked operations
OBJECTIVE 3

✓ Medium, $220

Based on the data presented in Exercise 12-16, assume that Blue Glass wanted to price all products so that they produced the same profit potential as the highest profit product. What would be the prices of all three products that would produce the largest profit?

Problems

PROBLEM 12 | 1
Differential analysis
report involving
opportunity costs
OBJECTIVE 1

✓ 3. $1,150,000

On July 1, Venus Stores Inc. is considering leasing a building and purchasing the necessary equipment to operate a retail store. The project would be financed by selling $800,000 of 9% U.S. Treasury bonds that mature in 18 years. The bonds were purchased at face value and are currently selling at face value. The following data have been assembled:

Cost of store equipment	$800,000
Life of store equipment	18 years
Estimated residual value of store equipment	$150,000
Yearly costs to operate the store, excluding	
depreciation of store equipment	$ 90,000
Yearly expected revenues—years 1–9	$260,000
Yearly expected revenues—years 10–18	$120,000

Instructions

1. Prepare a report as of July 1, 2006, presenting a differential analysis of the proposed operation of the store for the 18 years as compared with present conditions.
2. Based on the results disclosed by the differential analysis, should the proposal be accepted?
3. If the proposal is accepted, what would be the total estimated income from operations of the store for the 18 years?

PROBLEM 12 | 2
Differential analysis
report for machine
replacement decision
OBJECTIVE 1

Iowa Printing Company is considering replacing a machine that has been used in its factory for 2 years. Relevant data associated with the operations of the old machine and the new machine, neither of which has any estimated residual value, are as follows:

Old Machine

Cost of machine, 10-year life	$450,000
Annual depreciation (straight line)	45,000
Annual manufacturing costs, excluding depreciation	420,000
Annual nonmanufacturing operating expenses	265,000
Annual revenue	850,000
Current estimated selling price	220,000

New Machine

Cost of machine, 8-year life	$780,000
Annual depreciation (straight line)	97,500
Estimated annual manufacturing costs, exclusive of depreciation	300,000

Annual nonmanufacturing operating expenses and revenue are not expected to be affected by purchase of the new machine.

Instructions

1. Prepare a differential analysis report as of August 11, 2006, comparing operations utilizing the new machine with operations using the present equipment. The analysis should indicate the total differential income that would result over the 8-year period if the new machine is acquired.
2. List other factors that should be considered before a final decision is reached.

PROBLEM 12 | 3

Differential analysis report for sales promotion proposal

OBJECTIVE 1

✓ 1. Cologne differential income, $110,000

Rose Cosmetics Company is planning a one-month campaign for May to promote sales of one of its two cosmetics products. A total of $50,000 has been budgeted for advertising, contests, redeemable coupons, and other promotional activities. The following data have been assembled for their possible usefulness in deciding which of the products to select for the campaign:

	Cologne	Perfume
Unit selling price	$45	$55
Unit production costs:		
Direct materials	$ 9	$14
Direct labor	6	8
Variable factory overhead	4	4
Fixed factory overhead	5	2
Total unit production costs	$24	$28
Unit variable selling expenses	10	16
Unit fixed selling expenses	3	1
Total unit costs	$37	$45
Operating income per unit	$ 8	$10

No increase in facilities would be necessary to produce and sell the increased output. It is anticipated that 10,000 additional units of cologne or 10,500 additional units of perfume could be sold without changing the unit selling price of either product.

Instructions

1. Prepare a differential analysis report as of April 5, 2006, presenting the additional revenue and additional costs anticipated from the promotion of cologne and perfume.
2. The sales manager had tentatively decided to promote perfume, estimating that operating income would be increased by $55,000 ($10 operating income per unit for 10,500 units, less promotion expenses of $50,000). The manager also believed that the selection of cologne would increase operating income by only $30,000 ($8 operating income per unit for 10,000 units, less promotion expenses of $50,000). State briefly your reasons for supporting or opposing the tentative decision.

PROBLEM 12 | 4

Differential analysis report for further processing

OBJECTIVE 1

✓ Differential revenue, $4,500

The management of Sweet Sugar Company is considering whether to process raw sugar further into refined sugar. Refined sugar can be sold for $1.50 per pound, and raw sugar can be sold without further processing for $0.90 per pound. Raw sugar is produced in batches of 15,000 pounds by processing 18,000 pounds of sugar cane, which costs $0.20 per pound. Refined sugar will require additional processing costs of $0.25 per pound of raw sugar, and 1.25 pounds of raw sugar will produce 1 pound of refined sugar.

Instructions

1. Prepare a report as of May 30, 2006, presenting a differential analysis of the further processing of raw sugar to produce refined sugar.
2. Briefly report your recommendations.

PROBLEM 12 | 5

Product pricing using the cost-plus approach; differential analysis report for accepting additional business

OBJECTIVES 1, 2

✓ 2. (b) markup percentage, 5%

Presentation Labs Inc. recently began production of a new product, flat panel displays, which required the investment of $2,500,000 in assets. The costs of producing and selling 20,000 units of flat panel displays are estimated as follows:

Variable costs per unit:	
Direct materials	$210
Direct labor	40
Factory overhead	50
Selling and administrative expenses	20
Total	$320
Fixed costs:	
Factory overhead	$1,200,000
Selling and administrative expenses	400,000

Presentation Labs Inc. is currently considering the establishment of a selling price for flat panel displays. The president of Presentation Labs has decided to use the cost-plus approach to product pricing and has indicated that the displays must earn a 16% rate of return on invested assets.

Instructions

1. Determine the amount of desired profit from the production and sale of flat panel displays.
2. Using the total cost concept, determine (a) the cost amount per unit, (b) the markup percentage, and (c) the selling price of flat panel displays.
3. Comment on any additional considerations that could influence establishing the selling price for flat panel displays.
4. Assume that as of September 1, 2006, 12,000 units of flat panel displays have been produced and sold during the current year. Analysis of the domestic market indicates that 5,000 additional units are expected to be sold during the remainder of the year at the normal product price determined under the total cost concept. On September 3, Presentation Labs Inc. received an offer from Kane Company for 3,000 units of flat panel displays at $280 each. Kane Company will market the units in Canada under its own brand name, and no additional selling and administrative expenses associated with the sale will be incurred by Presentation Labs Inc. The additional business is not expected to affect the domestic sales of flat panel displays, and the additional units could be produced using existing capacity.
   a. Prepare a differential analysis report of the proposed sale to Kane Company.
   b. Based on the differential analysis report in (a), should the proposal be accepted?

PROBLEM 12 | 6

Product pricing and profit analysis with bottleneck operations

OBJECTIVES 1, 3

✓ 3. High grade price, $475

Indy Valley Steel Company produces three grades of steel: high, good, and regular. Each of these products (grades) has high demand in the market, and Indy Valley is able to sell as much as it can produce of all three. The furnace operation is a bottleneck in the process and is running at 100% of capacity. Indy Valley is attempting to determine how to improve profitability for the steel operations. The variable conversion cost is $5 per process hour. The fixed cost is $1,560,000. In addition, the cost analyst was able to determine the following information about the three products:

	High Grade	Good Grade	Regular Grade
Budgeted units produced	5,000	5,000	5,000
Total process hours per unit	15	15	12
Furnace hours per unit	10	8	6
Price per unit	$400	$370	$346
Direct materials cost per unit	$140	$135	$130

The furnace operation is part of the total process for each of these three products. So, for example, 10 of the 15 hours required to process high grade steel are associated with the furnace.

Instructions

1. Determine the contribution margin per unit for each product.
2. Provide an analysis to determine the relative product profitabilities, assuming that the furnace is a bottleneck.
3. Assume that management wishes to improve profitability by increasing prices on selected products. At what price would high and good grades need to be offered to produce the same relative profitability as regular grade steel?

Activities

Activity 12-1
Product pricing

Marcia Sanchez is a cost accountant for Hall Enterprises. Jan Foster, vice-president of marketing, has asked Marcia to meet with representatives of Hall's major competitor to discuss product cost data. Foster indicates that the sharing of these data will enable Hall to determine a fair and equitable price for its products.

Would it be ethical for Sanchez to attend the meeting and share the relevant cost data?

Activity 12-2
Decision on accepting additional business

A manager of Winner's Sporting Goods Company is considering accepting an order from an overseas customer. This customer has requested an order for 20,000 dozen golf balls at a price of $10 per dozen. The variable cost to manufacture a dozen golf balls is $8 per dozen. The full cost is $12 per dozen. Winner's has a normal selling price of $18 per dozen. The Winner's plant has just enough excess capacity on the second shift to make the overseas order.

What are some considerations in accepting or rejecting this order?

Activity 12-3
Accept business at a special price

If you are not familiar with **priceline.com**, go to its Web site. Assume that an individual bids $50 on priceline.com for a room in Dallas, Texas, on August 24. Assume that August 24 is a Saturday, with low expected room demand in Dallas at a **Marriott Hotel**, so there is room capacity expected. The fully allocated cost per room per day is assumed from hotel records as follows:

Housekeeping labor cost*	$25
Hotel depreciation expense	27
Cost of room supplies (soap, paper, etc.)	5
Laundry labor and material cost*	10
Cost of desk staff	4
Utility cost (mostly air conditioning)	3
Total cost per room per day	$74

*Both housekeeping and laundry staff include many part-time workers, so that workload can be matched to demand.

Should Marriott accept the customer bid for a night in Dallas on August 24 at a price of $50?

Activity 12-4
Product profitability with production constraints

Rich Company produces glass products for the automobile industry. The company produces three types of products: small, medium, and large windows. One of the process steps in glass making involves a furnace operation. Presently, the furnace runs 24 hours per day, 7 days per week. The following per-unit information is available about the three major product lines:

	Small Window	**Medium Window**	**Large Window**
Sales price	$14.00	$24.00	$32.00
Variable cost	6.00	14.00	18.00
Contribution margin	$ 8.00	$10.00	$14.00
Furnace hours	2	4	5

The product manager of Rich Company believes that the company should increase incremental sales effort on the large window since the contribution margin per unit is the highest.

Respond to this suggestion. What recommendations would you suggest to improve profitability?

Activity 12-5
Make or buy decision

The president of Red Hawk Company, Jason Sheppard, asked the controller, Gil Adkins, to provide an analysis of a make versus buy decision for material TS-101. The material is presently processed in Red Hawk's Roanoke facility. TS-101 is used in processing of final products in the facility. Adkins determined the following unit production costs for the material as of March 15, 2006:

Unit Production Costs

Direct materials	$ 6.70
Direct labor	2.50
Variable factory overhead	1.20
Fixed factory overhead	2.00
Total production costs per unit	$12.40

In addition, material TS-101 requires special hazardous material handling. This special handling adds an additional cost of $1.40 for each unit produced.

Material TS-101 can be purchased from an overseas supplier. The supplier does not presently do business with Red Hawk Company. This supplier promises monthly delivery of the material at a price of $9.00 per unit, plus transportation cost of $0.40 per unit. In addition, Red Hawk would need to incur additional administrative costs to satisfy import regulations for hazardous material handling. These additional administrative costs are estimated to be $0.80 per purchased unit. Each purchased unit would also require special hazardous material handling of $1.40 per unit.

a. Prepare a differential analysis report to support Adkins' recommendation on whether to continue making material TS-101 or whether to purchase the material from the overseas supplier.
b. What additional considerations should Adkins address in the recommendation?

Activity 12-6
Cost-plus and target costing concepts

The following conversation took place between Adam Myers, vice-president of marketing, and Jane Jacoby, controller of Francois Computer Company:

Adam: I am really excited about our new computer coming out. I think it will be a real market success.

Jane: I'm really glad you think so. I know that our price is one variable that will determine if it's a success. If our price is too high, our competitors will be the ones with the market success.

Adam: Don't worry about it. We'll just mark up our product cost by 25% and it will all work out. I know we'll make money at those markups. By the way, what does the estimated product cost look like?

Jane: Well, there's the rub. The product cost looks as if it's going to come in at around $2,400. With a 25% markup, that will give us a selling price of $3,000.

Adam: I see your concern. That's a little high. Our research indicates that computer prices are dropping by about 20% per year and that this type of computer should be selling for around $2,500 when we release it to the market.

Jane: I'm not sure what to do.

Adam: Let me see if I can help. How much of the $2,400 is fixed cost?

Jane: About $400.

Adam: There you go. The fixed cost is sunk. We don't need to consider it in our pricing decision. If we reduce the product cost by $400, the new price with a 25% markup would be right at $2,500. Boy, I was really worried for a minute there. I knew something wasn't right.

a. If you were Jane, how would you respond to Adam's solution to the pricing problem?
b. How might target costing be used to help solve this pricing dilemma?

Activity 12-7
Internet marketing

G R O U P

Many businesses are offering their products and services over the Internet. Some of these companies and their Internet addresses follow.

Company Name	Internet Address (URL)	Product
Delta Air Lines	http://www.delta.com	airline tickets
Amazon.com, Inc.	http://www.amazon.com	books
Dell Computer Company	http://www.dell.com	personal computers

a. In groups of three, assign each person in your group to one of these Internet sites. For each site, determine the following:
   1. A product (or service) description.
   2. A product price.
   3. A list of costs that are required to produce and sell the product selected in (1).
   4. Whether the costs identified in (3) are fixed costs or variable costs.
b. Which of the three products do you believe has the largest markup on variable cost?

Answers to Self-Study Questions

1. **A** Differential cost is the amount of increase or decrease in cost that is expected from a particular course of action compared with an alternative. For Marlo Company, the differential cost is $19,000 (answer A). This is the total of the variable product costs ($15,000) and the variable operating expenses ($4,000), which would not be incurred if the product is discontinued.

2. **A** A sunk cost is not affected by later decisions. For Victor Company, the sunk cost is the $50,000 (answer A) book value of the equipment, which is equal to the original cost of $200,000 (answer C) less the accumulated depreciation of $150,000 (answer B).

3. **C** The amount of income that could have been earned from the best available alternative to a proposed

use of cash is the opportunity cost. For Henry Company, the opportunity cost is 12% of $100,000, or $12,000 (answer C).

4. **B** The markup percentage for Product X is 25% (answer B) determined as follows:

$$\text{Markup percentage} = \frac{\text{Desired profit}}{\text{Total costs}}$$

$$= \frac{(\$600,000 \times 0.20)}{[(\$75 \times 5,000 \text{ units}) + \$80,000 + \$25,000]}$$

$$= \frac{\$120,000}{\$480,000} = 25\%$$

5. **C** Product 3 has the highest unit contribution margin per bottleneck hour ($14/2 = $7). Product 1 (answer A) has the largest contribution margin per unit but the lowest unit contribution per bottleneck hour ($20/4 = $5), so it is the least profitable product in the constrained environment. Product 2 (answer B) has the highest total profitability in March (1,500 units × $18), but this does not suggest that it has the highest profit potential. Product 2's unit contribution per bottleneck hour ($18/3 = $6) is between Products 1 and 3. Answer D is not true since the products all have different profit potential in terms of unit contribution margin per bottleneck hour.

13

LEARNING OBJECTIVES

OBJECTIVE 1

Describe the nature and objectives of budgeting.

OBJECTIVE 2

Describe the master budget for a manufacturing business.

OBJECTIVE 3

Describe the nature and use of standards.

OBJECTIVE 4

Explain and illustrate how standards are used in budgeting.

OBJECTIVE 5

Calculate and interpret the basic variances for direct materials and direct labor.

OBJECTIVE 6

Explain how standards can be used for nonmanufacturing expenses.

OBJECTIVE 7

Explain and provide examples of nonfinancial performance measures.

Budgeting and Standard Cost Systems

You could have financial goals for your life. To achieve these goals, it is necessary to plan for future expenses. For example, you could consider taking a part-time job to save money for school expenses for the coming school year. How much money would you need to earn and save to pay these expenses? One way to answer this question is to prepare a budget. For example, a budget would show an estimate of your expenses associated with school, such as tuition, fees, and books. In addition, you would have expenses for day-to-day living, such as rent, food, and clothing. You could also have expenses for travel and entertainment. Once the school year begins, you can use the budget as a tool for guiding your spending priorities during the year.

The budget is used in businesses in much the same way as it can be used in personal life. For example, **DaimlerChrysler** uses budgeting to determine the number of cars to produce, number of shifts to operate, number of people to employ, and amount of material to purchase. The budget provides the company a "game plan" for the year. In this chapter, you will see how budgets can be used for financial planning and control.

Nature and Objectives of Budgeting

OBJECTIVE   1

Describe the nature
and objectives of
budgeting.

If you were driving across the country, you could plan your trip with the aid of a road map. The road map would lay out your route across the country, identify stopovers, and reduce your chances of getting lost. In the same way, a **budget** charts a course for a business by outlining the plans of the business in financial terms. Like the road map, the budget can help a company navigate through the year and reduce negative outcomes.

Although budgets are normally associated with profit-making businesses, they also play an important role in operating most units of government. For example, budgets are important in managing rural school districts and small villages as well as agencies of the federal government. Budgets are also important for managing the operations of churches, hospitals, and other nonprofit institutions. Individuals and families also use budgeting techniques in managing their financial affairs. In this chapter, we discuss the principles of budgeting in the context of a business organized for profit.

Objectives of Budgeting

Budgeting involves (1) establishing specific goals, (2) executing plans to achieve the goals, and (3) periodically comparing actual results with the goals. These goals include both those of the overall business as well as the specific ones for the individual units

---

BUSINESS STRATEGY

The "Gap" at The Gap

During the 1990s, The Gap became the nation's largest specialty apparel retailer, with sales rising from $1.93 billion in 1990 to $11.64 billion in 1999. The Gap achieved this rapid growth by employing a strategy that emphasized simple, high-quality, casual clothing. Its strategy was aided by the shift in the 1990s to casual attire in the workplace. However, Gap's same-store sales and profits have plummeted over the past year and a half. Perhaps never before have so many shoppers stopped patronizing a retail chain so quickly. So what happened?

Many former customers blame Gap's changing fashion mix toward more far-fetched fashions, such as a denim trenchcoat with faux-fur collar, bleached graphic T-shirt, and fuschia-glittered disco jeans. In other words, The Gap has become too trendy for its targeted customer, who is between the ages of 20 and 30. In addition, as The Gap expanded its trendy fashions, it curtailed customer choices within its basic apparel. For example, one former customer visited a Gap store in search of Capri pants but wasn't pleased with what she found. "You can't take pink and baby-blue to work," she says.

Source: Adapted from Amy Merrick, "Gap's Image is Wearing Out," *The Wall Street Journal*, December 6, 2001.

within the business. Establishing specific goals for future operations is part of the *planning* function of management while executing actions to meet the goals is the *directing* function of management. Periodically comparing actual results with these goals and taking appropriate action is the *controlling* function of management. The relationships of these functions are illustrated in Exhibit 1.

EXHIBIT 1 *Planning, Directing, and Controlling*

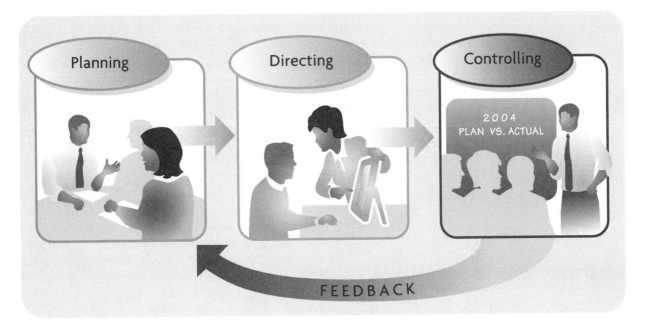

Human Behavior and Budgeting

In the budgeting process, business, team, and individual goals are established. Human behavior problems can arise if (1) the budget goal is unachievable (too tight), (2) the budget goal is very easy to achieve (too loose), or (3) the budget goals of the business conflict with the objectives of employees (goal conflict).

SETTING BUDGET GOALS TOO TIGHTLY   People can become discouraged if performance expectations are set too high. For example, would you be inspired or discouraged by a guitar instructor expecting you to play like Eric Clapton after only a few lessons? You'd probably be discouraged. This same kind of problem can occur in businesses if employees view budget goals as unrealistic or unachievable. In such a case, the budget discourages employees from achieving the goals. On the other hand, aggressive but attainable goals are likely to inspire employees to achieve them. Therefore, it is important that employees (managers and nonmanagers) be involved in establishing reasonable budget estimates.

Involving all employees encourages cooperation both within and among departments. It also increases awareness of each department's importance to the overall objectives of the company. Employees view budgeting more positively when they have an opportunity to participate in the budget-setting process. This is so because employees with a greater sense of control over the budget process will have a greater commitment to achieving its goals. In such cases, budgets are valuable planning tools that increase the possibility of achieving business goals.

SETTING BUDGET GOALS TOO LOOSELY   Although it is desirable to establish attainable goals, it is undesirable to plan lower goals than could be possible. Such budget "padding" is termed **budgetary slack**. An example is including spare employees in the plan. Managers could plan slack in the budget to provide a "cushion" for unexpected events or improve the appearance of operations. Budgetary slack can be avoided if lower- and mid-level managers are required to support their spending requirements with operational plans.

Slack budgets can cause employees to develop a "spend-it-or-lose-it" mentality. This often occurs at the end of the budget period when actual spending is much less than the budgeted amount. Employees can attempt to spend the remaining budget (purchase equipment, hire consultants, purchase supplies) to avoid having the budget cut next period. However, some evidence suggests that loose budgets can be appropriate in settings involving high uncertainty, such as research and development. The loose budget acts as a sort of "shock absorber," giving managers maneuvering room to minimize work disruptions.

SETTING CONFLICTING BUDGET GOALS   **Goal conflict** occurs when individual self-interest differs from business objectives. To illustrate, the manager of the Transportation Department of one company was instructed to stay within the department's budget. To meet the budget goal, the manager stopped transporting all shipments for the last two weeks of the period. Although the Transportation Department budget was met, customers were upset because they did not receive their orders. As a result, many customers stopped doing business with the company or demanded price discounts that far exceeded the additional transportation costs that should have been spent. In this example, the budget pressure caused the Transportation Department manager to make a decision that appeared correct from the department's view but was harmful to the business. Goal conflict can be avoided if budget goals are carefully designed for consistency across all areas of the organization.

ETHICS IN ACTION

In their public earnings announcements, companies have recently focused on reporting EBITDA (earnings before interest, taxes, depreciation, and amortization) to outside investors. This was done under the belief that EBITDA would be a more realistic measure of earning power in some industries with large depreciation expenses, such as telecommunications. However, alleged accounting fraud at Worldcom, Inc., has changed perceptions. Worldcom is alleged to have caused nearly $4 billion in costs to disappear when reporting EBITDA. As stated recently by one analyst, "I think the days of having EBITDA being the focus of an earnings release are probably numbered."

Budgeting Systems

Budgeting systems vary among businesses because of factors such as organizational structure, complexity of operations, and management philosophy. Differences in budget systems are even more significant among different types of businesses, such as manufacturers and service businesses. The details of a budgeting system used by an automobile manufacturer such as **Ford Motor Co.** would obviously differ from a service company such as **American Airlines**. However, the basic budgeting concepts illustrated in the following paragraphs apply to all types of businesses and organizations.

The budgetary period for operating activities normally includes the fiscal year of a business. A year is short enough that future operations can be estimated fairly accurately yet long enough that the future can be viewed in a broad context. However, to achieve effective control, the annual budgets are usually subdivided into shorter time periods, such as quarters of the year, months, or weeks. **Sprint Corporation** was spending twice as many resources producing budgets as it was analyzing them. As a result, Sprint reengineered its budget process by replacing its annual budget with quarterly reviews of six-quarter rolling forecasts of key business drivers, coupled with exception-based monitoring. The new process shortened the budget process from 137 days to less than 60 days and gave Sprint the ability to respond faster to changes in business conditions.

A variation of fiscal-year budgeting, called **continuous budgeting**, maintains a 12-month projection into the future. The 12-month budget is continually revised by removing the data for the period just ended and adding estimated budget data for the same period next year, as shown in Exhibit 2.

EXHIBIT 2 *Continuous Budgeting*

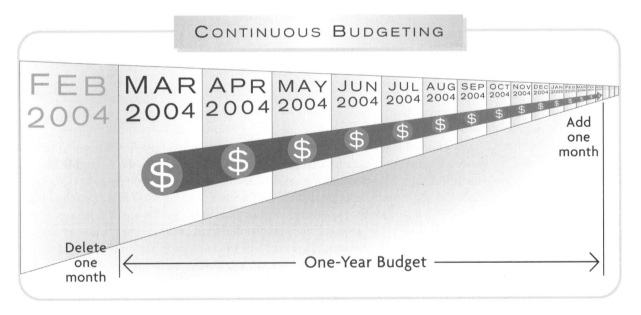

Developing budgets for the next fiscal year usually begins several months prior to the end of the current year. This responsibility is normally assigned to a budget committee. Such a committee often consists of the budget director and high-level executives such as the controller, the treasurer, the production manager, and the sales manager. Once the budget has been approved, the budget process is monitored and summarized by the Accounting Department, which reports to the committee.

There are several methods of developing budget estimates. One method, termed **zero-based budgeting**, requires managers to estimate sales, production, and other operating data as though operations are being started for the first time. This approach has the benefit of taking a fresh view of operations each year. **Lockheed Martin Corporation** used a zero-based budgeting approach, called *risk-based budgeting*, to identify cost savings during the downsizing of some of its military and weapons programs.

A more common approach is to start with last year's budget and revise it for actual results and expected changes for the coming year. Two major budgets using this approach are the *static budget* and the *flexible budget.*

Static Budget

A **static budget** shows the expected results of a responsibility center for only one activity level. Once the budget has been determined, it is not changed, even if the activity changes. Static budgeting is used by many service companies and for some administrative functions of manufacturing companies, such as purchasing, engineering, and accounting. For example, the Assembly Department manager for Colter Manufacturing Company prepared the static budget for the upcoming year, shown in Exhibit 3.

EXHIBIT 3
Static Budget

COLTER MANUFACTURING COMPANY Assembly Department Budget For the Year Ending July 31, 2004	
Direct labor	$40,000
Electric power	5,000
Supervisor salaries	15,000
Total department costs	$60,000

A disadvantage of static budgets is that they do not adjust for changes in activity levels. For example, assume that the actual amounts spent by the Assembly Department of Colter Manufacturing totaled $72,000, which is $12,000 or 20% ($12,000 ÷ $60,000) more than budgeted. Is this good news or bad news? At first you might think that this is a bad result. However, this conclusion may not be valid, since static budget results may be difficult to interpret. To illustrate, assume that the assembly manager constructed the budget based on plans to assemble 8,000 units during the year. However, 10,000 units were actually produced, which represents 25% (2,000 ÷ 8,000) more work than expected. Should the additional $12,000 in spending in excess of the budget be considered "bad news"? Maybe not. The Assembly Department provided 25% more output for only 20% additional cost.

Flexible Budget

Unlike static budgets, **flexible budgets** show the expected results of a responsibility center for several activity levels. You can think of a flexible budget as a series of static budgets for different levels of activity. Such budgets are especially useful in estimating and controlling factory costs and operating expenses. Exhibit 4 is a flexible budget for the annual manufacturing expense in the Assembly Department of Colter Manufacturing Company.

EXHIBIT 4
Flexible Budget

COLTER MANUFACTURING COMPANY Assembly Department Budget For the Year Ending July 31, 2004			
Units of production	8,000	9,000	10,000
Variable cost:			
Direct labor ($5 per unit)	$40,000	$45,000	$50,000
Electric power ($0.50 per unit)	4,000	4,500	5,000
Total variable cost	$44,000	$49,500	$55,000
Fixed cost:			
Electric power	$ 1,000	$ 1,000	$ 1,000
Supervisor salaries	15,000	15,000	15,000
Total fixed cost	$16,000	$16,000	$16,000
Total department costs	$60,000	$65,500	$71,000

Many hospitals use flexible budgeting to plan the number of nurses for patient floors. These budgets use a measure termed *relative value units*. A relative value unit is a measure of effort related to a nursing activity, such as feeding the patient or verifying vital signs. The total relative value units for a floor can be determined from a computer simulation based on the number of patients on the floor and the type of illnesses. Naturally, the more patients and the more severe their illnesses, the higher the total relative value units. The total relative units can then be translated into the number of nurses required to support the patients.

When constructing a flexible budget, we first identify the relevant activity levels. In Exhibit 4, there are 8,000, 9,000, and 10,000 units of production. Alternative activity bases, such as machine hours or direct labor hours, can be used in measuring the volume of activity. Second, we identify the fixed and variable components of the costs being budgeted. For example, in Exhibit 4, the electric power cost is separated into its fixed cost ($1,000 per month) and variable cost ($0.50 per unit). Lastly, we prepare the budget for each activity level by multiplying the variable cost per unit by the activity level and then adding the monthly fixed cost.

With a flexible budget, the department manager can be evaluated by comparing actual expenses to the budgeted amount for actual activity. For example, if Colter Manufacturing Company's Assembly Department actually spent $72,000 to produce 10,000 units, the manager would be considered over budget by $1,000 ($72,000 − $71,000). Under the static budget in Exhibit 3, the department was $12,000 over budget. This comparison is illustrated in Exhibit 5 on the following page. The flexible budget for the Assembly Department is much more accurate than the static budget because budget amounts adjust for changes in activity.

Computerized Budgeting Systems

In developing budgets, many firms use computerized budgeting systems. Such systems speed up and reduce the cost of preparing the budget. This is especially true when large amounts of data need to be processed. Computers are also useful in continuous budgeting. Reports that compare actual results with amounts budgeted can also be prepared on a timely basis through the use of computerized systems. For

EXHIBIT 5 *Static and Flexible Budgets*

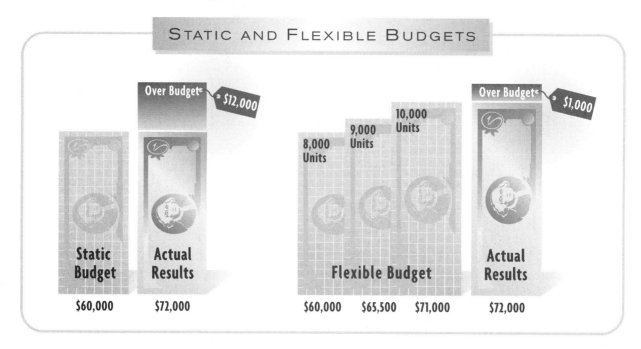

example, **Fujitsu** used Enterprise Resource Planning (ERP) software to streamline its budgeting process from 6 to 8 weeks down to 10 to 15 days.

Managers often use computer spreadsheets or simulation models to represent the operating and budget relationships. By using computer simulation models, the impact of various operating alternatives on the budget can be assessed. For example, the budget can be revised to show the impact of a proposed change in indirect labor wage rates. Likewise, the budgetary effect of a proposed product line can be determined.

A common objective of using computer-based budgeting is to tie all budgets of the organization together. In the next section, we illustrate how a company ties its budgets together to develop a complete plan.

Master Budget

OBJECTIVE   2

Describe the master budget for a manufacturing business.

Manufacturing operations require a series of budgets that are linked together in a **master budget**. The major parts of the master budget are as follows:

Budgeted Income Statement	Budgeted Balance Sheet
Sales budget	Cash budget
Cost of goods sold budget:	Capital expenditures budget
Production budget	
Direct materials purchases budget	
Direct labor cost budget	
Factory overhead cost budget	
Selling and administrative expenses budget	

Exhibit 6 shows the relationship among the income statement budgets. The budget process begins by estimating sales. The sales information is then provided to the various units for estimating the production and selling and administrative expenses budgets. The production budgets are used to prepare the direct materials purchases, direct labor cost, and factory overhead cost budgets. These three budgets are used to develop the cost of goods sold budget. Once these budgets and the selling and administrative expenses budget have been completed, the budgeted income statement can be prepared.

EXHIBIT 6
Income Statement
Budgets

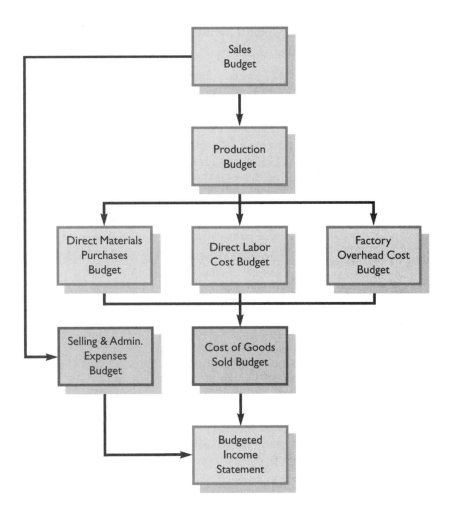

After the budgeted income statement has been developed, the budgeted balance sheet can be prepared. Two major budgets composing the budgeted balance sheet are the cash budget and the capital expenditures budget.

Income Statement Budgets

In the following sections, we illustrate the major elements of the income statement budget. We use a small manufacturing business, Elite Accessories Inc., as the basis for our illustration.

SALES BUDGET   The **sales budget** normally indicates for each product (1) the number of estimated sales and (2) the expected unit selling price. These data are often reported by region or by sales representative.

In estimating the quantity of sales for each product, past sales volumes are often used as a starting point. These amounts are revised for factors that are expected to affect future sales, such as the following factors:

- Backlog of unfilled sales orders

- Planned advertising and promotion

- Expected industry and general economic conditions

- Productive capacity

- Projected pricing policy

- Findings of market research studies

Once an estimate of the sales volume is obtained, the expected sales revenue can be determined by multiplying the volume by the expected unit sales price. Exhibit 7 is the sales budget for Elite Accessories Inc.

EXHIBIT 7
Sales Budget

ELITE ACCESSORIES INC.
Sales Budget
For the Year Ending December 31, 2004

Product and Region	Unit Sales Volume	Unit Selling Price	Total Sales
Wallet:			
East	287,000	$12.00	$ 3,444,000
West	241,000	12.00	2,892,000
Total	528,000		$ 6,336,000
Handbag:			
East	156,400	$25.00	$ 3,910,000
West	123,600	25.00	3,090,000
Total	280,000		$ 7,000,000
Total revenue from sales			$13,336,000

For control purposes, management can compare actual sales and budgeted sales by product, region, or sales representative. Management would investigate any significant differences and take possible corrective actions.

PRODUCTION BUDGET   Production should be carefully coordinated with the sales budget to ensure that production and sales are kept in balance during the period. The number of units to be manufactured to meet budgeted sales and inventory needs for each product is set forth in the **production budget**. The budgeted volume of production is determined as follows:

Expected units to be sold
+ Desired units in ending inventory
− Estimated units in beginning inventory
Total units to be produced

Exhibit 8 is the production budget for Elite Accessories Inc.

ELITE ACCESSORIES INC.
Production Budget
For the Year Ending December 31, 2004

	Units	
	Wallet	Handbag
Expected units to be sold (from Exhibit 7)	528,000	280,000
Plus desired ending inventory, December 31, 2004	80,000	60,000
Total	608,000	340,000
Less estimated beginning inventory, January 1, 2004	88,000	48,000
Total units to be produced	520,000	292,000

DIRECT MATERIALS PURCHASES BUDGET The production budget is the starting point for determining the estimated amounts of direct materials to be purchased. Multiplying these amounts by the expected unit purchase price determines the total cost of direct materials to be purchased.

Materials required for production
+ Desired ending materials inventory
− Estimated beginning materials inventory
Direct materials to be purchased

In Elite Accessories Inc.'s production operations, leather and lining are required for wallets and handbags. The number of square yards of direct materials expected to be used for each unit of product is as follows:

Wallet:
    Leather: 0.30 square yard per unit
    Lining: 0.10 square yard per unit

Handbag:
    Leather: 1.25 square yards per unit
    Lining: 0.50 square yard per unit

Based on these data and the production budget, the **direct materials purchases budget** is prepared. As shown in the budget in Exhibit 9 on the following page, for Elite Accessories Inc. to produce 520,000 wallets, 156,000 square yards (520,000 units × 0.30 square yard per unit) of leather are needed. Likewise, to produce 292,000 handbags, 365,000 square yards (292,000 units × 1.25 square yards per unit) of leather are needed. We can compute the needs for lining in a similar manner. Then adding the desired ending inventory for each material and deducting the estimated beginning inventory determines the amount of each material to be purchased. Multiplying these amounts by the estimated cost per square yard yields the total materials purchase cost.

EXHIBIT 9
*Direct Materials
Purchases Budget*

ELITE ACCESSORIES INC.
Direct Materials Purchases Budget
For the Year Ending December 31, 2004

| | Direct Materials | | |
	Leather	Lining	Total
Square yards required for production:			
Wallet (Note A)	156,000	52,000	
Handbag (Note B)	365,000	146,000	
Plus desired inventory, December 31, 2004	20,000	12,000	
Total	541,000	210,000	
Less estimated inventory, January 1, 2004	18,000	15,000	
Total square yards to be purchased	523,000	195,000	
Unit price (per square yard)	× $4.50	× $1.20	
Total direct materials to be purchased	$2,353,500	$234,000	$2,587,500

Note A: Leather: 520,000 units × 0.30 square yard per unit = 156,000 square yards
        Lining: 520,000 units × 0.10 square yard per unit = 52,000 square yards
Note B: Leather: 292,000 units × 1.25 square yards per unit = 365,000 square yards
        Lining: 292,000 units × 0.50 square yard per unit = 146,000 square yards

The direct materials purchases budget helps management maintain inventory levels within reasonable limits. For this purpose, the timing of the direct materials purchases should be coordinated between the purchasing and production departments.

DIRECT LABOR COST BUDGET   The production budget also provides the starting point for preparing the direct labor cost budget. For Elite Accessories Inc., the labor requirements for each unit of product are estimated as follows:

Wallet:
  Cutting Department: 0.10 hour per unit
  Sewing Department: 0.25 hour per unit

Handbag:
  Cutting Department: 0.15 hour per unit
  Sewing Department: 0.40 hour per unit

Based on these data and the production budget, Elite Accessories Inc. prepares the direct labor budget. As shown in the budget in Exhibit 10, for Elite Accessories Inc. to produce 520,000 wallets, 52,000 hours (520,000 units × 0.10 hour per unit) of labor in the Cutting Department are required. Likewise, to produce 292,000 handbags, 43,800 hours (292,000 units × 0.15 hour per unit) of labor in the Cutting Department are required. In a similar manner, we can determine the direct labor hours needed in the Sewing Department to meet the budgeted production. Multiplying the direct labor hours for each department by the estimated department hourly rate yields the total direct labor cost for each department.

The direct labor needs should be coordinated between the production and personnel departments. This ensures that there will be enough labor available for production.

FACTORY OVERHEAD COST BUDGET   The estimated factory overhead costs necessary for production make up the factory overhead cost budget. This budget usually includes the total estimated cost for each item of factory overhead, as shown in Exhibit 11.

EXHIBIT 10
Direct Labor Cost Budget

ELITE ACCESSORIES INC.
Direct Labor Cost Budget
For the Year Ending December 31, 2004

	Cutting	Sewing	Total
Hours required for production:			
Wallet (Note A)	52,000	130,000	
Handbag (Note B)	43,800	116,800	
Total	95,800	246,800	
Hourly rate	× $12.00	× $15.00	
Total direct labor cost	$1,149,600	$3,702,000	$4,851,600

Note A: Cutting Department: 520,000 units × 0.10 hour per unit = 52,000 hours
Sewing Department: 520,000 units × 0.25 hour per unit = 130,000 hours
Note B: Cutting Department: 292,000 units × 0.15 hour per unit = 43,800 hours
Sewing Department: 292,000 units × 0.40 hour per unit = 116,800 hours

EXHIBIT 11
Factory Overhead Cost Budget

ELITE ACCESSORIES INC.
Factory Overhead Cost Budget
For the Year Ending December 31, 2004

Indirect factory wages	$ 732,800
Supervisor salaries	360,000
Power and light	306,000
Depreciation of plant and equipment	288,000
Indirect materials	182,800
Maintenance	140,280
Insurance and property taxes	79,200
Total factory overhead cost	$2,089,080

A business can prepare supporting departmental schedules in which the factory overhead costs are separated into their fixed and variable cost elements. Such schedules enable department managers to direct their attention to those costs for which they are responsible and to evaluate performance.

COST OF GOODS SOLD BUDGET   The direct materials purchases budget, direct labor cost budget, and factory overhead cost budget are the starting point for preparing the **cost of goods sold budget**. To illustrate, these data are combined with the following desired ending inventory and the estimated beginning inventory data to determine the budgeted cost of goods sold shown in Exhibit 12 on the following page.

Estimated inventories on January 1, 2004:   Desired inventories on December 31, 2004:
Finished goods $1,095,600   Finished goods $1,565,000
Work in process   214,400   Work in process   220,000

SELLING AND ADMINISTRATIVE EXPENSES BUDGET   The sales budget is often used as the starting point for estimating the selling and administrative expenses.

EXHIBIT 12
*Cost of Goods Sold
Budget*

ELITE ACCESSORIES INC.
Cost of Goods Sold Budget
For the Year Ending December 31, 2004

Finished goods inventory, January 1, 2004			$ 1,095,600
Work in process inventory, January 1, 2004		$ 214,400	
Direct materials:			
Direct materials inventory,			
January 1, 2004 (Note A)	$ 99,000		
Direct materials purchases (from Exhibit 9)	2,587,500		
Cost of direct materials available for use	$2,686,500		
Less direct materials inventory,			
December 31, 2004 (Note B)	104,400		
Cost of direct materials placed			
in production	$2,582,100		
Direct labor (from Exhibit 10)	4,851,600		
Factory overhead (from Exhibit 11)	2,089,080		
Total manufacturing costs		9,522,780	
Total work in process during period		$9,737,180	
Less work in process inventory,			
December 31, 2004		220,000	
Cost of goods manufactured			9,517,180
Cost of finished goods available for sale			$10,612,780
Less finished goods inventory,			
December 31, 2004			1,565,000
Cost of goods sold			$ 9,047,780

Note A: Leather: 18,000 square yards × $4.50 per square yard		$ 81,000
Lining: 15,000 square yards × $1.20 per square yard		18,000
Direct materials inventory, January 1, 2004		$ 99,000
Note B: Leather: 20,000 square yards × $4.50 per square yard		$ 90,000
Lining: 12,000 square yards × $1.20 per square yard		14,400
Direct materials inventory, December 31, 2004		$104,400

For example, a budgeted increase in sales may require more advertising. Exhibit 13 is a selling and administrative expenses budget for Elite Accessories Inc.

Detailed supporting schedules are often prepared for major items in the selling and administrative expenses budget. For example, an advertising expense schedule for the Marketing Department should include the advertising media to be used (newspaper, direct mail, television), amounts (column inches, number of pieces, minutes), and the cost per unit. Attention to such details results in realistic budgets. Effective control results from assigning responsibility for achieving the budget to department supervisors.

BUDGETED INCOME STATEMENT   The budgets for sales, cost of goods sold, and selling and administrative expenses, combined with the data on other income,

EXHIBIT 13
Selling and Administrative Expenses Budget

ELITE ACCESSORIES INC.		
Selling and Administrative Expenses Budget		
For the Year Ending December 31, 2004		
Selling expenses:		
Sales salaries expense	$715,000	
Advertising expense	360,000	
Travel expense	115,000	
Total selling expenses		$1,190,000
Administrative expenses:		
Officers' salaries expense	$360,000	
Office salaries expense	258,000	
Office rent expense	34,500	
Office supplies expense	17,500	
Miscellaneous administrative expenses	25,000	
Total administrative expenses		695,000
Total selling and administrative expenses		$1,885,000

other expense, and income tax, are used to prepare the budgeted income statement. Exhibit 14 is a budgeted income statement for Elite Accessories Inc.

The budgeted income statement summarizes the estimates of all phases of operations. This allows management to assess the effects of the individual budgets on profits for the year. If the budgeted net income is too low, management could review and revise operating plans in an attempt to improve income.

EXHIBIT 14
Budgeted Income Statement

ELITE ACCESSORIES INC.		
Budgeted Income Statement		
For the Year Ending December 31, 2004		
Revenue from sales (from Exhibit 7)		$13,336,000
Cost of goods sold (from Exhibit 12)		9,047,780
Gross profit		4,288,220
Selling and administrative expenses:		
Selling expenses (from Exhibit 13)	$1,190,000	
Administrative expenses (from Exhibit 13)	695,000	
Total selling and administrative expenses		1,885,000
Income from operations		$ 2,403,220
Other income:		
Interest revenue	$ 98,000	
Other expense:		
Interest expense	90,000	8,000
Income before income tax		$ 2,411,220
Income tax		600,000
Net income		$ 1,811,220

Balance Sheet Budgets

Balance sheet budgets are used by managers to plan financing, investing, and cash objectives for the firm. The balance sheet budgets illustrated for Elite Accessories Inc. in the following sections are the cash budget and the capital expenditures budget.

CASH BUDGET   The **cash budget** is one of the most important elements of the budgeted balance sheet. The cash budget presents the expected receipts (inflows) and payments (outflows) of cash for a period of time.

Information from the various operating budgets, such as the sales budget, the direct materials purchases budget, and the selling and administrative expenses budget, affects the cash budget. In addition, the capital expenditures budget, dividend policies, and plans for equity or long-term debt financing also affect the cash budget.

We illustrate the monthly cash budget for January, February, and March 2004, for Elite Accessories Inc. We begin by developing the estimated cash receipts and estimated cash payments portion of the cash budget.

Estimated Cash Receipts.   Estimated cash receipts are planned additions to cash from sales and other sources, such as issuing securities or collecting interest. A supporting schedule can be used in determining the collections from sales. To illustrate this schedule, assume the following information for Elite Accessories Inc.:

Accounts receivable, January 1, 2004 . . . . $370,000

	January	February	March
Budgeted sales	$1,080,000	$1,240,000	$970,000

Elite Accessories Inc. expects to sell 10% of its merchandise for cash. Of the remaining 90% of the sales on account, 60% is expected to be collected in the month of the sale and the remainder in the next month.

Using this information, we prepare the schedule of collections from sales, shown in Exhibit 15. The cash receipts from sales on account are determined by adding the amounts collected from credit sales earned in the current period (60%) and the amounts accrued from sales in the previous period as accounts receivable (40%).

Estimated Cash Payments.   Estimated cash payments are planned reductions in cash from manufacturing costs, selling and administrative expenses, capital expenditures, and other sources, such as buying securities or paying interest or dividends. A supporting schedule can be used in estimating the cash payments for manufacturing costs. To illustrate, assume the following information for Elite Accessories Inc.:

Accounts payable, January 1, 2004 . . . . $190,000

	January	February	March
Manufacturing costs	$840,000	$780,000	$812,000

Depreciation expense on machines is estimated to be $24,000 per month and is included in the manufacturing costs. The accounts payable were incurred for manufacturing costs. Elite Accessories Inc. expects to pay 75% of the manufacturing costs in the month in which they are incurred and the balance in the next month.

EXHIBIT 15
*Schedule of Collections
from Sales*

ELITE ACCESSORIES INC.
Schedule of Collections from Sales
For the Three Months Ending March 31, 2004

	January	February	March
Receipts from cash sales:			
Cash sales (10% × current month's sales— Note A)	$108,000	$ 124,000	$ 97,000
Receipts from sales on account:			
Collections from prior month's sales (40% of previous month's credit sales—Note B)	$370,000	$ 388,800	$446,400
Collections from current month's sales (60% of current month's credit sales—Note C)	583,200	669,600	523,800
Total receipts from sales on account	$953,200	$1,058,400	$970,200

Note A: $108,000 = $1,080,000 × 10%
$124,000 = $1,240,000 × 10%
$ 97,000 = $ 970,000 × 10%

Note B: $370,000, given as January 1, 2003, Accounts Receivable balance
$388,800 = $1,080,000 × 90% × 40%
$446,400 = $1,240,000 × 90% × 40%

Note C: $583,200 = $1,080,000 × 90% × 60%
$669,600 = $1,240,000 × 90% × 60%
$523,800 = $ 970,000 × 90% × 60%

Using this information, we can prepare the schedule of payments for manufacturing costs, as shown in Exhibit 16.

EXHIBIT 16
*Schedule of Payments
for Manufacturing Costs*

ELITE ACCESSORIES INC.
Schedule of Payments for Manufacturing Costs
For the Three Months Ending March 31, 2004

	January	February	March
Payments of prior month's manufacturing costs {[0.25 × previous month's manufacturing costs (less depreciation)]—Note A}	$190,000	$204,000	$189,000
Payments of current month's manufacturing costs {[0.75 × current month's manufacturing costs (less depreciation)]—Note B}	612,000	567,000	591,000
Total payments	$802,000	$771,000	$780,000

Note A: $190,000, given as January 1, 2003, Accounts Payable balance
$204,000 = ($840,000 − $24,000) × 25%
$189,000 = ($780,000 − $24,000) × 25%

Note B: $612,000 = ($840,000 − $24,000) × 75%
$567,000 = ($780,000 − $24,000) × 75%
$591,000 = ($812,000 − $24,000) × 75%

In Exhibit 16, the cash payments are determined by adding the amounts paid from costs incurred in the current period (75%) and the amounts accrued as a liability from costs in the previous period (25%). The $24,000 of depreciation must be excluded from all calculations since depreciation is a noncash expense that should not be included in the cash budget.

Completing the Cash Budget.   To complete the cash budget for Elite Accessories Inc., as shown in Exhibit 17, assume that Elite Accessories Inc. is expecting the following:

Cash balance on January 1	$280,000
Quarterly taxes paid on March 31	150,000
Quarterly interest expense paid on January 10	22,500
Quarterly interest revenue received on March 21	24,500
Sewing equipment purchased in February	274,000

In addition, monthly selling and administrative expenses, which are paid in the month incurred, are estimated as follows:

	January	February	March
Selling and administrative expenses	$160,000	$165,000	$145,000

We can compare the estimated cash balance at the end of the period with the minimum balance required by operations. Assuming that the minimum cash bal-

EXHIBIT 17
Cash Budget

ELITE ACCESSORIES INC.
Cash Budget
For the Three Months Ending March 31, 2004

	January	February	March
Estimated cash receipts from:			
Cash sales (from Exhibit 15)	$ 108,000	$ 124,000	$ 97,000
Collections of accounts receivable			
(from Exhibit 15)	953,200	1,058,400	970,200
Interest revenue			24,500
Total cash receipts	$1,061,200	$1,182,400	$1,091,700
Estimated cash payments for:			
Manufacturing costs (from Exhibit 16)	$ 802,000	$ 771,000	$ 780,000
Selling and administrative expenses	160,000	165,000	145,000
Capital additions		274,000	
Interest expense	22,500		
Income taxes			150,000
Total cash payments	$ 984,500	$1,210,000	$1,075,000
Cash increase (decrease)	$ 76,700	$ (27,600)	$ 16,700
Cash balance at beginning of month	280,000	356,700	329,100
Cash balance at end of month	$ 356,700	$ 329,100	$ 345,800
Minimum cash balance	340,000	340,000	340,000
Excess (deficiency)	$ 16,700	$ (10,900)	$ 5,800

ance for Elite Accessories Inc. is $340,000, we can determine any expected excess or deficiency.

The minimum cash balance protects against variations in estimates and for unexpected cash emergencies. For effective cash management, much of the minimum cash balance should be deposited in income-producing securities that can be readily converted to cash. U.S. Treasury bills or notes are examples of such securities.

CAPITAL EXPENDITURES BUDGET   The **capital expenditures budget** summarizes plans for acquiring fixed assets. Such expenditures are necessary as machinery and other fixed assets wear out, become obsolete, or for other reasons need to be replaced. In addition, expanding plant facilities could be necessary to meet increasing demand for a company's product.

The useful life of many fixed assets extends over long periods of time. In addition, the amount of the expenditures for such assets can vary from year to year. It is normal to project the plans for a number of periods into the future in preparing the capital expenditures budget. Exhibit 18 is a five-year capital expenditures budget for Elite Accessories Inc.

EXHIBIT 18
Capital Expenditures Budget

ELITE ACCESSORIES INC. Capital Expenditures Budget For the Five Years Ending December 31, 2008					
Item	2004	2005	2006	2007	2008
Machinery—Cutting Department	$400,000			$280,000	$360,000
Machinery—Sewing Department	274,000	$260,000	$560,000	200,000	
Office equipment		90,000			60,000
Total	$674,000	$350,000	$560,000	$480,000	$420,000

The capital expenditures budget should be considered in preparing the other operating budgets. For example, the estimated depreciation of new equipment affects the factory overhead cost budget and the selling and administrative expenses budget. The plans for financing the capital expenditures can also affect the cash budget.

BUDGETED BALANCE SHEET   The budgeted balance sheet estimates the financial condition at the end of a budget period. The budgeted balance sheet assumes that all operating budgets and financing plans are met. It is similar to a balance sheet based on actual data in the accounts. For this reason, we do not illustrate a budgeted balance sheet for Elite Accessories Inc. If the budgeted balance sheet indicates a weakness in financial position, revising the financing plans or other plans could be necessary. For example, a large amount of long-term debt in relation to stockholders' equity might require revising financing plans for capital expenditures. Such revisions could include issuing equity rather than debt.

Standards

What are standards? **Standards** are performance goals. Service, merchandising, and manufacturing businesses can use standards to evaluate and control operations. For example, long-haul drivers for **United Parcel Service** are expected to drive a standard distance per day. Salespersons for **The Limited** are expected to meet sales standards.

Manufacturers normally use standard costs for each of the three manufacturing costs: direct materials, direct labor, and factory overhead. Accounting systems that use standards for these costs are called **standard cost systems**. These systems enable management to determine how much a product should cost (**standard cost**), how much it does cost (actual cost), and the causes of any difference (**cost variances**). When actual costs are compared with standard costs, only the exceptions, or variances, are reported for cost control. This reporting by the *principle of exceptions* allows management to focus on correcting the variances. Thus, using standard costs assists management in controlling costs and in motivating employees to focus on costs.

Standard cost systems are commonly used with job order and process systems. Automated manufacturing operations can also integrate standard cost data with the computerized system that directs operations. Such systems detect and report variances automatically and make adjustments to operations in progress.

Setting Standards

Setting standards is both an art and a science. The standard-setting process normally requires the joint efforts of accountants, engineers, and other management personnel. The accountant plays an essential role by expressing in dollars and cents the results of judgments and studies. Engineers contribute to the standard-setting process by identifying the materials, labor, and machine requirements needed to produce the product. For example, engineers determine the direct materials requirements by studying the materials specifications for products and estimating normal spoilage in production. Time and motion studies can be used to determine the length of time required for each manufacturing operation. Engineering studies can also be used to determine standards for factory overhead, such as the amount of power needed to operate machinery.

Setting standards often begins with analyzing past operations. However, standards are not just an extension of past costs, and caution must be used in relying on past cost data. For example, inefficiencies could be contained within past costs. In addition, changes in technology, machinery, or production methods could make past costs irrelevant for future operations.

Types of Standards

Standards imply an acceptable level of production efficiency. One of the major objectives in setting standards is to motivate workers to achieve efficient operations.

Like the budgets we discussed earlier, tight, unrealistic standards can have a negative impact on performance. This happens because workers can become frustrated with an inability to meet the standards and can give up trying to do their best. Such standards can be achieved only under perfect operating conditions, such as no idle time, no machine breakdowns, and no materials spoilage. These standards are called **theoretical standards** or **ideal standards**. Although ideal standards are not widely used, a few firms use them to motivate changes and improvement. For example, **Mohawk Forest Products** had a normal standard cost for a premium grade paper of $2,900 per ton and an ideal cost of $1,342 per ton. The company used the ideal standard to motivate cost improvement. The resulting improvements allowed the company to reduce the normal standard cost to $1,738 per ton.

Standards that are too loose might not motivate employees to perform at their best. This happens because the standard level of performance can be reached too easily. As a result, operating performance could be lower than what could be achieved.

Most companies use **currently attainable standards** (sometimes called **normal standards**). These standards can be attained with reasonable effort. Such standards allow for normal production difficulties and mistakes, such as materials spoilage and machine breakdowns. When reasonable standards are used, employees become more focused on cost and are more likely to put forth their best efforts.

An example from the game of golf illustrates the distinction between ideal and normal standards. In golf, *par* is an *ideal* standard for most players. Each player's **United States Golf Association** handicap is the player's *normal* standard. The motivation of average players is to beat their handicaps because they could view beating par as unrealistic.

Reviewing and Revising Standards

Standard costs should be continuously reviewed and should be revised when they no longer reflect operating conditions. Inaccurate standards can distort management decision making and could weaken management's ability to plan and control operations.

Standards should not be revised, however, just because they differ from actual costs. They should be revised only when they no longer reflect the operating conditions that they were intended to measure. For example, the direct labor standard would not be revised simply because workers were unable to meet properly determined standards. On the other hand, standards should be revised when prices, product designs, labor rates, or manufacturing methods change. For example, when aluminum beverage cans were redesigned to taper slightly at the top of the can, manufacturers reduced the standard amount of aluminum per can because less aluminum was required for the top piece of the tapered can.

Support and Criticism of Standards

Standards are used to value inventory and to plan and control costs. Companies are also using standards to assess performance at lower levels of the organization, for shorter accounting periods, and for an increasing number of costs.

Using standards for performance evaluation has been criticized by some. For example, critics assert that standards limit improvement of operations by discouraging improvement beyond the standard. Regardless of this criticism, standards are widely used. One survey reports that managers strongly support standard cost systems and that they regard standards as critical for running large businesses efficiently.

Budgetary Performance Evaluation

As we discussed earlier in this chapter, the master budget assists a company in planning, directing, and controlling performance. In the remainder of this chapter, we discuss using the master budget for control purposes. The control function, or budgetary performance evaluation, compares the actual performance against the budget.

We illustrate budget performance evaluation using Western Rider Inc., a manufacturer of blue jeans. Western Rider Inc. uses standard manufacturing costs in its budgets. The standards for direct materials, direct labor, and factory overhead are separated into two components: (1) a price standard and (2) a quantity standard. Multiplying these two elements together yields the standard cost per unit for a given manufacturing cost category, as shown for style XL jeans in Exhibit 19.

EXHIBIT 19

*Standard Cost for XL
Jeans*

Manufacturing Costs	Standard Price	×	Standard Quantity per Pair	=	Standard Cost per Pair of XL Jeans
Direct materials	$5 per square yard		1.50 square yards		$ 7.50
Direct labor	$9 per hour		0.80 hour per pair		7.20
Factory overhead	$6 per hour		0.80 hour per pair		4.80
Total standard cost per pair					$19.50

The standard price and quantity are separated because the means of controlling them are normally different. For example, the direct materials price per square yard is controlled by the Purchasing Department, and the direct materials quantity per pair is controlled by the Production Department.

As we illustrated earlier in this chapter, the budgeted costs at planned volumes are included in the master budget at the beginning of the period. The standard amounts budgeted for materials purchases, direct labor, and factory overhead are determined by multiplying the standard costs per unit by the planned level of production. At the end of the month, the standard costs per unit are multiplied by the actual production and compared to the actual costs. To illustrate, assume that Western Rider produced and sold 5,000 pairs of XL jeans. It incurred direct materials costs of $40,150, direct labor costs of $38,500, and factory overhead costs of $22,400. The **budget performance report** shown in Exhibit 20 summarizes the actual costs, the standard amounts for the actual level of production achieved, and the differences between the two amounts. These differences are called **cost variances**. A *favorable* cost variance occurs when the actual cost is less than the standard cost (at actual volumes). An *unfavorable* variance occurs when the actual cost exceeds the standard cost (at actual volumes).

Based on the information in the budget performance report, management can investigate major differences and take corrective action. In Exhibit 20, for example, the direct materials cost variance is an unfavorable $2,650. There are two possible explanations for this variance: (1) the amount of blue denim used per pair of blue jeans was different than expected and/or (2) the purchase price of blue denim was different than expected. In the next sections, we illustrate how to separate and analyze these variances for direct materials and direct labor.

EXHIBIT 20
*Budget Performance
Report*

WESTERN RIDER INC.
Budget Performance Report
For the Month Ended June 30, 2004

Manufacturing Costs	Actual Costs	Standard Cost at Actual Volume (5,000 pairs of XL Jeans)*	Cost Variance— (Favorable) Unfavorable
Direct materials	$ 40,150	$37,500	$ 2,650
Direct labor	38,500	36,000	2,500
Factory overhead	22,400	24,000	(1,600)
Total manufacturing costs	$101,050	$97,500	$ 3,550

*5,000 pairs × $7.50 per pair = $37,500
5,000 pairs × $7.20 per pair = $36,000
5,000 pairs × $4.80 per pair = $24,000

Variances from Standards

OBJECTIVE   5

Calculate and interpret
the basic variances for
direct materials and
direct labor.

The total difference between actual costs and standard costs for a period is normally made up of several variances, some of which can be favorable and some unfavorable. There can be variances from standards in direct materials costs, in direct labor costs, and in factory overhead costs. The relationship of these variances to the total manufacturing cost variance is shown here. Illustrations and analyses of these variances for Western Rider Inc. are presented in the following paragraphs.[1]

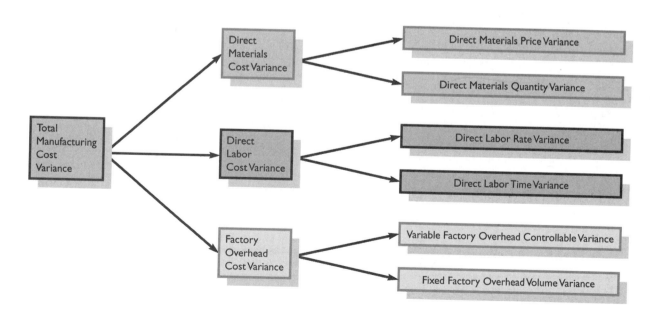

[1]Factory overhead variances are described and illustrated in the appendix at the end of this chapter.

Direct Materials Variances

What caused Western Rider Inc.'s unfavorable materials variance of $2,650? Recall that the direct materials standards from Exhibit 19 are as follows:

Price standard: $5 per square yard
Quantity standard: 1.5 square yards per pair of XL jeans

To determine the number of standard square yards of denim budgeted, multiply the actual production for June 2003 (5,000 pairs) by the quantity standard (1.5 square yards per pair). Then multiply the standard square yards by the standard price per square yard ($5.00) to determine the *standard* budgeted cost at the actual volume. The calculation is shown as follows:

Standard square yards per pair of jeans	1.5 square yards
Actual units produced	× 5,000 pairs of jeans
Standard square yards of denim budgeted for actual production	7,500 square yards
Standard price per square yard	× $5.00
Standard direct materials cost at actual production (same as Exhibit 20)	$ 37,500

This calculation assumes that there is no change in the beginning and ending materials inventories. Thus, the amount of materials budgeted for production equals the amount purchased.

Assume that the *actual* total cost for denim used during June 2004 was as follows:

Actual quantity of denim used in production	7,300 square yards
Actual price per square yard	× $5.50
Total actual direct materials cost (same as Exhibit 20)	$40,150

The total unfavorable cost variance of $2,650 ($40,150 − $37,500) results from an excess price per square yard of $0.50 and using 200 fewer square yards of denim. These two reasons can be reported as two separate variances, as shown in the next sections.

DIRECT MATERIALS PRICE VARIANCE   The **direct materials price variance** is the difference between the actual price per unit ($5.50) and the standard price per unit ($5.00), multiplied by the actual quantity used (7,300 square yards). If the actual price per unit exceeds the standard price per unit, the variance is unfavorable, as shown for Western Rider Inc. If the actual price per unit is less than the standard price per unit, the variance is favorable. The calculation for Western Rider Inc. is as follows:

Price variance:	
Actual price per unit	$5.50 per square yard
Standard price per unit	5.00 per square yard
Price variance—unfavorable	$0.50 per square yard × Actual quantity, 7,300 square yards = $3,650 U

DIRECT MATERIALS QUANTITY VARIANCE   The **direct materials quantity variance** is the difference between the actual quantity used (7,300 square yards) and the standard quantity at actual production (7,500 square yards), multiplied by the standard price per unit ($5.00). If the actual quantity of materials used exceeds the standard quantity budgeted, the variance is unfavorable. If the actual quantity of materials used is less than the standard quantity, the variance is favorable, as shown for Western Rider Inc.:

Quantity variance:
Actual quantity   7,300 square yards
Standard quantity at
   actual production   7,500
Quantity variance—favorable   (200) square yards × Standard price, $5.00 = ($1,000) F

DIRECT MATERIALS VARIANCE RELATIONSHIPS   The direct materials variances can be illustrated by making the three calculations shown in Exhibit 21.

EXHIBIT 21
Direct Materials
Variance Relationships

Actual cost:
Actual quantity
× Actual price
7,300 × $5.50 =
$40,150

Actual quantity ×
Standard price
7,300 × $5.00 =
$36,500

Standard cost:
Standard quantity
× Standard price
7,500 × $5.00 =
$37,500

Materials price variance

$40,150 − $36,500 =
$3,650 U

Materials quantity variance

$36,500 − $37,500 =
$(1,000) F

Total direct materials cost variance

$40,150 − $37,500 = $2,650 U

REPORTING DIRECT MATERIALS VARIANCES   The direct materials quantity variance should be reported to the proper operating management level for corrective action. For example, an unfavorable quantity variance could have been caused by malfunctioning equipment that has not been properly maintained or operated. However, unfavorable materials quantity variances are not always caused by operating departments. For example, the excess materials usage could be caused by purchasing inferior raw materials. In this case, the Purchasing Department should be held responsible for the variance.

The materials price variance should normally be reported to the Purchasing Department, which is or is not able to control this variance. If materials of the same quality could have been purchased from another supplier at the standard price, the variance was controllable. On the other hand, if the variance resulted from a marketwide price increase, the variance could not be controllable.

Direct Labor Variances

Western Rider Inc.'s direct labor cost variance can also be separated into two parts. Recall that the direct labor standards from Exhibit 19 are as follows:

Rate standard: $9 per hour
Time standard: 0.80 hour per pair of XL jeans

The actual production (5,000 pairs) is multiplied by the time standard (0.80 hour per pair) to determine the number of standard direct labor hours budgeted. The standard direct labor hours are then multiplied by the standard rate per hour ($9) to determine the *standard* direct labor cost at actual volumes. These calculations follow.

Standard direct labor hours per pair of XL jeans	0.80 direct labor hours
Actual units produced	× 5,000 pairs of jeans
Standard direct labor hours budgeted for actual production	4,000 direct labor hours
Standard rate per direct labor hour	× $9
Standard direct labor cost at actual production (same as Exhibit 20)	$ 36,000

Assume that the actual total cost for direct labor during June 2003 was as follows:

Actual direct labor hours used in production	3,850 direct labor hours
Actual rate per direct labor hour	× $10
Total actual direct labor cost (same as Exhibit 20)	$ 38,500

The total unfavorable cost variance $2,500 ($38,500 − $36,000) results from an excess rate of $1 per direct labor hour and using 150 fewer direct labor hours. These two reasons can be reported as two separate variances, as we discuss next.

DIRECT LABOR RATE VARIANCE   The **direct labor rate variance** is the difference between the actual rate per hour ($10) and the standard rate per hour ($9), multiplied by the actual hours worked (3,850 hours). If the actual rate per hour is less than the standard rate per hour, the variance is favorable. If the actual rate per hour exceeds the standard rate per hour, the variance is unfavorable, as shown here for Western Rider Inc.

Rate variance:	
Actual rate	$10 per hour
Standard rate	9
Rate variance—unfavorable	$ 1 per hour × Actual time, 3,850 hours = $3,850 U

DIRECT LABOR TIME VARIANCE   The **direct labor time variance** is the difference between the actual hours worked (3,850 hours) and the standard hours at actual production (4,000 hours), multiplied by the standard rate per hour ($9). If the actual hours worked exceed the standard hours, the variance is unfavorable. If the actual hours worked are less than the standard hours, the variance is favorable, as shown here for Western Rider Inc.:

Time variance:	
Actual hours	3,850 direct labor hours
Standard hours at actual production	4,000
Time variance—favorable	(150) direct labor hours × Standard rate, $9 = ($1,350) F

DIRECT LABOR VARIANCE RELATIONSHIPS   The direct labor variances can be illustrated by making the three calculations shown in Exhibit 22.

EXHIBIT 22
Direct Labor Variance Relationships

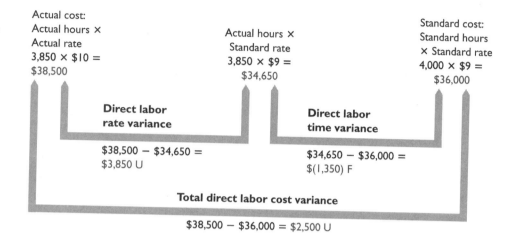

REPORTING DIRECT LABOR VARIANCES   Controlling direct labor cost is normally the responsibility of the production supervisors. To aid them, reports analyzing the cause of any direct labor variance can be prepared. Differences between standard direct labor hours and actual direct labor hours can be investigated. For example, a time variance could be incurred because of the shortage of skilled workers. Such variances could be uncontrollable unless they are related to high turnover rates among employees in which case the cause of the high turnover should be investigated.

Likewise, differences between the rates paid for direct labor and the standard rates can be investigated. For example, unfavorable rate variances could be caused by the improper scheduling and use of workers. In such cases, skilled, highly paid workers could be used in jobs that are normally performed by unskilled, lower-paid workers. In this case, the unfavorable rate variance should be reported for corrective action to the managers who schedule work assignments.

Standards for Nonmanufacturing Expenses

OBJECTIVE   6

Explain how standards can be used for nonmanufacturing expenses.

Using standards for nonmanufacturing expenses, such as service, selling, and administrative expenses, is not as common as using standards for manufacturing costs. The reason for this is that few nonmanufacturing expenses are directly related to a unit of output or other measure of activity. For example, the administrative expenses associated with the work of the office manager are not easily related to a measurable output. In these cases, nonmanufacturing expenses are normally controlled by using static budgets.

However, when nonmanufacturing activities are repetitive and produce a common output, standards can be applied. In these cases, the use of standards is similar to that described for a manufactured product. For example, standards can be applied to the work of office personnel who process sales orders. A standard cost for processing a sales order (the output) could be developed. The variance between the actual cost of processing a sales order and the standard cost could then be used to control sales order processing costs.

Nonfinancial Performance Measures

OBJECTIVE   7

Explain and provide examples of nonfinancial performance measures.

Many managers believe that financial performance measures, such as variances from standard, should be supplemented with nonfinancial measures of performance. Measuring both financial and nonfinancial performance helps employees consider multiple—and sometimes conflicting—performance objectives. For example, one company had a machining operation that was measured according to a direct labor time standard. Employees did their work quickly to create favorable direct labor time variances. Unfortunately, the fast work resulted in poor quality that, in turn, created difficulty in the assembly operation. The company decided to use both a labor time standard *and* a quality standard to encourage employees to consider both the speed and quality of their work.

U.S. airlines use a variety of nonfinancial measures, such as on-time performance, lost baggage, and customer complaints. These nonfinancial measures are used to balance customer satisfaction with cost reduction. Many airlines have admitted going too far in cutting costs. As a result, **Northwest Airlines** increased the frequency of steam-cleaning its planes' lavatories from every 14 days to every 9 days. **America West** upgraded food and installed in-flight phones. **Delta Air Lines** added baggage handlers and gate agents to reduce waiting time during arrivals and departures.

In the preceding examples, nonfinancial performance measures brought additional perspectives, such as quality of work, to evaluating performance. Some additional examples of nonfinancial performance measures are as follows:

Nonfinancial Performance Measures*

Inventory turnover (82%)
On-time delivery (41%)
Elapsed time between a customer order and product delivery (35%)
Customer preference rankings compared to competitors
Response time to a service call
Time to develop new products
Employee satisfaction
Number of customer complaints

*The first three examples indicate the percentage of firms using the nonfinancial performance measure, taken from a survey by Forrest B. Green and Felix E. Amenkhienan, "Accounting Innovations: A Cross-Sectional Survey of Manufacturing Firms," *Journal of Cost Management*, Spring 1992, pp. 58–64.

Nonfinancial measures can relate to either inputs or outputs to an activity or process, shown as follows:

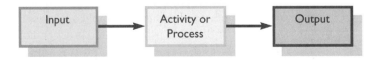

For example, consider the counter service activity of a fast-food restaurant. The following input/output relationship could be identified:

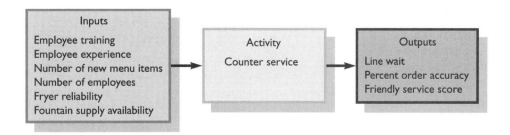

The outputs of the counter service activity include the customer line wait, order accuracy, and service experience. The inputs that impact these outputs include the number of employees, level of employee experience and training, reliability of the french fryer, menu complexity, fountain drink supply, and the like. Additionally, note that the inputs for one activity could be the outputs of another. For example, fryer reliability is an input to the counter service activity but is an output of the french frying activity. Moving back, fryer maintenance would be an input to the french frying activity. Thus, a chain of inputs and outputs can be developed between a set of connected activities or processes. The fast-food restaurant can develop a set of linked nonfinancial performance measures across the chain of inputs and outputs. The output measures tell management how the activity is performing, such as keeping the line wait to a minimum. The input measures are the *levers* that impact the activity's performance. Thus, if the fast-food restaurant line wait is too long, the input measures could indicate the need for more training, more employees, or better fryer reliability.

APPENDIX

Factory Overhead Cost Variances

Factory overhead costs are more difficult to manage than are direct labor and materials costs. This is so because the relationship between production volume and indirect costs is not easy to determine. For example, when production is increased, direct materials also will increase. But what about the Engineering Department overhead? The relationship between production volume and cost is less clear for the Engineering Department. Companies normally respond to this difficulty by separating factory overhead into variable and fixed costs. For example, manufacturing supplies are considered variable to production volume, whereas straight-line plant depreciation is considered fixed. In the following sections, we discuss the approaches used to budget and control factory overhead by separating overhead into fixed and variable components.

The Factory Overhead Flexible Budget

A flexible budget can be used to determine the impact of changing production on fixed and variable factory overhead costs. The standard overhead rate is determined by dividing the budgeted factory overhead costs by the standard amount of productive activity, such as direct labor hours. Exhibit 23 is a flexible factory overhead budget for Western Rider Inc.

WESTERN RIDER INC
Factory Overhead Cost Budget
For the Month Ending June 30, 2004

	80%	90%	100%	110%
Percent of normal capacity	80%	90%	100%	110%
Units produced	5,000	5,625	6,250	6,875
Direct labor hours (0.80 hour per unit)	4,000	4,500	5,000	5,500
Budgeted factory overhead:				
Variable costs:				
Indirect factory wages	$ 8,000	$ 9,000	$10,000	$11,000
Power and light	4,000	4,500	5,000	5,500
Indirect materials	2,400	2,700	3,000	3,300
Total variable cost	$14,400	$16,200	$18,000	$19,800
Fixed costs:				
Supervisory salaries	$ 5,500	$ 5,500	$ 5,500	$ 5,500
Depreciation of plant and equipment	4,500	4,500	4,500	4,500
Insurance and property taxes	2,000	2,000	2,000	2,000
Total fixed cost	$12,000	$12,000	$12,000	$12,000
Total factory overhead cost	$26,400	$28,200	$30,000	$31,800

Factory overhead rate per direct labor hour, $30,000/5,000 = $6.00

In Exhibit 23, the standard factory overhead cost rate is $6.00. It is determined by dividing the total budgeted cost of 100% of normal capacity by the standard hours required at 100% of normal capacity, or $30,000/5,000 hours = $6.00 per hour. This rate can be subdivided into $3.60 per hour for variable factory overhead ($18,000/5,000 hours) and $2.40 per hour for fixed factory overhead ($12,000/5,000 hours).

Variances from standard for factory overhead cost result from the following:

1. Actual variable factory overhead cost greater or less than budgeted variable factory overhead for actual production.
2. Actual production at a level above or below 100% of normal capacity.

The first factor results in the controllable variance for variable overhead costs. The second factor results in a volume variance for fixed overhead costs. We discuss each of these variances next.

Variable Factory Overhead Controllable Variance

The variable factory overhead **controllable variance** is the difference between the actual variable overhead incurred and the budgeted variable overhead for actual production. The controllable variance measures the *efficiency* of using variable overhead resources. Thus, if the actual variable overhead is less than the budgeted variable overhead, the variance is favorable. If the actual variable overhead exceeds the budgeted variable overhead, the variance is unfavorable.

To illustrate, recall that Western Rider Inc. produced 5,000 pairs of XL jeans in June. Each pair requires 0.80 standard labor hour for production. As a result, Western Rider Inc. had 4,000 standard hours at actual production (5,000 jeans × 0.80 hour). This represents 80% of normal productive capacity (4,000 hours/5,000 hours). The standard variable overhead at 4,000 hours worked, according to the budget in Exhibit 23, was $14,400 (4,000 direct labor hours × $3.60). The following actual factory overhead costs were incurred in June:

Actual costs:	
Variable factory overhead	$10,400
Fixed factory overhead	12,000
Total actual factory overhead	$22,400

The controllable variance can be calculated as follows:

Controllable variance:	
Actual variable factory overhead	$10,400
Budgeted variable factory overhead for	
actual amount produced (4,000 hours × $3.60)	14,400
Variance—favorable	$ (4,000) F

The variable factory overhead controllable variance indicates management's ability to keep the factory overhead costs within the budget limits. Since variable factory overhead costs are normally controllable at the department level, responsibility for controlling this variance usually rests with department supervisors.

Fixed Factory Overhead Volume Variance

Using currently attainable standards, Western Rider Inc. set its budgeted normal capacity at 5,000 direct labor hours. This is the amount of expected capacity that management believes will be used under normal business conditions. You should note that this amount could be much less than the total available capacity if management believes demand will be low.

The fixed factory overhead *volume variance* is the difference between the budgeted fixed overhead at 100% of normal capacity and the standard fixed overhead for the actual production achieved during the period. The volume variance measures the use of fixed overhead resources. If the standard fixed overhead exceeds the budgeted overhead at 100% of normal capacity, the variance is favorable. Thus, the firm used its plant and equipment more than would be expected under normal operating conditions. If the standard fixed overhead is less than the budgeted overhead at 100% of normal capacity, the variance is unfavorable. Thus, the company used its plant and equipment less than would be expected under normal operating conditions.

The volume variance for Western Rider Inc. is shown in the following calculation:

100% of normal capacity	5,000 direct labor hours
Standard hours at actual production	4,000
Capacity not used	1,000 direct labor hours
Standard fixed overhead rate	× $2.40
Volume variance—unfavorable	$ 2,400 U

Exhibit 24 illustrates the volume variance graphically. For Western Rider Inc., the budgeted fixed overhead is $12,000 at all levels. The standard fixed overhead at 5,000 hours is also $12,000. This is the point at which the standard fixed overhead line intersects the budgeted fixed cost line. For actual volume more than 100% of normal capacity, the volume variance is favorable. For volume at less than 100% of normal volume, the volume variance is unfavorable. For Western Rider Inc., the volume variance is unfavorable because the actual production is 4,000 standard hours, or 80% of normal volume. The amount of the volume variance, $2,400, can be viewed as the cost of the unused capacity (1,000 hours).

EXHIBIT 24

Graph of Fixed Overhead Volume Variance

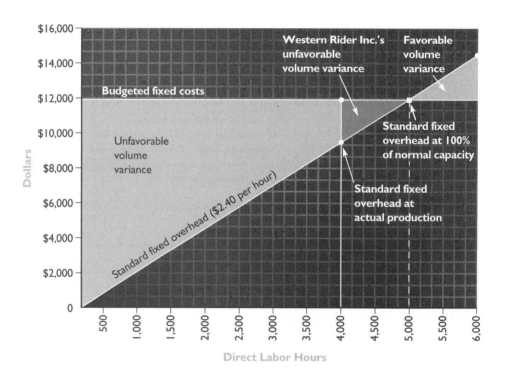

An unfavorable volume variance could be due to factors such as failure to maintain an even flow of work, machine breakdowns, repairs causing work stoppages, and failure to obtain enough sales orders to keep the factory operating at normal capacity. Management should determine the causes of the unfavorable variance and consider taking corrective action. A volume variance caused by an uneven flow of work, for example, can be remedied by changing operating procedures. Volume variances caused by lack of sales orders can be corrected through increased advertising or other sales effort.

Volume variances tend to encourage manufacturing managers to run the factory above the normal capacity. This is favorable when the additional production can be sold. However, if the additional production cannot be sold and must be stored as inventory, favorable volume variances could actually be harmful. For example, one paper company ran paper machines above normal volume to create favorable volume variances. Unfortunately, this created a 6-month supply of finished goods inventory that had to be stored in public warehouses. The "savings" from the favorable volume variances were exceeded by the additional inventory carrying costs. By creating incentives for manufacturing managers to overproduce, the volume variances produced *goal conflicts*, as we described earlier in the chapter.

Reporting Factory Overhead Variances

The total factory overhead cost variance is the difference between the actual factory overhead and the total overhead applied to production. This calculation is as follows:

Total actual factory overhead	$22,400
Factory overhead applied (4,000 hours × $6.00 per hour)	24,000
Total factory overhead cost variance—favorable	$ (1,600) F

The factory overhead cost variance can be broken down by each variable factory overhead cost and fixed factory overhead cost element in a **factory overhead cost variance report**. Such a report, which is useful to management in controlling costs, is shown in Exhibit 25. The report indicates both the controllable variance and the volume variance.

EXHIBIT 25 *Factory Overhead Cost Variance Report*

WESTERN RIDER INC.
Factory Overhead Cost Variance Report
For the Month Ended June 30, 2004

	Budget (at actual production)	Actual	Variances Favorable	Variances Unfavorable
Productive capacity for the month (100% of normal)	5,000 hours			
Actual production for the month	4,000 hours			
Variable factory overhead costs:				
Indirect factory wages	$ 8,000	$ 5,100	$2,900	
Power and light	4,000	4,200		$ 200
Indirect materials	2,400	1,100	1,300	
Total variable factory overhead cost	$14,400	$10,400		
Fixed factory overhead costs:				
Supervisory salaries	$ 5,500	$ 5,500		
Depreciation of plant and equipment	4,500	4,500		
Insurance and property taxes	2,000	2,000		
Total fixed factory overhead cost	$12,000	$12,000		
Total factory overhead cost	$26,400	$22,400		
Total controllable variances			$4,200	$ 200
Net controllable variance—favorable				$4,000
Volume variance—unfavorable:				
Capacity not used at the standard rate for fixed factory overhead—1,000 × $2.40				2,400
Total factory overhead cost variance—favorable				$1,600

It is also possible to break down many of the individual factory overhead cost variances into quantity and price variances, as is done for direct materials and direct labor. For example, the indirect factory wages variance could include both time and rate variances. Likewise, the indirect materials variance could include both a quantity variance and a price variance. Such variances are illustrated in advanced textbooks.

Key Points

1. Describe the nature and objectives of budgeting.

Budgeting involves (1) establishing specific goals, (2) executing plans to achieve the goals, and (3) periodically comparing actual results with these goals. In addition, budget goals should be established to avoid problems in human behavior. Thus, budgets should not be set too tightly, too loosely, or to cause goal conflict. Budgeting systems can use fiscal-year budgeting, continuous budgeting, or zero-based budgeting. Two major types of budgets are the static budget and the flexible budget. The static budget does not adjust with changes in activity while the flexible budget does adjust with changes in activity. Computers can be useful in speeding the budgetary process and in preparing timely budget performance reports. In addition, simulation models can be used to determine the impact of operating alternatives on various budgets.

2. Describe the master budget for a manufacturing business.

The master budget consists of the budgeted income statement and budgeted balance sheet. These two budgets are developed from detailed supporting budgets. The income statement supporting budgets are the sales budget, production budget, direct materials purchases budget, direct labor cost budget, factory overhead cost budget, cost of goods sold budget, and selling and administrative expenses budget. Both the cash budget and the capital expenditures budget support the budgeted balance sheet. The cash budget consists of budgeted cash receipts and budgeted cash payments. The capital expenditures budget is an important tool for planning expenditures for fixed assets.

3. Describe the nature and use of standards.

Standards represent performance benchmarks that can be compared to actual results in evaluating performance. Standards are developed, reviewed, and revised by accountants and engineers based on studies of operations. Standards are established so that they are neither too high nor too low but are attainable.

4. Explain and illustrate how standards are used in budgeting.

Budgets are prepared by multiplying the standard cost per unit by the planned production. To measure performance, the standard cost per unit is multiplied by the actual number of units produced, and the actual results are compared with the standard cost at actual volumes (cost variance).

5. Calculate and interpret the basic variances for direct materials and direct labor.

The direct materials cost variance can be separated into a direct materials price and a quantity variance. The direct materials price variance is calculated by multiplying the actual quantity by the difference between the actual and standard price. The direct materials quantity variance is calculated by multiplying the standard price by the difference between the actual materials used and the standard materials at actual volumes.

The direct labor cost variance can be separated into a direct labor rate and time variance. The direct labor rate variance is calculated by multiplying the actual hours worked by the difference between the actual labor rate and the standard labor rate. The direct labor time variance is calculated by multiplying the standard labor rate by the difference between the actual labor hours worked and the standard labor hours at actual volumes.

6. Explain how standards can be used for nonmanufacturing expenses.

Standards can be used for nonmanufacturing expenses when nonmanufacturing activities are repetitive and related to an activity base. Such standards can be useful to managers in planning, directing, and controlling nonmanufacturing expenses.

7. **Explain and provide examples of nonfinancial performance measures.**

Many companies use a combination of financial and nonfinancial measures in order for multiple perspec-

tives to be incorporated in evaluating performance. Combining financial and nonfinancial measures helps employees balance cost efficiency with quality and customer service performance.

Glossary

Budget: An accounting device used to plan and control resources of operational departments and divisions.

Budget performance report: A report comparing actual results with budget figures.

Capital expenditures budget: The budget summarizing future plans for acquiring plant facilities and equipment.

Cash budget: A budget of estimated cash receipts and payments.

Continuous budgeting: A method of budgeting that provides for maintaining a 12-month projection into the future.

Cost of goods sold budget: A budget of the estimated direct materials, direct labor, and factory overhead consumed by sold products.

Cost variance: The difference between the actual cost and the standard cost at actual volumes.

Currently attainable standards: Standards that represent levels of operation that can be obtained with reasonable effort.

Direct labor rate variance: The cost associated with the difference between

the standard rate and the actual rate paid for direct labor used in producing a commodity.

Direct labor time variance: The cost associated with the difference between the standard hours and the actual hours of direct labor spent producing a commodity.

Direct materials price variance: The cost associated with the difference between the standard price and the actual price of direct materials used in producing a commodity.

Direct materials purchases budget: A budget that uses the production budget as a starting point for determining the estimated amounts of direct materials to be purchased.

Direct materials quantity variance: The cost associated with the difference between the standard quantity and the actual quantity of direct materials used in producing a commodity.

Flexible budget: A budget that adjusts for varying rates of activity.

Goal conflict: Situation when individual self-interest differs from business objectives.

Master budget: The comprehensive budget plan linking the individual

budgets related to sales, cost of goods sold, operating expenses, projects, capital expenditures, and cash.

Production budget: A budget of estimated unit production.

Sales budget: A budget that indicates for each product (1) the quantity of estimated sales and (2) the expected unit selling price.

Standard cost: A detailed estimate of what a product should cost.

Standard cost systems: Accounting systems that use standards for each manufacturing cost entering into the finished product.

Static budget: A budget that does not adjust to changes in activity levels.

Theoretical standards: Standards that represent levels of performance that can be achieved only under perfect operating conditions.

Zero-based budgeting: A concept of budgeting that requires all levels of management to start from zero and estimate budget data as if there had been no previous activities in their units.

Self-Study Questions

(Answers appear at end of chapter.)

1. Static budgets are often used by:
   A. production departments.
   B. administrative departments.
   C. sales departments.
   D. capital projects.

2. The total estimated sales for the coming year is 250,000 units. The estimated inventory at the beginning of the year is 22,500 units, and the desired inventory at the end of the year is 30,000 units. The total production indicated in the production budget is:
   A. 242,500 units.   C. 280,000 units.
   B. 257,500 units.   D. 302,500 units.

3. Dixon Company expects $650,000 of credit sales in March and $800,000 of credit sales in April. Dixon historically collects 70% of its sales in the month of sale and 30% in the following month. How much cash does Dixon expect to collect in April?
   A. $800,000   C. $755,000
   B. $560,000   D. $1,015,000

4. The actual and standard direct materials costs for producing a specified quantity of product are as follows:

   Actual: 51,000 pounds at $5.05, $257,550.
   Standard: 50,000 pounds at $5.00, $250,000.

   The direct materials price variance is:
   A. $50 unfavorable.   C. $2,550 unfavorable.
   B. $2,500 unfavorable.   D. $7,550 unfavorable.

5. Bower Company produced 4,000 units of product. Each unit requires 0.5 standard hour. The standard labor rate is $12 per hour. Actual direct labor for the period was $22,000 (2,200 hours × $10 per hour). The direct labor time variance is:
   A. 200 hours unfavorable.
   B. $2,000 unfavorable.
   C. $4,000 favorable.
   D. $2,400 unfavorable.

Discussion Questions

1. Briefly describe the type of human behavior problems that could arise if budget goals are set too tightly.

2. Why should all levels of management and all departments participate in preparing and submitting budget estimates?

3. What behavioral problems are associated with setting a budget too loosely?

4. What behavioral problems are associated with establishing conflicting goals within the budget?

5. When would a company use zero-based budgeting?

6. Under what circumstances would a static budget be appropriate?

7. How do computerized budgeting systems aid firms in the budgeting process?

8. What is the first step in preparing a master budget?

9. Why should the production requirements set forth in the production budget be carefully coordinated with the sales budget?

10. Why should the timing of direct materials purchases be closely coordinated with the production budget?

11. In preparing the budget for the cost of goods sold, what are the three budgets from which data on relevant estimates of quantities and costs are combined with data on estimated inventories?

12. Give an example of the effect of the capital expenditures budget on other operating budgets.

13. How can standards be used by management to help control costs?

14. a. What are the two variances between the actual cost and the standard cost for direct materials?
    b. Discuss some possible causes of these variances.

15. The materials cost variance report for Nickols Inc. indicates a large favorable materials price variance and a significant unfavorable materials quantity variance. What could have caused these offsetting variances?

16. a. What are the two variances between the actual cost and the standard cost for direct labor?
    b. Who generally has control over the direct labor cost?

17. A new assistant controller recently was heard to remark, "All the assembly workers in this plant are covered by union contracts, so there should be no labor variances." Was the controller's remark correct? Discuss.

18. Would the use of standards be appropriate in a non-manufacturing setting, such as a fast-food restaurant?

19. Briefly explain why firms would use nonfinancial performance measures.

Exercises

EXERCISE 13-1
Flexible budget for selling and administrative expenses
OBJECTIVES 1, 2

✓ Total selling and administrative expenses at $200,000 sales, $56,500

Medico Medical Supply Company uses flexible budgets that are based on the following data:

Sales commissions	5% of sales
Advertising expense	12% of sales
Miscellaneous selling expense	$2,000 plus 3% of sales
Office salaries expense	$8,000 per month
Office supplies expense	2% of sales
Miscellaneous administrative expense	$500 per month plus 1% of sales

Prepare a flexible selling and administrative expenses budget for May 2004, for sales volumes of $120,000, $160,000, and $200,000. (Use Exhibit 4 as a model.)

EXERCISE 13-2
Sales and production budgets
OBJECTIVE 2

✓ b. Model CRI total production, 8,160 units

Grand Electronics Company manufactures two models of clock radios, CR1 and CR2. Based on the following production and sales data for September 2004, prepare (a) a sales budget and (b) a production budget.

	CR1	CR2
Estimated inventory (units), September 1	350	120
Desired inventory (units), September 30	410	100
Expected sales volume (units):		
East Region	4,700	3,200
West Region	3,400	2,400
Unit sales price	$65.00	$80.00

EXERCISE 13-3
Professional fees budget
OBJECTIVE 2

✓ Total professional fees, $15,259,500

Garcia and Berry, CPAs, offer three types of services to clients: auditing, tax, and computer consulting. Based on experience and projected growth, the following billable hours have been estimated for the year ending December 31, 2004:

	Billable Hours
Audit Department:	
Staff	36,000
Partners	5,200
Tax Department:	
Staff	30,600
Partners	4,100
Computer Consulting Department:	
Staff	40,200
Partners	15,800

The average billing rate for staff is $90 per hour, and the average billing rate for partners is $225 per hour. Prepare a professional fees budget for Garcia and Berry, CPAs, for the year ending December 31, 2004, using the following column headings and showing the estimated professional fees by type of service rendered:

Billable Hours	Hourly Rate	Total Revenue

EXERCISE 13-4
Professional labor cost budget
OBJECTIVE 2

✓ Staff total labor cost, $4,272,000

Based on the data in Exercise 13-3 and assuming that the average compensation per hour for staff is $40 and for partners is $120, prepare a professional labor cost budget for Garcia and Berry, CPAs, for the year ending December 31, 2004. Use the following column headings:

Billable Hours Required	
Staff	Partners

EXERCISE 13-5
Direct materials purchases budget
OBJECTIVE 2

✓ Total cheese purchases, $157,992

Mama Leona's Frozen Pizza Inc. has determined from its production budget the following estimated production volumes for 12″ and 16″ frozen pizzas for August 2004:

	Units	
	12″ Pizza	16″ Pizza
Budgeted production volume	28,500	41,800

There are three direct materials used in producing the two types of pizza. The amounts of direct materials expected to be used for each pizza are as follows:

	12″ Pizza	16″ Pizza
Direct materials:		
Dough	1.00 pound per unit	1.50 pounds per unit
Tomato	0.50	0.80
Cheese	0.70	1.10

In addition, Mama Leona's has determined the following information about each material:

	Dough	Tomato	Cheese
Estimated inventory, August 1, 2004	500 pounds	200 pounds	450 pounds
Desired inventory, August 31, 2004	450 pounds	240 pounds	350 pounds
Price per pound	$1.30	$2.10	$2.40

Prepare August's direct materials purchases budget for Mama Leona's Frozen Pizza Inc.

EXERCISE 13-6
Direct materials purchases budget
OBJECTIVE 2

✓ Concentrate budgeted purchases, $89,820

Coca-Cola Enterprises is the largest bottler of Coca-Cola® in North America. The company purchases Coke® and Sprite® concentrate from **The Coca-Cola Company**, dilutes and mixes the concentrate with carbonated water, and then fills the blended beverage into cans or plastic 2-liter bottles. Assume the estimated production for Coke and Sprite 2-liter bottles at the Chattanooga, Tennessee, bottling plant are as follows for the month of September:

Coke	155,000 2-liter bottles
Sprite	126,000 2-liter bottles

In addition, assume that the concentrate costs $90 per pound for both Coke and Sprite and is used at a rate of 0.2 pound per 100 liters of carbonated water in blending Coke and 0.15 pound per 100 liters of carbonated water in blending Sprite. Assume that 2-liter bottles cost $0.09 per bottle and carbonated water costs $0.04 per liter.

Prepare a direct materials purchases budget for September 2004, assuming no changes between beginning and ending inventories for all three materials.

EXERCISE 13-7
Direct labor cost budget
OBJECTIVE 2

✓ Total direct labor cost, Finishing, $154,620

Ace Racket Company manufactures two types of tennis rackets, the Junior and Pro-Striker models. The production budget for August for the two rackets is as follows:

	Junior	Pro-Striker
Production budget	4,300 units	14,600 units

Both rackets are produced in two departments, Molding and Finishing. The direct labor hours required for each racket are estimated as follows:

	Molding Department	Finishing Department
Junior	0.20 hour per unit	0.30 hour per unit
Pro-Striker	0.30 hour per unit	0.50 hour per unit

The direct labor rate for each department is as follows:

Molding Department	$15 per hour
Finishing Department	$18 per hour

Prepare the direct labor cost budget for August 2004.

EXERCISE 13-8
Production and direct labor cost budgets
OBJECTIVE 2

✓ a. Total production of 501 Jeans, 49,560

Levi Strauss & Co. manufactures jeans and slacks under a variety of brand names, such as Dockers® and 501 Jeans®. Slacks and jeans are assembled by a variety of different sewing operations. Assume that the sales budget for Dockers and 501 Jeans shows estimated sales of 25,400 and 49,600 pairs, respectively, for March 2004. The finished goods inventory is assumed as follows:

	Dockers	501 Jeans
March 1 estimated inventory	300	140
March 31 desired inventory	250	100

Assume the following direct labor data per 10 pairs of Dockers and 501 Jeans for four different sewing operations:

Direct Labor per 10 Pairs		
	Dockers	501 Jeans
Inseam	15 minutes	12 minutes
Outerseam	20	14
Pockets	5	8
Zipper	6	6
Total	46 minutes	40 minutes

a. Prepare a production budget for March.
b. Prepare the March direct labor cost budget for the four sewing operations, assuming a $9 wage per hour for the inseam and outerseam sewing operations and a $10 wage per hour for the pocket and zipper sewing operations.

EXERCISE 13-9
*Factory overhead cost
budget*
OBJECTIVE 2

✓ Total variable factory
overhead costs, $237,000

Hans Watch Company budgeted the following costs for anticipated production for January 2004:

Advertising expenses	$260,000
Manufacturing supplies	12,000
Power and light	45,000
Sales commissions	280,000
Factory insurance	20,000
Supervisor wages	123,000
Production control salaries	32,000
Executive officer salaries	210,000
Materials management salaries	25,000
Factory depreciation	19,000

Prepare a factory overhead cost budget, separating variable and fixed costs. Assume that factory insurance and depreciation are the only fixed costs.

EXERCISE 13-10
*Cost of goods sold
budget*
OBJECTIVE 2

✓ Cost of goods sold,
$342,050

The controller of Model Ceramic Company wishes to prepare a cost of goods sold budget for June. The controller assembled the following information for constructing the cost of goods sold budget:

Direct materials:

	Enamel	Paint	Porcelain	Total
Total direct materials purchases budgeted for June	$28,580	$5,340	$96,400	$130,320
Estimated inventory, June 1, 2004	1,250	2,400	4,540	8,190
Desired inventory, June 30, 2004	2,000	2,150	5,000	9,150

Direct labor cost:

	Kiln Department	Decorating Department	Total
Total direct labor cost budgeted for June	$36,500	$105,800	$142,300

Finished goods inventories:

	Dish	Bowl	Figurine	Total
Estimated inventory, June 1, 2004	$4,180	$3,270	$2,580	$10,030
Desired inventory, June 30, 2004	3,250	3,940	3,100	10,290

Work in process inventories:
Estimated inventory, June 1, 2004	$ 2,900
Desired inventory, June 30, 2004	1,350

Budgeted factory overhead costs for June:
Indirect factory wages	$45,800
Depreciation of plant and equipment	14,600
Power and light	5,300
Indirect materials	3,400
Total	$69,100

Use the preceding information to prepare a cost of goods sold budget for June 2004.

EXERCISE 13-11

Schedule of cash collections of accounts receivable

OBJECTIVE 2

✓ Total cash collected in May, $525,700

Trevor Company was organized on March 1, 2004. Projected sales for each of the first three months of operations are as follows:

March	$480,000
April	590,000
May	505,000

The company expects to sell 10% of its merchandise for cash. Of sales on account, 60% are expected to be collected in the month of the sale, 30% in the month following the sale, and the remainder in the second month following the sale.

Prepare a schedule indicating cash collections from sales for March, April, and May.

EXERCISE 13-12

Schedule of cash payments

OBJECTIVE 2

✓ Total cash payments in August, $136,925

Tutor.com Inc. was organized on May 31, 2004. Projected selling and administrative expenses for each of the first three months of operations are as follows:

June	$ 95,400
July	126,800
August	156,300

Depreciation, insurance, and property taxes represent $12,000 of the estimated monthly expenses. The annual insurance premium was paid on May 31, and property taxes for the year will be paid in December. Three-fourths of the remainder of the expenses are expected to be paid in the month in which they are incurred with the balance to be paid in the following month.

Prepare a schedule indicating cash payments for selling and administrative expenses for June, July, and August.

EXERCISE 13-13

Schedule of cash payments

OBJECTIVE 2

✓ Total cash payments in December, $123,980

The Sea Breeze Hotel is planning its cash payments for operations for the fourth quarter (October–December) of 2004. The Accrued Expenses Payable balance on October 1 is $18,400. The budgeted expenses for the next three months are as follows:

	October	November	December
Salaries	$ 57,400	$ 68,900	$ 75,600
Utilities	5,000	5,400	6,100
Other operating expenses	43,200	51,300	62,300
Total	$105,600	$125,600	$144,000

Other operating expenses include $13,500 of monthly depreciation expense and $1,000 of monthly insurance expense that was prepaid for the year on March 1 of the current year. Of the remaining expenses, 70% are paid in the month in which they are incurred with the remainder paid in the following month. The Accrued Expenses Payable balance on October 1 relates to the expenses incurred in September.

Prepare a schedule of cash payments for operations for October, November, and December.

EXERCISE 13-14

Capital expenditures budget

OBJECTIVE 2

✓ Total capital expenditures in 2007, $5,000,000

On January 1, 2004, the controller of Minter Manufacturing Company is planning capital expenditures for the years 2004–2007. The following interviews helped the controller collect the necessary information for the capital expenditures budget.

Director of Facilities: A construction contract was signed in late 2003 for the construction of a new factory building at a contract cost of $10,000,000. The construction is scheduled to begin in 2004 and be completed in 2005.

Vice-President of Manufacturing: Once the new factory building is finished, we plan to purchase $1.6 million in equipment in late 2005. I expect that an additional $300,000 will be needed early in the following year (2006) to test and install the equipment before we can begin production. If sales continue to grow, I expect we'll need to invest another million in equipment in 2007.

Vice-President of Marketing: We have really been growing lately. I wouldn't be surprised if we need to expand the size of our new factory building in 2007 by at least 40%. Fortunately, we expect inflation to have minimal impact on construction costs over the next four years.

Director of Information Systems: We need to upgrade our information systems to local area network (LAN) technology. It doesn't make sense to do this until after the new factory building is completed and producing product. During 2006, once the factory is up and running, we should equip the whole facility with LAN technology. I think it would cost us $1,800,000 today to install the technology. However, prices have been dropping by 20% per year, so it should be less expensive at a later date.

President: I'm excited about our long-term prospects. My only short-term concern is financing the $6,000,000 of construction costs on the portion of the new factory building scheduled to be completed in 2004.

Use this interview information to prepare a capital expenditures budget for Minter Manufacturing Company for the years 2004–2007.

EXERCISE 13-15
Standard product cost
OBJECTIVES 3, 4

Pine Hill Furniture Company manufactures unfinished oak furniture. Pine Hill uses a standard cost system. The direct labor, direct materials, and factory overhead standards for an unfinished dining room table are as follows:

Direct labor:	Standard rate	$12.00 per hour
	Standard time per unit	4.80 hours
Direct materials (oak):	Standard price	$24.00 per board foot
	Standard quantity	20 board feet
Variable factory overhead:	Standard rate	$4.00 per direct labor hour
Fixed factory overhead:	Standard rate	$1.50 per direct labor hour

Determine the standard cost per dining room table.

EXERCISE 13-16
Direct materials variances
OBJECTIVE 5

✓ a. Price variance, $12,680 F

The following data relate to the direct materials cost for the production of 4,000 automobile tires:

| Actual: | 126,800 pounds at $1.90 | $240,920 |
| Standard: | 125,000 pounds at $2.00 | $250,000 |

a. Determine the price variance, quantity variance, and total direct materials cost variance.
b. To whom should the variances be reported for analysis and control?

EXERCISE 13-17
Standard direct materials cost per unit from variance data
OBJECTIVE 5

The following data relating to direct materials cost for August of the current year are taken from the records of Big Toys Inc., a manufacturer of plastic toys:

Amount of direct materials used	40,000 pounds
Actual unit price of direct materials	$1.40 per pound
Units of finished product manufactured	6,000 units
Standard direct materials per unit of finished product	6.25 pounds
Direct materials quantity variance—unfavorable	$3,400
Direct materials price variance—unfavorable	$1,600

Determine the standard direct materials cost per unit of finished product, assuming that there was no inventory of work in process at either the beginning or the end of the month.

EXERCISE 13-18

Standard product cost, direct materials variance

OBJECTIVE 5

✓ a. $0.80 per pound

H.J. Heinz Company uses standards to control its materials costs. Assume that a batch of ketchup (1,500 pounds) has the following standards:

	Standard Quantity	Standard Price
Whole tomatoes	2,000 pounds	$0.35 per pound
Vinegar	104 gallons	2.50 per gallon
Corn syrup	15 gallons	8.50 per gallon
Salt	50 pounds	2.25 per pound

The actual materials in a batch can vary from the standard due to tomato characteristics. Assume that the actual quantity of materials for batch A-24 were as follows:

2,050 pounds of tomatoes
100 gallons of vinegar
16 gallons of corn syrup
48 pounds of salt

a. Determine the standard unit materials cost per pound for a standard batch.
b. Determine the direct materials quantity variance for batch A-24.

EXERCISE 13-19

Direct labor variances

OBJECTIVE 5

✓ a. Rate variance, $3,360 U

The following data relate to labor cost for production of 6,000 cellular telephones:

Actual:	8,400 hours at $16.40	$137,760
Standard:	9,000 hours at $16.00	$144,000

a. Determine the rate variance, time variance, and total direct labor cost variance.
b. Discuss what could have caused these variances.

EXERCISE 13-20

Direct labor variances

OBJECTIVE 5

✓ Time variance, $500 F

High Mountain Bicycle Company manufactures mountain bikes. The following data for March of the current year are available:

Amount of direct labor used	1,860 hours
Actual rate for direct labor	$13.00 per hour
Bicycles completed in March	250
Standard direct labor per bicycle	7.60 hours
Standard rate for direct labor	$12.50 per hour
Planned bicycles for March	200

Determine the direct labor rate and time variance.

EXERCISE 13-21

Direct materials and direct labor variances

OBJECTIVE 5

✓ Direct materials quantity variance, $1,250 F

At the beginning of September, Academic Printers Company budgeted 22,000 books to be printed in September at standard direct materials and direct labor costs as follows:

Direct materials	$28,600
Direct labor	24,200
Total	$52,800

The standard materials price is $0.50 per pound. The standard direct labor rate is $11 per hour. At the end of September, the actual direct materials and direct labor costs were as follows:

Actual direct materials	$31,250	
Actual direct labor	28,100	
Total	$59,350	

There were no direct materials price or direct labor rate variances for September. In addition, assume no changes in the direct materials inventory balances in September. Academic Printers Company actually produced 25,000 units during September.

Determine the direct materials quantity and direct labor time variances.

EXERCISE 13-22
Standards for nonmanufacturing expenses
OBJECTIVE 6

✓ a. $1,200

Mercy Hospital began using standards to evaluate its Admissions Department. The standard was broken into two types of admissions as follows:

Type of Admission	Standard Time to Complete Admission Record
Unscheduled admission	36 minutes
Scheduled admission	18 minutes

The unscheduled admission took longer since name, address, and insurance information needed to be determined at the time of admission. Information normally is collected on scheduled admissions in advance, which is less time consuming.

The Admissions Department employs two full-time people (40 productive hours per week, with no overtime) at $15 per hour. For the most recent week, the department handled 45 unscheduled and 180 scheduled admissions.

a. How much was the actual cost of labor for the week?
b. What were the standard hours for the actual volume for the week?
c. Calculate a time variance, and report how well the department performed for the week.

EXERCISE 13-23
Nonfinancial performance measures
OBJECTIVE 7

Concord University wishes to monitor the efficiency and quality of its course registration process.

a. Identify three input and three output measures for this process.
b. Why would Concord University use nonfinancial measures for monitoring this process?

EXERCISE 13-24
Nonfinancial performance measures
OBJECTIVE 7

WinnersEdge.com is an Internet retailer of sporting good products. Customers order sporting goods from the company, using an online catalog. The company processes these orders and delivers the requested product from the company's warehouse. The company wants to provide customers with an excellent purchase experience to expand its business with favorable word of mouth and to drive repeat business. To help monitor performance, the company developed this set of performance measures for its order placement and delivery process:

Number of misfilled orders
Average computer response time to customer "clicks"
System capacity divided by customer demands
Elapsed time between customer order and product delivery
Number of page faults or errors due to software programming errors
Server (computer) downtime
Training dollars per programmer
Dollar amount of returned goods
Number of orders per warehouse employee
Number of customer complaints divided by the number of orders
Maintenance dollars divided by hardware investment

From this list, classify the measures as either input or output related to the order placement and delivery process.

EXERCISE 13-25

Factory overhead cost variances

APPENDIX

✓ Volume variance, $19,200 U

The following data relate to factory overhead cost for the production of 20,000 micro-computers:

Actual:	Variable factory overhead	$448,000
	Fixed factory overhead	115,200
Standard:	30,000 hours at $18.80	564,000

If productive capacity of 100% was 36,000 hours and the factory overhead cost budgeted at the level of 30,000 standard hours was $583,200, determine the variable factory overhead controllable variance, fixed factory overhead volume variance, and total factory overhead cost variance. The fixed factory overhead rate was $3.20 per hour.

EXERCISE 13-26

Factory overhead cost variances

APPENDIX

✓ a. $400 U

Tennessee Textiles Corporation began March with a budget for 40,000 hours of production in the Weaving Department. The department has a full capacity of 50,000 hours under normal business conditions. The budgeted overhead at the planned volumes at the beginning of March was as follows:

Variable overhead	$164,000
Fixed overhead	77,500
Total	$241,500

The actual factory overhead was $262,400 for March. The actual fixed factory overhead was as budgeted. During March, the Weaving Department had standard hours at actual production volume of 45,000 hours.

a. Determine the variable factory overhead controllable variance.
b. Determine the fixed factory overhead volume variance.

EXERCISE 13-27

Factory overhead cost variance report

APPENDIX

✓ Net controllable variance, $13,300 F

Murphy Molded Products Inc. prepared the following factory overhead cost budget for the Trim Department for May 2004, during which it expected to use 12,000 hours for production:

Variable overhead cost:		
Indirect factory labor	$ 33,600	
Power and light	4,200	
Indirect materials	22,200	
Total variable cost		$ 60,000
Fixed overhead cost:		
Supervisory salaries	$114,200	
Depreciation of plant and equipment	39,200	
Insurance and property taxes	6,600	
Total fixed cost		160,000
Total factory overhead cost		$220,000

Murphy Molded Products has available 20,000 hours of monthly productive capacity in the Trim Department under normal business conditions. During May, the Trim Department actually used 15,000 hours for production. The actual fixed costs were as budgeted. The actual variable overhead for May was as follows:

Actual variable factory overhead cost:	
Indirect factory labor	$35,200
Power and light	4,000
Indirect materials	22,500
Total variable cost	$61,700

Construct a factory overhead cost variance report for the Trim Department for May.

EXERCISE 13-28
Variance calculations
APPENDIX

The data related to Big Fish Sporting Goods Company's factory overhead cost for the production of 70,000 units of product are as follows:

Actual:	Variable factory overhead	$385,700
	Fixed factory overhead	280,000
Standard:	60,000 hours at $10 ($6.50 for variable factory overhead)	600,000

Productive capacity at 100% of normal was 80,000 hours, and the factory overhead cost budgeted at the level of 60,000 standard hours was $670,000. Based on these data, the chief cost accountant prepared the following variance analysis:

Variable factory overhead controllable variance:			
Actual variable factory overhead cost incurred		$385,700	
Budgeted variable factory overhead for 60,000 hours		390,000	
Variance—favorable			$ (4,300)
Fixed factory overhead volume variance:			
Normal productive capacity at 100%		$ 80,000 hours	
Standard for amount produced		60,000	
Productive capacity not used		20,000 hours	
Standard variable factory overhead rate		× $6.50	
Variance—unfavorable			130,000
Total factory overhead cost variance—unfavorable			$125,700

Identify the errors in the factory overhead cost variance analysis.

Problems

PROBLEM 13 | 1
Sales, production, direct materials, and direct labor budgets
OBJECTIVE 2

✓ 3. Total direct materials purchases, $5,662,360

The budget director of Summertime Grill Company requests estimates of sales, production, and other operating data from the various administrative units every month. Selected information concerning sales and production for May 2004 is summarized as follows:

a. Estimated sales for May by sales territory:

Maine:
    Backyard Chef   3,500 units at $550 per unit
    Master Chef   1,800 units at $1,300 per unit
Vermont:
    Backyard Chef   2,800 units at $500 per unit
    Master Chef   1,500 units at $1,200 per unit
New Hampshire:
    Backyard Chef   4,000 units at $600 per unit
    Master Chef   2,900 units at $1,500 per unit

b. Estimated inventories at May 1:

Direct materials:
    Grates   1,000 units
    Stainless steel   2,500 lbs.
    Burner subassemblies 600 units
    Shelves   400 units
Finished products:
    Backyard Chef   1,500 units
    Master Chef   400 units

c. Desired inventories at May 31:

Direct materials:
Grates	800 units
Stainless steel	1,900 lbs.
Burner subassemblies	800 units
Shelves	480 units

Finished products:
Backyard Chef	1,200 units
Master Chef	500 units

d. Direct materials used in production:

To manufacture Backyard Chef:
Grates	2 units per unit of product
Stainless steel	25 pounds per unit of product
Burner subassemblies	1 unit per unit of product
Shelves	2 units per unit of product

To manufacture Master Chef:
Grates	6 units per unit of product
Stainless steel	65 pounds per unit of product
Burner subassemblies	4 units per unit of product
Shelves	3 units per unit of product

e. Anticipated purchase price for direct materials:

Grates	$15 per unit
Stainless steel	$3 per pound
Burner subassemblies	$72 per unit
Shelves	$7 per unit

f. Direct labor requirements:

Backyard Chef:
Stamping Department	0.50 hour at $12 per hour
Forming Department	0.75 hour at $10 per hour
Assembly Department	1.50 hours at $9 per hour

Master Chef:
Stamping Department	0.60 hour at $12 per hour
Forming Department	1.50 hours at $10 per hour
Assembly Department	2.50 hours at $9 per hour

Instructions

1. Prepare a sales budget for May.
2. Prepare a production budget for May.
3. Prepare a direct materials purchases budget for May.
4. Prepare a direct labor cost budget for May.

PROBLEM 13 | 2
Budgeted income statement and supporting budgets
OBJECTIVE 2

✓ 4. Total direct labor cost in Slitting Dept., $205,120

With the assistance of the controller, treasurer, production manager, and sales manager, the budget director of Instant Memories Film Company has gathered the following data for use in developing the budgeted income statement for October 2004:

a. Estimated sales for October:

Instant Image	26,800 units at $65 per unit
Pro Image	20,400 units at $90 per unit

b. Estimated inventories at October 1:

Direct materials:		Finished products:	
Celluloid	2,700 pounds	Instant Image	4,800 units at $35 per unit
Silver	3,000 ounces	Pro Image	2,400 units at $55 per unit

c. Desired inventories at October 31:

Direct materials:		Finished products:	
Celluloid	3,400 pounds	Instant Image	5,400 units at $35 per unit
Silver	2,900 ounces	Pro Image	1,900 units at $55 per unit

d. Direct materials used in production:

In manufacture of Instant Image:	
Celluloid	0.40 pound per unit of product
Silver	2.50 ounces per unit of product
In manufacture of Pro Image:	
Celluloid	0.60 pound per unit of product
Silver	4.00 ounces per unit of product

e. Anticipated cost of purchases and beginning and ending inventory of direct materials:

Celluloid $1.50 per pound   Silver $6 per ounce

f. Direct labor requirements:

Instant Image:	
Coating Department	0.20 hour at $14 per hour
Slitting Department	0.25 hour at $16 per hour
Pro Image:	
Coating Department	0.40 hour at $14 per hour
Slitting Department	0.30 hour at $16 per hour

g. Estimated factory overhead costs for October:

Indirect factory wages	$525,000
Depreciation of plant and equipment	145,000
Power and light	46,000
Insurance and property tax	18,400

h. Estimated operating expenses for October:

Sales salaries expense	$225,000
Advertising expense	146,500
Office salaries expense	120,800
Depreciation expense—office equipment	5,300
Telephone expense—selling	5,000
Telephone expense—administrative	1,900
Travel expense—selling	38,500
Office supplies expense	3,000
Miscellaneous administrative expense	4,200

i. Estimated other income and expense for October:

Interest revenue	$16,700
Interest expense	12,300

j. Estimated tax rate: 40%

Instructions

1. Prepare a sales budget for October.
2. Prepare a production budget for October.
3. Prepare a direct materials purchases budget for October.
4. Prepare a direct labor cost budget for October.
5. Prepare a factory overhead cost budget for October.
6. Prepare a cost of goods sold budget for October. Work in Process at the beginning of October is estimated to be $28,500, and Work in Process at the end of October is estimated to be $34,200.
7. Prepare a selling and administrative expenses budget for October.
8. Prepare a budgeted income statement for October.

PROBLEM 13 | 3

Cash budget

OBJECTIVE 2

✓ 1. October deficiency, $41,000

The controller of Butler Boat Company instructs you to prepare a monthly cash budget for the next three months. You are presented with the following budget information for August, September, and October 2004:

	August	**September**	**October**
Sales	$590,000	$650,000	$750,000
Manufacturing costs	300,000	340,000	390,000
Selling and administrative expenses	150,000	170,000	200,000
Capital expenditures			120,000

The company expects to sell about 10% of its merchandise for cash. Of sales on account, 60% are expected to be collected in full in the month following the sale and the remainder the following month. Depreciation, insurance, and property tax expense represent $30,000 of the estimated monthly manufacturing costs. The annual insurance premium is paid in July, and the annual property taxes are paid in November. Of the remainder of the manufacturing costs, 80% are expected to be paid in the month in which they are incurred and the balance in the following month.

Current assets as of August 1 include cash of $55,000, marketable securities of $85,000, and accounts receivable of $594,000 ($442,000 from July sales and $152,000 from June sales). Current liabilities as of August 1 include a $100,000, 10%, 90-day note payable due October 20 and $60,000 of accounts payable incurred in July for manufacturing costs. All selling and administrative expenses are paid in cash in the period they are incurred. It is expected that $1,500 in dividends will be received in August. An estimated income tax payment of $42,000 will be made in September. Butler's regular quarterly dividend of $15,000 is expected to be declared in September and paid in October. Management desires to maintain a minimum cash balance of $45,000.

Instructions

1. Prepare a monthly cash budget and supporting schedules for August, September, and October.
2. On the basis of the cash budget prepared in (1), what recommendation should be made to the controller?

PROBLEM 13 | 4

Direct materials and direct labor variance analysis

OBJECTIVES 4, 5

Dresses by Linda, Inc., manufactures silk dresses in a small manufacturing facility. Manufacturing has 13 employees. Each employee presently provides 36 hours of productive labor per week. Information about a production week is as follows:

✓ c. Rate variance, $351 U

Standard wage per hour	$10.00
Standard labor time per dress	18 minutes
Standard number of yards of silk per dress	4.2 yards
Standard price per yard of silk	$6.00
Actual price per yard of silk	$6.20
Actual yards of silk used during the week	6,100 yards
Number of dresses produced during the week	1,500
Actual wage per hour	$10.75
Actual hours per week	468 hours

Instructions

Determine (a) the standard cost per dress for direct materials and direct labor, (b) the price variance, quantity variance, and total direct materials cost variance, and (c) the rate variance, time variance, and total direct labor cost variance.

PROBLEM 13 | 5

Direct materials, direct labor, and factory overhead cost variance analysis

OBJECTIVE 5

✓ 3. Controllable variance, $150 F

Bayou Resins Company processes a base chemical into plastic. Standard costs and actual costs for direct materials, direct labor, and factory overhead incurred for the manufacture of 1,500 units of product were as follows:

	Standard Costs	**Actual Costs**
Direct materials	6,000 pounds at $3.40	5,930 pounds at $3.50
Direct labor	1,125 hours at $18.00	1,140 hours at $18.50
Factory overhead	Rates per direct labor hour, based on 100% of normal capacity of 1,100 direct labor hours:	
	Variable cost, $4.80	$5,250 variable cost
	Fixed cost, $12.00	$13,200 fixed cost

Each unit requires 0.75 hours of direct labor.

Instructions

1. Determine the price variance, quantity variance, and total direct materials cost variance.
2. Determine the rate variance, time variance, and total direct labor cost variance.
3. Appendix: Determine the variable factory overhead controllable variance, the fixed factory overhead volume variance, and total factory overhead cost variance.

PROBLEM 13 | 6

Standard factory overhead variance report

APPENDIX

✓ Volume variance, $3,300 F

Wells Inc., a manufacturer of construction equipment, prepared the following factory overhead cost budget for the Welding Department for May 2004. The company expected to operate the department at 100% of normal capacity of 3,000 hours.

Variable costs:		
Indirect factory wages	$22,800	
Power and light	3,750	
Indirect materials	10,200	
Total variable cost		$ 36,750
Fixed costs:		
Supervisory salaries	$67,500	
Depreciation of plant and equipment	26,400	
Insurance and property taxes	5,100	
Total fixed cost		99,000
Total factory overhead cost		$135,750

During May, the department operated at 3,100 hours, and the factory overhead costs incurred were indirect factory wages, $23,450; power and light, $3,980; indirect materials, $10,600; supervisory salaries, $67,500; depreciation of plant and equipment, $26,400; and insurance and property taxes, $5,100.

Instructions

Prepare a factory overhead cost variance report for May. To be useful for cost control, the budgeted amounts should be based on 3,100 hours.

Activities

Activity 13-1
Ethics and professional conduct in business
ETHICS

The director of marketing for Apex Software Company, Connie Keller, had the following discussion with the company controller, Josh Johnson, on July 26 of the current year:

Connie: Josh, it looks like I'm going to spend much less than indicated on my July budget.

Josh: I'm glad to hear it.

Connie: Well, I'm not so sure it's good news. I'm concerned that the president will see that I'm under budget and reduce my budget in the future. The only reason that I look good is that we've delayed an advertising campaign. Once the campaign hits in September, I'm sure my actual expenditures will go up. You see, we are also having our sales convention in September. Having the advertising campaign and the convention at the same time is going to kill my September numbers.

Josh: I don't think that's anything to worry about. We all expect some variation in actual spending month to month. What's really important is staying within the budgeted targets for the year. Does that look as if it's going to be a problem?

Connie: I don't think so, but just the same, I'd like to be on the safe side.

Josh: What do you mean?

Connie: Well, this is what I'd like to do. I want to pay the convention-related costs in advance this month. I'll pay the hotel for room and convention space and purchase the airline tickets in advance. In this way, I can charge all these expenditures to July's budget. This would cause my actual expenses to come close to budget for July. Moreover, when the big advertising campaign hits in September, I won't have to worry about expenditures for the convention on my September budget as well. The convention costs will already be paid. Thus, my September expenses should be pretty close to budget.

Josh: I can't tell you when to make your convention purchases, but I'm not too sure that it should be expensed on July's budget.

Connie: What's the problem? It looks like "no harm, no foul" to me. I can't see that there's anything wrong with this—it's just smart management.

How should Josh Johnson respond to Connie Keller's request to expense the advanced payments for convention-related costs against July's budget?

Activity 13-2
Evaluating budgeting systems

Elgin Sweeper Company began an overhaul of its planning and control system. This overhaul is described in the following excerpt from an article in *Management Accounting*:

How could we bring responsibility for and management of costs to the individual department managers? For two years before we began our efforts, the annual budget had been prepared substantially by the accounting department with little ownership for results felt by persons outside top management.

Our first step was to modify the budget responsibility reports to reflect only those costs controllable by the department manager. . . . The next step was the actual budget preparation. . . . [Expense] accounts did not segregate variable and fixed costs. When volume-adjusted numbers were required for either budget preparation or budget-to-actual comparison, we merely would use an "executive judgment" percentage to adjust the appropriate expenses. Needless to say, this system resulted in some unusual variations, which sometimes required "innovative" explanations.

Source: J. P. Callan, W. N. Tredup, and R. S. Wisinger, "Elgin Sweeper Company's Journey Toward Cost Management," *Management Accounting*, July 1991, pp. 24–27.

What are the behavioral ramifications of including expenses within a responsibility report for which a manager has no control? Did Elgin previously use static budgeting or flexible budgeting? What type of budgeting will Elgin use in the future?

Activity 13-3
Service company static decision making

The Acorn Bancorp manager uses the managerial accounting system to track the costs of operating the various departments within the bank. The departments include Cash Management, Trust Commercial Loans, Mortgage Loans, Operations, Credit Card, and Branch Services. The budget and actual results for the Operations Department are as follows:

Resources	Budget	Actual
Salaries	$150,000	$150,000
Benefits	30,000	30,000
Supplies	45,000	42,000
Travel	20,000	30,000
Training	25,000	30,000
Overtime	25,000	20,000
Total	$295,000	$302,000
Excess of actual over budget	$ 7,000	

a. What information is provided by the budget? Specifically, what questions can the bank manager ask of the Operations Department manager?
b. What information does the budget fail to provide? Specifically, could the budget information be presented differently to provide even more insight for the bank manager?

Activity 13-4
Behavioral aspects of financial goals

One aspect of motivating line employees is to provide them financial improvement targets. The following excerpt describes this approach:

For managers and line workers to be similarly focused on bottom-line issues, it's critical that all employees are first well-trained in understanding the financials. . . . While training is important, what makes Bottom Line Powered Management so powerful is that financial and performance data are presented to employees to be used as direct, practical feedback for operations. At **SRC**, for example, financial and performance data become critical to individual performance when the profit-and-loss statement is broken down for all operations—that is, for all employee teams and work groups. Each employee team then knows if it is on target and can make the appropriate corrections. If sales to a particular customer are off track, that is immediately investigated. If the team's overhead is above the projection, that is attacked. Moreover, this information is provided weekly, letting the employees quickly pounce on any problem. . . . To ensure that financial data are actually used, [they are given] numbers the employees can understand and influence.

Source: Willard I. Zangwill, "Focusing All Eyes on the Bottom Line," *The Wall Street Journal*, March 21, 1994, p. A12.

Identify the critical characteristics of the Bottom Line Powered Management (BLPM) approach and explain how they appear to affect human behavior.

Activity 13-5
Ethics and professional conduct in business

E T H I C S

Dan Hendrix is a cost analyst with Cambridge Insurance Company. Cambridge is applying standards to its claims payment operation. Claims payment is a repetitive operation that could be evaluated with standards. Dan used time and motion studies to identify a theoretical standard of 25 claims processed per hour. The Claims Processing Department manager, Angie Street, has rejected this standard and has argued that the standard should be 20 claims processed per hour. Angie and Dan were unable to agree, so they decided to discuss this matter openly at a joint meeting with the vice-president of operations, who would arbitrate a final decision. Prior to the meeting, Dan wrote the following memo to the VP:

To: Kim Jan, Vice-President of Operations
From: Dan Hendrix
Re: Standards in the Claims Processing Department

As you know, Angie and I are scheduled to meet with you to discuss our disagreement with respect to the appropriate standards for the Claims Processing Department. I have conducted time and motion studies and have determined that the theoretical standard is 25 claims processed per hour. Angie argues that 20 claims processed per hour would be more appropriate. I believe she is trying to "pad" the budget with some slack. I'm not sure what she is trying to get away with, but I believe a tight standard will drive efficiency up in her area. I hope you will agree when we meet with you next week.

Discuss the ethical and professional issues in this situation.

Activity 13-6
Nonfinancial performance measures

The senior management of Lang Company has proposed the following three performance measures for the company:

1. Net income as a percentage of stockholders' equity
2. Revenue growth
3. Employee satisfaction

Management believes these three measures combine both financial and nonfinancial measures and are thus superior to using just financial measures.

What advice would you give Lang Company for improving its performance measurement system?

Activity 13-7
Nonfinancial performance measures

At the Soladyne Division of **Rogers Corporation**, the controller used a number of measures to provide managers information about the performance of a just-in-time (JIT) manufacturing operation. Three measures used by the company follow:

- *Orders Past Due:* Sales dollar value of orders that were scheduled for shipment but were not shipped during the period.
- *Buyer Misery Index:* Number of different customers that have orders that are late (scheduled for shipment but not shipped).
- *Scrap Index:* The sales dollar value of scrap for the period.

1. How is the orders past due measure different from the buyer's misery index, or are the two measures just measuring the same thing?
2. Why do you think the scrap index is measured at sales dollar value rather than at cost?

Source: John W. Schmitthenner, "Metrics," *Management Accounting*, May 1993, pp. 27–30.

Activity 13-8
Variance interpretation
APPENDIX

TruNote Company is a small manufacturer of electronic musical instruments. The plant manager received the following variable factory overhead report for the period:

	Actual	Budgeted Variable Factory Overhead at Actual Production
Supplies	$21,000	$20,000
Power and light	9,000	8,000
Indirect factory wages	50,000	40,000
Total	$80,000	$68,000

Actual units produced: 4,000 (90% of practical capacity)

The plant manager is not pleased with the $12,000 unfavorable variable factory overhead controllable variance and has come to discuss the matter with the controller. The following discussion occurred:

Plant Manager: I just received this factory report for the latest month of operation. I'm not very pleased with these figures. Before these numbers go to headquarters, you and I will need to reach an understanding.

Controller: Go ahead, what's the problem?

Plant Manager: What's the problem? Well, everything. Look at the variance. It's too large. If I understand the accounting approach being used here, you are assuming that my costs are variable to the units produced. Thus, as the production volume declines, so should these costs. Well, I don't believe that these costs are variable at all. I think they are fixed costs. As a result, when we operate below capacity, the costs really don't go down at all. I'm being penalized for costs I have no control over at all. I need this report to be redone to reflect this fact. If anything, the difference between actual and budget is essentially a volume variance. Listen, I know that you're a team player. You really need to reconsider your assumptions on this one.

If you were in the controller's position, how would you respond to the plant manager?

Answers to Self-Study Questions

1. **B** Administrative departments (answer B), such as Purchasing or Human Resources, often use static budgeting. Production departments (answer A) frequently use flexible budgets. Sales departments (answer C) can use either static or flexible budgeting. Capital expenditure budgets are used to plan capital projects (answer D).

2. **B** The total production indicated in the production budget is 257,500 units (answer B), which is computed as follows:

Sales	250,000 units
Plus desired ending inventory	30,000
Total	280,000 units
Less estimated beginning inventory	22,500
Total production	257,500 units

3. **C** Dixon expects to collect 70% of April sales ($560,000) plus 30% of the March sales ($195,000) in April, for a total of $755,000 (answer C). Answer A is 100% of April sales. Answer B is 70% of April sales. Answer D adds 70% of both March and April sales.

4. **C** The unfavorable direct materials price variance of $2,550 is determined as follows:

Actual price	$5.05 per pound
Standard price	5.00
Price variance—unfavorable	$0.05 per pound

$0.05 × 51,000 actual pounds = $2,550

5.   **D** The unfavorable direct labor time variance of
$2,400 is determined as follows:

Actual direct labor time	2,200
Standard direct labor time	<u>2,000</u>
Direct labor time variance—unfavorable	200 × $12 standard rate = <u>$2,400</u>

14

LEARNING OBJECTIVES

OBJECTIVE 1
List and explain the advantages and disadvantages of decentralized operations.

OBJECTIVE 2
Prepare a responsibility accounting report for a cost center.

OBJECTIVE 3
Prepare responsibility accounting reports for a profit center.

OBJECTIVE 4
Compute and interpret the rate of return on investment, the residual income, and the balanced scorecard for an investment center.

OBJECTIVE 5
Explain how the market price, negotiated price, and cost price approaches to transfer pricing can be used by decentralized segments of a business.

Performance Evaluation for Decentralized Operations

Have you ever wondered if there is an economic reason that large retail stores, such as JC Penney Co. and Sears, are divided into departments? Typically, these stores include a Men's Department, Women's Department, Appliances Department, Home Entertainment Department, and Sporting Goods Department. Each department usually has a manager who is responsible for the financial performance of the department. The store can be the responsibility of a store manager, and a group of stores within a particular geographic area can be the responsibility of a division or district manager. If you were to be hired by a department store chain, you would probably begin your career in a department. Running a department would be a valuable experience before becoming responsible for a complete store. Likewise, responsibility for a complete store provides excellent training for other management positions.

In this chapter, we focus on the role of accounting in assisting managers in planning and controlling organizational units, such as divisions, stores, and departments.

Centralized and Decentralized Operations

OBJECTIVE   1

List and explain the advantages and disadvantages of decentralized operations.

A **centralized** business is one in which all major planning and operating decisions are made by top management. For example, a one-person, owner/manager-operated business is centralized because all plans and decisions are made by one person. In a small owner/manager-operated business, centralization can be desirable because the owner/manager's close supervision ensures that the business will be operated in the way the owner/manager wishes.

Separating a business into **divisions** or operating units and delegating responsibility to unit managers is called **decentralization**. In a decentralized business, the unit managers are responsible for planning and controlling the operations of their units.

A trend among large international companies is to decentralize into smaller customer-focused units while maintaining the advantage of a big company. For example, **Siemens**, the giant $60 billion German electronics company, divided responsibility into 16 minicorporations, each with its own CEO and board of directors. To streamline decision making and enhance financial accountability, **Aluminum Company of America (Alcoa)** restructured its centrally managed divisions into 26 autonomous business units.

Divisions are often structured around common functions, products, customers, or regions. For example, **Delta Air Lines** is organized around *functions*, such as the Flight Operations Division. The **Procter & Gamble Company** is organized around common *products*, such as the Soap Division, which sells a wide array of cleaning products.

There is no one best amount of decentralization for all businesses. In some companies, division managers have authority over all operations, including fixed asset acquisitions and retirements. In other companies, division managers have authority over profits but not fixed asset acquisitions and retirements. The proper amount of decentralization for a company depends on its advantages and disadvantages for the company's unique circumstances.

Advantages of Decentralization

As a business grows, it becomes more difficult for top management to maintain close daily contact with all operations. In such cases, delegating authority to managers closest to the operations usually results in better decisions. These managers often anticipate and react to operating data more quickly than could top management. In addition, as a company expands into a wide range of products and services, it becomes more difficult for top management to maintain operating expertise in all product lines and services. Decentralization allows managers to focus on acquiring expertise in their areas of responsibility. For example, in a company that maintains operations in insurance, banking, and health care, managers could become "experts" in their area of operation and responsibility.

AOL Time Warner is a major media and entertainment empire that is decentralized into net services, publishing, cable networks, music, and movie production units. The net services division is AOL. The publishing division produces a number of popular magazines, including *Time, People, Sports Illustrated,* and *Money.* The cable network division consists of Turner Broadcasting, which produces CNN. The music division records and distributes music for artists such as Sugar Ray, Red Hot Chili Peppers, and GooGoo Dolls. The movie production division produces Warner Brothers films, such as *The Matrix.* These divisions are treated as separate units with their own financial performance targets.

Decentralized decision making also provides excellent training for managers. This could be a factor in helping a company retain quality managers. Since the art of management is best acquired through experience, delegating responsibility allows managers to acquire and develop managerial expertise early in their careers.

Businesses that work closely with customers, such as hotels, are often decentralized. This helps managers create good customer relations by responding quickly to customers' needs. In addition, because managers of decentralized operations tend to identify with customers and with operations, they are often more creative in suggesting operating and product improvements.

Disadvantages of Decentralization

A primary disadvantage of decentralized operations is that decisions made by one manager can negatively affect the profitability of the entire company. For example, the Pizza Hut chain added chicken to its menu and ended up taking business away from KFC. Then KFC retaliated with a blistering ad campaign against Pizza Hut. This happened even though both chains are part of the same company, **Tricon Global Restaurants**!

ETHICS IN ACTION

Enron Corporation, once the seventh largest company in the United States, crashed into bankruptcy in a matter of months. Much of Enron's travails were related to undisclosed losses from complex financial transactions with certain partnerships that were run by its own officers, including the CFO. Enron management came under severe criticism for (1) providing minimum disclosure about these partnership investments to the investing public and (2) allowing senior officers to hold significant individual investments in these partnerships. Regarding the potential conflict of interest, Wayne Shaw, a professor of accounting stated, "If it was the CFO, why was he put in a position where no one knew what he was doing? If the blame's being placed on one party, you have to wonder about the internal controls of the company. There's got to be checks and balances, and they weren't there." The lesson from Enron is that unconsolidated investments can require significant additional disclosures in the footnotes and that senior officers should avoid a conflict of interest caused by holding individual interests in the investee while being an officer of the investor.

Another potential disadvantage of decentralized operations is duplicating assets and costs in operating divisions. For example, each manager of a product line could have a separate sales force and administrative office staff. Centralizing these personnel could save money.

Responsibility Accounting

In a decentralized business, an important function of accounting is to assist unit managers in evaluating and controlling their areas of responsibility, called **responsibility centers**. **Responsibility accounting** is the process of measuring and reporting operating data by responsibility center. Three common types of responsibility centers are cost centers, profit centers, and investment centers. These three responsibility centers differ in their scope of responsibility, as shown:

Cost Center	Profit Center	Investment Center
	Revenue	Revenue
Cost	− Cost	− Cost
	Profit	Profit
		Investment in assets

Responsibility Accounting for Cost Centers

OBJECTIVE   2

Prepare a responsibility accounting report for a cost center.

In a **cost center**, the unit manager has responsibility and authority for controlling the costs incurred. For example, the supervisor of the Power Department has responsibility for the costs incurred in providing power. A cost center manager does not make decisions concerning sales or the amount of fixed assets invested in the center. Cost centers vary in size from a small department to an entire manufacturing plant. In addition, cost centers can exist within other cost centers. For example, we could view an entire university as a cost center, and each college and department within the university could also be a cost center, as shown in Exhibit 1.

EXHIBIT 1   *Cost Centers in a University*

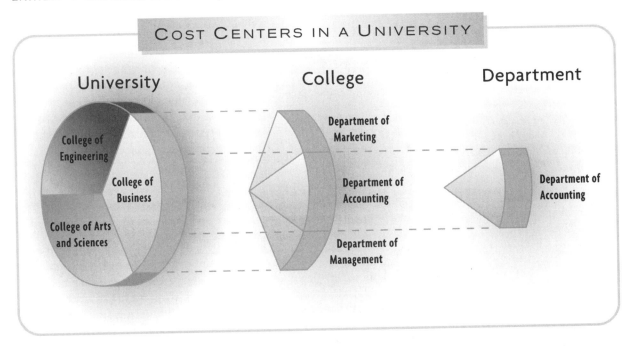

Since managers of cost centers have responsibility and authority over costs, responsibility accounting for cost centers focuses on costs. To illustrate, the budget performance reports in Exhibit 2 are part of a responsibility accounting system. These reports aid the managers in controlling costs.

EXHIBIT 2
*Responsibility
Accounting Reports for
Cost Centers*

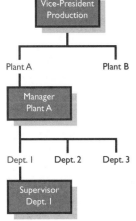

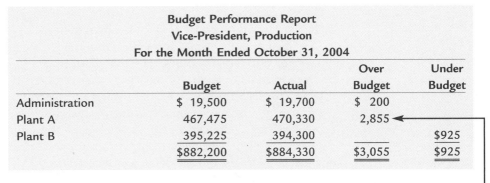

Budget Performance Report
Vice-President, Production
For the Month Ended October 31, 2004

	Budget	Actual	Over Budget	Under Budget
Administration	$ 19,500	$ 19,700	$ 200	
Plant A	467,475	470,330	2,855	
Plant B	395,225	394,300		$925
	$882,200	$884,330	$3,055	$925

Budget Performance Report
Manager, Plant A
For the Month Ended October 31, 2004

	Budget	Actual	Over Budget	Under Budget
Administration	$ 17,500	$ 17,350		$150
Department 1	109,725	111,280	$1,555	
Department 2	190,500	192,600	2,100	
Department 3	149,750	149,100		650
	$467,475	$470,330	$3,655	$800

Budget Performance Report
Supervisor, Department 1—Plant A
For the Month Ended October 31, 2004

	Budget	Actual	Over Budget	Under Budget
Factory wages	$ 58,100	$ 58,000		$100
Materials	32,500	34,225	$1,725	
Supervisory salaries	6,400	6,400		
Power and light	5,750	5,690		60
Depreciation of plant and equipment	4,000	4,000		
Maintenance	2,000	1,990		10
Insurance and property taxes	975	975		
	$109,725	$111,280	$1,725	$170

In Exhibit 2, the reports prepared for the department supervisors show the budgeted and actual manufacturing costs for their departments. The supervisors can use these reports to focus on areas of significant difference, such as the difference between the budgeted and actual materials cost. The supervisor of Department 1 in Plant A can use additional information from a scrap report to determine why materials are over budget. Such a report could show that materials were scrapped as a result of machine malfunctions, improper use of machines by employees, or low quality materials.

For higher levels of management, responsibility accounting reports are usually more summarized than for lower levels of management. In Exhibit 2, for example, the budget performance report for the plant manager summarizes budget and actual cost data for the departments under the manager's supervision. This report enables the plant manager to identify the department supervisors responsible for major differences. Likewise, the report for the vice-president of production summarizes the cost data for each plant. The plant managers can thus be held responsible for major differences in budgeted and actual costs in their plants.

Responsibility Accounting for Profit Centers

OBJECTIVE   3

Prepare responsibility accounting reports for a profit center.

In a **profit center**, the unit manager has the responsibility and the authority to make decisions that affect both costs and revenues (and thus profits). Profit centers can be divisions, departments, or products. For example, a consumer products company could organize its brands (product lines) as divisional profit centers. The manager of each brand could have responsibility for product cost and decisions regarding revenues, such as setting sales prices. The manager of a profit center does not make decisions concerning the fixed assets invested in the center. For example, the brand manager of a consumer products company does not make the decision to expand the plant capacity for the brand.

Profit centers are often viewed as an excellent training assignment for new managers. For example, Lester B. Korn, chairman and chief executive officer of **Korn/Ferry International**, offered the following strategy for young executives en route to top management positions:

> Get Profit-Center Responsibility—Obtain a position where you can prove yourself as both a specialist with particular expertise and a generalist who can exercise leadership, authority, and inspire enthusiasm among colleagues and subordinates.

Responsibility accounting reports usually show the revenues, expenses, and income from operations for the profit center. The profit center income statement should include only revenues and expenses that are controlled by the manager. **Controllable revenues** are revenues earned by the profit center. **Controllable expenses** are costs that can be influenced (controlled) by the decisions of profit center managers. For example, the manager of the Men's Department at **Nordstrom** most likely controls the salaries of department personnel but does not control the property taxes of the store.

Service Department Charges

We illustrate profit center income reporting for the Nova Entertainment Group (NEG). Assume that NEG is a diversified entertainment company with two operating divisions organized as profit centers: the Theme Park Division and the Movie Production Division. The revenues and operating expenses for the two divisions are shown below. The operating expenses consist of the direct expenses, such as the wages and salaries of a division's employees.

	Theme Park Division	Movie Production Division
Revenues	$6,000,000	$2,500,000
Operating expenses	2,495,000	405,000

In addition to direct expenses, divisions can also have expenses for services provided by internal centralized **service departments**. These service departments are often more efficient at providing service than are outside service providers. Examples of such service departments include the following:

- Research and Development
- Government Relations
- Telecommunications
- Publications and Graphics
- Facilities Management
- Purchasing
- Information Systems
- Payroll Accounting
- Transportation
- Personnel Administration

A profit center's income from operations should reflect the cost of any internal services used by the center. To illustrate, assume that NEG established a Payroll Accounting Department. The costs of the payroll services, called service department charges, are charged to NEG's profit centers, as shown in Exhibit 3.

EXHIBIT 3

Payroll Accounting Department Charges to NEG's Theme Park and Movie Production Divisions

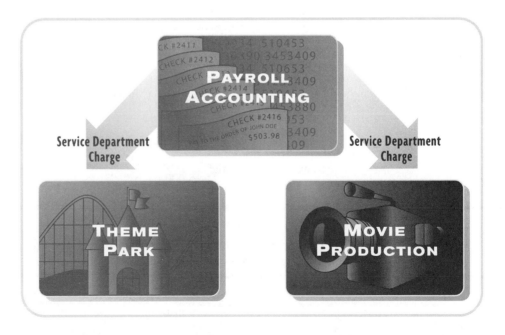

Service department charges are *indirect expenses* to a profit center. They are similar to the expenses that would be incurred if the profit center had purchased the services from a source outside the company. A profit center manager has control over such expenses if he or she is free to choose *how much* service is used from the service department.

To illustrate service department charges, assume that NEG has two other service departments—Purchasing and Legal—in addition to Payroll Accounting. The expenses for the year ended December 31, 2003, for each service department are as follows:

Purchasing	$400,000
Payroll Accounting	255,000
Legal	250,000
Total	$905,000

An **activity base** for each service department is used to charge service department expenses to the Theme Park and Movie Production Divisions. The activity base for each service department is a measure of the services performed. For NEG, the service department activity bases are as follows:

Department	Activity Base
Purchasing	Number of purchase requisitions
Payroll Accounting	Number of payroll checks
Legal	Number of billed hours

The use of services by the Theme Park and Movie Production Divisions is as follows:

	Service Usage		
	Purchasing	**Payroll Accounting**	**Legal**
Theme Park Division	25,000 purchase requisitions	12,000 payroll checks	100 billed hours
Movie Production Division	15,000	3,000	900
Total	40,000 purchase requisitions	15,000 payroll checks	1,000 billed hours

The rates at which services are charged to each division are called **service department charge rates**. These rates are determined by dividing each service department's expenses by the total service usage as follows:

$$\text{Purchasing: } \frac{\$400,000}{40,000 \text{ purchase requisitions}} = \$10 \text{ per purchase requisition}$$

$$\text{Payroll Accounting: } \frac{\$255,000}{15,000 \text{ payroll checks}} = \$17 \text{ per payroll check}$$

$$\text{Legal: } \frac{\$250,000}{1,000 \text{ hours}} = \$250 \text{ per hour}$$

The use of services by the Theme Park and Movie Production Divisions is multiplied by the service department charge rates to determine the charges to each division, as shown in Exhibit 4.

The Theme Park Division employs many temporary and part-time employees who are paid weekly. This is in contrast to the Movie Production Division, which has a

EXHIBIT 4
Service Department Charges to NEG Divisions

NOVA ENTERTAINMENT GROUP
Service Department Charges to NEG Divisions
For the Year Ended December 31, 2004

Service Department	Theme Park Division	Movie Production Division
Purchasing (Note A)	$250,000	$150,000
Payroll Accounting (Note B)	204,000	51,000
Legal (Note C)	25,000	225,000
Total service department charges	$479,000	$426,000

Note A:

25,000 purchase requisitions × $10 per purchase requisition = $250,000
15,000 purchase requisitions × $10 per purchase requisition = $150,000

Note B:

12,000 payroll checks × $17 per check = $204,000
3,000 payroll checks × $17 per check = $51,000

Note C:

100 hours × $250 per hour = $25,000
900 hours × $250 per hour = $225,000

more permanent payroll that is paid on a monthly basis. As a result, the Theme Park Division requires 12,000 payroll checks. This results in a large service charge from Payroll Accounting to the Theme Park Division. In contrast, the Movie Production Division uses many legal services for contract negotiations. Thus, there is a large service charge from Legal to the Movie Production Division.

Some companies require service departments to measure the quality of their service. For example, the **Weyerhaeuser** human resource, accounting, and quality control service departments must measure the quality of their services to line departments, such as sales, marketing, and production. So while the internal line departments "pay" for service in the form of service department charges, they also provide feedback on the service quality. In this way, the line departments are treated as customers.

Profit Center Reporting

The divisional income statements for NEG are presented in Exhibit 5. These statements show the service department charges to the divisions.

The **income from operations** is a measure of a manager's performance. In evaluating the profit center manager, the income from operations should be compared over time to a budget. It should not be compared across profit centers since the profit centers are usually different in terms of size, products, and customers.

EXHIBIT 5
*Divisional Income
Statements—NEG*

NOVA ENTERTAINMENT GROUP Divisional Income Statements For the Year Ended December 31, 2004		
	Theme Park Division	**Movie Production Division**
Revenues*	$6,000,000	$2,500,000
Operating expenses	2,495,000	405,000
Income from operations before service department charges	$3,505,000	$2,095,000
Less service department charges:		
Purchasing	$ 250,000	$ 150,000
Payroll Accounting	204,000	51,000
Legal	25,000	225,000
Total service department charges	$ 479,000	$ 426,000
Income from operations	$3,026,000	$1,669,000

*For a profit center that sells products, the income statement would show Net sales − Cost of goods sold = Gross profit. The operating expenses would be deducted from the gross profit to get the income from operations before service department charges.

Responsibility Accounting for Investment Centers

OBJECTIVE   4
Compute and interpret
the rate of return on
investment, the
residual income, and
the balanced scorecard
for an investment
center.

In an **investment center**, the unit manager has the responsibility and the authority to make decisions that affect not only costs and revenues but also the assets invested in the center. Investment centers are widely used in highly diversified companies organized by divisions.

The manager of an investment center has more authority and responsibility than the manager of a cost center or a profit center. The manager of an investment center occupies a position similar to that of a chief operating officer or president of a company and is evaluated in much the same way.

Since investment center managers have responsibility for revenues and expenses, income from operations is an important part of investment center reporting. In addition, because the manager has responsibility for the assets invested in the center, two additional measures of performance are often used. These measures are the *rate of return on investment* and *residual income*. Top management often compares these measures across investment centers to reward performance and assess investment in the centers.

To illustrate, assume that DataLink Inc. is a cellular phone company that has three regional divisions, Northern, Central, and Southern. Condensed divisional income statements for the investment centers are shown in Exhibit 6.

Using only income from operations, the Central Division is the most profitable division. However, income from operations does not reflect the amount of assets invested in each center. For example, if the amount of assets invested in the Central Division is twice that of the other divisions, the Central Division would be the least profitable in terms of the rate of return on these assets.

EXHIBIT 6
*Divisional Income
Statements—DataLink
Inc.*

DATALINK INC.
Divisional Income Statements
For the Year Ended December 31, 2004

	Northern Division	Central Division	Southern Division
Revenues	$560,000	$672,000	$750,000
Operating expenses	336,000	470,400	562,500
Income from operations before service department charges	$224,000	$201,600	$187,500
Service department charges	154,000	117,600	112,500
Income from operations	$ 70,000	$ 84,000	$ 75,000

Rate of Return on Investment

Since investment center managers also control the amount of assets invested in their centers, they should be held accountable for the use of these assets. One measure that considers the amount of assets invested is the **rate of return on investment** (ROI) or **rate of return on assets**. It is one of the most widely used measures for investment centers and is computed as follows:

$$\text{Rate of return on investment (ROI)} = \frac{\text{Income from operations}}{\text{Invested assets}}$$

The rate of return on investment is useful because the three factors subject to control by divisional managers (revenues, expenses, and invested assets) are used in its computation. By measuring profitability relative to the amount of assets invested in each division, the rate of return on investment can be used to compare divisions. The higher the rate of return on investment, the better the division utilizes its assets to generate income. To illustrate, the rate of return on investment for each division of DataLink Inc., based on the book value of invested assets, is as follows:

	Northern Division	Central Division	Southern Division
Income from operations	$ 70,000	$ 84,000	$ 75,000
Invested assets	$350,000	$700,000	$500,000
Rate of return on investment	20%	12%	15%

Although the Central Division generated the highest income from operations, its rate of return on investment (12%) is the lowest. Hence, relative to the assets invested, the Central Division is the least profitable division. In comparison, the rate of return on investment of the Northern Division is 20% and the Southern Division is 15%. These differences in the rates of return on investment can be further analyzed using an expanded formula for the rate of return on investment.

In the expanded formula, the rate of return on investment is the product of two factors. The first factor is the ratio of income from operations to sales, often called

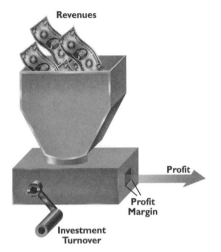

Revenues

Profit

Profit Margin

Investment Turnover

the **profit margin**. The second factor is the ratio of sales to invested assets, often called the **investment turnover**. In the illustration at the left, profits can be earned by either increasing the investment turnover (turning the crank faster), by increasing the profit margin (increasing the size of the opening), or both.

Using the expanded expression yields the same rate of return on investment for the Northern Division, 20%, as computed previously.

$$\text{Rate of return on investment (ROI)} = \textbf{Profit margin} \times \textbf{Investment turnover}$$

$$\text{Rate of return on investment (ROI)} = \frac{\text{Income from operations}}{\text{Sales}} \times \frac{\text{Sales}}{\text{Invested assets}}$$

$$\text{ROI} = \frac{\$70,000}{\$560,000} \times \frac{\$560,000}{\$350,000}$$

$$\text{ROI} = 12.5\% \times 1.6$$

$$\text{ROI} = 20\%$$

The expanded expression for the rate of return on investment is useful in evaluating and controlling divisions. This is so because the profit margin and the investment turnover focus on the underlying operating relationships of each division.

The profit margin component focuses on profitability by indicating the rate of profit earned on each sales dollar. If a division's profit margin increases and all other factors remain the same, the division's rate of return on investment also increases. For example, a division could add more profitable products to its sales mix and thereby increase its overall profit margin and rate of return on investment.

The investment turnover component focuses on efficiency in using assets and indicates the rate at which sales are generated for each dollar of invested assets. The more sales per dollar invested, the greater the efficiency in using the assets. If a division's investment turnover increases and all other factors remain the same, the division's rate of return on investment also increases. For example, a division could attempt to increase sales through special promotions or reduce inventory assets by using just-in-time principles, either of which would increase investment turnover.

The rate of return on investment, using the expanded expression for each division of DataLink Inc., is summarized as follows:

$$\textbf{Rate of return on investment (ROI)} = \frac{\textbf{Income from operations}}{\textbf{Sales}} \times \frac{\textbf{Sales}}{\textbf{Invested assets}}$$

$$\textbf{Northern Division ROI} = \frac{\$70,000}{\$560,000} \times \frac{\$560,000}{\$350,000}$$

$$\text{ROI} = 12.5\% \times 1.6$$

$$\text{ROI} = 20\%$$

$$\textbf{Central Division ROI} = \frac{\$84,000}{\$672,000} \times \frac{\$672,000}{\$700,000}$$

$$\text{ROI} = 12.5\% \times 0.96$$

$$\text{ROI} = 12\%$$

$$\text{Southern Division ROI} = \frac{\$75,000}{\$750,000} \times \frac{\$750,000}{\$500,000}$$

$$\text{ROI} = 10\% \times 1.5$$

$$\text{ROI} = 15\%$$

Although the Northern and Central Divisions have the same profit margins, the Northern Division investment turnover (1.6) is larger than that of the Central Division (0.96). Thus, by using its invested assets more efficiently, the Northern Division's rate of return on investment is higher than the Central Division's. The Southern Division's profit margin of 10% and investment turnover of 1.5 are lower than those of the Northern Division. The product of these factors results in a return on investment of 15% for the Southern Division compared to 20% for the Northern Division.

To determine possible ways of increasing the rate of return on investment, the profit margin and investment turnover for a division can be analyzed. For example, if the Northern Division is in a highly competitive industry in which the profit margin cannot be easily increased, the division manager could focus on increasing the investment turnover. To illustrate, assume that the revenues of the Northern Division could be increased by $56,000 through increasing operating expenses, such as advertising, to $385,000. The Northern Division's income from operations will increase from $70,000 to $77,000, as shown here:

Revenues ($560,000 + $56,000)	$616,000
Operating expenses	385,000
Income from operations before service department charges	$231,000
Service department charges	154,000
Income from operations	$ 77,000

The rate of return on investment for the Northern Division, using the expanded expression, is recomputed as follows:

$$\text{Rate of return on investment (ROI)} = \frac{\text{Income from operations}}{\text{Sales}} \times \frac{\text{Sales}}{\text{Invested assets}}$$

$$\text{Northern Division revised ROI} = \frac{\$77,000}{\$616,000} \times \frac{\$616,000}{\$350,000}$$

$$\text{ROI} = 12.5\% \times 1.76$$

$$\text{ROI} = 22\%$$

Although the Northern Division's profit margin remains the same (12.5%), the investment turnover has increased from 1.6 to 1.76, an increase of 10% (0.16/1.6). The 10% increase in investment turnover also increases the rate of return on investment by 10% (from 20% to 22%).

In addition to using it as a performance measure, the rate of return on investment can assist management in other ways. For example, in considering a decision to expand the operations of DataLink Inc., management could consider giving priority to the Northern Division because it earns the highest rate of return on investment. If the current rates of return on investment are maintained in the future, an investment in the Northern Division will return $0.20 (20%) on each dollar invested. In contrast, investments in the Central Division will earn only $0.12 per dollar invested, and investments in the Southern Division will return only $0.15 per dollar.

A disadvantage of the rate of return on investment as a performance measure is that it could lead divisional managers to reject new investments that could be profitable for the company as a whole. For example, the Northern Division of DataLink Inc. has an overall rate of return on investment of 20%. The minimum acceptable rate of return on investment for DataLink Inc. is 10%. The manager of the Northern Division has the opportunity of investing in a new project that is estimated to earn a 17% rate of return. If the manager of the Northern Division invests in the project, however, the Northern Division's overall rate of return will decrease from 20%. Thus, the division manager could decide to reject the project, even though the investment would exceed DataLink's minimum acceptable rate of return on investment. The CFO of **Millennium Chemicals Inc.** referred to a similar situation by stating: "We had too many divisional executives who failed to spend money on capital projects with more than satisfactory returns because those projects would have lowered the average return on assets of their particular business."

BUSINESS STRATEGY

The Lowest Prices

Amazon.com built its online business strategy on offering books at significant discounts that traditional chains couldn't match. Over the years, Amazon has expanded its online offerings to include DVDs, toys, electronics, and even kitchen appliances. But can its low-cost, discount strategy continue to work across a variety of products? Some have their doubts. The electronics business has lower margins and more competition than books. For example, **Dell Computers** is already an established low-cost provider of personal computers and software. In addition, some electronic manufacturers such as **Sony** are protective of their prices and have refused to make Amazon.com an authorized dealer. As Lauren Levitan, a noted financial analyst recently said, "It's hard to be the low-cost retailer. You have to execute flawlessly on a very consistent basis. Most people who try a low-price strategy fail." This risk of failing at the low-cost strategy was validated by **Kmart**'s filing for bankruptcy protection because of its inability to compete with **Wal-Mart**'s low prices.

Source: Saul Hansell, "A Profitable Amazon Looks to Do an Encore," *The New York Times,* January 26, 2002.

Residual Income

An additional measure of evaluating divisional performance—residual income—is useful in overcoming some of the disadvantages associated with the rate of return on investment. **Residual income** is the excess of income from operations over a minimum acceptable income from operations, as illustrated at the top of the next page.

The minimum acceptable income from operations is normally computed by multiplying a minimum rate of return by the amount of divisional assets. The minimum rate is set by top management based on such factors as the cost of financing the busi-

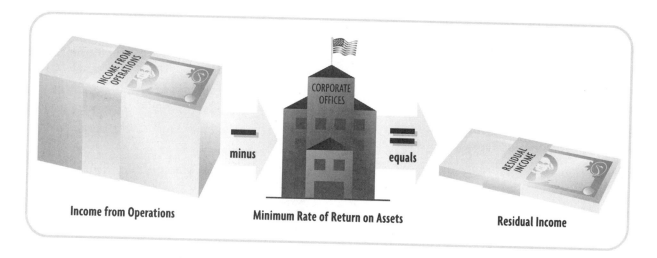

| | Income from Operations | minus | Minimum Rate of Return on Assets | equals | Residual Income |

ness operations. To illustrate, assume that DataLink Inc. has established 10% as the minimum acceptable rate of return on divisional assets. The residual incomes for the three divisions are as follows:

	Northern Division	Central Division	Southern Division
Income from operations	$70,000	$84,000	$75,000
Minimum acceptable income from operations as a percent of assets:			
$350,000 × 10%	35,000		
$700,000 × 10%		70,000	
$500,000 × 10%			50,000
Residual income	$35,000	$14,000	$25,000

The Northern Division has more residual income than the other divisions, even though it generates the lowest amount of income from operations. This happens because the assets on which to earn a minimum acceptable rate of return are less for the Northern Division than for the other divisions.

The major advantage of residual income as a performance measure is that it considers both the minimum acceptable rate of return and the total amount of income from operations earned by each division. Residual income encourages division managers to maximize income from operations in excess of the minimum. This provides an incentive to accept any project that is expected to have a rate of return in excess of the minimum. Thus, the residual income number supports both divisional and overall company objectives.

Companies such as **Quaker Oats Company** and **The Coca-Cola Company** are using residual income (sometimes called *economic value added*) to guide their investment decisions and to measure managers' abilities to return profits from the assets entrusted to them.

The Balanced Scorecard

In addition to financial divisional performance measures, many companies are also relying on nonfinancial divisional measures. One popular evaluation approach is the balanced scorecard.[1] The balanced scorecard is a set of financial and nonfinancial measures that reflect multiple performance dimensions of a business. A common balanced scorecard design measures performance in the innovation and learning, customer, internal, and financial dimensions of a business. These four areas can be diagrammed as shown in Exhibit 7.

EXHIBIT 7
The Balanced Scorecard

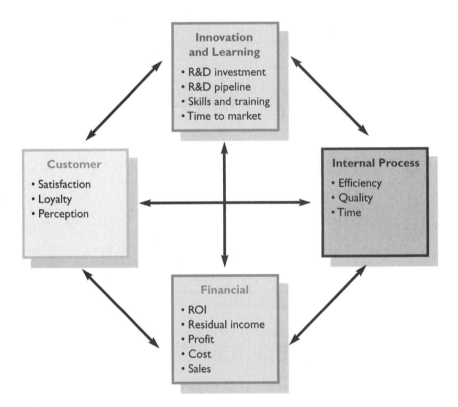

The *innovation* and *learning* perspective measures the amount of innovation in an organization. For example, a drug company, such as **Merck**, would measure the number of drugs in its **Food and Drug Administration** approval pipeline, the amount of research and development (R&D) spending per period, and the length of time it takes to turn ideas into marketable products. Managing the performance of its R&D processes is critical to Merck's longer-term prospects and thus would be an additional performance perspective beyond the financial numbers. The *customer* perspective would measure customer satisfaction, loyalty, and perceptions. For example, **Amazon.com** measures the number of repeat visitors to its Web site as a measure of customer loyalty. Amazon.com needs repeat business because the costs to acquire a new customer are very high. The *internal process* perspective measures the effectiveness and efficiency of internal business processes. For example, **DaimlerChrysler**

[1]The balanced scorecard was developed by R. S. Kaplan and D. P. Norton and is explained in *The Balanced Scorecard: Translating Strategy into Action* (Cambridge: Harvard Business School Press, 1996).

measures quality by the average warranty claims per automobile, measures efficiency by the average labor hours per automobile, and measures the average time to assemble each automobile. The *financial* perspective measures the economic performance of the responsibility center as we have illustrated in the previous sections of this chapter. All companies will use financial measures. For example, one survey found that more than 70% of companies use income from operations as a percentage of sales, 62% use rate of return on investment, and 13% use residual income as financial performance measures.[2]

Sears designed its balanced scorecard using measures targeted to three themes: Sears as a compelling place to work, a compelling place to shop, and a compelling place to invest. A Sears senior executive stated that "there are some leading indicators that predict what financial performance will be. In our case, they turn out to be things like employee attitudes and whether customers see our stores as fun places to shop."

The balanced scorecard is designed to reveal the underlying nonfinancial drivers, or causes, of financial performance. For example, if a business improves customer satisfaction, this will likely lead to improved financial performance. In addition, the balanced scorecard helps managers consider trade-offs between short- and long-term performance. For example, additional investment in R&D would penalize the short-term financial perspective, because R&D is an expense that reduces income from operations. However, the innovation perspective would measure additional R&D expenditures favorably because current R&D expenditures can lead to future profits from new products. The balanced scorecard motivates the manager to invest in new R&D, even though it is recognized as a current period expense. A recent survey has indicated that 40% of the companies use or are planning to use the balanced scorecard.[3] Thus, the balanced scorecard is gaining acceptance because of its ability to reveal the underlying causes of financial performance while helping managers consider the short- and long-term implications of their decisions.

ETHICS IN ACTION

The Sarbanes-Oxley Act of 2002 was enacted in response to the perceived abuses in accounting, corporate responsibility, and public disclosure at the beginning of this century. One of the provisions of this act is to require the principal executive and financial officers to certify under oath and penalty of law that the financial statements have been personally reviewed, contain no material omissions, and present fairly the financial condition and results of operations.

Transfer Pricing

OBJECTIVE   5

Explain how the market price, negotiated price, and cost price approaches to transfer pricing can be used by decentralized segments of a business.

When divisions transfer products or render services to each other, a **transfer price** is used to charge for them. Since transfer prices affect the goals for both divisions, setting these prices is a sensitive matter for division managers.

[2]Robert A. Howell, James D. Brown, Stephen R. Soucy, and Allen H. Seed, *Management Accounting in the New Manufacturing Environment* (Montvale, NJ: National Association of Accountants, 1987).
[3]Mark L. Frigo and Kip R. Krumwiede, "The Balanced Scorecard," *Strategic Finance* (January 2000), pp. 50–54.

Transfer prices should be set so that overall company income is increased when goods are transferred between divisions. As we illustrate, however, transfer prices can be misused in such a way that overall company income suffers.

In the following paragraphs, we discuss various approaches to setting transfer prices. Exhibit 8 shows the range of prices that results from common approaches to setting transfer prices.[4] Transfer prices can be set as low as the variable cost per unit or as high as the market price. Often, transfer prices are negotiated at some point between the two.

EXHIBIT 8
Commonly Used Transfer Prices

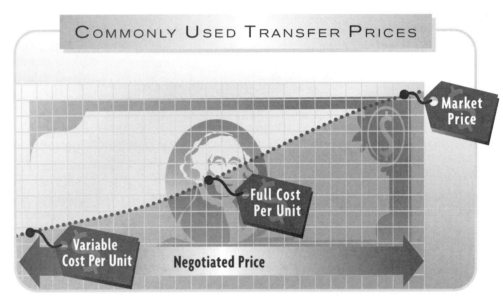

A survey of transfer pricing practices has reported the following usage:

Cost price (variable or full)	46%
Market price	37
Negotiated price	17

Source: Roger Y. W. Tang, "Transfer Pricing in the 1990's," *Management Accounting*, February 1992, pp. 22–26.

Transfer prices can be used when decentralized units are organized as cost, profit, or investment centers. To illustrate, we use a packaged snack food company (Wilson Company) with no service departments and two operating divisions (Eastern and Western) organized as investment centers. Condensed divisional income statements for Wilson Company, assuming no transfers between divisions, are shown in Exhibit 9.

---

[4]The discussion in this chapter highlights the essential concepts of transfer pricing. In-depth discussion of transfer pricing can be found in advanced texts.

EXHIBIT 9
Income Statement—No Transfers between Divisions

WILSON COMPANY
Divisional Income Statements
For the Year Ended December 31, 2004

	Eastern Division	Western Division	Total
Sales:			
50,000 units × $20 per unit	$1,000,000		$1,000,000
20,000 units × $40 per unit		$800,000	800,000
			$1,800,000
Expenses:			
Variable:			
50,000 units × $10 per unit	$ 500,000		$ 500,000
20,000 units × $30* per unit		$600,000	600,000
Fixed	300,000	100,000	400,000
Total expenses	$ 800,000	$700,000	$1,500,000
Income from operations	$ 200,000	$100,000	$ 300,000

*$20 of the $30 per unit represents materials costs, and the remaining $10 per unit represents other variable conversion expenses incurred within the Western Division.

Market Price Approach

Using the **market price approach**, the transfer price is the price at which the product or service transferred could be sold to outside buyers. If an outside market exists for the product or service transferred, the current market price can be a proper transfer price.

To illustrate, assume that materials used by Wilson Company in producing snack food in the Western Division are currently purchased from an outside supplier at $20 per unit. The same materials are produced by the Eastern Division. The Eastern Division is operating at full capacity of 50,000 units and can sell all it produces to either the Western Division or to outside buyers. A transfer price of $20 per unit (the market price) has no effect on the Eastern Division's income or total company income. The Eastern Division will earn revenues of $20 per unit on all its production and sales, regardless of who buys its product. Likewise, the Western Division will pay $20 per unit for materials (the market price). Thus, the use of the market price as the transfer price has no effect on the Eastern Division's income or total company income. In this situation, the use of the market price as the transfer price is proper. The condensed divisional income statements for Wilson Company in this case are also shown in Exhibit 9.

Negotiated Price Approach

If unused or excess capacity exists in the supplying division (the Eastern Division) and the transfer price is equal to the market price, total company profit is not necessarily maximized. This happens because the manager of the Western Division will be indifferent to purchasing materials from the Eastern Division or from outside suppliers. Thus, the Western Division can purchase the materials from outside suppliers. If, however, the Western Division purchases the materials from the Eastern Division, the difference between the market price of $20 and the variable costs of the Eastern

Division can cover fixed costs and contribute to company profits. When the negotiated price approach is used in this situation, the manager of the Western Division is encouraged to purchase the materials from the Eastern Division.

The **negotiated price approach** allows the managers of decentralized units to agree (negotiate) among themselves as to the transfer price. The only constraint on the negotiations is that the transfer price be less than the market price but more than the supplying division's variable costs per unit.

To illustrate the use of the negotiated price approach, assume that instead of a capacity of 50,000 units, the Eastern Division's capacity is 70,000 units. In addition, assume that the Eastern Division can continue to sell only 50,000 units to outside buyers. A transfer price less than $20 would encourage the manager of the Western Division to purchase from the Eastern Division. This happens because the Western Division's materials cost per unit would decrease and its income from operations would increase. At the same time, a transfer price above the Eastern Division's variable costs per unit of $10 (from Exhibit 9) would encourage the manager of the Eastern Division to use the excess capacity to supply materials to the Western Division. In doing so, the Eastern Division's income from operations would increase.

We continue the illustration with the aid of Exhibit 10, assuming that Wilson Company's division managers agree to a transfer price of $15 for the Eastern Division's product. By purchasing from the Eastern Division, the Western Division's materials cost decreases by $5 per unit. At the same time, the Eastern Division increases its sales by $300,000 (20,000 units × $15 per unit) and increase its income by $100,000 ($300,000 sales − $200,000 variable costs). The effect of reducing the Western Division's materials cost by $100,000 (20,000 units × $5 per unit) is to increase its income by $100,000. Therefore, Wilson Company's income is increased by $200,000 ($100,000 reported by the Eastern Division and $100,000 reported by the Western Division), as shown in the condensed income statements in Exhibit 10.

EXHIBIT 10
*Income Statements—
Negotiated Transfer
Price*

		Eastern Division	Western Division	Total
WILSON COMPANY				
Divisional Income Statements				
For the Year Ended December 31, 2004				
Sales:				
50,000 units × $20 per unit		$1,000,000		$1,000,000
20,000 units × $15 per unit		300,000		300,000
20,000 units × $40 per unit			$800,000	800,000
		$1,300,000	$800,000	$2,100,000
Expenses:				
Variable:				
70,000 units × $10 per unit		$ 700,000		$ 700,000
20,000 units × $25* per unit			$500,000	500,000
Fixed		300,000	100,000	400,000
Total expenses		$1,000,000	$600,000	$1,600,000
Income from operations		$ 300,000	$200,000	$ 500,000

*$10 of the $25 are variable conversion expenses incurred solely within the Western Division, and $15 per unit represents the transfer price per unit from the Eastern Division.

In this illustration, any transfer price less than the market price of $20 but more than the Eastern Division's unit variable costs of $10 would increase each division's income. In addition, overall company profit would increase by $200,000. By establishing a range of $20 to $10 for the transfer price, each division manager has an incentive to negotiate the transfer of the materials.

Cost Price Approach

Under the **cost price approach**, cost is used to set transfer prices. With this approach, a variety of cost concepts can be used. For example, *cost* can refer to either total product cost per unit or variable product cost per unit. If total product cost per unit is used, direct materials, direct labor, and factory overhead are included in the transfer price. If variable product cost per unit is used, the fixed factory overhead component of total product cost is excluded from the transfer price.

Either actual costs or standard (budgeted) costs can be used in applying the cost price approach. If actual costs are used, inefficiencies of the producing division are transferred to the purchasing division. Thus, there is little incentive for the producing division to control costs carefully. For this reason, most companies use standard costs in the cost price approach. In this way, differences between actual and standard costs remain with the producing division for cost control purposes.

When division managers have responsibility for cost centers, the cost price approach to transfer pricing is proper and is often used. The cost price approach could not be proper, however, for decentralized operations organized as profit or investment centers. In profit and investment centers, division managers have responsibility for both revenues and expenses. The use of cost as a transfer price ignores the supplying division manager's responsibility for revenues. When a supplying division's sales are all intracompany transfers, for example, using the cost price approach prevents the supplying division from reporting any income from operations. A cost-based transfer price could therefore not motivate the division manager to make intracompany transfers even though they are in the best interests of the company.

Key Points

1. **List and explain the advantages and disadvantages of decentralized operations.**

The advantages of decentralization include better decisions by the managers closest to the operations, more time for top management to focus on strategic planning, training for managers, improved ability to serve customers and respond to their needs, and improved manager morale. The disadvantages of decentralization include failure of the company to maximize profits because decisions made by one manager can affect other managers in such a way that the profitability of the entire company could suffer.

2. **Prepare a responsibility accounting report for a cost center.**

Since managers of cost centers have responsibility and authority to make decisions regarding costs, responsibility accounting for cost centers focuses on costs. The primary accounting tools for planning and controlling costs for a cost center are budgets and budget performance reports. An example of a budget performance report is shown in Exhibit 2.

3. Prepare responsibility accounting reports for a profit center.

In preparing a profitability report for a profit center, operating expenses are subtracted from revenues to determine the income from operations before service department charges. Service department charges are then subtracted to determine the income from operations of the profit center. An example of a divisional income statement is shown in Exhibit 5.

4. Compute and interpret the rate of return on investment, the residual income, and the balanced scorecard for an investment center.

The rate of return on investment for an investment center is the income from operations divided by invested assets. The rate of return on investment can also be computed as the product of (1) the profit margin and (2) the investment turnover. Residual income for an investment center is the excess of income from operations over a minimum amount of desired income from operations. The balanced scorecard combines nonfinancial measures to help managers consider the underlying causes of financial performance and trade-offs between short-term and long-term performance.

5. Explain how the market price, negotiated price, and cost price approaches to transfer pricing can be used by decentralized segments of a business.

Under the market price approach, the transfer price is the price at which the product or service transferred could be sold to outside buyers. Market price should be used when the supplier division is able to sell to outsiders and is operating at capacity.

Under the negotiated price approach, the managers of decentralized units agree (negotiate) among themselves as to the transfer price. Negotiated prices should be used when the supplier division is operating below capacity.

Under the cost price approach, cost is used as the basis for setting transfer prices. A variety of cost concepts can be used, such as total product cost per unit or variable product cost per unit. In addition, actual costs or standard (budgeted) costs can be used. The cost price approach should be used for supplier divisions that are organized as cost centers.

Glossary

Balanced scorecard: A performance evaluation approach that incorporates multiple performance dimensions by combining financial and nonfinancial measures.

Controllable expenses: Costs that can be influenced by the decisions of a manager.

Cost center: A decentralized unit in which the department or division manager has responsibility for the control of costs incurred and the authority to make decisions that affect these costs.

Cost price approach: An approach to transfer pricing that uses cost as the basis for setting the transfer price.

Decentralization: The separation of a business into more manageable operating units.

Division: A decentralized unit that is structured around a common function, product, customer, or geographical territory.

Income from operations: Revenues less operating expenses and service department charges for a profit or investment center.

Investment center: A decentralized unit in which the manager has the responsibility and authority to make decisions that affect not only costs and revenues but also the fixed assets available to the center.

Investment turnover: A component of the rate of return on investment computed as the ratio of sales to invested assets.

Market price approach: An approach to transfer pricing that uses the price at which the product or service transferred could be sold to outside buyers as the transfer price.

Negotiated price approach: An approach to transfer pricing that allows managers of decentralized units to agree (negotiate) among themselves as to the transfer price.

Profit center: A decentralized unit in which the manager has the responsibility and the authority to make decisions that affect both costs and revenues (and thus profits).

Profit margin: A component of the rate of return on investment computed as the ratio of income from operations to sales.

Rate of return on investment: A measure of managerial efficiency in the use of investments in assets computed as income from operations divided by invested assets.

Residual income: The excess of divisional income from operations over a "minimum" acceptable income from operations.

Responsibility accounting: The process of measuring and reporting operating data by areas of responsibility.

Service department charges: The costs of services provided by an internal service department and transferred to a responsibility center.

Transfer price: The price charged one decentralized unit by another for the goods or services provided.

Self-Study Questions

(Answers appear at end of chapter.)

1. When the manager has the responsibility and authority to make decisions that affect costs and revenues but no responsibility for or authority over assets invested in the department, the department is called:
   A. a cost center.
   B. a profit center.
   C. an investment center.
   D. a service department.

2. The Accounts Payable Department has expenses of $600,000 and makes 150,000 payments to the various vendors who provide products and services to the divisions. Division A has income from operations of $900,000, before service department charges, and requires 60,000 payments to vendors. If the Accounts Payable Department is treated as a service department, what is Division A's income from operations?
   A. $300,000
   B. $900,000
   C. $660,000
   D. $540,000

3. Division A of Kern Co. has sales of $350,000, cost of goods sold of $200,000, operating expenses of

$30,000, and invested assets of $600,000. What is the rate of return on investment for Division A?
   A. 20%
   B. 25%
   C. 33%
   D. 40%

4. Division L of Liddy Co. has a rate of return on investment of 24% and an investment turnover of 1.6. What is the profit margin?
   A. 6%
   B. 15%
   C. 24%
   D. 38%

5. Which approach to transfer pricing uses the price at which the product or service transferred could be sold to outside buyers?
   A. Cost price approach
   B. Negotiated price approach
   C. Market price approach
   D. Standard cost approach

Discussion Questions

1. Differentiate between the manager's responsibility for a cost center and a profit center.

2. Differentiate between the manager's responsibility for a profit center and an investment center.

3. In what major respect would budget performance reports prepared for the use of plant managers of a manufacturing business with cost centers differ from

those prepared for the use of the various department supervisors who report to the plant managers?

4. For what decisions is the manager of a cost center *not* responsible?

5. How are service department costs charged to responsibility centers?

6. How is a service department charge rate determined?

7. **Weyerhaeuser Company** developed a system that assigns service department expenses to user divisions on the basis of actual services consumed by the division. Several of Weyerhaeuser's activities in its central financial services department follow:

- Payroll
- Accounts payable
- Accounts receivable
- Database administration—report preparation

For each activity, identify an output measure that could be used to charge user divisions for the service.

8. What is the major shortcoming of using income from operations as a performance measure for investment centers?

9. Why should the factors under the control of the investment center manager (revenues, expenses, and invested assets) be considered in computing the rate of return on investment?

10. In a decentralized company in which the divisions are organized as investment centers, how could a division be considered the least profitable even though it earned the largest amount of income from operations?

11. Which component of the rate of return on investment (profit margin or investment turnover) focuses on efficiency in the use of assets and indicates the rate at which sales are generated for each dollar of invested assets?

12. How does using the rate of return on investment facilitate comparability between divisions of decentralized companies?

13. The rates of return on investment for Harmon Co.'s three divisions, A, B, and C, are 20%, 17%, and 15%, respectively. In expanding operations, which of Harmon Co.'s divisions should be given priority? Explain.

14. Why would a firm use a balanced scorecard in evaluating divisional performance?

15. What is the objective of transfer pricing?

16. When is the negotiated price approach preferred over the market price approach in setting transfer prices?

17. When using the negotiated price approach to transfer pricing, within what range should the transfer price be established?

Exercises

EXERCISE 14-1
Budget performance reports for cost centers
OBJECTIVE 2

✓ c. $2,300

Partially completed budget performance reports for Handy Company, a manufacturer of air conditioners, follow.

HANDY COMPANY
Budget Performance Report—Vice-President, Production
For the Month Ended April 30, 2004

Plant	Budget	Actual	Over Budget	Under Budget
St. Louis Plant	$523,700	$521,400		$2,300
Tempe Plant	810,000	805,200		4,800
Syracuse Plant	(g)	(h)	$ (i)	
	$ (j)	$ (k)	$ (l)	$7,100

HANDY COMPANY
Budget Performance Report—Manager, Syracuse Plant
For the Month Ended April 30, 2004

Department	Budget	Actual	Over Budget	Under Budget
Compressor Assembly	$ (a)	$ (b)	$ (c)	
Electronic Assembly	125,700	125,750	50	
Final Assembly	204,800	204,500		$300
	$ (d)	$ (e)	$ (f)	$300

HANDY COMPANY
Budget Performance Report—Supervisor, Compressor Assembly
For the Month Ended April 30, 2004

Costs	Budget	Actual	Over Budget	Under Budget
Factory wages	$ 34,800	$ 36,300	$1,500	
Materials	93,600	93,300		$300
Power and light	8,400	8,900	500	
Maintenance	14,800	15,400	600	
	$151,600	$153,900	$2,600	$300

a. Complete the budget performance reports by determining the correct amounts for the lettered spaces.

b. Compose a memo to Karen Poling, vice-president of production for Handy Company, explaining the performance of the production division for April.

EXERCISE 14-2
Divisional income statements
OBJECTIVE 3

✓ Residential Division Income from operations, $53,700

The following data were summarized from the accounting records for Circle D Electrical Equipment Company for the year ended June 30, 2004:

Cost of goods sold:	
Residential Division	$305,000
Industrial Division	425,000
Administrative expenses:	
Residential Division	90,500
Industrial Division	164,800
Service department charges:	
Residential Division	25,800
Industrial Division	75,200
Net sales:	
Residential Division	475,000
Industrial Division	825,000

Prepare divisional income statements for Circle D Electrical Equipment Company.

EXERCISE 14-3
Service department charges
OBJECTIVE 3

✓ a. Commercial payroll, $34,650

In divisional income statements prepared for Owen Paving Company, the Payroll Department costs are charged back to user divisions on the basis of the number of payroll checks, and the Purchasing Department costs are charged back on the basis of the number of purchase requisitions. The Payroll Department had expenses of $149,520, and the Purchasing Department had expenses of $59,640 for the year. The following annual data for Residential, Commercial, and Highway Divisions were obtained from corporate records:

	Residential	Commercial	Highway
Sales	$2,400,000	$2,600,000	$3,000,000
Number of employees:			
Weekly payroll (52 weeks per year)	120	60	80
Monthly payroll	20	15	25
Number of purchase requisitions per year	1,600	1,400	1,200

a. Determine the annual amount of payroll and purchasing costs charged back to the Residential, Commercial, and Highway Divisions from payroll and purchasing services.

b. Why does the Residential Division have a larger service department charge than the other two divisions even though its sales are lower?

EXERCISE 14-4
Service department charges and activity bases
OBJECTIVE 3

For each of the following service departments, identify an activity base that could be used for charging the expense to the profit center.

a. Duplication Services
b. Accounts Receivable
c. Electronic Data Processing
d. Central Purchasing
e. Legal
f. Telecommunications

EXERCISE 14-5
Activity bases for service department charges
OBJECTIVE 3

For each of the following service departments, select the activity base listed that is most appropriate for charging service expenses to responsible units.

	Service Department		Activity Base
a.	Accounts Receivable	1.	Number of purchase requisitions
b.	Conferences	2.	Number of travel claims
c.	Payroll Accounting	3.	Number of conference attendees
d.	Telecommunications	4.	Number of payroll checks
e.	Employee Travel	5.	Number of telephone lines
f.	Computer Support	6.	Number of computers
g.	Training	7.	Number of employees trained
h.	Central Purchasing	8.	Number of sales invoices

EXERCISE 14-6
Service department charges and activity bases
OBJECTIVE 3

✓ b. Help Desk, $16,704

Harris Corporation, a manufacturer of electronics and communications systems, uses a service department charge system to charge profit centers with Computing and Communications Services (CCS) service department costs. The following table identifies an abbreviated list of service categories and activity bases used by the CCS department. The table also includes some assumed cost and activity base quantity information for each service for March.

CCS Service Category	Activity Base	Assumed Cost	Assumed Activity Base Quantity
Help desk	Number of calls	$156,000	6,500
Network center	Number of devices monitored	547,560	10,800
Electronic mail	Number of user accounts	180,000	30,000
Local voice support	Number of phone extensions	416,560	25,400

One of the profit centers for Harris Corporation is the Communication Systems (COMM) sector. Assume the following information for the COMM sector:

- The sector has 5,800 employees, of whom 50% are office employees.
- All the office employees have a phone, and 80% of them have a computer on the network.
- Of the employees with a computer, 90% also have an e-mail account.
- The average number of help desk calls for March was 0.30 calls per individual with a computer.
- There are 300 additional printers, servers, and peripherals on the network in addition to the personal computers.

a. Determine the service charge rate for the four CCS service categories for March.
b. Determine the charges to the COMM sector for the four CCS service categories for March.

EXERCISE 14-7
Divisional income statements with service department charges
OBJECTIVE 3

Acadia Electronics Company has two divisions, Video and Audio, and two corporate service departments, Computer Support and Accounts Payable. The corporate expenses for the year ended December 31, 2004, are as follows:

✓ Audio income from
operations, $655,250

Computer Support Department	$360,000
Accounts Payable Department	125,000
Other corporate administrative expenses	215,000
Total corporate expense	$700,000

The other corporate administrative expenses include officers' salaries and other expenses required by the corporation. The Computer Support Department charges the divisions for services rendered based on the number of computers in the department, and the Accounts Payable Department charges divisions for services based on the number of checks issued. The usage of service by the two divisions is as follows:

Video Division	325 computers	4,500 checks
Audio Division	175	5,500
Total	500 computers	10,000 checks

The service department charges of the Computer Support Department and the Accounts Payable Department are considered controllable by the divisions. Corporate administrative expenses are not considered controllable by the divisions. The revenues, cost of goods sold, and operating expenses for the two divisions are as follows:

	Video	Audio
Revenues	$3,500,000	$2,750,000
Cost of goods sold	2,800,000	1,500,000
Operating expenses	250,000	400,000

Prepare the divisional income statements for the two divisions.

EXERCISE 14-8
Corrections to service department charges
OBJECTIVE 3

✓ b. Income from
operations, Cargo Division,
$1,184,000

Atlantic Airlines Inc. has two divisions organized as profit centers, the Passenger Division and the Cargo Division. The following divisional income statements were prepared:

ATLANTIC AIRLINES INC.
Divisional Income Statements
For the Year Ended October 31, 2004

	Passenger Division		Cargo Division	
Revenues		$6,500,000		$6,500,000
Operating expenses		5,500,000		5,000,000
Income from operations before				
service department charges		$1,000,000		$1,500,000
Less service department charges:				
Training	$150,000		$150,000	
Flight scheduling	200,000		200,000	
Reservations	300,000	650,000	300,000	650,000
Income from operations		$ 350,000		$ 850,000

The service department charge rate for the service department costs was based on revenues. Since the revenues of the two divisions were the same, the service department charges to each division were also the same.

The following additional information is available:

	Passenger Division	Cargo Division	Total
Number of flight personnel trained	160	40	200
Number of flights	180	320	500
Number of reservations requested	30,000	—	30,000

(continued)

a. Does the income from operations for the two divisions accurately measure performance?

b. Correct the divisional income statements using the activity bases provided in revising the service department charges.

EXERCISE 14-9
*Profit center
responsibility reporting*
OBJECTIVES 3, 5

✓ Income from
operations, Camping
Equipment Division,
$70,250

Tahoe Sporting Goods Co. operates two divisions, the Camping Equipment Division and the Ski Equipment Division. The following income and expense accounts were provided from the trial balance as of June 30, 2004, the end of the current fiscal year, after all adjustments, including those for inventories, were recorded and posted:

Sales—Camping Equipment Division	$460,000
Sales—Ski Equipment Division	745,000
Cost of Goods Sold—Camping Equipment Division	215,000
Cost of Goods Sold—Ski Equipment Division	385,000
Sales Expense—Camping Equipment Division	80,000
Sales Expense—Ski Equipment Division	105,000
Administrative Expense—Camping Equipment Division	45,400
Administrative Expense—Ski Equipment Division	66,800
Advertising Expense	19,900
Transportation Expense	22,050
Accounts Receivable Collection Expense	3,600
Warehouse Expense	45,000

The bases to be used in allocating expenses and other essential information are as follows:

a. Advertising expense—incurred at headquarters, charged back to divisions on the basis of usage: Camping Equipment Division, $7,400; Ski Equipment Division, $12,500.

b. Transportation expense—charged back to divisions at a transfer price of $4.50 per bill of lading: Camping Equipment Division, 2,300 bills of lading; Ski Equipment Division, 2,600 bills of lading.

c. Accounts receivable collection expense—incurred at headquarters, charged back to divisions at a transfer price of $0.80 per invoice: Camping Equipment Division, 2,000 sales invoices; Ski Equipment Division, 2,500 sales invoices.

d. Warehouse expense—charged back to divisions on the basis of floor space used in storing division products: Camping Equipment Division, 10,000 square feet; Ski Equipment Division, 5,000 square feet.

Prepare a divisional income statement with two column headings, Camping Equipment Division and Ski Equipment Division. Provide supporting schedules for determining service department charges.

EXERCISE 14-10
*Rate of return on
investment*
OBJECTIVE 4

✓ a. Milk Division, 20%

The income from operations and the amount of invested assets in each division of Green Bay Dairy Company are as follows:

	Income from Operations	Invested Assets
Cheese Division	$133,000	$ 950,000
Milk Division	104,000	520,000
Butter Division	182,400	1,140,000

a. Compute the rate of return on investment for each division.

b. Which division is the most profitable per dollar invested?

EXERCISE 14-11
Residual income
OBJECTIVE 4

✓ a. Cheese Division, $19,000

Based on the data in Exercise 14-10, assume that management has established a 12% minimum acceptable rate of return for invested assets.

a. Determine the residual income for each division.
b. Which division has the most residual income?

EXERCISE 14-12
Rate of return on investment
OBJECTIVE 4

The **Walt Disney Corporation** has three major sectors, as follows:

- **Creative Content:** produces live action and animated motion pictures, manages licensing, and operates the Disney Stores.
- **Broadcasting:** operates the ABC broadcasting network.
- **Theme Parks and Resorts:** operates the Disney entertainment and vacation properties, including Disney World and Disney Land.

Disney recently reported sector income from operations, revenue, and invested assets (in millions) as follows:

	Income from Operations	Revenue	Invested Assets
Creative Content	$1,403	$10,302	$ 9,509
Broadcasting	1,325	7,142	20,099
Theme Parks and Resorts	1,287	5,532	9,214

a. Use the expanded formula to determine the rate of return on investment for the three Disney sectors. Round to two decimal places.
b. How do the three sectors differ in their profit margin, investment turnover, and rate of return on investment?

EXERCISE 14-13
Determining missing items in rate of return computation
OBJECTIVE 4

✓ d. 1.4

One item is omitted from each of the following computations of the rate of return on investment:

Rate of return on investment	=	Profit margin	×	Investment turnover
27%	=	18%	×	(a)
(b)	=	12%	×	2.0
18%	=	(c)	×	0.75
21%	=	15%	×	(d)
(e)	=	8%	×	1.75

Determine the missing items, identifying each by the appropriate letter.

EXERCISE 14-14
Profit margin, investment turnover, and rate of return on investment
OBJECTIVE 4

✓ a. ROI, 18.4%

The condensed income statement for the New England Division of CinePlex Cinemas Inc. is as follows (assuming no service department charges):

Sales	$500,000
Cost of goods sold	320,000
Gross profit	$180,000
Administrative expenses	65,000
Income from operations	$115,000

The manager of the New England Division is considering ways to increase the rate of return on investment.

(continued)

a. Using the expanded formula for rate of return on investment, determine the profit margin, investment turnover, and rate of return on investment of the New England Division, assuming that $625,000 of assets have been invested in the New England Division.
b. If expenses could be reduced by $20,000 without decreasing sales, what would be the impact on the profit margin, investment turnover, and rate of return on investment for the New England Division?

EXERCISE 14-15
Determining missing items in rate of return and residual income computations
OBJECTIVE 4

✓ c. $9,000

Data for Black Gold Drilling Company is presented in the following table of rates of return on investment and residual incomes:

Invested Assets	Income from Operations	Rate of Return on Investment	Minimum Rate of Return	Minimum Acceptable Income from Operations	Residual Income
$450,000	$54,000	(a)	10%	(b)	(c)
220,000	(d)	14%	(e)	$35,200	$(4,400)
335,000	(f)	(g)	(h)	$50,250	$16,750
515,000	$77,250	(i)	12%	(j)	(k)

Determine the missing items, identifying each item by the appropriate letter.

EXERCISE 14-16
Determining missing items from computations
OBJECTIVE 4

✓ a. (e) 15%

Data for the North, East, South, and West Divisions of Mountain Power and Light Company are as follows:

	Sales	Income from Operations	Invested Assets	Rate of Return on Investment	Profit Margin	Investment Turnover
North	$850,000	$119,000	$680,000	(a)	(b)	(c)
East	$326,000	(d)	$407,500	12%	(e)	(f)
South	(g)	$60,000	(h)	(i)	12.5%	0.64
West	$365,000	(j)	(k)	20%	16%	(l)

a. Determine the missing items, identifying each by the letters (a) through (l).
b. Determine the residual income for each division, assuming that the minimum acceptable rate of return established by management is 10%.
c. Which division is the most profitable in terms of (a) return on investment and (b) residual income?

EXERCISE 14-17
Balanced scorecard
OBJECTIVE 4

American Express Company is a major financial services company noted for its American Express® card. Following are some of the performance measures used by the company in its balanced scorecard:

Average card member spending
Cards in force
Earnings growth
Hours of credit consultant training
Investment in information technology
Number of Internet features
Number of merchant signings
Number of card choices
Number of new card launches
Return on equity
Revenue growth

For each measure, identify whether the measure best fits the innovation, customer, internal process, or financial perspective of the balanced scorecard.

EXERCISE 14-18
Balanced scorecard
OBJECTIVE 4

Several years ago, **United Parcel Service (UPS)** believed that the Internet was going to change the parcel delivery market and would require UPS to become a more nimble and customer-focused organization. As a result, UPS replaced its old measurement system, which was 90% oriented toward financial performance, with a balanced scorecard. The scorecard emphasized four "point of arrival" measures, as follows:

1. Customer satisfaction index—a measure of customer satisfaction.
2. Employee relations index—a measure of employee sentiment and morale.
3. Competitive position—delivery performance relative to competition.
4. Time in transit—the time from order entry to delivery.

a. Why did UPS introduce a balanced scorecard and nonfinancial measures in its new performance measurement system?
b. Why do you think UPS included a factor measuring employee sentiment?

EXERCISE 14-19
Decision on transfer pricing
OBJECTIVE 5

✓ a. $2,800,000

Materials used by the Truck Division of Structure Motors are currently purchased from outside suppliers at a cost of $260 per unit. However, the same materials are available from the Component Division. The Component Division has unused capacity and can produce the materials needed by the Truck Division at a variable cost of $190 per unit.

a. If a transfer price of $230 per unit is established and 40,000 units of materials are transferred with no reduction in the Component Division's current sales, how much would Structure Motors' total income from operations increase?
b. How much would the Truck Division's income from operations increase?
c. How much would the Component Division's income from operations increase?

EXERCISE 14-20
Decision on transfer pricing
OBJECTIVE 5

✓ b. $400,000

Based on the Structure Motors data in Exercise 14-19, assume that a transfer price of $250 has been established and that 40,000 units of materials have been transferred with no reduction in the Component Division's current sales.

a. How much would Structure Motors' total income from operations increase?
b. How much would the Truck Division's income from operations increase?
c. How much would the Component Division's income from operations increase?
d. If the negotiated price approach is used, what would be the range of acceptable transfer prices and why?

Problems

PROBLEM 14 | 1
Budget performance report for a cost center
OBJECTIVE 2

The Eastern District of Mobile-One Communications Inc. is organized as a cost center. Its budget for the month ended September 30, 2004, is as follows:

Sales salaries	$ 625,700
Network administration salaries	321,900
Customer service salaries	173,400
Billing salaries	61,300
Maintenance	162,000
Depreciation of plant and equipment	58,000
Insurance and property taxes	31,400
Total	$1,433,700

During September, the costs incurred in the Eastern District were as follows:

Sales salaries	$ 623,700
Network administration salaries	320,100
Customer service salaries	189,200
Billing salaries	60,800
Maintenance	162,800
Depreciation of plant and equipment	58,000
Insurance and property taxes	31,600
Total	$1,446,200

Instructions

1. Prepare a budget performance report for the manager of the Eastern District of Mobile-One Communications Inc. for the month of September.
2. For which costs might the supervisor be expected to request supplemental reports?

PROBLEM 14 | 2

Profit center responsibility reporting

OBJECTIVE 3

✓ 1. Income from operations, Northern Division, $444,000

Continental Railroad Company organizes its three divisions, the Northwestern (NW), Western (W), and Northern (N) Regions, as profit centers. The CEO evaluates divisional performance using income from operations as a percentage of revenues. The following quarterly income and expense accounts were provided from the trial balance as of December 31, 2004:

Revenues—NW Region	$1,850,000
Revenues—W Region	2,830,000
Revenues—N Region	2,180,000
Operating Expenses—NW Region	900,000
Operating Expenses—W Region	1,750,000
Operating Expenses—N Region	1,430,000
Corporate Expenses—Dispatching	420,000
Corporate Expenses—Equipment	510,000
Corporate Expenses—Officers' Salaries	650,000
Corporate Expenses—Internal Auditing	350,000

The company operates three service departments, Dispatching, Equipment, and Internal Auditing. The Dispatching Department manages the scheduling and releasing of complete trains. The Equipment Department manages the railroad car inventories. It makes sure the right freight cars are at the right place at the right time. The Internal Auditing Department conducts a variety of audit services for the company as a whole. The following additional information has been gathered:

	Northwestern	Western	Northern
Number of scheduled trains	550	850	600
Number of railroad cars in inventory	5,000	6,000	6,000

Instructions

1. Prepare quarterly income statements showing income from operations for the three divisions. Use three column headings, Northwestern, Western, and Northern.
2. Which division would the CEO identify as the most successful? Round to two decimal places.
3. Recommend to the CEO a better method for evaluating the performance of the divisions. In your recommendation, identify the major weakness of the present method.

PROBLEM 14 | 3

Divisional income statements and rate of return on investment analysis

OBJECTIVE 4

✓ 2. Retail Broker Division ROI, 8.8%

Union Trust Inc. is a diversified financial services company with three operating divisions organized as investment centers. Condensed data taken from the records of the three divisions for the year ended December 31, 2004, are as follows:

	Retail Broker Division	E-trade Division	Mutual Fund Division
Fee revenue	$ 625,000	$250,000	$ 860,000
Operating expenses	350,000	225,000	705,200
Invested assets	3,125,000	125,000	1,000,000

The management of Union Trust Inc. is evaluating each division as a basis for planning a future expansion of operations.

Instructions

1. Prepare condensed divisional income statements for the three divisions, assuming that there were no service department charges.
2. Using the expanded formula for rate of return on investment, compute the profit margin, investment turnover, and rate of return on investment for each division.
3. If available funds permit the expansion of operations of only one division, which of the divisions would you recommend for expansion based on (1) and (2)? Explain.

PROBLEM 14 | 4

Effect of proposals on divisional performance

OBJECTIVE 4

✓ 3. Proposal 3 ROI, 18%

A condensed income statement for the Golf Equipment Division of St. Andrews Inc. for the year ended January 31, 2004, is as follows:

Sales	$4,800,000
Cost of goods sold	2,650,000
Gross profit	$2,150,000
Operating expenses	1,454,000
Income from operations	$ 696,000

Assume that the Golf Equipment Division received no charges from service departments. The president of St. Andrews Inc. has indicated that the division's rate of return on a $4,000,000 investment must be increased to at least 20% by the end of the next year if operations are to continue. The division manager is considering the following three proposals:

Proposal 1: Reduce invested assets by discontinuing a product line. This action would eliminate sales of $500,000, cost of goods sold of $323,000, and operating expenses of $40,000. Assets of $560,000 would be transferred to other divisions at no gain or loss.

Proposal 2: Transfer equipment with a book value of $1,000,000 to other divisions at no gain or loss and lease similar equipment. The annual lease payments would exceed the amount of depreciation expense on the old equipment by $72,000. This increase in expense would be included as part of the cost of goods sold. Sales would remain unchanged.

Proposal 3: Purchase new and more efficient machinery and thereby reduce the cost of goods sold by $168,000. Sales would remain unchanged, and the old machinery, which has no remaining book value, would be scrapped at no gain or loss. The new machinery would increase invested assets by $800,000 for the year.

Instructions

1. Using the expanded formula for rate of return on investment, determine the profit margin, investment turnover, and rate of return on investment for the Golf Equipment Division for the past year.
2. Prepare condensed estimated income statements and calculate the invested assets for each proposal.

(continued)

3. Using the expanded formula for rate of return on investment, determine the profit margin, investment turnover, and rate of return on investment for each proposal.
4. Which of the three proposals would meet the required 20% rate of return on investment?
5. If the Golf Equipment Division were in an industry in which the profit margin could not be increased, how much would the investment turnover have to increase to meet the president's required 20% rate of return on investment?

PROBLEM 14 | 5
Divisional performance analysis and evaluation
OBJECTIVE 4

✓ 2. Office Division ROI, 12%

The vice-president of operations of Van Horne Commercial Furniture Company is evaluating the performance of two divisions organized as investment centers. Invested assets and condensed income statement data for the past year for each division are as follows:

	Office Division	**Hotel Division**
Sales	$ 6,500,000	$5,000,000
Cost of goods sold	3,200,000	2,200,000
Operating expenses	1,350,000	1,300,000
Invested assets	16,250,000	6,250,000

Instructions

1. Prepare condensed divisional income statements for the year ended July 31, 2004, assuming that there were no service department charges.
2. Using the expanded expression for rate of return on investment, determine the profit margin, investment turnover, and rate of return on investment for each division.
3. If management's minimum acceptable rate of return is 10%, determine the residual income for each division.
4. Discuss the evaluation of the two divisions using the performance measures determined in (1), (2), and (3).

PROBLEM 14 | 6
Transfer pricing
OBJECTIVE 5

✓ 4. Instruments Division, $140,000

Fisher Instrument Company is a diversified aerospace company with two operating divisions, Electronics and Instruments Divisions. Condensed divisional income statements, which involve no intracompany transfers and include a breakdown of expenses into variable and fixed components, are as follows:

FISHER INSTRUMENT COMPANY
Divisional Income Statements
For the Year Ended December 31, 2004

	Electronics Division	Instruments Division	Total
Sales:			
700 units × $2,500 per unit	$1,750,000		$1,750,000
1,200 units × $5,500 per unit		$6,600,000	6,600,000
			$8,350,000
Expenses:			
Variable:			
700 units × $1,570 per unit	$1,099,000		$1,099,000
1,200 units × $4,200* per unit		$5,040,000	5,040,000
Fixed	430,000	735,000	1,165,000
Total expenses	$1,529,000	$5,775,000	$7,304,000
Income from operations	$ 221,000	$ 825,000	$1,046,000

*$2,500 of the $4,200 per unit represents materials costs, and the remaining $1,700 per unit represents other variable conversion expenses incurred within the Instruments Division.

The Electronics Division is presently producing 700 units of a total capacity of 900 units. Materials used in producing the Instruments Division's product are currently purchased from outside suppliers at a price of $2,500 per unit. The Electronics Division is able to produce the components used by the Instruments Division. Except for the possible transfer of materials between divisions, no changes are expected in sales and expenses.

Instructions

1. Would the market price of $2,500 per unit be an appropriate transfer price for Fisher Instrument Company? Explain.
2. If the Instruments Division purchases 200 units from the Electronics Division rather than externally at a negotiated transfer price of $2,000 per unit, how much would the income from operations of each division and total company income from operations increase?
3. Prepare condensed divisional income statements for Fisher Instrument Company based on the data in (2).
4. If a transfer price of $1,800 per unit is negotiated, how much would the income from operations of each division and total company income from operations increase?
5. a. What is the range of possible negotiated transfer prices that would be acceptable for Fisher Instrument Company?
   b. Assuming that the managers of the two divisions cannot agree on a transfer price, what price would you suggest as the transfer price?

Activities

Activity 14–1
Ethics and professional conduct in business

E T H I C S

Jolly Giant Company has two divisions, the Can Division and the Food Division. The Food Division can purchase cans from the Can Division or from outside suppliers. The Can Division sells can products both internally and externally. The market price for cans is $100 per 1,000 cans. Lee Tazwell is the controller of the Food Division, and Tracy Ford is the controller of the Can Division. The following conversation took place between them:

Lee: I hear you are having problems selling cans out of your division. Maybe I can help.
Tracy: You've got that right. We're producing and selling at only 70% of our capacity to outsiders. Last year we were selling all we could make. It would help a great deal if your division would divert some of your purchases to our division so we could use up our capacity. After all, we are part of the same company.
Lee: What kind of price could you give me?
Tracy: Well, you know as well as I that we are under strict profit responsibility in our divisions, so I would expect to get market price, $100 for 1,000 cans.
Lee: I'm not so sure we can swing that. I was expecting a price break from a "sister" division.
Tracy: Hey, I can only take this "sister" stuff so far. If I give you a price break, our profits will fall from last year's levels. I don't think I could explain that. I'm sorry, but I must remain firm—market price. After all, it's only fair. That's what you would have to pay from an external supplier.
Lee: Fair or not, I think we'll pass. Sorry we couldn't have helped.

Was Lee behaving ethically by trying to force the Can Division into a price break? Comment on Tracy's reactions.

Activity 14–2
Service department charges

The Accounting Department of Milford University asked the Publications Department to prepare a brochure for the Masters of Accountancy program. The Publications Department delivered the brochures and charged the Accounting Department a rate that was 20% higher than could be obtained from an outside printing company. The university policy required the Accounting Department to use the internal Publications Department for brochures. The Publications Department claimed that it had a drop in demand for its services during the fiscal year, so it had to charge higher prices to recover its payroll and fixed costs.

Should the cost of the brochure be transferred to the Accounting Department to hold the department head accountable for the cost of the brochure? What changes in policy would you recommend?

Activity 14-3
Evaluating divisional performance

The three divisions of World Media Enterprises are Broadcasting, Music, and Publications. The divisions are structured as investment centers. The following responsibility reports were prepared for the three divisions for the prior year:

	Broadcasting	Music	Publications
Revenues	$ 600,000	$1,400,000	$500,000
Operating expenses	240,000	800,000	100,000
Income from operations before service department charges	$ 360,000	$ 600,000	$400,000
Service department charges:			
Promotion	$ 100,000	$ 200,000	$200,000
Legal	50,000	40,000	80,000
	$ 150,000	$ 240,000	$280,000
Income from operations	$ 210,000	$ 360,000	$120,000
Invested assets	$1,500,000	$3,000,000	$800,000

1. Which division is making the best use of invested assets and thus should be given priority for future capital investments?
2. Assuming that the minimum acceptable rate of return on new projects is 10%, would all investments that produce a return in excess of 10% be accepted by the divisions?
3. Can you identify opportunities for improving the company's financial performance?

Activity 14-4
Evaluating division performance over time

The Snack Foods Division of Nature's Garden Food Co. has been experiencing revenue and profit growth during the years 2003–2005. The divisional income statements follow:

NATURE'S GARDEN FOOD CO.
Divisional Income Statements, Snack Foods Division
For the Years Ended December 31, 2003-2005

	2003	2004	2005
Sales	$420,000	$540,000	$650,000
Cost of goods sold	264,000	310,000	342,500
Gross profit	$156,000	$230,000	$307,500
Operating expenses	93,000	116,600	145,000
Income from operations	$ 63,000	$113,400	$162,500

Assume that there are no charges from service departments. The vice-president of the division, Harlan Tyson, is proud of his division's performance over the last three years. The president of Nature's Garden Food Co., Janice Gleason, discussed the division's performance with Harlan:

Harlan: As you can see, we've had a successful three years in the Snack Foods Division.
Janice: I'm not too sure.
Harlan: What do you mean? Look at our results. Our income from operations has nearly tripled, and our profit margins are improving.

Janice: I am looking at your results. However, your income statements fail to include one very important piece of information, namely, the invested assets. You have been investing a great deal of assets into the division. You had $210,000 in invested assets in 2003, $540,000 in 2004, and $1,000,000 in 2005.

Harlan: You are right. I've needed the assets to upgrade our technologies and expand our operations. The additional assets represent one reason we have been able to grow and improve our profit margins. I don't see that this is a problem.

Janice: The problem is that we must maintain a 20% rate of return on invested assets.

1. Determine the profit margins for the Snack Foods Division for 2003–2005.
2. Calculate the investment turnover for the Snack Foods Division for 2003–2005.
3. Calculate the rate of return on investment for the Snack Foods Division for 2003–2005.
4. Evaluate the division's performance over the 2003–2005 time period. Why was Janice concerned about the performance?

Activity 14–5
Evaluating division performance

Your father is president of Outdoor Life Inc., a privately held diversified company with five separate divisions organized as investment centers. A condensed income statement for the Sporting Goods Division for the past year, assuming no service department charges, is as follows:

OUTDOOR LIFE INC.—SPORTING GOODS DIVISION
Income Statement
For the Year Ended December 31, 2004

Sales	$16,000,000
Cost of goods sold	10,100,000
Gross profit	$ 5,900,000
Operating expenses	1,900,000
Income from operations	$ 4,000,000

The manager of the Sporting Goods Division recently had the opportunity to add an additional product line that would require invested assets of $12,000,000. A projected income statement for the new product line is as follows:

NEW PRODUCT LINE
Projected Income Statement
For the Year Ended December 31, 2004

Sales	$7,500,000
Cost of goods sold	4,200,000
Gross profit	$3,300,000
Operating expenses	2,100,000
Income from operations	$1,200,000

The Sporting Goods Division currently has $20,000,000 in invested assets. Outdoor Life Inc.'s overall rate of return on investment, including all divisions, is 8%. Each division manager is evaluated on the basis of divisional rate of return on investment, and a bonus equal to $5,000 for each percentage point by which the division's rate of return on investment exceeds the company average is awarded each year.

Your father is concerned that the manager of the Sporting Goods Division rejected the addition of the new product line although all estimates indicated that the product line would be profitable and would increase overall company income. You have been asked to analyze the possible reasons that the Sporting Goods Division manager rejected the new product line.

1. Determine the rate of return on investment for the Sporting Goods Division for the past year.

(continued)

2. Determine the Sporting Goods Division manager's bonus for the past year.
3. Determine the estimated rate of return on investment for the new product line.
4. Why might the manager of the Sporting Goods Division decide to reject the new product line?
5. Can you suggest an alternative performance measure for motivating division managers to accept new investment opportunities that would increase the overall company income and rate of return on investment?

Activity 14-6
The balanced scoreboard and EVA

G R O U P

Go to the home page of **Stern Stewart & Co.** at http://www.eva.com. Stern Stewart & Co. is a consulting firm that developed the concept of economic value added (EVA®), another method of measuring corporate and divisional performance similar to residual income.

Use links in the home page of Stern Stewart & Co. to learn about EVA. Prepare a brief report describing EVA and its claimed advantages. After preparing the report, discuss your research and prepare a brief analysis of this approach to corporate and divisional performance measurement.

Answers to Self-Study Questions

1. **B** The manager of a profit center (answer B) has responsibility for and authority over costs and revenues. If the manager has responsibility only for costs, the department is called a *cost center* (answer A). If the responsibility and authority extend to the investment in assets as well as costs and revenues, it is called an *investment center* (answer C). A service department (answer D) provides services to other departments. A service department could be a cost center, profit center, or investment center.

2. **C** $600,000/150,000 = $4 per payment. Division A anticipates 60,000 payments, or $240,000 (60,000 × $4), in service department charges from the Accounts Payable Department. Income from operations is thus $900,000 − $240,000, or $660,000. Answer A assumes that all of the service department overhead is assigned to Division A, which would be incorrect since Division A does not use all of the accounts payable service. Answer B incorrectly assumes that there are no service department charges from Accounts Payable. Answer D incorrectly determines the accounts payable transfer rate from Division A's income from operations.

3. **A** The rate of return on investment for Division A is 20% (answer A), computed as follows:

$$\text{Rate of return on investment (ROI)} = \frac{\text{Income from operations}}{\text{Invested assets}}$$

$$\text{ROI} = \frac{\$350,000 - \$200,000 - \$30,000}{\$600,000}$$

$$= 20\%$$

4. **B** The profit margin for Division L of Liddy Co. is 15% (answer B), computed as follows:

$$\text{Rate of return on investment (ROI)} = \text{Profit margin} \times \text{Investment turnover}$$

$$24\% = \text{Profit margin} \times 1.6$$

$$15\% = \text{Profit margin}$$

5. **C** The market price approach (answer C) to transfer pricing uses the price at which the product or service transferred could be sold to outside buyers. The cost price approach (answer A) uses cost as the basis for setting transfer prices. The negotiated price approach (answer B) allows managers of decentralized units to agree (negotiate) among themselves as to the proper transfer price. The standard cost approach (answer D) is a version of the cost price approach that uses standard costs in setting transfer prices.

15

LEARNING OBJECTIVES

OBJECTIVE 1
Explain the nature and importance of capital investment analysis.

OBJECTIVE 2
Evaluate capital investment proposals using the following methods: average rate of return, cash payback, net present value, and internal rate of return.

OBJECTIVE 3
List and describe factors that complicate capital investment analysis.

OBJECTIVE 4
Diagram the capital rationing process.

Capital Investment Analysis

Why are you paying tuition, studying this text, and spending time and money on a higher education? Most people believe that the money and time spent now will return them more income in the future. In other words, a higher education is an investment in future earning ability. How would you know if this investment is worth it? One method would be to compare the cost of a higher education against the estimated future increased earning power. The more your future increased earnings exceed the investment, the more attractive the investment. As you will see in this chapter, the same is true for business investments in fixed assets. Business organizations analyze potential capital investments by using various methods that compare investment costs to future earnings and cash flows.

In this chapter, we describe analyses useful for making investment decisions, which can involve thousands, millions, or even billions of dollars. We emphasize the similarities and differences among the most commonly used methods of evaluating investment proposals, as well as the uses of each method. We also discuss qualitative considerations affecting investment analyses. Finally, we discuss considerations complicating investment analyses and the process of allocating available investment funds among competing proposals.

Nature of Capital Investment Analysis

OBJECTIVE   1

Explain the nature
and importance of
capital investment
analysis.

How do companies decide to make significant investments such as the following?

- **Toyota Motor Company** doubles its annual production capacity to 400,000 cars at its Georgetown, Kentucky assembly plant.

- **General Electric** invests over $1 billion in plant and equipment to build new kitchen appliance products.

- **The Walt Disney Company** invests $320 million to build a new theme park in Hong Kong.

Companies use capital investment analysis to help evaluate long-term investments. **Capital investment analysis** (or **capital budgeting**) is the process by which management plans, evaluates, and controls investments in fixed assets. Capital investments involve the long-term commitment of funds and affect operations for many years. Thus, these investments must earn a reasonable rate of return so that the business can meet its obligations to creditors and provide dividends to stockholders. Because capital investment decisions are some of the most important decisions that management makes, capital investment analysis must be carefully developed and implemented.

A capital investment program should encourage employees to submit proposals for capital investments. It should communicate to employees the long-range goals of the business so that useful proposals are submitted. All reasonable proposals should be considered and evaluated with respect to economic costs and benefits. The program can reward employees whose proposals are accepted.

BUSINESS STRATEGY

Cannibalization: Is It Desirable?

Since it began operating in the late 1970s, **Home Depot** has grown from one store to more than 1,000 stores throughout the United States and Canada. Where should Home Depot build its stores? Does it make sense to build a new store near an existing store? Home Depot thinks so. Home Depot concedes that this strategy of building a new store on the edge of the market area of an existing store could initially "cannibalize" sales in the existing store. However, management believes that such a strategy ultimately increases customer service levels and in the long term will increase overall sales and enhance market penetration. During a recent year, approximately 30% of Home Depot's existing stores were near new stores.

Source: Home Depot, Inc., Securities and Exchange Commission 10-K filing for the fiscal year ended January 28, 2001.

Methods of Evaluating Capital Investment Proposals

OBJECTIVE   2

Evaluate capital investment proposals using the following methods: average rate of return, cash payback, net present value, and internal rate of return.

Capital investment evaluation methods can be grouped into the following two categories:

1. Methods that do not use present values
2. Methods that use present values

Two methods that do not use present values are (1) the average rate of return method and (2) the cash payback method. Two methods that use present values are (1) the net present value method and (2) the internal rate of return method. These methods consider the **time value of money concept**, which recognizes that an amount of cash invested today will earn income and therefore has value over time.

Management often uses a combination of methods in evaluating capital investment proposals. Each method has advantages and disadvantages. In addition, some of the computations are complex. Computers, however, can perform the computations quickly and easily. Computers can also be used to analyze the impact of changes in key estimates in evaluating capital investment proposals.

Methods That Ignore Present Value

The average rate of return and the cash payback methods are easy to use. These methods are often initially used to screen proposals. Management normally sets minimum standards for accepting proposals, and those not meeting these standards are dropped from further consideration. If a proposal meets the minimum standards, it is often subject to further analysis.

The methods that ignore present value are often useful in evaluating capital investment proposals that have relatively short useful lives. In such cases, the timing of the cash flows is less important.

AVERAGE RATE OF RETURN METHOD   The **average rate of return**, sometimes called the **accounting rate of return**, is a measure of the average income as a percentage of the average investment in fixed assets. The average rate of return is determined by using the following equation:

$$\text{Average rate of return} = \frac{\text{Estimated average annual income}}{\text{Average investment}}$$

The numerator is the average of the annual income expected to be earned from the investment over its life after deducting depreciation. The denominator is the average book value over the investment life. Thus, if straight-line depreciation and no residual value are assumed, the average investment over the useful life is equal to one-half of the original cost.[1]

To illustrate, assume that management is considering the purchase of a machine at a cost of $500,000. The machine is expected to have a useful life of 4 years with no

---

[1]The average investment is the midpoint of the depreciable cost of the asset. Since a fixed asset is never depreciated below its residual value, this midpoint is determined by adding the original cost of the asset to the estimated residual value and dividing by 2.

residual value and to yield total income of $200,000. The estimated average annual income is therefore $50,000 ($200,000/4), and the average investment is $250,000 [($500,000 + $0 residual value)/2]. Thus, the average rate of return on the average investment is 20%, computed as follows:

$$\textbf{Average rate of return} = \frac{\textbf{Estimated average annual income}}{\textbf{Average investment}}$$

$$\text{Average rate of return} = \frac{\$200,000/4}{(\$500,000 + \$0)/2} = 20\%$$

The average rate of return of 20% should be compared with the minimum rate for such investments. If the average rate of return equals or exceeds the minimum rate, the machine should be purchased.

When several capital investment proposals are considered, the proposals can be ranked by their average rates of return. The higher the average rate of return, the more desirable the proposal. For example, assume that management is considering two capital investment proposals and has computed the following average rates of return:

	Proposal A	Proposal B
Estimated average annual income	$ 30,000	$ 36,000
Average investment	$120,000	$180,000
Average rate of return:		
$30,000/$120,000	25%	
$36,000/$180,000		20%

If only the average rate of return is considered, Proposal A, with an average rate of return of 25%, would be preferred over Proposal B.

In addition to being easy to compute, the average rate of return method has several advantages. One advantage is that it includes the amount of income earned over the entire life of the proposal. In addition, it emphasizes accounting income, which is often used by investors and creditors in evaluating management performance. Its main disadvantage is that it does not directly consider the expected cash flows from the proposal and the timing of these cash flows.

CASH PAYBACK METHOD   Cash flows are important because cash can be reinvested. Very simply, the capital investment uses cash and must therefore return cash in the future to be successful.

The expected period of time that passes between the date of an investment and the complete recovery in cash (or equivalent) of the amount invested is the **cash payback period**. To simplify the analysis, the revenues and expenses other than depreciation related to operating fixed assets are assumed to be all in the form of cash. The excess of the cash flowing in from revenue over the cash flowing out for expenses is termed **net cash flow**. The time required for the net cash flow to equal the initial outlay for the fixed asset is the payback period.

To illustrate, assume that the proposed investment in a fixed asset with an 8-year life is $200,000. The annual cash revenue from the investment is $50,000, and the annual cash expense is $10,000. Thus, the annual net cash flow is expected to be $40,000 ($50,000 − $10,000). The estimated cash payback period for the investment is 5 years, computed as follows:

$$\frac{\$200,000}{\$40,000} = \text{5-year cash payback period}$$

In this illustration, the annual net cash flows are equal ($40,000 per year). If these annual net cash flows are *not* equal, the cash payback period is determined by adding the annual net cash flows until the cumulative sum equals the amount of the proposed investment. To illustrate, assume that for a proposed investment of $400,000, the annual net cash flows and the cumulative net cash flows over the proposal's 6-year life are as follows:

Year	Net Cash Flow	Cumulative Net Cash Flow
1	$ 60,000	$ 60,000
2	80,000	140,000
3	105,000	245,000
4	155,000	400,000
5	100,000	500,000
6	90,000	590,000

The cumulative net cash flow at the end of the fourth year equals the amount of the investment, $400,000. Thus, the payback period is 4 years. If the amount of the proposed investment had been $450,000, the cash payback period would occur during the fifth year. If the net cash flows are uniform during the period, the cash payback period would be 4$\frac{1}{2}$ years.

The cash payback method is widely used in evaluating proposals for investments in new projects. A short payback period is desirable because the sooner the cash is recovered, the sooner it becomes available for reinvestment in other projects. In addition, there is less possibility of losses from economic conditions, out-of-date assets, and other unavoidable risks when the payback period is short. The cash payback period is also important to bankers and other creditors who depend on net cash flow for repaying debt related to the capital investment. The sooner the cash is recovered, the sooner the debt or other liabilities can be paid. Thus, the cash payback method is especially useful to managers whose primary concern is liquidity.

One of the disadvantages of the cash payback method is that it ignores cash flows occurring after the payback period. In addition, the cash payback method does not use present value concepts in valuing cash flows occurring in different periods. In the next section, we review present value concepts and introduce capital investment methods that use present value.

Present Value Methods

An investment in fixed assets can be viewed as acquiring a series of net cash flows over a period of time. The period of time over which these net cash flows will be received can be an important factor in determining the value of an investment. Present value methods use both the amount and the timing of net cash flows in evaluating an investment. Before illustrating how these methods are used in capital investment analysis, we review basic present value concepts.

PRESENT VALUE CONCEPTS   **Present value concepts** can be divided into the *present value of an amount* and the *present value of an annuity*. We describe and illustrate these two concepts next.

Present Value of an Amount.   If you were given the choice, would you prefer to receive $1 now or $1 three years from now? You should prefer to receive $1 now because you could invest the $1 and earn interest for three years. As a result, the amount you would have after three years would be more than $1.

To illustrate, assume that on January 1, 2004, you invest $1 in an account that earns 12% interest compounded annually. After one year, the $1 has grown to $1.12 ($1 × 1.12) because interest of 12¢ is added to the investment. The $1.12 earns 12% interest for the second year. Interest earning interest is called **compounding**. By the end of the second year, the investment has grown to $1.254 ($1.12 × 1.12). By the end of the third year, the investment has grown to $1.404 ($1.254 × 1.12). Thus, if money is worth 12%, you would be equally satisfied with $1 on January 1, 2004, or $1.404 three years later.

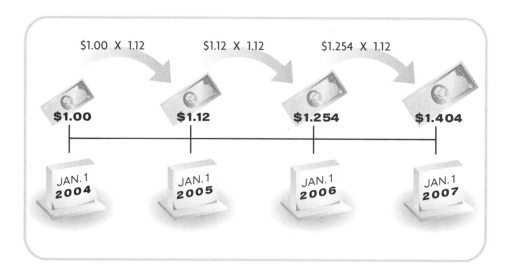

On January 1, 2004, what is the present value of $1.404 to be received on January 1, 2007? The answer can be determined with the aid of a present value of $1 table. For example, the partial table in Exhibit 1 indicates that the present value of $1 to be received three years hence, with earnings compounded at the rate of 12% a year, is 0.712. Multiplying 0.712 by $1.404 yields $1, which is the present value that started the compounding process.

Present Value of an Annuity.   An **annuity** is a series of equal net cash flows at fixed time intervals. Annuities are very common in business. For example, monthly

EXHIBIT 1

Partial Present Value of $1 Table

	Present Value of $1 at Compound Interest				
Year	6%	10%	12%	15%	20%
1	0.943	0.909	0.893	0.870	0.833
2	0.890	0.826	0.797	0.756	0.694
3	0.840	0.751	0.712	0.658	0.579
4	0.792	0.683	0.636	0.572	0.482
5	0.747	0.621	0.567	0.497	0.402
6	0.705	0.564	0.507	0.432	0.335
7	0.665	0.513	0.452	0.376	0.279
8	0.627	0.467	0.404	0.327	0.233
9	0.592	0.424	0.361	0.284	0.194
10	0.558	0.386	0.322	0.247	0.162

rental, salary, and bond interest cash flows are all examples of annuities. The **present value of an annuity** is the sum of the present values of each cash flow. In other words, the present value of an annuity is the amount of cash that is needed today to yield a series of equal net cash flows at fixed time intervals in the future.

To illustrate, the present value of a $100 annuity for five periods at 12% could be determined by using the present value factors in Exhibit 1. Each $100 net cash flow could be multiplied by the present value of $1 at 12% factor for the appropriate period and summed to determine a present value of $360.50, as shown in the following timeline:

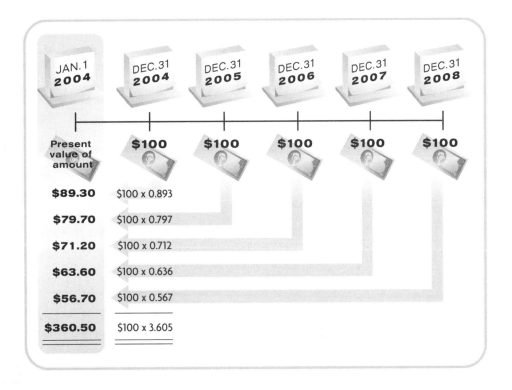

Using a present value of an annuity table is a simpler approach. Exhibit 2 is a partial table of present value of annuity factors. These factors are merely the sum of the present value of $1 factors in Exhibit 1 for the number of annuity periods. Thus, 3.605 in the annuity table (Exhibit 2) is the sum of the five individual present value of $1 factors at 12%. Multiplying $100 by 3.605 yields the same amount ($360.50) that was determined in the preceding illustration by five successive multiplications.

EXHIBIT 2

Partial Present Value of an Annuity Table

Present Value of an Annuity of $1 at Compound Interest					
Year	6%	10%	12%	15%	20%
1	0.943	0.909	0.893	0.870	0.833
2	1.833	1.736	1.690	1.626	1.528
3	2.673	2.487	2.402	2.283	2.106
4	3.465	3.170	3.037	2.855	2.589
5	4.212	3.791	3.605	3.353	2.991
6	4.917	4.355	4.111	3.785	3.326
7	5.582	4.868	4.564	4.160	3.605
8	6.210	5.335	4.968	4.487	3.837
9	6.802	5.759	5.328	4.772	4.031
10	7.360	6.145	5.650	5.019	4.192

NET PRESENT VALUE METHOD   The **net present value method** analyzes capital investment proposals by comparing the initial cash investment with the present value of the net cash flows. It is sometimes called the **discounted cash flow method**. The interest rate (return) used in net present value analysis is set by management. This rate is often based on factors such as the nature of the business, the purpose of the investment, the cost of securing funds for the investment, and the minimum desired rate of return. If the net present value of the cash flows expected from a proposed investment equals or exceeds the amount of the initial investment, the proposal is desirable.

To illustrate, assume a proposal to acquire $200,000 of equipment with an expected useful life of 5 years (no residual value) and a minimum desired rate of return of 10%. As shown at the top of the next page, the present value of the net cash flow for each year is computed by multiplying the net cash flow for the year by the present value factor of $1 for that year. For example, the $70,000 net cash flow to be received on December 31, 2004, is multiplied by the present value of $1 for one year at 10% (0.909). Thus, the present value of the $70,000 is $63,630. Likewise, the $60,000 net cash flow on December 31, 2005, is multiplied by the present value of $1 for two years at 10% (0.826) to yield $49,560, and so on. The amount to be invested, $200,000, is then subtracted from the total present value of the net cash flows, $202,900, to determine the net present value, $2,900, as shown in the following illustration. The net present value indicates that the proposal is expected to recover the investment and provide more than the minimum rate of return of 10%.

When capital investment funds are limited and the alternative proposals involve different amounts of investment, it is useful to prepare a ranking of the proposals by using a present value index. The **present value index** is calculated by dividing the

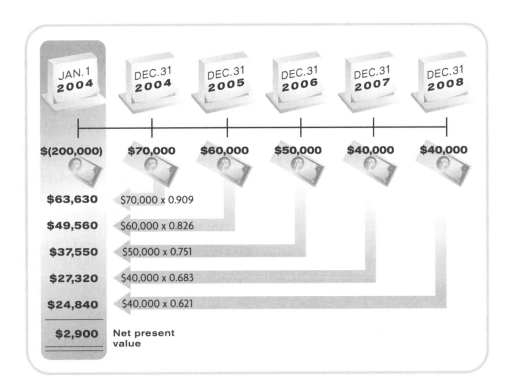

total present value of the net cash flow by the amount to be invested. The present value index for the investment in the previous illustration is calculated as follows:

$$\text{Present value index} = \frac{\textbf{Total present value of net cash flow}}{\textbf{Amount to be invested}}$$

$$= \frac{\$202,900}{\$200,000} = 1.0145$$

If a business is considering three alternative proposals and has determined their net present values, the present value index for each proposal is as follows:

	Proposal A	Proposal B	Proposal C
Total present value of net cash flow	$107,000	$86,400	$93,600
Amount to be invested	100,000	80,000	90,000
Net present value	$ 7,000	$ 6,400	$ 3,600
Present value index	1.07 ($107,000/$100,000)	1.08 ($86,400/$80,000)	1.04 ($93,600/$90,000)

Although Proposal A has the highest net present value, the present value indices show that it is not as desirable as Proposal B. In other words, Proposal B returns $1.08 present value per dollar invested, whereas Proposal A returns only $1.07. Proposal B requires an investment of $80,000 compared to an investment of $100,000 for Proposal A. Management should consider the possible use of the $20,000 difference in Proposal A and Proposal B investments before making a final decision.

An advantage of the net present value method is that it considers the time value of money. A disadvantage is that the computations are more complex than those for the methods that ignore present value. In addition, the net present value method assumes that the cash received from the proposal during its useful life can be reinvested at the rate of return used in computing the present value of the proposal. Because of changing economic conditions, this assumption is not always reasonable.

INTERNAL RATE OF RETURN METHOD   The **internal rate of return method** uses present value concepts to compute the rate of return from the net cash flows expected from capital investment proposals. This method is sometimes called the **time-adjusted rate of return method**. It is similar to the net present value method in that it focuses on the present value of the net cash flows. However, the internal rate of return method starts with the net cash flows and, in a sense, works backward to determine the rate of return expected from the proposal.

To illustrate, assume that management is evaluating a proposal to acquire equipment costing $33,530. The equipment is expected to provide annual net cash flows of $10,000 per year for 5 years. If we assume a rate of return of 12%, we can calculate the present value of the net cash flows using the present value of an annuity table in Exhibit 2. These calculations are shown in Exhibit 3.

EXHIBIT 3
Net Present Value Analysis at 12%

Annual net cash flow (at the end of each of 5 years)	$10,000
Present value of an annuity of $1 at 12% for 5 years (Exhibit 2)	× 3.605
Present value of annual net cash flows	$36,050
Less amount to be invested	33,530
Net present value	$ 2,520

In Exhibit 3, the $36,050 present value of the cash inflows based on a 12% rate of return is more than the $33,530 to be invested. Therefore, the internal rate of return must be more than 12%. Through trial-and-error procedures, the rate of return that equates the $33,530 cost of the investment with the present value of the net cash flows is determined to be 15%, as the following graphic shows.

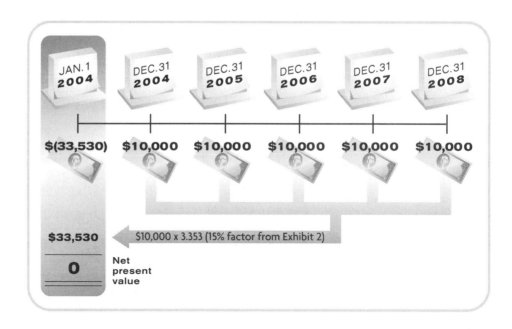

Such trial-and-error procedures are time consuming. However, when equal annual net cash flows are expected from a proposal, as in the illustration, the calculations are simplified by using the following procedures:[2]

1. Determine a present value factor for an annuity of $1 by dividing the amount to be invested by the equal annual net cash flows, as follows:

$$\textbf{Present value factor for an annuity of \$1} = \frac{\textbf{Amount to be invested}}{\textbf{Equal annual net cash flows}}$$

2. In the present value of an annuity of $1 table, locate the present value factor determined in (1). First locate the number of years of expected useful life of the investment in the Year column, and then proceed horizontally across the table until you find the present value factor computed in (1).
3. Identify the internal rate of return by the heading of the column in which the present value factor in (2) is located.

To illustrate, assume that management is considering a proposal to acquire equipment costing $97,360. The equipment is expected to provide equal annual net cash flows of $20,000 for seven years. The present value factor for an annuity of $1 is **4.868**, calculated as follows:

$$\textbf{Present value factor for an annuity of \$1} = \frac{\textbf{Amount to be invested}}{\textbf{Equal annual net cash flows}}$$

$$= \frac{\$97,360}{\$20,000} = \textbf{4.868}$$

For a period of seven years, the partial present value of an annuity of $1 table indicates that the factor **4.868** is related to a percentage of **10%**, as shown below. Thus, 10% is the internal rate of return for this proposal.

Year	Present Value of an Annuity of $1 at Compound Interest		
	6%	10% ←	12%
1	0.943	0.909	0.893
2	1.833	1.736	1.690
3	2.673	2.487	2.402
4	3.465	3.170	3.037
5	4.212	3.791	3.605
6	4.917	4.355	4.111
7	5.582	4.868	4.564
8	6.210	5.335	4.968
9	6.802	5.759	5.328
10	7.360	6.145	5.650

If the minimum acceptable rate of return for similar proposals is 10% or less, the proposed investment should be considered acceptable. When several proposals are considered, management often ranks the proposals by their internal rates of return.

---

[2]Equal annual net cash flows are assumed to simplify the illustration. If the annual net cash flows are not equal, the calculations are more complex, but the basic concepts are the same.

The proposal with the highest rate is considered the most desirable. The minimum acceptable rate of return (often termed the *hurdle rate*) for **Owens Corning** is 18%; for **General Electric**, it is 20%.

The primary advantage of the internal rate of return method is that it considers the present values of the net cash flows over the entire useful life of the proposal. In addition, by determining a rate of return for each proposal, all proposals are compared on a common basis. The primary disadvantage of the internal rate of return method is that the computations are more complex than for some of the other methods. However, spreadsheet software programs have internal rate of return functions that simplify the calculation. Also, like the net present value method, the internal rate of return method assumes that the cash received from a proposal during its useful life will be reinvested at the internal rate of return. Because of changing economic conditions, this assumption is not always reasonable.

Factors That Complicate Capital Investment Analysis

OBJECTIVE   3

List and describe factors that complicate capital investment analysis.

In the preceding discussion, we described four widely used methods of evaluating capital investment proposals. In practice, additional factors can have an impact on the outcome of a capital investment decision. In the following paragraphs, we discuss some of the most important of these factors: the federal income tax, unequal lives of alternative proposals, leasing, uncertainty, changes in price levels, and qualitative factors.

Federal Income Tax

In many cases, the impact of the federal income tax on capital investment decisions can be material. For example, in determining depreciation for federal income tax purposes, useful lives that are much shorter than the actual useful lives are often used. Also, depreciation can be calculated by methods that approximate the 200% declining-balance method. Thus, depreciation for tax purposes often exceeds the depreciation for financial statement purposes in the early years of an asset's use. The tax reduction in these early years is offset by higher taxes in the later years so that accelerated depreciation does not result in a long-run saving in taxes. However, the timing of the cash outflows for income taxes can have a significant impact on capital investment analysis.[3]

Unequal Proposal Lives

In the preceding discussion, the illustrations of the methods of analyzing capital investment proposals were based on the assumption that alternative proposals had the same useful lives. In practice, however, alternative proposals can have unequal lives. To illustrate, assume that alternative investments, a truck and computers, are being compared. The truck has a useful life of 8 years, and the computer network has a use-

---

[3]The impact of income taxes on capital investment analysis is described and illustrated in advanced textbooks.

ful life of 5 years. Each proposal requires an initial investment of $100,000, and the company desires a rate of return of 10%. The expected cash flows and net present value of each alternative are shown in Exhibit 4. Because of the unequal useful lives of the two proposals, however, the net present values in Exhibit 4 are not comparable.

Adjusting the proposals to end at the same time makes them comparable for the analysis. This can be done by assuming that the truck is to be sold at the end of 5 years. The residual value of the truck must be estimated at the end of 5 years, and this value must then be included as a cash flow at that date. Both proposals will then cover 5 years, and net present value analysis can be used to compare the two proposals over the same 5-year period. If the truck's estimated residual value is $40,000 at the end of year 5, the net present value for the truck exceeds the net present value for the computers by $1,835 ($18,640 − $16,805), as shown in Exhibit 5. Therefore, the truck can be viewed as the more attractive of the two proposals.

EXHIBIT 4 *Net Present Value Analysis*

Truck				Computers			
Year	Present Value of $1 at 10%	Net Cash Flow	Present Value of Net Cash Flow	Year	Present Value of $1 at 10%	Net Cash Flow	Present Value of Net Cash Flow
1	0.909	$ 30,000	$ 27,270	1	0.909	$ 30,000	$ 27,270
2	0.826	30,000	24,780	2	0.826	30,000	24,780
3	0.751	25,000	18,775	3	0.751	30,000	22,530
4	0.683	20,000	13,660	4	0.683	30,000	20,490
5	0.621	15,000	9,315	5	0.621	35,000	21,735
6	0.564	15,000	8,460	Total		$155,000	$116,805
7	0.513	10,000	5,130	Amount to be invested			100,000
8	0.467	10,000	4,670	Net present value			$ 16,805
Total		$155,000	$112,060				
Amount to be invested			100,000				
Net present value			$ 12,060				

EXHIBIT 5
Net Present Value Analysis

Truck—Revised to 5-Year Life			
Year	Present Value of $1 at 10%	Net Cash Flow	Present Value of Net Cash Flow
1	0.909	$ 30,000	$ 27,270
2	0.826	30,000	24,780
3	0.751	25,000	18,775
4	0.683	20,000	13,660
5	0.621	15,000	9,315
5 (Residual value)	0.621	40,000	24,840
Total		$160,000	$118,640
Amount to be invested			100,000
Net present value			$ 18,640

Truck NPV > Computers NPV

Lease versus Capital Investment

Leasing fixed assets has become common in many industries. For example, hospitals often lease diagnostic and other medical equipment. Leasing allows a business to use fixed assets without spending large amounts of cash to purchase them. In addition, management could believe that a fixed asset has a high risk of becoming obsolete. This risk can be reduced by leasing rather than purchasing the asset. Also, the *Internal Revenue Code* allows the lessor (the owner of the asset) to pass tax deductions on to the lessee (the party leasing the asset). These provisions of the tax law have made leasing assets more attractive. For example, a company that pays $50,000 per year for leasing a $200,000 fixed asset with a life of 8 years is permitted to deduct from taxable income the annual lease payments.

In many cases, before a final decision is made, management should consider leasing assets instead of purchasing them. Normally, leasing assets is more costly than purchasing because the lessor must include in the rental price not only the costs associated with owning the assets but also a profit. Nevertheless, using the methods of evaluating capital investment proposals, management should consider whether it is more profitable to lease rather than purchase an asset.

Uncertainty

All capital investment analyses rely on factors that are uncertain. For example, the estimates related to revenues, expenses, and cash flows are uncertain. The long-term nature of capital investments suggests that some estimates are likely to involve uncertainty. Errors in one or more of the estimates could lead to incorrect decisions.

Merck, a major pharmaceutical company, uses uncertainty in analyzing drugs under research and development. Management understands that a single hit would pay for the investment costs of many failures. As a result, Merck uses a technique in probability theory, called *Monte Carlo analysis*, which shows that the drugs under development will actually be very profitable.

Changes in Price Levels

In performing investment analysis, management must be concerned about changes in price levels. Price levels can change due to **inflation**, which occurs when general price levels are rising. Thus, while general prices are rising, the returns on an investment must exceed the rising price level, or the cash returned on the investment becomes less valuable over time.

Price levels also can change for foreign investments as the result of currency exchange rates. **Currency exchange rates** are the rates at which currency in another country can be exchanged for U.S. dollars. If the amount of local dollars that can be exchanged for one U.S. dollar increases, the local currency is said to be "weakening to the dollar." Thus, if a company made an investment in another country whose local currency was weakening, it would adversely impact the return on that investment as expressed in U.S. dollars. This happens because the expected amount of local currency returned on the investment would purchase fewer U.S. dollars.

Management should attempt to anticipate future price levels and consider their effects on the estimates used in capital investment analyses. Changes in anticipated price levels could significantly affect the analyses.

Qualitative Considerations

Some benefits of capital investments are qualitative in nature and cannot be easily estimated in dollar terms. If management does not consider these qualitative considerations, the quantitative analyses can suggest rejecting a worthy investment.

Qualitative considerations in capital investment analysis are most appropriate for strategic investments. Strategic investments are those that are designed to affect a company's long-term ability to generate profits. Strategic investments often have many uncertainties and intangible benefits. Unlike capital investments that are designed to cut costs, strategic investments have very few "hard" savings. Instead, they can affect future revenues, which are difficult to estimate. An example of a strategic investment is **Nucor's** decision to be the first to invest in a new continuous casting technology that had the potential to make thin gauge sheet steel and thus open new product markets. Nucor's new investment was justified more on the strategic importance of the investment than on the economic analysis. As it turned out, the investment was very successful.

Qualitative considerations that can influence capital investment analysis include product quality, manufacturing flexibility, employee morale, manufacturing productivity, and market opportunity. Many of these qualitative factors could be as important, if not more important, than the results of quantitative analysis.

ETHICS IN ACTION

One of the largest alleged accounting frauds in history involved the improper accounting for capital expenditures. **Worldcom, Inc.**, the second largest telecommunications company in the United States, improperly treated maintenance expenditures on its telecommunications network as capital expenditures. As a result, the company had to restate its prior years' earnings downward by nearly $4 billion to correct this error. The company declared bankruptcy within months of disclosing the error.

Capital Rationing

OBJECTIVE 4

Diagram the capital rationing process.

Funding for capital projects can be obtained from issuing bonds or stock or from operating cash. **Capital rationing** is the process by which management allocates these funds among competing capital investment proposals. In this process, management often uses a combination of the methods described in this chapter. Exhibit 6 on the following page portrays the capital rationing decision process.

In capital rationing, alternative proposals are initially screened by establishing minimum standards for the cash payback and the average rate of return. The proposals that survive this screening are further analyzed using the net present value and internal rate of return methods. Throughout the capital rationing process, qualitative factors related to each proposal should also be considered. For example, the acquisition of new, more efficient equipment that eliminates several jobs could lower employee morale to a level that could decrease overall plant productivity. Alternatively, new equipment could improve the quality of the product and thus increase consumer satisfaction and sales.

EXHIBIT 6
*Capital Rationing
Decision Process*

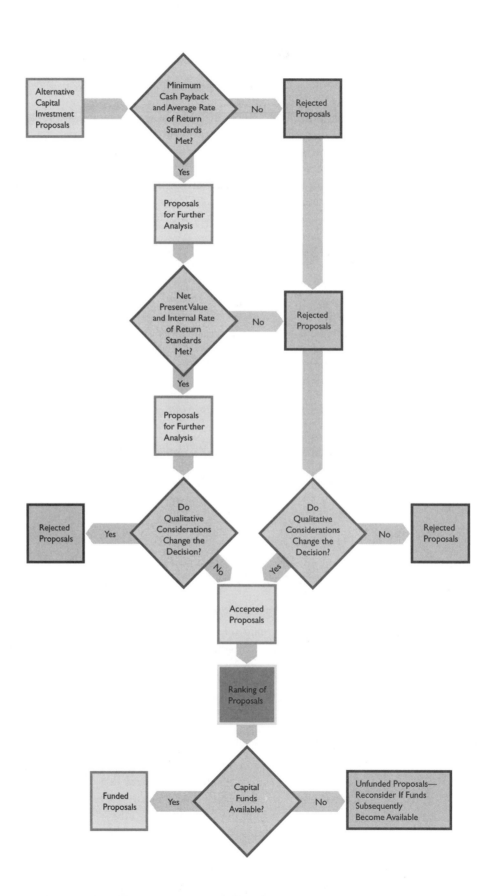

The final steps in the capital rationing process are ranking the proposals according to management's criteria, comparing the proposals with the funds available, and selecting the proposals to be funded. Funded proposals are included in the **capital expenditures budget** to aid the planning and financing of operations. Unfunded proposals can be reconsidered if funds later become available.

Key Points

1. **Explain the nature and importance of capital investment analysis.**

   Capital investment analysis is the process by which management plans, evaluates, and controls investments involving fixed assets. Capital investment analysis is important to a business because such investments affect profitability for a long period of time.

2. **Evaluate capital investment proposals using the following methods: average rate of return, cash payback, net present value, and internal rate of return.**

   The average rate of return method measures the expected profitability of an investment in fixed assets. It is calculated using the following formula:

   $$\text{Average rate of return} = \frac{\text{Estimated average annual income}}{\text{Average investment}}$$

   The expected period of time that will pass between the date of an investment and the complete recovery in cash (or equivalent) of the amount invested is the cash payback period. Investment proposals with the shortest cash payback are considered the most desirable.

   The net present value method uses present values to compute the net present value of the cash flows expected from a proposal. The net present value of the cash flows is then compared across proposals. The present value of a cash flow is computed by looking up the present value of $1 from a table of present values and multiplying it by the amount of the future cash flow, as shown in the text.

   The internal rate of return method uses present values to compute the rate of return from the net cash flows expected from capital investment proposals. When equal annual net cash flows are expected from a proposal, the computations are simplified by using a table of the present value of an annuity, also as shown in the text.

3. **List and describe factors that complicate capital investment analysis.**

   Factors that can complicate capital investment analysis include the impact of the federal income tax, unequal lives of alternative proposals, leasing, uncertainty, changes in price levels, and qualitative considerations. A brief description of the effect of each of these factors appears in the text.

4. **Diagram the capital rationing process.**

   Capital rationing refers to the process by which management allocates available investment funds among competing capital investment proposals. A diagram of the capital rationing process appears in Exhibit 6.

Glossary

Annuity: A series of equal cash flows at fixed intervals.

Average rate of return: A method of evaluating capital investment proposals that focuses on the expected profitability of the investment.

Capital investment analysis: The process by which management plans, evaluates, and controls long-term capital investments involving fixed assets.

Capital rationing: The process by which management allocates available investment funds among competing capital investment proposals.

Cash payback period: The expected period of time that will elapse between the date of a capital expenditure and the complete recovery in cash (or equivalent) of the amount invested.

Currency exchange rate: The rate at which currency in another country can be exchanged for local currency.

Inflation: A period when prices in general are rising and the purchasing power of money is declining.

Internal rate of return method: A method of analyzing proposed capital investments that focuses on using present value concepts to compute

the rate of return from the net cash flows expected from the investment.

Net present value method: A method of analyzing proposed capital investments that focuses on the present value of the cash flows expected from the investments.

Present value concept: Cash today is not the equivalent of the same amount of money to be received in the future.

Present value index: An index computed by dividing the total present value of the net cash flow to be received from a proposed capital investment by the amount to be invested.

Present value of an annuity: The sum of the present values of a series of equal cash flows to be received at fixed intervals.

Time value of money concept: The concept that an amount of money invested today will earn interest.

Self-Study Questions

(Answers appear at end of chapter.)

1. Methods of evaluating capital investment proposals that ignore present value include:
   A. average rate of return.
   B. cash payback.
   C. both A and B.
   D. neither A nor B.

2. Management is considering a $100,000 investment in a project with a 5-year life and no residual value. If the total income from the project is expected to be $60,000 and recognition is given to the effect of straight-line depreciation on the investment, the average rate of return is:
   A. 12%.   C. 60%.
   B. 24%.   D. 75%.

3. The expected period of time that will elapse between the date of a capital investment and the complete recovery of the amount of cash invested is called:

   A. the average rate of return period.
   B. the cash payback period.
   C. the net present value period.
   D. the internal rate of return period.

4. A project that will cost $120,000 is estimated to generate cash flows of $25,000 per year for 8 years. What is the net present value of the project, assuming an 11% required rate of return? (Use the present value tables in the chapter.)
   A. $(38,214)   C. $55,180
   B. $8,653   D. $75,000

5. A project is estimated to generate cash flows of $40,000 per year for 10 years. The cost of the project is $226,009. What is the internal rate of return for this project?
   A. 8%   C. 12%
   B. 10%   D. 14%

Discussion Questions

1. Which two methods of capital investment analysis ignore present value?

2. Which two methods of capital investment analysis can be described as present value methods?

3. How is the average rate of return computed for capital investment analysis, assuming that the effect of

straight-line depreciation on the amount of the investment is considered?

4. What are the principal objections to the use of the average rate of return method in evaluating capital investment proposals?

5. Discuss the principal limitations of the cash payback method for evaluating capital investment proposals.

6. Which method of evaluating capital investment proposals reduces their expected future net cash flows to present values and compares the total present values to the amount of the investment?

7. A net present value analysis used to evaluate a proposed equipment acquisition indicated a $9,750 net present value. What is the meaning of the $9,750 as it relates to the desirability of the proposal?

8. How is the present value index for a proposal determined?

9. What are the major disadvantages of the use of the net present value method of analyzing capital investment proposals?

10. What are the major disadvantages of the use of the internal rate of return method of analyzing capital investment proposals?

11. What provision of the *Internal Revenue Code* is especially important to consider in analyzing capital investment proposals?

12. What method can be used to place two capital investment proposals with unequal useful lives on a comparable basis?

13. What are the major advantages of leasing a fixed asset rather than purchasing it?

14. Give an example of a qualitative factor that should be considered in a capital investment analysis related to acquiring automated factory equipment.

15. **Monsanto**, a large chemical and fibers company, invested $37 million in state-of-the-art systems to improve process control, laboratory automation, and local area network (LAN) communications. The investment was not justified merely on cost savings but was also on the basis of qualitative considerations. Monsanto management viewed the investment as a critical element toward achieving its vision of the future. What qualitative and quantitative considerations do you believe Monsanto would have considered in its strategic evaluation of these investments?

Exercises

EXERCISE 15–1
Average rate of return
OBJECTIVE 2

✓ Turning machine, 12.5%

The following data are accumulated by Mora Machining Company in evaluating two competing capital investment proposals:

	Turning Machine	Milling Machine
Amount of investment	$36,000	$48,000
Useful life	4 years	5 years
Estimated residual value	0	0
Estimated total income over the useful life	$ 9,000	$12,000

Determine the expected average rate of return for each proposal.

EXERCISE 15–2
Average rate of return—cost savings
OBJECTIVE 2

Millwood Company is considering an investment in equipment that will replace direct labor. The equipment has a cost of $61,000 with a $6,000 residual value and an 11-year life. The equipment will replace one employee who has an average wage of $18,000 per year. In addition, the equipment will have operating and energy costs of $9,315 per year.

Determine the average rate of return on the equipment, considering straight-line depreciation on the investment.

EXERCISE 15–3
Average rate of return—new product
OBJECTIVE 2

Portable Communications Inc. is considering an investment in new equipment that will be used to manufacture a pager. The pager is expected to generate additional annual sales of 18,000 units at $75 per unit. The equipment has a cost of $870,000, residual value of $30,000, and a 10-year life. The equipment can be used to manufacture only the pager. The cost to manufacture it follows.

✓ Average annual income, $360,000

Cost per unit:

Direct labor	$15.00
Direct materials	22.00
Factory overhead (including depreciation)	18.00
Total cost per unit	$55.00

Determine the average rate of return on the equipment.

EXERCISE 15-4
Calculate cash flows
OBJECTIVE 2

✓ Year 1: $(141,600)

Cornucopia Inc. is planning to invest $206,000 in a new garden tool expected to generate additional sales of 8,000 units at $24 each. The $206,000 investment includes $46,000 for initial launch-related expenses and $160,000 for equipment that has a 15-year life and a $10,000 residual value. Selling expenses related to the new product are expected to be 5% of sales revenue. The cost to manufacture the product includes the following per unit costs:

Direct labor	$ 5.00
Direct materials	8.25
Fixed factory overhead-depreciation	1.25
Variable factory overhead	1.50
Total	$16.00

Determine the net cash flows for the first year of the project, years 2–14, and for the last year of the project.

EXERCISE 15-5
Cash payback period
OBJECTIVE 2

✓ Proposal 1: 5 years

United Security Bank Corporation is evaluating two capital investment proposals for a drive-up ATM. Each requires an investment of $200,000 and each has an 8-year life and expected total net cash flows of $320,000. Location 1 is expected to provide equal annual net cash flows of $40,000, and Location 2 is expected to have the following unequal annual net cash flows:

Year 1	$70,000	Year 5	$30,000
Year 2	50,000	Year 6	30,000
Year 3	40,000	Year 7	30,000
Year 4	40,000	Year 8	30,000

Determine the cash payback period for both proposals.

EXERCISE 15-6
Cash payback method
OBJECTIVE 2

✓ a. Cosmetics: 4 years

Johnson Consumer Products Company is considering an investment in one of two new product lines. The investment required for either product line is $360,000. The net cash flows associated with each product are as follows:

	Liquid Soap	Cosmetics
Year 1	$ 50,000	$ 90,000
2	60,000	90,000
3	70,000	90,000
4	80,000	90,000
5	100,000	90,000
6	120,000	90,000
7	120,000	90,000
8	120,000	90,000
Total	$720,000	$720,000

a. Recommend a product offering to Johnson Consumer Products Company based on the cash payback period for each product line.
b. Why is one product line preferred over the other even though both have the same total net cash flows through eight periods?

EXERCISE 15-7
Net present value method
OBJECTIVE 2

✓ a. NPV $12,560

The following data are accumulated by Markon Container Company in evaluating the purchase of $300,000 of equipment with a 4-year useful life:

	Net Income	Net Cash Flow
Year 1	$65,000	$140,000
Year 2	25,000	100,000
Year 3	5,000	80,000
Year 4	5,000	80,000

a. Assuming that the desired rate of return is 12%, determine the net present value for the proposal. Use the table of the present value of $1 in this chapter.
b. Would management be likely to look with favor on the proposal? Explain.

EXERCISE 15-8
Net present value method
OBJECTIVE 2

✓ a. $62,956

Corcoran Group, Inc., a New York real estate broker, determined that its new Web site generated $120,000,000 of real estate sales for the year. Corcoran estimated that the Web site should be credited with revenue equal to 0.6% of sales, which is the rate Corcoran ordinarily pays individuals who pass along sales leads. In addition, the annual cash expenses for supporting the Web site were approximately $670,000 for the year. Assume that the initial cost to set up the Web site was $100,000 and that annual net cash flow is expected to increase by 10% per year for three more years.

a. Determine the net present value of the Web site investment if the desired rate of return is 15%. Use the table of the present value of $1 in Exhibit 1 of this chapter. Round to the nearest dollar.
b. Under the assumptions provided here, is the Web site expected to be an acceptable investment?

EXERCISE 15-9
Net present value method–annuity
OBJECTIVE 2

✓ a. $41,500

Laidlow Excavation Company is planning an investment of $160,000 for a bulldozer. The bulldozer is expected to operate for 1,500 hours per year for 5 years. Customers will be charged $90 per hour for bulldozer work. The bulldozer operator is paid an hourly wage of $32 per hour. The bulldozer is expected to require annual maintenance costing $8,000. The bulldozer uses fuel that is expected to cost $25 per hour of bulldozer operation.

a. Determine the equal annual net cash flows from operating the bulldozer.
b. Determine the net present value of the investment, assuming that the desired rate of return is 10%. Use the table of present values of an annuity of $1 in the chapter. Round to the nearest dollar.
c. Should Laidlow invest in the bulldozer based on this analysis?

EXERCISE 15-10
Net present value– unequal lives
OBJECTIVES 2, 3

✓ Net present value, Apartment Complex, $8,840

Crider Development Company has two competing projects, an apartment complex and an office building. Both projects have an initial investment of $460,000. The net cash flows estimated for the two projects are as follows:

	Net Cash Flow	
Year	Apartment Complex	Office Building
1	$160,000	$180,000
2	150,000	180,000
3	120,000	150,000
4	100,000	150,000
5	100,000	
6	90,000	
7	80,000	
8	60,000	

The estimated residual value of the Apartment Complex at the end of year 4 is $140,000.

Determine which project should be favored by comparing the net present values of the two and assuming a minimum rate of return of 15%. Use the table of present values in the chapter.

The **Royal Caribbean Cruise Line (RCCL)** recently placed into service the largest cruise ship in the world. The *Eagle Class* ship, which can hold up to 3,100 passengers, cost $600 million to build. Assume the following additional information:

- The average occupancy rate for the new ship is estimated to be 70% of capacity.
- There will be 300 cruise days per year.
- The variable expenses per passenger are estimated to be $50 per day.
- The revenue per passenger is expected to be $245 per day.
- The fixed expenses for running the ship other than depreciation are estimated to be $21,000,000 per year.
- The ship has a service life of 10 years, with a salvage value of $50,000,000 at the end of 10 years.

a. Determine the annual net cash flow from operating the cruise ship.
b. Determine the net present value of this investment, assuming a 12% minimum rate of return. Use the present value tables in the chapter in determining your answer.
c. Assume that RCCL decided to increase its price so that the revenue increased to $260 per passenger per day. Would this allow RCCL to earn a 15% rate of return on the cruise ship investment? Use the present value tables in the chapter in determining your answer.

Panorama Glass Company has computed the net present value for capital expenditure proposals A and B by using the net present value method. Relevant data related to the computation are as follows:

	Proposal A	Proposal B
Total present value of net cash flow	$267,240	$321,750
Amount to be invested	262,000	325,000
Net present value	$ 5,240	$ (3,250)

Determine the present value index for each proposal.

AllStar Sporting Goods Company is considering an investment in one of two machines. The sewing machine will increase productivity from sewing 120 baseballs per hour to sewing 160 per hour. The contribution margin is $0.70 per baseball. Assume that any increased production of baseballs can be sold. The second machine is an automatic packaging machine for the golf ball line. The packaging machine will reduce packing labor cost equivalent to $21 per hour. The sewing machine will cost $230,525, have an 8-year life, and will operate for 2,000 hours per year. The packing machine will cost $136,027, have an 8-year life, and will operate for 1,600 hours per year. AllStar seeks a minimum rate of return of 15% on its investments.

a. Determine the net present value for the two machines. Use the table of present values of an annuity of $1 in the chapter. Round to the nearest dollar.
b. Determine the present value index for the two machines. Round to 2 decimal places.
c. If AllStar has sufficient funds for only one of the machines and qualitative factors for the two machines are equal, in which machine should it invest?

EXERCISE 15-14
Average rate of return, cash payback period, net present value method
OBJECTIVE 2

✓ b. 4 years

Hi-Temper Forging Company is considering the acquisition of equipment at a cost of $375,000. The equipment has an estimated life of 10 years and no residual value. It is expected to provide yearly net cash flows of $93,750. The company's minimum desired rate of return for net present value analysis is 12%.

Compute the following:

a. The average rate of return, giving effect to straight-line depreciation on the investment.
b. The cash payback period.
c. The net present value. Use the table of the present value of an annuity of $1 in this chapter. Round to the nearest dollar.

EXERCISE 15-15
Internal rate of return method
OBJECTIVE 2

✓ a. 4.487

The internal rate of return method is used by Ace Storage and Moving Company in analyzing a capital expenditure proposal that involves an investment of $62,818 and annual net cash flows of $14,000 for each of the 8 years of its useful life.

a. Determine a present value factor for an annuity of $1 that can be used in determining the internal rate of return.
b. Using the factor determined in (a) and the present value of an annuity of $1 table in this chapter, determine the internal rate of return for the proposal.

EXERCISE 15-16
Internal rate of return method
OBJECTIVE 2

IBM Corporation recently saved $250 million over three years by implementing supply chain software that reduced the cost of components used in its manufacture of computers. If we assume that the savings occurred equally over the 3 years and the cost of implementing the new software was $175,500,000, what would be the internal rate of return for this investment? Use the present value of an annuity of $1 table in Exhibit 2 in determining your answer.

EXERCISE 15-17
Internal rate of return method—two projects
OBJECTIVE 2

✓ a. Delivery truck, 12%

Salty Popcorn Company is considering two possible investments, a delivery truck and a bagging machine. The delivery truck would cost $28,777 and could be used to deliver an additional 35,000 bags of popcorn per year. Each bag of popcorn can be sold for a contribution margin of $0.30. The delivery truck operating expenses, excluding depreciation, are $0.25 per mile for 14,000 miles per year. The bagging machine would replace an old bagging machine, and its net investment cost would be $22,710. The new machine would require 2 fewer hours of direct labor per day. Direct labor is $12 per hour. There are 250 operating days in the year. Both the truck and the bagging machine are estimated to have 6-year lives. The minimum rate of return is 11%. However, Salty has funds to invest in only one of the projects.

a. Compute the internal rate of return for each investment. Use the table of present values of an annuity of $1 in the chapter.
b. Prepare a memo to management with a recommendation.

EXERCISE 15-18
Net present value method and internal rate of return method
OBJECTIVE 2

✓ a. ($8,080)

Janitor Supply Co. is proposing to spend $91,280 on a 7-year project whose estimated net cash flows are $20,000 for each of the 7 years.

a. Compute the net present value using a rate of return of 15%. Use the table of present values of an annuity of $1 in the chapter.
b. Based on the analysis prepared in (a), is the rate of return (1) more than 15%, (2) 15%, or (3) less than 15%? Explain.
c. Determine the internal rate of return by computing a present value factor for an annuity of $1 and using the table of the present value of an annuity of $1 in the text.

EXERCISE 15-19
Identify error in capital investment analysis calculations
OBJECTIVE 2

Fastex Computer Company is considering the purchase of automated machinery that is expected to have a useful life of 4 years and no residual value. The average rate of return on the average investment has been computed to be 25%, and the cash payback period was computed to be 4.5 years.

Do you see any reason to question the validity of the data presented? Explain.

EXERCISE 15-20
Changing prices
OBJECTIVE 3

Hardy Company invested $1,000,000 to build a plant in a foreign country. The labor and materials used in production are purchased locally. The plant expansion was estimated to produce an internal rate of return of 20% in U.S. dollar terms. Due to a currency crisis, the exchange rate between the local currency and the U.S. dollar doubled from 4 local units per U.S. dollar to 8 local units per U.S. dollar.

a. Assume that the plant produced and sold product in the local economy. Explain what impact this change in the currency exchange rate would have on the project's internal rate of return.
b. Assume that the plant produced product in the local economy but exported it back to the United States for sale. Explain what impact the change in the currency exchange rate would have on the project's internal rate of return under this assumption.

Problems

PROBLEM 15 | 1
Average rate of return method, net present value method, and analysis
OBJECTIVE 2

✓ 1. a. 20%

The capital investment committee of Beautify Landscaping Company is considering two capital investments. The estimated income from operations and net cash flows from each investment are as follows:

| Year | Greenhouse | | Skid Loader | |
	Income from Operations	Net Cash Flow	Income from Operations	Net Cash Flow
1	$ 5,000	$15,000	$15,000	$25,000
2	5,000	15,000	10,000	20,000
3	5,000	15,000	5,000	15,000
4	5,000	15,000	0	10,000
5	5,000	15,000	(5,000)	5,000
	$25,000	$75,000	$25,000	$75,000

Each project requires an investment of $50,000. Straight-line depreciation will be used, and no residual value is expected. The committee has selected a rate of 10% for purposes of the net present value analysis.

Instructions

1. Compute the following:
   a. The average rate of return for each investment.
   b. The net present value for each investment. Use the present value of $1 table in this chapter.
2. Prepare a brief report for the capital investment committee to advise it on the relative merits of the two investments.

PROBLEM 15 | 2
Cash payback period, net present value method, and analysis
OBJECTIVE 2

✓ 1. b. Plant Expansion, $11,370

Echo Clothes Company is considering two investment projects. The estimated net cash flows from each project follow:

Year	Plant Expansion	Retail Store Expansion
1	$100,000	$150,000
2	130,000	120,000
3	150,000	110,000
4	130,000	110,000
5	170,000	190,000
Total	$680,000	$680,000

Each project requires an investment of $380,000. A rate of 20% has been selected for the net present value analysis.

Instructions

1. Compute the following for each project:
   a. Cash payback period.
   b. The net present value. Use the present value of $1 table in this chapter.
2. Prepare a brief report advising management on the relative merits of each of the two projects.

PROBLEM 15 | 3
Net present value method, present value index, and analysis
OBJECTIVE 2

✓ 2. Railcars, 1.08

Rocky Mountain Railroad Company wishes to evaluate three capital investment proposals by using the net present value method. Relevant data related to the proposals are summarized as follows:

	Route Expansion	Acquire Railcars	New Maintenance Yard
Amount to be invested	$560,000	$280,000	$425,000
Annual net cash flows:			
Year 1	200,000	140,000	175,000
Year 2	250,000	130,000	175,000
Year 3	350,000	125,000	200,000

Instructions

1. Assuming that the desired rate of return is 15%, prepare a net present value analysis for each proposal. Use the present value of $1 table in this chapter.
2. Determine a present value index for each proposal. Round to two decimal places.
3. Which proposal offers the highest present value per dollar of investment? Explain.

PROBLEM 15 | 4
Net present value method, rate of return method, and analysis
OBJECTIVE 2

✓ 1. a. Generating unit, $34,580

The management of Western Utilities Inc. is considering two capital investment projects. The estimated net cash flows from each project are as follows:

Year	Generating Unit	Distribution Network Expansion
1	$260,000	$90,000
2	260,000	90,000
3	260,000	90,000
4	260,000	90,000

The generating unit requires an investment of $789,620, and the distribution network expansion requires an investment of $256,950. No residual value is expected from either project.

Instructions

1. Compute the following for each project:
   a. The net present value. Use a rate of 10% and the present value of an annuity of $1 table appearing in this chapter.
   b. A present value index. Round to 2 decimal places.
2. Determine the internal rate of return for each project by (a) computing a present value factor for an annuity of $1 and (b) using the present value of an annuity of $1 table in this chapter.
3. What advantage does the internal rate of return method have over the net present value method in comparing projects?

PROBLEM 15 | 5

Evaluate alternative capital investment decisions

OBJECTIVES 2, 3

✓ 2. Project II, $12,080

The investment committee of Jake's Brewery Inc. is evaluating two projects. Each has a different useful life, but each requires an investment of $145,000. The estimated net cash flows from each project are as follows:

	Net Cash Flows	
Year	Project I	Project II
1	$40,000	$55,000
2	40,000	55,000
3	40,000	55,000
4	40,000	55,000
5	40,000	
6	40,000	

The committee has selected a rate of 15% for purposes of net present value analysis. It also estimates that the residual value at the end of each project's useful life is $0, but at the end of the fourth year, Project I's residual value would be $60,000.

Instructions

1. For each project, compute the net present value. Use the present value of an annuity of $1 table in this chapter. (Ignore the unequal lives of the projects.)
2. For each project, compute the net present value, assuming that Project I is adjusted to a 4-year life for purposes of analysis. Use the present value of $1 table in this chapter.
3. Prepare a report to the investment committee, providing your advice on the relative merits of the two projects.

PROBLEM 15 | 6

Capital rationing decision involving four proposals

OBJECTIVES 2, 4

✓ 5. Proposal B, 1.23

Columbus Capital Group is considering the allocation of a limited amount of capital investment funds among four proposals. The amount of proposed investment, estimated income from operations, and net cash flow for each proposal are as follows:

	Investment	Year	Income from Operations	Net Cash Flow
Proposal A:	$600,000	1	$ 40,000	$160,000
		2	40,000	160,000
		3	40,000	160,000
		4	0	120,000
		5	0	120,000

	Investment	Year	Income from Operations	Net Cash Flow
Proposal B:	$520,000	1	$ 96,000	$200,000
		2	56,000	160,000
		3	56,000	160,000
		4	56,000	160,000
		5	48,000	152,000
Proposal C:	$180,000	1	$ 44,000	$ 80,000
		2	24,000	60,000
		3	24,000	60,000
		4	24,000	60,000
		5	22,500	58,500
Proposal D:	$250,000	1	$ 50,000	$100,000
		2	50,000	100,000
		3	(10,000)	40,000
		4	(10,000)	40,000
		5	(10,000)	40,000

The company's capital rationing policy requires a maximum cash payback period of three years. In addition, a minimum average rate of return of 10% is required on all projects. If the preceding standards are met, the net present value method and present value indexes are used to rank the remaining proposals.

Instructions

1. Compute the cash payback period for each of the four proposals.
2. Considering straight-line depreciation on the investments and assuming no estimated residual value, compute the average rate of return for each of the four proposals. Round to one decimal place.
3. Using the following format, summarize the results of your computations in (1) and (2). By placing a check mark in the appropriate column at the right, indicate which proposals should be accepted for further analysis and which should be rejected.

Proposal	Cash Payback Period	Average Rate of Return	Accept for Further Analysis	Reject
A				
B				
C				
D				

4. For the proposals accepted for further analysis in (3), compute the net present value. Use a rate of 10% and the present value of $1 table in this chapter. Round to the nearest dollar.
5. Compute the present value index for each of the proposals in (4). Round to two decimal places.
6. Rank the proposals from most attractive to least attractive based on the present values of net cash flows computed in (4).
7. Rank the proposals from most attractive to least attractive based on the present value indexes computed in (5). Round to two decimal places.
8. Based on the analyses, comment on the relative attractiveness of the proposals ranked in (6) and (7).

Activities

Activity 15-1
Ethics and professional conduct in business

E T H I C S

Sherry Dale was recently hired as a cost analyst by Converse Company. One of Sherry's first assignments was to perform a net present value analysis for a new warehouse. Sherry performed the analysis and calculated a present value index of 0.75. The plant manager, I. M. Madd, is very intent on purchasing the warehouse because he believes that more storage space is needed. I. M. Madd asks Sherry into his office, and the following conversation takes place.

I. M.: Dale, you're new here, aren't you?

Sherry: Yes, sir.

I. M.: Well, Dale, let me tell you something. I'm not at all pleased with the capital investment analysis that you performed on this new warehouse. I need that warehouse for my production. If I don't get it, where am I going to place our output?

Sherry: We hope with the customer, sir.

I. M.: Now don't get smart with me, young woman.

Sherry: No, really, I was being serious. My analysis does not support constructing a new warehouse. There is no way that I can get the numbers to make this a favorable investment. In fact, it seems to me that purchasing a warehouse does not add much value to the business. We need to be producing product to satisfy customer orders, not to fill a warehouse.

I. M.: Listen, you need to understand something. The headquarters people will not allow me to build the warehouse if the numbers don't add up. I know as well as you that many assumptions go into your net present value analysis. Why don't you relax some of your assumptions so that the financial savings will offset the cost?

Sherry: I'm willing to discuss my assumptions with you. Maybe I overlooked something.

I. M.: Good. Here's what I want you to do. I see in your analysis that you don't project increased sales as a result of the warehouse. It seems to me if we can store more goods, we will have more to sell. Thus, logically, a larger warehouse translates into more sales. If you incorporate this into your analysis, I think you'll see that the numbers will work out. Why don't you work it through and come back with a new analysis? I'm really counting on you on this one. Let's get off to a good start together and see if we can get this project accepted.

What is your advice to Sherry?

Activity 15-2
Qualitative considerations

Some companies have attempted to respond to competitive pressure by relying solely on automation. For example, **Federal Mogul**, a parts supplier to the automotive industry, invested in robots, production line computers, and automated materials movement systems to regain a cost advantage that it lost to Japanese competitors. Unfortunately, this automation not only failed to lower costs but also caused the plant to become much less flexible than required by its customers. The high technology could not be "changed over" quickly from one product to another. In addition, Federal Mogul found that the new automation reduced employee motivation. As indicated by one of the managers, "Very clearly, we made some poor decisions. One of them was that high-tech was the answer."

Why might relying solely on automation lead to lower profits?

Activity 15-3
Investment analysis and qualitative considerations

The plant manager of Celco Power Equipment Company is considering the purchase of a new robotic assembly plant. The new robotic line will cost $1,250,000. The manager believes that the new investment will result in direct labor savings of $250,000 per year for 10 years.

1. What is the payback period on this project?
2. What is the net present value, assuming a 10% rate of return?
3. What else should the manager consider in the analysis?

Activity 15-4
Qualitative issues in investment analysis

The following are some selected quotes from senior executives:

John H. McConnel, CEO, Worthington Industries (a high-technology steel company): *"We try to find the best technology, stay ahead of the competition, and serve the customer.... We'll make any investment that will pay back quickly ... but if it is something that we really see as a must down the road, payback is not going to be that important."*

George Rathmann, Chairman Emeritus of Amgen (a biotech company): *"You cannot really run the numbers, do net present value calculations, because the uncertainties are really gigantic ... You decide on a project you want to run, and then you run the numbers [as a reality check on your assumptions]. Success in a business like this is much more dependent on tracking rather than on predicting, much more dependent on seeing results over time, tracking and adjusting and readjusting, much more dynamic, much more flexible."*

Judy Lewent, Chief Financial Officer of Merck & Co. (a pharmaceutical company): *"at the individual product level—the development of a successful new product requires on the order of $230 million in R&D, spread over more than a decade—discounted cash flow style analysis does not become a factor until development is near the point of manufacturing scale-up effort. Prior to that point, given the uncertainties associated with new product development, it would be lunacy in our business to decide that we know exactly what's going to happen to a product once it gets out."*

Explain the role of capital investment analysis for these companies.

Activity 15-5
Analyze cash flows

You are considering an investment of $360,000 in either Project A or Project B for Wonder Studios Inc. In discussing the two projects with an advisor, you decided that, for the risk involved, a return of 12% on the cash investment would be required. For this purpose, you estimated the following economic factors for the projects:

	Project A	**Project B**
Useful life	4 years	4 years
Residual value	-0-	-0-
Net income:		
Year 1	$ 65,000	$ 25,000
2	50,000	40,000
3	40,000	58,000
4	25,000	64,200
Net cash flows:		
Year 1	$155,000	$115,000
2	140,000	130,000
3	130,000	148,000
4	115,000	154,200

Although the average rate of return exceeds 12% on both projects, you have tentatively decided to invest in Project B because its rate was higher. Its total net cash flow is $547,200, which exceeds that of Project A by $7,200.

1. Determine the average rate of return for both projects.
2. Why is the timing of cash flows important in evaluating capital investments? Calculate the net present value of the two projects at a minimum rate of return of 12% to demonstrate the importance of net cash flows and their timing to these two projects. Round to the nearest dollar.

Activity 15-6
Capital investment analysis

GROUP

The class members will work in two groups. One should find a local business, such as a copy shop, that rents time on microcomputers for an hourly rate. Determine the hourly rate. The other group should determine the price of a mid-range microcomputer at http://www.dell.com. Combine this information from the two groups and perform a capital budgeting analysis. Assume that one student will use the computer for 35 hours per semester for the next 3 years.

Also assume that the minimum rate of return is 10%. (*Hint:* Use the appropriate present value factor for 5% compounded for six semiannual periods.)

Does your analysis support the student purchasing the computer or using one on an hourly rental rate?

Answers to Self-Study Questions

1. **C** Methods of evaluating capital investment proposals that ignore the time value of money are categorized as methods that ignore present value. This category includes the average rate of return method (answer A) and the cash payback method (answer B).

2. **B** The average rate of return is 24% (answer B), determined by dividing the expected average annual earnings by the average investment, as follows:

$$\frac{\$60,000/5}{(\$100,000 - \$0)/2} = 24\%$$

3. **B** Of the four methods of analyzing proposals for capital investments, the cash payback period (answer B) refers to the expected period of time required to recover the amount of cash to be invested. The average rate of return (answer A) is a measure of the anticipated profitability of a proposal. The net present value method (answer C) reduces the expected future net cash flows originating from a proposal to their present values. The

internal rate of return method (answer D) uses present value concepts to compute the rate of return from the net cash flows expected from the investment.

4. **B** The net present value is determined as follows:

Present value of $25,000 for 8 years at 11%	
($25,000 × 5.14612)	$128,653
Less: Project cost	120,000
Net present value	$ 8,653

5. **C** The internal rate of return for this project is determined by solving for the present value of an annuity factor that when multiplied by $40,000 will equal $226,009. By division, the factor is as follows:

$$\frac{\$226,009}{\$40,000} = 5.65$$

In Exhibit 2, scan along the n = 10 years row until finding the 5.650 factor. The column for this factor is 12%.

Appendix A
Double-Entry Accounting Systems

Throughout this text, we recorded and summarized transactions by using the accounting equation. Each financial statement item was represented in the equation. Transactions were recorded as pluses or minuses for each item affected by the transaction. Monitoring the equality of the accounting equation facilitated the detection and prevention of errors in processing transactions. That is, total assets must equal total liabilities plus stockholders' equity.

Double-entry accounting systems use these same concepts. In addition, double-entry accounting systems use debit and credit rules as an additional control on the accuracy of recording transactions. In this appendix, we describe the basic elements of double-entry accounting systems.

In a double-entry accounting system, transactions are recorded in accounts. An **account**, in its simplest form, has three parts. First, each account has a title, which is the name of the item recorded in the account. Second, each account has a space for recording increases in the amount of the item. Third, each account has a space for recording decreases in the amount of the item. The account form presented here is called a **T account** because it resembles the letter *T*. The left side of the account is called the *debit* side, and the right side is called the *credit* side.[1]

Title	
Left side	Right Side
debit	*credit*

Amounts entered on the left side of an account, regardless of the account title, are called **debits** to the account. When debits are entered in an account, the account is said to be *debited* (or charged). Amounts entered on the right side of an account are called **credits**, and the account is said to be *credited*. Debits and credits are sometimes abbreviated as *Dr.* and *Cr.*

In the T account for the cash account that follows, transactions involving cash receipts are listed on the debit side of the account. The transactions involving cash payments are listed on the credit side. If at any time the amount of the total cash

---

[1]The terms *debit* and *credit* are derived from the Latin *debere* and *credere*.

receipts ($10,950) is needed, the entries on the debit side of the account are added. The total of the cash payments on the credit side, $6,850 in the example, is determined in a similar manner. Subtracting the payments from the receipts, $10,950 − $6,850, determines the amount of cash on hand, $4,100. This amount is called the **balance of the account**. This balance should be identified as a *debit balance* in some way, such as showing the balance on the debit side of the account or simply listing it as a debit balance.

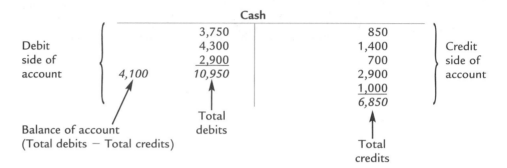

Rules of Debit and Credit

Why did we record increases in the cash account as debits and decreases as credits? The simple answer is to follow convention. That is, a standardized method of recording increases and decreases in accounts is essential so that businesses record transactions in a similar manner. If each business recorded transactions differently, the result would be chaotic and comparability between and among companies would be lost.

The standardized **rules of debit and credit** are shown in Exhibit 1. These rules are used by all businesses—from the corner gas station to the largest public corporation.

Exhibit 1 shows several important characteristics of the rules of debit and credit. First, the normal balance of an account is the side of the account used to record increases. Thus, the normal balance of an asset account is a debit balance, and the normal balance of a liability account is a credit balance. This characteristic is often useful in detecting errors in the recording process. That is, when an account normally hav-

EXHIBIT 1   *Rules of Debit and Credit*

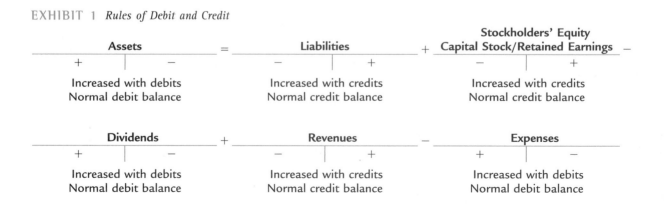

ing a debit balance actually has a credit balance, or vice versa, an error could have occurred or an unusual situation could exist.

To illustrate, assume that at the end of the period, the cash account has a credit balance. In this case, either an error has occurred or the company has overdrawn its bank account. Likewise, if accounts payable has a debit balance, an error has occurred or the company has overpaid its accounts payable. On the other hand, a credit balance in the office equipment or land account can result only from an error in the recording process. That is, a company cannot have negative office equipment or land. Thus, the normal balances of accounts provide a degree of control in the recording process.

The second characteristic shown in Exhibit 1 is that accounts on the left side of the accounting equation (the assets side) are increased by debits and have normal debit balances while accounts on the right side of the accounting equation (liability and stockholders' equity side) are increased by credits and have normal credit balances. On the asset (left-hand) side of the equation, the only exception to the preceding relationship is that some asset accounts, called *contra asset accounts*, are normally increased by credits and have normal credit balances. As the words *contra asset* imply, these accounts offset the normal debit balances of asset accounts. For example, accumulated depreciation, an offset to plant assets, is increased by credits and has a normal credit balance. Thus, accumulated depreciation is a contra asset account.

On the liability and stockholders' equity (right-hand) side of the equation, the only exceptions to the preceding relationship are the dividend and expense accounts. The payment of dividends decreases stockholders' equity (retained earnings); thus, the dividends account is increased by debits and has a normal debit balance. In this sense, the dividends account can be thought of as a type of contra account to retained earnings. However, unlike contra asset accounts, the dividends account is closed to Retained Earnings at the end of the period. In this way, dividends for each period are recorded and accounted for separately.

Revenue increases stockholders' equity (retained earnings); thus, revenue accounts are increased by credits and have normal credit balances. In contrast, expenses decrease stockholders' equity (retained earnings). Thus, expense accounts are increased by debits and have a normal debit balance. Like dividends, expense accounts can be thought of as a type of contra account. In this case, expenses can be thought of as contra accounts to revenues. Like dividends, expense accounts are closed at the end of the period.

The third characteristic of the rules of debit and credit is that for each transaction, the total debits equal the total credits. That is, each transaction must be recorded so that the total debits for the transaction equal the total credits. For example, assume that a company pays cash of $500 for supplies. The asset account Supplies is debited (increased) by $500 and Cash is credited (decreased) by $500. Likewise, if the company provides services and receives $2,000 from customers, Cash is debited (increased) and Fees Earned is credited (increased) by $2,000. Debits equaling the credits for each transaction provides a degree of control in the recording process.

To summarize, each transaction is recorded under the rules shown in Exhibit 1. Under these rules, the total debits equal the total credits for each transaction. In addition, the equality of the debits and credits is built into the accounting equation: Assets = Liabilities + Stockholders' Equity.

The Journal

Each transaction is initially entered in chronological order in a record called a **journal**. In this way, the journal documents the history of the company. The process of recording transactions in the journal is called **journalizing**. The specific transaction record entered in the journal is called a **journal entry**.

In practice, a business can use a variety of formats for recording journal entries. It can use one all-purpose journal, sometimes called a *general journal*, or several journals. In the latter case, a *special journal* is designed to record a single type of transaction that occurs frequently. To simplify, we will use a basic, two-column general journal in the remainder of this appendix to illustrate the journalizing of transactions.

Assume that on November 1, 2004, Shannon Pence organizes a corporation that will be known as Online Solutions. The first phase of Shannon's business plan is to operate Online Solutions as a service business that provides assistance to individuals and small businesses in developing Web pages and in configuring and installing application software. Shannon expects this initial phase of the business to last 1 to 2 years. During this period, Online Solutions will gather information on the software and hardware needs of customers. During the second phase of the business plan, Online Solutions will expand into an Internet-based retailer of software and hardware to individuals and small businesses.

To start the business, Shannon deposits $25,000 in a bank account in the name of Online Solutions in return for shares of stock in the corporation. This first transaction increases Cash and Capital Stock by $25,000. The transaction is entered in the general journal by first listing the date, the title of the account to be debited, and then the amount of the debit. Next, the title of the account to be credited is listed below and to the right of the debit, followed by the amount to be credited. The resulting journal entry follows.

2004				
Nov.	1	Cash	25 000 00	
		Capital Stock		25 000 00

The increase in the asset is debited to the cash account. The increase in stockholders' equity (capital stock) is credited to the capital stock account. As other assets are acquired, the increases are also recorded as debits to asset accounts. Likewise, other increases in stockholders' equity will be recorded as credits to stockholders' equity accounts.

Online Solutions entered into the following additional transactions during the remainder of November:

Nov. 5 Purchased land for $20,000, paying cash. The land is located in a new business park with convenient access to transportation facilities. Online Solutions plans to rent office space and equipment during the first phase of its business plan. During the second phase, the company plans to build an office and warehouse on the land.

   10 Purchased supplies on account for $1,350.

   18 Received $7,500 for services provided to customers for cash.

   30 Paid expenses as follows: wages, $2,125; rent, $800; utilities, $450; and miscellaneous, $275.

   30 Paid creditors on account, $950.

   30 Paid stockholder (Shannon Pence) dividends of $2,000.

The journal entries to record these transactions follow.

Nov.	5	Land	20 000 00	
		Cash		20 000 00
	10	Supplies	1 350 00	
		Accounts Payable		1 350 00
	18	Cash	7 500 00	
		Fees Earned		7 500 00
	30	Wages Expense	2 125 00	
		Rent Expense	800 00	
		Utilities Expense	450 00	
		Miscellaneous Expense	275 00	
		Cash		3 650 00
	30	Accounts Payable	950 00	
		Cash		950 00
	30	Dividends	2 000 00	
		Cash		2 000 00

Posting to the Ledger

As we discussed in the preceding section, a transaction is first recorded in the journal. The journal thus provides a chronological history of transactions. Periodically, the journal entries must be transferred to the accounts. The group of accounts for a business is called its **general ledger**. The list of accounts in the general ledger is called the **chart of accounts**. The accounts are normally listed in the order in which they appear in the financial statements, beginning with the balance sheet and concluding with the income statement. The chart of accounts for Online Solutions is shown in Exhibit 2.

EXHIBIT 2
Chart of Accounts for Online Solutions

Balance Sheet Accounts	Income Statement Accounts
Assets	Revenue
Cash	Fees Earned
Accounts Receivable	Rent Revenue
Supplies	Expenses
Prepaid Insurance	Wages Expense
Office Equipment	Rent Expense
Accumulated Depreciation	Depreciation Expense
Land	Utilities Expense
Liabilities	Supplies Expense
Accounts Payable	Insurance Expense
Wages Payable	Miscellaneous Expense
Unearned Rent	
Stockholders' Equity	
Capital Stock	
Retained Earnings	
Dividends	

The process of transferring the debits and credits from the journal entries to the accounts in the ledger is called **posting**. To illustrate the posting process, Online Solutions' November 1 transaction, along with its posting to the cash and capital stock accounts, is shown in Exhibit 3.

EXHIBIT 3
Posting a Journal Entry

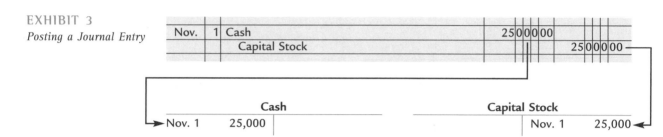

The debits and credits for each journal entry are posted to the accounts in the order in which they occur in the journal. In posting to the accounts, the date is entered followed by the amount of the entry. After the journal entries have been posted, the ledger becomes a chronological history of transactions by account. The posting of Online Solutions' remaining journal entries is shown later in Exhibit 7.

Trial Balance and Financial Statements

How can you be sure that you have not made an error in posting the debits and credits to the ledger? One way is to determine the equality of the debit and credit balances of accounts in the ledger. This equality should be proved at the end of each accounting period, if not more often. Such a proof, called a **trial balance**, can be in the form of a computer printout or as shown in Exhibit 4.

EXHIBIT 4
Trial Balance

ONLINE SOLUTIONS Trial Balance November 30, 2004		
Cash	5,900	
Supplies	1,350	
Land	20,000	
Accounts Payable		400
Capital Stock		25,000
Dividends	2,000	
Fees Earned		7,500
Wages Expense	2,125	
Rent Expense	800	
Utilities Expense	450	
Miscellaneous Expense	275	
	32,900	32,900

The trial balance does not provide complete proof of accuracy of the ledger. It indicates only that the debits and the credits are equal. This proof is of value, however, because errors often affect the equality of debits and credits. If the two totals of a trial balance are not equal, an error has occurred. In such a case, the error must be located and corrected before financial statements are prepared. This ability to detect errors in recording when the trial balance totals are not equal is the primary control feature and advantage of the double-entry accounting system.

The trial balance can be used as the source of data for preparing financial statements. The financial statements prepared in a double-entry accounting system are similar to those we described and illustrated in the text. For this reason, the financial statements are not illustrated in this appendix.

Review of Double-Entry Accounting

As a review of the double-entry accounting financial reporting system, we continue our illustration of Online Solutions. During December, assume that Online Solutions entered into the following transactions:

Dec. 1 Paid a premium of $2,400 for a comprehensive insurance policy covering liability, theft, and fire. The policy covers a two-year period.

1 Paid rent for December, $800. The company from which Online Solutions is renting its store space now requires the payment of rent on the first day of each month rather than at the end of the month.

1 Received an offer from a local retailer to rent the land purchased on November 5. The retailer plans to use the land as a parking lot for its employees and customers. Online Solutions agreed to rent the land to the retailer for three months with the rent payable in advance. Online Solutions received $360 for three months' rent beginning December 1.

4 Purchased office equipment on account from Executive Supply Co. for $1,800.

6 Paid $180 for a newspaper advertisement.

11 Paid creditors $400.

13 Paid a receptionist and a part-time assistant $950 for two weeks' wages.

16 Received $3,100 from fees earned for the first half of December.

16 Earned fees on account totaling $1,750 for the first half of December.

20 Paid $1,800 to Executive Supply Co. on the debt owed from the December 4 transaction.

21 Received $650 from customers in payment of their accounts.

23 Purchased $1,450 of supplies by paying $550 cash and charging the remainder on account.

27 Paid the receptionist and the part-time assistant $1,200 for two weeks' wages.

31 Paid $310 telephone bill for the month.

31 Paid $225 electric bill for the month.

31 Received $2,870 from fees earned for the second half of December.

31 Earned fees on account totaling $1,120 for the second half of December.

31 Paid dividends of $2,000 to stockholders.

The journal entries for the December transactions are shown in Exhibit 5. The posting of the journal entries to the ledger accounts is shown later in Exhibit 7.

				Debit	Credit
Dec.	1	Prepaid Insurance		2 400 00	
		Cash			2 400 00
	1	Rent Expense		800 00	
		Cash			800 00
	1	Cash		360 00	
		Unearned Rent			360 00
	4	Office Equipment		1 800 00	
		Accounts Payable			1 800 00
	6	Miscellaneous Expense		180 00	
		Cash			180 00
	11	Accounts Payable		400 00	
		Cash			400 00
	13	Wages Expense		950 00	
		Cash			950 00
	16	Cash		3 100 00	
		Fees Earned			3 100 00
	16	Accounts Receivable		1 750 00	
		Fees Earned			1 750 00
	20	Accounts Payable		1 800 00	
		Cash			1 800 00
	21	Cash		650 00	
		Accounts Receivable			650 00
	23	Supplies		1 450 00	
		Cash			550 00
		Accounts Payable			900 00
	27	Wages Expense		1 200 00	
		Cash			1 200 00
	31	Utilities Expense		310 00	
		Cash			310 00
	31	Utilities Expense		225 00	
		Cash			225 00
	31	Cash		2 870 00	
		Fees Earned			2 870 00
	31	Accounts Receivable		1 120 00	
		Fees Earned			1 120 00
	31	Dividends		2 000 00	
		Cash			2 000 00

The trial balance shown in Exhibit 6 indicates that after posting December transactions to the general ledger, the total of the debit balances of accounts equals the total of the credit balances. Exhibit 7 shows the journal entries posted to the ledger accounts of Online Solutions.

EXHIBIT 6

Trial Balance for Online Solutions

ONLINE SOLUTIONS
Trial Balance
December 31, 2004

Cash	2,065	
Accounts Receivable	2,220	
Supplies	2,800	
Prepaid Insurance	2,400	
Office Equipment	1,800	
Land	20,000	
Accounts Payable		900
Unearned Rent		360
Capital Stock		25,000
Dividends	4,000	
Fees Earned		16,340
Wages Expense	4,275	
Rent Expense	1,600	
Utilities Expense	985	
Miscellaneous Expense	455	
	42,600	42,600

EXHIBIT 7

Ledger for Online Solutions

Cash

Nov.	1	25,000	Nov.	5	20,000
	18	7,500		30	3,650
				30	950
				30	2,000
		32,500			26,600
Nov. 30 Bal.		5,900	Dec.	1	2,400
Dec.	1	360		1	800
	16	3,100		6	180
	21	650		11	400
	31	2,870		13	950
				20	1,800
				23	550
				27	1,200
				31	310
				31	225
				31	2,000
		12,880			10,815
Dec. 31 Bal.		2,065			

Accounts Receivable

Dec.	16	1,750	Dec.	21	650
	31	1,120			
Dec. 31 Bal.		2,220			

Supplies

Nov. 10	1,350		
Dec. 23	1,450		
Dec. 31 Bal.	2,800		

Prepaid Insurance

Dec.	1	2,400	

Land

Nov.	5	20,000	

Office Equipment

Dec.	4	1,800	

Accounts Payable

Nov. 30	950	Nov. 10		1,350
		Nov. 30 Bal.		400
Dec. 11	400	Dec.	4	1,800
20	1,800		23	900
	2,200			3,100
		Dec. 31 Bal.		900

EXHIBIT 7
(concluded)

Unearned Rent

	Dec. 1	360

Capital Stock

	Nov. 1	25,000

Dividends

Nov. 30	2,000	
Dec. 31	2,000	
Dec. 31 Bal.	4,000	

Fees Earned

	Nov. 18	7,500
	Dec. 16	3,100
	16	1,750
	31	2,870
	31	1,120
	Dec. 31 Bal.	16,340

Wages Expense

Nov. 30	2,125	
Dec. 13	950	
27	1,200	
Dec. 31 Bal.	4,275	

Rent Expense

Nov. 30	800	
Dec. 1	800	
Dec. 31 Bal.	1,600	

Utilities Expense

Nov. 30	450	
Dec. 31	310	
31	225	
Dec. 31 Bal.	985	

Miscellaneous Expense

Nov. 30	275	
Dec. 6	180	
Dec. 31 Bal.	455	

Exercises

EXERCISE 1
Rules of debit and credit

The following table summarizes the rules of debit and credit. For each item (a) through (n), indicate whether the proper answer is a debit or a credit.

	Increase	Decrease	Normal Balance
Balance sheet accounts:			
Asset	Debit	Credit	(a)
Liability	(b)	(c)	(d)
Stockholders' Equity:			
Capital Stock	(e)	(f)	Credit
Retained Earnings	Credit	(g)	(h)
Dividends	(i)	Credit	(j)
Income statement accounts:			
Revenue	(k)	Debit	(l)
Expense	(m)	Credit	(n)

EXERCISE 2
Identifying transactions

World Co. is a travel agency. The nine transactions recorded by World during April, its first month of operations, are indicated in the following T accounts:

Cash

(1)	30,000	(2)	1,500
(7)	9,500	(3)	10,000
		(4)	4,050
		(6)	7,500
		(8)	3,000

Equipment

(3)	30,000	

Dividends

(8)	3,000	

Accounts Receivable		Accounts Payable		Service Revenue	
(5) 13,000	(7) 9,500	(6) 7,500	(3) 20,000		(5) 13,000

Supplies		Capital Stock		Operating Expenses	
(2) 1,500	(9) 1,050		(1) 30,000	(4) 4,050 (9) 1,050	

Indicate for each debit and each credit (a) whether an asset, liability, stockholders' equity, dividends, revenue, or expense account was affected and (b) whether the account was increased (+) or decreased (−). Present your answers in the following form, with transaction (1) given as an example:

	Account Debited		Account Credited	
Transaction	Type	Effect	Type	Effect
(1)	asset	+	stockholders' equity	+

EXERCISE 3
Journal entries

Based on the T accounts in Exercise 2, prepare the nine journal entries from which the postings were made.

EXERCISE 4
Trial balance

Based on the data in Exercise 2, prepare a trial balance listing the accounts in their proper order.

EXERCISE 5
Classification of accounts, normal balances

The following accounts (in millions) were adapted from the financial statements of **Apple Computer, Inc.**, for the year ending September 29, 2001:

Accounts Payable	$ 801
Accounts Receivable	466
Accrued Expenses Payable	717
Capital Stock	1,660
Cash	2,310
Cost of Sales	4,128
Inventories	11
Investments	2,154
Long-Term Debt	317
Other Assets	516
Other Income (net)	319
Other Liabilities	266
Other Operating Expenses	11
Property, Plant, and Equipment	564
Retained Earnings, September 30, 2000	2,285
Sales	5,363
Selling, General, and Administrative Expenses	1,138
Research and Development Expenses	430

(continued)

a. Identify each account as either a balance sheet account or an income statement account.
b. For each balance sheet account, identify it as an asset, a liability, or stockholders' equity. For each income statement account, identify it as a revenue or an expense.
c. Indicate the normal balance of the account.

EXERCISE 6
Trial Balance

Using the data from Exercise 5, prepare a trial balance for **Apple Computer, Inc.**, as of September 29, 2001. List the accounts in the order they would appear in Apple Computer's ledger.

EXERCISE 7
Account balances

a. On June 1, the cash account balance was $3,850. During June, cash receipts totaled $11,850, and the June 30 balance was $4,150. Determine the cash payments made during June.
b. On May 1, the accounts receivable account balance was $18,500. During May, $21,000 was collected from customers on account. Assuming that the May 31 balance was $27,500, determine the fees billed to customers on account during May.
c. During January, $60,500 was paid to creditors on account, and purchases on account were $77,700. Assuming that the January 31 balance of Accounts Payable was $31,000, determine the account balance on January 1.

EXERCISE 8
Transactions

Wildcat Co. has the following accounts in its ledger: Cash, Accounts Receivable, Supplies, Office Equipment, Accounts Payable, Capital Stock, Dividends, Fees Earned, Rent Expense, Advertising Expense, Utilities Expense, and Miscellaneous Expense.

Journalize the following selected transactions in a journal:

Mar. 1 Paid rent for the month, $2,500.
     2 Paid advertising expense, $600.
     4 Paid cash for supplies, $1,050.
     6 Purchased office equipment on account, $4,500.
     8 Received cash from customers on account, $3,600.
    12 Paid creditor on account, $2,150.
    20 Paid dividends, $1,000.
    25 Paid cash for repairs to office equipment, $120.
    30 Paid telephone bill for the month, $195.
    31 Earned fees for the month and billed to customers, $11,150.
    31 Paid electricity bill for the month, $280.

EXERCISE 9
Journalizing and posting

On November 12, 2004, Trux Co. purchased $1,720 of supplies on account.

a. Journalize the November 12, 2004 transaction.
b. Prepare a T account for Supplies. Enter a debit balance of $390 as of November 1, 2004.
c. Prepare a T account for Accounts Payable. Enter a credit balance of $9,681 as of November 1, 2004.
d. Post the November 12, 2004 transaction to the accounts and determine the balances of the accounts.

EXERCISE 10
Trial balance

The accounts in the ledger of Bogart Park Co. as of August 31 of the current year are listed as follows in alphabetical order. All accounts have normal balances. The balance of the cash account has been intentionally omitted.

Accounts Payable	$ 13,710
Accounts Receivable	27,500
Capital Stock	75,000
Cash	?
Dividends	25,000
Fees Earned	333,500
Insurance Expense	5,000
Land	125,000
Miscellaneous Expense	9,900
Notes Payable	40,000
Prepaid Insurance	3,150
Rent Expense	58,000
Retained Earnings	35,290
Supplies	4,100
Supplies Expense	5,900
Unearned Rent	6,000
Utilities Expense	41,500
Wages Expense	175,000

Prepare a trial balance listing the accounts in their proper order and inserting the missing figure for cash.

Problems

PROBLEM | 1

Journal entries and trial balance

On May 1, 2004, Jim Lindley established Homestead Realty, which completed the following transactions during the month:

(a) Transferred cash from Jim Lindley's personal bank account to an account to be used for the business in exchange for capital stock, $7,500.
(b) Paid rent on office and equipment for the month, $2,500.
(c) Purchased supplies on account, $1,200.
(d) Paid creditor on account, $900.
(e) Earned sales commissions, receiving cash, $15,750.
(f) Paid automobile expenses (including rental charge) for month, $2,400, and miscellaneous expenses, $1,250.
(g) Paid office salaries, $4,500.
(h) Determined that the cost of supplies used was $875.
(i) Paid dividends, $2,500.

Instructions

1. Journalize entries for transactions (a) through (i) using the following accounts: Cash, Supplies, Accounts Payable, Capital Stock, Dividends, Sales Commissions, Office Salaries Expense, Rent Expense, Automobile Expense, Supplies Expense, Miscellaneous Expense.
2. Post the journal entries to T accounts by placing the appropriate letter to the left of each amount to identify the transactions. Determine the account balances after all posting is complete.
3. Prepare a trial balance as of May 31, 2004.

PROBLEM | 2

Journal entries and trial balance

Eastside Realty acts as an agent in buying, selling, renting, and managing real estate. Its account balances at the end of March 2004 of the current year are as follows:

Cash	8,150	
Accounts Receivable	28,750	
Prepaid Insurance	1,100	
Office Supplies	1,050	
Land	0	
Office Equipment	8,500	
Accumulated Depreciation		2,400
Accounts Payable		900
Salary and Commissions Payable		0
Unearned Fees		1,500
Notes Payable		0
Capital Stock		10,000
Retained Earnings		32,750
Dividends	0	
Fees Earned		0
Salary and Commission Expense	0	
Rent Expense	0	
Office Supplies Expense	0	
Advertising Expense	0	
Automobile Expense	0	
Insurance Expense	0	
Depreciation Expense	0	
Miscellaneous Expense	0	
	47,550	47,550

The following business transactions were completed by Eastside Realty during April 2004:

Apr.   1   Paid rent on office for April, $4,000.
    2   Purchased office supplies on account, $1,375.
    5   Paid annual insurance premiums, $1,650.
    8   Received cash from clients on account, $27,500.
  15   Purchased land for a future building site for $75,000, paying $7,500 in cash and giving a noninterest-bearing note payable due in 2006 for the remainder.
  17   Paid creditors on account, $900.
  20   Returned a portion of the office supplies purchased on April 2, receiving full credit for their cost, $275.
  24   Paid advertising expense, $1,100.
  25   Billed clients for fees earned, $38,400.
  27   Paid salaries and commissions, $11,500.
  28   Paid automobile expense (including rental charges for an automobile), $715.
  29   Paid miscellaneous expenses, $215.
  30   Received cash from client for fees earned, $5,000.
  30   Paid dividends, $2,000.

Instructions

1.   Record the April 1 balance of each account in the appropriate column of a T account. Write *Balance* to identify the opening amounts.
2.   Journalize the transactions for April in a two-column journal.
3.   Post the journal entries to the T accounts, placing the date to the left of each amount to identify the transaction. Determine the balances for all accounts with more than one posting.
4.   Prepare an unadjusted trial balance of the ledger as of April 30.

Appendix B
Process Cost Systems

As we discussed in Chapter 10, the job order cost system is best suited to industries that make special orders for customers or manufacture different products in groups. Industries that use job order cost systems include special-order printing, custom-made tailoring, furniture manufacturing, shipbuilding, aircraft building, and construction. Process manufacturing is different from job order manufacturing. Process manufacturers typically use large machines to process a flow of raw materials into a finished state. For example, a petrochemical business processes crude oil through numerous refining steps to produce higher grades of oil until gasoline is produced. The cost accounting system used by process manufacturers is called the **process cost system**.

In some ways, the process cost and job order cost systems are similar. Both systems accumulate product costs—for direct materials, direct labor, and factory overhead—and allocate these costs to the units produced. Both systems maintain perpetual inventory accounts with subsidiary ledgers for materials, work in process, and finished goods. Both systems also provide product cost data to management for planning, directing, improving, controlling, and decision making. The main difference in the two systems is the form in which the product costs are accumulated and reported.

Exhibit 1 on the following page illustrates the main differences between the job order and process cost systems. In a job order cost system, product costs are accumulated by job and are summarized on job cost sheets. The job cost sheets provide unit cost information and can be used by management for product pricing, cost control, and inventory valuation. The process manufacturer does not manufacture according to "jobs." Thus, costs are accumulated by department. Each unit of product that passes through the department is similar. Thus, the production costs reported by each department provide unit cost information that can be used by management for cost control. In a job order cost system, the work in process inventory at the end of the accounting period is the sum of the job cost sheets for partially completed jobs. In a process cost system, the amount of work in process inventory is determined by allocating costs between completed and partially completed units within a department.

EXHIBIT 1   *Job Order and Process Cost Systems Compared*

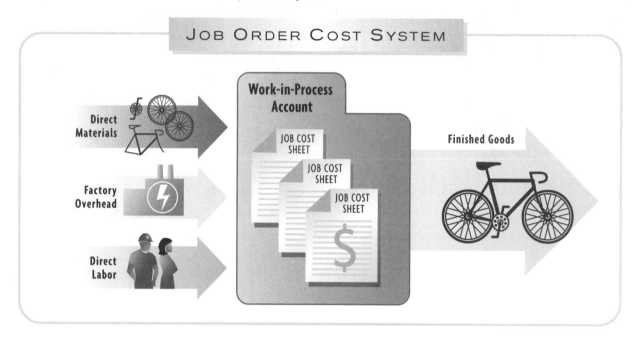

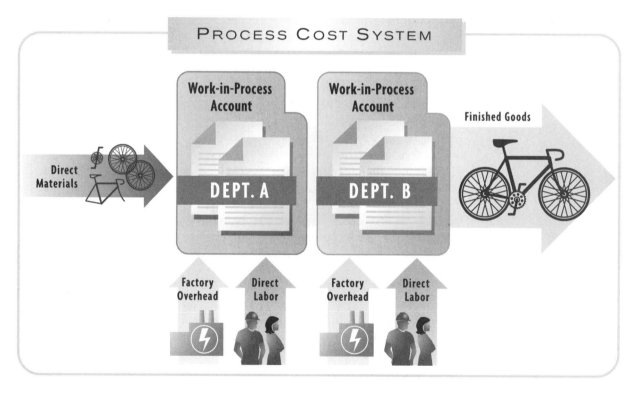

Physical Flows and Cost Flows for a Process Manufacturer

Exhibit 2 illustrates the physical flow of materials for a steel processor. Direct materials in the form of scrap metal are placed into a furnace in the Melting Department. The Melting Department uses conversion costs (direct labor and factory overhead) during the melting process. The molten metal is then transferred to the Casting Department, where it is poured into an ingot casting. The Casting Department also uses conversion costs during the casting process. The ingot castings are transferred to the finished goods inventory for shipment to customers.

EXHIBIT 2 *Physical Flows for a Process Manufacturer*

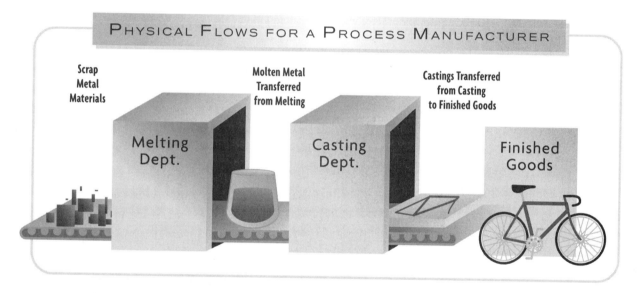

The cost flows in a process cost system reflect the physical materials flows and are illustrated in Exhibit 3 on the following page. Purchased materials increase Materials (a) and Accounts Payable (not shown). Direct materials (scrap metal) used by the Melting Department increase Work in Process—Melting and decrease Materials (b). In addition, indirect materials and other overhead incurred increase department factory overhead accounts and decrease Materials (d) and other accounts. Direct labor in the Melting Department increases the department's work in process account (c) and Wages Payable (not shown). Applied factory overhead increases Work in Process—Melting using a predetermined overhead rate (e). The cost of completed production from the Melting Department is transferred to the Casting Department by increasing Work in Process—Casting and decreasing Work in Process—Melting (f). The transferred costs include the direct materials and conversion costs for completed production of the Melting Department. The direct labor and applied factory overhead costs in the Casting Department increase Work in Process—Casting (g and h). The cost of the finished ingots is transferred out of the Casting Department by

EXHIBIT 3   *Cost Flows for a Process Manufacturer*

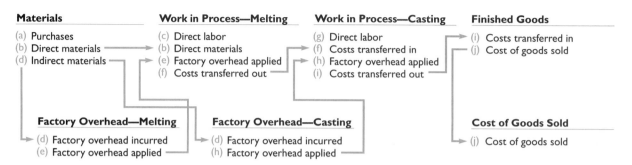

increasing Finished Goods and decreasing Work in Process—Casting (i). The cost of ingots sold to customers is transferred out of finished goods with increase to Cost of Goods Sold and a decrease to Finished Goods (j).

The Average Cost Method

In a process cost system, the costs transferred in and out of each department must be determined. The costs transferred in minus the cost transferred out determine the ending work in process for each department. Like a merchandising business, a manufacturer uses a cost flow assumption in determining the costs flowing into, out of, and remaining in each manufacturing department. The manufacturer can use a **first-in, first-out**; **last-in, first-out**; or **average cost flow assumption**. To simplify, we use the average cost flow assumption.[1]

Most process manufacturers have more than one department. In the illustrations that follow, McDermott Steel Inc. has two departments, Melting and Casting. McDermott melts scrap metal and then pours the molten metal into an ingot casting.

To illustrate the average cost method, we simplify by using only the Melting Department of McDermott Steel Inc. The following data for the Melting Department are for July of the current year:

Work in process inventory, July 1, 500 tons (70% completed)	$28,050
Direct materials cost incurred in July, 1,000 tons @ $50	50,000
Direct labor cost incurred in July	4,000
Factory overhead applied in July	4,350
Total production costs to account for	$86,400
Cost of goods transferred to Casting in July (includes units in process on July 1), 1,100 tons	?
Cost of work in process inventory, July 31, 400 tons, 25% completed as to conversion costs	?

Using the average cost system, our objective is to allocate the total costs of production of $86,400 to the 1,100 tons completed and transferred to the Casting De-

---

[1]The first-in, first-out and last-in, first-out cost flow assumptions are described and illustrated in advanced cost accounting textbooks and courses.

partment and the costs of the remaining 400 tons in the ending work in process inventory. These costs are represented in the preceding table by two question marks. We determine these amounts by using the following four steps:

1. Determine the units to be assigned costs.
2. Calculate equivalent units of production.
3. Determine the cost per equivalent unit.
4. Allocate costs to transferred and partially completed units.

Step 1: Determine the Units to Be Assigned Costs

The first step in our illustration is to determine the units to be assigned costs. A unit can be any measure of completed production, such as tons, gallons, pounds, barrels, or cases. We use tons as the definition for units in McDermott Steel.

McDermott Steel's Melting Department had 1,500 tons of direct materials to account for during July, as shown here:

Total tons to account for:	
Work in process, July 1	500 tons
Received from materials storeroom	1,000
Total units to account for by the Melting Department	1,500 tons

As we noted earlier, there are two categories of units to be assigned costs for the period: (1) units completed and transferred out and (2) units in the ending work in process inventory. During July, the Melting Department completed and transferred 1,100 tons to the Casting Department. Of the 1,000 tons started in July, 600 tons were completed and transferred to the Casting Department. Thus, the ending work in process inventory consists of 400 tons.

The total units (tons) to be assigned costs for McDermott Steel can be summarized as follows:

(1) Transferred out to the Casting Department in July	1,100 tons
(2) Work in process inventory, July 31	400
Total tons to be assigned costs	1,500 tons

Note that the total units (tons) to be assigned costs (1,500 tons) equals the total units to account for (1,500 tons).

Step 2: Calculate Equivalent Units of Production

Process manufacturers often have some partially processed units remaining in production at the end of a period. When this happens, the costs of production must be allocated between the units that have been completed and transferred to the next process (or finished goods) and those that are only partially completed and remain within the department. This allocation is determined by using equivalent units of production.

Equivalent units of production are the number of units that *could* have been completed within a given period. In contrast, **whole units** represent the number of units in production during a period whether completed or not. For example, 400 tons of whole units are in the work in process inventory for the Melting Department on July 31. Since these units are 25% complete, the number of equivalent units in process in the Melting Department on July 31 is 100 tons (400 tons × 0.25).

Since the units transferred to the Casting Department have been completed, the whole units (1,100 tons) transferred are the same as the equivalent units transferred.

The total equivalent units of production for the Melting Department is determined by adding the equivalent units in the ending work in process inventory to the units transferred and completed during the period as shown here:

Equivalent units completed and transferred to the Casting Department during July	1,100 tons
Equivalent units in ending work in process, July 31	100
Total equivalent units	1,200 tons

Step 3: Determine the Cost per Equivalent Unit

In step 3, we calculate the cost per equivalent unit. The **cost per equivalent unit** is determined by dividing the total production costs by the total equivalent units of production as follows:

$$\text{Cost per equivalent unit} = \frac{\text{Total production costs}}{\text{Total equivalent units}} = \frac{\$86,400}{1,200 \text{ tons}} = \$72$$

We use the cost per equivalent unit in step 4 to allocate the production costs to the completed and partially completed units.

Step 4: Allocate Costs to Transferred and Partially Completed Units

In step 4, we multiply the cost per equivalent unit by the equivalent units of production to determine the cost of transferred and partially completed units. For the Melting Department, these costs are determined as shown:

(1) Transferred out to the Casting Department:	
1,100 tons × $72	$79,200
(2) Work in Process Inventory, July 31:	
400 tons × 0.25 complete × $72	7,200
Total production costs assigned	$86,400

The Cost of Production Report

A **cost of production report** is normally prepared for each processing department at periodic intervals. The July cost of production report for McDermott Steel's Melting Department is shown in Exhibit 4. The cost of production report in Exhibit 4 summarizes the following:

1. The units for which the department is accountable and the disposition of those units.
2. The production costs incurred by the department and the allocation of those costs between completed and partially completed units.

EXHIBIT 4
*Cost of Production
Report for McDermott
Steel's Melting
Department—FIFO*

MCDERMOTT STEEL INC.
Cost of Production Report—Melting Department
For the Month Ended July 31, 2004

Units	Whole Units (step 1)	Equivalent Units of Production (step 2)
Units to account for during production:		
Work in process inventory, July 1	500	
Received from materials storeroom	1,000	
Total units accounted for by the Melting Dept.	1,500	
Units to be assigned cost:		
Transferred to Casting Department in July	1,100	1,100
Inventory in process, July 31 (25% complete)	400	100
Total units to be assigned cost	1,500	1,200

Costs	
Cost per Equivalent Unit **(step 3):**	
Total production costs for July in Melting Dept.	$86,400
Total equivalent units (from Step 2 above)	÷ 1,200
Cost per equivalent unit	$ 72
Costs assigned to production:	
Inventory in process, July 1	$28,050
Direct materials costs incurred in July	50,000
Direct labor cost incurred in July	4,000
Factory overhead applied in July	4,350
Total production costs accounted for by the Melting Dept.	$86,400
Costs allocated to transferred and partially completed units **(step 4):**	
Transferred to Casting Dept. in July (1,100 units × $72)	$79,200
Inventory in process, July 31 (400 units × 0.25 × $72)	7,200
Total costs assigned by the Melting Dept.	$86,400

The cost of production report is also used to control costs. Each department manager is responsible for the units entering production and the costs incurred in the department. Any failure to account for all costs and any significant differences in unit product costs from one month to another should be investigated.

Cost Flows for a Process Cost System

Exhibit 5 shows the flow of costs for each transaction. Note that the highlighted amounts in Exhibit 5 were determined from assigning the costs charged to production in the Melting Department. These amounts were computed and are shown at the bottom of the cost of production report for the Melting Department in Exhibit 4. Likewise, the amount transferred out of the Casting Department to Finished Goods would have also been determined from a cost of production report for the Casting Department.

EXHIBIT 5 *McDermott Steel's Cost Flows*

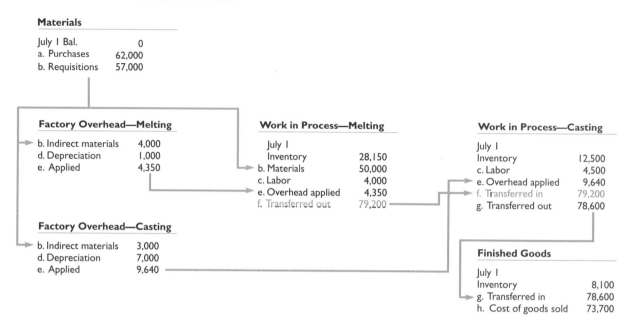

Using the Cost of Production Report for Decision Making

The cost of production report is one source of information that can be used by managers to control and improve operations. A cost of production report normally lists costs in more detail than the one in Exhibit 4. This increased detail helps management isolate problems and opportunities. To illustrate, assume that the Blending Department of Holland Beverage Company prepared cost of production reports for April and May. In addition, assume that the Blending Department had no beginning or ending work in process inventory either month. Thus, in this simple case, there is no need to determine equivalent units of production for allocating costs between completed and partially completed units. The cost of production reports for April and May in the Blending Department are as follows:

Cost of Production Reports
Holland Beverage Company—Blending
Department For the Months Ended April 30
and May 31, 2004

	April	May
Direct materials	$ 20,000	$ 40,600
Direct labor	15,000	29,400
Energy	8,000	20,000
Repairs	4,000	8,000
Tank cleaning	3,000	8,000
Total	$ 50,000	$ 106,000
Units completed	÷ 100,000	÷ 200,000
Cost per unit	$ 0.50	$ 0.53

Note that the preceding reports provide more cost detail than simply reporting direct materials and conversion costs. The May results indicate that total unit costs have increased from $0.50 to $0.53, or 6 from the previous month. What caused this increase? To determine its possible causes, the cost of production report can be restated in per-unit terms, as shown here.

Blending Department
Per-Unit Expense Comparisons

	April	May	% Change
Direct materials	$0.200	$0.203	1.50%
Direct labor	0.150	0.147	(2.00)
Energy	0.080	0.100	25.00
Repairs	0.040	0.040	0.00
Tank cleaning	0.030	0.040	33.33
Total	$0.500	$0.530	6.00%

Both energy and tank cleaning per-unit costs increased dramatically in May. Further investigation should focus on these costs. For example, a trend indicating increased energy costs could indicate that the machines are losing fuel efficiency, thereby requiring the company to purchase an increasing amount of fuel. This unfavorable trend could motivate management to repair the machines. The tank-cleaning costs could be investigated in a similar fashion.

In addition to unit production cost trends, managers of process manufacturers are also concerned about yield trends. **Yield** is the ratio of the materials output quantity to the input quantity. A yield of less than 1.0 occurs when the output quantity is less than the input quantity due to materials losses during the process. For example, if 1,000 pounds of sugar entered the packing operation but only 980 pounds of sugar were packed, the yield is 98%. During the packing process, 2% or 20 pounds of sugar were lost or spilled.

Exercises

EXERCISE 1

Flowchart of accounts related to service and processing departments

Alcoa Inc. is the world's largest producer of aluminum products. Alcoa manufactures aluminum sheet products for the aerospace industry among others. The entire output of the Smelting Department is transferred to the Rolling Department. Part of the fully processed goods from the Rolling Department is sold as rolled sheet, and the remainder of the goods is transferred to the Converting Department for further processing into sheared sheet.

Prepare a chart of the flow of costs from the processing department accounts into the finished goods accounts and then into the cost of goods sold account. The relevant accounts are as follows:

Cost of Goods Sold	Finished Goods—Rolled Sheet
Materials	Finished Goods—Sheared Sheet
Factory Overhead—Smelting Department	Work in Process—Smelting Department
Factory Overhead—Rolling Department	Work in Process—Rolling Department
Factory Overhead—Converting Department	Work in Process—Converting Department

EXERCISE 2

Equivalent units of production

✓ a. 11,100

The Converting Department of Zhao Napkin Company had 1,200 units in work in process that were 60% complete at the beginning of the period. During the period, 10,500 units were completed and transferred to the Packing Department. There were 600 units in process that were 30% complete at the end of the period.

a. Determine the number of whole units to be accounted for and to be assigned costs for the period.
b. Determine the number of equivalent units of production for the period.

EXERCISE 3

Equivalent units of production

✓ a. 77,600 units to be accounted for

Units of production data for the two departments of Southern Cable and Wire Company for October of the current fiscal year are as follows:

	Drawing Department	Winding Department
Work in process, October 1	2,000 units, 65% completed	1,400 units, 30% completed
Completed and transferred to next processing department during October	74,000 units	73,000 units
Work in process, October 31	3,600 units, 75% completed	2,400 units, 20% completed

a. Determine the number of whole units to be accounted for and to be assigned costs and the equivalent units of production for the Drawing Department.
b. Determine the number of whole units to be accounted for and to be assigned costs and the equivalent units of production for Winding Department.

EXERCISE 4

Equivalent units of production

✓ a. 27,500

The following information concerns production in the Finishing Department for March.

ACCOUNT Work in Process—Finishing Department

Date	Item	
Mar. 1	Bal., 14,000 units, 40% completed	38,000
31	Direct materials, 103,000 units	240,000
31	Direct labor	68,000
31	Factory overhead	40,800
31	Goods finished, 89,500 units	(304,842)
31	Bal. ? units, 60% completed	81,958

a. Determine the number of units in work in process inventory at the end of the month.
b. Determine the number of whole units to be accounted for and to be assigned costs and the equivalent units of production for March.

EXERCISE 5

Equivalent units of production and related costs

✓ b. 71,080 units

The charges to Work in Process—Baking Department for a period as well as information concerning production are as follows. All direct materials are placed in process at the beginning of production.

Work in Process—Baking Department	
Bal., 8,000 units, 70% completed	75,000
Direct materials, 67,400 units @ $2.20	148,280
Direct labor	35,000
Factory overhead	18,932
To Finished Goods, 70,000 units	?
Bal., 5,400 units, 20% completed	?

Determine the following:

a. Determine the number of whole units to be accounted for and to be assigned costs.
b. Determine the number of equivalent units of production.
c. Determine the costs per equivalent unit.
d. Determine the cost of the units transferred to Finished Goods.
e. Determine the cost of ending Work in Process.

EXERCISE 6
Cost per equivalent unit

✓ a. $12.85

The following information concerns production in the Forging Department for September.

ACCOUNT Work in Process—Forging Department

Date		Item	
Sept.	1	Bal., 5,500 units, 40% completed	53,000
	30	Direct materials, 36,000 units	284,400
	30	Direct labor	83,385
	30	Factory overhead	83,706
	30	Goods transferred, 38,300 units	?
	30	Bal., 3,200 units, 30% completed	?

a. Determine the cost per equivalent unit.
b. Determine the cost of the units transferred to Finished Goods.
c. Determine the cost of ending Work in Process.

EXERCISE 7
Cost of production report

✓ Cost per equivalent unit, $1.72

The increases to Work in Process—Cooking Department for Better Beans Company for January 2004 as well as information concerning production are as follows:

Work in process, January 1, 800 pounds, 30% complete	$ 1,050
Beans added during January, 48,600 pounds	58,320
Conversion costs during January	25,254
Work in process, January 31, 500 pounds, 60% completed	—
Goods finished during January, 48,900 pounds	—

Prepare a cost of production report.

EXERCISE 8
Cost of production report

✓ Cost per equivalent unit, $5.58

Prepare a cost of production report for the Cutting Department of Arizona Carpet Company for July 2004 using the following data and assuming that all materials are added at the beginning of the process:

Work in process, July 1, 10,000 units, 70% complete	$ 50,000
Materials added during July from Weaving Dept., 182,000 units	837,200
Direct labor for July	71,160
Factory overhead for July	50,504
Goods finished during July (includes goods in process, July 1), 178,000 units	—
Work in process, July 31, 14,000 units, 20% completed	—

EXERCISE 9
Decision making

Denver Bottling Company bottles popular beverages. The beverages are produced by blending concentrate with water and sugar. The concentrate is purchased from a concentrate producer that sets higher prices for the more popular concentrate flavors. The following is a simplified cost of production report separating the cost of bottling the four flavors.

	Orange	Cola	Lemon-Lime	Root Beer
Concentrate	$ 3,600	$33,000	$21,000	$1,800
Water	1,200	9,000	6,000	600
Sugar	2,000	15,000	10,000	1,000
Bottles	4,400	33,000	22,000	2,200
Flavor changeover	3,000	1,800	1,200	3,000
Conversion cost	1,600	7,500	5,000	800
Total cost	$15,800	$99,300	$65,200	$9,400
Number of cases	2,000	15,000	10,000	1,000

Beginning and ending work in process inventories are negligible and are omitted from the cost of production report. The flavor changeover cost represents the cost of cleaning the bottling machines between production runs of different flavors.

Prepare a memo to the production manager analyzing this comparative cost information. In your memo, provide recommendations for further action as well as supporting schedules showing the total cost per case and cost per case by cost element.

Problems

PROBLEM | 1

Cost of production report

✓ Cost per equivalent unit, $9.35

Valdez Coffee Company roasts and packs coffee beans. The process begins in the Roasting Department. From the Roasting Department, the coffee beans are transferred to the Packing Department. The following is a partial work in process account of the Roasting Department at March 31, 2004:

ACCOUNT Work in Process—Roasting Department

Date	Item	
Mar. 1	Bal., 13,800 units, 80% completed	114,600
31	Direct materials, 258,000 units	1,444,800
31	Direct labor	335,000
31	Factory overhead	562,406
31	Goods finished, 260,500 units	?
31	Bal. ? units, 20% completed	?

Instructions

Prepare a cost of production report, and identify the missing amounts for the Work in Process—Roasting Department account.

PROBLEM | 2

Equivalent units and related costs; cost of production report

✓ Transferred to Packaging Dept., $1,014,000

Baker's Choice Flour Company manufactures flour by a series of three processes, beginning in the Milling Department. From the Milling Department, the materials pass through the Sifting and Packaging Departments, emerging as packaged refined flour.

The balance in the account Work in Process—Sifting Department was as follows on July 1, 2004:

Work in Process—Sifting Department (25,800 units, 75% completed) $38,700

The following costs were charged to Work in Process—Sifting Department during July:

Direct materials transferred from Milling Department: 640,000 units
    at $1.15 a unit $736,000
Direct labor   148,742
Factory overhead   96,720

During July, 650,000 units of flour were completed. Work in Process—Sifting Department on July 31 was 15,800 units, 25% completed.

Instructions

1. Prepare a cost of production report for the Sifting Department for July.
2. Discuss the uses of the cost of production report.

Glossary

A

Accelerated depreciation method: A depreciation method that provides for a higher depreciation amount in the first year of the asset's use, followed by a gradually declining amount of depreciation.

Account: A record in which increases and decreases in a financial statement element are recorded.

Accounting: An information system that provides reports to stakeholders about the economic activities and condition of a business.

Accounting cycle: The process that begins with the analysis of transactions and ends with the preparation of the accounting records for the next accounting period.

Accounting equation: Assets = Liabilities + Stockholders' Equity.

Accounting period concept: An accounting concept in which accounting data are recorded and summarized in a period process.

Accounts payable: Liabilities for amounts incurred from purchases of products or services in the normal operations of a business.

Accounts receivable: Receivables created by selling merchandise or services on credit.

Accounts receivable turnover: Measures how frequently during the year the accounts receivable are being converted to cash by dividing net sales by the average net accounts receivable.

Accrual basis of accounting: A system of accounting in which revenue is recorded as it is earned and expenses are recorded when they generate revenue.

Accruals: Revenues or expenses that have not been recorded.

Accrued expenses: Expenses that have been incurred at the end of an accounting period but have not been recorded in the accounts; sometimes called *accrued liabilities*.

Accrued revenues: Revenues that have been earned at the end of an accounting period but have not been recorded in the accounts; sometimes called *accrued assets*.

Accumulated depreciation: An offsetting or contra asset account used to record depreciation on a fixed asset.

Acid-test ratio: The ratio of the sum of cash, receivables, and marketable securities to current liabilities.

Activity base: A measure of activity that is related to changes in cost and is used in the denominator in calculating the predetermined factory overhead rate to assign factory overhead costs to cost objects.

Activity cost pools: Cost accumulations that are associated with a given activity, such as machine usage, inspections, moving, and production setups.

Activity-based costing: A cost allocation method that identifies activities causing the incurrence of costs and allocates these costs to products (or other cost objects) based on activity drivers (bases).

Activity-based costing (ABC) method: An accounting framework based on determining the cost of activities and allocating these costs to products using activity rates.

Adequate disclosure concept: An accounting concept that requires financial statements to include all relevant data a reader needs to understand the financial condition and performance of a business.

Adjustment process: A process required by the accrual basis of accounting in which the accounts are updated prior to preparing financial statements.

Administrative expenses: Expenses incurred in the administration or general operations of the business.

Aging-of-receivables method: The process of analyzing the accounts receivable and classifying them according to various age groupings, with the due date being the base point for determining age.

Allowance for doubtful accounts: The contra asset account for accounts receivable.

Amortization: The periodic transfer of the cost of an intangible asset to expense.

Annuity: A series of equal cash flows at fixed intervals.

Assets: The resources owned by a business.

Average cost method: The method of inventory costing that is based upon the assumption that costs should be charged against revenue by using the weighted average unit cost of the items sold.

Average rate of return: A method of evaluating capital investment proposals that focuses on the expected profitability of the investment.

B

Balance sheet: A list of the assets, liabilities, and owner's equity *as of a specific date*, usually at the close of the last day of a month or a year.

Balanced scorecard: A performance evaluation approach that incorporates multiple performance dimensions by combining financial and nonfinancial measures.

Bank reconciliation: The analysis that details the items responsible for the difference between the cash balance reported in the bank statement and the balance of the cash account in the ledger.

Bank statement: A summary of all transactions mailed to the depositor by the bank each month.

Bond: A form of interest-bearing note used by corporations to borrow on a long-term basis.

Bond indenture: The contract between a corporation issuing bonds and the bondholders.

Bonds payable: A type of long-term debt financing with a face amount that is in the future with interest that is normally paid semiannually.

Book inventory: The amount of inventory recorded in the accounting records.

Book value: The cost of a fixed asset minus accumulated depreciation on the asset.

Bottleneck: A condition that occurs when product demand exceeds production capacity.

Break-even point: The level of business operations at which revenues and expired costs are equal.

Budget: An accounting device used to plan and control resources of operational departments and divisions.

Budget performance report: A report comparing actual results with budget figures.

Business: An organization in which basic resources (inputs), such as materials and labor, are assembled and processed to provide goods or services (outputs) to customers.

Business entity concept: An accounting concept that limits the economic data in the accounting system of a specific business or entity to data related directly to the activities of that business or entity.

Business stakeholder: A person or entity who has an interest in the economic performance of a business.

Business strategy: An integrated set of plans and actions designed to enable the business to gain an advantage over its competitors and in doing so, maximize its profits.

C

Capital expenditures: The costs of acquiring fixed assets, adding a component, or replacing a component of fixed assets.

Capital expenditures budget: The budget summarizing future plans for acquiring plant facilities and equipment.

Capital investment analysis: The process by which management plans, evaluates, and controls long-term capital investments involving fixed assets.

Capital rationing: The process by which management allocates available investment funds among competing capital investment proposals.

Capital stock: Types of stock a corporation may issue.

Cash: Coins, currency (paper money), checks, money orders, and money on deposit available for unrestricted withdrawal from banks and other financial institutions.

Cash basis of accounting: A system of accounting in which only transactions involving increases or decreases of the entity's cash are recorded.

Cash budget: A budget of estimated cash receipts and payments.

Cash dividend: A cash distribution of earnings by a corporation to its shareholders.

Cash equivalents: Highly liquid investments that are usually reported with cash on the balance sheet.

Cash payback period: The expected period of time that will elapse between the date of a capital expenditure and the complete recovery in cash (or equivalent) of the amount invested.

Cash short and over account: The account used to record the difference between the amount of cash in a cash register and the amount of cash that should be on hand according to the records.

Classified balance sheet: A balance sheet prepared with various sections, subsections, and captions that aid in its interpretation and analysis.

Closing process: The process of transferring the balances of the revenue, expense, and dividends accounts to retained earnings in preparation for the next accounting period.

Combination strategy: A business strategy that includes elements of both the low-cost and differentiation strategies.

Common stock: The basic type of stock issued to stockholders of a corporation when a corporation has issued only one class of stock.

Common-size financial statement: A financial statement in which all items are expressed in percentages.

Contingent liabilities: Potential liabilities if certain events occur in the future.

Continuous budgeting: A method of budgeting that provides for maintaining a 12-month projection into the future.

Contract rate: The periodic interest to be paid on the bonds that is identified in the bond indenture; expressed as a percentage of the face amount of the bond.

Contribution margin: Sales less variable cost of goods sold and variable selling and administrative expenses.

Contribution margin ratio: The percentage of each sales dollar that is available to cover the fixed costs and provide income from operations.

Controllable expenses: Costs that can be influenced by the decisions of a manager.

Controlling account: The account in the general ledger that summarizes the balances of the accounts in a subsidiary ledger.

Conversion costs: The combination of direct labor and factory overhead costs.

Copyright: An exclusive right to publish and sell a literary, artistic, or musical composition.

Corporation: A business organized under state or federal statutes as a separate legal entity.

Cost: A payment of cash (or a commitment to pay cash in the future) for the purpose of generating revenues.

Cost accounting system: A system used to accumulate manufacturing costs for decision-making and financial reporting purposes.

Cost allocation: The process of assigning indirect costs to a cost object, such as a job.

Cost behavior: The manner in which a cost changes in relation to its activity base (driver).

Cost center: A decentralized unit in which the department or division manager has responsibility for the control of costs incurred and the authority to make decisions that affect these costs.

Cost concept: An accounting concept that determines the amount initially entered into the accounting records for purchases.

Cost of goods sold: The cost of the manufactured product sold.

Cost of goods sold budget: A budget of the estimated direct materials, direct labor, and factory overhead consumed by sold products.

Cost of merchandise sold: The cost that is reported as an expense when merchandise or a manufactured product is sold; also called *cost of goods sold*.

Cost price approach: An approach to transfer pricing that uses cost as the basis for setting the transfer price.

Cost variance: The difference between the actual cost and the standard cost at actual volumes.

Cost-volume-profit analysis: The systematic examination of the relationships among costs, expenses, sales, and operating profit or loss.

Cost-volume-profit chart: A chart used to assist management in understanding the relationships among costs, expenses, sales, and operating profit or loss.

Credit memorandum: A form used by a seller to inform the buyer of the amount the seller proposes to decrease the account receivable due from the buyer.

Credit period: The amount of time the buyer is allowed in which to pay the seller.

Credit terms: Terms for payment on account by the buyer to the seller.

Cumulative preferred stock: A class of preferred stock that has a right to receive regular dividends that have been passed (not declared) before any common stock dividends are paid.

Currency exchange rate: The rate at which currency in another country can be exchanged for local currency.

Current assets: Cash and other assets that are expected to be converted to cash or sold or used up through the normal operations of the business within one year or less.

Current liabilities: Liabilities that will be due within a short time (usually one year or less) and that are to be paid out of current assets.

Current ratio: The ratio of current assets to current liabilities.

Currently attainable standards: Standards that represent levels of operation that can be obtained with reasonable effort.

D

Debit memorandum: A form used by a buyer to inform the seller of the amount the buyer proposes to decrease the account payable due the seller.

Decentralization: The separation of a business into more manageable operating units.

Declining-balance method: A method of depreciation that provides periodic expense based on the declining book value of a fixed asset over the estimated life.

Deferrals: Delayed recordings of expenses or revenues.

Deferred expenses: Items that are initially recorded as assets but are expected to become expenses over time or through the normal operations of the business; sometimes called *prepaid expenses*.

Deferred revenues: Items that are initially recorded as liabilities but are expected to become revenues over time or through the normal operations of the business; sometimes called *unearned revenues*.

Deflation: A period when prices in general are falling and the purchasing power of money is increasing.

Depletion: The process of transferring the cost of natural resources to an expense account.

Depreciation: The systematic periodic transfer of the cost of a fixed asset to an expense account during its expected useful life.

Differential analysis: The area of accounting concerned with the effect of alternative courses of action on revenues and costs.

Differential cost: The amount of increase or decrease in cost expected from a particular course of action compared with an alternative.

Differential revenue: The amount of increase or decrease in revenue expected from a particular course of action as compared with an alternative.

Differentiation strategy: A business strategy in which a business designs and produces products or services that possess unique attributes or characteristics for which customers are willing to pay a premium price.

Direct labor cost: Wages of factory workers who are directly involved in converting materials into a finished product.

Direct labor time variance: The cost associated with the difference between the standard hours and the actual hours of direct labor spent producing a commodity.

Direct labor rate variance: The cost associated with the difference between the standard rate and the actual rate paid for direct labor used in producing a commodity.

Direct materials cost: The cost of materials that are an integral part of the finished product.

Direct materials price variance: The cost associated with the difference between the standard price and the actual price of direct materials used in producing a commodity.

Direct materials purchases budget: A budget that uses the production budget as a starting point.

Direct materials quantity variance: The cost associated with the difference between the standard quantity and the actual quantity of direct materials used in producing a commodity.

Discount on bonds payable: The excess of the face amount of bonds over their issue price.

Dividend yield: A profitability measure that is computed by dividing the annual dividends paid per share of common stock by the market price per share on a specific date.

Dividends: Distributions of the earnings of a corporation to stockholders.

Dividends per share: The ratio of dividends paid to common stockholders divided by the number of common shares outstanding.

Division: A decentralized unit that is structured around a common function, product, customer, or geographical territory.

E

Earnings per share: A measure of profitability computed by dividing net income, reduced by preferred dividends, by the number of common shares outstanding.

Electronic data interchange (EDI): An information technology that allows different business organizations to use computers to communicate orders, relay information, and make or receive payments.

Electronic funds transfer (EFT): A system in which computers rather than paper (money, checks, etc.) are used to effect cash transactions.

Elements of internal control: The control environment, risk assessment, control activities, information and communication, and monitoring.

Employee fraud: The intentional act of deceiving an employer for personal gain.

Employee involvement: A philosophy that grants employees the responsibility and authority to make their own decisions about their operations.

Expenses: Costs used to earn revenues.

F

Factory overhead cost: All of the costs of operating the factory except for direct materials and direct labor.

Financial Accounting Standards Board (FASB): The authoritative body that has the primary responsibility for developing accounting principles.

Financial accounting system: A system that includes (1) a set of rules for determining what, when, and the amount that should be recorded for economic events, (2) a framework for facilitating preparing financial statements, and (3)

one or more controls to determine whether errors could have arisen in the recording process.

Financial statements: Financial reports that summarize the effects of events on a business.

Financing activities: Business activities that involve obtaining funds to begin and operate a business.

Finished goods inventory: The cost of finished products on hand that have not been sold.

Finished goods ledger: The subsidiary ledger that contains the individual accounts for each kind of commodity or product produced.

First-in, first-out (fifo) method: A method of inventory costing based on the assumption that the costs of merchandise sold should be charged against revenue in the order in which the costs were incurred.

Fixed asset turnover ratio: A ratio that measures the number of dollars of revenue earned per dollar of fixed assets, and is calculated as total revenue divided by the average book value of fixed assets.

Fixed assets: Long-lived or relatively permanent tangible assets that are used in the normal business operations; sometimes called *plant assets.*

Fixed costs: Costs that tend to remain the same in amount, regardless of variations in the level of activity.

Flexible budget: A budget that adjusts for varying rates of activity.

Fringe benefits: Benefits provided to employees in addition to wages and salaries.

FOB (free on board) destination: Freight terms in which the seller pays the transportation costs from the shipping point to the final destination.

FOB (free on board) shipping point: Freight terms in which the buyer pays the transportation costs from the shipping point to the final destination.

G

Generally accepted accounting principles (GAAP): Rules for the way financial statements should be prepared.

Goal conflict: Situation when individual self-interest differs from business objectives.

Going concern concept: An accounting concept that assumes a business will continue operating for an indefinite period of time.

Goodwill: An intangible asset of a business that is created from favorable factors such as location, product quality, reputation, and managerial skill, as verified from a merger transaction.

Gross pay: The total earnings of an employee for a payroll period.

Gross profit: Sales minus the cost of merchandise sold.

H

High-low method: A technique that uses the highest and lowest total cost as a basis for estimating the variable cost per unit and the fixed cost component of a mixed cost.

Horizontal analysis: A method of analyzing financial performance that computes the percentage of increases and decreases in related items in comparative financial statements.

I

Income from operations (operating income): The excess of gross profit over total operating expenses.

Income statement: A summary of the revenue and expenses *for a specific period of time,* such as a month or a year.

Indirect method: A method of preparing the statement of cash flows that reconciles net income with net cash flows from operating activities.

Inflation: A period when prices in general are rising and the purchasing power of money is declining.

Intangible assets: Long-lived assets that are useful in the operations of a business, are not held for sale, and are without physical qualities.

Interest payable: A liability to pay interest on a due date.

Internal control: The policies and procedures used to safeguard assets, ensure accurate business information, and ensure compliance with laws and regulations.

Internal rate of return method: A method of analyzing proposed capital investments that focuses on using present value concepts to compute the rate of return from the net cash flows expected from the investment.

Inventory shrinkage: The amount by which the merchandise for sale, as indicated by the balance of the merchandise inventory account, is larger than the total amount of merchandise counted during the physical inventory.

Inventory turnover: Measures the relationship between the volume of goods (merchandise) sold and the amount of inventory carried during the period.

Investing activities: Business activities that involve obtaining the necessary resources to start and operate the business.

Investment center: A decentralized unit in which the manager has the responsibility and authority to make decisions that affect not only costs and revenues but also the fixed assets available to the center.

Investment turnover: A component of the rate of return on investment computed as the ratio of sales to invested assets.

Invoice: The bill that the seller sends to the buyer.

J

Job cost sheet: An account in the work in process subsidiary ledger in which the costs charged to a particular job order are recorded.

Job order cost system: A type of cost accounting system that provides for a separate record of the cost of each particular quantity of product that passes through the factory.

Just-in-time manufacturing: A business philosophy that focuses on eliminating time, cost, and poor quality within manufacturing processes.

L

Last-in, first-out (lifo) method: A method of inventory costing based on the assumption that the most recent merchandise inventory costs should be charged against revenue.

Lead time: The elapsed time between starting a unit of product into the beginning of a process and its completion.

Leverage: The tendency of the rate earned on stockholders' equity to vary from the rate earned on total assets because the amount earned on assets acquired through the use of funds provided by creditors varies from the interest paid to these creditors.

Liability: The right of a creditor that represents a legal obligation to repay an amount borrowed according to terms of the borrowing agreement.

Lifo conformity rule: A financial reporting rule requiring a firm that elects to use lifo inventory valuation for tax purposes to also use lifo for external financial reporting.

Long-term liabilities: Liabilities that will not be due for a long time (usually more than one year).

Loss from operations: The excess of operating expenses over gross profit.

Low-cost strategy: A business strategy in which a business designs and produces products of acceptable quality at a cost lower than that of competitors.

Lower-of-cost-or-market (LCM) method: A method of valuing inventory that reports the inventory at the lower of its cost or current market value (replacement cost).

M

Management discussion and analysis: An annual report disclosure that provides management's analysis of the results of operations and financial condition.

Manufacturing: A type of business that changes basic inputs into products that are sold to individual customers.

Margin of safety: The difference between current sales revenue and the sales at the break-even point.

Market price approach: An approach to transfer pricing that uses the price at which the product or service transferred could be sold to outside buyers as the transfer price.

Market rate of interest: The effective rate of interest at the time bonds are issued.

Markup: An amount that is added to a "cost" amount to determine product price.

Master budget: The comprehensive budget plan linking the individual budgets related to sales, cost of goods sold, operating expenses, projects, capital expenditures, and cash.

Matching concept: An accounting concept that requires expenses of a period to be matched with the revenue generated during that period.

Materials inventory: The cost of materials that have not yet entered into the manufacturing process.

Materials ledger: The subsidiary ledger containing the individual accounts for each type of material.

Materials requisitions: The form or electronic transmission used by a manufacturing department to authorize the issuance of materials from the storeroom.

Maturity: The time period that the liability is outstanding prior to its due date.

Maturity value: The amount that is due at the maturity or due date of a note.

Merchandise available for sale: The cost of merchandise available for sale to customers.

Merchandise inventory: Merchandise on hand (not sold) at the end of an accounting period.

Merchandising: A type of business that purchases products from other businesses and sells them to customers.

Mixed cost: A cost with both variable and fixed characteristics.

Multiple-step income statement: A form of income statement that contains several sections, subsections, and subtotals.

N

Negotiated price approach: An approach to transfer pricing that allows managers of decentralized units to agree (negotiate) among themselves as to the transfer price.

Net income: The excess of revenues over expenses.

Net loss: The excess of expenses over revenues.

Net pay: Gross pay less payroll deductions; the amount the employer is obligated to pay the employee.

Net present value method: A method of analyzing proposed capital investments that focuses on the present value of the cash flows expected from the investments.

Net realizable value: For a receivable, the amount of cash expected to be realized in the future. For inventory, the estimated selling price of an item of inventory less any direct costs of disposal, such as sales commissions.

Net sales: Gross sales less sales returns and allowances and sales discounts.

Nonvalue-added lead time: The time that units wait in inventories, move unnecessarily, and wait during machine breakdowns.

Note payable: A type of short- or long-term financing that requires payment of the amount borrowed plus interest.

Notes receivable: Written claims against debtors who promise to pay the amount of the note plus interest at an agreed-upon rate.

Number of days' sales in inventory: The relationship between the volume of sales and inventory, computed by dividing the inventory at the end of the year by the average daily cost of goods sold.

Number of days' sales in receivables: The relationship between sales and accounts receivable, computed by dividing the net accounts receivable at the end of the year by the average daily sales.

Number of times interest charges are earned: A ratio that measures the risk that interest payments to debt holders will continue to be made if earnings decrease.

O

Objectivity concept: An accounting concept that requires accounting records and data reported in financial statements be based on objective evidence.

Operating activities: Business activities that involve using the business's resources to implement its business strategy.

Operating leverage: A measure of the relative mix of a business's variable costs and fixed costs, computed as contribution margin divided by income from operations.

Opportunity cost: The amount of income forgone from an alternative to a proposed use of cash or its equivalent.

Other expense: Expenses that cannot be traced directly to operations.

Other income: Revenue from sources other than the primary operating activity of a business.

Outstanding stock: The stock in the hands of stockholders.

Overapplied factory overhead: The amount of factory overhead applied in excess of the actual factory overhead costs incurred for production during a period.

Owner's equity: The financial rights of the owner.

P

Par: The monetary amount printed on a stock certificate.

Partnership: A business owned by two or more individuals.

Patents: Exclusive rights to produce and sell goods with one or more unique features.

Payroll: The total amount paid to employees for a certain period.

Period costs: Those costs that are used up in generating revenue during the current period and that are not involved in the manufacturing process.

Periodic inventory method: The inventory method in which the inventory records do not show the amount available for sale or sold during the period.

Perpetual inventory method: The inventory system in which each purchase and sale of merchandise is recorded in an inventory account.

Petty cash fund: A special-purpose cash fund to pay relatively small amounts.

Physical inventory: A detailed listing of the merchandise for sale at the end of an accounting period.

Predetermined factory overhead rate: The rate used to apply factory overhead costs to the goods manufactured. The rate is determined from budgeted overhead cost and estimated activity usage data at the beginning of the fiscal period.

Preferred stock: A class of stock with preferential rights over common stock.

Premium on bonds payable: The excess of the issue price of bonds over their face amount.

Premium on stock: The excess of the issue price of a stock over its par value.

Prepaid expenses: Assets resulting from the prepayment of future expenses such as insurance or rent that are expected to become expenses over time or through the normal operations of the business; often called *deferred expenses*.

Present value concept: Cash today is not the equivalent of the same amount of money to be received in the future.

Present value index: An index computed by dividing the total present value of the net cash flow to be received from a pro-

posed capital investment by the amount to be invested.

Present value of an annuity: The sum of the present values of a series of equal cash flows to be received at fixed intervals.

Price-earnings (P/E) ratio: The ratio of the market price per share of common stock at a specific date to the annual earnings per share.

Process cost system: A type of cost accounting system in which costs are accumulated by department or process within a factory.

Process-oriented layout: Organizing work in a plant or administrative function around processes (tasks).

Product costs: The three components of manufacturing cost: direct materials, direct labor, and factory overhead costs.

Production budget: A budget of estimated unit production.

Product-oriented layout: Organizing work in a plant or administrative function around products; sometimes referred to as *product cells*.

Profit center: A decentralized unit in which the manager has the responsibility and the authority to make decisions that affect both costs and revenues (and thus profits).

Profit margin: A component of the rate of return on investment computed as the ratio of income from operations to sales.

Profitability: The ability of a firm to earn income.

Profit-volume chart: A chart used to assist management in understanding the relationship between profit and volume.

Proprietorship: A business owned by one individual.

Pull manufacturing: A just-in-time method wherein customer orders trigger the release of finished goods, which trigger production, which triggers release of materials from suppliers.

Purchase discounts: Discounts taken by the buyer for early payment of an invoice.

Purchase return or allowance: From the buyer's perspective, returned merchandise or an adjustment for defective merchandise.

Push manufacturing: Materials are released into production and work in process is released into finished goods in anticipation of future sales.

Q

Quick assets: The sum of cash, receivables, and marketable securities.

R

Rate earned on common stockholders' equity: A measure of profitability computed by dividing net income, reduced by preferred dividend requirements, by common stockholders' equity.

Rate earned on stockholders' equity: A measure of profitability computed by dividing net income by total stockholders' equity.

Rate earned on total assets: A measure of the profitability of assets without regard to the equity of creditors and stockholders in the assets.

Rate of return on investment: A measure of managerial efficiency in the use of investments in assets computed as income from operations divided by invested assets.

Ratio of fixed assets to long-term liabilities: A solvency measure that indicates the margin of safety of the noteholders or bondholders.

Ratio of liabilities to stockholders' equity: A solvency measure that indicates the margin of safety for creditors.

Ratio of net sales to assets: A profitability measure that measures how effectively a firm utilizes its assets.

Receivables: All money claims against other entities, including people, business firms, and other organizations.

Receiving report: The form or electronic transmission used by the receiving personnel to indicate that materials have been received and inspected.

Relevant range: The range of activity over which changes in cost are of interest to management.

Report form: The form of balance sheet in which assets, liabilities, and stockholders' equity are reported in a downward sequence.

Residual income: The excess of divisional income from operations over a "minimum" acceptable income from operations.

Residual value: The estimated value of a fixed asset at the end of its useful life.

Responsibility accounting: The process of measuring and reporting operating data by areas of responsibility.

Responsibility center: An organizational unit for which a manager is assigned responsibility over costs, revenues, or assets.

Retained earnings: Net income retained in a corporation.

Retained earnings statement: A summary of the changes in the retained earnings in a corporation *for a specific period of time*, such as a month or a year.

Revenue: The increase in assets from selling products or services to customers.

Revenue expenditures: Costs that benefit only the current period or costs incurred for normal maintenance and repairs of fixed assets.

S

Sales: The total amount charged to customers for merchandise sold, including cash sales and sales on account.

Sales budget: A budget that indicates for each product (1) the quantity of estimated sales and (2) the expected unit selling price.

Sales discounts: From the seller's perspective, discounts that a seller can offer the buyer for early payment.

Sales mix: The relative distribution of sales among the various products available for sale.

Sales returns and allowances: From the seller's perspective, returned merchandise or an adjustment for damaged or defective merchandise.

Selling expenses: Expenses that are incurred directly in the selling of merchandise.

Service: A type of business that provides services rather than products to customers.

Service department charges: The costs of services provided by an internal service department and transferred to a responsibility center.

Setup: The effort required to prepare an operation for a new production run.

Single-step income statement: A form of income statement in which the total of all expenses is deducted from the total of all revenues.

Solvency: The ability of a firm to pay its debts as they come due.

Special-purpose fund: A cash fund used for a special business need.

Standard cost: A detailed estimate of what a product should cost.

Standard cost systems: Accounting systems that use standards for each manufacturing cost entering into the finished product.

Stated value: A value, similar to par value, approved by the board of directors of a corporation for no-par stock.

Statement of cash flows: A summary of the cash receipts and cash payments *for a specific period of time*, such as a month or a year.

Static budget: A budget that does not adjust to changes in activity levels.

Stock dividend: A distribution of shares of stock to its stockholders.

Stock split: The reduction in the par or stated value of common stock and issuance of a proportionate number of additional shares.

Stockholders: Investors who purchase stock in a corporation.

Stockholders' equity: The stockholders' rights to the assets of a business.

Straight-line method: A method of depreciation that provides for equal periodic depreciation expense over the estimated life of a fixed asset.

Subsidiary ledger: A ledger containing individual accounts with a common characteristic.

Sunk cost: A cost that is not affected by subsequent decisions.

Supplier partnering: A just-in-time method that views suppliers as a valuable contributor to the overall success of the business.

T

Target cost concept: A concept used to design and manufacture a product at a cost that will deliver a target profit for a given market-determined price.

Taxable income: The income of a corporation that is subject to taxes as determined according to the tax laws.

Temporary differences: Differences between taxable income and income before income taxes that are created because items are recognized in one period for tax purposes and in another period for income statement purposes.

Theoretical standards: Standards that represent levels of performance that can be achieved only under perfect operating conditions.

Theory of constraints (TOC): A manufacturing strategy that attempts to remove the influence of bottlenecks (constraints) on a process.

Time tickets: The form on which the amount of time spent by each employee and the labor cost incurred for each individual job, or for factory overhead, are recorded.

Time value of money concept: The concept that an amount of money invested today will earn interest.

Total cost concept: A concept used in applying the cost-plus approach to product pricing in which all the costs of manufacturing the product plus the selling and administrative expenses are included in the cost amount to which the markup is added.

Total liabilities to total assets ratio: A solvency ratio that measures the percentage of total assets financed by debt.

Trademark: A name, term, or symbol used to identify a business and its products.

Transaction: An economic event that under generally accepted accounting principles affects an element of the accounting equation and, therefore, must be recorded.

Transfer price: The price charged one decentralized unit by another for the goods or services provided.

Treasury stock: Stock that a corporation has once issued and then reacquires.

U

Uncollectible accounts expense: The operating expense incurred because of the failure to collect receivables.

Underapplied factory overhead: The actual factory overhead costs incurred in excess of the amount of factory overhead applied for production during a period.

Unearned revenues: Items that are initially recorded as liabilities but are expected to become revenues over time or through the normal operation of the business; often called *deferred revenues.*

Unit contribution margin: The dollars available from each unit of sales to cover fixed costs and provide income from operations.

Unit of measure concept: An accounting concept requiring that economic data be recorded in dollars.

V

Value chain: The way a business adds value for its customers by processing inputs into a product or service.

Value-added lead time: The time required to manufacture a unit of product or other output.

Variable costing: A method of reporting variable and fixed costs that includes only the variable manufacturing costs in the cost of the product.

Variable costs: Costs that vary in total dollar amount as the level of activity changes.

Vertical analysis: A method of analyzing comparative financial statements in which percentages are computed for each item within a statement to a total within the statement.

Voucher: Any document that serves as proof of authority to pay cash.

Voucher system: A set of procedures for authorizing and recording liabilities and cash payments.

W

Work in process inventory: The direct materials costs, the direct labor costs, and the factory overhead costs that have entered into the manufacturing process but are associated with products that have not been finished.

Working capital: The excess of total current assets over total current liabilities at some point in time.

Z

Zero-based budgeting: A concept of budgeting that requires all levels of management to start from zero and estimate budget data as if there had been no previous activities in their units.

Index

Company Index